Statistics and Research Design in the Behavioral Sciences

Statistics and Research Design in the Behavioral Sciences

Richard S. Lehman

FRANKLIN & MARSHALL COLLEGE

Wadsworth Publishing Company

Belmont, California

A Division of Wadsworth, Inc.

Psychology Editor: Kenneth King
Editorial Assistant: Cynthia Campbell
Production Editor: Donna Linden
Managing Designer: Kaelin Chappell
Print Buyer: Barbara Britton
Permissions Editor: Robert Kauser
Cover and Text Designer: Al Burkhardt
Copy Editor: Joan Pendleton
Art Editor: Mary Burkhardt
Technical Illustrator: Judith Ogus/Random Arts
Compositor: Asco Trade Typesetting Ltd., Hong Kong
Cover Photo: © 1988 Larry Hamill
Signing Representative: Jim Brace Thompson

Credits appear on page 562.

Printed in the United States of America 18

2 3 4 5 6 7 8 9 10—95 94 93 92 91

Library of Congress Cataloging-in-Publication Data

Lehman, Richard S.
    Statistics and research design in the behavioral sciences / Richard S. Lehman.
        p.   cm.
    Includes bibliographical references and index.
    ISBN 0-534-13878-0
    1. Psychology—Statistical methods.   2. Psychology—Research—Methodology.
I. Title.
BF39.L34   1991
150′.72—dc20   90-36704

BRIEF CONTENTS

CONTENTS

PART TWO

Describing Data 97

CHAPTER 5

Frequencies and Frequency Distributions 99

CHAPTER 6

Measures of Center 119

CHAPTER 7

Measures of Spread and Form 135

CHAPTER 8

Standardized Variables and the Normal Distribution 154

PART THREE

Statistical Inference and Classical Experimental Design 215

PART FOUR

Other Research Techniques 473

PREFACE

Many years ago, when I was finishing graduate school and interviewing for faculty positions, I was often asked whether I would prefer to teach a course in statistics or one in research methods. I have always had trouble answering that question, because to me the two topics are so completely intertwined as to make their separation difficult and confusing to students. In the traditional curriculum, the "methods" course presents ways to set up research, and the "statistics" course addresses how to analyze the data that come from research. Why not, I wondered, just have a single course that teaches students both how to ask questions by using good research design and how to answer questions by using the appropriate statistics? Fortunately, I found a faculty position that didn't force me to decide between the two courses, and I have been teaching a single combined course for 25 years.

I've always had to use two texts to teach my combined course, because no single book has adequately presented research methods and statistics. I hope that *Statistics and Research Design in the Behavioral Sciences* addresses that problem. Here you will find all of the usual topics from the "methods" course, as well as all those from the "statistics" course. They are combined into a single volume in a way that makes sense to me and to my students. Presenting the complementary topics of research design and analysis together helps students learn that the research enterprise is a unified undertaking and that it is not separate processes of collecting data and then analyzing them.

Features

- Research methods and statistics are developed together. The emphasis is on how each method addresses certain kinds of research questions and how the statistics help answer those questions. In every case, the logic of a particular method is discussed first, and then the appropriate analysis is presented conceptually and computationally.
- The mechanics of doing research—from getting ideas to analyzing data to interpreting and presenting the results—are developed in an integrated way.
- Classical experimental designs are developed in a logical progression, from the simplest single-sample procedure through complex analysis of variance designs, showing how the different designs are interrelated.
- Survey research, quasi-experiments, and other research strategies are covered, and their strengths and weaknesses outlined.
- Measurement theory is developed carefully and its relationship to both research questions and statistical answers is clarified.
- Analysis of variance is presented thoroughly, because it is the most widely

used general research strategy in the behavioral sciences. One-way designs, both between and within subjects, and two-factor designs (between subjects, within subjects, and mixed) are given full treatment. Follow-up tests are given for all ANOVA computations.
- The anxiety with which many students approach the design and statistics course is directly addressed. The writing is relaxed, informal, and non-mathematical in style. In addition, many of the illustrations use sets of actual data addressing nontrivial questions, supplied by my colleagues. Each researcher is introduced by a short biography so that students are exposed to real research workers in a personal way.

Organization

The book is arranged in four major sections. Part One begins with a discussion of the nature of research and theory in the behavioral sciences. Chapters 2–4 are devoted to research methods, measurement theory and procedures, and ways of controlling and manipulating variables. The underlying theme in Part One is how to ask questions by establishing the setting in which data can be collected.

Part Two introduces univariate and bivariate descriptive statistics. These statistics are presented as ways of finding answers, in data, to the questions posed by virtue of the research design. Graphic methods are presented first, and then the usual univariate descriptive statistics are given careful treatment. Correlation and regression are developed as descriptive methods for two variables.

When the classical experimental designs are developed in Part Three, they are shown to provide a structured way of posing questions and analyzing data. The presentation of experimental design begins with single-group studies, progresses through single-factor experiments, and concludes with the full treatment of factorial designs.

Part Four presents alternative ways of carrying out research. The treatment of categorical data is covered fully here. In addition, research using single subjects, quasi-experiments, case studies, surveys, and archival and small-N research are discussed.

Order of Presentation

Anyone who writes a textbook must choose an order for the topics; the users must then decide whether to use the author's order or provide their own. Some parts of this book offer flexibility in reordering the material, while others are more rigidly ordered. Chapters 1–4 are written cumulatively, so that each chapter depends critically upon previous material. Similarly, the univariate descriptive statistics (Chapters 5–8) are developed cumulatively. But the correlation and regression material, presented here as bivariate descriptive statistics (Chapters 9 and 10), could easily be studied out of sequence.

The classical design material (Part Three) is tightly integrated, and most instructors will probably want to teach this unit in the order presented, with one exception. The one-way within-subjects design (Chapter 17) is presented *before* the between-subjects factorial experiment (Chapters 18 and 19). This nonstandard ordering permits complete development of the single-factor experimental design in all of its guises *before* the factorial is introduced. The order of those chapters can easily be changed to put the between-subjects factorial in its customary place—before the first repeated-measures design.

The final two chapters are self-contained and may easily be moved. Some instructors may wish to introduce the material on other research methods (Chapter 22) earlier, perhaps following Chapters 1–4, so that all of the methods material is together. Similarly, the Chi-square topics in Chapter 21 can easily be moved from their present position to anywhere after the development of inferential logic in Chapters 12 and 13.

Some Pedagogical Matters

The book is intended for a 5- or 6-credit one-semester course, or for a two-quarter or a two-semester sequence in research methods and statistics. It presupposes no background in mathematics beyond high school algebra and geometry and does not rely upon any content prerequisite. It can profitably be used by students who have had only an introductory course in psychology.

Nearly every chapter includes exercises. Solutions to roughly half of the exercises are provided at the back of the book, and a supplementary answer book provides the rest. Since I believe that students don't really understand a set of data and its analysis if they can't describe it, many of the exercises ask that the results be communicated in written form, often using the American Psychological Association format.

This book recognizes that most statistical arithmetic is done by computer in the "real" research world. But it is not a computer-dependent text. No computer is necessary for any of the material, except for some optional exercises, and no computer output is pictured. Complete computations are given and illustrated for all statistics. Statistical materials are always first presented conceptually and then the computations are illustrated. In this way, instructors who choose to have their students use computers may omit the hand calculations with no loss of continuity.

For the student with access to a computer, there are numerous computer-based exercises. Some of them merely ask that the student repeat a previous analysis using a computer. Others, though, use the computer to expand on illustrations and concepts. No particular computer program is assumed by these optional exercises, and no instruction in computer use is offered.

The book offers somewhat more statistical coverage than is the norm for an undergraduate first course. Among the more unusual topics covered are tests for correlations, variances, medians, and proportions. Also slightly unusual are the extensive treatments given to within-subjects and mixed-factorial designs and to follow-up tests for every analysis of variance design. In addition, the chapter on regression offers careful development of residuals and the logic of r^2, as well as a brief conceptual introduction to multiple regression. Although no detail is provided on multiple regression, the student is introduced to the concept and may be motivated to further explore it on an available computer program.

Acknowledgments

I want to recognize assistance from several sources. First, Franklin & Marshall College, through its sabbatical leave program, made it possible for me to accomplish the bulk of the actual writing free of many academic duties. Alan Levine helped me plot several distribution forms. N. John Castellan Jr. advised me on some of the materials in Chapter 21. My departmental colleagues Chuck Stewart, Don Tyrrell, Tim Hubbard, Ed Hass, John Campbell, and Fred Owens all provided data sets.

I want to thank three authors for setting good examples of clear, readable, technical writing: Donald Knuth, Geoffrey Keppel, and David Howell. All have written beautiful expositions of difficult material—in computer science and in statistics. They offer proof that despite difficult subject matter, writing can still be understandable, graceful, and, yes, even humorous. In addition, the late Richard V. Andree taught me more about good writing in a one-page handout than any number of courses could have. If the writing in this book rises above the stuffy prose that's common in this kind of material, those men are due some of the credit.

Over the years, my family has learned to understand the writer in the house. My wife, Jean, has endured late hours, no weekends, abbreviated summer vacations, scant help in her studio, and endless uncompleted home repairs, all in the name of progress on The Book. My daughter, Barbara, has grown from a child, drawing with flowchart templates while I was writing an early simulation book, to a young adult, complaining that this book comes a semester too late for her to use it as a text. I very much appreciate their love, tolerance, and support.

Several reviewers of early versions of the manuscript helped to shape it in various ways. I especially want to thank Cole Barton, Davidson College, University of California, San Francisco; Fred Fidura, SUNY, Geneseo; Timothy Goldsmith, University of New Mexico; Donald Kendrick, Middle Tennessee State University; Willard Larkin, University of Maryland, College Park; Lee Sechrest, University of Arizona; Kirk Smith, Bowling Green State University; and Michael Wogalter, Rensselaer Polytechnic Institute. I wish I could blame them for inadequacies in the book, but those are my responsibility, sometimes because I ignored their advice. Ken King at Wadsworth recognized the worth of this project (if not its original expression) and he, together with production editor Donna Linden, worked hard to help me bring it into shape. Thank you.

Richard Lehman
Lancaster, PA

PART ONE

Some Research Fundamentals

Psychology is the science that studies behavior. It seeks to understand why we behave as we do and why others behave as they do. It asks questions about behavior in an attempt to understand and explain it. And it seeks answers to its questions by conducting research. In broader terms, science is the process of asking questions and answering them. This book is about that process as it is used in psychology.

Doing research—the process of asking and answering questions—relies on certain skills. Among those skills are the understanding of and the ability to use a variety of research methods and techniques. Many of those methods and techniques are statistical—they allow us to describe research results and to make inferences about similar behavior in similar situations.

In Part One of this book, we begin the study of research methods in psychology by looking at some fundamental considerations. Chapter 1 discusses the nature of science and scientific research. Chapter 2 introduces most of the common research strategies in psychology and discusses some of the mechanics of actually doing research. Then Chapter 3 discusses measurement, which is a fundamental for all research.

Finally, Chapter 4 discusses ways psychologists design and conduct experiments by controlling and manipulating variables.

The remaining three parts of the book deal with descriptive statistics (Part Two), inference and classical experimental design (Part Three), and other research techniques (Part Four).

CHAPTER 1

An Overview of Research in Psychology

Research in psychology is remarkably diverse. Here are four short examples. As you read the descriptions and the questions they raise, see if you can anticipate how a researcher might approach this area and try to answer the questions.

Problem 1 What can a young infant perceive? Can a two-day-old child, for example, tell the difference between a visual pattern that it has seen before and a novel one? Can it recognize that a photograph and a drawing of an adult are the same person? Could it tell if they were different people? Can an infant tell the difference between the patterns of movement made by running and walking adults? Is there an age at which infants cannot make these distinctions and later an age when they can? Since an infant can't respond verbally, is there any way to obtain the answers to these questions? What would the answers to these questions tell us about the way that humans develop? Can they help us to determine an answer to the old question of nature and nurture—what capabilities do humans have at birth, and which are acquired by experience? Can we use the child's innate abilities, if they exist, to make predictions about later intelligence? About possible developmental disabilities, brain injury, or retardation?

Problem 2 Suppose that you became violently ill immediately after drinking a can of your favorite diet soda. After you recovered, how would you feel about your old favorite soda? Would you still like it? Would you switch brands? Or might you even avoid most sweet drinks in the future? Could you induce the same kind of experience in animals? If you could, might you be able to devise a way for animals to learn to avoid consuming certain toxic chemicals?

Problem 3   The human personality is extremely complex. One hears, for example, about introverts and extraverts. Do these two types of people actually exist? Or are those two categories extremes on a dimension along which people might vary? If introversion/extraversion represents a dimension of personality, what are some other dimensions? How are the dimensions related to each other? Can any of them help us to understand how people get along with others, succeed in careers, select friends, or adjust to the problems of daily life?

Problem 4   Is the process of vision different in darkness and in light? If so, what does the difference tell us about the way the visual system operates? Can the difference help to explain why so many motor vehicle accidents happen after dark? Could we find ways to improve night vision and thereby save some of the lives that are now lost in nighttime highway accidents?

The four research areas described illustrate the broad range of questions raised by research psychologists. They also illustrate the research conducted by four of my colleagues, whom we will meet in more detail as we proceed. We'll use their research, as well as that by others, to illustrate the discussion. When we begin a detailed study of one of these research areas, we'll introduce the researcher, discuss what his or her interests are, show how the research has both theoretical and practical sides, and point out how the experimenter collaborates with students. Indeed, all of the research conducted by these psychologists is conducted with undergraduate students as research associates and partners. These student researchers have completed a course in research methods and statistics like the one that you're taking right now. In their research, they put the principles that we'll present in this book into action.

An Example: Conditioned Taste Aversion

Let's pursue the soft drink problem further as an example of the process of research.

If you let a rat consume some substance (saccharin, for example) and then administer a small dose of lithium chloride, the animal will become violently ill. After the animal recovers from its brief sickness, it will avoid the substance that it tasted immediately before getting sick. This phenomenon is known as a conditioned taste aversion and is usually learned very quickly—normally in one experience. Conditioned taste aversion is uncommon among humans (despite our earlier suggestions about diet sodas), but can easily be induced in animals. Conditioned aversion provides a valuable tool for studying animals' perceptual abilities.

While humans certainly are more complex in most ways than other animals, our taste system is very similar to that of the laboratory rat. As a result, the rat often makes an ideal organism for researchers studying the chemical senses of taste and smell. Not only are animals more dependable than humans (rats almost never forget to show up for an experiment, for example), but also we can ask

Our taste researcher is Dr. Charles N. Stewart. Dr. Stewart holds a Ph.D. in psychology from the University of Oregon and has taught at Franklin & Marshall College since 1963. His research interests are in the senses of taste and smell and in the physiology that underlies behavior, especially the effects of nutritional deficiency on salt preference and the processes related to taste preferences in humans. He is currently involved in research on the chemistry of the sweet taste, collaborating with a colleague in the chemistry department. Dr. Stewart publishes his research in journals such as *Chemical Senses*. His coauthors are often undergraduate students, as well as colleagues from Franklin & Marshall or the Monnell Chemical Sciences Center.

them to taste and smell substances that might be distasteful or injurious to humans. Using animals, taste researchers have discovered some facts about the chemical senses that, while they may not all apply to humans, are interesting and possibly useful because they illuminate the basic processes of taste that seem to be shared by humans and other animals.

Lest you think that such an unusual phenomenon as conditioned taste aversion in the animal world has no interest to you, consider the fate of the California condor. Their numbers reduced to the point of near extinction, condors now exist only in breeding programs in zoos. What killed them? It was the pesticide DDT, which was in wide use until banned a few years ago. The DDT entered the condor's food chain from agricultural spraying and weakened the shells of the condor eggs so badly that the parents' weight crushed them and few hatched. The result? The condors are extinct in the wild. If only they could have been given a conditioned taste aversion, they would have avoided anything containing DDT. A number of researchers are currently investigating the taste preferences and aversions of a large number of species. One of their goals is to develop pesticide flavors that are specific to the target species and that will be avoided by the animals that are not targeted. Dr. Stewart's research in taste is closely related to this pesticide research.

Saccharin is a common sweetener in many dietetic beverages. It is used because it tastes sweet and has many fewer calories than does sugar. Rats and humans both seem to like its taste, at least in moderation. Given a choice between plain water and water containing saccharin, rats will prefer the saccharin-water.

Chemically, saccharin and sugar are quite different, yet they both taste sweet. An important question for a taste researcher to ask is whether sugar and saccharin seem behaviorally the same. One way to find out would be to present a choice between sugar-water and saccharin-water and observe how much of each solution the animals drank in a test period. If the rats chose them in roughly the same proportions, then we would conclude that the two sweet substances were the same behaviorally. (And in fact they are, at least for reasonable concentrations.)

Another indication of behavioral similarity might make use of conditioned taste aversion. If sugar and saccharin are behaviorally the same, then a conditioned taste aversion to one of them should lead animals to avoid the other. In other words, suppose we were to induce a conditioned taste aversion to saccharin. We know that animals with such an aversion will avoid saccharin in the future.

But will they also avoid sugar-water? If they do, then the aversion to saccharin has generalized to sugar, another sweet taste, indicating that the two are behaviorally the same for the animals. To verify that only the sweet taste has generalized, we might present some other taste substances as well. If the consumption of, say, a salty tasting solution doesn't change after the aversion training, then we know that the aversion to saccharin hasn't generalized to salt. One of Dr. Stewart's experiments investigated just those questions.

Twenty laboratory rats were used in the experiment. Dr. Stewart randomly divided his animals into two groups of 10 rats each. In one group, which we can call the *experimental group*, the animals were given saccharin-water and then administered lithium chloride to induce a conditioned taste aversion. The other group, the *control group*, was given plain water, followed by lithium chloride. After recovery, all animals were offered four taste solutions: sugar, salt, quinine (bitter), and hydrochloric acid (sour). The overall plan of the experiment is illustrated in Figure 1.1. If the rats treat sugar and saccharin behaviorally the same, the conditioned taste aversion to a sweet taste in the experimental group should lead to less consumption of sugar and to no change in the consumption of the other solutions. Did it?

In a 15-minute test period, Dr. Stewart measured the amount of each taste solution consumed (in milliliters). On the average, the experimental group drank 4.05 milliliters of sugar water, while the control animals drank 20.35 milliliters. On the basis of those values, and ignoring for the moment the other three taste solutions, it certainly looks like the taste aversion generalized to sugar. We can probably conclude that, by this test, saccharin and sugar are behaviorally the

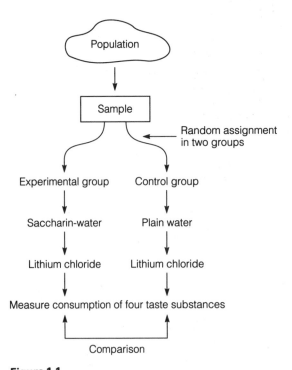

Figure 1.1

same. We can't be absolutely certain, since the results could be due just to chance and a second experiment might not confirm this finding; but the difference between 4 and 20 milliliters certainly suggests that the animals have avoided the sweet taste of sugar.

How about the effect of the aversion training on the other three taste substances? The average amounts consumed for all four of the taste solutions follow.

Condition	Sugar	Salt	Sour	Bitter
Experimental	4.05	19.70	10.20	9.00
Control	20.35	19.80	8.75	5.55

Graphically, the results are striking (see Figure 1.2). There are practically no differences between the two groups of animals, *except* for their consumption of sugar. Slight variations exist between the groups in their consumption of the sour and the bitter solutions, but these are nothing like the magnitude of the variation for sugar. Our conclusion, without further analysis at least, is that the sweet taste of saccharin generalizes to sugar. The aversion conditioning may have slightly increased the consumption of sour and bitter, but a conclusion concerning that question can wait for a later analysis.

This example illustrates several features of the scientific method. We began with a question—are the tastes of saccharin and sugar behaviorally the same for rats? Dr. Stewart devised a method for answering the question, collected data, looked at the data, and then drew a conclusion.

More is involved in the research. The question about the similarity of the tastes of sugar and saccharin didn't arise in a vacuum. It fits into a broader context of the research area that Dr. Stewart studies. Establishing the equivalence of two taste substances may not appear earthshaking, and perhaps it's not all by itself. But suppose that Dr. Stewart were searching for a way to teach California condors to avoid DDT. He might proceed the same way, this time looking for a harmless substance that tasted like DDT. He could use the same taste aversion

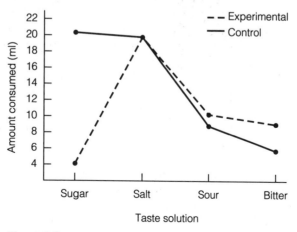

Figure 1.2

procedure we've described; but in the larger context, the methodology seems more important and useful.

In addition to illustrating a context for research, our example shows the empirical nature of science. As scientists, psychologists seek evidence in data collected in experimental situations to provide support for their theories about the nature of behavior. In this case, rather than speculate on the possible similarity or simply assume that sugar and saccharin should be behaviorally the same, Dr. Stewart looked for the evidence.

Finally, our example illustrated a well-conducted experiment and the handling of data. We didn't describe the research in detail, but a great deal of care went into it. The situation where the data were collected was carefully controlled to avoid the disturbing influences of outside factors. The amounts and administration of the saccharin and the lithium chloride were controlled and followed standard laboratory practices. The concentrations of the taste solutions were appropriate for the animals and for the question being asked. (This is an important point in this research—at too high a concentration, saccharin tastes bitter.) The measurement of the amount consumed was made properly and the data were analyzed appropriately, allowing an inference to be drawn about the behavior of the rats. In our study of research design and statistics, all of these matters are of concern.

This book focuses on the procedures for doing research. We discuss the proper techniques for measuring behavior, for describing results of that measurement, and for making inferences. We're not particularly interested in exactly how Dr. Stewart's 20 (long-since-dead) animals behaved; what is of interest is the phenomenon of behavioral similarity in the tastes of sugar and saccharin. We expect that rats in general, and perhaps even humans (since our sensory systems are so similar), will show the same taste equivalences as those demonstrated by Stewart's animals. We expect that, if we repeated the experiment, we would obtain essentially the same results, indicating that sugar and saccharin are similar in taste. In other words, we want to be able to generalize beyond the data and draw more general conclusions.

Our major aim throughout this book is to show how research questions lead to research projects, how research projects lead to data, and how proper handling of data allows conclusions to be drawn, thereby answering the initial question posed by the investigator. The focus always is, or should be, on asking and answering questions and on advancing knowledge. Unfortunately, that focus frequently gets lost for students in the welter of detail that necessarily accompanies actual research. Many factors must be considered in designing research studies, in collecting the data, and in conducting the analysis and making the inferences. Some of that detail can be reduced by letting a computer do a lot of the arithmetic; even so, the researcher has much work to do. And that's why this book is as long as it is.

The Nature of Science

Many scientists and philosophers have written about the scientific method, and we won't spend a great deal of time on the matter here except to provide a framework. Most working scientists don't really think much about what they're doing on a philosophical level; but as a foundation for understanding the nature of the scientific enterprise, a brief overview of some of psychology's scientific underpinnings is helpful.

Ways of Knowing   Philosophers tell us that science is one of several ways in which we may gain knowledge. Kerlinger (1986), summarizing considerable philosophical thought, suggests that the most commonly cited methods of gaining knowledge are tenacity, intuition, authority, and science. Let's look at them briefly.

In the *method of tenacity*, we believe or know something because we have always believed it and hold tightly to it. Tenacity is actually more a method of holding a belief than a method of gaining new knowledge, but nonetheless it is a way in which we define our knowledge. You may have seen the novelty sign reading

> **My mind's made up.**
> **Don't confuse**
> **me with facts.**

That's the method of tenacity.

In the *method of intuition* we develop or hold to a belief because it seems intuitively reasonable and correct. If you've never paid much attention to some problem, then intuition will most likely be one of the primary ways in which you form initial ideas. Probably many of our attitudes and beliefs have been developed by the method of intuition.

The *method of authority* holds that we develop knowledge by accepting information as the truth because a respected authority says it is so. Common authority figures in all of our lives include parents, religious leaders, and teachers. A great deal of our knowledge must necessarily be acquired in this way. Otherwise each of us would have to rediscover everything, and surely we don't have time enough in our lives to do that. Parents, teachers, professors, and even textbook authors attempt to communicate knowledge by establishing themselves as respected authorities. Students are expected to learn from them because of authority. (But note that one oft-stated goal of higher education is to foster independent learning, the questioning of authority. There's no real conflict here, for mature adults should recognize how they are gaining knowledge and question whether or not that method seems best for the material at hand.)

In the *method of science*, truth is found by external reference; that is, empirically. Truth, in the scientific sense, is available externally to the observer. It is not established by the application of some internal standard or logic, but by an appeal to external data. Thus scientific truth is established in such a way that all people can find the same truth in the same way. In other words, the methods of science are public and are thus repeatable by others; we'll return to these points shortly. Philosophers rarely place value judgments on their conclusions, and we won't either. Any or all of the ways of knowing are of value, and which one we use at any particular time is determined by a large number of factors. But since this is a book on the scientific method, we will expand on its features to the exclusion of the other ways in which we may gain and hold knowledge.

The Scientific Approach	No single way of gaining knowledge can properly be called *the* scientific method. Instead, there is a collection of methods and approaches that, when taken together, could be used to define the scientific approach to gaining knowledge. While there may be as many different lists of the distinguishing features of science as there are philosophers of science, several characteristics appear in nearly every definition. First, all definitions agree that there is actually a "world" to be understood. That is, the external world actually exists and is not a creation of our own minds, as some philosophical schools of thought hold. Second, laws in that external world explain the events that take place there. That is, behavior does not occur randomly but occurs for distinct reasons, and those reasons may be discovered. Third, the means for finding the explanatory laws in the world is empirical—meaning through our senses. Together, these three assumptions underlie and provide the reason for the methods that science uses. Let's look briefly at some major features of "the scientific method" and see how they are related to these three assumptions.

Science Is Empirical. To say that the scientific approach is distinguished by being *empirical* means that it looks for answers to questions by collecting data. Indeed, it is empiricism that most clearly distinguishes between science and all other methods. In science, the appeal is not to authority or to intuition but to the external reality provided in the actual world. The empirical nature of science stems directly from the third assumption that scientists share—that the route to understanding the laws of the external world is through the appeal to direct sensory knowledge.

Science Is Repeatable and Public. Science shares its knowledge. Since the world that we seek to understand is "out there," so too is our knowledge of it. By sharing knowledge of the external world, scientists can build upon previous findings. For a scientific fact to have permanent standing in the literature of the discipline, it must be capable of being replicated. The assumption of a single external "real world" isn't compatible with research results that are limited to one person or to one research laboratory. For truth to be scientifically acceptable, it must be established in such a way that someone else can follow the same methods and arrive at the same view of the world. Thus an important aspect of keeping science public is making certain that research methods are available for everyone so that others may have the information necessary to replicate research findings.

An example of the need to replicate important findings in other laboratories made world news while this book was being written. Two Utah scientists announced that they had achieved the long-sought goal of a sustained nuclear fusion reaction at room temperature and had done so with comparatively simple apparatus. That announcement set off a worldwide flurry of attempts to replicate the Utah experiment. The process of replication was made difficult because the original investigators had not used the normal means of publicizing and describing their results, and so other scientists had a great deal of trouble obtaining the necessary details of the project. Books, monographs, and journals fulfill any discipline's requirement of keeping its methods and results public. In addition, they represent in a tangible way a discipline's knowledge as gathered by the scientific approach. An important implication of the requirement that science be public is that merely studying the methods of research, of data collection, and of analysis won't be sufficient; we'll also have to pay attention to the communication of results and written interpretations as well.*

Science Is Explanatory, Predictive, and Theoretical. Scientific knowledge is more than just the published collection of facts and data. Science integrates individual facts by developing theories that interrelate and interpret the facts. Theory building and testing follow directly from the second of the three assumptions we listed. The scientist views the world as governed by understandable laws, and theoretical explanations express those laws in words and formulas. A *theory* explains behavior by postulating an account of why the behavior occurs, usually in terms of the conditions under which the behavior happens. Since theory explains behavior in the world, an obvious test of theory is to let it predict behavior in a situation other than the setting where the theory was developed. If a theory adequately predicts behavior, then that theory is strengthened. Theories that have stood repeated tests and that subsume and organize numerous facts become a part of science's understanding of the laws of the external world.

The Nature of Theory in Psychology	By one definition, "A theory is a set of interrelated constructs (concepts), definitions, and propositions that present a systematic view of phenomena by specifying relations among variables, with the purpose of explaining and predicting the phenomena" (Kerlinger, 1986, p. 9). This definition, from a respected author in psychology, would satisfy most psychologists. The definition has several components that need elaboration if we are to understand the nature of psychological theory.

Theories Subsume and Organize Facts. Theories may be judged on their ability to subsume facts. A theory that claims to explain some behavioral phenomenon should be able to account for all of the facts about that behavior. For example, many theories of learning propose that all learning occurs over a series of experiences and that it decays over time. Conditioned taste aversion, though, has caused difficulty for such theories; taste aversions are typically learned in a single exposure and often last a lifetime. Any theory of learning, then, must be

---

*We might note that all sciences have a literature that may not meet all of the requirements of the scientific method. Psychology, in particular, lends itself to nonscientific writing that often masquerades as science. Is that "pop-psych" theorist that you particularly like really writing as a scientist? Or was his or her "knowledge" and world understanding acquired by some other means, such as faith or intuition? The skeptical reader will frequently question how knowledge was acquired and will demand empirical justification before accepting conclusions as scientific fact.

able to account for both typical learning over time and sudden learning phenomena like conditioned taste aversion.

Theory plays an important organizing role in a scientific discipline. It provides the logical structure that helps to make sense of facts. A general theory of the functioning of taste receptors, for example, will provide a framework that interrelates many facts about the behavior of humans and animals. It will deal not only with facts about the similarity of the taste of sugar and saccharin, but also with facts about conditioned taste aversions, the similar tastes of chemically dissimilar substances, and the interrelations between taste and smell. By describing the relationships among empirical observations, a theory can attempt to explain how the processes under consideration operate.

Theories Are Descriptive. Theories offer concise descriptions of processes and data. By describing situations and behaviors, they perform their role of organizing facts into coherent patterns. Several chapters of this book are related to descriptive statistical procedures. The aim of those descriptions will be to simplify and summarize individual data values so that patterns emerge more clearly. Theory serves the same role in describing and simplifying many possibly diverse facts into an organized whole.

Kerlinger's definition says that the purpose of theory is both explanation in the sense of summarizing relationships and facts *and* prediction. Prediction is a necessary consequence of the ability to explain; if you can explain, you can probably also predict. Just as a physicist can explain the effects of temperature change on water, he can predict that if water is cooled to a certain temperature, it will freeze. Similarly, a psychologist might predict that if a rat is given lithium chloride after drinking a saccharin solution, the rat will avoid sweet substances in the future.

Theories Are Testable. The ability of a theory to predict gives investigators the ability to test a theory. A theory should fit with the facts that it attempts to explain and also should generate testable predictions. Theories that don't generate testable predictions generally do not last long in the scientific community, regardless of how otherwise appealing they might be. For example, Freud's theories concerning the structure of personality may explain and subsume a great many facts, but do not readily generate testable predictions and therefore are not held in high regard by the scientific community.

Variables in Theory. Within certain limits, if you make a laboratory rat hungry, it will learn faster. That is, if you vary the number of hours of food deprivation for a group of animals, you'll find that those with the longer deprivation (within limits of starvation, naturally) learn a new task in fewer trials. In other words, there is a relationship between the variables "hours of food deprivation" and "trials to learn."

Theories usually state their predictions and explanations in terms of variables. The concept of a variable and definition and measurement of variables are sufficiently important that we devote Chapters 3 and 4 to them. For now, we'll note that there are observable (sometimes called *overt*) variables and nonobservable (*latent* or *intervening*) variables. Observable variables are those that can be measured and manipulated, such as weight, running time, number of words recalled, hours since the last feeding, and so on. Intervening variables are employed in theory, often as explanatory concepts or mechanisms that connect two observable variables.

Learning provides an excellent example of both kinds of variables. As an organism learns, there is presumably some change in the underlying neural organization and/or chemistry. We can't observe those changes directly (indeed, we don't even know just where to look for them), but we can theorize about them. Such theoretical explanations involve intervening variables and processes that link together observable variables. For example, if we manipulate the overt variable of hunger, we will find that the overt variable of "trials to learn" changes. A theory of learning will have to relate the facts about those two variables. To do so, it will probably make use of some hypothetical intervening variable, perhaps concerning internal "drive states" and how they relate to physiological states in the animal that can't be directly observed.

Theory provides the foundation of any science, and psychology is no exception. Psychology's theories are typically limited in scope and do not attempt to explain all aspects of the behavior of animals or humans. As we proceed, we'll find several small theories, having to do with limited areas of behavior such as taste phenomena, infant perception, and a few personality traits. What is important to keep in mind as we proceed is that theory underlies research. The real reason why psychologists do research and learn about experimental design and statistics is to enhance their understanding of the behavior of organisms. That understanding—the explanation and prediction of behavior—is contained within the discipline's theories. And those theories are our best understanding of the laws that govern the universe of behavior.

Statistics and Research Design in Psychology

Research in any science represents a blending of theory and data collection. Research typically proceeds from theory, often to test predictions or to explore the consequences of a new theoretical explanation. Very often, the underlying question in research is something like "If my understanding of the situation is correct, then I expect certain things to be the case. Am I correct?" For example, if our theoretical understanding of the mechanism of taste leads us to believe that sugar and saccharin are behaviorally the same, then the question is "Are they really the same?"

In other words, research typically asks a question, and the answer to the question helps us to understand the situation better. Descriptive statistics help us to see the answer in the data, while research design helps us to ask the right question. If a set of data does not conform to predictions, there can be only two possible explanations—either the theory is incorrect, or the data are erroneous. One of the roles of research design is to ensure that data are collected so that the latter explanation is not likely to be the case.

Research Design   Proper research design involves defining a situation so that it "asks the right question." By this we mean that if the theory suggests a certain relationship between variables, the research setting must let us manipulate and measure those variables clearly and unambiguously. In Dr. Stewart's taste aversion study, for example, the question posed is whether the aversion established to the taste of saccharin will generalize to sugar. (More broadly, we are interested in whether sugar and saccharin are the same insofar as the animal's behavior is concerned.) Dr. Stewart chose a particular experimental procedure to investigate his question. He selected what we will come to know as a two-condition experimental design because it was the most appropriate setting to address the question. He could have used just one group of animals and measured their consumption of saccharin before and after a lithium dosage, but that wouldn't really have answered the question as precisely. In particular, if just one group had been used, how would Dr. Stewart know if it was just the lithium or the pairing of lithium with saccharin that changed the consumption? Perhaps the lithium administration merely led to less overall consumption. He needed the control group and other substances to establish that it was the lithium-saccharin combination that led to the reduction of consumption in only the "sweet" condition.

Not all research questions are best addressed by a two-condition experiment like the one that Dr. Stewart used. In some cases, a single group of observations is best, while multiple groups are best in other circumstances. Part Three of this book is organized around different forms of experimental design. For each design, we take special note of the kinds of questions it can address and of what kinds of analyses are and are not appropriate for the design and research questions.

Statistics in Research

Regardless of the experimental design and questions, research involves measuring and interpreting variables. In an experiment, we manipulate one or more variables, measure at least one other, and control all the rest. Research design is concerned primarily with establishing rules for manipulation and control of variables, while the discipline of statistics is concerned with measurement and interpretation of variables. More specifically, statistics serve three purposes in research: description, inference, and communication.

Description. Descriptive statistics make the results of a research investigation understandable. It's usually very difficult to draw any conclusions from a mass of raw numbers. Statistics offer ways to condense raw data so that their important features stand out clearly. Without descriptive statistics, we would have to rely on hunches and "impressions" derived from an inefficient inspection of the data.

Inference. We're rarely interested in only the particular set of data that comes from a single research project. Rather, we hope that the results of one project will apply to other similar situations and groups of subjects. The particular group of observations in a research project is a *sample* of the potentially much larger group of observations that we didn't observe. The data from Dr. Stewart's 20 animals constitute a sample from all of the possible sets of such data that might ever be available—a very large set of observations. The large set of observations is called the *population*, and it's normally the real interest in research.

The population in Dr. Stewart's experiment is the performance of *all* rats, past, present, and future, in such a taste preference situation. Obviously, we can't hope to ever be able to determine the performance of that population by actual test. But the population of all rats is the important population. We don't want the results limited only to the 20 animals in the experiment; we want the results to hold *in general*. Drawing these kinds of conclusions makes use of inferential statistical methods. The inferential methods, which we will begin to introduce in Chapter 11, allow us to make estimates of *parameters* (characteristics of populations) on the basis of sample *statistics* (characteristics of samples). Without introducing any of the logic, you can already make a guess about some parameters. From the table on page 7, we can see that the average amount of sweet solution consumed by the control group animals in 15 minutes is 20.35 ml. That value is a statistic, since it is based on a sample of subjects. It is also our best guess as to how much any other group of rats treated the same way would drink in the same situation. Our estimate of the parameter is thus 20.35 ml, and we have just made a simple inference. Inferential statistics are normally more complex than our example, but their aim is the same—using a sample statistic to make some statement about the probable value of a population parameter.

Not only will we want to be able to make inferences about the behavior of people and animals that we haven't seen, but we will also want to predict behavior in situations other than those tested. This ability to *generalize* or go beyond the specific situation is important in science, since it makes development of general theoretical statements possible.

Inference fills an important role in science—it gives us a way to have confidence in the conclusion that we draw from a sample. Since science tries to understand the laws that govern the external world and since we want those laws to be as broadly applicable as possible, we don't want the results of a single experiment to be limited to only the participants in a single project. The methods of inferential statistics provide us with a means of generalizing the results beyond the particular sample.

Communication. Finally, we'll use both descriptive and inferential statistics in communications with others. The literature of psychology is filled with research results (and the theory derived from it, of course). Those results are communicated by descriptive and inferential statistics. The figures, tables, and other data presentations in the literature are intended to communicate with other scholars. Thus statistics are invaluable to the public nature of science and its discoveries. Along with the written word, they communicate the findings of research.

A Note of Caution

The study of statistics and research design suffers from at least two difficulties. First, students normally dread the course and the material, fearing that it will be difficult, mathematical, and/or boring. And second, the real nature of the material is often obscured by details. Neither of these common problems needs be the case.

While mathematics certainly provides the foundation for the statistical methods that we'll study, the presentation here will not be mathematical. Students who go into a stupor at the first mathematical symbol (like a simple Σ, for example) can be assured that, while symbols will be unavoidable, there is nothing difficult about them. Understanding sentences containing Greek letters and formulas is not hard, but reading the material will take longer than if it were ordinary prose. This book is written in simple English sentences, and even symbols and formulas can be read as a part of a sentence. Consider the following sentence: "Most students know that the formula for the arithmetic mean,

$$\frac{\Sigma X}{N},$$

says to add up all of the values and divide by the number of values added." Note the comma following the formula: it suggests that the full sentence should be read as "Most students know that the formula for the arithmetic mean, 'sigma X over N,' says to add up all of the values and divide by the number of values summed." Formulas in this book are usually presented in just this way and invite being read as a part of a sentence. Don't skip over the symbols; they're a part of the sentence, and the sentence usually explains the symbol.* In addition, your instructor may assume that you'll have a computer do most computation. If that's the case, much of the arithmetic part of mathematics is no longer to be dreaded.

By and large, the material in this book isn't inherently difficult. It will be unfamiliar, but then so is the content of any new subject area. You will be forced to think about the logic of question asking and answering carefully, and you will be expected to think and write clearly and critically; but again, that's not difficult.

The material may appear boring at times. At least in part, that's because of the second problem (losing track of what's important). But it's also due in part to the nature of the book and the course. Most of the "interesting stuff" in psychology is not to be found in the "stat and design" course but in the content courses (learning, personality, motivation, cognition, etc.). The "stat course" is normally moderately content-free, because it tries to teach methods that are relevant to many subfields of the discipline. This book will be content-light, too, and for the same reason. But we will follow several different research areas as examples. We have already introduced Dr. Stewart's research area of taste, and others will appear soon. In addition, you should begin developing your own research interests. If you have some special interest within psychology, start becoming familiar with the area in more detail by learning about the resources at your library. As new topics are introduced in the book, try to apply them to your own area by developing your own research proposals or by looking for published studies that use the technique. In short, getting involved with research of your own, as you progress through this material, will greatly aid your understanding of statistics and design.

The second difficulty with statistical and design material is that we may easily lose track of what's really important under a mass of detail. There are so many ways of summarizing data, for example, that it might be easy to forget that we're really interested in whether or not taste avoidance generalizes to similar

---

*I normally tell my students on the first class day that they will have to memorize four formulas during the semester and that they already know one (the mean). The others are the standard deviation, the z score, and the standard error of the mean. Your instructor will, of course, have his or her own rules about memorizing formulas.

substances. That is a constant problem in studying this material. We will try to fight that difficulty by putting the techniques in the context of actual research to show how research questions arise, how they are addressed by the research methods, and how the statistical methods allow conclusions to be drawn.

Some Recurring Themes

While it may not always be obvious, the underlying theme of this book is science. We have already pointed out that science is empirical, and this book addresses the methods of empiricism in psychology quite directly. As we've also just noted, though, our presentation of empirical methods will be quite general. Don't expect any thorough presentation of methods appropriate to visual depth perception or to surgical manipulation of the adrenal gland; that level of detail is appropriate to more advanced, content-oriented courses. What we will cover, though, are general research strategies and methods. But we'll be addressing the empirical method, and that's a fundamental part of science.

We noted that science is systematic and theoretical. Again, because of the "methods" nature of the material, our coverage of the theory underlying research will be somewhat superficial. But we'll always include enough context so that our example results will be meaningful, and we will illustrate the in-context interpretation of statistical data. The chapter exercises encourage verbal interpretation of results, since numbers alone don't provide a satisfactory answer to an empirical question.

A second recurring theme will be science as an exploratory endeavor. Research design provides a framework in which empirical exploration can take place. Statistical methods provide the tools to aid in exploration. The attitude taken here is that there isn't usually one "correct" technique for a given set of data, and we will emphasize using any tools available to extract the maximum meaning from a set of results.

A final theme of the book is communication. Science is a public enterprise, and communication is an important element of it. Students are sometimes surprised to learn that they are expected to interpret (in complete sentences!) the results of a data-analysis problem. But that shouldn't be a surprise. The numeric solution to a problem is rarely the most important thing; rather, it's the words that interpret the solution that communicate best.

A Note on Exercises

Exercises are scattered throughout this book. Do take the time to work them. As with most subjects, mastering the skills in this book requires practice. Your instructor will probably assign certain exercises for you to complete or will provide you with other problem sets. Do *all* of the problems provided, those in the book and those given by your instructor.

Every statistics and methods instructor has stories of the students who claimed that they had mastered the material by reading, only to find that they couldn't apply their "knowledge" on an exam or when confronted with "real" data. The computational exercises are intended to give you practice in the skills needed to analyze and describe the results of an investigation. By working the exercises, you'll derive maximum benefit from them. The solutions to roughly half of the exercises appear in the back of the book.

You'll notice that many of the computational questions ask you to summarize the conclusions in words as well as in numbers. This reflects my belief that if you can't state the results of a research project or a data analysis in words, then perhaps you haven't understood either the question being asked in the research or the answer provided by the data.

SUMMARY

- The aim of research is to ask and answer questions and thereby advance knowledge.
- "Science" assumes that there is a "world" to be understood, that the world is governed by certain laws, and that the empirical method is the means by which we learn the nature of those laws.
- Science is explanatory, predictive, and theoretical; its data are repeatable and public.
- A *theory* postulates an explanatory principle by attempting to explain the circumstances under which a behavior occurs.
- A successful *theory* organizes and subsumes facts, describes the process underlying behavior, and is testable.
- If a theory has withstood repeated tests, it may become a part of our understanding of the laws of the behavioral world.
- *Descriptive statistics* summarize data and may help us to see an answer in research results.
- *Inferential statistics* let us generalize beyond a particular set of data.
- Both descriptive and inferential statistics are used to communicate the results of a research study.
- Research design defines a situation in which a question is asked.
- An experiment manipulates one or more variables, measures at least one variable, and controls other variables.
- A *population* is a large set of observations; a *sample* is a small set of observations taken from a population.
- A *parameter* is a characteristic of a population; a *statistic* is a characteristic of a sample.
- The best (indeed, the only) way to learn the material in this book is to do the exercises faithfully.

KEY TERMS

Descriptive statistics	**Method of tenacity**
Empirical	**Observable (overt) variables**
Generalization	**Parameter**
Inferential statistics	**Population**
Latent (intervening) variables	**Sample**
Method of authority	**Statistic**
Method of intuition	**Theory**
Method of science	

CHAPTER 2

Research Strategies

Most of current personality theory centers on the identification and measurement of specific personality traits. A trait is a measurable dimension, like heat or weight in the physical world, along which individuals may differ. Identifying traits or dimensions is often done using a powerful statistical technique called factor analysis. The final result of such an analysis is a personality test or scale that measures the dimension of interest. The following items illustrate typical questions on such a test. These are drawn from a common personality scale (Zuckerman, Eysenck, & Eysenck, 1978):

- I often wish I could be a mountain climber.
- I would like to go scuba diving.
- I like to have new and exciting experiences and sensations even if they are a little unconventional or illegal.
- I like to try out new foods that I have never tasted before.

By following the scoring rules that accompany the personality scale, the researcher can obtain the value for the person being tested on the personality dimension (or dimensions) measured.

In his research, Dr. Campbell focuses on a personality trait called introversion/extraversion. People who score toward one end of the scale (the introversion end) tend to be reserved and cautious, emotionally controlled, and not sociable. Those individuals who score at the other end, on the contrary, tend to be daring and expressive. active, and very sociable. Notice that the scale is not either-or, but allows a person to be placed anywhere along a continuum from extreme introversion to extreme extraversion.

There are several theoretical treatments of introversion/extraversion. One theory suggests that individuals who score toward the introversion end of the scale derive a great deal of stimulation internally and thus need not be particularly outgoing in seeking stimulation. On the other hand, according to this

Dr. John B. Campbell holds a Ph.D. from the University of Michigan and an undergraduate degree from the College of Wooster. He is interested in personality theory and measurement, with a particular focus on the introversion/extraversion dimension hypothesized by Eysenck and his coworkers. Dr. Campbell often works with student colleagues; his work has been published in the *Journal of Research in Personality* and in *Personality and Individual Differences*.

theory, extraverts should tend to seek outside stimulation. This theoretical position leads to the prediction that, if we were to measure both introversion/ extraversion and "experience seeking," introverts should score low on "experience seeking" while extraverts should score high. Dr. Campbell and others have carried out exactly that research study. He obtained a group of college students to serve as his subjects and gave them a personality scale that measured introversion/extraversion and another that measured experience seeking. To measure introversion/extraversion, Dr. Campbell used the Eysenck Personality Inventory (Eysenck & Eysenck, 1968); for his measure of experience seeking, he chose the total score on Zuckerman's Sensation Seeking Scale (Version 5) (Zuckerman et al., 1978). By plotting the two sets of values as shown in Figure 2.1, Dr. Campbell could visualize the relationship between the two variables.

In the illustration, each point represents one of Dr. Campbell's subjects, so that the lowest (left-most) point indicates a person who scored 2 on the introversion/extraversion scale, and about 9 on the sensation-seeking scale. In general, the illustration shows that, as predicted, people toward the introversion end of the introversion/extraversion scale tend to have lower values on the sensation-seeking scale, while the opposite is true of of individuals scoring toward the extraversion end of the scale. (See Figure 2.2.)

In Chapter 9 we'll learn more about constructing illustrations like that in

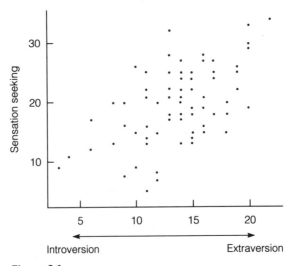

Figure 2.1

Figure 2.1 (it's called a scatterplot) and about a precise numeric measure of the relationship between two variables (it's the Pearson *r*). For now, it's sufficient for us to conclude that the illustration shows that the relationship between the two variables is what we expected from the theoretical interpretation of a relationship between introversion/extraversion and sensation seeking.

Dr. Campbell's personality research is quite different from Dr. Stewart's investigations in conditioned taste aversion (described in Chapter 1). Their experimental subjects are from different species, their theoretical interests are quite different, and certainly their actual laboratory procedures were different. But what do they have in common? Both follow the scientific method, for both have interests in the theoretical *and* empirical aspects of behavior. Each is interested in understanding certain features of the behavior of their chosen organisms. They take a theoretical approach and follow it with empirical data collection. Both followed the characteristic steps in scientific research. Dr. Stewart began his research with a theoretical question in taste; Dr. Campbell began with a theoretical question in personality theory. In both cases, theory suggested certain consequences that could be tested in research. They next decided upon a research strategy, selected subjects, measured the appropriate variable or variables, and finally were able to draw conclusions about the adequacy of their theoretical understanding of behavior.

These two researchers illustrate the nature of scientific activity. A theory, a hunch, or simply curiosity led to collection and then into interpretation of data. The goal of the interpretation and explanation was to better understand and explain the behavior of interest. That is, the interpretation was cast in theoretical terms—do the results confirm the initial understanding, disconfirm it, or perhaps invite an expanded theory?

Of course, real research is never quite as simple as we've just made it appear in the two research descriptions, but the basic scheme of science that they illustrate is correct.

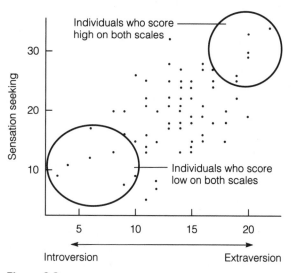

Figure 2.2

You may have noticed that there is a fundamental difference between Dr. Campbell's research strategy and the way that Dr. Stewart proceeded. Both were interested in exploring the relationship between two variables—introversion/extraversion and sensation seeking for Dr. Campbell, and taste aversion and taste consumption for Dr. Stewart. But Dr. Stewart *manipulated* a variable, and Dr. Campbell didn't. Dr. Stewart did something to his experimental subjects, but Dr. Campbell simply measured personality traits that already existed in his subjects. These approaches to research illustrate two of the several ways that a psychologist can proceed in doing research.

Research Strategies

Dr. Stewart and Dr. Campbell both investigated questions dealing with the relationship between two things—personality scales in one case, and a manipulated aversion variable and liquid consumption in the other. In each case, something was being measured. Something that is measured is known as a variable—it can take on various values. The variable or variables that are measured are normally called *dependent* variables. Descriptive and inferential statistics normally deal with the values of dependent variables. That is, we usually summarize the dependent variable and make inferences about its probable values in other situations.

In an experiment, but not in some other forms of research, we also use at least one *independent* variable. An independent variable is controlled by the experimenter to see how changing it causes a change in the dependent variable. (Most instructors advise using the memory trick phrase "The dependent variable depends on the independent variable" as an aid in remembering which variable is which.) In Dr. Stewart's research, the independent variable was taste aversion—some of the animals were given the aversion while others were not. Dr. Stewart's dependent variable was the amount of each taste solution consumed. The presence of an independent variable—the variable that is manipulated by the researcher—is one of the defining characteristics of an experiment and sets that research strategy apart from the others.

In designing experiments, researchers also need to identify variables that might confuse interpretation of their results. In Dr. Stewart's research, for example, the sex of the animals might have an effect on how they respond to the taste aversion conditioning. In order not to complicate his results with a possible sex effect, he might decide to test only female (or male) animals, or he might make sure that he had equal numbers of males and females in each of his two groups. The variable of sex in Dr. Stewart's research is neither an independent variable nor a dependent variable. Instead, it is an example of a large category of variables that can pose problems for a researcher. Any variable that is neither independent nor dependent is called an *extraneous* variable. These variables, which may (or may not) have an impact on the outcome of the research, either are left to vary or are controlled somehow within the research plan. Sex is an extraneous variable in Dr. Stewart's research; he might choose to ignore its possible effects, or he might deal with it in one of the two ways just suggested.

Sex of the subjects can also be an important variable for Dr. Campbell. But he is likely to deal with it in a different way. Dr. Campbell would probably treat it as another dependent variable and look at its relationship to his measure of introversion/extraversion and sensation seeking.

The difference between how Dr. Stewart and Dr. Campbell would handle the extraneous variable of sex indicates yet another difference between their overall approaches to research. In fact, the way a research strategy deals with extraneous variables is a key feature that distinguishes one research method from another.

Having introduced the three important kinds of variables (independent, dependent, and extraneous), let's look now at the kinds of research plans used by psychologists in seeking answers to research questions. The strategies fall into three broad groups that may be differentiated by their treatment of independent and extraneous variables. There are several different kinds of *observational methods*. They don't have an independent variable and usually involve numerous dependent variables. They're primarily descriptive in the answers that they can provide. *Correlational methods* are useful in investigating questions about the relationships among dependent variables or in developing procedures for predicting one variable when you know the value of another variable. Like the observational methods, correlational methods have no independent variable. Finally, the *experiment* is the most powerful of the techniques and also the most restrictive; it is the only research method that permits inference about cause and effect. An experiment is marked by having at least one independent variable and typically one dependent variable.

The Experiment

Dr. Stewart's research is an example of an experiment. In an experiment, the investigator manipulates one or more independent variables. In Dr. Stewart's case, he manipulated the taste aversion independent variable by giving one group the conditioning while the other group did not receive it. In addition, the research situation in an experiment is controlled very tightly to eliminate or minimize the effect of extraneous variables. Dr. Stewart, for example, used male and female animals in each group to control the extraneous variable of sex. Other extraneous variables were dealt with by making sure that all of the animals were of the same genetic strain, were of roughly the same age, and were handled in the same fashion since birth.

The dependent variable, naturally, is the indicator of the effect that the independent variable has. In Dr. Stewart's case, the amount of each test solution consumed shows the effect of the taste conditioning and provides the means for drawing a conclusion about the similarity in taste between sugar and saccharin.

In the experiment, all subjects are treated alike during the experiment except, of course, for the manipulation of the independent variable. In the taste aversion example, the animals were treated just the same except for the substance given before the lithium injection. Note that the control animals—those that received plain water followed by lithium—provide a control for the extraneous variable of receiving lithium. This controls for a possible effect of lithium alone, since all animals receive it. The control animals, though, are given plain water before their injection and thus acquire a conditioned aversion to it; plain water isn't one of the test solutions. Had Dr. Stewart used a control group that did not receive an injection at all, then any difference between the groups could have been injection-caused, since you would be comparing a saccharin/injected group with a non-saccharin/non-injected group.

As we suggested earlier, the sex of the animal is an important extraneous variable in Dr. Stewart's study, as it is in most studies that involve drug effects. You certainly wouldn't want all females in the experimental group and all males in the control; if you found a difference, there would be no way to know whether it was a sex-caused difference or a treatment-caused difference. Dr. Stewart balanced the numbers of males and females in each group, thus ensuring that the sexes were equally represented in each experimental condition.

In an experiment, all variables, except for the independent variable, are controlled. The only element of the situation that is allowed to change is under control of the researcher; thus any change seen in the dependent variable must be attributable to the independent variable. The experiment, with its tight control, is the only situation in which clear inferences of cause and effect may be drawn.* The experiment is thus preferable when the question being asked is one of causality.

For all of its strengths, there are weaknesses in the experiment that prevent it from being used in all research situations. Almost by definition, the experiment requires an artificial environment; some critics argue that, especially in psychology, the situations are so unnatural that the results cannot possibly apply to any real-world behaviors. Certainly, some experimental situations are so far removed from reality that their applicability can be questioned. But the fact that real-world objects rarely fall in a complete vacuum hasn't deterred physicists from building theories based on the results of vacuum chamber experiments. In the same way, the absence of pure solutions in the real world of biochemistry has not made laboratory experiments less relevant to medicine. We'll return to this topic in Chapter 4 when we discuss the topic of external validity, the extent to which we may generalize results beyond the immediate research setting.

In addition to its possible artificiality, there are other difficulties with the experiment as a way to proceed in every research setting. Some experiments simply cannot be conducted due to practical or ethical limitations. It is considered unethical to apply any treatment to humans that will possibly cause long-term damage or distress to the individual. For example, research ethics would prohibit depriving children of an education in an effort to establish a no-education control condition.

The experiment stands as the most important of the methods of science, primarily because it is the only method that allows us to make cause-effect inferences. Since a major goal of science is to make causal inferences, the experiment will form the basis of much of the content of this book.

The Quasi-Experiment. When an independent variable is present in a research investigation but is not directly controlled by the experimenter, the procedure is often called a *quasi-experiment*. In a quasi-experiment, the independent variable

---

* Recent developments have established certain carefully prescribed procedures under which causal inferences may sometimes be based on correlational data. These techniques are well beyond the scope of this book.

is "manipulated" externally. If a group of individuals with a particular brain injury were available, they could serve as an "experimental group" in an investigation on the effects of brain injury. But they wouldn't be an "experimental group" in the same sense as if the experimenter were able to randomly assign rats to an experimental group and surgically cause brain injury. Since the subjects in the human brain injury study cannot be assigned to a group and their injury directly controlled by the experimenter, they could conceivably differ in some other unknown fashion. Thus the inferences that may be drawn in a quasi-experiment are less certain and less sound in their causal inference than in a true experiment. Chapter 22 presents quasi-experiments in some detail.

Observational Methods

Several varieties of research strategy can be categorized as observational. They differ among themselves, but all are distinguished from the experiment in not having an independent variable to be manipulated; they have only dependent variables to be measured or observed. The degree of interaction between the subjects in the study and the researcher varies in the different observational techniques, as does the amount of the structure and control in the situation.

Naturalistic Observation. In naturalistic observation, sometimes called "field study," there is little or no interaction with the subjects under study. Indeed, most naturalistic research is conducted with scrupulous care not to disturb the behavior at all. Much of the animal research reported by such workers as Mech (1987), or as depicted in the motion picture *Gorillas in the Mist*, consists of naturalistic observation. Naturalistic observation as a strategy need not be limited to work with animals in the wild. For example, both von Cranach, Foppa, Lepenies, and Ploog (1979) and Bakeman and Gottman (1986) show the application of observational techniques to human behavior.

Simple observation is often useful in the beginning stages of research work, when the investigator has very little idea of what variables might be involved. The questions best addressed by the method are often poorly formed and center on trying to identify fundamental behavior types, social patterns, and the variables that seem to be related to certain kinds of behaviors. An excellent introduction to the field may be found in Martin and Bateson (1986).

The major strength of naturalistic observation is its realism. Behavior is studied in its context, with great pains taken to avoid any actions that might change the situation. Naturalistic observation and the experiment are thus at the opposite ends of the realism-artificiality dimension, and many people find this to be a powerful argument in its behalf. But the realism is bought at a considerable cost—control. In a natural setting, the investigator cannot modify the situation, introduce new stimuli or animals, or change the physical surroundings. In short, manipulation of variables is impossible. If wolf researchers like Mech (1987) want to learn about the effect of a new wolf entering the area, they must wait, perhaps for a very long time, for a new wolf to enter the pack's territory. An experimenter could simply introduce a new animal.

The major weaknesses of the naturalistic observation research strategy are the risk of observer bias in data recording, lack of control of the research situation, and the inability to draw causal conclusions. Since naturalistic observation often begins with little or no understanding of the patterns of behavior that may be observed, a standardized measurement procedure is often difficult to establish. In the process of establishing categories of behaviors, it is very easy for the researcher to be blinded by preconceptions about what is to be expected and not be able to recognize new and unexpected behaviors.

Without the ability to manipulate variables in an observational research study, the investigator is left to explore and record only those situations that naturally present themselves. While artificially structured environments are sometimes used, this lack of control results in observation being used primarily at early stages of research. But more important, without the ability to control extraneous variables and manipulate an independent variable, naturalistic observation cannot establish cause-effect relationships.

In naturalistic observation studies data are usually collected through copious notes taken in the field and reduced to summary paragraphs and sometimes simple counts of the frequency of various behaviors.

Case Study. Case study, sometimes called the "clinical method," involves the detailed study of a single subject. Perhaps the best known example of this kind of research is the classic study of multiple personality by Thigpen and Cleckley (1957). These two clinicians describe, in detail, the case of "Eve," one of the first documented cases of multiple personality. Some of the literature in psychology consists of such studies, but little useful scientific research is conducted as case studies. The technique is especially useful in early stages of the study in an unexplored area, or in a very unusual occurrence or phenomenon. The detailed information provided by a case study will often suggest variables to be explored in more depth by using different research methods.

An interesting case study is presented by Baron-Cohen, Wyke, and Binnie (1987). They describe an individual with color-word synesthesia (that is, a word elicits a vivid color image). They report that a long-term study of the individual shows that the color associations are perfectly consistent over time—for example, "fear is mottled light grey, with a touch of soft green and purple" (p. 763). Baron-Cohen et al. relate their results with their single subject to a theory of synesthesia that suggests that such phenomena can be explained by assuming that the sensory systems are a unified perceptual system at some level in perceptual processing.

Case studies are severely limited in several respects. They clearly can suffer from the same sorts of observer bias that we mentioned for naturalistic observation. Baron-Cohen et al. (1987) used a small experiment with their subject in an attempt to avoid observer bias in their demonstration of the consistency of color associations over time. In clinical case studies, though, the risk of theoretical bias is strong, since practicing clinicians often have strong attachments to their theories.

In addition to possible observer bias, a subject bias is possible in case studies as well. The subject being studied is not likely to have been randomly selected from any larger group, and so generalization beyond the specific case at hand is risky at best. Indeed, case studies usually arise because a very unusual individual becomes available for study. In some cases, like that of Baron-Cohen et al. (1987), the concern over the bias is negligible, since synesthesia cases are rare and any individual is worthy of study alone. But in clinical case studies, it may not be clear just why an individual was selected for study. The reader is often left to judge whether or not a case was chosen for description merely because it supported a clinician's "pet" theory.

Finally, case studies do not permit making causal inferences. The investigator may be able to conclude that, for this patient, a particular therapy was successful; but since there was no control of extraneous variables and no manipulation of an independent variable, cause and effect can't be inferred. As a result, there's no way to infer that the treatment might have a like effect on another patient, no matter how similar the two might be.

A popular research strategy in some subareas of psychology appears similar to the case study, but is really different. This is the so-called "$N = 1$" study, where there is a single subject and an identifiable dependent variable. This strategy is very useful in investigating the effects of various kinds of treatments on certain behaviors.

Both $N = 1$ and case studies are considered in more detail in Chapter 22.

Self-Report. Introspection, simply observing one's own thoughts and feelings, was the earliest of the methods of psychology and certainly the one that we all use frequently. As a method for scientific inquiry, though, introspection has been out of favor for many years. Clearly, there is observer bias present, and data collected introspectively are difficult to verify independently and replicate. Since that's the case, pure introspection can't really be admitted as a scientific method. Still, a similar technique serves a valuable role in scientific investigation as a source of ideas and hunches, and as a check on whether a hypothesis seems plausible.

Recently, several studies have been published that use self-report introspective data. There is a small and growing body of literature in cognitive psychology that relies on very long term memory. Many of these studies are conducted using surveys and ask participants to recall events from their past (see, for example, Fitzgerald, 1988; and Pillemer, Goldsmith, Panter, & White, 1988). Essentially autobiographical in nature, studies like these are bringing the old technique of self-report back into the array of tools that a psychologist may use.

Surveys and Interviews. A survey is a technique for collecting information on a range of variables rather quickly by using a standard data-collection form. Kerlinger (1986) distinguishes between surveys whose goal is to assess the status quo (*status surveys*) and those whose purpose is to assess the relationships between variables (*research surveys*). Status surveys are sometimes conducted by national polling agencies such as Roper or Gallup, but they can also be conducted by local groups. In either case, their aim is to determine current attitudes and opinions. For scientific research, though, we are usually more interested in the relationships that are predicted on the basis of some theory. A survey that stems from a theoretical question is a research survey.

Some surveys combine both status and research goals, as an example of mine illustrates. Lehman (1988) polled members of the Society for Computers in Psychology about their use of computer programming languages. The aim was partly for status purposes (to document which computers and languages are actually used and for what purposes), but also to explore the relationship between formal training in programming and the use of certain programming techniques as well as to look at the reasons why certain computer languages are chosen for particular tasks. The results documented heavy use of the Basic and Pascal languages in psychology laboratories, along with a number of other languages. In addition, the results helped answer a research question about the relationship between the features of programming languages and which languages were chosen for what kinds of programs. The survey concluded that, while professional research psychologists may often know that other languages are better suited for some tasks, a language is usually chosen for convenience and not for its particular features.

A survey is a standardized observational procedure in which all respondents are confronted with the same survey document and with the same instructions, under the same general conditions. The major advantage of the survey is that it can quickly, and generally quite accurately, assess a number of variables for a large number of individuals.

A major weakness of the survey is the possibility for self-selection by the respondents. Some individuals will simply refuse to respond to requests to complete a survey. The characteristics of the nonrespondents are unknown, and they may differ in important ways from those who do respond. This problem is especially difficult with mail surveys, where the return rate is typically below 50% (it was 46% in Lehman, 1988). Sometimes it is possible to obtain some follow-up information from nonrespondents that can establish whether they differ substantially from respondents; if they don't, the results can probably be believed.

Another weakness of the survey is its ability to collect only relationship data, thus precluding causal inference. We'll encounter this same difficulty in correlational studies, which we'll discuss shortly.

An interview is best thought of as a survey that is conducted individually and face-to-face. Many interviews are just that—the interviewer has a set list of questions to ask, and the responses are typically coded into one of a group of predefined categories, just as if the respondent were given a set of multiple-choice questions. Both surveys and interviews may, naturally, include open-ended questions ("Tell me what you think of . . .") as well.

Surveys are considered in detail in Chapter 22.

Correlational Research

Correlational research studies relationships between variables. Dr. Campbell's research is correlational. He is interested in the relationship between the personality variables of introversion/extraversion and experience seeking. He is not trying to establish a causal connection between the two variables, but rather is trying to determine that there is a relationship. Such an aim is typical of correlational research. Dr. Campbell doesn't think that if he could artificially increase someone's extraversion, that person would become more stimulus-seeking (that's causality), but only that the two characteristics are related in a particular way. Dr. Campbell suspects that both introversion/extraversion and stimulus seeking are themselves caused by some underlying personality trait that he can't measure directly. But he can nevertheless gain an understanding of the personality process by observing the predicted relationship between the two variables he can measure.

Causality The history of science is filled with debate over the nature and meaning of the word *cause*. Some current opinion suggests that the concept of a "cause" for an event is a meaningless concept (see Kerlinger, 1986, p. 361 for one illustration). Whether or not they agree with that position, scientists clearly act as if they are searching for causal explanations of behavior. We have talked about causality several times in the past few pages and have pointed out that only the experiment can clearly establish a causal connection. Now let's explore the concept of causation a little more carefully.

Many philosophers and scientists would agree with Kenny (1979) that there are three requirements to be met before a causal connection between two events can be inferred:

1. Covariation
2. Temporal ordering
3. No confounding

The requirement of covariation means that two events must vary together; if there's no change in one, it can't be a cause of change in the other. For example, if the level of lighting in a room remains constant, but the ability to see a visual stimulus changes, we can't argue that illumination level is a cause of the change in vision.

Second, in order for a variable to cause a change in another, the cause must precede the effect. If a change in room illumination not only occurs, but also regularly precedes a change in visual acuity, then it could be a cause of the change in vision.

Third, there must be no variables confounded with the proposed relationship. All other possible causal variables must be ruled out. We might begin by measuring visual acuity under one set of conditions and then change conditions (an independent variable) to see what the effect is on acuity (the dependent variable). If we were to increase the room illumination, for example, and at the same time increase the size of the visual stimulus, then we have confounded two variables—size and illumination. When variables vary together in this way, they are said to be confounded. As a result of the confounding, we can't infer that *either* the change in illumination *or* the change in stimulus size causes a change in acuity. Since the two variables changed together, the effect could have been caused by either one of them or perhaps by the combination.

This third requirement for causal inference, then, requires that variables be unconfounded in order to make causal inferences about them. This last requirement gives the experiment its particular strength. But the same requirement also fuels the argument that causality is a meaningless concept. The very act of controlling the situation carefully enough to eliminate confounding may also make the situation so far removed from the real world that the results have no meaning.

The experiment, with its tight control over extraneous variables and its limitation of the variation to only the independent variable, comes closest to meeting the requirements for making a causal inference. For this reason, the experiment is the technique that lets us make causal inferences from data. At the same time, though, we must acknowledge that we can never be absolutely certain that all extraneous confounding variables have been eliminated from even the best-controlled experiment.

With that said, where are we left with respect to making inferences about cause and effect? As a practical matter, scientists continue to think about causality, even if they may secretly acknowledge that causal inference is impossible in the strictest sense. After all, scientists see prediction of behavior as a part of their

Table 2.1 Summary of Research Strategies

Technique	Features	Strengths	Weaknesses
OBSERVATIONAL METHODS			
Naturalistic	Nonintrusive and "natural"	Realistic situation	Possible intrusion Observer bias Lack of control No causal inference
Case study and $N = 1$ research	Interactive	In-depth study Realistic situation	Observer bias Clearly intrusive Subject bias No causal inference
Self-report	Highly personal	In-depth study	Subjectivity Observer bias Lack of generality No causal inference
Survey	Structured	Objective	Purely descriptive No causal inference
CORRELATIONAL METHODS			
	Structured testing	Relationships Widely applicable	Possible confounding No causal inference
EXPERIMENTAL METHODS			
Quasi-experiment	Can't manipulate independent variable	Only way to do some experiments	Loss of control Possible confounding
Experiment	Full control of variables	Economy Causal inference	Artificial Possible lack of generality

goal, and prediction certainly implies the ability to make a causal inference. Recognizing the elements necessary to make causal inference helps us to evaluate research and also helps us to understand the reluctance of many philosophers to acknowledge that causal inferences are even possible.

Table 2.1 summarizes the essential features, strengths, and weaknesses of the research strategies that we have surveyed.

The Research Process

As you have probably surmised by now, being a scientist involves several kinds of activity, and actually collecting the data is only one of them. Now that we have looked briefly at the major research strategies used in psychology, we may turn to the details of conducting research. There are two aspects to our description. First, we'll look at the "textbook" description of how research is conducted. It emphasizes the order of the activities and the logic underlying the process. It will seem straightforward and sensible, the way that scientists would say that their discipline proceeds. But that isn't the way we actually do research! As we'll point out after we look at the textbook description, real research is much less structured than this overview makes it seem.

What We Say We Do

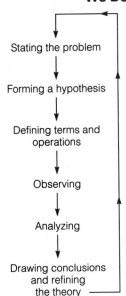

Figure 2.3

The process of doing research can be summarized by the idealized circular diagram in Figure 2.3. Presenting all of the different activities summarized in Figure 2.3 will occupy the rest of this book. But to begin to understand what we're suggesting here, let's consider Dr. Stewart's research. He began with a question about how similar two tastes are to animals. He knew about the conditioned aversion procedure, and he reasoned that using conditioned aversion would allow him to address his question. Briefly stated, the problem that Dr. Stewart addressed was "Is the taste of sugar and the taste of saccharin the same to rats?" This question led him to form a hypothesis: If the tastes are the same, then forming a conditioned aversion to one substance will lead to reduced ingestion of the other one. This hypothesis was followed by the development of the actual experimental procedures, where he carefully defined his terms and the operations that he would use to test his hypothesis. Then he conducted the experiment and collected the data; next came the analysis stage, where Dr. Stewart compared the amounts consumed. Finally, he was able to draw a conclusion from the data—did the taste of saccharin generalize to sugar?

But note the line leading back to the top of Figure 2.3; it suggests that the process is never really complete. Each new set of results may suggest additional new problems and questions, which will suggest new theoretical understanding about the process, which will lead to new research, and so on. Let's now look at the steps in more depth.

Getting Ideas

Novice researchers, particularly undergraduate students, often have trouble finding a topic for their first project. Longtime, active researchers have a different problem—what to do first. Scientists get their ideas in a number of ways, typically

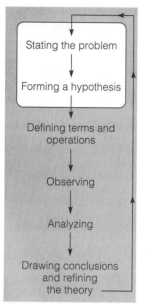

Stating the problem

Forming a hypothesis

Defining terms and
operations

Observing

Analyzing

Drawing conclusions
and refining
the theory

as a result of studying previous research—their own or others'. Once an area and a general topic is located, then the scientist (or the student) must narrow down the area of interest into a focused statement, a hypothesis or research question.

Locating Subject Areas. Research ideas should follow from your interests in psychology. If you're interested in personality, psychotherapy, animal learning, or thinking, your interests will naturally steer you in those directions. Ideas can strike you while reading varieties of the "popular" science magazines such as *Scientific American, Psychology Today, American Scientist*, or sometimes even the daily newspaper. When you read such accounts of research, be alert for variables that look interesting to you or that seem to need further exploration. Sometimes authors conclude an article with a series of unanswered questions.

The broader the audience of the magazine, the less detailed will be the coverage of the area. Most magazine articles, but not newspapers, will include references where you can find additional information. In fact, the references found in articles and journals are an important tool in becoming familiar with the literature in a field, a point that we'll explore further shortly.

Books are another way to explore interesting research areas. Your old introductory psychology textbook offers a broad survey of the discipline. It introduces all of the areas of psychology and provides references to more detailed sources. The text in a content area course such as perception or cognition can also suggest many ideas and places to look.

All libraries have sets of encyclopedias. You might find some ideas to stimulate your thinking in one of the general sets such as the *Encyclopedia Britannica* or the *Encyclopedia Americana*, but you will probably have better luck with one of the more specialized sets like the *Encyclopedia of Psychology* (Corsini, 1984) or the *International Encyclopedia of Psychiatry, Psychology, Psychoanalysis, and Neurology* (Wolman, 1977). In any of these general sources, be alert to what seem to be the current trends in research, areas where more work is needed, or areas where there seem to be contradictory findings. These are all clues to places where research can be profitably applied. But remember that by the time research gets reported in textbooks or encyclopedias, it is several years old; you will have to check in the more current literature to be sure that your literature review is up to date.

Don't overlook your psychology instructors as possible sources of information. Many of the examples that your instructor uses in lecture may come from his or her own research. If something you hear in class intrigues you, ask your instructor where to look for more information.

At some point, you will need to get into the actual research literature of psychology. Before you do, or perhaps even after you have made your first efforts, you should understand a bit about the structure and organization of the literature in the field and how best to use it. Remembering that science is both a process and an accumulation of facts and theories, we need to consider briefly how you can find your way through that stockpile of information to focus on your interests.

The Research Literature. The research literature in any discipline (and psychology is certainly no exception) consists of several kinds of materials. Several levels of library materials serve different purposes and are accessed in different ways. At the broadest level, we have already mentioned encyclopedias and dictionaries. These serve as very broad introductions to areas within the discipline. They are typically written by well-known scholars and survey the area. By nature, they are dated because it takes current literature several years to find its way into such sources.

Current popular literature, such as magazines, may be accessed through the *Reader's Guide to Periodical Literature.* Textbooks and various survey journals make up another level of the literature of psychology. Journals such as *Psychological Bulletin* and the annual series books such as *Annual Reviews of Psychology* offer integrating views of the recent literature, written by active researchers in the subfields of psychology.

The basic, or primary, literature in psychology is made up of the research journals, and there are many of them. The following list illustrates the range of research journals in the field:

> *American Journal of Psychology*
> *Behavior Research Methods, Instruments, and Computers*
> *British Journal of Psychology*
> *Bulletin of the Psychonomic Society*
> *Cognition*
> *Developmental Psychology*
> *Journal of Abnormal Psychology*
> *Journal of Applied Psychology*
> *Journal of Consulting and Clinical Psychology*
> *Journal of Experimental Psychology: Animal Behavior Processes*
> *Journal of Experimental Psychology: General*
> *Journal of Experimental Psychology: Human Learning and Memory*
> *Journal of Experimental Psychology: Human Perception and Performance*
> *Journal of Social Psychology*
> *Perception and Psychophysics*
> *Psychological Bulletin*
> *Psychological Review*
> *Psychometrika*

There are many more journals that cover the discipline of psychology; *Psychological Abstracts* lists approximately 1,300 journals.

Because there are so many journals and so much primary literature, no one person could possibly keep up in all of the areas. Fortunately, several tools can help us locate what we want to read. A short summary of a research paper, called the abstract, forms an important part of one major research tool, *Psychological Abstracts.* The *Abstracts* is published monthly by the American Psychological Association and is usually bound into six-month accumulations. The abstracts from all of the articles in the roughly 1,300 journals that *Abstracts* covers are numbered and printed. The abstract number is indexed by both subject and author indices in each six-month volume of *Abstracts.* Each abstract also shows where to find the original article—the journal title, the year of publication, and the volume and page numbers.

An important companion to the *Psychological Abstracts* that many students overlook is the *Thesaurus of Psychological Index Terms* (American Psychological Association, 1988). In developing the *Abstracts*, a fixed terminology is used to categorize the subject matter of psychology. This book lists all of the subject category terms that are used in *Psychological Abstracts*, gives synonyms so that if you start looking under the wrong word you will be directed to the correct subject heading, and also suggests "broader" and "narrower" subject headings. Suppose, for example, that you want to study a phenomenon in verbal learning. You might look under "Learning" in the *Thesaurus*, finding an entry like that in Figure 2.4.

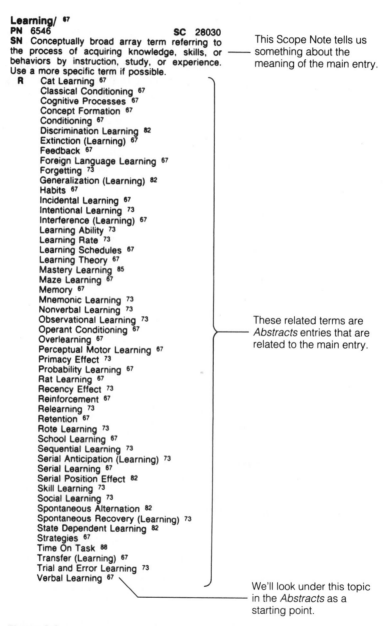

Learning/ 67
PN 6546   **SC** 28030
SN Conceptually broad array term referring to the process of acquiring knowledge, skills, or behaviors by instruction, study, or experience. Use a more specific term if possible.

This Scope Note tells us something about the meaning of the main entry.

    R   Cat Learning 67
        Classical Conditioning 67
        Cognitive Processes 67
        Concept Formation 67
        Conditioning 67
        Discrimination Learning 82
        Extinction (Learning) 67
        Feedback 67
        Foreign Language Learning 67
        Forgetting 73
        Generalization (Learning) 82
        Habits 67
        Incidental Learning 67
        Intentional Learning 73
        Interference (Learning) 67
        Learning Ability 73
        Learning Rate 73
        Learning Schedules 67
        Learning Theory 67
        Mastery Learning 85
        Maze Learning 67
        Memory 67
        Mnemonic Learning 73
        Nonverbal Learning 73
        Observational Learning 73
        Operant Conditioning 67
        Overlearning 67
        Perceptual Motor Learning 67
        Primacy Effect 73
        Probability Learning 67
        Rat Learning 67
        Recency Effect 73
        Reinforcement 67
        Relearning 73
        Retention 67
        Rote Learning 73
        School Learning 67
        Sequential Learning 73
        Serial Anticipation (Learning) 73
        Serial Learning 67
        Serial Position Effect 82
        Skill Learning 73
        Social Learning 73
        Spontaneous Alternation 82
        Spontaneous Recovery (Learning) 73
        State Dependent Learning 82
        Strategies 67
        Time On Task 88
        Transfer (Learning) 67
        Trial and Error Learning 73
        Verbal Learning 67

These related terms are *Abstracts* entries that are related to the main entry.

We'll look under this topic in the *Abstracts* as a starting point.

Figure 2.4

Let's look at the entry. There are several features that we can ignore, but note the "Scope Note" (SN) and "Related" (R) entries. Notice also that "Verbal Learning" is a related category, indicating that it will be found in the *Abstracts* themselves.

To see how "*Psych Abstracts*," as it's popularly called, works, let's pursue the "Verbal Learning" entry in the Subject Index in the 1987 volume. There we will find the listing in Figure 2.5.

Moving to the main entries in the same volume of the *Abstracts*, we find the entry in Figure 2.6. From this point, you may wish to locate the bound copies of *Bulletin of the Psychonomic Society* and read the entire paper. In addition, once you're into the primary literature through the *Abstracts*, you can use the references in the papers to locate additional sources.

Another useful tool, although more complex than *Psychological Abstracts*, is the *Social Science Citation Index* (*SSCI*). The *SSCI* is a complex tool, but it

Verbal Learning [See Also Nonsense Syllable Learning, Paired —— Note the "See also" list.
Associate Learning, Serial Anticipation (Learning), Serial Learning]
adjunct questions & objectives, retention of verbatim & semantic information & concepts & principles in prose learning setting, literature review, 4847
auditory vs visual presentation of words, word learning & immediate & delayed recall, medical students, 21169 ———————— Each abstract has a number that will allow us to find it in the main volume.

serial anticipation vs complete presentation method, retention of erroneous responses in verbal learning, 4th–6th graders, 8688
single exposure of new word in conversation vs story vs paired with definition, initial phase of word learning, 4–11 yr olds, 816
subjective organization, temporal contiguity of recall in multitrial —— This one, sequence, male college students, 13688   Abstract #13688,
verbal memory failure, individuals with mild vs moderate Alz- looks interesting.
heimer-type dementia, 1616

Figure 2.5

Authors and their
13688. **Puff, C. Richard & Van Slyke, Deborah A.** (Franklin & —— affiliation
Marshall Coll, Whitely Psychology Labs) **The temporal relation-**
ship between recall and subjective organization. *Bulletin of the* —— Title and complete
Psychonomic Society, 1985(Jan), Vol 23(1), 21–24. —24 male reference
undergraduates were presented with a list of unrelated words in a
multitrial free-recall paradigm. Items were correctly recalled significantly earlier in the sequence of trials than they were first entered
into units of intertrial repetition (ITR). These findings corroborate
E. C. Carterette and E. A. Coleman's (1963) conclusion and imply
that subjective organization has little to do with making items
initially accessible for recall. However, other findings suggest that Abstract
subjective organization may be important in making items more
reliably accessible. Additional analyses showed that, unlike "forward" ITR units, "reverse" ITR units remained significantly below
chance across all trials. Implications for the use of the bidirectional
ITR measure are discussed, and it is suggested that the bidirectional
measure defines a different phenomenon and is not a better measure
of the tendency to develop a fixed order of recall. (11 ref) —*Journal*
abstract.

The paper contains 11 references.

Figure 2.6

allows something that the *Abstracts* do not—a forward search from a single publication. Suppose that in your reading, you find an interesting paper by J. F. Fagan that was published in *Child Development* in 1976. We want to know what has been done since that time. Looking in *SSCI* under J. F. Fagan, we find the partial listing shown in Figure 2.7. Each of the three papers listed under the 1976 *Child Development* papers referred to it. Looking at the author entry in *SSCI* for just one of these (the Tyrrell paper), we find the entry shown in Figure 2.8. The

These are the papers by J. F. Fagan that were referred to in other papers.

Here is the one that we want.

During the time covered by this issue of *SSCI*, these are papers that referred to the Fagan paper.

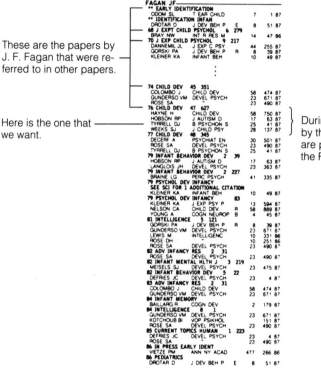

Figure 2.7

There were several coauthors.

Title and complete reference

Author's address

The paper refers to these other papers. (Note that there are several references to papers by Fagan, including the 1976 paper that led us here.)

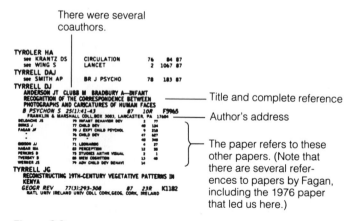

Figure 2.8

ability to use a single reference and follow it forward by locating papers that referenced the original (like the Fagan paper here) makes the *SSCI* a unique and powerful tool for searching the literature.

Becoming familiar with the literature in an area that holds your interest is a fundamental step in the research process. If you have located some interesting variables to investigate or if you have found some confusions or questions in the literature, you're well on your way. Your next step should be to begin to develop a hypothesis for investigation.

Developing and Evaluating a Hypothesis. When confronted with their first "develop a research proposal" assignment, most students' first reaction is panic. The panic comes from two sources—lack of knowledge of the field and lack of originality. At the beginning of any study, lack of knowledge is a normal condition, not a pathological one, as students seem to believe. We have just offered a number of suggestions for how to deal with psychology's research literature. Admittedly, the literature of the discipline is large and complex, and initially at least *Psychological Abstracts* seems imposing. But once you begin doing the library work, you will become familiar with the area fairly quickly. In fact, you will learn about so many variables and research possibilities that you will have to learn to scale back proposals to include fewer variables.

The other difficulty, fearing lack of originality, is a constant problem. Undergraduates feel that they must come up with a completely original, highly sophisticated, and theoretically important research hypothesis and theory right away. But that's difficult even for established scientists to accomplish routinely. A reasonable aspiration level for a student is to come up with a research proposal that asks an interesting question, one that is derived logically from past literature, but that is not expected to be a new idea or hypothesis of great importance. By insisting that the research be derived from previous literature we eliminate frivolous or just-for-fun research ideas (for example, "What would happen if I gave my roommate's pet fish a different food?" or "Are fraternity members really better beer drinkers than nonmembers?"). While such "experiments" may be interesting and even amusing, they're not good starting points for a budding scientist. Instead, developing an idea, even a simple one, from existing ideas provides good practice in logical thinking.

How, then, do you begin? First, follow your interests through the literature. If you're planning to pursue a career in psychology, you must find at least some part of it interesting. Explore that area in the literature. Second, take notes as you read and keep track of interesting variables and the relationships between them. Are there relationships that surprise you? Can you locate studies that explore the same relationship and find conflicting results? If so, there's a hot area to pursue; you might even be able to do something original. Have you come across research findings that you find hard to believe for reasons of experimental control? Perhaps an investigator failed to consider something that you think might be important. Are there relationships that seem to be unexplored? Sometimes it's because they've been explored and there was nothing to report, but other times the research may not have been done.

Third, start to formulate a research hypothesis involving an independent variable, a dependent variable, and a logical connection between them. By this point, you probably have information on many more variables than you can possibly consider. A common student problem is to have so many variables that seem interesting that it seems impossible to narrow your focus to just a couple. But you can't possibly investigate everything of interest in one research project, and you need to begin to narrow your focus somewhat. Once you're to this stage, then perhaps you are ready to spend a little time in evaluating your hypothesis; in doing so you may be able to clarify your interests and narrow your focus.

Evaluating research hypotheses. The first question to ask about your research hypothesis is whether it is explicit. Have you defined your independent variable clearly? Just what do you mean by "an introvert" or "a hungry animal"? By "people" do you mean college students? All humans? Adult English-speakers? Kindergarten children? How about your dependent variable? Have you made it equally explicit?

A second evaluative question asks whether the logic linking the independent variable with the dependent variable is sound and clear. Does the connection between the two make sense in terms of your theoretical explanation? Can you express your theory and its predictions clearly in words? (Try writing it. Then have someone read it. If their reaction is "Huh?" then you probably haven't made your logic clear; try it again.) Does the hypothesized relationship between the independent variable and dependent variable ask the question that you are interested in asking? It's not uncommon to find that in the process of identifying variables, you've lost all track of what you were curious about in the first place.

Third, is your hypothesis testable? Does it allow you to make a prediction of the form "If I do *this*, then *that* should happen"? If not, then maybe your understanding of the process is less clear than you think it is.

Finally, is it practical to think that you can do the research in the time and with the resources that you have available? Some projects are best reserved for a senior research project, while others may demand the time and concentration that a Ph.D. candidate could bring to them. Others may demand investment of a number of years in the project; file them away for future reference.

The research hypothesis asks a specific question or group of questions. The literature review that led to the hypothesis surveys the empirical studies and the theoretical discussions that form the background of your research project. Many instructors advise (or insist) that the first draft of the introduction section of the research report be written as soon as the hypothesis is defined. That's not a bad idea because it forces you to put down all of your thinking and logic, not to mention the hypothesis itself, while it's fresh in your memory. You will probably revise the introduction later, but a draft can be written before you begin to define the actual research procedures, which is normally the next step in the process.

Setting Up Research

Once the hypothesis is defined, the next logical step is to develop the general research strategy, define the variables and how they are measured, and determine the various control procedures. (The latter two matters are considered in depth in Chapters 3 and 4.) As we said earlier in this chapter, the research question will often suggest a particular strategy to be followed. If you want to be able to draw firm causal inferences, then an observational method is not the approach to take.

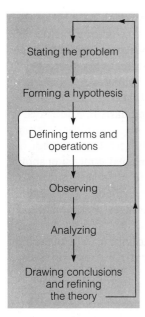

Stating the problem

Forming a hypothesis

Defining terms and operations

Observing

Analyzing

Drawing conclusions and refining the theory

On the other hand, if you want to explore a number of variables quickly, perhaps a survey would be best, or even a case study if you're trying to explore a particular situation in some depth.

Operational Definitions. Before actually beginning to collect data, the exact operations to be used in conducting the research must be specified. The independent variable must be defined, not just verbally but also by a specification of just how it is to be manipulated. Dr. Stewart must decide not only that his independent variable is the presence or absence of lithium chloride, but he must define how it is to be administered, in what dosage, and at what length of time after the exposure to the saccharin or water. In a research report of his study you might read "Lithium chloride was administered by intraperitoneal injection of .003 mg/kg of body weight in a saline solution five minutes after the exposure to water or saccharin solution." That's explicit enough for someone else to replicate the procedure. But that level of detail must be specified before Dr. Stewart can begin his investigation. Similarly, Dr. Campbell must define the exact procedures that he will use to measure the introversion/extraversion and sensation-seeking tendencies that interest him.

What we've just described is an *operational definition,* a definition in terms of the exact operations that are used to manipulate or measure each variable. Dr. Stewart shouldn't decide for each rat how to administer the lithium, any more than Dr. Campbell should change his introversion/extraversion test for each subject in his research. The procedures for measuring, manipulating, and controlling variables need to be established beforehand, as a part of the process of setting up the project.

Careful definition of the operations serves several purposes in research. For one, it often will force the investigator to clarify his or her thinking. It's one thing to say "I think that alcohol consumption makes people clumsy," but something else to specify exactly what you mean by alcohol consumption and exactly what you mean by clumsy. You might define alcohol consumption as "3 ounces of 80-proof vodka mixed with orange juice and consumed within a 30-minute period," or alternatively as a specific blood alcohol level as determined by a breathalyzer, or something similar. You might define clumsiness to be performance on a standardized manual dexterity test or perhaps as performance on a particular video game.

A second important reason for using operational definitions is that they make communication easier. Once the operations are defined and published, procedures can be repeated by other investigators, making replication possible. Such precise communication is essential to the goal of replication (see Chapter 1, p. 10).

Operational definitions clarify exactly what is intended by a particular word or phrase in the research. Readers of a research report thus have an agreed-upon meaning for the variables. When you have defined exactly what you mean by "alcohol consumption" in your research, there is little room for debate over your meaning. Other investigators might disagree with whether you should define alcohol consumption in the way that you did, but they can't misunderstand what you meant.

Definitions in terms of operations are an important part of research, but you should be careful that the variables so defined don't take on a life of their own. You may have heard the quip that "intelligence is what intelligence tests measure." If you find that operational definition of intelligence less than satisfying, then you can see the problem. There are two aspects to this difficulty: the narrowness of the operational definition and its logical connection to the underlying concept. An operational definition specifies a set of procedures to manipulate or measure an experimental variable. That variable, in turn, is intended to be the representation of some underlying concept or process, and it's sometimes easy to lose track of that relationship. Dr. Campbell is really interested in a particular personality dimension that is thought to exist; that dimension should be revealed by a subject's score on a specific introversion/extraversion test, and the interest is not on the specific test scores but on the underlying personality process. Likewise, Dr. Stewart is not particularly interested in lithium per se, but uses it to establish a conditioned avoidance that will let him ask the really important questions about the similarity of tastes. You don't want interest to focus on just the test scores or on just the lithium; the broader behavioral processes are what is of interest, and narrow operational definitions sometimes obscure them.

One of the most important questions to ask in evaluating research (including your own) is whether the variables are adequate reflections of the underlying processes. Clearly, you wouldn't try to measure intelligence by asking your subjects to stand on a scale, but it's sometimes difficult to evaluate the relationship between a hypothetical variable and its measurement. The question here is one of the validity of a measurement technique (the extent to which it measures what it should); we'll return to validity in some detail in Chapter 3.

Manipulating and Measuring. An important part of the planning for a research project is defining the procedures for manipulating the independent variable in an experiment and for measuring the dependent variable. Although these are the central core of an experiment, we won't spend much time on them here. As far as manipulating an independent variable is concerned, we won't spend much time on that topic in the entire book. Independent variables are highly specific to particular research. This book is devoted to general considerations that cut across all content areas of psychology, and so we can't devote the time necessary to fully understand experimental manipulations. Chapter 4 presents some important material on manipulating variables, but you will learn which variables are important and how they are manipulated during library research on a topic of interest to you.

To some extent, the measurement of a dependent variable is similar to the manipulation of an independent variable—it too is highly specific to a particular experimental context. However, in contrast to independent variables, a number of very general principles about measurement can be presented in the abstract. We will devote Chapter 3 to a broad consideration of the principles of measurement.

| Conducting Research | When you carry out a piece of empirical research, what do you actually do? Basically, you carry out the plans that you have already made. You solicit or |

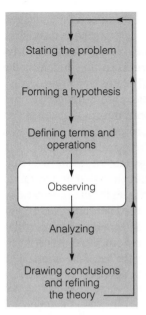

Stating the problem

Forming a hypothesis

Defining terms and operations

Observing

Analyzing

Drawing conclusions and refining the theory

otherwise obtain subjects and treat them as required by your research. You measure the dependent variable. You repair broken apparatus, remind subjects of their appointments, and generally try to keep body and soul together during what is often a rather fast-paced and trying period. And you keep doing all of that until you have collected the data that your design requires. It all sounds fairly simple, and we've covered all of those elements to some extent. All but one topic, that is—dealing with subjects.

Some Ethical Considerations. Any piece of research presumably has some value. Perhaps it promises an advance in the theoretical understanding of some small domain of behavior. Or perhaps it promises to help to solve a problem in psychotherapy. Perhaps it serves only to meet a requirement in a course. Or perhaps it promises nothing but to satisfy the scientist's curiosity. But it has some anticipated benefit; if it doesn't, then the research won't get done.

Any piece of research has costs associated with it and also certain responsibilities on the part of the researcher. Psychologists have spent much time and effort studying research ethics for both human and animal subjects, and the American Psychological Association (APA) has published guidelines regarding subjects. We'll explore them in a bit more detail in the following sections.

A primary rule in planning a piece of research, one that forms the basis for APA's guidelines, is a risk/benefit analysis that tries to strike a balance between the subject's rights and the possible benefits that will result from the research. In other words, before beginning any research, the investigator is expected to analyze all of the procedures that will be used during the research with an eye to anything that might put the subjects "at risk." Risk in this context refers not just to physical risk, but also to any possible long-term psychological damage that might be caused by the procedure. Any such risks must be balanced against the possible benefits to be derived from the study.

All institutions involved in research have various review committees that oversee research involving living organisms. Student research is usually conducted under the overview of a faculty review panel, often within the department. Other research is probably reviewed by an institutional group. Any research that is funded by the federal government must have its procedures reviewed by an Institutional Review Board if it involves living organisms.

The APA, along with other organizations, has established guidelines for ethical conduct in research with humans and animals. Summaries of those guidelines follow. For additional information, you should consult the published document and also make yourself aware of institutional regulations that will pertain to your research.

Dealing with human subjects. In addition to the risk/benefit analysis that is a part of all research planning, any research using humans must be based on the principle of *minimal risk*. In this context, minimal risk means that participating in research does not increase the subject's chance of injury. As a companion requirement, the researcher has an obligation to protect the subject from physical or mental harm, danger, or discomfort throughout the research.

A major requirement of research with humans is *informed consent*. Before a subject agrees to serve in the research, he or she must be given full information about the procedures that will be used. The investigator is particularly obligated to communicate any information that might influence a participant's decision to participate. The potential research subject must be given a clear opportunity to decline to participate without penalty. The subject must also be free to terminate participation at any time, also without penalty. Before the research begins, the experimenter and the subject should have a very clear understanding of the obligations and responsibilities of each, which is often confirmed in a simple written agreement.

The principle of informed consent can be in conflict with the research plan in cases where advance knowledge could influence the subject's behavior. For example, studies in interpersonal perception sometimes require that two research subjects meet to work together on some task; later, each rates the other on certain characteristics. Often, one of the two "strangers" is a confederate of the experimenter, who plays a certain role (helpful, perhaps, or belligerent, or even hostile) as a part of an independent variable manipulation. Where deception is necessary in the experimental procedure, it is permitted under very carefully controlled circumstances. The APA guidelines require that two questions be addressed specifically before any study involving deception may be conducted:

1. Is the deception justified? That is, is it really necessary to keep some aspects of the procedure secret from the subject?
2. Are there alternatives to using deception?

Once those questions have been considered, if the deception is still deemed necessary, it may be used.

Subjects must be debriefed immediately after the experiment. During the debriefing, they are given an overview of the research project, including its procedures and expected benefits. The debriefing should remove any misconceptions that the subject has about the research and provide an opportunity for him or her to ask questions. In any deception study, the investigator is obligated to explain the deception and why it was necessary to the subject as soon as is possible, normally during the debriefing.

Finally, all information gathered during the research is to be kept confidential with regard to the subject's identity. The subject must be assured of confidentiality during the initial explanation of the research in the informed consent discussions. For the full text of the APA guidelines see APA (1990).

Dealing with animal subjects. Since animal subjects cannot give informed consent to the research nor can they elect to leave during the research, special care must be taken to guard their welfare. It is the investigator's responsibility to assure that all research animals receive humane treatment during and after the research. Animal researchers have a responsibility to minimize discomfort, illness, and pain in the animals. The researcher must also assure that all individuals who assist with animal care and research are explicitly instructed in the techniques to be used and that they are carefully supervised throughout the research. Finally, when animals must be killed during or after the research, the sacrificing must be done quickly and painlessly. APA's full policy on the ethics of research using animal subjects may be found in its official statement (APA, 1990).

Analyzing and Interpreting Results

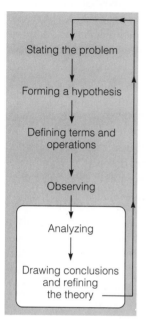

Stating the problem

↓

Forming a hypothesis

↓

Defining terms and operations

↓

Observing

↓

Analyzing

↓

Drawing conclusions and refining the theory

The final stages in the research process are analyzing the data and interpreting them in light of their theoretical context. Analyzing and presenting results are the major topics of Chapters 5 through 10, and we needn't discuss them further just now. The processes of interpreting the results and selecting the appropriate research design occupy the balance of the book, so we don't need to consider those topics any further in this chapter.

The APA Writing Style. The American Psychological Association (APA) publishes an extensive guide to scientific writing (American Psychological Association, 1983) that is followed by nearly all journals in the discipline and by many related disciplines as well. The outline suggested by the APA publication manual parallels the research outline that we just described. We'll discuss the sections of an APA report here and show how they mirror the phases of research. In addition, understanding the organization of research publications will help you to read the basic literature in the field.

The APA format dictates four sections for a typical research report: Introduction, Method, Results, and Discussion. In addition, the paper begins with an Abstract and ends with References. The precise style of writing, referencing, typing, drawing figures, and constructing tables, and a wealth of other technical details are addressed in the APA *Manual*. Many psychology instructors require that all assignments be written according to the APA rules of style.

Introduction. The Introduction section surveys relevant literature and summarizes past research. Interpretations and inferences from the literature are introduced here. In this section the investigator develops the theory underlying the present research. The Introduction section typically ends with a clear statement of the independent and dependent variables to be used in the current research, as well as a statement of the hypothesis being investigated. The Introduction to a scientific paper differs from a "term paper" in that it doesn't normally attempt to survey a broad area of literature, nor does it attempt to provide an exhaustive bibliography of the area. Rather, it is narrowly focused and ties directly to the research that will be reported in the rest of the paper. The Introduction corresponds to the "Stating the problem" and the "Forming a hypothesis" sections of our earlier outline.

Method. The Method section defines the actual operations that were carried out in the research. This section sometimes has several subsections. (One common set of subtopics includes Subjects, Apparatus, and Procedure.) The Method section describes what was done in the research in sufficient detail that an experienced researcher familiar with the area could repeat the study. The operational definitions appear here, as does the description of the overall research strategy, the instructions to the subjects, and all other mechanical elements of the research. The Method section describes the activities that we discussed earlier as "Defining terms and operations."

Results. The outline suggested "Observing" and "Analyzing" as the next two activities. While "observing" is rarely illustrated in a research report (except in rare instances where sections of raw data are presented for illustrative purposes), the analyses of the data certainly are. One of the major goals of statistical analysis is to communicate the results of the research. The descriptive techniques in Chapters 5 through 10, and the inferential ones in Chapters 11 through 21, are intended for use in Results sections of research papers. Along with the publication of the methods of research in the Methods section of a research report, the publication of the results is the on-paper evidence of science as a public endeavor. A Results section contains only the results of data analysis and does not offer any interpretation of their meaning; that role is served by the Discussion section.

Discussion. The results are interpreted in this final section. Typically, the literature described in the introduction is discussed in light of the results. Since science and its theories advance by continuing research, this section is an important one because it is used to refine, to modify, or perhaps to discard previous theories. It draws conclusions and refines theory, as our outline suggests. It also suggests future research and thus completes the circle shown in the outline.

The APA-prescribed outline of a report, like our outline of research, suggests a chronology. As we'll point out in the following section, that chronology is often illusory. While many researchers actually begin a project by writing an introduction, most don't really do it until later. Usually some hazy ideas and hypotheses are formed at the outset and perhaps written down. But the full logical justification for the experiment that is contained in the introduction is typically written later, after the data are in and analyzed and the report is being prepared.

By necessity, our study in this book will focus on the latter two points of the outline and thus on the Results and Discussion sections of an APA research paper. But we remind ourselves once more that the entire purpose of research is to gain knowledge and that knowledge is best expressed in words, typically in the Introduction and Discussion sections of reports.

What We Really Do

The neat cycle of research activities just described is fine as a summary of the general activities of a scientist doing research. It makes a great deal of sense and implies a nice, orderly chronology of activities. But that's not the way it really is. If you were to observe a scientist in action, day in and day out (using a naturalistic observation procedure, of course), you would find that the activities don't seem to follow that precise chronology at all. The scientist jumps back and forth between analyzing data, collecting data, fixing broken equipment, reading journals, talking with colleagues, and writing—all in no apparent order. Only by taking a long view of the process could you determine that the patterns of activity fall into several different groups and that those activity groups could be given the names suggested previously—stating the problem, forming a hypothesis, and so forth.

One writer (Bachrach, 1962) opens the preface to his little book on research methods by stating his "First Law":

> People don't usually do research the way people who write books about research say that people do research (p. vii).

This law is as true now as when Bachrach first formulated it. The process of research is complicated and confusing to the observer (and often to the participant!), and books about research simplify and abstract to the extent that all that students sometimes see is the clean and neat summary. The real process is much less well-organized and polished. Students are sometimes frustrated when they sit down to begin actually "doing" research. They expect, because that's what the books on research tell them, to be able to start "from the top," as it were, and carry a research project all the way through by following the outline. That's not how it's done. (For an interesting description of the way an actual program of research appears to an insider, read Dethier's delightful little book on his research with house flies [Dethier, 1962]).

SUMMARY

- Variables that are measured are called *dependent variables*.
- An *independent variable* is manipulated by the experimenter in order to study its effect on a dependent variable.
- *Extraneous variables* are all other possible sources of variability.
- An experiment is the only research procedure that lets us draw causal conclusions.
- A *quasi-experiment* has an independent variable, but it isn't manipulated by the investigator.
- In *naturalistic observation*, there is no manipulation of an independent variable, and there is little or no interaction with the subjects; it is often useful at the beginning of research.
- A *case study* is a detailed investigation of a single individual.
- *Self-report* is sometimes used to study long-term memory.
- *Surveys* and *interviews* are standardized ways of collecting information from a large number of individuals.
- *Correlational research* studies the relationships among measured variables.
- To infer causality, we must establish (1) covariation, (2) temporal ordering, and (3) no confounding.
- Research proceeds through several stages, from stating the problem through drawing conclusions.
- Books, newspapers, magazines, texts, encyclopedias, instructors, and research journals are all good sources for research ideas.
- The literature of psychology has several levels, with the research literature as the foundation.
- The *Psychological Abstracts* summarizes and indexes the literature of the field.
- The *Social Science Citation Index* (*SSCI*) allows searches forward in time from a selected research paper.
- A research hypothesis should be (1) clearly defined, (2) logically sound, (3) testable, and (4) practical.
- An *operational definition* defines a variable in terms of the operations used to manipulate or measure it.

- An important step in planning an investigation is a risk-benefit analysis that helps to define the ethics of the project.
- Minimal risk and informed consent are crucial principles in an investigation using humans.
- The APA writing style shows four sections in a typical report: Introduction, Method, Results, and Discussion.

KEY TERMS

APA writing style	Informed consent
Case study	Interview
Causality	Minimal risk
Confounding	Naturalistic observation
Correlational research	Operational definition
Covariation	*Psychological Abstracts*
Dependent variable	Quasi-experiment
Experiment	Risk-benefit analysis
Extraneous variable	Self-report
Independent variable	Survey

EXERCISES

Solutions to asterisked (*) exercises appear at the back of the book.

1. For each of the following research questions, select one of the observational methods, and suggest how you would apply it.
   *a. Do pet dogs have distinct territories?
   b. What are the effects of music during study periods on test scores?
   *c. Do certain sounds have color associations for some people?
   d. How are hours of study related to grade point average?
   *e. Can behavior modification techniques help to control disruptive behavior in a sheltered workshop?
   f. Do people have strategies that help them to remember items for a test?
   *g. How do people describe how they find their way from one building to another on campus?
   h. Is there a relationship between training in art and appreciation of various kinds of paintings?
   *i. Is there a relationship between family background and the amount of time the individual volunteers to help in hospitals and social agencies?
   j. Are there personality factors that differentiate between drug abusers and tobacco smokers?

*2. For each of the questions listed in Exercise 1, suggest an experiment that is related to the topic by indicating a possible independent variable and a possible dependent variable.

CHAPTER 3

Measuring Variables

Stating the problem

Forming a hypothesis

Defining terms and
operations

Observing

Analyzing

Drawing conclusions
and refining
the theory

In this chapter, we begin to consider the actual conduct of a research investigation, the "Observing" part of the process. "Observing" typically consists of measuring some action or, more likely, a dependent variable.

When Dr. Campbell administers the introversion/extraversion personality scale to his subjects, he is measuring his subjects' scores. The correlational research method that Dr. Campbell uses measures variables and assesses their relationships, and so the measurement of his variables is very important.

More specifically, the personality scales that Dr. Campbell uses are made up of specific questions and are presented to individuals following specific instructions. He follows the instructions for administering the personality test and then follows additional scoring rules for the introversion/extraversion scale that let him assign a numeric value to each person. When Dr. Campbell was designing his research project, he decided what personality tests to use; the administration and scoring rules for those tests constitute the operational definitions of the variables in his research. In fact, as you pursue the research literature in an area, you'll find that many operational definitions have to do with measuring variables.

When Dr. Stewart places his animals into the test chamber and records the amount of each of the four test solutions that they drink in a fixed time period, he too is measuring variables. His measurement procedure differs from Dr. Campbell's, but he is measuring quite different variables and has quite different aims. But both Dr. Campbell and Dr. Stewart assign numbers to a behavior by following certain rules, with the aim of using the results to make inferences about underlying psychological processes.

Just what do we mean by the word *variable*? Without further qualifiers, we're referring to anything that can vary or that can exist in more than one condition. That might not seem like a satisfying definition; but, in the broadest sense, it's exactly what we do mean. We've just described two measured variables: score on introversion/extraversion scale and the amount of test solutions consumed. Some other examples might include:

- running time in a maze
- running time in the 440-yard dash
- number of errors on a true-false test
- number of errors made in a maze
- amount of a drug administered
- kind of reading instruction given to first-grade children
- brightness of the room illumination
- kind of psychotherapy administered to patients
- score on an IQ test

In this chapter, we'll deal specifically with variables that are measured. But the word *variable* is also correctly applied to an independent variable in an experiment (for example, whether an animal receives water or saccharin before the lithium injection). Independent variables are not usually measured, but rather are manipulated by the experimenter; they'll be a major focus in Chapter 4. This chapter is concerned with variables that are measured and not manipulated.

Fundamentals of Measurement

Most recent discussions of the nature of measurement rely on a fundamental statement by Stevens (1951): "In its broadest sense, measurement is the assignment of numerals to objects or events according to rules" (p. 1). We might also add that often the aim of measurement is to assign the numerals in such a way that they represent the quantity of some attribute in the object being measured. Strictly speaking, we don't ever really *measure* an object, person, or animal, but instead measure its properties. We don't really measure Fred, Peter, or Sara, but we can measure their height, weight, IQ, running speed, or perhaps their recall of definitions in a statistics course.

The "rules" by which numerals are assigned define the process of measurement and vary from very simple to quite complex. The rules for measuring the length of a table with a steel tape can be explained easily, as can those for weighing fruit in a grocery store. But the rules that Dr. Stewart uses for measuring the amount of sugar solution consumed are a bit more complicated. The rules that Dr. Campbell uses for his introversion/extraversion test are even more complex, and those that are used by other researchers can be very complicated. The point of the rules (and they constitute the operational definition of the variable being measured) is to ensure objectivity and communication in research. Dr. Campbell needs to be sure that his subjects are treated in the same way throughout his research so that variations in measurement don't become an extraneous variable in his project. In addition, Dr. Campbell uses a standard measure of introversion/extraversion, so that following each test's rules exactly assures that his scores will be comparable to those of some other researcher who uses the same introversion/extraversion scale.

The result of any measurement operation is a numeral. Just what meaning to place on those numerals is not always clear—for at least two reasons. In the first place, numerals carry with them certain properties that we're familiar with and invite certain operations like adding and subtracting, but those operations and properties may not always be meaningful. And second, we're not always sure that the numbers actually measure what they purport to measure. The latter problem concerns validity, a second important topic in this chapter. The first concern, though, leads us directly to considering the several "measurement scales" and their properties.

Scales of Measurement

You may never have thought much about it, but some of the most common ways of measuring everyday objects are really quite different. Consider the weather and sports reports on the evening news. Suppose that the news reports that the high temperature for the day had been 62°, that a high wind had been clocked at 86 miles per hour, and that your friend Fred had finished third in a race. Think about those three numbers—temperature, wind speed, and place of finish in the race—for a moment. Other than the fact that they are measuring different phenomena and that they are in different units, the numbers differ in several other important ways; and those differences have an effect on what we may sensibly do with the numbers. The race results contained only the order of finish, and the "measurement" of the runners was accomplished by applying the rule "Assign '1' to the first person across the line, assign '2' to the second, and so on." (Does that rule constitute a measurement procedure? Certainly it does, according to Stevens's definition.) Notice that there is no information in the finish-position numbers to tell you how long the interval was between Fred and the person ahead of or behind him, only that there were two people ahead of him. And notice that there's no use of a zero value in the race finish order; what would a "zero" position in the race mean, anyway?

The other two numbers, wind speed and temperature, differ from the order-of-finish value too. At least you know that today's 62° is exactly 10° colder than if the high for the day had been 72°, and that the 10-degree difference is the same as the difference between 90° and 100° (although it may not seem the same!). And as for wind speed, you can also feel comfortable that 86 mph is 10 mph harder than a wind clocked at a breezy 76 mph; you also know that a 10-mph difference in wind speed is the same whether it's between 76 and 86 or between 25 and 35.

You also know that a wind speed of 86 mph means a pretty windy day, and that a wind speed of 0 mph means that there was no wind at all. And you know that a high temperature of 62° means a relatively cool day. But does a 0 on either the Fahrenheit or the Celsius temperature scale indicate that there was no temperature at all? No, it doesn't mean that, since the zero in either of the temperature scales in common use doesn't correspond to the absence of the property being measured.

What have we just suggested? That the measurement rules and the scales of measurement that come from them differ in how they assign numerals. It also suggests that there are differences between the scales in how they make use of some of the properties of numbers and in how we interpret the meanings of the values.

The System of Real Numbers. Torgerson (1958) identified three properties of the mathematical system of real numbers that are important for measurement purposes and also pointed out that the various scales of measurement may be distinguished by whether or not they accommodate those properties. He listed these properties of the real numbers:

1. The numbers are in an order.
2. Differences between pairs of numbers may themselves be ordered (that is, some differences between numbers are larger than are other differences).
3. The number series has an origin value at zero.

To Torgerson's list, we might add the self-evident—that each number is different from every other. These four properties of the number system have a relationship to the rules of measurement that may be used to assign the numbers to objects in attempting to measure properties of the objects.

Same–different (nominal) measurement. Suppose that you're studying attitudes among university employees and need a way to categorize individuals' employment. You might devise the scheme:

1. Tenured faculty
2. Untenured faculty
3. Administrator
4. Secretary
5. Technician
6. Facility maintenance
7. Grounds maintenance
8. Other

Armed with this list, you could interview each employee and "measure" him or her by assigning a number according to your list. The process is certainly a measurement operation in that it assigns numerals to objects according to rules and does so in such a fashion that the numerals represent an important property of each person. But just what do the numerals mean? Only that someone that is assigned a "3" has a different kind of job from one assigned a "7." It certainly does not mean that a "7" person is necessarily larger, heavier, older, or better than a "3" person. All they mean is that "3" and "7" people have different jobs. In short, this measurement scheme doesn't make use of any of the properties of the real number system except that of the numbers being different.

We have just described what is usually known as a *nominal* measurement scale. A nominal scale is constructed by using a set of rules that employ only the "uniqueness" property of the number system. The numbers are really nothing more than names (hence the designation "nominal") for the various groups or categories into which the objects may be placed. In fact, we'll sometimes refer to nominal measurement as *category* measurement.

If you were to poll your friends about their postgraduation plans, you might find that their choices fell into several categories:

1. Teach high school
2. Attend graduate school
3. Teach elementary school
4. Attend medical or professional school
5. Get some other kind of job
6. Undecided

You might assign category numbers to the choices as suggested; if you did, then you would have measured your friends' postgraduation plans.

Suppose that you measure 50 people on the nominal measurement scale that we have for jobs or that you measure 50 of your friends on their postgraduation plans. In either case, you'll have a collection of 50 numbers, representing 50 employees or 50 students' plans. Suppose you were to compute the average of those 50 values? What kind of sense could you make of the result? If you found that the "average" employee scored 4.3, what could you do with that number? Or if the average postgraduation plan was 4.6, what does that mean? Actually, it means almost nothing, except that (if you did the computation right) it represents the average of a set of 50 numbers. But beyond that, knowing the average doesn't help you to understand anything about the employees or about your friends either. Are there any arithmetic operations that we might use on category data that make any sense at all? About the only operation that can be meaningfully applied to nominal data is simple counting, but sometimes that's quite informative. Suppose that we found that the job categories occurred with different frequencies, such as

Category	Job	Number of employees
1	Tenured faculty	10
2	Untenured faculty	8
3	Administrator	5
4	Secretary	7
5	Technician	3
6	Facility maintenance	8
7	Grounds maintenance	6
8	Other	3

The counting operation has shown a pattern—there are more people employed as tenured faculty than any other category, and there are very few technicians and "other" workers. So counting is a useful and meaningful thing to do to nominal data. In fact, it's the only useful arithmetic operation for such data, as we'll point out later.

More-of (ordinal) measurement. The order of finish in a race assigns numerals in the order in which racers cross the finish line. The first person across receives a "1," the second a "2," and so forth. Such a measurement rule takes advantage of not only the fact that the numbers are different, but also the fact that they have an order implied. In this kind of measurement, the larger value implies more of the quantity being measured (in the case of a race, it's actually the time taken to complete the prescribed distance).

The measurement scale that we call *ordinal* makes use of the different and the ordered properties of the number system. When we have measured on the ordinal scale, we can tell which objects have more or less of the property, but not how much more or less. If we were to line up all of the members of a high school gym class in order from shortest to tallest and give the number "1" to the shortest, then all we know for sure is that "18" is taller than "10" and shorter

Ordered differences?

	No	Yes
No (True zero point?)	Ordinal measurement	Interval measurement
Yes (True zero point?)	Ordinal measurement with origin	Ratio measurement

Figure 3.1

Ordered differences?

	No	Yes
No (True zero point?)	Ordinal	Interval
Yes (True zero point?)	Ordinal with origin	Ratio

Figure 3.2

than "22." We don't know whether the difference between a score of "16" and "18" is the same as the difference between "6" and "8."

If a measurement procedure makes use of the order property of the number system, it might or might not also make use of the remaining properties, namely the ordering of differences and the use of the zero point. Following Torgerson (1958), we may construct an illustration of the ways in which measurement procedures do or do not use the remaining properties (see Figure 3.1). Ordinal measurement, as we have just presented it, falls in the upper left corner of the illustration in Figure 3.2, indicating that it makes use of the order property of numbers, but not the ordered differences or the zero-point property. A very common ordinal value is high school rank in class. It is often used by college admissions officers as one of the measures that they collect on applicants.

Beyond rank-in-class measurements, several common psychological procedures produce ordinal scales. In aesthetic research, subjects are frequently asked to arrange artistic stimuli in order from most preferred to least preferred, or from least to most beautiful. Most subjects can handle such tasks easily. For example, you probably could arrange steak, baked fish, fried chicken, meat loaf, steamed shrimp, and roast turkey in order of preference without much difficulty. You might have more trouble if asked to assign each a number reflecting your choice, other than merely an order-of-preference number ("my first choice, my second choice . . ."). The ease with which humans can produce preference orderings among stimulus items has led to a rapid development within the past decade or so of procedures for dealing with ordinal data. We'll introduce a few of the descriptive measures for ordinal data in the next several chapters.

Ordinal measurement with a zero point. One consequence of Torgerson's fourfold arrangement of measurement procedures is that it highlights a special case of ordinal measurement where a zero value is assigned to represent neutrality (Figure 3.3). Suppose that you were asked to rate the statement "The University should include student rating of faculty teaching as a part of the annual salary determination process" using the categories:

I strongly disagree
I somewhat disagree
I disagree a little

Ordered differences?

	No	Yes
No	Ordinal	Interval
Yes	Ordinal with origin	Ratio

True zero point?

Figure 3.3

I don't care one way or the other
I agree a little
I somewhat agree
I strongly agree

We could score the answers using any values we wished—1, 2, 3, 4, 5, 6, and 7, for example; or 10, 20, 30, 40, 50, 60, and 70; or even 3, 5, 9, 17, 22, 55, and 67, from strongly disagree to strongly agree. All of those assignments are reasonable and result in ordinal measurement. (We probably wouldn't necessarily want to use consecutive numbers, since that implies equal intervals, and the verbal statements are probably not equally spaced for everyone.) We could also use a set of numbers that equate the value of zero with the "neutral" phrase, as for example the series −10, −8, −3, 0, 7, 15, 20. These values still represent an ordinal series, since the higher value indicates a more positive attitude; but we have now aligned the zero value with neutral or "zero" on the dimension of negative-to-positive attitude that we're measuring. An ordinal scale that places the zero value at some neutral or zero value on the dimension being measured fits into the lower left-hand cell in Torgerson's scheme and might be called *ordinal measurement with origin*. Such scales are infrequent but do appear from time to time in attitude studies and in similar situations where we could conceive of a true neutral in what is being measured.

How-much-more (interval) measurement. The Fahrenheit and the Celsius temperature scales represent *interval* measurement. Interval measurement, as Figure 3.4 shows, adds the use of equal intervals to the order property of the

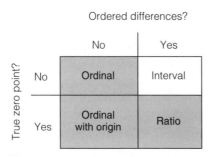

Ordered differences?

	No	Yes
No	Ordinal	Interval
Yes	Ordinal with origin	Ratio

True zero point?

Figure 3.4

number system. In interval measurement, the intervals between values may themselves be arranged in order, but the value of 0 in the number system isn't aligned with the absence of the property that is being measured. Neither of the two common temperature scales align the zero value with absence of temperature as defined by a physicist, although the Kelvin (or absolute) temperature scale does. In either the Fahrenheit or the Celsius scale, though, differences between pairs of temperatures can be compared. Thus on a day when it's 95° Fahrenheit, it's 10° warmer than when it's 85°. That difference of 10° is the same 10-degree difference as that between 20° and 30°. This statement might or might not be true if the measurement had been made on an ordinal scale.

When the measurement procedure takes advantage of the equal spacing of the number system, then the measurement is interval in nature. Interval measurement is probably the most common scale in psychology (although some writers claim that we really can measure only orders). The great bulk of the tests and scales that psychologists use, including the introversion/extraversion and sensation-seeking scales that Dr. Campbell employs, appear to be interval scales.

We used the "weasel word" *appear* because it's often difficult to determine just whether or not the intervals are actually equal. Consider an experiment in human learning, where a common dependent variable is the number of words recalled. When a subject in a learning experiment recalls 10 words from a list one time and 14 words the next, we normally use those numbers as values on the dependent variable. Of course, we have no real way of knowing whether, in fact, the difference between 10 and 14 words recalled is *really* the same difference in amount learned as for a subject who recalled 5 words on one trial and 9 on the next. Are those equivalent amounts of actual *learning*? Is there any way that we can really know the answer to that question? The answer is no—until we can develop a way to measure the biochemical changes that underlie learning, we can't really know. But in the absence of clear evidence to the contrary, psychologists usually assume that such measurements are at an interval level.

A common measurement technique for some areas in psychology is the rating scale. Instead of having subjects indicate their agreement with the statement "The University should include student rating of faculty teaching as a part of the annual salary determination process" using the categories listed earlier, we might ask people to indicate their level of agreement by marking along the scale

We could then score the attitude rating by using the numeric scale equivalents

Many measurement authorities would agree now that we had probably measured with an interval procedure, for when the subjects made the ratings, they

would subjectively define the intervals along the scale as equal. Note that only the extremes of the scale are labeled. That labeling avoids the difficulty of trying to develop verbal descriptions for a seven-point scale where (everyone would agree) the points represent equal steps in attitude. This technique, known as a bipolar *equal-appearing intervals* scaling procedure, is widely used in psychology and the behavioral sciences. We should also comment, though, that data from a measurement procedure using equal-appearing intervals aren't universally regarded as interval values. Some psychologists would argue that such measurement is actually ordinal.

With interval measurement, we can talk about the equality or inequality of differences along the scale. With an IQ test, for example, we can feel confident that the difference of 10 points between 75 and 85 represents roughly the same difference in intelligence as the 10 points between 100 and 110. We can also talk about relative differences, indicating, for example, that the difference between two children with IQ scores of 95 and 103 is less than the difference between two other children with scores of 110 and 125. (As we'll note later, though, while it's meaningful to talk about differences, and even ratios of differences, it's not meaningful to talk about ratios of scores; Johnny, with an IQ of 120, is not twice as intelligent as his brother Sam with an IQ of 60).

Ratios of scores. IQ tests are frequently constructed so that a child who scores average for his age group will receive an IQ score of 100. The anchor point of an IQ scale is thus the "normal" or average individual, and the performance of that individual is equated with a score of 100 on the test. Does an interval measuring scale like IQ have a meaningful or "true" zero point? That is, is zero aligned with "absence" of the property being measured? No—the fact that the number system has a zero point doesn't mean that it corresponds to "0" quantity. Just what does an IQ score of 0 mean? Nothing, actually—the scale doesn't go that far down. A zero could only mean that the individual taking the test was so far off the scale as to be untestable, but not that there was no intelligence to be measured.

When measurement rules take advantage of order, equal intervals, and also align the zero point in the number system with absence of the property being measured, then we are measuring on a *ratio* measurement scale (Figure 3.5). The absolute (Kelvin) temperature scale is a ratio scale, since a 0° temperature is applied only to a substance when there is no molecular motion (and that's the physical definition of absence of heat).

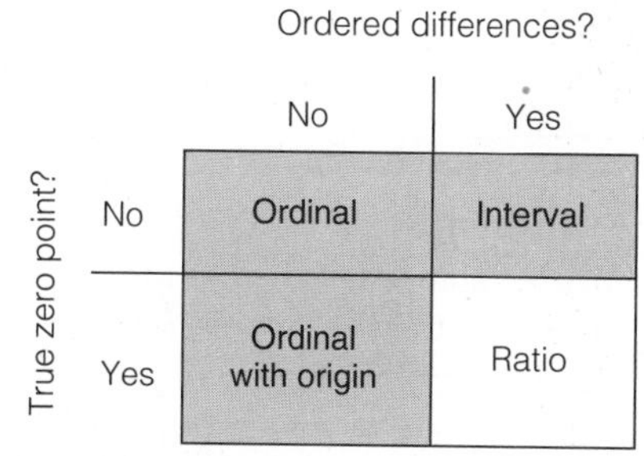

Ordered differences?

	No	Yes
No	Ordinal	Interval
Yes	Ordinal with origin	Ratio

True zero point? (No / Yes — rows)

Figure 3.5

Psychologists have comparatively few ratio measurement scales. Elapsed time is a ratio scale, as are such countable variables as trials to criterion, number of errors or correct responses, and so on, as well as clearly physical variables such as body weight or stimulus distance. But most psychological variables yield measurement that is either ordinal or interval. And in fact, that's probably appropriate in most instances. Do we have any concept of what zero intelligence really means? Does it matter that the number zero that's present in the number system doesn't line up with "zero intelligence," even if we could understand what that meant? No, it really makes little difference. What's important in IQ measurement is generally establishing differences in level between groups or individuals, and interval measurement is certainly satisfactory for that purpose.

The Importance of Measurement Scales. Why is all of this consideration of measurement scales important? Because the scale of measurement for a variable has an important effect on the kinds of operations that we can meaningfully apply to the data. And that, in turn, influences the choice of descriptive and inferential measures that we may use.

Arithmetic operations. Sometimes during data analysis it's convenient to apply various arithmetic operations to the data. We might want to add or subtract a value from every data value (for example, to make them all positive) or to multiply or divide each value by some other value (to change some characteristics of the data). Such operations are often called *transformations*. While the data are always "just numbers" and we can do any arithmetic operation to any numbers, some transformations are sensible with some kinds of measurement and some are not. We already mentioned the possibility of calculating the average of a set of numbers; for any collection of numbers, we can compute the average, but whether the average has an interpretable meaning is quite another matter.

For nominal data, the only aspect of the number system that matters is the uniqueness. We may do anything that we like to the numbers from nominal measurement so long as we preserve the uniqueness. In our example of categories of employees, it really doesn't matter at all whether we call tenured faculty 1, 63, or 528, just as long as we don't use its number for any other category. If we did, then we wouldn't even be using the uniqueness property of the number system, and our data would be difficult or impossible to interpret; if both administrator and technician were assigned the value 88, we'd never know exactly what a score of 88 represented, and data analysis would be very difficult.

Ordinal measurement takes advantage of the fact that the numbers have an order defined for them. When the measurement is at the ordinal level, assigning a large value indicates more of the property being measured. With ordinal data, we may do any operation that preserves the order property of the values without losing the meaning of the measurement. All that is required for meaning to be preserved is that a larger value is assigned to the object with more of the property being measured. In fact, most of the techniques for handling ordinal data simply convert the data from their original values to the values 1, 2, 3, ... for analysis. But it makes no difference whether we use the values 1, 2, 3, 4, 5, and 6 to describe food preferences, or values of 3, 8, 12, 13, 22, and 53. All that's important for the meaningfulness of the data is that a higher value indicates greater preference.

Changes that preserve the order of the data are referred to as *monotonic transformations*, a phrase that you may stumble across in the research literature from time to time. In a monotonic transformation, there are two rules, the uniqueness rule and the order rule. That is, individuals or objects that have different initial values must receive different transformed values, and two individuals or objects that are measured differently must appear in the same order in the transformed data. In other words, if you put steak ahead of fried chicken, it doesn't matter whether steak is given the value "2" and chicken "1," or whether steak is "32" and chicken is "25." What's important is that the ordering is preserved—higher values mean more of the property measured.

Ordinal data with an origin are very similar to ordinal data with respect to what we may do with the values and still preserve their meaning as measurements. Any monotonic transformation maintains the meaning of the data. So it doesn't matter whether we score our attitude data as $-10, -8, -3, 0, 7, 15, 20$, or as $-99, -18, -1, 0, 17, 18, 525$, or as $-3, -2, -1, 0, 1, 2, 3$ as long as we keep them in ascending order and attach the zero to the neutral category.

For interval data, meaningful operations must preserve the relationships among the intervals between data values. For example, if we had the interval values 34, 42, and 46, an operation should maintain the relationships between pairs of values. For these three values, the difference between the smallest pair $(42 - 34 = 8)$ is twice that between the largest pair $(46 - 42 = 4)$, and any operations applied to the values must preserve that relationship or the interval property of the measurement scale is lost.

What kinds of transformations will preserve the interval measurement? Certainly we could simply add the same value to each number and the differences would be the same: adding 50 produces the numbers 84, 92, and 96, and the differences between pairs are exactly the same. We might also multiply each value by the same number; multiplying by 3 gives 102, 126, and 138, and the difference between the smallest pair $(126 - 102 = 24)$ is still twice that between the largest $(138 - 126 = 12)$. We could even add and multiply. For example, if we multiplied each value by 3 and added 50, we would have the transformed values 152, 176, and 188. Again, with these values, the interval relationship is still maintained because the difference between the smallest values $(176 - 152 = 24)$ is still twice that between the larger two $(188 - 176 = 12)$.

In fact, any *linear transformation* applied to interval data preserves the ratios of differences. A linear transformation is one that multiplies and adds. That is, it follows the formula

$$Y = aX + b,$$

where Y is a new value and X is an original value. In the formula, a is any value and b is any real value. For example, in the first illustration (adding 50 to each value), $a = 1$ and $b = 50$, so that the formula is

$$Y = 1X + 50$$
$$= X + 50.$$

In the second example, we would have $a = 3$ and $b = 0$, or

$$Y = 3X + 0$$
$$= 3X.$$

Combining the two, using $a = 3$ and $b = 50$, with a formula of

$$Y = 3X + 50,$$

results in values of 152, 176, and 188. In each case, the linear transformation has preserved essential information concerning the relationships between the data values.

Any linear transformation will preserve the interval nature of the data. Since those ratios are maintained in interval measurement, it makes sense to talk about differences, and even ratios of differences, between pairs of measured values. With interval measurement, then, we can make computations that involve the difference between pairs of values without losing the underlying meaning in the data.

While we may meaningfully talk about ratios of differences for values measured on an interval scale, we can't talk about ratios of values themselves and be sure that we have preserved the meaning in the data. For example, IQ scores are generally regarded as being interval measurements, at least in the middle ranges.* Thus we can reasonably talk about a difference of 20 IQ points as being twice as large as a difference of 10 points, but we shouldn't claim that an IQ of 120 is twice that of an IQ of 60.

When the measurement is ratio, the interval property of the number system is employed. In addition, the value "0" is applied to the absence of the property measured. Numerous physical scales represent ratio measures—elapsed time, mass, and length are three examples. On a ratio scale, ratios between data values themselves are meaningful. Thus if Dan takes 10 minutes to complete a problem-solving task and Sara requires 15 minutes, then we may meaningfully say that Dan completed the task in two-thirds of Sara's time.

With ratio data, we may apply any scale change that preserves both the interval ratios and also the meaning of the zero point. Adding a value to all measurement obviously changes the zero point and so is an operation that changes the meaning of the values. If we've used a stopwatch to measure elapsed time to solve a problem, for example, the zero point in the measurement coincides with zero time taken. We can talk about Dan's requiring two-thirds as long as Sara to solve a problem. But we couldn't make that statement about Dan and Sara if we were to add a constant to both of their times. If we were to arbitrarily add 20 to both time scores, then we would have Dan measured at 30 and Sara at 35. It's still true that Dan completed the problem five minutes faster than did Sara, but Dan's score is no longer two-thirds of Sara's.

With ratio measurement, then, to preserve the relationship among the elements of the data, we may apply a multiplicative transformation but not an additive one. What this means is that we may apply any linear transformation where $b = 0$. Consider a common dependent variable in psychology—reaction time. Reaction time is commonly measured in milliseconds (.001 seconds). Reaction time is clearly a ratio measurement, since 0 corresponds to no elapsed time. The transformation of milliseconds to seconds is a simple one—multiply milli-

---

*In the extremes of IQ measurement, the scale is probably only ordinal. That is, while we can say that a retarded individual with an IQ of 60 is less intelligent than one with an IQ of 70, most psychologists wouldn't feel comfortable claiming that the 10-point difference here is equivalent to the 10-point difference between scores of 95 and 105, for example.

Table 3.1   Transformations that Preserve Meaning

Measurement scale	Transformation that preserves meaning	Example
Nominal	Any relabeling	Secretary = 1 Technician = 3 etc. becomes Secretary = 78 Technician = 46 etc.
Ordinal and ordinal with origin	Monotonic	Steak = 1 Shrimp = 2 etc. becomes Steak = 17 Shrimp = 28 etc.
Interval	Linear	$C° = (5/9)(F° − 32)$ $C° = (5/9)(70° − 32)$ $= 21.1°$
Ratio	Linear where $b = 0$	Sec = .001 × Msec Sec = .001 × 25,000 $= 25.0$

seconds by .001. The formula, then, is

Sec = .001 × Msec,

which is a linear equation where $b = 0$; we could just as easily write the formula as

Sec = .001 × Msec + 0.

Transformations can be applied to any set of numbers. The numbers "don't care" what is done to them; we've just applied mathematically permissible operations to the values. But we have stressed our concern with preserving the meaning that the numbers convey. Certainly, we can apply a monotonic, but nonlinear, transformation to values measured on an interval scale if we want. But the results of that transformation will have meaning only insofar as the order is concerned. We would no longer be confident that the intervals between values had the same meaning as originally.

Table 3.1 summarizes the transformations that preserve the meaning of the several measurement scales that we have discussed.

Statistical operations. Over the years, statisticians and writers of books like this one have taken varying positions on the importance, or lack of importance, of the measurement scale on the kinds of statistical operations that may be performed on data. Lord (1953), in a classic paper, pointed out that the numbers don't know or care what operations are done to them. His example is the numbers on football jerseys. Football numbers are best regarded as representing a nominal scale because they serve primarily to distinguish one player from another. If we want to, Lord points out, we could calculate the average of the football numbers; nothing prevents us from doing so. The numbers that come from football jerseys follow the properties of the number system, and statistics based on those numbers follow known properties of the statistics.

But the problem is in the meaning of the average that we computed, not in whether or not the operation is "permitted" by the system of numbers. If we calculate a value based on a nominal scale, any transformation that preserves the scores' uniqueness is permissible, but could change the statistic dramatically. Thus the interpretation of the average becomes meaningless.

For ordinal data, where any monotonic transformation preserves the meaning of the data, the average also doesn't make much sense. Suppose that Dan, Sara, and Peter run a race, and we record their order of finish. It doesn't matter whether we assign the values 1, 2, and 3 to the first, second, and third finishers, or 21, 28, and 44—the lowest number is still the lowest, the highest is still the highest, and the score in the middle is still in the middle. But the average changes from 2 to 31 after the transformation is made. Again, the mathematics gods can't complain about finding the average. But we can—the transformation, which is permissible for ordinal data, has made computing an average a nonsensical operation as far as interpretation is concerned.

On the other hand, with interval and ratio measurement, we can meaningfully talk about ratios of differences, and the average makes a great deal of sense, as do many other common statistical operations. As we proceed, we'll be alert to the measurement characteristics of the data, because they influence the choice of procedures that we might use for describing the data. Stine (1989) presents an excellent review of the considerations involved in measurement and statistics; the reader is referred there for additional detail.

Reliability and Validity

Two important characteristics of any measurement procedure are reliability and validity. When we say that a measuring instrument is reliable, we mean that we can count on it to assign the same numeric value each time we measure the same object. A reliable yardstick will measure the length of your desk the same today as it did yesterday, and the same today as it will tomorrow. A valid measurement procedure, as mentioned in Chapter 2, is one that measures the property that it claims to measure. Reliability and validity are related topics but address rather separate aspects of the measurement process. You might decide to measure an individual's intelligence by recording the number of words read per minute. You'd probably find that the number of words read was fairly constant over time, assuming you gave the individual similar material each time; in other words, the number of words per minute is a reliable measurement, since you tend to get similar measurements every time. But does the number of words read per minute really provide a good measure of intelligence? Probably not; the relationship between them is most likely quite weak. In this case, the number of words read per minute isn't a valid measure of intelligence. And that's the case even if the measurement of words per minute is reliable.

Assessing Validity   Earlier in this chapter we quoted Stevens (1951) as saying that "... measurement is the assignment of numerals to objects or events according to rules." We added that the aim of measurement is to assign the numerals so that they represent the quantity of some attribute. This relationship between the measured value and its underlying attribute is important in research. For Dr. Campbell, the attribute is the hypothetical personality dimension of introversion/extraversion, and the test that he uses purports to measure it. Naturally, he wants his measured value to reflect the underlying dimension. Evaluating the validity of a measurement means to assess how accurate the relationship between the measure and its underlying trait actually is.

    Validity is often confined to a particular context. Dr. Campbell's measurement of introversion/extraversion is confined to his research, and he is content to establish the validity of his measurement in that context. Whether the scores are related to the more "popular" meanings of introversion and extraversion as it concerns an individual's style of relating to others isn't important for Dr. Campbell's research. Of course, a social psychologist might want to establish the validity of the same introversion/extraversion scale that Dr. Campbell uses in another context.

    Some attributes that we might want to measure are readily available for validity checks. To assure ourselves that a timer that measures reaction time in subjects is valid, we can use external time standards to verify our equipment. Establishing the validity of a timer, then, is a simple matter of comparing its output measurements against known input time intervals or the measurements from other, known timers. For some other variables that psychologists use, establishing validity is a straightforward matter. But for many psychological variables, there is no "Bureau of Standards" to provide external validation; for this reason, psychology has probably directed more attention to developing validation procedures than has any other scientific discipline.

    A first consideration for many people is whether or not a measurement procedure "looks like" it's measuring what it should. That is, a test of introversion/extraversion should contain items that ask whether the person is outgoing and sociable. A test of reading ability should require reading, and so forth. In other words, does the measuring device look, on the face of it, as if it is measuring the correct characteristics? This criterion, called *face validity*, usually isn't considered important by measurement experts. Measurement procedures that meet the other criteria of validity often have face validity, but they need not. A valid measure of introversion/extraversion might not even ask about sociability, for example, but might instead ask about hobbies or even about leisure-reading habits. While those kinds of questions might not *seem* closely related to introversion/extraversion, other criteria might well establish that they are better measures than they appear. These other, more useful, criteria for validity are those involving prediction, content, and theoretical relationships. More specifically, the most important aspects of validity are predictive validity, content validity, and construct validity.

Predictive Validity. The term *predictive validity* means that a measurement should correlate with other measures of the same thing. If a test is designed to select good candidates for a particular job, then it should be able to predict how well employees will succeed in the job. If you're developing a test to predict how well a word-processor operator will succeed on the job, you'll want your test to correlate highly with standard measures of job success. Establishing the validity of a measurement scale is of special importance in applied settings where just such predictions are routinely needed. Industrial placement and education are two of the situations where predictive validity is important. In those situations, it is also relatively easy to assess a test's validity, because there are known criteria for success.

Predictive validity of a measurement is demonstrated by a strong correlation between the measurement and the criterion. That is, individuals who score highly on the test for word-processor operators should turn out to be the best at their task. On the other hand, individuals who score poorly on the test should be poor word-processor operators.

The criterion used for a predictive validity test need not actually be a "future" one, like job success or educational achievement. Any external referent will suffice, because a strong correlation between two measures implies that we could, if we wanted, accurately predict the values of one variable from the other. We needn't wait to assess the actual performance of potential word-processor operators, for example. We could test a range of operators already at work and look at the relationship between their test scores and their on-the-job performance. Since we needn't actually predict a variable to establish validity, the term *predictive validity* is more commonly called "concurrent" or "criterion-related" in the current literature.

A major problem with predictive or concurrent validity is that, as we've suggested, for a great many important variables in psychology there is simply no external criterion variable available. While performance variables—like the performance of word-processing employees—are common in applied situations, much psychological research concerns variables like motivation, drive, attitude, personality, and so forth for which there aren't agreed-upon external criteria. For that reason, criterion-based approaches to establishing measurement validity are often of lesser importance than the two remaining approaches to validation, content validity and construct validity.

Content Validity. For some variables, it's possible to define a set of behaviors characteristic of situations or knowledge that is relevant to the behavior to be measured. The validity of the measurement then is established by the extent to which it adequately samples the content. The most obvious situations where content validity is useful are those where knowledge of a particular set of information is to be measured, as in an achievement test or course examination. When an instructor develops an examination for a course, he or she first defines what the students are expected to know (that is, the domain of knowledge to be covered by the test). Then the instructor samples from the content of the domain and develops the test items. The test may be said to have content validity if it samples the domain representatively. The student's scores on the test are then regarded as valid measurements of the knowledge of the material.

In predictive or criterion-related validity, a correlation coefficient is generally used to define the degree to which a test relates to other measures of the same or related variables. In content validation, though, there is no external referent and a correlation is meaningless. Therefore content validation is a judgmental process, with the investigator or others deciding if the test seems well constructed and samples its domain adequately.

Construct Validity. Construct validation is the technique that is applied to most measurement in psychology, and it is the area in which psychology has contributed the most to the theory of measurement. Essentially, construct validity looks for patterns of relationships among variables that are expected on the basis of theory. Dr. Campbell's research might very well be regarded as trying to establish the validity of the scale of introversion/extraversion that he is using. The theory of introversion and extraversion that Dr. Campbell is investigating suggests that those individuals who score toward the introversion end of the scale derive much of their stimulation internally, while those who score at the opposite end of the scale seek external stimulation. That suggestion, coming from theory, prompted Dr. Campbell to measure two variables, using an introversion/extraversion test and a measure of sensation seeking. When he finds a relationship between those two variables, he is validating not only the theory but also the measures of introversion/extraversion and sensation seeking, since the variables relate as predicted.

Construct validation doesn't stop with two variables and a relationship predicted by a theory. A measurement that has good construct validity is expected to relate highly with measures of other variables that the theory says should be related and, in addition, to not relate to variables that should be unrelated. These two requirements are sometimes known as *convergence* (measures that should be related "converge" on the same behaviors) and *divergence* (a variable should discriminate its behaviors from others that it is not expected to measure).

Convergence suggests that Dr. Campbell should find strong correlations between his introversion/extraversion measure and other measures of sensation seeking, openness to others, social outgoingness, and so forth. Divergence requires that Dr. Campbell's measures show no correlation with such other personal attributes as intelligence, attitude toward socialized medicine, and marital status, all of which are predicted by the theory to be unrelated to introversion/extraversion.

As should be clear, construct validity is established both by judgment and by correlation. Judgment decides how the validation procedures are related to the theory; the correlations are used to evaluate convergence and discrimination. Without both components, the process is incomplete. It's not enough for Dr. Campbell to reason that measures of sensation seeking and introversion/extraversion logically vary together and that neither varies with intelligence; the data must support the logic. Conversely, he can't just look at a pattern of correlations and infer validity—the pattern of correlations must fit with the logic of the theory.

| Assessing Reliability | Reliability is the extent to which you may expect to find the same result when you measure the same thing again. As such, it is a measure of the "repeatability" |

of the measurement process, the extent to which we may expect to find that repeated measurements of the same individual or object will give essentially the same results. A classical definition of reliability is the test-retest definition: if the measurement results in the same answer upon retest, then the test is reliable. This form of reliability is established by measuring the same objects twice and correlating the results. A high correlation is evidence of reliability.

It's very difficult to actually obtain test-retest reliability directly, since once a human (or animal) subject has been tested or subjected to some measurement procedure, it's not the "same" organism any longer; certainly your instructor couldn't establish the reliability of the final examination by giving it to your class twice! Several techniques have been devised to assess reliability in ways other than the classical test-retest manner. One procedure involves the use of *parallel forms* of the same test, in which two tests are given that contain different but equivalent items. Another procedure, the *split-half* procedure, divides a test into two halves and correlates them with each other. The result is the same as a parallel-forms reliability check except that the two forms are given together.

| **The Importance of Validity and Reliability** | When you listen to the evening news and hear reports of temperature, wind speed, and race results, you now know that there are two features of those numbers that you need to take account of in interpreting the reports. The numbers may represent different measurement scales, certainly, but you can also be concerned about their reliability and validity. Perhaps you wouldn't make the mistake of trying to interpret the average of the order-of-finish positions in the races that are reported, but you might be tempted to conclude that today's high of 90° is twice the record low of 45° for this date. In addition to the sorts of interpretations you might make, you can also think about the reliability and validity of the newscaster's values. While weather values have probably been measured with accurate (that is, reliable and valid) instruments and while the order of racers crossing the finish line is probably valid, how about statements like "Nine out of ten doctors surveyed . . . ," or "72.6% of those questioned . . . ," or "The polls show . . ."? |

Earlier in this chapter, we used an example of measuring intelligence by measuring the number of words read per minute. It's likely that the number of words per minute would be a reliable measurement. That is, if we kept the reading material fairly constant, an individual would probably read at roughly the same rate. But reading rate wouldn't meet most criteria for a valid measure of intelligence. It probably correlates only weakly with academic success or teacher ratings of ability (predictive or concurrent validity). It doesn't sample the domain of activities that we would regard as "intelligent" behaviors (content validity). And it doesn't fit well with the current theoretical understanding of intelligence. It wouldn't be expected to correlate well with other measures of intelligence, nor to differentiate reading speed from other behaviors that aren't related to intelligence (construct validity). In short, just because a measurement (like reading speed, for example) is reliable, it's not necessarily valid.

Just as it's important to understand whether variables are measured on an interval or ordinal scale, it is important to understand that measurements used in research should be evaluated for their reliability and validity. If invalid measures are used, then any conclusions that might be drawn are meaningless, just as if an inappropriate descriptive procedure were used for nominal data. Likewise, if measurements are unreliable, we have little confidence that the same results would be obtained if the research were repeated.

SUMMARY

- Measuring assigns numerals to objects or events according to certain rules.
- Nominal measurement uses only the "uniqueness" property of the number system.
- If larger values represent "more" of the property measured, the measurement is at least ordinal.
- Ordinal measurement scales are sometimes aligned with the zero point in the number system, making an "ordinal with origin" scale.
- In interval measurement, the differences between values may themselves be meaningfully ordered.
- Interval measurement is probably the most common scale in psychology.
- Ratio measurement makes use of the equal-interval and the zero-point properties of the number system.
- The scale of measurement influences the operations that we can meaningfully do with data.
- *Reliability* is the extent to which the same value would be obtained if the measurement were repeated.
- A valid measuring instrument measures what it claims to measure.

KEY TERMS

Concurrent validity

Construct validity

Content validity

Face validity

Interval measurement

Linear transformation

Monotonic transformation

Nominal measurement

Ordinal measurement

Ordinal with origin measurement

Predictive validity

Ratio measurement

Reliability

Validity

EXERCISES

Solutions to asterisked (∗) exercises appear at the back of the book.

1. The following list gives some measurement rules. For each, indicate what scale of measurement (nominal, ordinal, ordinal with origin, interval, or ratio) is represented

   ∗a. The experimenter starts a stopwatch when the subject begins a task and stops it when the task is completed.

   b. A child is given an IQ test.

   ∗c. Subjects are asked to arrange a set of five soft drinks in order of preference.

   d. Subjects are asked to indicate whether they agree or disagree with each of a series of statements. The experimenter then counts how many statements are checked for agreement.

*e. Subjects are shown a pattern of letters for a brief flash and asked to recall as many as possible; the experimenter counts how many are correctly recalled.

f. A rat is placed in a Skinner box; the number of bar presses per minute is recorded.

*g. People are asked to indicate their political party preference.

h. Participants in an experiment are asked to indicate their degree of agreement/disagreement with various political statements on a −10 to +10 scale.

*i. Subjects manipulate a switch that moves a visual pattern back and forth until it appears clearest. The experimenter measures the distance between the stimulus and the subject's eyes using a steel tape measure.

j. Observers classify the behavior patterns of free-ranging gorillas into 15 categories.

*k. Students are asked to estimate the percent of their time spent in different activities during a typical week.

l. Participants are asked to arrange a series of photographs of people in order of attractiveness.

*m. Animals are given a choice of two substances to eat. The food items are weighed before being placed in the cages. After a two-hour period, the food is weighed again and the amount of each consumed is determined.

*2. Some athletic events (for example, diving in the Olympics) are scored by having a panel of expert judges rate each performance on a 0–10 scale, where a 10 represents a perfect performance. What scale of measurement does each judge's rating represent?

3. In Exercise 2, the individual score is computed by dropping the highest and the lowest of the individual ratings and then summing the remaining values. Based on your answer to Exercise 2, is that a reasonable operation to do with the ratings? Why or why not?

*4. In some events (diving, for example), the judges' total (from Exercise 3) is multiplied by a "difficulty rating" for the particular performance; the product becomes the final score. Based on your answer to Exercise 2, is that a reasonable operation to do with the ratings? Why or why not?

5. You have developed a test that you claim can predict final grades in a statistics class. How would you convince someone that your test was valid using:
   a. Concurrent validation
   b. Content validation
   c. Construct validation

C H A P T E R   4

Controlling and Manipulating Variables

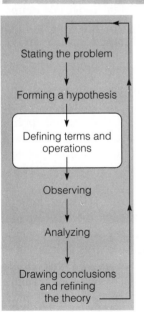

Stating the problem

Forming a hypothesis

Defining terms and operations

Observing

Analyzing

Drawing conclusions and refining the theory

Chapter 2 presented an overview of research and methods; we elaborated on some of that material, especially the part of research involving measurement, in Chapter 3. This chapter discusses more of the mechanics of conducting research, emphasizing the kinds of manipulation and control typical of experimental methods. By the end of this chapter, together with what we've learned in Chapters 2 and 3, we'll have a core of research methods that will serve us throughout the development of research designs in Chapters 11 through 20.

Most of the material in this chapter concerns decisions made before actual data collection begins. These decisions have to do with manipulating and controlling variables in the experiment. In particular, before data collection begins, extraneous variables that might compromise the results must be dealt with, and the independent variable manipulations operationally defined.

In this chapter we'll also discuss internal and external validity. Internal validity refers to the degree to which the experiment is logically consistent and allows causal inferences to be made, while external validity concerns the degree to which the results of one study may be generalized to other situations. Both of these topics are closely related to the actual conduct of the research, particularly the ways in which variables are measured, manipulated, and controlled. Chapter 3 talked about measurement, while this one covers manipulation and control.

Manipulating the Independent Variable

The essence of the experimental method can be summarized easily: manipulate the independent variable, and hold all other conditions constant; any observed changes can have been caused only by the changes in the independent variable. That sounds simple and straightforward, and so it is. But it's much more difficult to actually *do* an experiment than it is to define one.

Consider the phrase "manipulate the independent variable." Suppose that you want to study the effect of room illumination on factory productivity. How many levels of illumination should you use? What brightness levels should you use? How will you choose which factory workers work under which conditions? Or should all workers work under all conditions? Just these few simple questions suggest that the situation isn't as simple as you might think.

Some independent variables are quantifiable, like level of illumination in a room, amount of practice given, age of the subjects, and so forth. Others are not—Dr. Stewart's animals are either given a conditioned avoidance experience or they are not. Independent variables like Dr. Stewart's are called *qualitative*, since the experimental conditions differ in the kind of stimulus presented to the subject. A variable like illumination level, on the other hand, is known as a *quantitative* variable, since it varies in amount. In either case, we want to choose independent variable manipulations that maximize effect on the dependent variable.

Deciding whether an independent variable is quantitative or qualitative normally stems directly from the research question. In Dr. Stewart's experiment, the question is best addressed by the two conditions of aversion conditioning. Aversion conditioning seems to be an all-or-nothing phenomenon, and so there's no reason to explore several "amounts" or "levels" of it. A study of room illumination, on the other hand, invites a consideration of the range of illumination possible. The nature of the two variables—aversion conditioning and room illumination—thus dictates that one be qualitative and the other quantitative.

Manipulating a Quantitative Independent Variable

If an independent variable is a quantitative one, it may assume any of a large number of values. If you're planning to manipulate illumination level, for example, you can choose from a great many possible levels. Choosing the specific values to be used in the experiment is important. There are really two choices—how many different values of the independent variable to use (for example, how many different illumination levels will you use?) and just what those levels will be.

For some variables, using *extreme values* may be useful. For example, if you're interested in the effects of instruction in piano on musical pitch perception, you might choose some individuals who have been playing since a very young age and others of the same age who have never played. Note the specification of "others of the same age." You shouldn't merely choose those who have played less than a year and those who have played for more than 10 years, for example, since there might be a difference in age; if you found a difference in pitch perception, you wouldn't know whether it was due to the subject's age or to piano instruction. To investigate the effect of illumination level, we might choose "light" and "dark," instead of "dim" and "twilight."

Choice of levels is best based on some understanding of the relationship between the independent variable and the dependent variable. Sometimes it's effective to use extreme values of the independent variable, and sometimes it's not. For example, some variables are related by a U-shaped function across their full ranges. (See Figure 4.1.) Here, as the independent variable increases, the value of the dependent variable increases at first, then levels off, and then decreases.

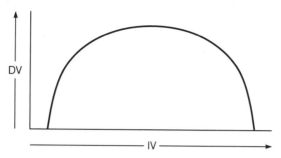

Figure 4.1

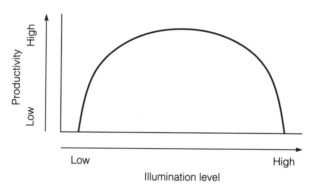

Figure 4.2

What variables might be related in this fashion? Illumination level and industrial productivity provide one example. At very low and at very high illumination levels, productivity would decrease, while the highest productivity would be found in the middle range of illumination. (See Figure 4.2.)

Think about using hours of food deprivation as an independent variable in an animal study with running speed as the dependent variable. With no food deprivation, animals are lethargic and inactive; increasing food deprivation increases their activity level, and thus running speed, at least up to a point. Once that point is reached, additional food deprivation has little effect until starvation and weakness begin; and then running speed slows again.

Or consider the independent variable of loudness of signal tone: too soft and it can't be heard, too loud and it could be extremely disruptive. Or how about a relationship between anxiety level in humans and test performance? At a low level, anxiety could have no effect; at a high level, the individual might be so crippled by anxiety that no effect could be seen.

Selecting the levels of the independent variable to present requires some thought, as well as some knowledge of the relationship between the variables under consideration. In many cases, using extreme levels will not show any effect on the dependent variable. Instead of using extremes, then, choosing *optimal levels* of the independent variable is a good strategy. If we were to choose to manipulate the independent variable in only two different ways, we want the differences between those two conditions to be as large as possible. We should,

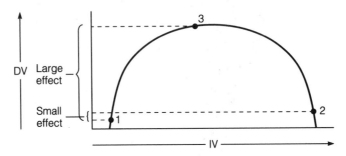

Figure 4.3

therefore, try to select points like those labeled 1 and 3 in Figure 4.3 and avoid those that are like points 1 and 2. In other words, the optimal levels of food deprivation for rats are probably closer to 0 and 24 hours than they are to 0 and 90 hours. Or the best illumination levels for studying the effect of illumination are probably "dim" and "moderately bright," but not "pitch black" and "blinding."

There is no assurance, of course, that the variables in a study are related in this U-shaped fashion. In fact, many quantitative independent variables have other forms of relationship with possible dependent variables. We'll illustrate some of the other possibilities when we turn to selecting the number of experimental conditions. In an experiment, there are normally two or more different treatments, or variations, of the independent variable.

Choosing the Number of Levels of the Independent Variable

In some cases, as in Dr. Stewart's experiment, only two variations of the independent variable are necessary (taste aversion or not, in his case). In that case, then, the decision on how many variations to use in the experiment is easily made. Fortunately, the question being addressed in a research project often provides the number of experimental conditions necessary. Dr. Stewart needed only two experimental conditions to address his question of sweetness generalization. In other cases, though, more conditions are necessary, and experimental designs expand to accommodate them.

The number of manipulations is generally dictated by the research question —does the number of experimental conditions permit a clear answer to the question being posed? In Dr. Stewart's case, two conditions are plenty. But if you were looking at the effects of several different drugs, at several different kinds of video presentations, or at several different kinds of words, two conditions wouldn't be enough.

Again, there's a difference between qualitative and quantitative independent variables in choosing the number of experimental conditions. While qualitative variables normally have their conditions dictated by the research question, quantitative variables require some additional consideration. For example, to address the question of the effect of illumination level on productivity would take several different levels of lighting. Using two could only establish that there might be differences, but to really understand the relationship might require a number of different lighting levels. An investigator who used only points 1 and 3 in

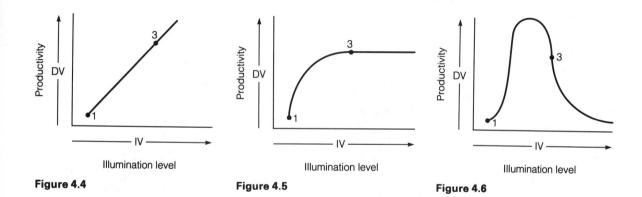

Figure 4.4 **Figure 4.5** **Figure 4.6**

Figures 4.4, 4.5, and 4.6, for example, would have an incomplete understanding. The figures illustrate three possible relationships. Thus with only two amounts of the independent variable, there is no way to explore a quantitative relationship adequately. This fact probably explains why experimental designs with multiple conditions are very pervasive in psychology.

Between and Within Subjects: Manipulating the Independent Variable. When Dr. Stewart induces a taste aversion to saccharin in some of his subjects and not in others, he is manipulating his independent variable. He then measures the sucrose* consumption of his animals and has two sets of measurements: consumption by aversion-conditioned animals and consumption by non-conditioned animals. By comparing those sets of data, he can draw a conclusion about the effect of the aversion conditioning and thereby decide whether or not the sweet taste of saccharin has generalized to another sweet substance.

Donald J. Tyrrell holds B.A. and Ph.D. degrees from the University of Connecticut. His current research interests focus on the cognitive and perceptual development of infants and very young children. He and his students regularly have infants and their parents visit the laboratory to participate in research projects. His research has been published in several developmental psychology journals such as *Child Development*. When not teaching and doing research, Dr. Tyrrell and his wife are avid white-water canoeists.

Another of our example researchers, Dr. Tyrrell, studies infant development. His work often makes use of a phenomenon known as "preference for novelty." When an infant is presented with two stimuli, it will normally spend more time looking at an unfamiliar object than at a familiar one. In a study that we'll explore in more detail later, Dr. Tyrrell shows an infant a videotape of a person walking. Later, he'll show that same tape to the child, alongside a tape of the same person jogging. If the infant spends more time looking at the jogging pictures, Dr. Tyrrell

---

*He also looks at the consumption of the other three taste solutions, as we noted earlier.

can infer that the child can tell the difference between walking and jogging since it preferred jogging as a novel pattern. Normally, Dr. Tyrrell shows a sequence like that just described and then reverses the pattern, giving a jogging pattern for a familiarization period followed by the presentation of the two patterns again. In that way, he records two amounts of time—walking and jogging—when each is a novel pattern.

When he shows a walking video and a jogging video to his subjects, Dr. Tyrrell is also manipulating his independent variable. Like Dr. Stewart, he has two sets of data, one set consisting of "looking times" to the walking pattern and the other set consisting of "looking times" to the jogging pattern. And, again like Dr. Stewart, by comparing those two sets of data, Dr. Tyrrell will draw a conclusion about the results. In this case, he'll make an inference about the perceptual ability of infants.

Notice that there's a difference in the way that Dr. Stewart and Dr. Tyrrell manipulated their independent variable with respect to their subjects. In Dr. Stewart's research, each individual rat either is given a taste aversion or it isn't. He uses two separate groups of animals, one corresponding to the aversion condition in the experimental design and the other to the non-aversion condition. Thus the two different independent variable conditions in the experiment correspond to two different experimental groups. A comparison of the data from the aversion condition with that from the non-aversion condition is a comparison *between* two separate groups of subjects (Figure 4.7)

On the other hand, Dr. Tyrrell shows each of his infants both the jogging

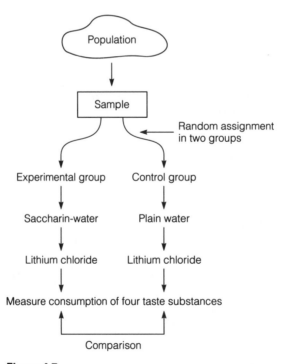

Figure 4.7

and the walking patterns. Some of the children see the walking pattern first followed by the jogging, and others see the reverse order; but all experience both of the conditions of the experiment. Thus, when Dr. Tyrrell compares his two sets of data, he is comparing the sets of data from his two experimental conditions, just like in Dr. Stewart's experiment, but now the comparison is *within* the same group of subjects.

The two forms of manipulation—all conditions applied to the same subjects, or all conditions applied to different subjects—lead to what are known as the *between-subjects experimental design* and the *within-subjects experimental design*. The phrase "between- or within-subjects" communicates the fact that comparisons between conditions are comparisons *between* different groups of subjects or *within* the same group of subjects. A simple between-subjects design with two conditions is illustrated in Figure 4.8. The figure makes it clear that there are two separate sets of subjects, each receiving one of two experimental treatments. Those treatments, of course, represent the manipulation of the independent variable. In Dr. Stewart's experiment, the two conditions were the two aversion treatments. It's also clear that there is a comparison between two sets of measurements, one following each experimental treatment.

Contrast the two-condition design in Figure 4.8 with a within-subjects manipulation, illustrated in Figure 4.9. Again, there is a comparison between two sets of dependent variable observations, each taken after one of the two experimental conditions. But in this case, the sets of data come from the same subjects.

The major difference in the *between* and *within* procedures is in the data

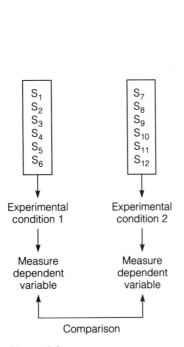

Figure 4.8

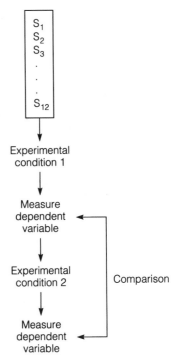

Figure 4.9

analysis, where slightly different statistical methods are used. But the question will be the same—are there differences among the sets of data derived from the different independent variable conditions? If there are, and if the experiment has internal validity (see p. 88), then we are able to infer that the change in the independent variable caused those differences.

Why did Dr. Stewart choose a between-subjects experimental design and Dr. Tyrrell use a within-subjects procedure? There are several possible reasons, but the short answer is that the within-subjects manipulation is often used because of certain control features that we'll discuss soon. A within-subjects procedure may also be chosen for reasons of economy, since a within-subjects manipulation obviously requires fewer subjects. Both kinds of experimental strategy have disadvantages and advantages that we'll learn about as we proceed, and each is better suited to certain purposes than is the other. Understanding the features of the two procedures requires that we address the matter of experimental control directly, a topic to which we now turn.

Experimental Control

A typical experiment has a single dependent variable that is measured and one (or sometimes more) independent variable that the experimenter manipulates. In addition, there are a large number of extraneous variables that are dealt with in various ways. An extraneous variable is any source of variation in the research setting that is not an independent or dependent variable. Sex of the subject, for example, could be an independent variable in an experiment that looked for sex differences (correctly, the experiment would be a quasi-experiment, since the independent variable isn't actually being manipulated), or it could be an extraneous variable in other situations. (Sex could even be a dependent variable, if you were doing a genetic experiment in sex determination!)

Confounded Variables

You surely wouldn't want all of Dr. Stewart's control animals to be one sex and all of his experimental animals to be the other, would you? If they were, and if there were a difference between the two sets of observations, was the difference caused by the sex of the animals in the groups, or was it caused by conditioned aversion given to one group? There's simply no way to tell.

Suppose that you're interested in the effect of the age of the experimenter on recall of information from a series of television commercials. The independent variable is the age of the experimenter who presents the commercials. You will assign subjects to two experimental groups; one group will have an older experimenter and the other a younger one. Subjects in both conditions will see a series of television commercials. The participants will then answer some questions about the products seen in the advertisements. As a matter of convenience, you decide to have all of the subjects arrive at the same time for the experiment and assign them to the two conditions. Also as a matter of convenience, the first 15 people who arrive are assigned to the older experimenter, and the last 15 to the younger. If you find a difference between the groups, can you infer that it is caused by the age of the experimenter? No, because you have also found a difference between the first and the last people to arrive. It's possible that the experimenter's age really has an effect, but there are alternative explanations. The groups could differ in at least the following ways, any of which is another possible explanation for the difference in performance:

1. The first arrivals are exceptionally responsible and compulsively punctual individuals who also always have everything completed well ahead of the deadline.
2. The first arrivals have somewhere else that they need to be and hope that by coming early they will be able to leave early.
3. The later arrivals rushed to get there and are anxious that they may not be included in the experiment.
4. The later arrivals are habitually disorganized and are there only because their roommates reminded them that they had an appointment.

Of course, there's no way to distinguish between any of the possible explanations for the difference, since it could be any of the listed possibilities (or others that you might think of yourself); it might even be that there's a difference between young and old experimenters. But you'll never know for sure.

Two variables whose relationships are completely entangled, like the age of the experimenter and the time of the subject's arrival, were defined in Chapter 2 as *confounded*. Confounding occurs when the two variables *covary*, meaning that they vary *together*. In the example, when the age of the experimenter changes, so does the time at which the subjects arrived at the experiment. If all of Dr. Stewart's control animals are female and all the experimental animals male, when sex of the animal changes, so does the aversion treatment. (Naturally, Dr. Stewart would be very careful to avoid such a confounding.)

In Chapter 2 we indicated that confounding must be avoided if we are to draw causal conclusions, and we point it out again here. When confounding involves an independent variable and an extraneous variable like sex of the animal or the time of arrival at the experiment, it's impossible to draw a conclusion about the effect of the independent variable. Since it could just as easily be either variable that caused the difference, the results are unclear, and causal inference is impossible.

In within-subjects research as we diagrammed it in Figure 4.9, did it occur to you to worry about the fact that the comparison between the two experimental conditions was also a comparison between the *first* and the *second* task presented to the subjects? If there was a difference, was it because of the treatment or because the first measurement was *made first*? The second time a subject is tested, it's in some ways not quite the same subject as it was the first time. Recall the first time you ever took an achievement test; you'd probably never seen a printed multiple-choice test before, especially not one that was administered with such strict time limits and with instructions read very precisely by the examiner. By your second such test, you had learned a lot about taking tests. Apart from the fact that you were also older and that the tests were different, some of the difference between your first and your second scores was probably due to the effect of the order in which you took the tests.

A within-subjects experimental design always opens the possibility that the order in which the tasks are presented can be an extraneous variable. If all of the subjects are given the tasks in exactly the same order, then the independent variable will certainly be confounded with the order of presentation. Special methods are needed to avoid order effects in within-subjects experiments; we'll discuss techniques for dealing with the extraneous variable in the following sections.

How did Dr. Stewart deal with the problem of sex as a confounded extraneous variable? One solution might have been to use only one sex in both groups. Another solution could have been to randomly assign animals to his two conditions in the hopes that the sex would "balance out," or at least not be a deliberately confounded variable. He could even have expanded his experimental design and used the sex of the subject as a second independent variable. (In fact, he assigned equal numbers of males and females to each experimental condition.) All of the techniques that we just suggested are possible solutions; let's look at them and at some others more closely.

| Sources of Extraneous Variables | Extraneous variables arise from a large number of sources. For sake of discussion, let's group them into general types of variables. |

Physical Factors. The most obvious sources of extraneous variables are *physical and situational*. Physical variables are those in the environment. Noise, room size, room color, and other environmental characteristics are physical factors that might vary. Likewise, time of day and day of the week are possible extraneous variables. Ways of handling, feeding, and housing animal subjects are also physical variables; they're generally simple to control. The instructions given to human subjects can also be an extraneous variable.

Intra-Subject Factors. Another class of extraneous variable includes the personal factors involving individual subjects that could cause confounds in the experiment. Obvious factors such as the sex, age, or education of the subjects may be relevant to the experiment and could cause confounding. *Selection* is a less obvious extraneous variable; we illustrated it in our example of assigning the first arrivals to one condition and the later subjects to the other. Selection need not be that obvious to cause trouble; volunteers may be different from nonvolunteers, and they may both be different from paid participants or from students taking part in an experiment as a part of a course requirement; all of these may differ from members of the military or from a prison population who may have little alternative to participating in the research.

Other intra-subject sources of extraneous variables include *order effects* in within-subjects designs, where one experimental condition in some way "changes" the way a subject responds to succeeding treatments. Long-term within-subjects investigations, as sometimes used in developmental studies, allow the possibility that individuals in the study will have different events occur in their lives between treatments or observations. This extraneous variable is often called *history*, since it refers to a sequence of events in a subject's life. Different histories help to explain why even identical twins behave somewhat differently from one another.

Finally, an extraneous variable called the *regression effect* is an easy intra-subject variable to overlook. Regression is a slippery concept, and we'll use an example to illustrate it. Suppose that you wanted to investigate the effect of a training program on running speed. To begin, you want to obtain two groups of athletes who differ with respect to their running speed in a 100-yard dash. You might have all of your possible subjects run 100 yards, time them, and then assign the fastest to the "fast" condition and the slowest to the "slow" condition. Then you give all of the people a training program and time them again in 100 yards. Suppose that you find that the "slow" group improved their speed more than did the "fast" group. Could you conclude that there is a difference in the amount of improvement? Unfortunately not. If you did *nothing* between the two timings of your subjects, you would probably find that your "slow" group ran faster and that your "fast" group was slower. Your results have been confounded with a regression effect, which describes why extreme pretest scores tend to change in the direction of an average score on retesting.

Why should this happen? Simply because, on the first race, some of the slow runners were slower than they "should have been." (Everyone has a bad day now and then; maybe some people lost sleep the night before; others didn't feel well; and so on.) When you retest those people, some of whom may have been classified into the "slow" group, their times are likely to improve. The same logic holds for the "fast" group; on rerunning the race, some of the individuals who were faster "than they should have been" the first time may run slower, so that the speed of the "fast" group decreases. This phenomenon, known as *regression to the mean*, or simply the *regression effect*, is an extraneous variable in many studies where groups are formed by pretesting.

Interpersonal Factors. Considerable evidence for interpersonal factors exists in psychological research. The very fact that they're being studied often changes people's behavior. The example of the effect of illumination on factory productivity is based on a real study, the famous "Hawthorne" studies reported by Roethlisberger and Dickson (1939). In the lighting-level study, conducted at the Hawthorne Plant of the Western Electric Company, production-line workers were tested under two conditions in a between-subjects design. In one condition, the lighting level remained constant; in the other condition, the illumination level was increased over several testing periods. The results showed increasing productivity in *both* conditions. That study and several others led to the conclusion that the very fact of participating in a research study increased productivity, regardless of other manipulations. As a result, the *Hawthorne effect* is a factor that must be kept in mind as a likely extraneous variable in any behavioral research.

But the Hawthorne effect isn't the only interpersonal extraneous variable. In some cases, especially where tests are being used, subjects may suffer from *evaluation apprehension*—a concern about being tested—and may change their responses so as not to appear "abnormal," or they may try to behave as they think the experimenter wants them to behave. In fact, there's evidence that subjects can feel constrained to act in certain ways, to be a "good subject," as it were (Weber & Cook, 1972). Subjects often try to figure out what the experimenter wants or expects, and many try to behave in ways that will support the experimenter's hypothesis.

In addition, Orne (1962) suggests that experimenters sometimes give cues as to what they expect. Orne calls these the *demand characteristics* of the experimental situation. Recent research, including that reported by Weber and Cook (1972), questions how pervasive such characteristics really are, but they remain a factor to be dealt with in setting up experimental situations.

Subjects aren't the only participants in a research experience—there are experimenters, too. Experimenters often have opinions and expectations about how the research should turn out. So the demand characteristics that Orne reports could be very real and could communicate what the experimenter "wants" to happen. Rosenthal (1976) summarized a great deal of research on experimenter expectancies.

Controlling Extraneous Variables

If the preceding discussion has left you with the feeling that we are beset by extraneous variables from every direction, take heart: many of the possible confounding factors in an experiment can be dealt with quite simply. While there are an infinite number of extraneous variables in any situation, we need normally worry only about those that might have an influence on the behavior that we're studying. The color of a car, for example, is probably irrelevant to its acceleration and can safely be ignored. Naturally, though, we wouldn't want to ignore color in a study of a car's sales appeal.

Even more important, while we won't be able to identify or explicitly control every extraneous variable, the main concern is that they not be confounded with an independent variable. For example, while Dr. Stewart can control the extraneous variable of sex in several ways, his main concern is that it not be confounded with aversion conditioning. While in an ideal experiment, we might control all possible extraneous variables, as a practical matter we can't hope to do so. So our goal, then, is to make sure that the extraneous variables don't influence different experimental conditions systematically.

Holding Conditions Constant. Some extraneous variables may be controlled by simply holding them at a constant level across all conditions of the independent variable. We could arrange that all of our cars be the same color, for example, or Dr. Stewart could use only male animals in his research. Many variables are typically controlled by keeping them constant. The instructions given to subjects provide one example; many investigators present instructions by videotape to assure that all subjects have exactly the same presentation. The experimental situation is kept the same throughout an experiment, thus controlling a great many possible extraneous variables and also making certain that the same demand characteristics are presented in each experimental condition.

Nonexperimental research strategies also benefit from careful attention to maintaining constant conditions. The surveys conducted by such organizations as Roper are carefully structured so that the instructions and questions given to the respondents are the same for everyone in the study. Classroom teachers and others who administer standardized tests are provided with detailed instructions on testing procedures, including exactly how to read instructions and how to respond to questions.

Eliminating Extraneous Variables. Many extraneous variables can be eliminated quite simply. One of the major benefits of conducting research in a laboratory is that the experimenter can close the door and hang a "Do not disturb" sign outside, thus eliminating many possible intrusions. Soundproof or isolated rooms are often available to keep outside sounds from disturbing the experiment.

Many experiments combine holding conditions constant and eliminating them. The sex of the subjects is effectively eliminated by holding it constant in all conditions; it's sometimes difficult to tell the two techniques apart.

Incorporating an Extraneous Variable into the Experimental Design. Sometimes you may be able to deal with an extraneous variable by turning it into an independent variable in your experiment. In Chapter 18 we will introduce the factorial experimental design, which permits exploring two or more independent variables in a single experiment. For example, we can picture Dr. Stewart's experiment as shown in Figure 4.10.

If we incorporate sex as a second independent variable, we might diagram the experiment as shown in Figure 4.11. This experimental design contains four separate groups and, as we will learn later, would allow Dr. Stewart to examine the effect of aversion conditioning alone, the effect of sex alone, and also whether the sexes react in the same way to the aversion conditioning. It is a very useful and powerful experimental design and is widely employed.

If we can deal with sex as an extraneous variable by building it into the experiment, why not do the same with other variables? If we want to control age of the animals, for example, why not construct an experimental design with three independent variables: aversion conditioning, sex, and age (perhaps using "young" and "old" animals)? This design would have groups like "Young males receiving aversion conditioning," "Young males not receiving aversion conditioning," and so on. We could certainly do that, and the result would be a three-way experimental design.

If three independent variables can be used, two of them controlling extraneous variables, why not four variables, perhaps adding two different strains of laboratory rats? We can certainly have four variables. If four, why not five, adding perhaps early rearing conditions, in which some animals are reared

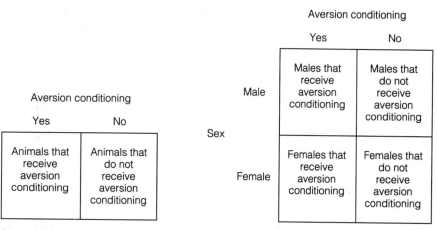

Figure 4.10

Figure 4.11

individually and some are reared in groups? Certainly. But we could continue this process indefinitely, leading to a very complicated experimental design. In the last example, we would have 32 different experimental groups ("Young, Sprague-Dawley strain, group-reared males receiving aversion conditioning," "Young, Sprague-Dawley strain, group-reared males not receiving aversion conditioning," and so on), making for a complicated experiment. In addition to the mechanics of conducting such an experiment, the data analysis, while certainly possible, is complicated and likely to be confusing to even an experienced investigator.

So there is a limit, and it's usually just one or two, to the number of extraneous variables that can reasonably be controlled by making them into independent variables.

Blinds and Placebos. When Dr. Tyrrell tests infants, there are two experimenters present. One experimenter controls which videotape is shown and in what position it's presented. The second experimenter watches the infant's eyes and controls the timers that record where the baby is looking. The second experimenter doesn't know what stimuli are being presented, and the experimenter who presents the stimuli doesn't record data. In this way, the measurement of the dependent variable—looking time—isn't open to experimenter expectancy; the "recording experimenter" simply records time, with no knowledge of the experimental situation being presented. If experimenters don't know what to expect at any point in the experiment, then their expectancies can't influence the recorded data. A procedure that keeps an experimenter in the dark with regard to condition presented is called an *experimenter-blind* condition, and that experiment is said to be conducted with a *single blind*.

Careful researchers use an experimenter-blind procedure whenever possible. The complication, of course, is that it increases the effort required to conduct the experiment, since two experimenters are usually needed. Sometimes a clever experimenter will figure out how to keep himself blind during data collection— usually by coding the data forms in some way that he can't remember easily.

Just as a blind procedure is good for eliminating experimenter expectancy effects, it can be used to control subject expectancies as well. In some situations, of course, it's impossible for the subjects not to know what's going on. Subjects who agree to participate in an experiment titled "The effect of list difficulty on learning nonsense syllables" and receive the list "GYX, KIQ, QAZ, . . ." may guess that they're in for a rough time. But it is often possible for a subject to be kept blind as to the experimental condition and certainly with regard to the anticipated outcome of the experiment.

A subject-blind study is often conducted by using a *placebo*, an apparent experimental manipulation that really has no effect, other than perhaps introducing a subject expectancy. A placebo is typically employed in drug studies, where two conditions are commonly used—with drug, and without drug. So that participants in each of the conditions in the study have the same expectations and are given the same treatment insofar as possible, the non-drug subjects are given a placebo, usually a sugar pill, a flavored beverage, or an injection of nonreactive saline solution. Naturally, the ethical requirement of informed consent requires that all participants in such a study be told that some people will receive a drug and that others will receive a placebo and that they won't know which they'll be getting.

Placebos are used in animal studies as well, but not to control for expectancies. Instead they're used for controlling the possible extraneous variable of receiving a treatment. Suppose that you're exploring the effect of a particular drug on memory in animals. You train all of your subjects to do some task (running a maze, for example, or learning to press a bar to receive food) to some criterion so that you're sure that all of the subjects know the task equally well. Then you select some animals to receive the experimental drug by injection. The other animals receive nothing. If you retest all of the animals after a period of time and find a difference, can you conclude that it was due to the drug? No, because you have confounded "receiving an injection" with "receiving the drug." Just the act of giving an animal an injection could be enough to cause a difference in behavior. To avoid that confound, you need to use a placebo injection of an inert solution of the same volume that is injected into the experimental animals.

Drug studies are often conducted using a *double-blind* procedure. In a double blind, neither the subject nor the experimenter doing the dependent-variable measurement knows which condition the subject is in. A double blind protects against both experimenter and subject expectancies. In a typical double-blind drug study, patients trying a new drug wouldn't know whether they were receiving the real drug or a placebo, and neither would the physicians who were diagnosing its effects. A third individual would keep the records of which patient was in which drug condition until all data were collected.

Unobtrusive Measures. A very effective way to avoid evaluation effects is to not let the subject know that he or she is being measured. While this is difficult in many situations, there are often unobtrusive measures that sometimes can be applied. One common technique is to develop a measuring procedure that misleads the subject in some way. A set of personality items might also include questions about eating habits (if that was the actual dependent variable). Another technique is to include so many different sorts of test items and measures that the subject is confused about what is actually the purpose of the research.

A variety of observational measures can be employed in many situations. The distance between people, the extent of physical contact, the time spent on various activities, and the choice of magazines in a waiting room are all possible dependent variables that can be observed without the subject's awareness.

Unobtrusive measures are sometimes called *nonreactive* measures, since they don't cause reactions in the subjects being tested. Nonreactive measurement is often used in environmental studies, where the measurements of interest are often patterns of use of doors, windows, pathways, and so on. Nonreactive measures are often used in the kinds of nonexperimental studies discussed in Chapter 22.

Matching. Suppose that you're interested in the effect of background sound on ability to distinguish between intervals on the musical scale. There are to be two experimental conditions: one presenting a series of musical intervals in a quiet room, and the other with the same sounds accompanied by a tape recording of construction noise. You elect to use a between-subjects design, so that each group of subjects will hear the tones in either a quiet room or a noisy room. In this experiment, the musical training of the subjects could very well be an extraneous variable. Clearly, having all subjects in one condition be trained musicians, while there are none in the other condition would confound noise with musical training. You could eliminate trained musicians from your study as a way of holding that variable constant, but there are better procedures.

Using a measure of musical training (which might be the number of years that someone played an instrument, for example), you can find pairs of subjects that are as similar as possible in their training. Then, within each pair, randomly (by coin-flip, perhaps) assign one to each of the two experimental conditions. Your two groups are now matched with respect to musical training, and you have eliminated training as an extraneous variable by making sure that it is distributed equally across the experimental conditions. This sort of matching can apply to any number of experimental conditions; it's not limited to two-condition experiments.

Matching produces sets of subjects, with one member of each pair assigned to each condition. This procedure is often called *precision matching*, since it matches by sets of identical pretest scores.

A close variant of precision matching is called *range matching*. Range matching defines a range of scores that are used in the match. To match on a variable like IQ, for example, it would probably be difficult to match subjects exactly; a range match would let a group of scores within 5 points, for example, define a matched set of subjects.

Matching can be done on a number of variables if they're important to control. In the example, you might try to match not only by years of musical experience, but also by kind of instrument, by sex, by age, and so on. Such matching is obviously intended to deal with a number of extraneous variables by matching, all at the same time. While in principle, that sort of matching sounds good, in practice, it's normally very difficult to accomplish without access to a very large pool of potential subjects.

Precision and range matching are often difficult to achieve with a single variable; adding more variables only compounds the difficulty. A common alternative to exact matching is *frequency-distribution matching*. In this procedure, the subjects are not sorted into pairs on the basis of a pretest. Instead, the pretest scores are used to assure that the experimental groups are equivalent. Thus we would not try to match our subjects on the basis of years of musical training, but just assure ourselves that the two experimental groups have roughly the same distribution of training. You wouldn't want the average musical training to be substantially different between the two groups of subjects any more than you'd be pleased with all of the trained musicians in the same group. In addition, a frequency distribution matching procedure assures that the range and the variability of musical training is roughly the same in the two groups.

Matching is usefully applied to extraneous variables that are closely related to the dependent variable. It makes little sense to match groups on the basis of body weight for a study of musical perception, but it might for a study of weight loss or running speed, for example. Matching in animal studies is sometimes done by assigning litter-mates to different conditions, thus assuring matching on a number of possibly important hereditary variables. In human studies, matching has occasionally been done by finding pairs of identical twins, but rarity of human twin births makes such research impractical for most purposes. Using a pretest of a variable related to the dependent variable is the most practical and the most widely used method.

To take matching to its logical extreme, the best match for any individual is that very same individual. To match in such a way requires a within-subjects design. These designs are normally used for any of several reasons; exact matching of the subjects under each experimental condition is obviously an important benefit.

Using the same subjects in more than one condition isn't possible in some cases (the same person can't learn the same list of words twice under two different conditions, for example), but many times it is. In the music perception task, for example, there's no reason why each subject couldn't be used in both the quiet and the noisy conditions. Naturally, you'd have to worry about order effects, a topic that we turn to next.

Balancing for Order and Carryover Effects. In within-subjects designs, you should always assume that anything that you do to a subject will have an influence on anything that you do later to the same subject. That is, you should assume that you will have effects that carry over from one experimental condition to the next. Such effects are almost always confounded with the independent variable unless something is done to eliminate the problem.

There are two kinds of such extraneous variables; and while the controls for them are the same, we should distinguish between them. An *order effect* is a difference in a treatment condition that is due to the position in the sequence of trials in the experiment. In a typical problem-solving experiment, for example, the third problem to be solved (regardless of exactly what the problem is) is probably solved more quickly than is the first or the second, simply because it's in the third position. An order effect of this sort is often caused by the subjects' having a chance to practice on the kinds of tasks being used, and so it is often called a *practice effect*.

Another kind of order effect, a *fatigue effect*, causes a decrease in a subject's performance, regardless of the specific task. Suppose that your instructor decides to give your class a 150-item true-false test. He uses a computer to generate a different ordering of questions for each member of your class. On scoring the tests, he will probably find that the students answer more questions correctly on the first half of the exam than they do on the last half, even though the test was structured so that any particular question was as likely to be in the first or the second half. That result is an order effect, specifically a fatigue effect.

A *carryover effect*, in contrast to an order effect, is a consequence of an experimental condition that directly influences a following condition. Thus if the first condition in an experiment involves the administration of some drug, as an example, there is likely to be a carryover of the drug's effect to the next condition. Carryover effects are common in drug studies, but can appear with other sorts of independent variables as well.

Orders Across Different Subjects. Suppose that you're conducting a study of problem solving in which your subjects are given a series of problems and the amount of time subjects used to solve the problems is measured. You should be concerned with the effect of the order of the tasks. We can develop a scheme in which every possible ordering of tasks occurs an equal number of times. If there are three different tasks, A, B, and C, there are six possible orders in which subjects might work on the three tasks:

Problem-solving task

		First	Second	Third
	1	Solve A	then B	and then C
	2	Solve A	then C	and then B
Possible order	3	Solve B	then A	and then C
	4	Solve B	then C	and then A
	5	Solve C	then A	and then B
	6	Solve C	then B	and then A

A subject assigned to order 1, for example, would solve the problems in the order A, B, and C. Someone in the third order would be confronted with the problems in the order B, A, and then C.

If you set up the experiment with a multiple of six subjects, each order can be used an equal number of times. This systematic presentation of all possible orders is called *complete counterbalancing*, and it controls order effects by assuring that all orders appear. In the listing, notice that each task is preceded by each other an equal number of times across the set of orders. In addition, each problem is used as the first, the second, and the third task an equal number of times. Finally, each problem precedes and follows each other at every position in the order. Thus each problem occurs in every possible context (as the first, second, and third task) and precedes and follows each other problem the same number of times.

Also note that each subject gets a different order so that, while an *individual subject* may experience an order effect, that effect will be balanced out when the data are analyzed over all of the subjects. When the data are summarized, the average solution time for problem A, for example, will not reflect an order effect since the average will be over all possible orders and positions.

As the number of different independent variable conditions increases, so does the number of orders. With four problems to solve, for example, there are 24 different orders; there are 120 different orders of five problems. In general, there are $N!$ possible orders of N objects; $N!$ is read N-factorial (and not as N!!!!!). It represents the product of the numbers $1, 2, 3, \ldots, N$. In our example, there are six orders of three problems, and $3! = 1 \times 2 \times 3 = 6$. For four objects, then, $N! = 4! = 1 \times 2 \times 3 \times 4 = 24$, and for 5, $N! = 5! = 1 \times 2 \times 3 \times 4 \times 5 = 120$.

Clearly, when there are a large number of experimental conditions, complete counterbalancing becomes impractical, and we can resort to some form of *incomplete counterbalancing*. There are several ways of setting up a design with incomplete balancing. In *partial counterbalancing*, a selection from the complete set of orders is made, making sure that—among the set of orders used—each condition appears in each position in the order the same number of times and that each condition precedes and follows each other the same number of times. A *random counterbalancing* procedure drops the two conditions and uses a random selection from the set of possible orders.

Finally, a *Latin square* design keeps only the requirement that each task appear at each position as close to the same number of times as possible. For example, with four experimental conditions (A, B, C, and D) the arrangement

Problem-solving task

	First	Second	Third	Fourth
1	A	B	C	D
2	B	D	A	C
3	C	A	D	B
4	D	C	B	A

(Possible order)

is a Latin square. Note that each condition appears exactly once in each position and that the number of possible orders is the same as the number of conditions. Using a multiple of four subjects will use each order an equal number of times.

Table 4.1 summarizes the across-subject counterbalancing procedures.

Table 4.1   Summary of Across-Subject Counterbalancing Procedures

Technique	Features
Complete counterbalancing	1. Each condition is at each position the same number of times 2. Each condition precedes and follows each other the same number of times 3. Each condition precedes and follows each other at each position the same number of times 4. All possible orders are presented
Latin square	1. Each condition is at each position the same number of times 2. Each condition precedes and follows each other the same number of times 3. The number of orders is equal to the number of conditions
Partial counterbalancing	1. Each condition is at each position the same number of times 2. Each condition precedes and follows each other the same number of times
Random counterbalancing	1. Random selection of orders

Orders Within the Same Subject. Counterbalancing may be applied within a single subject as well as across a group of individuals. Dr. Owens and some of his students (Leer, Salvador, Goldberg, & Owens, 1986) had subjects wear prism glasses that distorted their vision and then had them play a bean bag toss game from two different distances ("near" and "far"). The investigators were interested in the changes in subjects' visual convergence as a result of the bean bag toss exercise. Since there is probably an order effect, depending upon whether the subjects use the order "near-far" or "far-near," Dr. Owens and his students counterbalanced the order so that each subject received the tasks in either the order "far-near" or "near-far."

D. Alfred Owens received his undergraduate degree from Franklin & Marshall College in 1972 and his Ph.D. from Pennsylvania State University in 1976. He spent two years as a postdoctoral research fellow at MIT before returning to his alma mater as a faculty member. His research primarily concerns the differences between day and night vision, but he also studies the effects of fatigue and other factors on vision. His research has appeared in *Psychology Today* and in *Reader's Digest*, as well as in scientific journals such as *American Scientist, Vision Research, Science,* and *Perception.* Much of his research is supported by a grant from the National Eye Institute. In his spare time, Dr. Owens restores both his historic home and classic cars.

Dr. Owens used what is called an A-B, B-A counterbalancing procedure. This scheme, often applied within individual subjects, assures that both stimulus orders are present an equal number of times. Using this scheme, Dr. Owens and his students counterbalanced the order by assigning half of the subjects to the A-B (near-far) order, and the other half to the B-A (far-near) order.

Actually, the experiment was more complicated than just described. The investigators were interested in the effect on vision of switching from a far to a near position, and vice versa; and each subject did both distance changes. Since there is probably an order effect, depending upon whether the subjects use the order "near-far" or "far-near," Dr. Owens and his students counterbalanced, so that each subject received the tasks in either the order "far-near, rest period, near-far" or "near-far, rest period, far-near." This procedure counterbalanced the effects of distance change *within* each subject, as well as *across*, using the A-B–B-A order for half of the subjects, and B-A–A-B for the other half.

If there are three conditions to be counterbalanced within each subject, the orders A-B-C–C-B-A and C-B-A–A-B-C are normally employed. Regardless of the number of conditions, when the data have been collected, the A conditions are combined, the B's are combined, and so are the C conditions. That done, the conditions may be compared, with the order effect eliminated.

Random Assignment. Counterbalancing is probably second only to randomizing as the most widely used technique for dealing with extraneous variables. The two are often used together; one or two variables are dealt with by counterbalancing, and randomization is used for most others.

Randomly assigning subjects to experimental conditions is a common and valuable technique. It may be used alone, but it is often applied in conjunction with other control measures as well. In principle, randomly assigning subjects means that there is no systematic bias in the group selection. A given subject is as likely to be placed into any one group as into any other. There is no guarantee that randomizing will produce an "equal" representation of males and females across the groups, only that there is not systematic bias. Naturally, if an investigator found that a random assignment had resulted in assigning males and females to separate groups, that random assignment would probably be discarded in favor of a "more random" one. Such a procedure should properly be called "random assignment with constraints."

Another common constraint is that of equal-sized groups; Dr. Stewart might assign animals to his two groups by flipping a coin, but with a constraint on equal group sizes. Subjects are typically assigned at random to experimental conditions; and with two conditions, flipping a coin is hard to beat as a randomizing system.

While there is no guarantee that random assignment of subjects to conditions will eliminate confounded extraneous variables, in the long run, it does assure a balanced distribution of subjects into conditions. Randomizing is a "global" control technique that is best counted on for the control of unknown extraneous variables. If you can identify a potentially confounding extraneous variable, the techniques presented earlier are much more powerful for controlling it than just using randomization. Dr. Stewart might control for sex of his animals by using only males, but he would still assign them to experimental conditions randomly. He certainly wouldn't want to put the first 10 animals that he was able to catch into the experimental group any more than he would want all females there; the slow rats might differ in important ways from those that escaped capture for a longer time.

Some mechanics. Randomizing can be done in a number of ways, and the exact procedure is not very important as long as it meets the requirement that no one group assignment is any more likely to occur than is any other. Flipping a coin is a perfectly reasonable procedure when deciding between two conditions. If there are more than two, other procedures can be used. Appendix B is a table of random digits. If you have four experimental groups, for example, you might select the group for an animal by reading through the table until you find a digit between 1 and 4 and use that to define the group. In using a table, be sure that you don't get the same numbers every time you use the table. You might consider closing your eyes and pointing to a starting point, and then using the first number that you find at your fingertip to define which way to read (1 = read down the column, 2 = read up the column, 3 = read to the right, 4 = read to the left). Of course, you could decide upon which direction to go before you open the table. Exactly how you use the table isn't too important, as long as you don't use it in the same way every time.

Many statistical programs offer random number generation; you might use such a program to generate a set of numbers between 1 and 4, for example, to assign subjects to groups.

Randomizing isn't limited to assigning subjects to groups. It can be used to

Table 4.2   Extraneous-Variable Control Techniques

Extraneous variable	Technique
Physical (sound, light, etc.)	Hold constant, eliminate, build into experiment
Expectancies	Blind (single, double), placebo
Instructions	Tape record or read carefully
Order effects (across subjects)	Complete, partial, or random counterbalancing; Latin square
Order effects (within subjects)	Counterbalanced order (A-B–B-A)
All others	Randomization

select visual stimuli from a set of patterns, to select a musical selection from a set of possible compositions, to decide whether a pattern is to be presented on the left or the right, and so on. Nonexperiments use randomizing too. Consider the following hypothetical instructions to a survey-organization employee (the community being sampled and the starting intersection too were randomly selected by the polling group):

> Proceed to the corner of Dickinson and Temple Avenues. Flip a coin; if it's heads, you'll proceed along Dickinson, and if it's tails, you'll go along Temple. Flip the coin again. If it's heads, go to the north side of Temple or the east side of Dickinson, whichever you chose earlier. If it's tails, you'll work on the south side of Temple or the west side of Dickinson. Look at the second hand of your watch. If it's between 12 and 3, begin your polling at the first residence from the intersection in your chosen direction and side; if it's between 3 and 6, begin with the second house or apartment; between 6 and 9, the third; and between 9 and 12, the fourth. Continue polling. . . .

Table 4.2 summarizes the control procedures that we have presented. Obviously, not all of the techniques need to be used in every experiment. Some procedures, like holding constant and eliminating extraneous variables, can only be employed when the relevant variable(s) is known and can be manipulated. Randomization is routinely applied along with all other controls, though it is less powerful as a control technique than the others. But randomization has the advantage of balancing extraneous variables across conditions, even when you can't control (or even know) the variables directly.

Internal and External Validity

Manipulating and controlling variables is a topic closely related to the two important forms of validity in an experiment, internal and external. We close this chapter with some additional discussion of them.

Internal Validity   In Chapter 2, we discussed the prerequisites for making a cause-effect inference in an experiment. The three prerequisites were (1) covariation, (2) temporal ordering, and (3) no confounding. Setting up an experiment involves all three of those elements. An independent variable is chosen and manipulated so that it may covary with a dependent variable. The conduct of an experiment involves presenting the independent variable, and *then* testing to see if the dependent variable varied as expected, thus establishing the necessary temporal ordering. The third element in making the inference refers to the lack of confounding, that is, the degree to which extraneous variables have been eliminated. Internal validity refers to all of the three requirements, and is thus really asking "Is the connection between independent variable and dependent variable clear and unambiguous enough to make a causal inference?"

This chapter has been devoted to manipulating variables and to avoiding confounding by extraneous variables. Let's review those topics again, this time with an eye to how they influence internal validity.

Manipulating the Independent Variable. Manipulation of an independent variable is the key feature of the experiment. The manipulation is done so that the independent variable can precede, and perhaps covary with, a dependent variable. Since we're seeking to establish the relationship between the two variables, it's critical that the manipulation be done properly. That was the reason for the attention that we paid to choosing the levels of the independent variable. In evaluating the internal validity of an experiment, the operational definition of the independent variable needs to be clear so that its manipulation has appropriate construct validity. The manipulation of the variable must follow from the logic of the experiment. For example, if the independent variable of the experiment is the similarity of visual patterns, then the operational definition of similarity should follow from the theory. In addition, the operations that are proposed to manipulate similarity should do just that and should not manipulate a related, but theoretically unimportant, factor like size or shape.

Physical Factors. Certainly, physical variables that can be identified as confounding factors will render an experiment invalid. If time of day, background noise, differences in instructions, or any other identifiable variable is confounded with the independent variable, then a clear causal inference can't be drawn and the internal validity suffers.

The measurement used in an experiment should be adequate. In Chapter 3 we talked about the validity of measurement procedures. Measurement operations need to be scrutinized carefully in evaluating an experiment's internal validity. If the procedure used to measure the dependent variable isn't valid, there is no way for the experiment to have internal validity.

Personal Factors. The major extraneous variables that we discussed in this category were individual maturation and history, order effects, and the regression effect. To those we can add several other considerations related to internal validity. Did the subjects self-select themselves into groups? Or even into the experiment at all? If the experimenter didn't have sufficient control of the situation to assign subjects into experimental conditions, then the internal validity is questionable. In some cases, though, the researcher is not able to assign subjects randomly; much important research is done in the "real world" of education and industry when random assignment of students into certain classes, for example,

Table 4.3   Checklist for Internal Validity

PHYSICAL FACTORS

    Physical variables
       Time of day
       Noise
       Temperature, etc.
       Instructions
    Manipulation of the independent variable
       Operational definition
       Construct validity
    Measurement
       Reliability
       Validity

PERSONAL FACTORS

    Selection
    Maturation/history
    Order effects
    Regression
    Subject loss

INTERPERSONAL FACTORS

    The Hawthorne effect
    Evaluation effects
    Social desirability
    Demand characteristics

REPLICATION USING THE SAME CONDITIONS

---

simply can't be done. In Chapter 22 we'll talk about some quasi-experiments where this is the case, but for now, lack of experimental control means weakened internal validity, and thus less ability to draw causal conclusions.

What if Dr. Stewart reported that he began with 30 subjects in each of his two conditions; but when he tested animals for taste preference later, he had 27 animals in the non-aversion condition but only 12 in the aversion condition? Should you be suspicious of his conclusions? You sure should—why did he lose so many animals in the aversion condition? Did the experimental manipulation do something to them? If that's so, do his conclusions apply only to those rats that survive the experimental manipulation? Suppose that you were reading the results of a test of a new drug designed to assist people in quitting smoking. The investigators began with 150 subjects in a smoking clinic and randomly assigned 75 people each to drug and to placebo conditions. At the end of a six-week period, 10% of the people remaining in the drug group were still smokers, while in the placebo condition, 63% were still smokers, leading to the clear implication that the drug helped substantially in quitting smoking. (Pretty impressive, so far!) But then you read further and discover that when the final determinations were made, there were only 34 people in the drug group, and there were 71 in the placebo condition. Now what do you make of the results? Why did so many more "drug" participants drop out of the study than dropped out from the placebo condition? And what do you suppose might be the characteristics of the subjects who remained?

Loss of subjects, that is, subject attrition, is a very real threat to the internal validity in an experiment. If there are substantially different numbers of subjects in the various conditions in the experiment, internal validity is open to question.

Interpersonal Factors. Some of the easiest internal validity problems to overlook, as well as the most slippery to control, are those involving the interpersonal factors in the experiment itself. The effects of being in an experiment are very strong among humans. The Hawthorne effect is very difficult to control, although careful development of unobtrusive measures can be of some help. Other interpersonal effects, such as expectancies and demand characteristics are somewhat easier to control, once you know that they exist. Any experiment should be evaluated for its control of expectancies and other demand properties.

Replication. Fortunately, there's a check on the adequacy of the interval validity of an experiment: replication. If an experiment has internal validity, then its cause-effect conclusion is correct. If additional studies, using essentially the same variables and controls, confirm the original conclusion, then we may conclude that a cause-effect relationship has been established.

Table 4.3 presents a summary checklist for determining internal validity.

External Validity

Internal validity asks whether an experiment's conclusion is warranted. External validity, on the other hand, asks whether the results of an experiment can be generalized beyond the specific situation. Experiments, especially in psychology, are often criticized as having no relevance to "real life." And it's true that, in the attempt to control the variables tightly, as required to establish internal validity, much research is done in artificial environments, with artificial constraints, rules, and tasks. And it's also true that there is often a trade-off between internal and external validity—to make a situation more "real," we may have to give up some of the control that makes a study internally valid.

To evaluate external validity, we can look at three aspects of an experiment: the population of subjects sampled, the generality of the variables in the experiment, and the ability to generalize to other settings.

The Subject Population. If the subjects in an experiment were all anemic, color-blind, left-handed, orphaned identical-twin 13-year-old males raised separately from their brothers, you might rightfully question how general the results of the study might be. The question, clearly, is whether we can expect the same results to occur if we used different subjects.

When we present the statistics for making an inference about the generality of results, we'll view the data from an experiment as a sample from a larger population. Strictly speaking, we're limited to generalizing to the population that was sampled. So, if we use only anemic, color-blind, left-handed, orphaned identical-twin 13-year-old males raised separately from their brothers, then we can really generalize only to the larger population of anemic, color-blind, left-handed, 13-year-old orphaned identical-twin males raised separately.

That's an extreme example, of course, but it does make a point: the population sampled influences the external validity of an experiment. In fact, psychology has been accused of being the science of white rats and college sophomores, an indictment that recognizes the most common subjects in psychological research. In most cases, though, the experimenter wants to generalize beyond those two species.

The key question in generalizing is whether the subjects used differ in some way from the *real* population of interest. And if so, is that difference confounded with the independent variable? For example, Dr. Owens studies visual processes in humans. For his subjects, he uses college students. Are those subjects representative of humans in general? Or do they have characteristics that differ in ways that would confound his variables? Probably not; most visual variables are little influenced by social class, intelligence, motivation, and the other variables that might separate college students from the broader population of all people.

On the other hand, Dr. Campbell must be concerned with the extent to which the personality characteristics that he measures in his college students can be generalized. Not only are college students generally more intelligent than the overall population, but they certainly differ in other important ways as well, very possibly along some of the very introversion/extraversion dimensions that are Dr. Campbell's main interest.

In short, if there's an interaction between the variables studied and the subjects used, there's reason for concern about external validity (see, for example, Cook & Campbell, 1979, or Oakes, 1972). Checking for such an interaction can be done with only a little added effort. Use two or more different kinds of subject groups; if the results change with different groups, then there's an interaction. Both Dr. Campbell and Dr. Owens, for example, might use college students and other individuals of the same age selected from groups of local employees, choosing those of college age who are not in college. Complete demonstration of an interaction between the subjects and the situations requires the analysis-of-variance techniques that will be developed in Chapter 18.

The Variables and the Situations. Another often-heard complaint about research in psychology is that the experimental situation is so unrealistic that the results can have no possible application to "real life." There's often considerable truth to that accusation; and when it's raised, the critic is attacking external validity. In an attempt to control variables, eliminate confounding, and measure accurately, much research in psychology lacks external validity. At least, it lacks external face validity. Just as with a measurement procedure, the critical element in establishing external validity isn't the "appearance" of validity but whether or not the results can actually apply to other situations and variables.

Many of the variables measured in the laboratory have direct parallels in the "real world," though their measurement may be different. In the laboratory, the psychologist will measure attitudes through a written test, while in the real world attitudes are typically inferred from behavior. In the laboratory, the experimenter gives instructions and establishes specific tasks to be done, often contrived in ways to manipulate independent variables appropriately. In the world outside the lab, individuals are freer to set their own tasks and rules. But the test of validity is not whether the situation "looks like" an external environment but whether the results can generalize.

The variables in a research setting can be evaluated, and often are, by partial replications of the research. Most replications aren't exact re-creations but rather elaborations on the original. Dr. Stewart, or another researcher, might use different substances to represent the four tastes; Dr. Tyrrell might use different tapes or visual stimuli with his infants; or Dr. Campbell might even use different introversion/extraversion tests. If essentially the same results are obtained despite changes in the exact variables, then we can have some confidence in the external validity of the variables in the research.

There's often less of a problem with generalizing to other situations, since both humans and animals show a great deal of consistency in behavior across environments and tasks. Thus what Dr. Owens and his students learned about the effects of wearing prism glasses will almost certainly hold true in a different task from the one that they used. And once Dr. Stewart has established that an aversion to sugar will generalize to saccharin, it's very likely that it will generalize to similar sweet tastes as well.

The problem here has often been called *ecological validity*—the extent to which the situation adequately represents the "real world." Some researchers try to inject more of the real world into their studies. In another study, Dr. Owens (Owens & Leibowitz, 1976) made laboratory measures of the ways subjects' eyes focused in darkness and then simulated an automobile ride in darkness, measuring their ability to recognize traffic signs with various corrective lenses.

Evaluating External Validity. As with internal validity, external validity can be checked by using replication. For internal validity, the replication needed to be with the same operations and variables; the check on external validity demands more. Since external validity asks about generalization beyond the specific experiment, the replications should be with other settings, with other subject populations, and with other, but related, variables.

Finally, we might point out that there are instances when it may be argued that external validity is irrelevant. When the goal of an experiment is to test a theoretical prediction, then some people (see, for example, Mook, 1983) suggest that there is no need for external validity. In this case, the entire purpose of the experiment is to confirm a theoretical prediction. If that's the point, then generality across many different situations is unimportant.

Table 4.4 summarizes the factors in external validity.

What Is an Experimental Design?

An experimental design is an arrangement of conditions in a research situation, established to permit the answering of one or more specific research questions in such a way that alternative explanations of the results are ruled out. It's an overall plan for an investigation that involves an independent variable (perhaps more than one), a dependent variable (again, there might be more than one), and a procedure for manipulating the independent variable. Designs may be classified in several ways; we've suggested some already, but let's explore them a bit more.

Table 4.4   Checklist for External Validity

THE SUBJECTS

What population do they represent?
Can we generalize beyond that population?

THE VARIABLES

Can different independent variables be substituted for the original without disrupting the essence of the results?
Can different dependent variables be substituted for the original without seriously disrupting the results?
Can different control manipulations be substituted for the original while preserving the results?

THE SITUATIONS

Are "real" situations represented (ecological validity)?
Can the results generalize to other similar situations?

REPLICATION

Replication using different samples, different variables, and different settings is the major way to establish external validity.

In the simplest design, there is a single set of observations, and we ask whether they seem to come from a particular population. For example, Dr. Tyrrell needs only a single set of data because he can easily specify a population parameter that will allow him to make an inference about the ability of infants. That is, if his infants look at the familiar (a person walking) and the novel (the person jogging) for about the same proportion of time, then they can't tell the difference between them. On the other hand, if they watch one pattern or the other for more than 50% of the time, then they can distinguish between them. (And, infants being the way they are, they will watch the novel pattern for longer.) In his experiment, then, the question will become "Do the babies look at the new pattern for 50% of the time?" Questions of the kind that Dr. Tyrrell asks—are these data typical of what I know of the population?—are addressed by the *single-condition experimental design*.

Dr. Campbell's research design is somewhat different from Dr. Tyrrell's. Like Dr. Tyrrell, he uses only a single group of subjects, but he measures several different variables for each subject. As a consequence, Dr. Campbell can explore the relationships between his variables. But he can also consider each of his variables separately to address questions such as whether his subjects are "normal" in the introversion/extraversion scores. But his interest is primarily in looking at relationships; research of this kind is normally called *correlational research design*, since he makes extensive use of correlation coefficients for measuring relationships.

Professor Stewart's research, on the other hand, makes use of two different experimental conditions. In one condition, animals are given an aversion-conditioning treatment, while in the other condition, they are not. In a two-condition design like Dr. Stewart's, the two conditions differ only with regard to a single independent variable—aversion training. Dr. Stewart isn't interested in comparing his animals' performance with some hypothesized reference value (like Tyrrell's 50%), nor in the relationships between pairs of variables (as in Campbell's research), but in the difference between the two experimental conditions that was introduced by the aversion training. His inference will be about the differences in consumption of several taste substances by animals in the two conditions. Dr. Stewart manipulates an independent variable in a true experimental fashion, and his plan of research is called a *two-condition experimental design*.

It's possible for an experimental design to have multiple conditions or levels, as we suggested earlier. In an experiment of the effect of illumination level on productivity, for example, we might have a number of different levels of brightness. Such an arrangement of experimental conditions is called a *multiple-condition experimental design* or sometimes a *one-way ANOVA design* because of the inferential statistical technique (the analysis of variance or ANOVA) that is normally applied.

Earlier we suggested that a way to deal with an extraneous variable might be to build it into the experiment as another independent variable. That would result in a design with two (or even more) separate independent variables; such a design is called a *factorial experimental design* or sometimes a *factorial ANOVA design*. A factorial design is especially useful when the research question asks about the joint effects of the independent variables.

We also indicated earlier in this chapter that there are two ways of manipulating an independent variable—between subjects and within subjects. In the first procedure, there is a separate group of subjects for each condition in the experiment. In the second, there is a single group of subjects, and each subject receives each condition of the independent variable. In a between-subjects design, more subjects are required, and we may have to concern ourselves with matching the groups in some way. In the within-subjects design, we need to be concerned with order and carryover effects. In short, there are advantages, disadvantages, and trade-offs in the choice of experimental design. As we progress, we'll present the experimental designs in some detail and talk about their features, especially those of control and internal validity, in detail.

SUMMARY

- A quantitative independent variable may assume a very large number of possible values, while a qualitative one normally has only a few.
- A *between-subjects* variable has different subjects for each of the experimental conditions while a *within-subjects* variable presents each subject with all of the experimental conditions.
- When two variables covary, they are *confounded* and make it impossible to draw a conclusion about which has an effect.
- The most common sources of extraneous variables are physical, intrasubject, and interpersonal factors.
- Holding conditions constant is a common way to control extraneous variables.
- Sometimes an extraneous variable can be controlled by building it into the experimental design as an independent variable.

- Subjects are often matched as a control for some intra-subject variables.
- Balancing and counterbalancing are used to eliminate the effects of carryover and order.
- *Internal validity* refers to the experiment's ability to lead to causal inference, and external validity asks whether the results can be generalized

KEY TERMS

Balancing	**Latin square**
Between-subjects design	**Matching**
Carryover effect	**Order effect**
Complete counterbalancing	**Partial counterbalancing**
Confounded variables	**Placebo**
Counterbalancing	**Practice effect**
Demand characteristics	**Precision matching**
Double-blind experiment	**Qualitative variable**
Ecological validity	**Quantitative variable**
Evaluation apprehension	**Random assignment**
Experimenter expectancies	**Random counterbalancing**
External validity	**Range matching**
Extraneous variables	**Replication**
Frequency distribution matching	**Single-blind experiment**
Hawthorne effect	**Subject expectancies**
Incomplete counterbalancing	**Within-subjects design**
Internal validity	

EXERCISES

Solutions to asterisked (∗) exercises appear at the back of the book.

∗1. You're studying the effect of amount of practice on the time taken to solve problems. As an experimenter, you want to manipulate the number of practice trials to be given to your subjects. How would you decide on the number of practice trials to give?

2. Suppose that you decide to use two and five practice trials as the two experimental conditions in Exercise 1. Would you use a between-subjects or a within-subjects manipulation? Why?

∗3. List some possible confounding variables in an experiment that investigates the effect of practice on problem solving.

4. For each item listed in Exercise 3, suggest a way of controlling for that confounding variable.

∗5. You are convinced that more practice will lead to better problem solving in your subjects. You also believe that your expectations might influence the subject's behavior. How might you control for your own expectancies?

6. You want to explore the effect of the color of the first-grade classroom on color choice in children's art. You believe that being in a "warm-colored" room will influence children to choose to paint with "cooler" colors, and vice versa. List several possible confounding variables and suggest how you might deal with them.

7. You have three different paintings (A, B, and C) that you want your subjects to rate for attractiveness, but you're concerned about the order of presentation. Suggest how you might solve the problem using:
  ∗a. Complete counterbalancing
  b. Random counterbalancing
  ∗c. Latin square

Describing Data

Part One developed the logic of research and discussed some of the mechanical details involved in actually conducting research. As a result of a research investigation, we always have data. The data were collected to answer a research question or questions. If the research is an experiment, we are probably interested in drawing a causal inference from the data. If the research took some other form, we still need to summarize it and draw conclusions from it.

In Part Two, we develop ways for summarizing, describing, and presenting research results. In Chapter 5, we discuss the simplest of the summary procedures—counting. Here we'll learn how to summarize data in frequency distributions. Since an important goal of science is communication, we'll also learn how to present frequency summaries so that other investigators can understand our results. Chapter 6 continues the presentation of descriptive procedures with statistics that describe where an "average" or the center of the data is located. Then Chapter 7 introduces ways of describing and illustrating how spread out data are from their center. In Chapter 8, we'll learn how to use the normal distribution, an important and widely applicable statistical distribution. These first chapters of descriptive statistics focus on a single variable; Chapters

9 and 10 turn our attention to situations where two (or more) variables are measured at the same time. Chapter 9 presents descriptive methods for two variables, while Chapter 10 discusses how we can use the relationship between two variables to make predictions of cases that we haven't observed.

CHAPTER 5

Frequencies and Frequency Distributions

Following this paragraph are some numbers from Dr. Campbell's research. They are scores on the Eysenck Personality Inventory Extraversion (EPIE) scale for each of his 84 subjects. At a glance, what can we say about these scores? What is the range of their values? What's an "average" score? Are there two groups of people—introverts and extraverts—or does there seem to be a more-or-less continuous range of scores?

15	14	6	20	14	14	16	15	12	14
14	14	12	11	12	11	14	4	17	13
9	15	19	19	15	16	10	14	15	14
18	15	13	11	17	10	15	10	13	16
11	11	16	20	16	16	14	20	18	18
16	13	6	9	14	19	14	15	16	11
22	15	11	11	15	15	16	13	3	10
9	8	17	13	13	17	20	15	17	12
14	13	8	15						

If you claim that it's very difficult to answer those kinds of questions quickly when confronted by all those numbers, then you can see the problem with looking at raw data. The answers to the questions are there before our eyes, but we can't see them.

Here's an even worse question. Following are two groups of scores on the Bartlett Impulsivity Scale (BIS), another of the measures that Dr. Campbell often uses.

	Group 1					**Group 2**			
68	70	74	71	71	46	49	51	52	23
53	53	54	55	55	26	37	37	38	40
56	56	57	57	57	34	35	41	42	36
60	60	89	60	61	36	37	42	42	42
63	65	65	67	67	43	44	44	45	45
51	52	52	52	53	52	53	53	46	47
76	81	83	85	85	48	48	48	49	53
89	65				40	41	27	31	49
					49	52	46	33	54

Do these two groups differ, or are they the same? And just what do we mean by "differ"? If we mean "do the sets of data differ in size?" then we can obtain the answer by counting. But if we mean "do the groups differ in their performance on the BIS?" then it's not easy to answer the question just by looking at the raw numbers. We might have a vague impression that the scores in Group 1 look a little larger, but we haven't a really good way to document that hunch. We could also ask questions like "does one group tend to be more homogeneous in its scores than the other?" Or "does one group have more large (or small) scores than the other?"

As you can probably guess, the answers to all of these questions are in the data, but we need some special tools to make them stand out from the mass of raw numbers. And that's just what descriptive statistical tools are for—making visible an answer that's already in data.

Frequency Counting

The simplest, but sometimes the most helpful, approach to reducing a mass of values to something more manageable is simple counting. It's just about the only technique that we can use with nominal (category) measurement and will be very valuable for ordinal, interval, and ratio data as well.

Category Data Suppose that we have conducted a survey of employees* and tallied our counts as follows:

Category	Job	Number of employees
1	Tenured faculty	28
2	Untenured faculty	9
3	Administrator	12
4	Secretary	17
5	Technician	12
6	Facility maintenance	13
7	Grounds maintenance	10
8	Other	8
	Total	109

---

*It's a different survey from the one in Chapter 3, but we'll use the same categories as before.

This simple tally summarizes the data remarkably well. We can see that tenured faculty members and secretaries are the most well-represented. Since the measurement here is nominal, we wouldn't want to take the average of the categories, because the result would be meaningless. But we can certainly summarize the data by counting, and that summary shows some things that weren't obvious with raw data.

We could convert the raw frequency counts into percentages, because it's helpful to see the relative numbers of observations in each category. If we did that, we would have the data summary

Category	Job	Percentage of employees
1	Tenured faculty	25.69
2	Untenured faculty	8.26
3	Administrator	11.01
4	Secretary	15.60
5	Technician	11.01
6	Facility maintenance	11.93
7	Grounds maintenance	9.17
8	Other	7.34
	Total	100.01

This summary shows more clearly than do the raw counts just what percentage of the employees are tenured faculty members, secretaries, and so forth.

One more arrangement will bring out another aspect of the data:

Category	Job	Percentage of employees
1	Tenured faculty	25.69
4	Secretary	15.60
6	Facility maintenance	11.93
3	Administrator	11.01
5	Technician	11.01
7	Grounds maintenance	9.17
2	Untenured faculty	8.26
8	Other	7.34
	Total	100.01

This listing, in descending order by percent, highlights the sizes of the categories and shows their relative frequency. Note that in all of the preceding lists, the category number or "measurement" is really irrelevant to understanding the data.

Ordinal, Interval, and Ratio Data

When measurement is at least at the ordinal level—that is, where values are measured on an ordinal (with or without origin), interval, or ratio scale—we can be more sophisticated in our counting procedures. The principle will be roughly the same, though—count the number of occurrences of a value or of a group of values.

A common data summary is the frequency distribution. In this summary, the numbers of each value are counted and usually arranged in a table.

If there are only a few different values in the data, then a simple table will suffice nicely. Suppose that we give 75 students a seven-item quiz and tally the number of items correct as*

Number correct	Frequency
0	1
1	5
2	8
3	15
4	22
5	12
6	9
7	3

This arrangement shows the full range of values (0–7) and also illustrates that they tend to cluster in the middle range; most of the scores fall into the 3–5 range.

As we did with the category data, we can also express the frequencies as a percentage of the total number (75 in this example) of observations, leading to the arrangement

Number correct	Percent
0	1.3
1	6.7
2	10.7
3	20.0
4	29.3
5	16.0
6	12.0
7	4.0

Sometimes the proportions corresponding to the frequencies are used instead of the percentages. In this context, proportions are usually called relative frequencies, since they represent the frequency of each value, relative to the total number of values present. (For example, the score of 2 was represented by 8 of the 75 scores, and $8/75 = .107$.) For these data, the relative frequencies are

Number correct	Relative frequency
0	.013
1	.067
2	.107
3	.200
4	.293
5	.160
6	.120
7	.040

*There seems to be no general agreement among textbook authors on the arrangement of the distribution. Some authors present the values in ascending order going down the page as we show here, while others arrange the values in descending order. We'll follow the ascending-order rule; be sure that you know your instructor's requirements before you turn in frequency tables to be graded!

Another form of frequency distribution presents cumulative frequencies. Consider the following arrangement of the seven-item quiz data:

Number correct	Frequency	Cumulative frequency
0	1	1
1	5	6
2	8	14
3	15	29
4	22	51
5	12	63
6	9	72
7	3	75

What we have added is a column that shows how many scores in the data are equal to *or less than* each value. For example, it's easy to tell that there are 14 scores of 2 or less, that there are 63 of 5 or less, and so on. If the data were the scores that students made on a pop quiz, then it might be important (and interesting) to know how many people scored at or below your score on the quiz. In these data, if you had received a score of 5, for example, this data arrangement shows that 63 of the 75 students in the class received a score of 5 or less.

Data are often presented with cumulative relative frequencies or cumulative percentages. For this hypothetical set of data, the percentage and cumulative percentage distribution appears as

Number correct	Percent	Cumulative percent
0	1.3	1.3
1	6.7	8.0
2	10.7	18.7
3	20.0	38.7
4	29.3	68.0
5	16.0	84.0
6	12.0	96.0
7	4.0	100.0

Now we can clearly see that 84.0% of the students scored 5 or less. Expressing an individual's standing in a set of data is a very common practice in many testing situations ("You scored higher than 90% of the people who took the test"). Percentile scores, which we'll come to very soon, provide just this kind of information.

Score Intervals. When we have so many different values that listing them all becomes impractical or cumbersome (about 10 to 15 different values or so), it's best to group them into intervals. For example, Dr. Campbell's introversion/extraversion scores presented at the beginning of the chapter contain values ranging from 3 to 22. Since that is roughly 20 different values, these data are a good candidate for grouping into intervals. But how many intervals should we use? There's no number that's best for all data sets, but between 10 and 15 is usually a good choice.

Let's illustrate the process using the introversion/extraversion scores. Since the lowest value is 3 and the highest is 22, then the range of values is $22 - 3 = 19$, and if we want about 10 intervals, then each interval must be $19/10 \cong 2.0$ units wide.*

Intervals are usually defined so that the lowest one contains the smallest value and also has a lower value that is evenly divisible by the interval width. In this case, then, we might write the intervals as

    2– 3
    4– 5
    6– 7
    8– 9
    10–11
    12–13
    14–15
    16–17
    18–19
    20–21
    22–23

Our procedure gave us 11 score intervals or categories. We had planned on 10, the value by which we divided the range of scores; but to include the highest value, we had to use 11 intervals.

The set of intervals tells us that values of 2 or 3 will be counted into the first interval, 4 and 5 into the second, and so on. For the introversion/extraversion data, these intervals suffice nicely. But suppose that we had decimal values in the data. What would we do with a score of 3.5? To answer that question, we need to digress briefly and return to our discussion of measurement from Chapter 3.

Measurement (Again). Measurement assigns numerals to objects so that they represent an underlying property of the object being measured. In the case of the introversion/extraversion scale, that underlying personality dimension is assumed to be continuous, from very introverted to very extraverted. But the measurement scale assigns only whole numbers between 1 and 25. It's just as if we were measuring with a ruler that had only whole inches with no fractions allowed. When that's the case, as it is with most psychological scales, we assume that a score of 17 on the scale, for example, really represents an underlying value somewhere between 16.5 and 17.4999.... That is, the real psychological dimension is continuous, but is broken into whole-number chunks, like this

---

*Because the result is fractional, we round it to a whole number, since fractional intervals are cumbersome. The result may be one interval more or less than we wanted, but usually that's no problem.

In other words, the measured value is taken to be the midpoint of an interval that extends 0.5 units on each side of the measured value. The precision of measurement of this example scale is only to the nearest integer, while the underlying scale is continuous.

The same sort of consideration extends to other measurements, of course. If we are measuring reaction time, our timer will have a precision of measurement of perhaps 0.01 sec. Clearly, the underlying dimension of time is continuous, but the timer will give us only values of 5.23, 5.24, or 5.25.

Time, clearly, is a continuous variable. It is measured in discrete "chunks" that are determined by the precision of the timing instrument that we have. But some of the variables that psychologists often use seem to be clearly discrete and not representative of an underlying continuum. The number of errors made, or the number of problems solved, for example, appear to be discrete variables that don't necessarily reflect an underlying continuous variable. If we are *really* interested in just the numbers of errors or problems solved, then the variable is discrete. Usually, though, we're taking those apparently discrete values as measurement of an underlying variable that really might be conceived of as continuous. The number of errors, for example, often appears as a dependent variable in learning studies, where it is presumed to reflect learning. That is, if an animal or a human learns how to perform some task, and if we want evidence of that learning, we can observe a decline in the numbers of errors made on successive trials. Again, our "ruler" has only whole numbers used to measure what may be a continuous latent variable. (We'll ignore a debate among learning theorists concerning the continuous versus incremental nature of the learning process itself, which leaves the whole notion of an underlying continuum up in the air.) A similar argument might be made about many other apparently discrete variables, such as the number of problems solved, which might be taken as a measure of an underlying (continuous) skill.

How does all of this digression help us? For one thing, it leads to a rule about rounding, and for another it helps to explain the common procedure for dealing with scores that fall exactly on an apparent boundary between intervals.

First, the rounding rule. The results of most computations should be rounded. Computers typically carry the computation of an average, for example, to an unreasonably large number of digits. Do we want to use all of those digits? Certainly not; the data themselves have a precision that is determined by the measuring device, and using a large number of digits beyond the original values is meaningless. If we are measuring only to the nearest whole integer, as with the introversion/extraversion scores, for example, it makes little sense to have summary values with 10 digits following the decimal point. A reasonable rule, then, is to *round to two digits greater precision than are present in the data.* Following this rule, then, if we computed the average of the introversion/extraversion scores as 13.816735394, we should round the value to 13.82 when we report it.*

---

*Many psychologists follow an additional rounding rule when rounding a 0.5 value: round a 5 so that the result is an even number. Following this rule, 33.425663 would round to 33.42, but 33.43565 would round to 33.44. By following this rule consistently, we won't bias our computations either up or down.

Intervals with Decimals. Now, to come back to the earlier question—how do we handle the score of 3.5 when our intervals are 2–3, 4–5, etc.? Since the intervals are probably intended to represent a continuous underlying variable, the intervals really represent the values

1.5–3.499...
3.5–5.499...
5.5–7.499...

and a 3.5 should be scored into the interval 4–5. Note that the actual interval limits extend 0.5 above and below each interval. This illustrates a rule about constructing the intervals—the actual limits go one half of a measurement unit above and below. Since the data are measured to whole-number precision, the intervals are shown as ± 0.5.

Since it's awkward to produce tables and illustrations using intervals that are described with decimals, intervals are often labeled with just the midpoints, with the interval understood to extend equal distances on each side of the midpoint. With this agreed upon then, we can present the introversion/extraversion data as

Category midpoint	Frequency
2.5	1
4.5	1
6.5	2
8.5	5
10.5	12
12.5	12
14.5	26
16.5	14
18.5	6
20.5	4
22.5	1

This summary of the data is compact and easy to comprehend. It also tells us something important that was not apparent in the raw data—most of the people tested fall in the middle range of the introversion/extraversion scale rather than in two extreme groups. The fact that there don't seem to be two distinct groups of people is an important finding, and all we had to do was count the numbers to learn it. Like most traits, introversion/extraversion seems to be distributed across people so that most people are at neither one extreme nor the other but tend to fall into the middle range.

As another example using decimal values, consider these data, and use 15 intervals:

2.5	3.6	9.2	11.6
5.6	6.1	3.2	8.1
3.2	4.0	5.3	6.8
9.9	2.6	6.8	9.3

The scores range from 2.5 to 11.6. Dividing that range of values by 15, we calculate the width of each interval as $(11.6 - 2.5)/15 = 0.607$. Rounding, we'll use an interval width of 0.6. The first interval can start at 2.40 (it's lower than the lowest value, and is divisible by the interval width). Using these values, the intervals then become

```
2.40–  2.90
3.00–  3.50
3.60–  4.10
4.20–  4.70
4.80–  5.30
5.40–  5.90
6.00–  6.50
6.60–  7.10
7.20–  7.70
7.80–  8.30
8.40–  8.90
9.00–  9.50
9.60–10.10
10.20–10.70
10.80–11.30
11.40–11.90
```

To construct the intervals, we begin with 2.40 as a starting point and continue downward, each interval starting 0.60 larger than its predecessor, resulting in the numbers in the first column. The logic of the upper limit is as follows. Because the data are measured to 0.1 precision, the actual interval values extend 0.5 (one half of the measurement unit) below each starting value. Thus the first two lower limits are actually 2.35 and 2.95 (corresponding to the 2.40 and 3.00 shown). The actual upper limit of the first interval coincides with the actual lower limit of the second interval (2.95).

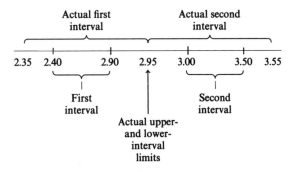

The top value given for the first interval is one-half measurement unit less than its actual upper limit of 2.95. This leads to 2.90 as the upper limit for the first interval. Once the limits of the first interval are found, all of the remaining upper values are determined by simply adding the interval width (0.60) to the successive values.

Computer programs that count frequencies have built-in rules that guide their formation of intervals, usually arriving at around 10 to 15 intervals, because those numbers seem to work best for most data. Using 10 to 15 intervals usually is sufficient to represent most data sets without becoming overwhelming. In addition, that's usually enough intervals so that important features of the data won't be obscured by too few intervals. But 10 to 15 intervals won't be best for all data, and you should experiment with various numbers of intervals. The ideal presentation will illuminate the important features of the data, and we'll talk later about what some of those are, but will also keep the detail at a minimum. After all, you're trying to summarize data, and too much detail, or too many intervals, won't help. Too few intervals won't help, either, because that distribution will mask too much of the data.

A Note on Cumulative Distributions. When cumulative frequencies, relative frequencies, or proportions are presented, the actual *upper limit* of each interval is used instead of the interval midpoint. Thus the introversion/extraversion data would be presented as follows.

Category upper limit	Frequency	Cumulative frequency
3.5	1	1
5.5	1	2
7.5	2	4
9.5	5	9
11.5	12	21
13.5	12	33
15.5	26	59
17.5	14	73
19.5	6	79
21.5	4	83
23.5	1	84

Outliers. A data value that is far away from the bulk of the values in the data is often called an *outlier*, since it lies outside of the usual values in the data. Outliers are important in data analysis for several reasons. Sometimes an extreme value appears as the result of an error—a decimal point out of place, perhaps, or the digits interchanged in recording the data. Other outliers, though, may indicate valid data points that are simply unusual. When an outlier is seen— usually a single value at the high or the low end of the data—it should be checked carefully. If it's an erroneous value, including it can distort the frequency distribution, as well as most descriptive statistics.

Presenting Frequencies. There are two ways to present frequencies—in tabular form or as an illustration (normally called a *figure*). We'll consider tables first, since we've already illustrated them.

Tables. A *table* is an orderly arrangement of numbers in rows and columns. For frequencies, the table nearly always has either two or three columns, and as many rows as there are intervals. As an example, here's the introversion/ extraversion data once again, formatted as you might type it in a research report: We'll digress here to look at the mechanics of this table in some detail. Mechanics are important in constructing both tables and figures for presenting

Table 1

Introversion/Extraversion Scores
(Eysenck Personality Inventory)

Category midpoint	Frequency
2.5	1
4.5	1
6.5	2
8.5	5
10.5	12
12.5	12
14.5	26
16.5	14
18.5	6
20.5	4
22.5	1

scientific data because there are certain standards for them that facilitate communication. Just as an APA research report follows a set outline, so too do the figures and tables that are contained within them. The reason for insisting that students learn how to prepare proper tables and figures is not to stifle their creativity (and students can be enormously creative in designing such things!), nor to insist that the APA standard is the only "right way" to do it, but to teach an accepted standard. A reader of an APA-style report knows roughly what to expect, and following a standard form for tables and figures likewise gives the audience a break; the reader doesn't have to figure out each author's own peculiarities. With that in mind, let's look carefully at the table and point out some important features of the APA table style.

First, notice that the table has a number and a title. When you write a research paper, the numbers of tables are assigned consecutively in the order that they are mentioned in the report. (Note that, while this book follows the APA style for some elements such as referencing, all of our illustrations aren't necessarily numbered or even given titles; books can follow different rules than do APA-style research reports.) Note that there is a single horizontal line separating the title and number from the body of the table, that the title and the

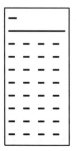

Vertical table

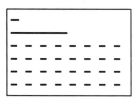

Horizontal table

Figure 5.1

number lines are underlined, aligned at the left margin, and separated by double spaces (as are the lines in the body of the table).

The columns of numbers are neatly spaced, and the column headings are underlined. If values in the table have been rounded, each column should have a consistent number of decimal digits. The numerals in each column are aligned neatly under their headings. The alignment of the numerals is on decimal position even though there are no decimals. (If you're preparing a table with a word processor and not a typewriter, use decimal tabs to align your numbers.) There are no vertical rules dividing the columns.*

The most common error in constructing a table isn't a construction error at all, but is using a table where one isn't needed. Students will often use a table to present only one or two numbers. That's overkill. Don't use a table unless you have at least four numbers to present; tables are at their best when you need a compact way of presenting a substantial number of values. On the other hand, a table that can't be fit onto a single sheet of typing paper and still maintain neat spacing and legibility is probably trying to present too much data and should be subdivided.

Another common error is that of transposing the table; that is, having more columns than rows. A table is best built vertically on a page (Figure 5.1).

Students tend to be sloppy in constructing tables, even when the rest of their work is very neat, and that sloppiness leads to tables that do not communicate effectively at all. The point of using a table for a set of frequencies, or any other set of numbers, is to communicate a mass of information easily. If the reader spends too much time trying to decipher a sloppy table, then the table isn't communicating as it should.

Graphics. The other way to present frequency data is graphically, using one of several kinds of illustrations. Line graphs and frequency polygons are the most common in scientific literature, while bar graphs and histograms are less common.

A histogram is constructed by drawing rectangles whose heights represent the frequencies of intervals. For example, the introversion/extraversion frequency data might appear as shown in Figure 5.2. The figure presents the same data as does our sample Table 1, but does so visually. The picture makes it clearer that there is a strong tendency for the scores to cluster in the middle range, but also that there is a straggle of individuals with very low scores.

While tables are best arranged vertically, figures are best horizontal, as illustrated in our sample Figure 1 (Figure 5.2). The usual rule is that a figure is best when it's a little wider than it is tall; two units high for each three units wide is a common rule of thumb, so that the proportion should generally be measured in whatever units are convenient (Figure 5.3). The vertical and horizontal axes should be calibrated so that the scale occupies the full length.

When prepared for a student paper, a figure is constructed on a separate sheet of paper and not merged with typewritten text. The figure is centered on

---

*For some reason, students love to put vertical rules in tables. Do like a graphic designer would instead—let the "white space" delimit the columns.

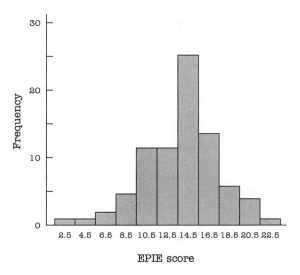

Figure 1. The distribution of EPIE scores for 84 subjects.

Figure 5.2

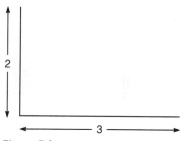

Figure 5.3

its page, which is placed in the report immediately following the page where the figure is mentioned. Figures are also numbered consecutively, and the figure number and caption should be placed below the figure.

The axes should be labeled with the name of the variable being shown—frequency and EPIE score, in this case. The rectangles representing the frequencies are drawn to the height of the frequency for each value of interval midpoint, and in width to the real midpoint between two intervals. Note that when frequency data are presented, they should *always* appear on the ordinate or vertical axis.

For continuous variables, most often those measured as interval or ratio, the rectangles are drawn so that they are connected, as illustrated in Figure 5.2. When the data present nominal or ordinal measurements, the rectangles are drawn individually, with space between them, showing graphically that they are not to be seen as continuous. A presentation like this is normally called a *bar chart*, to distinguish it from a histogram. Figure 5.4 illustrates the job category data using a bar chart.

Bar charts may be presented horizontally or vertically, so that you might see the same data as illustrated in Figure 5.5. Scientific graphics are nearly always drawn in black on white paper; unless your instructor says otherwise, you should follow that rule for all assignments.

While bar charts are frequently used for category and ordinal data and histograms are used to present data from interval and ratio measurement, other representations are usually used for the latter kinds of measurements. In particular, the frequency polygon, or line graph, is often found in journals and reports. A polygon is constructed by laying out a set of axes following the same proportions and other rules as for a histogram and placing a point to represent the frequency for each score interval. The points are then connected by straight lines, so that the EPIE score distribution would appear as shown in Figure 5.6. The

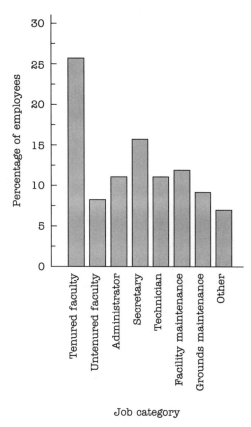

Figure 2. Percentage of employees in each job category.

Figure 5.4

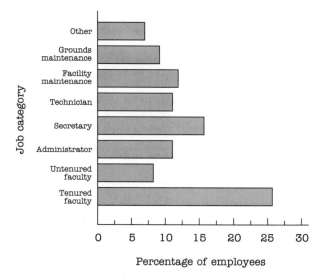

Figure 3. Percentage of employees in each job category.

Figure 5.5

rules for constructing polygons are similar to those for histograms, at least as far as the axes, labeling, and titles are concerned. In addition, note that the ends of the polygon are "tied down" to the abscissa (the bottom axis) by continuing the line to the baseline at each end. Polygons, like histograms, are drawn in black on white paper, so keep your colored pencils in your desk.

The same general format of the polygon may be used for over-time or over-trials data and may also show more than a single dependent variable. Shown in Figure 5.7, for example, are some hypothetical data for a subject learning a list of words over a series of trials. Two dependent variables were recorded: number of words correctly recalled and the time taken in recall. While these are *not* frequency polygon data, Figure 5.7 illustrates the application of the same graphic rules to a different kind of data. In a case like this one, a legend is used to distinguish one dependent variable from the other. The legend is placed within the axes of the figure and indicates the lines used.

Comparing the Use of Tables and Figures. Both tables and figures are exceptionally effective ways of communicating information about frequencies. They're also useful for showing other sorts of results, as we illustrated with the double-

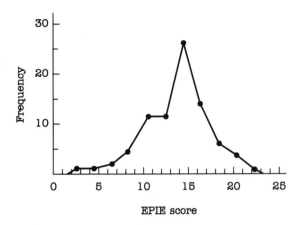

Figure 4. EPIE scores for Dr. Campbell's 84 subjects.

Figure 5.6

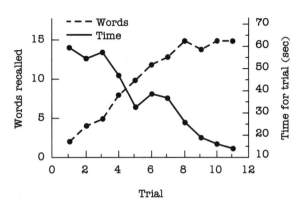

Figure 5. Words recalled and time required for the 11 learning trials.

Figure 5.7

axis plot of the learning data (Figure 5.7). But how do you decide whether a table or a figure is the best way of communicating, and when should you rely on words alone?

Tables and figures are at their best when they're used to communicate a substantial amount of information. Tables, we suggested earlier, should be used for more than four numbers, and they're usually best with many more than that. When there are only a few numbers, they are best communicated in sentence format in the text of a report. Tables are often chosen for their ability to show sets of frequencies or summary statistics side by side for ease of comparison. Figures are very good at showing the form of a distribution of data, but aren't normally used for that purpose unless you're trying to make a point about form and a picture seems easiest.

Both tables and figures are "costly" in some sense. For students, there is extra effort involved in making the illustration. For investigators submitting the research report for publication, the preparation of high-quality figures had been difficult and costly until the recent development of computer software that can produce publication-quality illustrations with very little effort. For journal editors, tables and figures present special and costly production problems.

Nevertheless, both tables and figures offer very effective ways to communicate. In deciding whether to use them, consider the amount of data that you have to communicate and what you want it to say. If you have only a few values, or an unremarkable frequency distribution that you can describe easily, then use words. On the other hand, if you have a lot of numbers, perhaps representing several groups, the compact, side-by-side format of a table might be the best way to communicate. If you want to make a point of the shape of the distribution, or if you want to show a trend over time or trials, then a figure may be the choice. In Chapter 18, we'll discuss how to present and interpret interactions in complicated experimental designs; the figure is the preferred way to present interaction data because it communicates visually what could be difficult to say as concisely in words.

Percentiles and Percentile Ranks

Suppose that you wanted to compare your relative standing on two exams in your German class. If your instructor happens to use the same grading scale on both exams, then you may be able to compare directly one score with the other. But if one exam had a possible high grade of 50, and the other a possible top score of 75, then comparing raw test scores might be difficult.

If you happen to receive perfect scores on both exams, you know exactly how you stand in the class. You can describe your position as being "first in the class," regardless of your actual test scores. Another way to describe your top position is to say that your score is higher than those of 100% of your classmates. You don't have to use actual test scores to describe where you are in class; you can do it all by citing the percentage of the scores that are below yours. If you say that "I did better than 75% of the class on the first test," you don't have to worry about whether the test was scored on a 50-point scale, on a 75-point scale, or on any arbitrary scale. In the same way, if your score is higher than 75% of the students on the first exam but exceeds 90% on the second, then you know that you have improved relative to your class, regardless of your actual scores.

What we have just described is a measure called the percentile rank. The *percentile rank* of a score is the percentage of the distribution below that score. Using such measures of relative standing in a set of data is a common procedure, especially in educational settings.

Suppose that there are 15 students in your German class and that you received a 33 on a weekly quiz. If you arranged the grades of all of the students in order, you might have

15　17　22　23　27　33　38　41　42　43　52　58　60　66　71
　　　　　　　　　　↑
　　　　　　　Your score

The percentile rank of your score of 33 is 40, since it exceeds 6/15, or 40%, of the data. If your friend John scored 66 on the same quiz, then the percentile rank of John's 66 is 93, since it exceeds 14/15 (93%) of the values in the data.

Approximate percentile ranks may be determined graphically from a plot of a frequency distribution. Suppose that we have the following distribution of errors in recalling a list of 32 words:

Words recalled	Frequency	Cumulative frequency
2	0	0
5	3	3
8	3	6
11	4	10
14	4	14
17	6	20
20	8	28
23	7	35
26	5	40
29	2	42
32	1	43

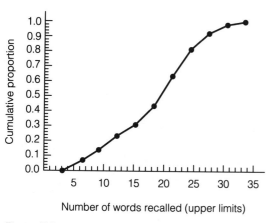

Figure 5.8

Figure 5.9

By calculating the relative frequencies corresponding to the cumulative frequencies and plotting the resulting cumulative distribution using the upper limits (Figure 5.8), we can determine approximate percentile ranks easily.

Words recalled	Frequency	Cumulative frequency	Cumulative proportion
3.5	0	0	.00
6.5	3	3	.07
9.5	3	6	.14
12.5	4	10	.23
15.5	4	14	.32
18.5	6	20	.46
21.5	8	28	.65
24.5	7	35	.81
27.5	5	40	.93
30.5	2	42	.98
33.5	1	43	1.00

To find the approximate percentile rank of a number of words recalled, find the value on the horizontal line of Figure 5.8 and draw a vertical from it to the cumulative curve. Then move to the left to find the percentile point. Figure 5.9 shows how to determine the approximate percentile rank for 6 words recalled; the rank is a little under 6. As another example, the percentile rank for 26 words recalled is about 86 (Figure 5.10).

The percentile rank provides a convenient means for comparing scores in dissimilar distributions since the comparison is on a standard 0–100% scale. It has the additional advantage of being readily understandable by people with no background in statistics or the quantitative treatment of data.

A closely related statistic (indeed, it's the mirror image of the percentile rank) is the *percentile*. A percentile gives the *score* that exceeds a given percentage of the distribution. For example, the score that is at the 50% point of the distribution would be called the 50th percentile. A score that is larger than 25% of the distribution is the 25th percentile; that exceeding 85% is the 85th percentile, and

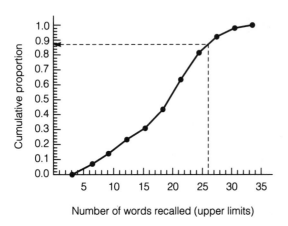

Figure 5.10

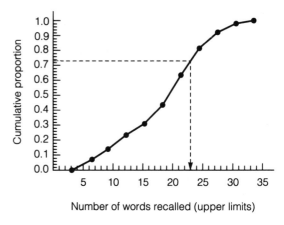

Figure 5.11

so forth. Scores that divide the distribution into four equal-sized segments are also known as *quartiles*, as we noted earlier, so that the 25th percentile is the same as the first quartile, the 50th percentile is the second quartile, and the 75th percentile is the third quartile.

Interpolation on a cumulative frequency plot may also be used to locate approximate percentiles. Using the words-recalled data set, to locate the 75th percentile, for example, you begin with the 75% (or 0.75) point on the vertical axis and move to the right until the cumulative frequency line is located, and then drop to the value scale to find the data value of approximately 23 (Figure 5.11).

The unfortunate similarity of the names *percentile* and *percentile rank* has caused untold confusion among generations of students, but they are really quite different, though related, values. The *percentile rank* is a value between 0 and 100% that shows the standing of a data value relative to the other scores in the distribution. The *percentile*, on the other hand, is a value from the range of the scores themselves; specifically, it is a value that exceeds a specific percentage of the distribution. If you keep the illustration in mind, the percentile is a value on the horizontal axis, while the percentile rank is a value on the vertical axis.

S U M M A R Y

- Counting frequencies is a simple and effective way to summarize data.
- A frequency distribution giving values and their frequencies can be presented as either a table or a figure.
- Ordinal, interval, and ratio measurements can be grouped into score intervals so that the range of scores is divided into 10–15 intervals.
- Computational results are typically rounded to two digits greater precision than were present in the data.
- An *outlier* is a value that is far away from the other data.

- Tables are used to present a large number of values and should be neatly arranged vertically on the page.
- Tables and figures are always numbered and have titles.
- There are no vertical rules in a table.
- Figures should be drawn wider than they are tall; 2 : 3 is a good ratio of height to width.
- The *percentile rank* of a score is the percentage of the distribution below that score.
- A *percentile* gives the score that exceeds a given percentage of the distribution.
- Scores that divide the distribution into four equal segments are called *quartiles*.

K E Y   T E R M S

Bar chart	**Percentile**
Cumulative frequencies	**Percentile rank**
Frequency distribution	**Quartile**
Frequency polygon	**Relative frequency**
Histogram	**Score interval**
Line graph	**Table**
Outlier	

E X E R C I S E S

Solutions to asterisked (∗) exercises appear at the back of the book. Exercises preceded by a section symbol (§) must be solved using a computer. Exercises preceded by a dagger (†) can be solved by hand.

∗†1. Here are the scores for a class of students on a midterm examination:

61	82	71	87
83	82	92	75
89	67	86	78
76	69	73	62
69	88	81	77
76	75	72	69
86	89	98	71
64	62	75	86

Construct a frequency distribution for these values and present it as a histogram. (*Hint:* Use an interval width of 3.0.)

†2. Using the Eysenck Personality Inventory Extraversion (EPIE) data from Dr. Campbell that were presented at the beginning of this chapter, construct the frequency distribution. Present it as a frequency polygon.

∗†3. The following is a set of 28 reaction times to a tone; the times are given in hundredths of seconds (that is, the value 31 = 0.31 sec):

80	19	18	17
82	22	119	22
89	28	148	20
94	31	149	60
21	42	38	72
21	53	23	38
25	55	26	105

Construct the frequency distribution for these data and present it as a frequency polygon and as a table.

†4. Here are the data giving the number of words recalled in a learning experiment for two groups of subjects, five-year-old children and college students. Find the two frequency distributions and plot them as frequency polygons on the same set of axes:

Children	College students	
26	28	25
21	23	21
14	25	25
12	18	30
29	20	21
17	24	19
7	23	32
28	21	24
14	16	31
13	15	27
8	27	27
27	21	26
11	19	23
20	26	17
17	24	31
18		
6		
6		
7		
16		

*†5. A study in cognitive psychology presented a group of subjects with a large list of words, consisting of equal numbers of verbs, nouns, adverbs, and adjectives. The total number of each kind of word recalled by a group of subjects was:

Verb	153
Noun	178
Adverb	121
Adjective	78

Present the data as a bar graph.

†6. Using the data from Exercise 1, plot the cumulative proportions. Use the plot to find the following:
   a. The 25th, 50th, and 75th percentiles.
   b. The percentile ranks of the following scores: 62, 92, 88, and 71.

*†7. Using the data from Exercise 2:
   a. Construct the cumulative relative frequency distribution.
   b. Using the plot, find the 50th, 40th, 25th, and 90th percentiles.
   c. Find the percentile rank for scores of 12, 16, 20, and 19.

*†8. Using the data from Exercise 3:
   a. Construct the cumulative frequency distribution and plot it.
   b. Find the 10th, 25th, 40th, 50th, 60th, 75th, and 90th percentiles.
   c. Find the percentile ranks for reaction times of 0.40, 1.25, 0.63, and 0.35 seconds.

CHAPTER 6

Measures of Center

Summarizing data by counting frequencies, as we did in Chapter 5, is a powerful technique for condensing a very large amount of information into a more manageable size. By inspecting the distribution of the frequencies, you can tell where the bulk of the observations fall, which are the unusual values, and so forth.

But there's more to summarizing data than just frequency counting. What if you wanted some *single* value that would characterize the data? What value best summarizes a set of data? If you answered "the average," then you're on the right track. Actually, there are several different summary statistics that we might use to describe where the "center" or the "typical" value in a set of data is, and the term *average* could correctly be applied to all of them. The choice among the measures of central tendency is influenced by a number of factors, including the nature of the measurement, the "shape" of the frequency distribution, and just what we want to show. Remember that we're always looking for an answer to some question (or questions) in the data, and some techniques give a clearer answer than do others.

"Averages"

You were probably in the fifth grade when you learned that the average was calculated by adding together all of the values and dividing by the number of values added. The result, the "average," was a measure that you could use to summarize your performance in school, perhaps, or maybe the number of stamps per country in your collection. At about the same time, you may have learned about another kind of average, the batting averages of baseball players; but those "averages" are computed by dividing the number of hits by the number of times at bat, and so the number is really a proportion. You may have also heard phrases like "the average family income," which is usually obtained by another sort of

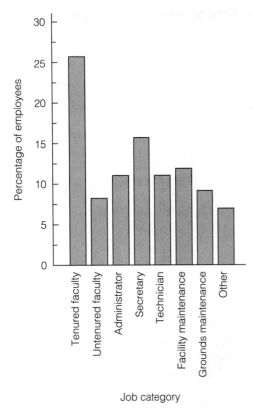

Figure 6.1

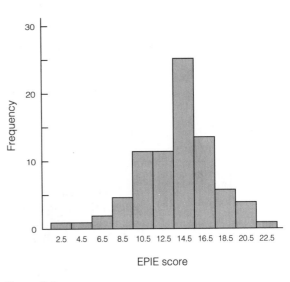

Figure 6.2

computation. And you've undoubtedly heard a phrase like "on the average, I like my stat class pretty well."

In short, the word *average* is imprecise. We have a sense of what it means as a summary statistic, but the word alone doesn't communicate very well. Let's look at some of the numerous measures of central tendency, or "average," that have been developed.

| The Mode | The mode is the score, or the score interval, that occurs most frequently in the data. As such, you can think of it as a popularity-contest measure. When the measurement is nominal, the mode is an appropriate measure to employ. Consider the category data from Chapter 5, as graphed in Figure 6.1.

The most frequent job category is tenured faculty. Notice that if you were to report only the mode, you wouldn't say anything about any other category, we don't even know whether "tenured faculty" is the winner by one person or by 100. Even so, the mode does offer a simple summary of the data, even though there's a lot of information in the frequency distribution that it doesn't communicate.

When ordinal, interval, or ratio data are counted into intervals for the frequency distribution, the mode is normally reported as the midpoint of the most frequent interval. Thus for the introversion/extraversion data graphed in Figure 6.2, the mode is reported as 14.5.

The Median The median is the score that's at the center of a distribution of data in the sense that one-half of the data values are less than the median, and one-half are larger. Thus it's much more likely to meet our expectation of an "average" in the middle of the data than is the mode. Since we must be able to at least arrange the data in order from smallest to largest in order to determine the median, it's not a useful statistic for nominal data. But it's very useful for ordinal, interval, and ratio data.

Calculating Simple Medians. The exact determination of the median is simple for a few values that are easily ordered, especially when there's an odd number of values, such as

17 23 45 46 83 84 96
↑
Median

Here the median is the center score, and the same number of values are above as are below the median.

For an even number of scores, the median is the midpoint between the two center values, as in

23 45 46 83 84 96
↑
Median = 64.5

The expression $(N + 1)/2$ will give the location of the median in the ordered data. In the first example, there are 7 values, and so the median is at the $(7 + 1)/2 = 4$th position. In the second illustration, the median is at the position halfway between 3 and 4, determined by $(6 + 1)/2 = 3.5$.

Calculating the Median with Grouped Data. When the data are grouped into intervals, the median frequently will fall within an interval. In that case, the median is that point within the interval where the $(N + 1)/2$ score is located. For example, consider the following simple frequency distribution, shown with individual and cumulative frequencies:

Upper limit	Frequency	Cumulative frequency
9.5	2	2
14.5	6	8
19.5	18	26
24.5	22	48
29.5	17	65
34.5	9	74
39.5	6	80
44.5	1	81

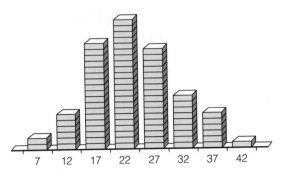

Figure 6.3

The lowest two scores are in the interval below 9.5, while the next larger 6 scores are in the interval below 14.5. There are a total of 81 scores in the data. If they were all written down in order, the median would be the $(81 + 1)/2 = 41$st score. We don't have the actual data values, but the median is still the 41st value. The 41st score must be in the interval with the upper limit of 24.5; there are 26 scores below that interval, and by the time we go to the next higher interval, we have counted 48 scores. Therefore, the 41st must be there:

Upper limit	Frequency	Cumulative frequency	
9.5	2	2	
14.5	6	8	Only 26 scores to this point
19.5	18	26	
24.5	22	48	Median is in this interval
29.5	17	65	But more than 41 to here
34.5	9	74	
39.5	6	80	
44.5	1	81	

We might picture the distribution as being made of bricks on a board, where each brick represents one individual score. (See Figure 6.3; for clarity, the histogram bars are not drawn immediately adjacent in this illustration, as they normally should be.) In Figure 6.3, it's clear that there are two scores in the interval centered on 7, six in the interval centered on 12, and so forth. The middle (that is, the 41st) score must certainly be one of those in the pile of bricks centered on a score of 22, but how do we decide which one?

Recalling the actual limits on the intervals, the interval with the median must be bounded by the values 19.5 and 24.5. In the median interval there are 22 scores, and they must be the 27th, 28th, 29th, . . . , 40th, 41st, 42nd, and so on through the 48th value in the data. If we spread out the 22 bricks evenly over that interval, we have a result like that shown in Figure 6.4. The median is the 41st score; it is also the 15th score in the interval. Since the median is the 15th "brick" above the start of the interval, and since there are 22 "bricks" in the interval, the median must be 15/22 of the way between the bottom of the interval and its top. The median thus can be found as the lower limit of the interval (that is, 19.5), plus 15/22 of the distance through the next interval, as shown in Figure 6.5. The interval (19.5 to 24.5) has a width of 5.0, so that 15/22 of it is

$$\frac{15}{22} \times 5 = 3.41,$$

and the median is thus $19.5 + 3.41 = 22.91$.

In general terms, the overall computation is

Lower real limit + As much of the next interval as needed
to reach the median.

To find the median, we determine the lower real limit from the frequency distribution. Then a simple computation gives the amount that must be added to the lower limit. We may express the entire process in the more precise formula

$$\text{Lower real limit} + \frac{0.5 \times N - \text{Cf}_{\text{below}}}{\text{Freq}_{\text{interval}}} \times \text{interval width.}$$

In the formula, "Cf_{below}" designates the cumulative frequency below the interval with the median, "$\text{Freq}_{\text{interval}}$" indicates the frequency in the median's interval, and N is the total number of scores in the data set. The quantity "$0.5 \times N$" is normally rounded up if N is an odd number.

For our example, the median is calculated as

$$\begin{aligned}
\text{Mdn} &= 19.5 + \frac{0.5 \times 81 - 26}{22} \times 5 \\
&= 19.5 + \frac{41 - 26}{22} \times 5 \\
&= 19.5 + 3.41 \\
&= 22.91.
\end{aligned}$$

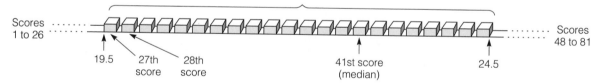

22 "bricks"
between 19.5 and 24.5

Scores 1 to 26   Scores 48 to 81

19.5   27th score   28th score   41st score (median)   24.5

Figure 6.4

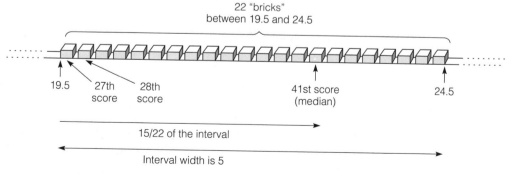

22 "bricks"
between 19.5 and 24.5

19.5   27th score   28th score   41st score (median)   24.5

15/22 of the interval

Interval width is 5

Figure 6.5

"Averages"

While the computation may seem a little confusing, it's actually quite simple to do. Most students make one (or sometimes both) of two mistakes. One mistake is to find the wrong interval for the median and thus base their calculations on the wrong frequencies and lower limit—the median interval is the one *just before* the interval where the cumulative frequency exceeds $(N + 1)/2$. The other error is to calculate the "as much of the next interval" part incorrectly, usually because they use the wrong frequencies.

The median computation that we have illustrated is also the procedure that most computer programs use, except that they don't normally do the rounding operation for the $0.5 \times N$ calculation.

Percentiles (Again). In Chapter 5 we illustrated a graphic method of determining approximate percentile points. Since the median is that score that exceeds 50% of the data, it's also the 50th percentile. We can easily modify the formula for the median to calculate any percentile value. Since the $0.5 \times N$ component of the median formula defines the 50% point in the data, by changing the decimal value, we may select any percentile. For example, we may calculate the 25th percentile as

$$\text{Lower real limit} + \frac{0.25 \times N - \text{Cf}_{\text{below}}}{\text{Freq}_{\text{interval}}} \times \text{interval width}.$$

In applying this formula, we use the lower limit and the frequencies appropriate to the 25th percentile. Because $0.25 \times 81 = 20.25$, the interval containing the 25th percentile must be the one in which the cumulative frequency exceeds 20.25. So in the example data, we have

Upper limit	Frequency	Cumulative frequency	
9.5	2	2	
14.5	6	8	
19.5	18	26	} ← 25th percentile is in this interval
24.5	22	48	
29.5	17	65	
34.5	9	74	
39.5	6	80	
44.5	1	81	

Applying the formula, we have

$$25\text{th percentile} = 14.5 + \frac{0.25 \times 81 - 8}{18} \times 5$$

$$= 17.90.$$

Using the graphic method from Chapter 5 (shown in Figure 6.6) as a check, we get an estimated value of slightly under 18; the computed value is more precise. Figure 6.6 uses grouped data. If there were a small number of values, then percentiles other than the 25th (the first quartile) and the 75th (the third quartile) are rarely useful. They are calculated as the medians of the lower and upper halves of the ordered data.

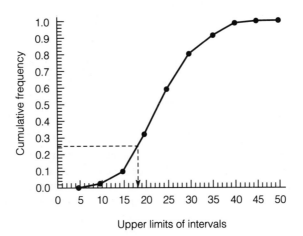

Upper limits of intervals

Figure 6.6

This is our old friend the "average," with its correct name. The arithmetic mean is nothing more than all of the scores added up and divided by the number of scores in the data set. You probably even know the formula,

$$\overline{X} = \frac{\Sigma X}{N}.$$

The uppercase Greek letter *sigma*, Σ is used in mathematics to stand for the *summation* or "add-'em-up" operation. We'll find the summation operation in a number of formulas as we proceed, and it will always mean the same thing, namely "add-'em-up." We have also used the standard symbol, $\overline{X}$ (pronounced "X bar"), to stand for the arithmetic mean. (You may encounter the letter M used for the mean in some books.)

The mean of the values 17, 23, 45, 46, 83, 84, and 96 is

$$\overline{X} = \frac{\Sigma X}{N}$$

$$= \frac{17 + 23 + 45 + 46 + 83 + 84 + 96}{7}$$

$$= 56.28.$$

Calculating the Mean with Grouped Data. If we have data in a grouped frequency distribution, the mean is calculated as

$$\overline{X} = \frac{\Sigma fX}{N}.$$

In this formula, "f" is the frequency in each interval, and "X" is the midpoint; for the example distribution from page 122, we then have

$$\bar{X} = \frac{\Sigma fX}{N}$$

$$= \frac{2(7) + 6(12) + 13(17) + 22(22) + 17(27) + 9(32) + 6(37) + 1(42)}{81}$$

$$= 22.25.$$

Other Measures of the Center

There are a number of other statistics that are sometimes used to describe the "center" of a set of data. Trimmed means, bimeans (also called biweighted means), geometric and harmonic means, and midranges and centile midpoints are all occasionally cited in the literature. (And we'll discuss two of them in very specialized situations later.) Many computer programs offer some of them, and we listed them here so that they'll look familiar if you find them in computer output. But in psychology, only the mode, the median, and the arithmetic mean are used with any regularity. We'll leave the others to more advanced texts.

Properties of the Measures of Center

All of the measures of the center have two important properties:

1. Adding or subtracting a constant does the same thing to the measure of the center.
2. Multiplying or dividing by a constant does the same thing to the measure of the center.

If we take the simple values 4, 6, 7, 8, and 16, with the arithmetic mean of 8.20 and the median of 7 and add the value 100 to each data value, we would have the new data set 104, 106, 107, 108, and 116. Clearly, the median of these numbers is 107. The arithmetic mean is 108.20; in both cases, the new value is the original value plus the constant 100. The rule holds for the addition or subtraction of any value.

In a similar way, if we were to multiply each value by, for example, the number 25, then we would have the new data set 100, 150, 175, 200, and 400. The median of these values is 175 (and $175 = 7 \times 25$), while the arithmetic mean is 205.0 (which is 8.20×25); the multiplication rule holds as well.

The Effect of Measurement Scale

Of the measures, the mode is the only one that is appropriate to use with category data. For category data, the data aren't ordered, and so the concept of a "center" is really meaningless. Nevertheless, the mode is often useful for communicating the most frequent choice.

The median is especially useful for ordinal data but is occasionally used with interval and ratio data as well.

The arithmetic mean requires arithmetic operations on intervals between values. For that reason, it is appropriately and meaningfully used only with data that have equal intervals—that is, interval and ratio data.

The Mode

We have already pointed out two properties of the mode that should be taken into account in deciding on a measure to describe the center of the data. First, the mode relies on none of the properties of the number system other than the fact that the numbers are different from one another. And second, even if the data *can* be arranged in order meaningfully, the mode may not be in the "center" of the data at all. To these two problems, we might also add that the mode may not be unique in a set of data. Suppose that our hypothetical frequency distribution had been

Midpoint	Frequency
7	2
12	6
17	18
22	13
27	17
32	18
37	6
42	1

Now we have two modes, and very nearly a third. Data sets with multiple modes are not at all unusual and highlight a serious problem with the mode as a descriptive measure.

The Arithmetic Mean

The arithmetic mean is the center of a data set in two important ways. First, the sum of the algebraic differences (that is, taking signs into account) between scores and their mean is zero. Second, the sum of the squares of the differences between scores and their mean is less than for any other number (that is, it is a minimum).

We can offer both arithmetic and graphic demonstrations of the first property. First, consider the simple data set for a variable (that we just call X for convenience); let's use the numbers 4, 6, 7, 8, 16 that we used before. Its mean is 8.20. If we find the differences $(X - \bar{X})$, then they should sum to zero. That is,

$\bar{X}$	$X - \bar{X}$	
4	−4.2	
6	−2.2	
7	−1.2	$\bar{X} = 8.2$
8	−0.2	
16	7.8	
	$0.0 = \Sigma(X - \bar{X})$	

The sum, $\Sigma(X - \bar{X})$, equals zero, meaning that the negative differences exactly offset the positive; the arithmetic mean is in the center of the distribution in terms of the algebraic differences.

This same property of $\bar{X}$ can be demonstrated visually. Let's look at the board and bricks again (Figure 6.7). The point at which the board would balance, that is, where the weight on one side is exactly offset by the weight on the other, is the arithmetic mean, illustrated in Figure 6.8. This "center of balance" property

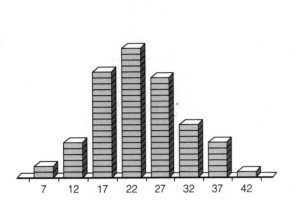

Figure 6.7

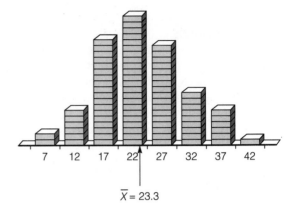

Figure 6.8

$\bar{X} = 23.3$

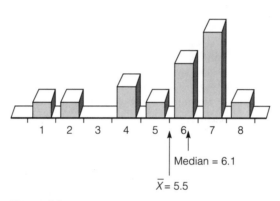

Median = 6.1

$\bar{X} = 5.5$

Figure 6.9

is not true of the median, since the median does not take distance from the center into account. To make a point that we'll return to in a later discussion relative to the median, the arithmetic mean of the distribution shown in Figure 6.9 is shifted toward the extreme values of the left of the board supporting the bricks. The shift of $\bar{X}$ keeps the histogram "in balance." The median, while it has 50% of the observations on each side of it, is not at the center of balance. We may see this easily if we make a single change in the data set: replace the smallest value (1) with a value of -5 (Figure 6.10). The arithmetic mean has been shifted to the left, compensating for the extremely low value; the median is unchanged, since all we did was to substitute one low value for another.

The second property of $\bar{X}$, that $\Sigma(X - \bar{X})^2 =$ a minimum, means that $\bar{X}$ "best fits" the data in an important mathematical sense. Remember that a measure of the center like the arithmetic mean is a summary value; in some sense, it is a "typical" value in the data. If we were to choose a single value to "represent" all of the data, it should come as close to all of the original values as it could. The quantity $(X - \bar{X})$ is the difference between a score and the mean. You may think of this difference as the amount by which the mean "misses" a value. The mean "fits" the data in the sense that it minimizes the squared "misses." The mean's property of minimizing squared differences means that the arithmetic mean is

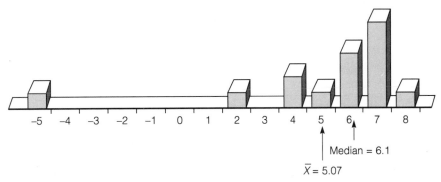

Figure 6.10

the "least squares" best fit to the data. Being a least squares best-fitting measure of center gives the arithmetic mean some desirable properties and relates it closely to some very powerful statistics that we'll meet soon.

The Median

The median is a measure of center that is, as we have seen, largely uninfluenced by extreme values in the data. It is the center of the data; there are equal numbers of scores above and below it, a property that it doesn't always share with the arithmetic mean. We might compute the median and then determine the difference between the median and each value in the original data, $(X - \text{Median})$. The sum of the squares of these "miss" values will probably be greater than for the mean. However, the sum of the *absolute values* of the differences will be smaller for the median than for any other other number. That is, the median is the "center" of the data in the sense that it is closest to all of the numbers in terms of absolute distance. The arithmetic mean, remember, is the closest in terms of squared differences. While this feature of the median may not strike you as especially exciting, or even important, it will be useful in a measure of the spread of the data, a topic that we'll cover in Chapter 7.

Choosing a Measure

A major consideration in selecting a measure of the center of the data is the scale of measurement. If the measurement is categories only, then the mode is the only appropriate choice. When the measurement is ordinal or ordinal with origin, we need a measure whose meaning is insensitive to monotonic transformations. The median is usually the preferred measure of center, since it continues to indicate the "middle" of the data even after a nonlinear, but monotonic, transformation.

When the measurement is interval or ratio, the arithmetic mean is normally preferred. But there are a number of circumstances where the median may be preferred, and we'll turn to those other considerations now.

The Mean and the Median. Earlier we noted that the arithmetic mean is pulled toward an extreme score in the data if there is one. While this preserves $\overline{X}$ as a good estimate of the center, it has a possibility of distorting the conclusions that we might draw. Look at the data graphed in Figure 6.11. Which statistic is

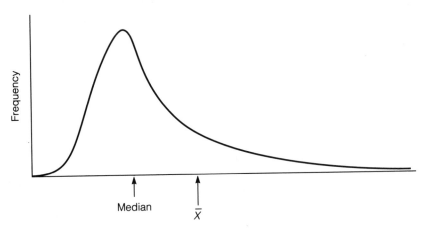

Figure 6.11

the better single indicator of the center? Data of this form, with a long tail of low frequencies extending in one direction or the other is called *skewed* and is often troublesome. A common illustration of the effect of skew on the mean and the median is the distribution of U.S. income. For the year 1987, the arithmetic mean U.S. household income was $32,144, while the median was $25,986.* Which statistic more accurately summarizes the income of most American households? Probably not the mean, which has been inflated by a comparatively few extremely high-income households; the vast majority of American households have an income less than the mean, and so the median is the preferred measure. (Incidentally, when income averages are presented, it is invariably the median that is used.)

A corollary to the mean's property of being pulled toward an extreme tail in the distribution is that if the values of the mean and the median are close, then you may conclude that the distribution is symmetrical, a topic that we'll return to in Chapter 7.

Choosing a Measure for "Symmetric" Data. If the mean and the median are about the same for a set of data—that is, if there's no skew—then the arithmetic mean is the usual statistic to employ unless there are extreme outlying scores at both ends of the distribution. If there are, then one of the other measures is sometimes recommended.

The general recommendation to use the arithmetic mean stems from the statistic's desirable properties as a measure of center, and also from its properties as an estimator. We normally use a statistic like $\overline{X}$ not just to describe a set of data but also to make an inference about a population value, and $\overline{X}$ has some very desirable properties as an estimator and as a descriptive statistic.

Choosing a Measure for "Unusual" Data. A frequency distribution with extreme data values, or with extreme skewness, is an unusual distribution, at least from the point of view of traditional statistical methods. Until recently, if you

---

*U.S. Department of Commerce (1989), p. 442.

Table 6.1 Effect of Measurement Level on Choice of Measure of Center

Level of measurement	Measure of center
Nominal	Mode
Ordinal	Median
Interval and ratio	
Symmetric data	Arithmetic mean
Skewed data	Median
Very long tails	Arithmetic mean
	Bimean

were a researcher confronted with an unusual distribution, you could generally follow one of four general strategies: (1) You could ignore the problem completely. (2) You could treat the offending data values (usually extremely large or small) as errors in coding or recording the data and either remove them or edit them into more "normal" values. (3) You could eliminate a few extreme values from both ends of the distribution and apply standard statistical procedures. (4) You could use the median as the measure of center. For all cases but the last, there are standard inferential procedures to accompany the arithmetic mean, and so the median is rarely used when inference is needed.

The past decade or so has seen the introduction of numerous new descriptive statistics for unusual distributions, as well as new inferential procedures to accompany them. The bimean is one such new statistic. In addition, the median has gained new respect with the development of inferential procedures for it. In fact, some authorities recommend the median even for data that are not skewed; in years past the arithmetic mean was often employed when it was inappropriate because appropriate inferential methods for the median were lacking. While consideration of many of the newer techniques is beyond the scope of this book, you should know that they exist.

Table 6.1 summarizes the recommendations related to choosing a measure of center.

Presenting Measures of Center

Measures of center are often presented verbally, in sentence form, when there are only a few. For example, we might find this sentence in a paper reporting on sex differences: "The mean running time for males was 38.62 sec, while that for the females was 35.41 sec." For one or two values, the sentence format is a compact and straightforward way to present the values. If there are too many values in a sentence, the reader can be confused: "The mean words recalled on trials 1, 2, 3, 4, 5, and 6 are 7.83, 9.44, 16.22, 18.72, 19.04, and 19.87, respectively." Not only is that sentence confusing, but it also doesn't communicate as effectively as it might. When several measures of center are presented, a table makes an effective presentation (Table 6.2).

Tabular presentation makes it very easy for the reader to compare adjacent entries. In addition, the tabular arrangement makes the similarities in the measures of center easy to see.

Table 6.2 Number of Items Recalled Under Three Different Cue Conditions

	Visual cue	Vocal cue	Tone cue
Mean	13.6	16.2	8.2
Median	12.9	16.8	9.0
Mode	13.4	16.3	8.5

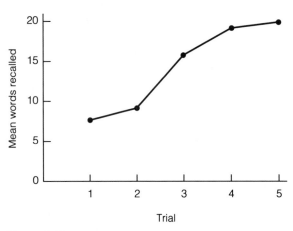

Figure 6.12

There are times when a figure is a good way to present measures of center. Consider the series of mean numbers of words recalled for a set of six trials: 7.83, 9.44, 16.22, 18.72, 19.04, and 19.87. There's a large "jump" in the number of words recalled between trials two and three, and a distinct leveling off between trials four and five; those features of the data become more evident if the means are presented in a graph (Figure 6.12).

Some Notes on Computer Use

This book presents computational formulas and examples, but recognizes that you may actually do most of your calculations by computer. We don't make any assumptions about what kind of computer or what specific software you'll use since that depends upon the facilities available to you.

When you use the computer, you're relieved of most of the drudgery of statistics—the arithmetic and deciphering the formulas—but you're left with three very important matters. First, you have to be able to get the data into your computer correctly. Second, you must be able to select the appropriate analysis for your experimental design and your data. And third, you must be able to interpret and communicate the results of your analysis. The latter two points are the major subject matter of this book, and much of our effort is directed toward teaching you to select the proper research techniques, choose the right analytic tools, and interpret results correctly.

The first point—getting the data in properly—calls for some simple guidelines. There's only one rule about entering data for computer analysis, and it should be posted prominently near every computer and terminal:

**Don't trust
the computer**

What we really mean is that, just because a computer did the computations, we shouldn't trust the results. Statistics programs are generally very accurate numerically, at least to the degree of precision that is demanded by most psychologists' data. In other words, given correct data, the programs will produce numerically correct answers. But notice that phrase "given correct data."

Apart from choosing an incorrect analysis procedure, the most common error in having the computer do your statistics is entering the data incorrectly. And it's easy to check on whether the data are entered properly. Two tests should be done every time data are entered into the computer. First, *always* print the data after you've entered it and check it against your data sheets. Be especially alert for transposing digits (typing 4353 instead of 5433) and too many (or few) digits. If your data are all two-digit numbers, a value with four digits probably means a forgotten "Return," and a single-digit number probably means a typing error as well.

Second, *always* check the computer's results. That doesn't mean that you have to redo everything that the computer does; checking two simple descriptive statistics is normally sufficient. Always check the mean and the standard deviation for each group of subjects. These two checks will almost always show whether or not you and the computer agree about the data. The mean and the standard deviation are common statistics, and many inexpensive calculators offer them as built-in functions.* The mean and standard deviation check should be done for each variable and group in your data set.

These two data checks are so simple that you'd think that everyone would do them, but students often don't. In fact, students (and others!) are so prone to believe what a computer says—just because it's a computer—that they omit even commonsense checks. So there's a third check—*always* check for the logical correctness of the results. The eyeball and simple logic provide checks that don't even require a calculator. If your data values are in the 20 to 40 range, for example, the mean should be too. A mean of 78.3 for a variable whose scores range from 20 to 40 should be a clear indicator that the computer isn't using the right numbers! But students often don't even notice such an obvious problem.

---

*In fact, if you don't already own a calculator with memory, square root, reciprocal, and elementary statistics, get one before you go much further in this book.

- "Averages" summarize the data by providing a "typical" or "representative" score.
- The mode is the most frequently occurring score or the midpoint of the most frequently occurring score interval.
- The median is in the center of the data in the sense that it is larger than half of the scores and smaller than half.
- The arithmetic mean is in the center of the data in the sense that the sum of the squares of the differences between the scores and their mean is a minimum.
- The median is the 50th percentile.
- The arithmetic mean is the sum of all of the scores divided by the number of scores in the data.
- Adding or subtracting a constant from the data, or multiplying by a constant, does the same thing to all of the measures of the center.
- The median is the most appropriate measure when ordinal data are used or when the distribution is skewed.
- The arithmetic mean is meaningfully used only with data measured on interval or ratio scales.
- A figure is often useful to show a trend over a series of measures of center.
- Computers will almost always produce numerically correct answers, but it is your responsibility to make sure that the computer has the correct data.

K E Y   T E R M S

Arithmetic mean	**Measures of center**
Average	**Median**
Least squares best fit	**Mode**

E X E R C I S E S

Solutions to asterisked (∗) exercises appear at the back of the book. Exercises preceded by a section symbol (§) must be solved using a computer. Exercises preceded by a dagger (†) can be solved by hand.

∗†1. Return to Exercise 5.1. Compute the mean and the median for those data.

†2. Compute the same statistics for the data in Exercise 5.2.

∗†3. Find the mean and the median for the data in Exercise 5.3.

†4. Using the data from Exercise 5.4, find the mean, the median, and the mode for both the children's and the college students' data. Describe in words what the differences between the groups seem to be.

§5. Repeat Exercise 1 using the computer.

§6. Repeat Exercise 2 using the computer.

§7. Repeat Exercise 3 using the computer.

§8. Repeat Exercise 4 using the computer.

CHAPTER 7

Measures of Spread and Form

Suppose that you've had two exams in your chemistry course. After taking the second exam, you learn that you have scored 63, exactly the same as you did on the first exam, and that the class mean, 52, is also the same for each exam. Should you be pleased with your consistent performance, since you exceeded the mean by 11 points each time? Not necessarily, for you really need to know more about how you stand relative to the other students.

Suppose that the frequency distribution for the first exam looked like the curve in Figure 7.1 and that for the second looked like the curve in Figure 7.2. The second distribution is much more compact, with more of the students' scores falling near the mean. Your score is still 11 points above the mean, but more of the distribution is now below your score. The difference could be expressed by using the percentile ranks of the two scores; your percentile rank is about 85 on the first exam, and about 97 on the second. In other words, relative to the others in the class, your second score is better; it exceeds 97% of the class scores, while the first score exceeds only 85% (still not a bad place to be!). The difference

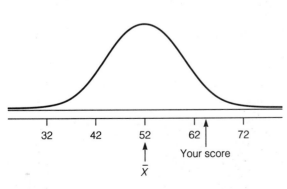

Figure 7.1

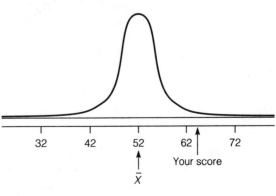

Figure 7.2

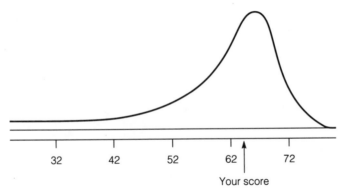

32   42   52   62   72

Your score

Figure 7.3

between the two sets of exam scores is not in their center, which is the same, but in the extent to which they cluster tightly around their center. This characteristic of a distribution of data is known as spread or variability; are the scores close to the center or spread out?

Suppose that there's a third exam in the class, again with a mean of 52, and that you happen to score 63 once more. But now the exam's grade distribution follows the curve shown in Figure 7.3. In this distribution, the mean has been pulled to the left by a very long tail of infrequent scores, while the bulk of the class has scored just about where you did or better. The difference between the first and second exams' distributions and this one is not one of variability but rather of the shape of the distribution. No longer are the exam's scores distributed more or less evenly about their mean, but instead they're piled up in the higher values, with a few scores in the low range. Since the mean is pulled toward the lower values to keep the frequency polygon "in balance" about its mean, your standing relative to the bulk of the class has changed once again. Now, even though you're still 11 points above the mean, so are a lot of your fellow students.

In this chapter, we deal with the descriptive techniques that summarize information about the spread or variability of a set of data. Several statistics are useful in describing the extent to which the data vary around their center point. In addition, we'll also show how to describe the form of a frequency distribution. Together with a measure of center, a measure of spread and a description of form completely characterize a distribution of data. If we're able to summarize those three features of a data set, then there's very little left to do with descriptive statistics.

Measures of Spread

Sources of Variability

Let's return to the chemistry classroom and suppose that you and your class-mates differ in your knowledge of the material covered on the exam. You shouldn't be surprised to find that your scores were different, should you?

Certainly not, and those differences in knowledge contribute to the variability in the scores on the exam. Each student in the class may come to the test with a different degree of chemistry knowledge. Since that's probably the case, there must be variability in the exam scores reflecting those differences in knowledge. In fact, a major source of variability in the class's test scores probably comes from individual differences in knowledge of chemistry.

But suppose that you and your roommate, as well as all of the other students in the class, actually know the material equally well. If that's the case, then you should all receive the same test score, right? Not necessarily, since there are at least three other sources of variation in the scores.

First, the instructor's exam probably is neither perfectly reliable nor perfectly valid. (That's not intended as a criticism of your chemistry instructor, or of any other instructor; it's an acknowledgement that no measuring instrument is perfect.) So even if you and your classmates are really identical in true knowledge, the chances are that your test scores won't be the same. Therefore, there will be some variability in the data due to measurement error.

A second source of differences among the scores can be called, for lack of any better word, randomness. Perhaps there was a question for which none of you knew the answer, and you all guessed. Perhaps the class flipped a coin (mentally, since most instructors take a dim view of flipping actual coins during exams). Your answers were probably different and resulted in a different total score. Or perhaps you were distracted when the student beside you dropped his pencil and you misread a question. That dropped pencil could have also contributed to the dropper's lack of attention and thus influenced both his grade and yours. Or maybe some students glanced out the window and, as a result, chose an incorrect alternative answer. These occurrences can lead to error that is due neither to validity, reliability, nor individual differences, but is best viewed as the result of extraneous variables. And such extraneous variables introduce variability into the test. You might argue that such variation is just as likely to make your score higher as it is to make it lower and so should really "balance out" across the class. Your argument is correct, and so the mean of the test shouldn't change much because of random variation; but the test's variability should, and variability is our concern here.

Finally, students vary in their ability to take tests, quite apart from their knowledge of the material. Some students do better at essay tests, some better at multiple choice, some better at short-answer questions, and so forth. These differences, along with other individual factors (intelligence, writing ability, amount of sleep, etc.) all contribute to variability in the test scores.

So far, then, we have variability in test scores that is due to individual differences in both knowledge and ability, to measurement error, and to extraneous variables. In some situations, there is yet a fourth source of variability. Suppose that your chemistry class was divided into two lab sections, and each lab section was using a different laboratory manual. This could happen if, unknown to the students, the instructor was conducting an experiment on the effect of the lab manual. Maybe he established a simple two-condition experiment; the version of the lab manual is the independent variable, and exam score is the dependent variable. In this case, there's yet another source of variability in the test scores—the effect of the lab manual. Even if everyone's knowledge of chemistry (from the text and lectures) were actually identical, the different lab manuals would be a source of variability. If there is an independent variable, then its effects add another source of variation to the data.

Now that we've suggested several possible sources of variation in data—measurement error, extraneous variables, individual differences, and maybe an independent variable—how shall we measure that variability?

Quantitative Measures of Variability

Quantitative measures of variability or spread can be grouped into two broad categories, those based on simple distances between certain scores and those based on differences from the center of all of the values. In the first category are various ranges, while the second group includes the variance and the standard deviation.

Distance Measures. Distance measures provide a quantitative description of variability by indicating how far it is between two specific points in the distribution.

The range. The simplest measure of the variability or the spread of a set of data is just the distance between the smallest and the largest values. This statistic, called the *range* or the *crude range*, is computed as

Range = Largest value − Smallest value.

The range is a handy statistic that can be obtained without much effort. It offers a crude but effective description of the variability of the values. If the first exam in our chemistry class has a mean of 52 with a range of 60, while the second exam has the same mean with a range of 30, you can tell right away that the class was less variable on the second test. But you'll also note that the range takes into account only two of the scores in the data, and a single extreme score in either direction can distort the range substantially.

The interquartile range. Since an extreme value can easily inflate a range, there are several procedures for producing a range that is shortened in some way. For example, if we find the 25th and 75th percentiles, the difference between them represents "how far" it is across the middle 50% of the data (Figure 7.4). This range, between the top and the bottom quarters of the data, is called the *interquartile range* and is a common measure of the spread of the data.

The semi-interquartile range. A value of one-half of the interquartile range is often used as a spread statistic. This statistic is called the semi-interquartile range and is roughly the distance across 25% of the distribution. If we take an interval of one semi-interquartile range on each side of a measure of center, we would then have an interval that includes the middle 50% of the data (Figure 7.5).* The statistic can be used easily in simple communication—for example, in

---

* This interpretation is strictly true only for a distribution that is not skewed, meaning that the scores are distributed roughly equally around their center.

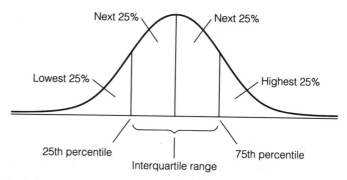

Figure 7.4

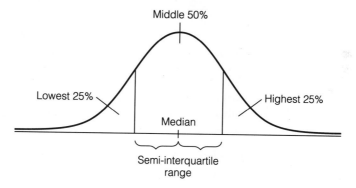

Figure 7.5

the statement "The interval 52 ± 6 contains the middle 50% of the data." In that sentence, the value 52 is some measure of center, such as a median, and the 6 represents a semi-interquartile range.

The range statistics provide a measure of the spread of the values by giving the distance between two points in the data. These statistics are particularly well suited for use as spread measures to accompany the median. The second general variety of spread statistics is based not on distances between two points, but on distances from the center of the data.

Center-Based Measures. Several statistics use the center of the data as a point of reference and reflect how data cluster around it. Of these statistics, the variance and the standard deviation are the most widely used and understood; both are based on the mean. In addition, the median absolute deviation (based on the median) is occasionally found in the literature.

Suppose that we take a set of scores and find some measure of center, such as the arithmetic mean. To the extent that the mean is in the center of the data, we would expect to find that the differences between the data values and their mean are small. A possible measure of the spread, then, might make use of the differences between scores and their mean. For example, with the simple set of numbers 5, 8, 13, 14, and 17, we might calculate

Measures of Spread

X	X − X̄
5	−6.4
8	−3.4
13	1.6
14	2.6
17	5.6

$$0.0 = \Sigma(X - \overline{X})$$

As we pointed out in Chapter 6, and as illustrated here, the sum of the differences between scores and their mean is zero, and so that quantity isn't useful as the basis for a measure of spread. But two related measures are.

If we were to take the absolute values of the differences, sum them, and then divide by the number of values added, we would have the mean of the absolute differences from the mean. (For the values listed, that value is 3.92.) This quantity is a measure of the spread of the data and is known as the *mean absolute deviation*, or more simply the *mean deviation*. The statistic, though, is rarely used.

The median absolute deviation. If we were to compute the median of the absolute deviations from the *median* instead of from the mean, we would have a statistic called the *median absolute deviation*; for the example data it is computed as

X	X − Mdn	|X − Mdn|
5	−8	8
8	−5	5
13	0	0
14	1	1
17	4	4

The median absolute deviation then is 4.0, the median of the values 0, 1, 4, 5, 8.

In Chapter 6 we pointed out that the median as a measure of center is closest to all of the data in terms of the absolute differences between scores and their center. In other words, the quantity $\Sigma|X - \text{Mdn}|$ is a minimum; using any number other than the median will result in a larger value for the sum. The median absolute deviation isn't a common measure for psychologists to use, but perhaps it should be. It is a perfectly acceptable measure to employ when the center is reported as the median.

The variance. While $\Sigma|X - \text{Mdn}|$ is a minimum, so too is $\Sigma(X - \overline{X})^2$. In other words, the arithmetic mean is the center in terms of the sum of the squared deviations, while the median is the center in terms of absolute deviations. Since that's the case, a mean of the squared differences might be a good measure of the spread around the mean. And the statistic computed as

$$s^2 = \frac{\Sigma(X - \overline{X})^2}{N}$$

is a useful measure called the *sample variance*. The sample variance is simply the arithmetic mean of the squared differences.

For the example set of data, the sample variance is computed as

X	$X - \bar{X}$	$(X - \bar{X})^2$
5	−6.4	40.96
8	−3.4	11.56
13	1.6	2.56
14	2.6	6.76
17	5.6	31.36
		93.20 $= \Sigma(X - \bar{X})^2$

$$s^2 = \frac{\Sigma(X - \bar{X})^2}{N} = \frac{93.20}{5} = 18.64.$$

Before we leave it, let's comment just a bit more on the quantity $\Sigma(X - \bar{X})^2$. This sum of squared deviations about the arithmetic mean is an important value in several statistics, and you may be sure that we'll encounter it again. It's so useful, in fact, that it's given a special name—sum of squares, or SS for short. When an SS is divided by some other number, typically the number of things added to get the SS itself (or often one less than the number summed), it becomes a variance. Variance is the foundation of the most widely used and powerful of the inferential statistics, the analysis of variance. An important part of developing the analysis of variance is examining the sum of squares, dividing it into segments that represent different sources of the variation in the data. For now, though, the important thing to remember is that the sum of squares represents differences between scores and their mean and thus represents the variation in the data.

The sample standard deviation. The sample variance is the mean of the squared differences between scores and their mean. As useful as it is as a way of describing the spread of data, it's an awkward statistic to use descriptively since it deals with squares of numbers. A much more useful measure of the spread is the square root of the variance, a quantity called the *sample standard deviation*. For the example data, the standard deviation, s, is

$$s = \sqrt{\frac{\Sigma(X - \bar{X})^2}{N}} = \sqrt{\frac{93.20}{5}} = \sqrt{18.64} = 4.32.$$

The sample standard deviation is by far the most commonly used measure of the spread of the data. You won't go far wrong in your understanding of it if you think of it as an average deviation around the arithmetic mean. A larger standard deviation means a more spread-out distribution (like the first exam at the beginning of this chapter), while a smaller value indicates that the data are more tightly clustered about their mean (as in the second hypothetical chemistry exam).

The formula just illustrated is a good definitional formula, but is often the difficult way to do the calculation. An equivalent formula that begins with raw data is

$$s = \sqrt{\frac{\Sigma X^2 - \dfrac{(\Sigma X)^2}{N}}{N}}.$$

Using this formula, we would calculate

X	X^2
5	25
8	64
13	169
14	196
17	289
$\Sigma X = 57$	$743 = \Sigma X^2$

so that

$$s = \sqrt{\frac{\Sigma X^2 - \frac{(\Sigma X)^2}{N}}{N}} = \sqrt{\frac{743 - \frac{(57)^2}{5}}{5}} = 4.32.$$

An even simpler formula, since you'll probably already have the mean, is

$$s = \sqrt{\frac{\Sigma X^2}{N} - \overline{X}^2}.$$

For the example, the mean is 11.4, and we would calculate

$$s = \sqrt{\frac{\Sigma X^2}{N} - \overline{X}^2} = \sqrt{\frac{743}{5} - 11.4^2} = 4.32.$$

Estimation statistics. In this chapter, we're discussing ways to describe the spread in a set of data. In Chapter 12, we'll look at these statistics as estimators for their respective population parameters. The variance and the standard deviation, as we have just defined them, are appropriate when we are merely describing the data or when we think of the data as comprising the entire population. They're *not* the best statistics to use when we're trying to *estimate* a population parameter. The two quantities that we just defined are called the *sample* standard deviation and variance, to emphasize that they're used purely for description. In Chapter 12, we'll make slight adjustments to both the variance and the standard deviation formulas to obtain better statistics for use in estimating parameters.*

Graphic Presentation of Variability

Group or experimental condition data are sometimes presented graphically to show a series of center statistics, often the arithmetic mean. For an example, see the hypothetical grade data showing an increase in means over years in Figure 7.6.

---

* Many calculators offer statistical functions, including the variance and the standard deviation. Since there are actually two formulas for each statistic, some calculators offer a choice. The standard deviation and variance as defined here may be indicated on the keys as "σ" and "σ^2," or perhaps "s_n" and "s_n^2." The modified formulas that will be presented in Chapter 12 may be labeled "s" and "s^2," or maybe "s_{n-1}" and "s_{n-1}^2." You should know which formula your calculator is using when you push a button. Here's an easy way to find out. Use the simple data set 2, 3, 4 and find the standard deviation on your calculator. If the answer is 0.82, the calculator uses the formula from this chapter; if the answer is 1.00, then it uses the formula from Chapter 12.

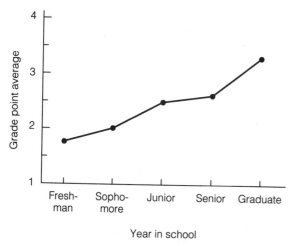

Figure 7.6

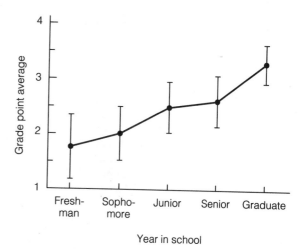

Figure 7.7

While the illustration shows the changes in grade point average as a function of year clearly enough, it provides no indication of the variability of the data. By adding vertical bars the length of the standard deviation for each year, we can enhance the presentation (see Figure 7.7). In this figure, the bar extends one full standard deviation on each side of the arithmetic mean, showing the spread of the data around each mean. Note how this presentation highlights a decrease in the standard deviation over time. We've used a standard deviation above and below the mean for drawing vertical bars; the bar's length is thus two standard deviations. There are several other ways to draw the vertical bars. Some plots are drawn so that the bar extends one-half standard deviation above and below the mean, so that the length of the bar represents one standard deviation. You may also find values other than the standard deviation represented as bars. One such number is the "standard error of the mean," a value common in inferential statistics. (When that statistic is shown, the vertical lines are often called "error bars.") The other use of the bar illustrates a confidence interval around the mean, a topic that we'll explore in Chapter 12. The title of a figure, or its reference in the surrounding text, should always tell you what the vertical bar means. Without explanation, you can't be sure what the vertical bars show.

Tabular Presentation of Variability

While graphic presentations of the measures of variability are important and useful, the statistics are most often presented in sentence or tabular form. In a research report you might find the sentence "The mean number of errors for the subjects was 13.62, with a standard deviation of 3.2." That sentence communicates both the mean and the standard deviation very simply and directly. When only a few values, typically a pair or two of measures of center and spread (such as mean and standard deviation, median and interquartile range) are being given, sentences are straightforward ways to communicate. If more than a few values are to be given, a tabular arrangement is often best. For example, Table 7.1 gives the grade point statistics that we've just plotted.

Table 7.1 Grade Point Averages for Five Classes of Students

| | Grade point average | |
Group	Mean	Standard deviation
Freshman	1.77	0.65
Sophomore	2.03	0.51
Junior	2.51	0.42
Senior	2.63	0.44
Graduate	3.33	0.24

Table 7.2 Presenting Variability

IN A FIGURE

Error bars — Used to show standard deviations when several measures of center are presented, often to show a trend

IN WORDS

Sentences — Best used when only a few values are to be presented
The measure of spread is usually given in the same sentence as the measure of center

IN A TABLE

Table entries — Best suited for presenting a number of values
Especially useful when you want to make it easy to compare adjacent values

A table is valuable when you have a number of values and also when you want to make it easy to compare adjacent numbers. In the example, it's simple to see the trend in grades because they are all listed together.

Table 7.2 summarizes recommendations on how to present measures of spread or variability.

Comparing the Variability Measures

As with measures of center, the scale of measurement is an important consideration in choosing a variability measure. All of the statistics that we've introduced rely on differences, either between data points or around a measure of center. For that reason, none of the measures that we have described is satisfactory for nominal measurement.[*]

If we're measuring on an interval or ratio scale, all of the statistics that we have discussed are meaningful. In interval and ratio measurement, the differences between pairs of values are meaningful, and so both the distance-based and the center-based spread statistics are useful.

---

[*]Hammond, Householder, and Castellan (1970, pp. 111–117) present a measure with some merit, but it has not been widely adopted.

Table 7.3   Effect of Measurement Level on Choice of Measure of Spread

Scale of measurement	Measure of spread
Nominal	None
Ordinal	None, though the standard deviation is often used
Interval and Ratio	
Symmetric data	Variance and/or standard deviation
Skewed data	
(What is used as center?)	
Median	Median absolute deviation
Arithmetic mean	Standard deviation
Mode	Range

If the measurement is ordinal, many psychologists would argue that at least the distance indices—the various ranges—are appropriate spread statistics. But there's no universal agreement with that position. The problem is that in ordinal measurement, it's best to not use measures that assume the equal-interval properties of numbers. The range statistics all use differences between two points in the distribution. With ordinal measurement, then, we really have no appropriate statistic for describing the spread of the data.

Now, having made the point about the lack of an appropriate measure of spread of ordinal data, we'll go on to say that ignoring the level of measurement probably won't cause serious errors in most cases. While it's really not meaningful to use differences in ordinal data, perhaps some measure of variability is better than none; so go right ahead and use means and sample standard deviations. If you do, though, remember that the measure is based upon differences and that differences are inherently meaningless in ordinal measurement.

Choosing a Statistic. The best measure of spread is one that is related to the measure of center that is used. This suggests that we should decide, following the guidelines given in Chapter 6, on a descriptive measure for center and then let that dictate a measure of spread. If the arithmetic mean is chosen, for example, then the variance or the sample standard deviation is the logical choice for spread. If the median is chosen, then the median absolute deviation is logical, as is the interquartile range. If the mode is used with numeric data, then present the range along with it. Table 7.3 summarizes the recommendations for a choice of spread measure.

You should know that this book makes a point of illustrating a variety of statistics for similar purposes, even though they may not be widely known and used. For example, any spread statistic other than the variance or the standard deviation is likely to be unfamiliar to many psychologists.* These are the "standard" spread statistics in psychology, and many instructors (and journal editors) insist on their use. One reason is simply familiarity, since many of the other measures are relatively infrequent in the literature. But, in addition, the variance

---

* Indeed, the very terminology of *center* and *spread* are recent additions to the statistical vocabulary; older terms are *central tendency* and *variability.*

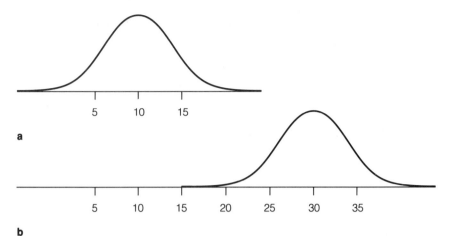

a

b

Figure 7.8

and the standard deviation have certain mathematical properties that make them very useful. For that reason, they are the measures preferred by most psychologists.

The Effects of Transformations

In Chapter 5 we discussed the effects of arithmetic operations, or transformations, on the measures of the center. In short, adding (or subtracting, or multiplying, or dividing) by a constant has the same effect on all of the measures of center. For example, if we add 100 to all values, then all measures of center also increase by 100. Or if we multiply each data value by 100, then all measures of center are also multiplied by 100.

For the spread measures these are the important properties:

1. Adding or subtracting a constant does nothing to any measure of the spread.
2. Multiplying or dividing by a constant does the same thing to all of the measures of the spread *except* the variance.
3. Multiplying or dividing by a constant multiplies or divides the variance by the square of the constant.

The first property can be illustrated easily; adding a value does nothing to a set of data except to shift it higher on the number scale. Add 20 to the values of Figure 7.8a and the result is the curve shown in Figure 7.8b.

To illustrate the second and third properties, let's take Dr. Stewart's aversion-conditioned animals' sucrose consumption data. The raw scores are 7, 9, 9, 9, 9, 10, 11, 12, 12, and 14. If we were to multiply each value by 10, we would have the transformed data values 70, 90, 90, 90, 90, 100, 110, 120, 120, and 140. The range of the original data is 7 and that for the second is 70, and thus the second rule holds for the range (as it would for all of the other distance-based measures). The standard deviation of the original data is 2.59; that for the transformed data is 25.9. For the original data, the variance is 6.71 and for the transformed scores the variance is 670.81, thus illustrating the second and third rules.

Descriptions of Form

Frequency distributions can differ not only with respect to the center and their spread, but also with respect to their shape. For example, there's something different about the two distributions in Figure 7.9, even though they might have the same mean and standard deviation.

In Figure 7.9a there is a larger frequency pile-up toward the higher end of the distribution, while in Figure 7.9b the scores are distributed symmetrically around their center. Figure 7.9a has a long "tail" of less frequent scores extending toward the left end of the number line. If we had the means and the medians of the two distributions, we would find that they would be about equal in Figure 7.9b, while the mean would be less than the median in Figure 7.9a since $\overline{X}$ is pulled toward the long tail.

A distribution may have a long tail—that is, be skewed—with the long tail toward either the low scores or the high scores. When the tail is to the left, with the bulk of the scores in the higher end of their range, the distribution is *negatively skewed*. If the long tail points toward the higher scores—to the right—then the distribution is *positively skewed*. Graphically, Figure 7.10a is negatively skewed, while Figure 7.10b is positively skewed. If you have trouble keeping positive and negative straight in your head, visualize the tail as a long arrow pointing toward either the positive or the negative end of the real number line (Figure 7.11).

The use of the words *negative* and *positive* in these descriptions comes from the numerical index frequently employed to quantify skewness. The most common skewness measure was developed by the early statistician Pearson and is thus known as the *Pearson coefficient of skew*. This statistic is easily computed as

$$Sk_\mathrm{p} = \frac{3(\overline{X} - \mathrm{Mdn})}{s}$$

a

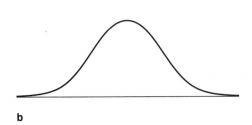

b

Figure 7.9

a

b

Figure 7.10

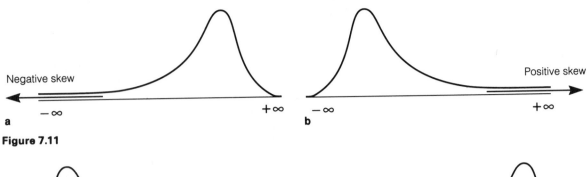

a

Figure 7.11

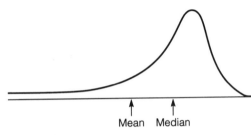

Median Mean

Figure 7.12

b

Mean Median

Figure 7.13

This statistic makes use of the difference between the mean and the median in a skewed distribution. In a symmetric distribution, the two centers are equal, so that the skewness statistic has a value of zero. Since the arithmetic mean is pulled in the direction of the skew, the two statistics are unequal unless the distribution is symmetric about its center. For a distribution with its long tail to the right (Figure 7.12), the mean is greater than the median, so that the difference $(\overline{X} - \text{Med})$ is positive, and the value of Sk_P is also positive. If the tail is to the left (Figure 7.13), the median is greater than the mean, so that the difference $(\overline{X} - \text{Mdn})$ and Sk_P is negative.

As an example of the skewness statistic, let's look at the amount of the sour solution consumed by Dr. Stewart's experimental animals. The histogram for these data is shown in Figure 7.14. The mean amount consumed is 10.2, the median is 9.5, and $s = 2.044$. The Pearson skewness statistic is thus

$$Sk_P = \frac{3(\overline{X} - \text{Mdn})}{s} = \frac{3(10.2 - 9.5)}{2.044} = 1.03.$$

The sign of the statistic tells us that the distribution is positively skewed. In addition, the magnitude of Sk_P tells us something about how severe the skew is. Values of Sk_P between -0.5 and 0.5 are usually accepted as showing no substantial departure from symmetry. A distribution with Sk_P greater than 0.5 in either direction is regarded as skewed. The example value thus indicates a moderate positive skew.

Apart from skewness, there are other differences in the form of distributions. For example, both curves in Figure 7.15 have a single peak at the mode. While we don't often use the mode as a measure of center, we frequently want to distinguish a distribution with a single mode from a distribution with two or

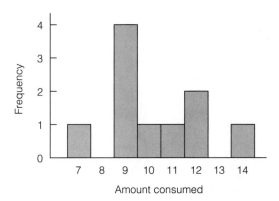

Figure 7.14

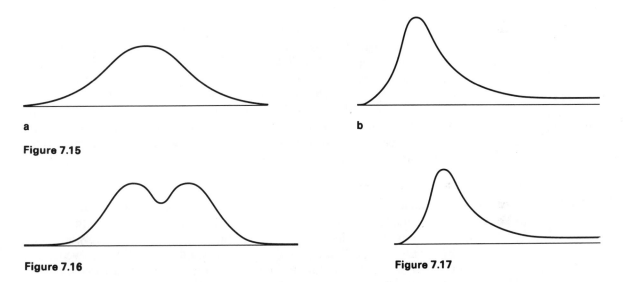

a   b

Figure 7.15

Figure 7.16   **Figure 7.17**

more. We would say that both curves in Figure 7.15 are *unimodal*, while the curve in Figure 7.16 is *bimodal*, but still symmetrical.

To describe the form of a distribution, then, we can apply terms to its skewness and to its modality. We might say that a distribution is unimodal and positively skewed, for example, to describe a distribution like that in Figure 7.17, or bimodal symmetric, to describe a distribution like that in Figure 7.18. We could even have a bimodal, negatively skewed distribution such as that in Figure 7.19. Note that it's not necessary to have the two modes at precisely the same height in order for the adjective *bimodal* to be applied, although there is, strictly, only a single mode in this distribution.

The modality of the distribution and its skewness or lack of it are important in describing the form of a distribution. One more characteristic of form is the relative "peakedness" or "flatness" of the distribution. The three distributions in Figure 7.20 all have the same symmetry, modality, center, and spread. Yet

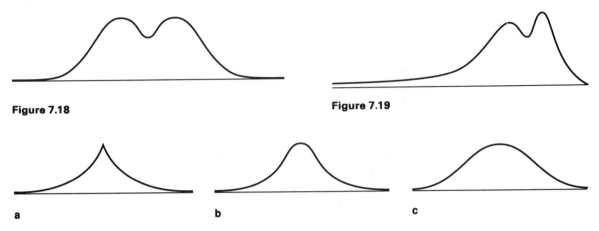

Figure 7.18

Figure 7.19

a   b   c

Figure 7.20

they still differ in *kurtosis*. We usually distinguish three varieties of kurtosis, as illustrated. Figure 7.20b is known as *mesokurtic*, while the more peaked distribution in Figure 7.20a is termed *leptokurtic*. The relatively more flattened distribution of Figure 7.20c is *platykurtic*. The descriptions are taken relative to a particular distribution form, the *normal distribution*, which defines a mesokurtic distribution. The normal is a symmetric, bell-shaped distribution, like Figure 7.20b. A great many variables (but certainly not all) follow the normal distribution, and we devote all of Chapter 8 to exploring it.

Transformations and Form

If we were to add a constant to all of the values in a set of data, the center of the values would change, but the spread would not, as we've pointed out. In addition, the form of the distribution would be unchanged. We could multiply all values by a constant, and the center and the spread would change; the form would not. In short, linear transformations don't change the form of a distribution at all. We are free to apply linear transformations to the data, and we won't change the distribution's shape.

Nonlinear transformations, on the other hand, do change the shape. Replacing each data value with its square root (a nonlinear operation), for example, will change the center, the spread, and the form of a distribution. The exercises at the end of this chapter ask you to explore the effect of some other nonlinear operations on form.

The three shape characteristics—skewness, modality, and kurtosis—complete our presentation of the ways to describe data. We defined a statistic for skewness; but for psychologists, verbal descriptions of form suffice. There are descriptive statistics for kurtosis, and some computer programs offer them.

When we want to describe a variable, offering a measure of the center, the spread, and the form is both necessary and sufficient. That is, a complete description of a data set must address all three elements. In practice, though, only the first two are regularly found in the research literature. The usual practice in reporting results is to describe form only if it is other than symmetric and bell-shaped (that is, other than normal).

- Measures of spread describe the extent to which the data values vary among themselves.
- Variability in data can come from measurement error, extraneous variables, individual differences, and independent variables.
- The *range* is the difference between the smallest and largest value in the data.
- The *interquartile range* is the difference between the first and third quartiles; it gives the "distance" across the middle 50% of the data.
- The *semi-interquartile range* is one-half of the interquartile range.
- The *median absolute deviation* is the median of the absolute values of the differences between the scores and their median.
- The *sample variance* is the mean of the squared differences between the scores and their arithmetic mean.
- The *sample standard deviation* is the square root of the variance; it is convenient to think of it as an "average" difference between scores and their mean.
- The sample variance and standard deviation as defined in this chapter are appropriate for use as descriptive statistics, but not as estimates of parameters.
- Measures of center and spread are often presented together—mean with the standard deviation, median with the median absolute deviation, and mode with the range.
- Adding or subtracting a constant does not change the spread of the data.
- Multiplying or dividing changes the measures of spread.
- A distribution with the long tail to the left is negatively skewed, while the long tail to the right indicates a positive skew.
- A distribution with a single mode is said to be *unimodal*.
- Distributions may be leptkokurtic (peaked in the center) or platykurtic (flattened) relative to the normal distribution (which is mesokurtic).
- Linear transformations do not change the form of the frequency distribution, while nonlinear transformations may.

K E Y   T E R M S

Bimodal	**Range**
Interquartile range	**Sample standard deviation**
Kurtosis	**Sample variance**
Median absolute deviation	**Semi-interquartile range**
Pearson coefficient of skew	**Unimodal**

E X E R C I S E S

Solutions to asterisked (∗) exercises appear at the back of the book. Exercises preceded by a section symbol (§) must be solved using a computer. Exercises preceded by a dagger (†) can be solved by hand.

*†1. Following are the data for three groups of students on the Barrett Impulsivity Scale. Find the mean, median, range, interquartile range, sample variance, and sample standard deviation for each of the three groups. Present the results in a table.

Group A	Group B	Group C
36	46	42
42	49	61
37	52	40
39	60	34
41	43	76
48	44	65
42	50	59
51	48	82
45	55	37
39	59	49
41	47	54
44	53	45

†2. Following are the results of a study on learning; the data are the number of errors made on each of six trials. For each trial, find the mean, median, sample variance and standard deviation, and interquartile range. Present the statistics in a table.

		Trial			
1	2	3	4	5	6
36	21	17	1	2	0
35	1	10	13	0	5
4	23	21	10	5	3
35	5	26	11	3	7
25	5	18	15	4	3
33	2	5	5	5	4
29	22	13	7	0	2
31	11	24	2	4	1
49	14	13	6	6	2
19	36	11	6	1	8
11	26	9	4	5	3
27	27	18	0	4	3
28	25	1	7	7	4
8	13	0	4	7	4
27	17	20	1	2	6
13	4	12	6	6	5
36	26	19	10	7	4
19	14	0	10	2	4
24	14	5	13	0	1
40	11	10	3	2	2
19	18	2	7	1	3
43	16	12	9	4	3

*†3. The following data give the scores earned by a class of students on four weekly exercise sets. For each exercise set, find the mean, median, sample variance, sample standard deviation, and interquartile range. Present the statistics in a table.

	Week					Week		
1	2	3	4		1	2	3	4
78	15	54	32		43	30	57	59
44	42	55	40		44	36	48	50
20	21	41	23		19	28	50	14
13	19	49	24		31	18	45	72
17	19	55	37		30	21	60	51
36	29	46	35		65	26	52	46
63	21	58	42		56	19	49	42
14	31	59	57		38	37	42	61
70	19	48	48		44	27	59	48
67	12	48	42		50	45	43	51
22	19	52	15		65	20	54	56
71	23	59	62		39	29	66	38
45	9	50	21					
56	24	60	59					
49	32	52	56					

§4. Generate 10 sets of 20 random numbers. (If you can, have them sampled from a distribution with a mean of 100 and a standard deviation of 25. If you can't specify those values, take any values that you can get.) Using the computer for as many as you can, find the mean, median, interquartile range, sample variance, and sample standard deviation for each group of data. Prepare a table showing the statistics.

§5. Having just finished Exercise 4, you should have 10 sample variances, 10 sample standard deviations, and 10 interquartile ranges. Now take each of those three sets of numbers (10 ranges, 10 standard deviations, and 10 variances) and find the standard deviation for each of them. (In other words, you're getting a measure of the variability of three measures of variability.) Which of the three has the greatest variability?

†6. Using the data from Exercise 1, present the data as a plot of the group means with standard deviation bars.

*†7. Present the means from Exercise 3 as a plot with error bars representing the standard deviations.

§8. Using your computer, generate a set of 30 data values with any characteristics you wish. Compute the mean, median, standard deviation, and interquartile range of the data.
  a. Transform the data by adding the constant 10.0 to each value. Find the same statistics as you did for

the original data. Do the measures of center and spread follow the rules that we stated earlier?

b. Transform the data by multiplying each value by 10.0. Find the same statistics as you did for the original data. Do the measures of center and spread follow the rules that we stated earlier?

c. Transform the data by multiplying each value by 25 and then adding the constant 10.0 to each. Find the same statistics as you did for the original data. Do the measures of center and spread follow the rules?

*†9. Using the following data, complete the questions.

8	8	8	8	8
9	9	9	10	10
7	7	7	7	8
1	2	3	4	5
5	5	6	6	6
8	8	8	8	8
9	9			

a. Construct the histogram and get the descriptive statistics, including the Pearson skewness statistic.

b. Transform the data by changing the signs (multiply each value by −1.0) and calculate the same measures as in (a). What do you conclude?

c. Transform each value in the original data again, replacing each number by its reciprocal. What happens to the skewness measure?

d. Transform each value in the original data again, replacing each number by its logarithm. What happens to the skewness measure?

†10. The following set of data represents reaction times (in seconds), a frequent measure in some fields of psy-

chology. Reaction times are typically positively skewed, and these are no exception.

0.293	0.391	0.195	0.195	0.195
0.293	0.586	0.684	0.586	0.684
0.195	0.195	0.195	0.293	0.195
0.195	0.293	0.391	0.488	0.489
0.391	0.293	0.391	0.489	0.586
0.488	0.391	0.293	0.879	0.782
0.195	0.195	0.097	0.097	0.195
0.293	0.293	0.195	0.195	0.195
0.195	0.097	0.097	0.097	0.097
0.097				

a. Construct the histogram and compute the descriptive statistics, including the skewness measure.

b. Transform the original data using a square root operation so that each number is replaced by its square root. What happens to the form of the distribution and to the skewness measure?

c. Transform the data using a log operation so that each number is replaced by its logarithm. What happens to the form of the distribution and to the skewness measure?

†11. Some statistical procedures assume that their data are normal in form or at least that the form is fairly symmetric, unimodal, and mesokurtic. For the data in Exercises 9 and 10, which of the transformed distributions comes the closest to meeting those requirements?

§12. Explore some of the other kinds of transformations (trigonometric functions, roots and powers, etc.) on the two data sets, with the goal of changing the distribution form to as close to symmetric and mesokurtic as you can get. What transformations seem to be successful for which data?

CHAPTER 8

Standardized Variables and the Normal Distribution

In Chapter 5 we described how percentile ranks are used to compare relative positions in two or more sets of data. Percentile ranks use order information within the data to describe positions. The percentile rank gives the percentage of the distribution below a particular score, without regard to the actual values of the data. In that way, it can provide a way of comparing positions in data sets that have different forms, centers, or spreads.

We can think of calculating the percentile ranks as a transformation applied to each score in a data set, changing the score from its raw value into a number that shows the percentage of the data below it. For example, if we have the scores

17   18   24   27   32,

we can think of the percentile ranks as resulting from this transformation as

Score	Percentile rank
17	20
18	40
24	60
27	80
32	100

The transformation is monotonic and uses only the ordinal position of the values within the data set. Thus it's appropriate for ordinal, interval, and ratio measurements. But if we have interval or ratio data, we can use the distance information in the data to transform the data in another way.

Standardizing

Suppose that we define the transformation operation $X - \overline{X}$. With the preceding example, where $\overline{X} = 23.6$, this transformation is

X	$X - \overline{X}$
17	−6.6
18	−5.6
24	0.4
27	3.4
32	8.4

Now we have a new set of values, each indicating how far an original score is from the mean. The transformation is a linear one, and so the meaning of distances between data values is preserved.

The $(X - \overline{X})$ transformation has another feature besides changing the scores to deviations from the mean. You'll recall that subtracting a constant ($\overline{X}$ in this case) from a set of data subtracts the same constant from each measure of center. In this case, the mean of the transformed data becomes $\overline{X} - \overline{X} = 0$.

We thus have a new variable $X - \overline{X}$, with the values

	Original	$(X - \overline{X})$
	17	−6.6
	18	−5.6
	24	0.4
	27	3.4
	32	8.4
Mean	23.60	0.00
Standard deviation	5.61	5.61

Notice that the transformation leaves the spread unchanged (since adding or subtracting a constant changes only the center). As a result, the transformed data values are just as spread out as they were originally.

Now we'll divide the $(X - \overline{X})$ scores by their standard deviation. Consider the consequences of that operation. If a score was, for example, one standard deviation below the mean in the original data, its transformed score will be −1.0, meaning that it is one standard deviation below the mean. A score that was located 1.5 standard deviations above the mean would likewise become a value of 1.5. In other words, the unit of measurement on the transformed variable becomes the standard deviation.

We accomplish the transformation by taking the previous transformation $(X - \overline{X})$ and dividing by the standard deviation, using the formula

$$z = \frac{X - \overline{X}}{s}.$$

We have given the new variable the name z. The z variable, always defined as the original data minus the mean and divided by the standard deviation, is known as a *standardized variable*. Since for the example data $s = 5.61$, the results of the standardizing transformation are

	Original	$z = (X - \bar{X})/s$
	17	−1.18
	18	−1.00
	24	0.07
	27	0.61
	32	1.50
Mean	23.60	0.00
Standard deviation	5.61	1.00

Standardizing is a linear transformation of the original data. Standardizing a variable preserves the distance information in the original data and is thus a meaning-preserving operation for interval and ratio data. In addition, a standardized variable has three important characteristics. First, its mean is always zero. This is so because we subtract $\bar{X}$ from each value; adding or subtracting a constant to each value adds or subtracts the constant from the mean. The mean of the original data was $\bar{X}$, and so the mean of the transformed variable is $\bar{X} - \bar{X} = 0.0$.

Second, the standard deviation of a standardized variable is always 1.0 (and so is the variance, since the variance is s^2, and $1.0^2 = 1.0$). This property of standardized scores derives from the operation of dividing a variable by a constant, in this case the standard deviation. Multiplying or dividing by a constant multiplies or divides the standard deviation by the same constant. Thus, since the standard deviation of the unstandardized variable is s, then the standard deviation of the variable divided by s will be $s/s = 1.0$.

The third important property of standardized variables also follows from the effects of linear transformation. A linear transformation does not change the form of the distribution, so the form of a z distribution is unchanged from the form of the original data.

We may summarize the z score, or standardizing, transformation by noting that

$\bar{z} = 0.0$

$s_z = 1.0$

The form of z is unchanged.

We mentioned earlier that the unit of the new standardized scale is the standard deviation. This means that a score that was located a standard deviation away from the mean in the original data will receive a z equal to 1.0 (or −1.0 if the score was below the mean). To see that this is the case, consider the score 18 in the example. The mean of the data is 23.6, and 18 is 5.6 units below the mean. But the standard deviation of the data happens to be exactly 5.6, so that 18 represents a data value one standard deviation below the mean. The z value corresponding to 18 becomes −1.0, since

$$z = \frac{X - \bar{X}}{s}$$

$$= \frac{18 - 23.6}{5.6}$$

$$= -1.0.$$

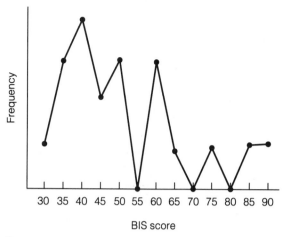

Figure 8.1

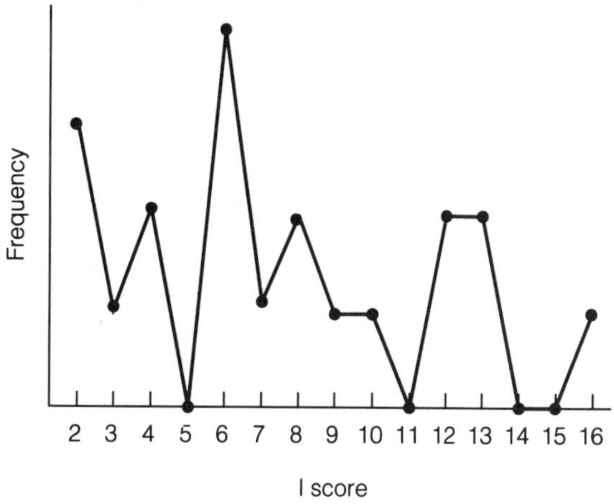

Figure 8.2

Let's illustrate the use of standardizing to compare an individual's position in two different distributions. Susan, a participant in Dr. Campbell's personality research, completed both the Barrett Impulsivity Scale (BIS) and Eysenck's Impulsivity scale (I). She scored 65 on the BIS and 13 on I. On which scale is she the more extreme? Figures 8.1 and 8.2 show the frequency polygons for all of Dr. Campbell's subjects on the two variables. The means for the two distributions are 51.70 for BIS and 7.45 for I, with standard deviations of 16.67 and 4.15, respectively.

Now suppose that you want to compare Susan's score of 65 on the BIS scale with her 13 on the Eysenck I scale. Clearly, the raw scores are quite different, and so we'll have to convert to the z scale to compare her positions. For the Barrett scale, Susan's score is

$$z = \frac{X - \overline{X}}{s}$$

$$= \frac{65 - 51.70}{16.67}$$

$$= 0.80,$$

meaning that her score of 65 is 0.80 standard deviations above the mean of all of the subjects in the research. Using the score of 13 on the Eysenck scale, we calculate

$$z = \frac{X - \overline{X}}{s}$$

$$= \frac{13 - 7.45}{4.15}$$

$$= 1.34.$$

The score of 13 on the I scale is 1.34 standard deviations above the mean of that variable. The z for the Eysenck Impulsivity score, 1.34, is considerably higher than is the 0.80 on the Barrett Impulsivity (BIS) test.

Standardizing **157**

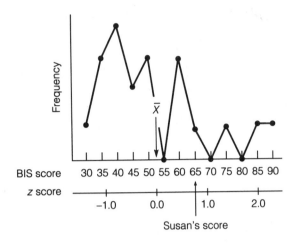

Figure 8.3

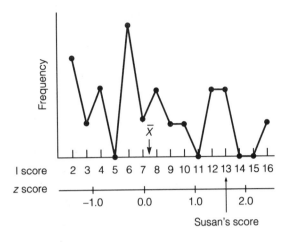

Figure 8.4

Sometimes it's helpful to visualize the standardizing transformation as putting a new measurement scale under the data. The new scale is a linear transformation of the original scale, so that all of the relationships between values have been preserved. The original scores have been standardized, meaning that they are measured in standard deviation units. Figure 8.3 illustrates the original and the standardized scales for the BIS scores, with Susan's score indicated. In this representation, the two means are aligned vertically, and the values representing one standard deviation above and below the mean (68.4 and 35.03) become 1.0 and −1.0 on the z scale, respectively. Looking at the frequency distribution in this way, it's clear that the form of the frequency distribution remains the same and that the distance information among the data is preserved.

Figure 8.4 illustrates the same information for the Barrett I scale. Again note that standardizing changed only the scale; the form of the distributions remains as it was at the beginning. We made this point earlier, but it is worth repeating here because as we move into the next section, it is easy to lose track of the form rule. When we standardize any variable, the form remains the same; if the data are skewed, standardizing won't change that fact. On the other hand, if the form of the distribution is unimodal, symmetric, and mesokurtic before standardizing, those properties remain after standardizing. And it's important that you remember these facts about form when we consider the normal distribution. Since we don't change the form, standardizing won't produce a normal distribution if it wasn't there to begin with. Some nonlinear transformations can make skewed distributions appear more symmetric since they do change the form. But standardizing does not do so.

Comparing z Scores and Percentile Ranks

Percentile ranks and z scores may both be used to compare the relative position of an individual within a group. How should we decide which to use? There are two major considerations—level of measurement and the audience with whom you want to communicate.

Percentile ranks deal only with the ordinal position. Transforming data to percentile ranks is a monotonic operation that relies only on position and is thus meaningful with ordinal, interval, or ratio measurements. Standardizing is a linear transformation that relies on differences between pairs of values for both its numerator and its denominator. The numerator of the z score formula gives the difference between a score and the mean; the denominator is the standard deviation, which is based on the differences between the data values and their mean. Thus standardizing is appropriate and preserves meaning for interval and ratio data, but not for ordinal data.

Beyond measurement level, there's another consideration in choosing a statistic that compares the position of an individual across variables—the audience for the data. Percentile ranks are relatively unsophisticated measures that don't take any of the data's distance information into account. But they describe an individual's position in the data in terms of the percent of scores exceeded, and that's easily understood by a lay audience.

On the other hand, z scores are confusing to people who are unfamiliar with their use. In scientific writing, standardized scores should be no problem, and they have some desirable properties for data manipulation and in inference. But try explaining to an irate parent why little Johnny received a negative score on a test!

The Normal Distribution

Let's explore a common use of standardizing, namely using it with tables of a very important distribution—the normal distribution.

The normal distribution is a specific distribution having a shape defined by the mathematical expression

$$f(x) = \frac{1}{\sqrt{2\pi\sigma^2}} e^{-\frac{(x-\mu)^2}{2\sigma^2}} .$$

This imposing formula defines the height of a curve as a function of two parameters, μ and σ^2. The Greek letter μ (mu) indicates the population mean, while σ^2 (sigma squared) gives the variance. The exact appearance of the distribution changes with different parameter values. For example, Figure 8.5 illustrates four curves that differ only in spread (σ^2) but not in center (μ).

Curves can also be located at different points, depending upon their center. Figure 8.6 illustrates two normal curves with the same variance that differ only in μ. There are an infinite number of normal curves, one for each possible pair of values for μ and σ^2. But for now we will worry about only a specific normal distribution, the standardized one. For that distribution, since $\mu = 0.0$ and $\sigma^2 = 1.0$, the defining equation simplifies to

$$f(z) = \frac{1}{\sqrt{2\pi}} e^{-\frac{z^2}{2}}.$$

The normal distribution is a symmetric, bell-shaped, unimodal distribution. It is important for two reasons. First, a very large number of the variables used

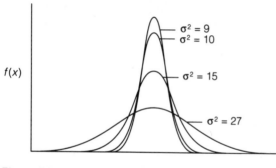

Figure 8.5

Figure 8.6

by psychologists appear to be normally distributed. IQ is normally distributed, as are many physical measurements, a great many scores on personality variables, and scores on other tests constructed for research purposes. Since so many variables in the natural world tend to be normally distributed, statisticians have devoted much attention to the distribution and its properties and have developed a large number of statistical procedures that rely on it. Second, the normal distribution is important because it provides a basis for some useful inferential statistics. This is so because in many cases the possible values of sample means follow the normal form.

While the normal is a very important distribution, many variables that are frequently used in psychology are not normally distributed. Reaction time is one very common non-normal variable, as is proportion of words recalled from a list of a fixed number of words. In addition to the fact that some variables don't follow the normal distribution form, we should also be aware that the normal is a continuous distribution. This isn't often a serious problem, since we can assume that it is our measurement that limits the precision of the data. But more importantly, we do need to assume interval or ratio measurement in order to employ the normal distribution.

Using a Normal Distribution

The standardized normal distribution shown in Figure 8.7 is but one representation of the curve. Normal distributions may be drawn in other proportions, but all represent the same distribution form.

Areas under the normal curve represent proportions of the data in regions of the distribution. For example, the proportion of the observations in a normal distribution between one and two standard deviations above the mean is shown in Figure 8.8. Likewise, the proportion between $z = -1.0$ and $z = 1.0$—that is, within a standard deviation either side of the mean—is shown in Figure 8.9. The entire area under the curve, theoretically from $-\infty$ to $+\infty$, can be taken as 100%, or the proportion 1.0.

In order to compute areas under a curve such as the normal, the method of integration from calculus must be applied. That is, to find the area between $z = -1.0$ and $z = 1.0$, we must compute the integral of the function between -1 and 1. In addition, if we wanted to find the area in a different normal distribution, with $\overline{X} = 50$ and $s^2 = 20$, for example, we'd have to compute an integral

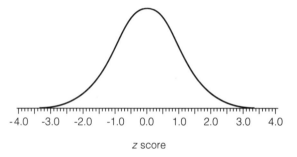

Figure 8.7

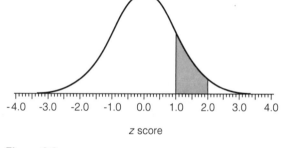

Figure 8.8

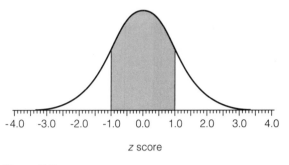

Figure 8.9

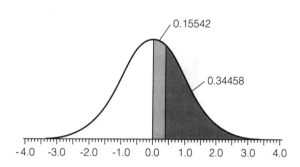

Figure 8.10

from that distribution. Fortunately for us, all of the integral computations have been done already and are summarized in tables of the normal curve such as the one in Appendix A.

Since any distribution may be standardized to have $\overline{X} = 0$ and $s = 1$, we may present a single table of the areas under the normal curve. Appendix A presents areas under a standardized distribution, and we can use it to find the areas in any normal distribution. And we won't have to compute a single integral. Standardizing, then, lets us use a single table of normal distribution values; if we couldn't standardize, then we really would have to compute the integral any time we wanted a normal curve value.

To see how to use the table, let's take a few examples. A glance at Appendix A shows that the table is arranged in three columns. The first column lists values of z, beginning with 0.00 and continuing upward in steps of 0.01. The next two columns give, for each value of z, the proportion under the curve between 0.00 and z, or beyond z, as illustrated by the column headings.

Reading down the z column to the value 0.40, for example, you will learn that between the z values of 0.00 and 0.40 there is 0.15542. Therefore, 0.15542, or 15.54%, of the area under the curve lies between a z value of 0.00 and a z value of 0.40. The third column gives the proportion of the area that is beyond 0.40, namely 0.34458 (or 34.46%). The areas are shown graphically in Figure 8.10. The normal curve is symmetrical, and so the left-hand side is just like the right; the proportion between 0.00 and -0.40, and the proportion below -0.40 are shown in Figure 8.11.

The Normal Distribution

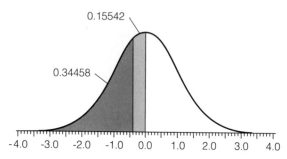

Figure 8.11

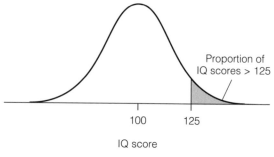

Proportion of
IQ scores > 125

IQ score

Figure 8.12

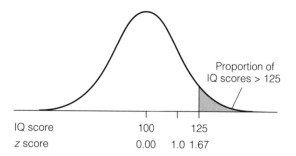

Proportion of
IQ scores > 125

IQ score
z score

Figure 8.13

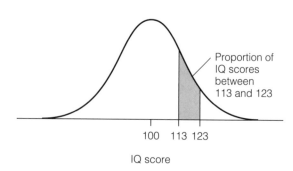

Proportion of
IQ scores
between
113 and 123

IQ score

Figure 8.14

Let's use the standardized normal distribution to find proportions of IQ scores that fall into particular ranges. IQ scores are normally distributed, and have a mean (μ) of 100 and population standard deviation (σ) of 15. What proportion of IQ scores is greater than 125? Figure 8.12 shows the proportion that we want in the distribution of IQ scores.

Since we don't really want to compute the integral from 125 to $+\infty$, we rely on the table in Appendix A. To do that, we'll have to convert from the IQ measurement scale to the z scale, but that's simple enough. Using the standardizing formula and the parameter values of 100 and 15 for the mean and standard deviation, we find that

$$z = \frac{X - \mu}{\sigma}$$

$$= \frac{125 - 100}{15}$$

$$= 1.67.$$

The distribution, with its original and standardized scales, is shown in Figure 8.13. In Appendix A, we find that the area under the curve beyond $z = 1.67$ is 0.0475; thus 4.75% of the scores in an IQ distribution are beyond 125. In a group of 100 people, then, we should expect to find about five people with IQs greater than 125.

What proportion of IQ scores lies between 113 and 123? This is a little more difficult to answer, but if we approach the problem graphically, we can see that we

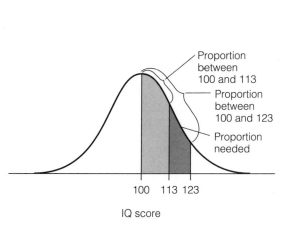

Figure 8.15

Proportion
between
100 and 113

Proportion
between
100 and 123

Proportion
needed

100 113 123

IQ score

Proportion
needed

IQ scale   100 113 123

z
scale   -3.0   -2.0   -1.0   0.0   1.0   2.0   3.0

Proportion between ⟶   0.87
100 and 113

Proportion between ⟶   1.53
100 and 123

Figure 8.16

need to find the area shown in Figure 8.14. To find the area, we'll need to find two proportions: that between 100 and 113, and that between 100 and 123. The difference between them will be the region that we need (Figure 8.15.). The two shaded regions represent the area between 100 and 123, while the lighter area is between 100 and 113, which overlaps. The difference between the two—the darker region—is what we need to find.

Computing the z values, we find that

$$z = \frac{X - \mu}{\sigma}$$
$$= \frac{113 - 100}{15}$$
$$= 0.87$$

and

$$z = \frac{X - \mu}{\sigma}$$
$$= \frac{123 - 100}{15}$$
$$= 1.53.$$

Figure 8.16 shows the z scale, the points, and their areas. In Appendix A, we find the two proportions needed to be 0.43700 and 0.30786 (Figure 8.17). And the answer that we want is $0.43700 - 0.30786 = 0.12914$, the proportion of IQ scores between 113 and 123.

As another example, what proportion of scores falls within 15 IQ points of the mean of 100? That is, what is the area shaded in Figure 8.18? Since the standard deviation of 15 corresponds to ± 1.0 on the z scale, we don't even need to compute anything and proceed directly to Appendix A where we find that the region between 0 and $z = 1.0$ is 0.34134. And since the region between 0 and -1.0 is also 0.34134, the proportion of IQ scores between 85 and 115 is $0.34134 + 0.34134 = 0.68268$ (Figure 8.19). In any normal distribution, then, approximately 68% of the data lies within a standard deviation each direction of the mean.

Finally, let's ask what proportion of IQ scores is in the region that is usually classified as "exceptional"—that is, more than two standard deviations from the mean in either direction. The areas are graphed in Figure 8.20. Notice that "exceptional" can be either high or low IQ, and so the regions of interest lie in the two tails of the curve. We don't need to calculate z scores; we know we're asking about the ± 2.0 points because we defined "exceptional" as two or more standard deviations away from the mean. So we can proceed directly to Appendix A to find the proportions under the curve more extreme than ± 2.00. This time, we look at the third column, because the region that we want is that beyond 2.0.

From the table we learn that 0.02275 of the curve is beyond 2.0. Since we have two tails of interest, the total area is $0.02275 + 0.02275 = 0.04550$; just a little under 5% of the IQ distribution is in the exceptional tails.

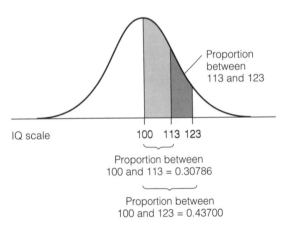

Figure 8.17

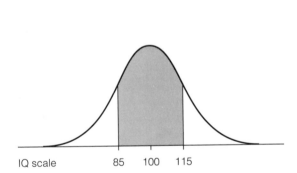

Figure 8.18

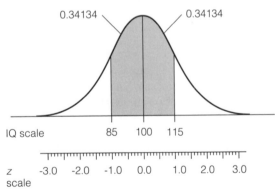

Figure 8.19

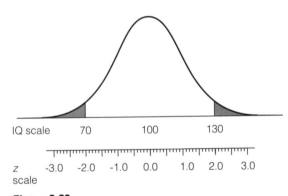

Figure 8.20

With a table of proportions of areas under the normal curve available, it's easy to locate percentile points in the normal distribution. For example, the 25th percentile, that point that exceeds 25% of the distribution, will be located along the z scale at the point where the proportion to the left is 0.25, namely at −0.67 (Figure 8.21). Applying the same logic, we find that the z value corresponding to the 10th percentile is −1.280, that for the 20th percentile is −0.840, and so forth for the remaining 10% points (Figure 8.22).

Finding the percentile rank corresponding to a score in a normal distribution is a straightforward matter of finding the cumulative percentage of the distribution below the score. For example, in a normal distribution with a mean of 125 and a standard deviation of 19, the percentile rank of a score of 132 corresponds to the area below the score (Figure 8.23). To find the area, we first calculate the standardized score corresponding to 132 as

$$z = \frac{X - \mu}{\sigma}$$

$$= \frac{132 - 125}{19}$$

$$= 0.37.$$

In Appendix A we find that the region between 0.00 and 0.37 is 0.14432 (Figure 8.24). Adding the 0.14432 to the 0.50 that represents the left half of the curve, we obtain a percentile rank of 64.43% for the score of 132.

For one last example, let's find the percentile rank of the score of 111 in the same distribution. The area that we want is shown in Figure 8.25. Computing the z score corresponding to 111, we find

$$z = \frac{X - \mu}{\sigma}$$

$$= \frac{111 - 125}{19}$$

$$= -0.74.$$

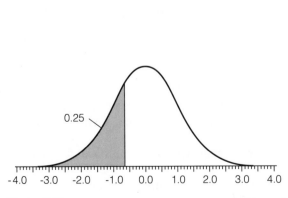

Figure 8.21

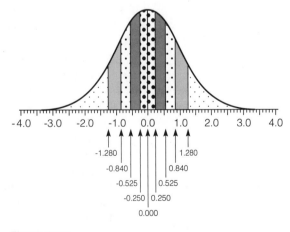

Figure 8.22

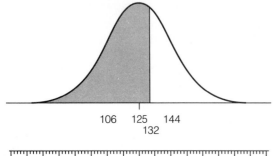

Figure 8.23

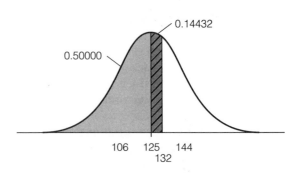

Figure 8.24

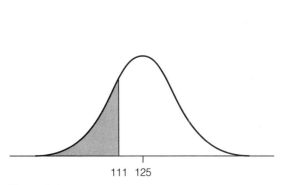

Figure 8.25

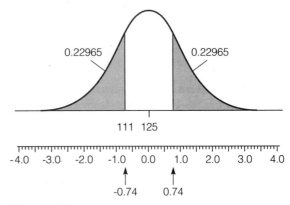

Figure 8.26

To find the area to the left of -0.74, we look in Appendix A for the value 0.74 and obtain the area of the curve that is more extreme; and since the curve is symmetric, the answer is 0.22965, or a percentile rank of nearly 23 (Figure 8.26).

SUMMARY

- Percentile ranks may be used to compare individuals' relative positions in different distributions.
- Standardizing a variable transforms it to a different scale, making it easier to compare across different variables.
- Standardized variables have a mean of zero and a standard deviation of 1.0.
- Standardizing is a linear transformation and so does not change the form of the distribution. (Specifically, it can't make a normal distribution out of data that aren't normally distributed.)
- The normal distribution is a bell-shaped, symmetric, unimodal distribution.
- A large number of (but not all) variables are normally distributed.
- The normal distribution is very useful in inferential statistics because sample means often are normally distributed.

- Tables of the normal distribution, like Appendix A, give proportions or areas under specific regions of the curve.

KEY TERMS

Normal distribution	μ
Standardized variable	σ
z score	σ^2

EXERCISES

Solutions to asterisked (∗) exercises appear at the back of the book. Exercises preceded by a section symbol (§) must be solved using a computer. Exercises preceded by a dagger (†) can be solved by hand.

∗†1. You scored 63 on each of two chemistry exams, and the class means were equal for the tests (52.0). Calculate your z scores on the two exams, assuming that the standard deviations are 8.5 and 3.6, respectively. On which test did you perform better?

†2. For the following set of data, compute the mean and the standard deviation, and then do the following operations:

4	6	2	8	7
8	9	8	7	6
5	6	6	5	5
1	4	5	6	9
3	3	4	9	8

a. Find the z score for each raw data value.
b. Check on your z computations by verifying that the mean and the standard deviation of the z scores are indeed 0 and 1.

∗†3. Use the data from Exercise 7.9 for this problem. Apply one more transformation to those data: the z score. Get all of the same descriptive statistics as you did originally. What changes when you do the z score transformation? And what doesn't change?

∗†4. Assume that the distributions for the two chemistry exams (both with means of 52) are normal in form. The standard deviations of the two exams, as given in Exercise 1, are 8.5 and 3.6. What proportion of the scores on the first exam
a. Are greater than 60?
b. Are less than 50?
c. Are between 52 and 57?
d. Are between 40 and 65?

†5. Using the second chemistry exam (mean = 52, standard deviation = 3.6), find the same proportions as in Exercise 4.

∗†6. Compute your percentile rank on each of the two chemistry exams (you scored 63 on each).

∗†7. Dr. Campbell wants to form two extreme groups of subjects with respect to the Barrett Impulsivity Scale (BIS). That is, he wants to have two specific values for the BIS, so that if someone scores below the lower point, that individual would be in the lowest 25% of scores; or if the individual scores above the higher point, then the score is in the highest 25%. If we assume that BIS is normally distributed with an overall mean of 50 and a standard deviation of 15, what should the two values be?

CHAPTER 9

Bivariate Descriptive Statistics

Chapters 5 through 8 presented a large number of statistical and graphic ways to describe the center, spread, and form of individual variables. In this chapter, we take the next logical step and discuss a few techniques for showing and describing the relationship between two variables.

Suppose that you were asked to guess someone's weight and were given no other information about the person. Your best strategy would be to guess what you know to be the mean weight of humans (around 150 pounds, for males and females together). (This is the best guess because the mean, as we know, minimizes the quantity $\Sigma(X - \overline{X})^2$, meaning that $\overline{X}$ is closest to the data points in terms of the squared differences between scores and their mean.) But if you were to learn that the individual whose weight you are guessing is a male and is 6′8″ tall, you'd probably want to revise your estimate upwards, because you know something about the relationship between sex and weight and between height and weight. We will say that the variables height and weight are positively correlated; people who are high on one variable (like height) tend to also be high on the other (weight). If you know that fact, you can probably do a better job of predicting one from the other. The prediction won't be perfect, of course; we all know tall people who weigh less than some short people of our acquaintance. But, on the average, we'll make better predictions if we can use relationship information; we'll err in our predictions sometimes, but knowledge of height certainly helps to predict weight. On the other hand, knowledge of height (or of sex, for that matter) probably won't help you predict a person's grade point average at all; there's no correlation between height (or sex) and GPA.

Our task in this chapter is to develop ways of describing the relationship between two variables. Chapter 10 discusses how to use information on that relationship to predict values on one variable from values on the other.

Let's take a second example of data on two variables. When Dr. Campbell collected his data, he measured a number of variables, all at roughly the same time. Each variable, of course, has its own center, spread, and form. But, in addition, each variable has a relationship with each other variable. A person with a score on the Experience-Seeking scale (ES), for example, also has a score on the Venturesomeness (V) scale of the Eysenck and Eysenck (1968) Impulsivity-Venturesomeness-Empathy (IPE) questionnaire. What we are concerned with in this chapter is not the mean, the median, the range, or the form of the V, the ES, or even the IPE scale. Instead, we are interested in the relationship between pairs of variables.

In particular, we are interested in questions like, "Are individuals who score high on the Venturesomeness scale also likely to score high on the Experience-Seeking scale? Are people who are low on one likely to be low on the other?" Note that these questions are unrelated to questions about the centers, spreads, and forms of the variables—they ask specifically about the *relationship* between the variables. Another kind of question might be, "If we had someone's score on the V scale, could we make a prediction or 'educated guess' about their value on ES? What confidence would we have in our estimate?" There are two kinds of questions about the *bivariate* (meaning, naturally, two-variable) relationship between the variables. The first question, that of the relationship between variables, is known as *correlation* and is discussed in this chapter. The second question, that of predicting one variable from another, is called *regression* and is presented in Chapter 10.

For now, we'll limit ourselves to two variables at a time. At the end of Chapter 10, though, we'll expand the discussion a little and briefly introduce the idea of multiple regression. These procedures expand our ability to deal with relationships among multiple variables.

Representing the Relationship Graphically

As we saw in the previous chapters, variables can be described numerically and graphically. And, as with single variables, the technique is strongly influenced by the measurement characteristics of the data. When the data on both variables are measured on nominal (category) scales, none of the techniques that we'll present in this chapter is appropriate. Chapter 21 is devoted entirely to category data. When the measurement is ordinal, interval, or ratio on at least one of the variables, then we have quantitative techniques as well as graphic ones.

Scatterplots   The basic graphic technique for representing the relationship between two interval or ratio variables is the scatterplot, an illustration that plots the values of one variable against those of another. Suppose, for example, that we had a set of data from Dr. Campbell's research, consisting of values on the V and the ES scales that we mentioned earlier. The first four subject's data look like

Subject	V	ES
1	5	16
2	15	18
3	9	13
4	12	19
.	.	.
.	.	.
.	.	.

We can begin a scatterplot by selecting one variable to be placed along the vertical axis and another along the horizontal and then calibrating the axes to represent the values (Figure 9.1). Now we place each individual subject's pair of scores on the figure, using the V value to locate the point vertically and the ES for the horizontal position. For subject 1, we place a point 5 units up and 16 units to the right. Figure 9.2 shows the first four points. We can't continue to place the subject numbers on the plot as we add the remainder of the data because the plot would become cluttered; we just let a single point represent each pair of values. Figure 9.3 is the finished scatterplot for 18 subjects.

When collisions arise because two or more subjects score the same on both variables, you can adopt several different strategies. One approach is to ignore the duplication and just use a single point regardless of the number of actual pairs of data values at that location. Alternatively, you might use a numeral to represent the number of values located there, or you might use some special symbol to stand for the number of value. Some computer programs plot the points with different symbols, while others may use numerals. Figure 9.4 shows several common ways to identify ties.

Interpreting Scatterplots

The scatterplot is a useful tool in understanding the relationship between two variables. For example, in a plot with an up-and-to-the-right pattern like Figure 9.4, we can tell that high scores on one variable tend to be associated with

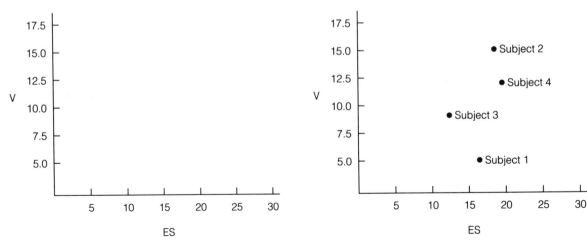

Figure 9.1

Figure 9.2

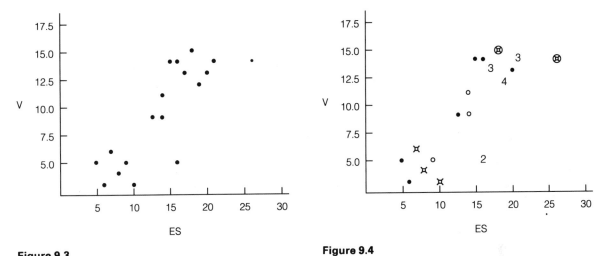

Figure 9.3

Figure 9.4

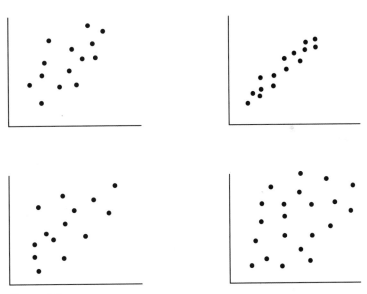

Figure 9.5

high scores on the other, while low scores also go together. The plots in Figure 9.5 all show this relationship to a greater or lesser degree. We say that plots showing this up-and-to-the-right orientation show a *positive* relationship; the numerical index of the relationship will have a positive sign (for example, 0.43).

The plots in Figure 9.6 show the opposite of a positive relationship, namely a *negative* one (for example, −0.61). Here, as one variable increases in value, the other decreases, and the pattern of the data points is down-and-to-the-right.

The scatterplot can also tell us about the form of the relationship between the two variables. Variables are sometimes related in a linear fashion, so that the points are more or less evenly spread about a straight line that you might draw,

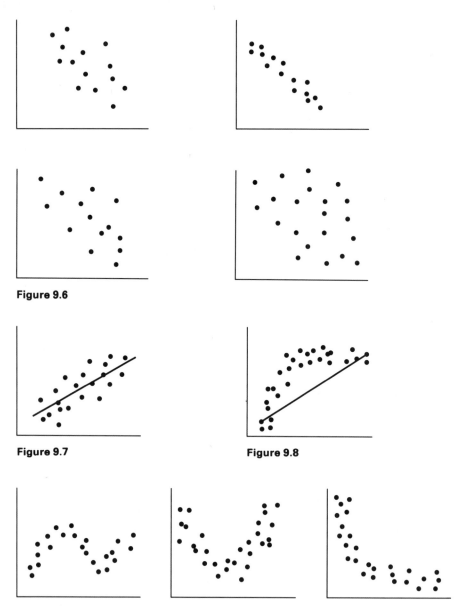

Figure 9.6

Figure 9.7

Figure 9.8

Figure 9.9

such as in Figure 9.7. For some pairs of variables, though, the relationship may be nonlinear, and the scatterplot is a very good, and very simple, way to find that out. Some variables may be related in the fashion shown in Figure 9.8, where a straight line "fits" the data only at the two end points in the scatterplot. Some other forms of nonlinear data are shown in Figure 9.9, but other patterns are certainly possible too.

For data that are linearly related, the tighter the cluster of the points around the line, the better the fit of the line. Consider the two plots in Figure 9.10. Certainly, the data in the left-hand scatterplot seem to represent a "stronger"

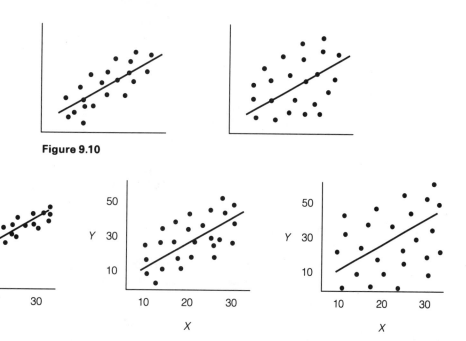

Figure 9.10

Figure 9.11

relationship between the two variables than do those in the right-hand plot, even though the line that seems to come the closest to the data points is the same in each plot.

If we take the line through the data as a two-dimensional "center" through the scatterplot, then we can think of a "spread" around that "center." In the right-hand plot of Figure 9.10, the points are more spread around their center. Now consider the three scatterplots in Figure 9.11. In all three plots, the data seem to be approximated by roughly the same line, yet the scatter about the line differs considerably. Suppose that you were given some X values and asked to predict the corresponding Y values for each by interpolating visually on the illustrations. In which plot would you feel the most comfortable? In Figure 9.11a, a low value of X—for example, 10—seems to be connected with a low range of Y values, perhaps in the range of about 8 to 18 or so. In Figure 9.11b, on the other hand, the same values of X are related to a wider range of Y values, roughly from 5 to 25. Figure 9.11c shows a great deal of variation; the lowest values of X are associated with a Y range of perhaps 5 to 40.

Presenting Scatterplots

A scatterplot presented in APA form follows the same rules as does any other figure. The "2 : 3" rule for the dimensions of the axes is often relaxed in favor of 1 : 1 when drawing scatterplots, especially when both of the variables have roughly the same range of values.

Scatterplots are expensive to reproduce in publications, so they're not often seen in published journals unless the author is trying to illustrate a specific

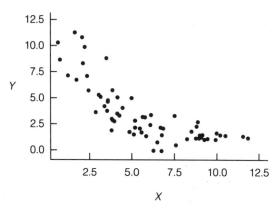

Figure 9.12

departure from linearity or the degree of "goodness" of the fit of a particular function. In student reports, though, they're perfectly appropriate and often expected by instructors.

Transformations and the Form of the Relationship

In the last two chapters we noted that addition/subtraction operations changed the center of a variable by the amount added or subtracted and that multiplication/division operations performed the same operation on both centers and spreads. We also noted that nonlinear transformations could change the form of a frequency distribution, but that a linear transformation would not. Similar rules hold for bivariate relationships. In general, a linear transformation of either or both of the variables in a bivariate relationship has no effect on the relationship at all. The scatterplot will remain unchanged after a linear transformation, as will any numeric indices of the relationship. The *scales* used to label the axes will change, naturally, since linear transformations may affect the centers and spreads of the variables. But the relationship between the two variables remains unchanged.

The same statements cannot be made about nonlinear transformations and bivariate relationships. Suppose that we have a pair of variables whose scatterplot looks quite nonlinear (Figure 9.12). If we were to try to fit a line through this plot, a curved line seems to fit better than would a straight one. While there is nothing inherently "better" or more "natural" about a straight line, having variables related linearly makes a wide range of powerful statistical tools easily available. Most of the statistics in this chapter assume that the relationship between the two variables is linear. While there are techniques for assessing whether the relationship actually is linear, the eyeball is a pretty good guide. If the scatterplot *looks* nonlinear, it probably is.

Representing the Relationship Numerically

There are several different measures for describing the relationship between two variables. The statistics differ primarily in the assumptions that they make regarding the measurement characteristics of the variables. Thus we will find procedures for use when both variables are measured with interval or ratio procedures, when both are measured as ordinal variables, when one variable is ordinal and the other is interval, and so forth. We'll defer the special case of two nominal variables until Chapter 21, but here we'll present procedures for describing the relationship between a nominal variable and an ordinal, interval, or ratio variable.

The measures of relationship are known generically as *correlation coefficients* and have several features in common. In particular, they all use the range -1.0 to 1.0 to describe the relationship between variables, where 0.0 indicates an absence of relationship and ± 1.0 indicates an identity relationship. Most correlation coefficients use the sign of the coefficient to indicate the "direction" of the relationship. As we noted before, a positive relationship means that high values of one variable go with high values of the other, while a negative relationship means that high values of one are associated with low values of the other. In other words, correlation coefficients range in values between -1.0 and $+1.0$, with the sign indicating the direction and the magnitude of the statistic indicating the strength of the relationship. The exception to the use of the sign occurs in the measure for relationship in nominal variables, where "high" and "low" are meaningless; correlation coefficients for these variables range between 0.0 and 1.0.

Interval and Ratio Data

As usual, we may treat data that were obtained with interval and ratio measurement procedures in the same way since the statistics make use of the equal-interval property of numbers that is shared by these two measurement systems.

The correlation coefficient that is appropriate for describing the relationship between interval and ratio data is a very important statistic, and we'll develop it rather carefully. Specifically, we will be presenting the *Pearson product-moment correlation coefficient*, often called *Pearson's r*, or simply *r*, the universal symbol for the statistic.

A statistic that measures the relationship between variables is an index of their tendency to vary together. That is, the statistic should be able to gauge the extent to which a high score on one is paired with a high score on the other, and vice versa for low scores. If we restate that goal a little, we can take the first step toward developing Pearson's *r*. A score that is high on a variable is also one that is above the mean for that variable, and a low score is below its mean. Thus we can talk about deviations above and below the mean in the same way that we could talk about high and low scores. So the task of measuring the relationship now becomes one of assessing the agreement between pairs of deviations from the means of the two variables.

Let's take a simple example.* The following data present five subjects' scores on two variables that we'll just call X and Y.

---

*If you haven't noticed, people who write statistics books love simple examples because they're easy to present on paper. Naturally, real data are more complicated than book examples, if for no other reason than that there are usually more values. In general, this book tries to use real data when possible. In this case, though, as in a number of others, we'll make an exception. Simple, artificial data really are better for some illustrations!

X	Y
6	3
9	10
4	7
2	4
4	6

$$\overline{X} = 5.0$$

$$\overline{Y} = 6.0$$

The scatterplot of these simple variables shows a positive relationship (Figure 9.13). From the plot, we can see that, in general, low scores on X go with low on Y, and high scores on X go with high on Y. To see that this is the case for the deviation scores as well, we can calculate the differences from the means of the two variables as

X	Y	$(X - \overline{X})$	$(Y - \overline{Y})$
6	3	1	−3
9	10	4	4
4	7	−1	1
2	4	−3	−2
4	6	−1	0

If we were to plot the two sets of deviation scores, we would find that the transformation hasn't changed the form of the relationship (see Figure 9.14). Indeed, the form of the relationship—the scatterplot—shouldn't change. We applied a linear transformation to each variable, and linear transformations don't change the form.

When the variance was first introduced in Chapter 7, we defined it as a measure of spread based on the differences between the values and their mean, namely the quantities $(X - \overline{X})$. We squared the differences, summed and divided

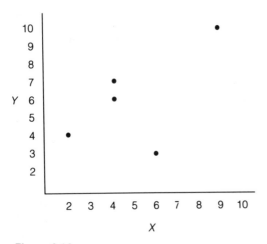

Figure 9.13

Figure 9.14

by N to give the sample variance. We are now ready to define a comparable quantity, called the *covariance*, which is related to the association between a pair of variables.

The covariance of two variables, X and Y, is defined as

$$\text{cov}(X, Y) = \frac{\Sigma(X - \bar{X})(Y - \bar{Y})}{N}.$$

To see the parallel with the variance, we could rewrite the variance as

$$\text{var}(X) = \frac{\Sigma(X - \bar{X})(X - \bar{X})}{N}.$$

The numerator of each expression is the sum of a series of products of deviations from a mean. In the variance, of course, the products are actually squares, while in the covariance the products are those of an X deviation times a Y deviation. In both cases, the sum of deviation products is divided by N, the number of subjects.

Completing the computation of $\text{cov}(X, Y)$ for our example, we have

X	Y	$(X - \bar{X})$	$(Y - \bar{Y})$	$(X - \bar{X})(Y - \bar{Y})$
6	3	1	-3	-3
9	10	4	4	16
4	7	-1	1	-1
2	4	-3	-2	6
4	6	-1	0	0
				$18 = \Sigma(X - \bar{X})(Y - \bar{Y})$

so that

$$\text{cov}(X, Y) = \frac{18}{5} = 3.6.$$

The value of the covariance is closely related to the relationship between X and Y. The larger the absolute value of $\text{cov}(X, Y)$, the stronger the relationship. This is so because as data values are farther from their respective means, their products will be also. If an X deviation is large (the X score is far from its mean) and so is the Y deviation, their product will be large. On the other hand, if an X deviation is large and the corresponding Y deviation is small, then their product will be proportionally less.

In addition, the sign of the covariance behaves as we want. If a pair of deviations from the X and Y means are in the same direction (which indicates that the scores the deviations are based on are both either above or below their respective means), then their product will be positive. On the other hand, if one score is above its mean and the other below, the deviations will have different signs and their product will be negative. When the cross-products are summed, then, the sign of the sum will indicate whether the relationship is, on balance, a positive or a negative one.

But the covariance can't be the measure of correlation that we desire, because its magnitude is heavily dependent upon the spread of the variables.

Variables with larger ranges will have larger deviations to enter into the cross-product computations, making the covariance larger than it would be with a smaller range. Thus the covariance of widely spread variables will be greater than for variables with smaller spreads, even though the degree of association might be equal. We can see this effect easily in our example data set by manipulating the spread. Multiply Y by 10 to get the "new" Y values. The new Y variable has a mean and a spread increased by a factor of 10. Now calculate the covariance:

X	Y	$(X - \bar{X})$	$(Y - \bar{Y})$	$(X - \bar{X})(Y - \bar{Y})$
6	30	1	−30	−30
9	100	4	40	160
4	70	−1	10	−10
2	40	−3	−20	60
4	60	−1	0	0
				$180 = \Sigma(X - \bar{X})(Y - \bar{Y})$

$$\text{cov}(X, Y) = \frac{180}{5} = 36.0.$$

The original covariance was 3.6; now it's 36. Multiplying one variable by a constant multiplies the covariance by the same constant.

Suppose that we multiply the other variable by a constant also. We might suppose that doing so would multiply the covariance by the product of the two constants; and it does, as the following computation of the covariance of the example data shows. Here, we multiplied Y by 10 and multiplied X by 5. The result illustrates that the covariance is multiplied by the product of the two constants:

X	Y	$(X - \bar{X})$	$(Y - \bar{Y})$	$(X - \bar{X})(Y - \bar{Y})$
30	30	5	−30	−150
45	100	20	40	800
20	70	−5	10	−50
10	40	−15	−20	300
20	60	−5	0	0
				$900 = \Sigma(X - \bar{X})(Y - \bar{Y})$

$$\text{cov}(X, Y) = \frac{900}{5} = 180 = 3.6 \times 5 \times 10.$$

If we happen to pick two very special constants and multiply the covariance by their product, we finally come to the measure that we want. The two constants that will do the job are the reciprocals of the standard deviations of the two original variables. We might calculate

$$\text{cov}(X, Y) \times \frac{1}{s_X} \times \frac{1}{s_Y}.$$

Since multiplying by the reciprocal is the same as dividing, the formula then becomes

$$r = \frac{\text{cov}(X, Y)}{s_X s_Y},$$

which is one definition of the Pearson product-moment correlation coefficient, or Pearson's r, for short. You might think of this formula as representing the sort of "standardizing" operation for the covariance. And, in fact, that's very much what it is. The largest absolute magnitude that the covariance can have is the product of the standard deviations of the two variables, and so dividing by that product limits the value of Pearson's r to ± 1.0. That maximum of ± 1.0 can be reached only when the covariance reaches the largest absolute value that it can for the data.

There are many other formulas for Pearson's r. For example, it is a short algebraic step from the Pearson's r definition just shown to this one:

$$r = \frac{\Sigma(X - \bar{X})(Y - \bar{Y})}{\sqrt{\Sigma(X - \bar{X})^2 \Sigma(Y - \bar{Y})^2}}.$$

This formula emphasizes a connection between the variance and Pearson's r. Note that the numerator of the expression is the sum of cross-products that we defined earlier and that the denominator involves sums of squares (or SSs). In Chapter 7 we learned that when an SS is divided by the appropriate number, it becomes a variance. And, indeed, those sums of squares in the denominator can become variances since

$$s_X^2 = \frac{\Sigma(X - \bar{X})^2}{N}$$

and

$$s_Y^2 = \frac{\Sigma(Y - \bar{Y})^2}{N}.$$

This close tie between Pearson's r and variance shows that they are similar statistics; we'll explore that similarity further a little later.

Computing Pearson's r. There are a number of formulas for computing Pearson's product-moment correlation coefficient, some of them quite complex. We'll look at only a couple of them, since the statistic is available in every statistics package.

The formula that we just presented,

$$r = \frac{\Sigma(X - \bar{X})(Y - \bar{Y})}{\sqrt{\Sigma(X - \bar{X})^2 \Sigma(Y - \bar{Y})^2}},$$

provides one means of calculating r (the initial calculations are shown in Table 9.1):

$$r = \frac{\Sigma(X - \bar{X})(Y - \bar{Y})}{\sqrt{\Sigma(X - \bar{X})^2 \Sigma(Y - \bar{Y})^2}} = \frac{18}{\sqrt{28 \times 30}} = 0.62.$$

This computation requires that the two variable means be computed first and then subtracted from each data value.

Table 9.1

X	Y	$(X - \bar{X})$	$(Y - \bar{Y})$	$(X - \bar{X})(Y - \bar{Y})$	$(X - \bar{X})^2$	$(Y - \bar{Y})^2$
6	3	1	−3	−3	1	9
9	10	4	4	16	16	16
4	7	−1	1	−1	1	1
2	4	−3	−2	6	9	4
4	6	−1	0	0	1	0
$\bar{X} = 5.0$	$\bar{Y} = 6.0$			18	28	30

Table 9.2

X	Y	X^2	Y^2	XY
6	3	36	9	18
9	10	81	100	90
4	7	16	49	28
2	4	4	16	8
4	6	16	36	24
25	30	153	210	168
↑	↑	↑	↑	↑
ΣX	ΣY	ΣX^2	ΣY^2	ΣXY

A common formula for Pearson's r, beginning with raw data values so that it avoids the need to compute means and subtract, is

$$r = \frac{N\Sigma XY - (\Sigma X)(\Sigma Y)}{\sqrt{[N\Sigma X^2 - (\Sigma X)^2][N\Sigma Y^2 - (\Sigma Y)^2]}}.$$

While the formula looks cumbersome, it is actually a simple way to make the computation. Return to the raw data and obtain the sums of both X and Y, the sum of squared values of X and Y, and the sum of the products of the X and Y values (Table 9.2). The computation is now completed as

$$r = \frac{N\Sigma XY - (\Sigma X)(\Sigma Y)}{\sqrt{[N\Sigma X^2 - (\Sigma X)^2][N\Sigma Y^2 - (\Sigma Y)^2]}}$$

$$= \frac{5 \times 168 - 25 \times 30}{\sqrt{[5 \times 153 - 25^2][5 \times 210 - 30^2]}}$$

$$= \frac{840 - 750}{\sqrt{140 \times 150}}$$

$$= \frac{90}{144.91}$$

$$= 0.62.$$

Interpreting Pearson's r. When used together with a scatterplot, Pearson's r is a good indicator of the relationship between a pair of variables. The correlation

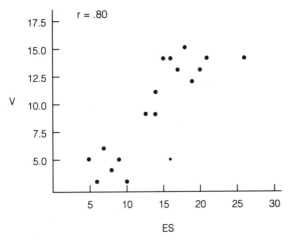

Figure 9.15

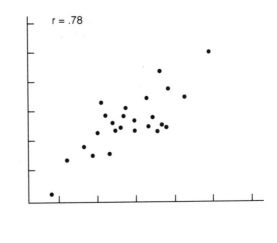

Figure 9.16

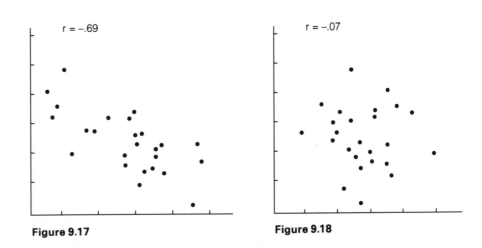

Figure 9.17

Figure 9.18

coefficient provides a quantitative measure of the extent of the covariation, while the scatterplot provides a good visual check on the linearity of the relationship. The magnitude of *r* gives an easy-to-grasp measure of the relationship—the closer to 1.0 the stronger the relationship—while the sign indicates the direction of that relationship.

Some practice in interpreting correlation coefficients will be developed by using them. Figures 9.15–9.18 are examples of scatterplots with the correlations, beginning with the plot of V against ES that we saw earlier (Figure 9.15). Figure 9.16 shows another fairly strong, positive relationship, while Figure 9.17 shows a negative correlation of roughly the same magnitude. The correlation in Figure 9.18 is essentially zero.

To illustrate that the Pearson product-moment correlation coefficient reflects both the relationship and the scatter about the best-fitting straight line through the scatterplot, consider the pair of plots in Figure 9.19. These two sets of data were carefully constructed so that they have the same best-fitting line.

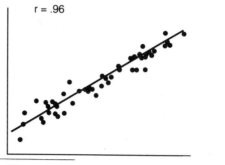

r = .96

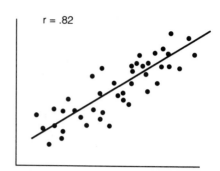

r = .82

Figure 9.19

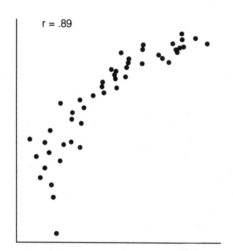

r = .89

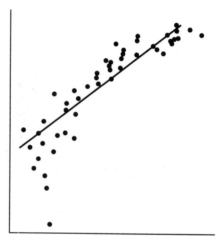

Figure 9.20   **Figure 9.21**

Both of the *r* values are high and positive, yet the plots clearly differ in the degree to which the points are clustered about the best-fitting line. The Pearson's *r* reflects that difference. In Chapter 10 we'll introduce the measure for the variability about the best-fitting line, and we will see that the value of Pearson's *r* is directly related to that value.

Several times we've mentioned the requirement of a linear relationship between the two variables in a correlation. Two illustrations will demonstrate the inability of Pearson's *r* to deal with curvilinear data. Consider the scatterplot in Figure 9.20. While *r* is respectably large, the line of best fit clearly misses many of the data values, being too high at both extremes of the *X* values, and too low in the midrange (see Figure 9.21). If we had a procedure for fitting a curve to the data (which we won't develop in this book) we could do substantially better, as Figure 9.22 shows.

Pearson's *r* is applicable only to data that have linear relationships. While this seems to be a serious limitation, often it is not. Many variables are in fact linearly related and so the problem solves itself. In other cases, replacing the values of one or both variables with, for example, their square roots or logarithms

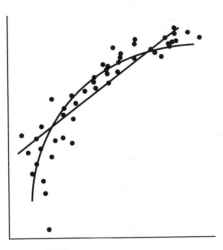

Figure 9.22

will solve the problem. While we won't explore these operations here, you should keep them in mind.

A frequent constraint on applying Pearson's *r* is that it requires that both variables be measured with interval or ratio measurement procedures. A number of alternative correlation measures address this problem, and we turn to them now. We won't spend nearly the time on them as we have on Pearson's *r*, but they are important and widely used.

Ordinal Data   When both variables are measured on an ordinal scale or when one is ordinal and the other either interval or ratio, the Pearson product-moment correlation coefficient isn't appropriate. The Pearson *r* is based on differences between scores and their means, and those differences aren't really meaningful with ordinal measurement. Fortunately, there are two good, and commonly used, measures of relationship for ordinal data—*Spearman's rank-order correlation*, often called *Spearman's rho*, and *Kendall's tau* (τ). There are differences between the two measures in their assumptions and in their computations, but both are designed for the situation where one or both of the variables is measured on an ordinal scale.

Spearman's Rho. A very common measure of the relationship between two ordinal variables, or variables that have been converted to ranks, is Spearman's rho, r_s. Converting an interval or ratio variable to ranks is a simple matter, especially if your computer program can convert a set of scores to their rank orders. Or, even if your program can't, ranking isn't difficult. Sort, or have your program sort, the data from smallest to largest value. Then assign the rank 1 to the smallest, 2 to the next, and so on. If you have sets of tied scores, assign each value the mean rank. Thus if your data are 5, 7, 12, 15, 15, 18, 22, then the ranks would be

Raw score	5	7	12	15	15	18	22
Rank	1	2	3	4.5	4.5	6	7

Once the data are in ranks for both variables, computation for r_s is simple; compute Pearson's r *using the ranks*. While there are a number of computational formulas for r_s, they may be more trouble than they're worth, especially when you have data containing ties. Since we already have formulas for r, and since every computer program worth its salt will compute Pearson's r, why not do it the easy way?

Kendall's Tau (τ). Kendall's tau is an alternative correlational procedure for two ordinal variables. Not many computer programs offer τ; some do. The computations are not difficult. In any event, we'll illustrate them here.

Kendall's τ is often used to describe the relationship between the rankings or orderings made by two individuals. Suppose that, as part of a study in experimental esthetics, you ask two people to arrange a group of ten paintings in order from most to least attractive. This is an easy task for most people, although they might not be able to tell you exactly how they arrived at their judgments. If the two people ranked the paintings in exactly the same order, then we would say that there's perfect agreement, or correlation, between them. On the other hand, suppose that they arranged the paintings in exactly opposite orders. This defines the other extreme—complete disagreement. Tau is based on the number of times that a painting is ranked the same for each of the two judges; more precisely, it is based on the number of inversions in ranking. If Fred and Mary rank paintings B and C in the same order, there is no inversion in order. On the other hand, if Fred ranks them in the order B–C and if Mary ranks them as C–B, then the ordering contains an inversion.

The easy way to count the number of inversions is to use a graphic method. Name the paintings A, B, C, and so forth. Then we list the paintings and Fred and Mary's rank orderings as

Painting	Ranking by Fred	Mary
A	1	1
B	3	3
C	2	2
D	6	5
E	5	7
F	7	6
G	4	4
H	10	10
I	8	9
J	9	8

In this example, Fred and Mary agreed that painting A was most attractive, that C was second, and that B was third. They disagreed on painting D, with Fred ranking it in sixth place and Mary in fifth, and so forth.

Painting	Ranking by Fred	Mary
A	1	1
B	3	3
C	2	2
D	6	5
E	5	7
F	7	6
G	4	4
H	10	10
I	8	9
J	9	8

With the data arranged in this fashion, the number of inversions can be found graphically by connecting the pairs of rank values, as shown and counting the crossings. (For clarity, the drawing shows only the lines that cross; there's little point in cluttering the picture by connecting 1 to 1, 3 to 3, and so on when they're across from each other.) Each crossed pair of lines represents an inversion in the subject's orderings. The value of τ is calculated easily as

$$\tau = 1 - \frac{2(\text{number of inversions})}{\text{number of pairs of objects ranked}}$$

or, since the number of pairs of m objects is $m(m-1)/2$,

$$\tau = 1 - \frac{2(\text{number of inversions})}{m(m-1)/2},$$

where m is the number of objects ranked (the 10 paintings in our example). For our data,

$$\tau = 1 - \frac{2(3)}{10(9)/2}$$

$$= 1 - .13$$

$$= 0.87.$$

When there are ties in the data, as might occur if one or both of the variables are converted to ranks, the calculation of τ is more complicated and we'll leave it to the computer. (Hays, 1981, pp. 202–205, illustrates the calculation.)

The maximum value that τ can attain is 1.0, when there are no reversals. When there are the maximum possible reversals (the two ranks are in reverse order), the value of τ is 0.0.

Choosing Between r_s and τ. Both r_s and τ are used to describe the relationship between sets of ordinal data. How should you decide which one to use? The answer isn't simple (how many statistical answers are?) and depends partly on the data and partly on the questions that you want to ask of the data. Spearman's rho is probably most appropriate when one or both variables have been converted to ranks from interval or ratio measurement. Kendall's tau is most often employed in the situation that we just illustrated—two subjects (often called "judges") have ranked the same set of objects.

Beyond those considerations, though, you'll note that τ does not yield negative values, which may be a disadvantage. On the other hand, it has a straightforward interpretation based on probability theory. It represents a probability (actually, an estimate of the probability) that, upon repeated rankings, any pair of objects will remain in the same relative ordering. More specifically, a τ of .87 as in the example suggests that the chances of any pair of paintings being ranked in the same order is 87% greater than the chance of their appearing in some other order. In other words, the higher the value of τ, the greater the chance that the objects will be ranked in the same order again.

Other Coefficients for Other Purposes

Suppose that you have a numeric variable, either interval or ratio, and a two-category nominal variable (such as male-female, single-married, or college graduate-nongraduate) and you want to calculate a measure of relationship? One approach would be to code the category variable as 0 and 1 (or any two different values) and then compute Pearson's r. If you did that, the result would be a special coefficient known as the *point biserial correlation coefficient*, often symbolized as r_{pb}. The point biserial coefficient is widely used when one variable is a true two-category (dichotomous) variable. Clearly, the sign of the coefficient is meaningless since it can be switched by reversing the 0-1 variable. Suppose that we have the following results of a statistics quiz taken by juniors and seniors. Is there a correlation between year in school and grade on the quiz?

Juniors	Seniors
35	26
41	22
39	22
28	46
37	33
17	41
68	30
65	54
19	45
42	32
	20
	40

Recoding juniors as 0 and seniors as 1, we have

Class	Quiz grade	Class	Quiz grade
0	35	1	22
0	41	1	22
0	39	1	46
0	28	1	33
0	37	1	41
0	17	1	30
0	68	1	54
0	65	1	45
0	19	1	32
0	42	1	20
1	26	1	40

The Pearson r (actually the point biserial correlation coefficient) for these data is $-.179$, indicating virtually no correlation. Had we coded the classes as 1-0 for juniors and seniors, the correlation would be .179, illustrating that the sign is meaningless with the category variable.

In the examples we have cited, it is clear that there were only two categories (male-female, single-married) and that there was no underlying continuous variable beneath the category coding. In many cases, though, you can think of groups that have been formed through an "artificial" dichotomy. Passing-failing on an exam, for example, can form two groups by using a cutoff on a numerical grade variable. Dr. Campbell might pick two groups of people, which he might choose to call introverts and extraverts, by picking some score on the introversion/ extraversion scale and categorizing the subjects according to their test value. In either case, the result would be a dichotomy, pass-fail, or introvert-extravert, but a dichotomy that was formed by dividing an underlying continuous variable into two categories. In this case, applying the point biserial correlation is inappropriate. The measure to use with one continuous variable and one "artificial" dichotomy is the *biserial correlation coefficient* (r_b), and it is computed differently. We won't develop the coefficient any further here since it's not used very frequently. Howell (1987, pp. 257–259) discusses the coefficient and gives an example of computation.

Another class of correlation measures are those involving two category variables; we're deferring these until Chapter 21. That leaves us with just a single statistic left to present here, the *Kendall coefficient of concordance*. Strictly speaking, the measure is not one of correlation between two variables; rather, it is a measure of the agreement of a set of individuals who have ordered the same set of stimuli or objects. In our discussion of Kendall's τ, we used an example of two people who rated 10 paintings. Suppose that instead of two people, or judges, we used five, so that our data are

Painting	Judge 1	2	3	4	5
A	1	1	2	4	3
B	3	3	1	1	2
C	2	2	4	5	4
D	6	5	3	3	1
E	5	7	5	2	5
F	7	6	6	9	7
G	4	4	7	10	6
H	10	10	8	8	9
I	8	9	10	6	10
J	9	8	9	7	8

Now how may we assess the degree of agreement among the judges? The Kendall coefficient of concordance, W, provides a good measure. Few computer packages offer W, but we can easily demonstrate how it's calculated here. We begin by finding the sum of the ranks for each object ranked, paintings in our case:

Painting	Judge 1	2	3	4	5	Sum of ranks
A	1	1	2	4	3	11
B	3	3	1	1	2	10
C	2	2	4	5	4	17
D	6	5	3	3	1	18
E	5	7	5	2	5	24
F	7	6	6	9	7	35
G	4	4	7	10	6	31
H	10	10	8	8	9	45
I	8	9	10	6	10	43
J	9	8	9	7	8	41

Now the computation is done using the formula

$$W = \frac{12\Sigma T^2}{N^2 m(m^2 - 1)} - \frac{3(m + 1)}{m - 1},$$

where T is a total sum of ranks for a painting, m is the number of items ranked (paintings), and N is the number of judges. Completing the calculation:

$$W = \frac{12(11^2 + 10^2 + 17^2 + \cdots + 41^2)}{5^2 \times 10 \times (10^2 - 1)} - \frac{3(10 + 1)}{10 - 1}$$

$$= 4.437 - 3.667$$

$$= .770.$$

W can be thought of as the ratio of the variability in the ranking totals to the maximum possible variability. In our example, if all subjects had rated the 10 paintings in the same order, then the total for painting 1 would have been 5, that for painting 2 would have been 10, and so on, with painting 10 having a total ranking of 100; in short, the painting totals would have been as variable as they could possibly be. If the judges ranked all the paintings as differently as possible, on the other hand, the totals would have been much more alike since each painting would have a mix of high and low rankings. In fact, when there is maximum possible disagreement in ranking, the variance of the totals is at its minimum. The statistic W is the ratio

$$W = \frac{\text{variance of rank totals}}{\text{maximum possible variance of rank totals}}.$$

Our obtained value of .770, then, indicates that 77% of the possible variability—that is, total agreement—was obtained with our data. This indicates a substantial agreement among our five judges.

With this interpretation, it should be clear that W is not a correlation coefficient in the sense that we have had before now. W's value may range from 0.0 to 1.0, but a negative value is impossible. W is a proportion of variability, but not exactly a correlation.

Table 9.3 summarizes the measures of relationship presented in this chapter.

Table 9.3   Choosing a Measure of Linear Relationship

If one variable is . . .	Nominal	And the other is . . . Ordinal	Interval or ratio
Nominal	See Chapter 21		Point biserial Biserial
Ordinal	No appropriate statistic	Spearman's rho Kendall's tau (for two rankings) Kendall's coefficient of concordance	
Interval or ratio	Point biserial (for true dichotomy) Biserial (for artificial dichotomy)	Spearman's rho	Pearson's product-moment correlation

SUMMARY

- Bivariate statistics describe the relationship between pairs of variables.
- A scatterplot pictures the relationship between variables.
- Linear transformations of the variables do not change the form of the relationship between variables.
- The Pearson product-moment correlation coefficient (r) ranges from -1.0 to $+1.0$; its sign shows the direction of the relationship, and its magnitude shows the strength of the linear relationship.
- When one or both variables are measured on an ordinal scale, the appropriate correlational measure is Spearman's rho.
- Kendall's tau may be used to describe the relationship between a pair of ranks.
- When one variable is a true dichotomy, the correlation between it and an interval or ratio variable is a point biserial correlation coefficient.
- The Kendall coefficient of concordance describes the relationship among a set of rankings.

KEY TERMS

Bivariate

Correlation

Covariance

Kendall coefficient of concordance

Kendall's tau

Point biserial correlation coefficient

Regression

Scatterplot

Spearman's rho

Solutions to asterisked (*) exercises appear at the back of the book. Exercises preceded by a section symbol (§) must be solved using a computer. Exercises preceded by a dagger (†) can be solved by hand.

*†1. The following table gives the scores for 16 students on two statistics quizzes. Obtain the appropriate descriptive measures for each quiz and construct the scatterplot showing the relationship between Quiz 1 and 2.

Student	Quiz 1	Quiz 2
1	20	13
2	30	27
3	23	22
4	27	23
5	23	24
6	15	17
7	30	29
8	20	20
9	26	24
10	27	20
11	19	13
12	18	25
13	21	20
14	26	26
15	25	24
16	26	24

†2. Here is a set of data on variables X and Y. Using the Y values on the ordinate, construct the scatterplot.

X	Y	X	Y
2	103	12	121
2	98	12	123
4	109	8	128
3	105	18	123
4	103	7	115
3	111	23	131
13	112	14	133
5	113	17	130
12	116	17	133
10	125	17	136

*†3. Use the following data for this series of questions.

X	Y	X	Y
81	9	52	11
19	8	80	10
52	8	6	3
33	6	4	3
33	8	79	11
4	4	23	6
6	7	33	6
33	7	5	4
5	4	9	5
1	2	21	8
2	1	2	1
15	7	13	6
9	5	1	1
13	6	3	2
51	7	14	6
51	10	82	9
2	3	8	7
23	7	2	1
3	2	2	3
6	4	3	3

a. Find the univariate descriptive statistics, including the Pearson skewness statistic, and frequency distributions for each variable.

b. Construct the scatterplot, with Y on the ordinate.

c. In words, how do you describe the relationship between X and Y?

d. Try several transformations on each variable, constructing the scatterplot after each. Be sure that you use at least the square root, square, reciprocal, and log transformations on variables singly and together. Which transformation(s) seem to make the relationship the most linear?

*†**4.** For the data given in Exercise 1, compute Pearson's *r*.

†**5.** Compute Pearson's *r* for the data given in Exercise 2.

†**6.** Using the same data as for Exercise 2, convert both X and Y to ranks and obtain Spearman's rho.

*†**7.** The SuperCola company is developing a new drink. As a part of its taste research, the company obtains a group of six professional tasters. Each taster is asked to rank, in order of preference, eight beverages, including the "old" SuperCola, three competing drinks, and four formulas for the "new" SuperCola. The data follow:

Beverage	Taster					
	1	2	3	4	5	6
Old SuperCola	2	4	7	2	1	2
Brand X Cola	1	2	1	3	8	3
Brand Y Cola	4	1	5	1	5	1
Brand Z Cola	8	8	8	6	7	6
New #1	3	3	2	7	2	5
New #2	7	7	6	8	6	8
New #3	5	5	2	5	3	4
New #4	6	6	3	4	4	7

a. Compute Kendall's W for the data.
b. Compute Spearman's rho between the rankings of judges 1 and 2, 2 and 5, and 4 and 6.
c. Calculate Kendall's tau for the same pairs of judges as you did in part (b).

§**8.** Returning to Exercise 3, compute the Pearson product-moment correlation coefficient for the original variables and the values after you made what you found were the most effective transformations. What is the effect of the transformation on r?

*†**9.** Following is a set of data for men and women giving the amount of change they had in their pocket or purse when stopped randomly on the street. Using the point biserial, is there a relationship between sex and amount of change?

Men	Women
$1.42	$.55
.52	.91
1.02	.00
.23	1.54
.00	.67
.41	.85
.13	.92
.04	.29
.85	2.61
.00	.36
.93	.88
	.77
	1.04
	.46

CHAPTER 10

Regression and Linear Prediction

Chapter 9 discussed ways to describe the relationship between two variables and introduced several correlation coefficients. If there's a relationship between two variables, then knowing the value of one variable lets you do a better job predicting a value on the other one. If you know that you're to guess the weight of a male, you might guess 165 pounds, because that's close to the mean for American males. But if you also know that the male whose weight you are to guess is only 4'8" tall, you'll certainly want to adjust your guess downward. Your adjustment of the "predicted" weight takes advantage of your knowledge of the relationship between height and weight. It's not a perfect relationship—there are, after all, very short people who are also heavy, just as there are tall people who are very thin—but on the whole, there is a strong, positive correlation between weight and height.

In Chapter 9 we referred repeatedly to a hypothetical best-fitting straight line through a scatterplot. In this chapter we'll develop the best-fitting line as a model of the relationship between two variables and use it to predict values on one variable from another.

Linear Prediction

Statistical prediction relies upon the relationship between variables; the correlation coefficients described in Chapter 9 measure that relationship, but by themselves don't offer a way to make a prediction. Nevertheless, the fact that two variables are correlated suggests that knowledge of one tells something about the other. For example, if you are asked to guess a person's weight and are given no additional information, your best guess is the mean weight of humans. If you are also given the individual's height, you could revise your weight estimate appropriately because you know something about the relationship between height and weight. Of course, you can't expect that the prediction will be perfect, but you'll make better predictions if you can use correlational information.

Predicting one variable from another is generally known as *regression*, a term with various meanings. In this context, the word is shorthand for "regression to the mean," a tendency for children to have (or "regress to") a height close to the mean height of the population. The early statistician Sir Francis Galton, who did much of the pioneering work leading to the development of correlation techniques, first noted the tendency and published a report around 1885 (see Tankard, 1984). Since his time, the procedures for predicting one variable from another have been termed *regression*.

Statistical prediction is done by establishing a simplified statement, or a model, of the relationship between two variables. Like all models, a statistical model is an approximation and simplification, one that loses some of the richness and complexity present in the real situation. But, in return, a statistical model may let us predict the values of one variable from another.

While there are many different forms that the relationship between two variables might take, we'll concentrate on just one—the linear model. A linear model simplifies the relationship between two variables by representing the scatterplot as a straight line. The straight line has a well-known mathematical representation, and its use is supported by a long tradition of linear modeling in the behavioral sciences.

The Linear Equation

A linear equation has the general mathematical form

$$Y = bX + a,$$

where X and Y are two variables, with Y normally represented on the ordinate of a graph and X on the abscissa. The two constants, b and a, are the slope of the line and the Y intercept, respectively. The equation

$$Y = 0.67X + 2,$$

for example, describes the line graphed in Figure 10.1.

The Y intercept (a), 2 in Figure 10.1, shows where the line crosses the Y axis, that is, the value of Y when X is 0. Changing the value of a shifts the line vertically without changing its slope. With $a = -5$, for example, the line looks like that in Figure 10.2. The slope of the line (b) gives the rate of climb of the line per unit of X. In the example, the slope of 0.67 means that for every increase of 1.0 in X, the Y value increases 0.67. For example, suppose that, instead of a slope of 0.67 as in Figure 10.2, the slope were 1.5. Then, to construct the line, we'd start by drawing the axes (Figure 10.3) and then calculate the value of Y for any two X values. Suppose that we picked $X = 10$. To find the corresponding Y value, just substitute 10 into the equation as

$$Y = 1.5X + 2$$
$$= 1.5(10) + 2 = 17.$$

This tells us that when $X = 10$, $Y = 17$; the point $X = 10$, $Y = 17$ is thus on the line, as is the point corresponding to $X = -15$:

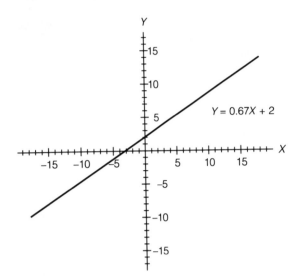

Figure 10.1

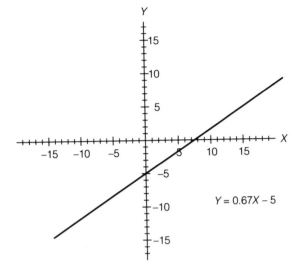

Figure 10.2

$$Y = 1.5X + 2$$
$$= 1.5(-15) + 2 = -20.5.$$

Now we have determined that when $X = -15$, $Y = -20.5$. Since two points are all that are needed to define a straight line, we can now plot the line by locating the points for the two pairs of X, Y values, and connecting them with a line, as in Figure 10.4. Here the line rises more steeply than did that in the Figure 10.1 (where the slope was 0.67), 1.5 units for every unit of X, but the intercepts are equal ($a = 2.0$) so that both lines pass through the Y axis at the same point.

A slope may be negative, or it may be zero. A line with zero slope means that Y does not change for any change in X. For example, if the slope were zero and the intercept were -7, the line would look like the one in Figure 10.5. A negative slope indicates that for every increase in the value of X, Y decreases in value. A line with a slope of -0.9 and an intercept of 6, for example, appears in Figure 10.6.

We encountered linear functions earlier in talking about the kinds of operations that can be applied to measurements and preserve the meaning in the data. But how are they related to statistical prediction? If we assume that the association between two variables is linear, then the linear equation can serve as the model of the relationship. If we can find an appropriate line—and that means finding the appropriate values of the slope and the intercept—then we can use that equation for prediction. In particular, we'll have a linear equation just like the ones we've been using to describe (or model) the relationship between two variables. For any two variables, X and Y, then, the linear model describing them can be written as

$$\hat{Y} = bX + a,$$

where $\hat{Y}$ will be our symbol for a predicted Y value.

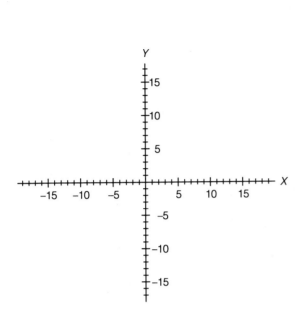

Figure 10.3

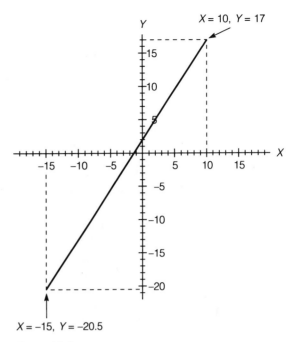

$X = 10, \ Y = 17$

$X = -15, \ Y = -20.5$

Figure 10.4

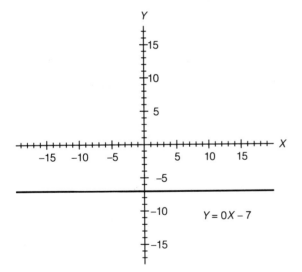

$Y = 0X - 7$

Figure 10.5

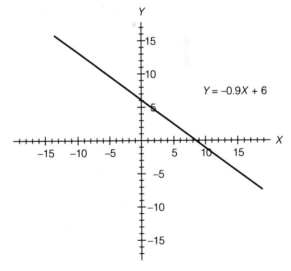

$Y = -0.9X + 6$

Figure 10.6

Having proposed the linear equation as the model for predicting, the next matter is seeing how we might determine the slope and the intercept, since those two values will determine the line.

Fitting the Line

The line through the scatterplot will serve as a kind of two-dimensional "center" for the data. That is, we want a line that comes close to, and summarizes, the data points in the same way the measures of center did. We would like the line to have roughly the same number of data points on each side of it, and we would like the points to, in some sense, balance around the line.

There are several ways that we might define the line to serve as the model of the relationship between two variables. We'll present just one of them, the classic "least squares" procedure. The procedure has two goals: (1) to reduce the scatterplot to a single straight line described by a linear equation and (2) to arrange that the line comes closest to the data values according to some "best-fitting" criterion.

For our example, here's another artificial data set, with two variables that we'll just call X and Y. The data, from 21 hypothetical subjects, are

X	Y
3	4
5	4
1	1
4	3
1	2
8	8
2	1
7	3
2	2
6	4
4	7
3	2
7	6
5	3
7	5
2	3
6	6
4	5
8	7
4	6
4	2

The scatterplot for these data indicates a strong linear relationship; in fact, $r = .72$ (see Figure 10.7).

To develop a "best fit" criterion, recall that the arithmetic mean is the center of its data set in the sense that it minimizes the sum of the squared differences between it and the scores; that is, $\Sigma(X - \overline{X})^2$ is a minimum. Since this sum of

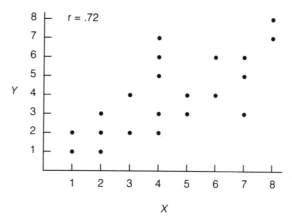

Figure 10.7

squared deviations is a minimum, the arithmetic mean is said to be a *least squares* measure of the center of the data.

The least squares logic can be applied in two dimensions to fit a line to a scatterplot. In this case, the linear equation that describes the line is to minimize the errors of prediction. These values are symbolized $(Y - \hat{Y})$, and represent the difference between actual values (Y) and those predicted by the model $(\hat{Y})$. We could use calculus to find the formulas for slope and intercept that would minimize the quantity $\Sigma(Y - \hat{Y})^2$. Since we don't assume that calculus is part of your background, we'll let someone else worry about the mathematics and merely present the formulas for a line that best fits the data using the least squares criterion.

The slope of the best-fitting least squares line is

$$b = \frac{\text{cov}(X, Y)}{s_X^2};$$

that is, the ratio of covariance to the variance of the Y variable. Alternatively, the slope of the line may be defined as

$$b = r\frac{s_Y}{s_X},$$

where r is the Pearson product-moment correlation coefficient.

If the two standard deviations and the correlation between the two variables are available from a separate computation, the second formula for slope is very convenient. For the example data, where the two standard deviations are $s_X = 2.15$ and $s_Y = 2.02$ and $r = .72$, the slope is

$$b = r\frac{s_Y}{s_X}$$

$$= .72\frac{2.02}{2.15}$$

$$= 0.68.$$

A convenient raw data formula for the slope is

$$b = \frac{N\Sigma XY - (\Sigma X)(\Sigma Y)}{N\Sigma X^2 - (\Sigma X)^2}.$$

The necessary summary values from the raw data are

X	Y	X²	Y²	XY
3	4	9	16	12
5	4	25	16	20
1	1	1	1	1
.	.	.	.	.
.	.	.	.	.
.	.	.	.	.
4	6	16	36	24
4	2	16	4	8
93	84	509	422	438
↑	↑	↑	↑	↑
ΣX	ΣY	ΣX^2	ΣY^2	ΣXY

Using the raw score formula, the calculation is

$$
\begin{aligned}
b &= \frac{N\Sigma XY - (\Sigma X)(\Sigma Y)}{N\Sigma X^2 - (\Sigma X)^2} \\
&= \frac{21 \times 438 - 93 \times 84}{21 \times 509 - 93^2} \\
&= \frac{9198 - 7812}{10689 - 8649} \\
&= \frac{1386}{2040} \\
&= 0.68.
\end{aligned}
$$

The formula for the intercept is

$$a = \overline{Y} - b\overline{X},$$

and so the intercept may be calculated as

$$
\begin{aligned}
a &= \overline{Y} - b\overline{X} \\
&= 4.00 - 0.68 \times 4.43 \\
&= 0.99,
\end{aligned}
$$

using the example data.

In our example, then, the values $b = 0.68$ and $a = 0.99$ define the best-fitting (in the least squares sense) linear model for the data as

$$\hat{Y} = 0.68X + 0.99.$$

This linear equation describes the least squares best-fitting line for predicting Y from X. We can use it to compute predicted Y values for any X value. For example, suppose that we want to predict the Y value corresponding to an X

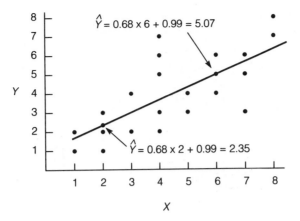

Figure 10.8

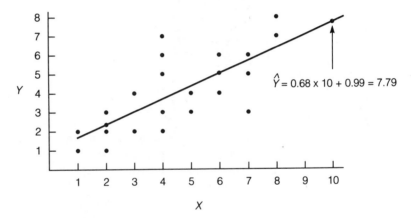

Figure 10.9

value of 6. Substituting the value 6 into the equation, we have

$$\widehat{Y} = 0.68 \times 6 + 0.99 = 5.07.$$

Or, for an X value of 2, we would have

$$\widehat{Y} = 0.68 \times 2 + 0.99 = 2.35.$$

Both of these predicted Y values fall along the line described by the equation. By plotting the two points just calculated and connecting them with a straight line, we may superimpose the regression line on the scatterplot in Figure 10.8. Any other predicted value will also fall directly on the line; for $X = 10$, we have

$$\widehat{Y} = 0.68 \times 10 + 0.99 = 7.79,$$

as illustrated in Figure 10.9.

Note that the predicted Y values for an X of 6 or 10 (or for any other X value) don't agree precisely with any of the actual values in the data. This shouldn't be surprising, since the relationship between X and Y is being modeled

Table 10.1   Residuals for Least Squares Line

X	Y	Ŷ	Y − Ŷ
3	4	3.03	0.97
5	4	4.39	−0.39
1	1	1.67	−0.67
4	3	3.71	−0.71
1	2	1.67	0.33
8	8	6.43	1.57
2	1	2.35	−1.35
7	3	5.75	−2.75
2	2	2.35	−0.35
6	4	5.07	−1.07
4	7	3.71	3.29
3	2	3.03	−1.03
7	6	5.75	0.25
5	3	4.39	−1.39
7	5	5.75	−0.75
2	3	2.35	0.65
6	6	5.07	0.93
4	5	3.71	1.29
8	7	6.43	0.57
4	6	3.71	2.29
4	2	3.71	−1.71

by the linear equation, and models rarely agree precisely with reality. But what we have accomplished is to present an equation that fits the data according to a criterion that minimizes the squared differences between the predicted and the actual Y values.

Residuals

The differences between actual and predicted values of the Y variable—often called residuals—are important figures because they can help to illustrate several features of the linear prediction process. Earlier we illustrated several residuals; Table 10.1 shows all of them for our hypothetical data.

Here we have the original X and Y values, and a set of predicted and residual values coming from the linear model. The residuals can be used to tell us quite a bit about the data and also something about the fit of the line to the data.

Spread Around the Line

The sample variance, as you recall, is defined as the mean of the squared deviations about the mean. That is,

$$s^2 = \frac{\Sigma(X - \bar{X})^2}{N}.$$

You'll also remember that since the mean is the least squares center of the data,

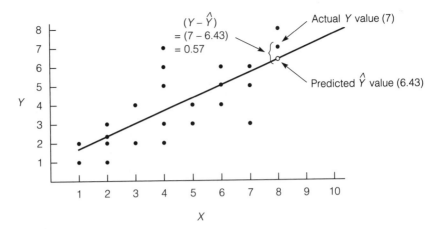

Figure 10.10

$\Sigma(X - \overline{X})^2$ is a minimum. The variance, a very useful measure of spread, is therefore computed by dividing the quantity minimized by an appropriate value. Applying the same logic to similar quantities in least squares regression, we have a comparable measure of variability. But this time the variability is measured around the regression line instead of the mean. Thus we can think of the quantity

$$s^2_{\text{Error}} = \frac{\Sigma(Y - \widehat{Y})^2}{N - 2}$$

as the variance around the best-fitting line. There's a small but important difference here—the appropriate divisor in this case is $N - 2$, where N is the number of pairs of X, Y scores.

As we've mentioned before, any expression that represents a sum of squared differences—like $\Sigma(X - \overline{X})^2$ or $\Sigma(Y - \widehat{Y})^2$—is called a *sum of squares* (SS). So the numerator of the s^2_{Error} formula is a sum of squares. Specifically, it is the sum of the squared differences between the actual values of the Y variables and the values predicted by the linear model. The quantities represent the amount of error in the prediction—with perfect prediction, all of the $(Y - \widehat{Y})$ values would be zero. Graphically, Figure 10.10 is the scatterplot showing the difference between the actual and the predicted scores for the third subject from the bottom in the data (whose actual X and Y scores were 8 and 7).

This value, $(Y - \widehat{Y}) = (7 - 6.43) = 0.57$, represents the amount by which the linear model "missed" the actual Y score. In this case, the "miss" was an underestimate. For some other cases in the data—the third subject, for example—the prediction overestimated the actual value (Figure 10.11).

The denominator of the s^2_{Error} formula is the number of pairs of data values, less two. It is known as a *degrees of freedom* (df) value. (Degrees of freedom is a term from inferential statistics; we'll return to it in later chapters.) A variance is sometimes defined as an SS divided by an appropriate df. Using SS and df notation, then, we might write

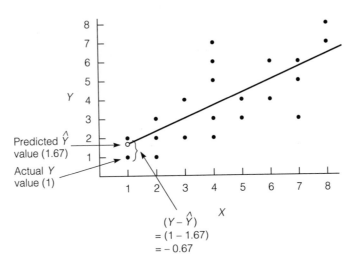

Figure 10.11

$$s^2_{\text{Error}} = \frac{\Sigma(Y - \hat{Y})^2}{N - 2} = \frac{\text{SS}_{\text{Error}}}{\text{df}_{\text{Error}}}$$

and define "error" variance. The term *error* is used here since, as indicated earlier, the residuals are the errors that result from using the linear model to predict Y values from X.

For the example data, the computations are

X	Y	$\hat{Y}$	$Y - \hat{Y}$	$(Y - \hat{Y})^2$
3	4	3.03	0.97	0.94
5	4	4.39	−0.39	0.15
1	1	1.67	−0.67	0.45
.	.	.	.	.
.	.	.	.	.
.	.	.	.	.
8	7	6.43	0.57	0.32
4	6	3.71	2.29	5.24
4	2	3.71	−1.71	2.92

$$41.16 = \Sigma(Y - \hat{Y})^2$$
$$= \text{SS}_{\text{Error}}$$

so that

$$s^2_{\text{Error}} = \frac{\Sigma(Y - \hat{Y})^2}{N - 2} = \frac{\text{SS}_{\text{Error}}}{\text{df}_{\text{Error}}}$$

$$= \frac{41.16}{21 - 2}$$

$$= 2.17.$$

The square root of the variance, the standard deviation, is the preferred measure of spread for describing a single variable. In the same way, the square root of the error variance is a much more useful measure. The quantity

$$s_{est} = \sqrt{s^2{}_{Error}} = \sqrt{\frac{\Sigma(Y - \widehat{Y})^2}{N - 2}} = \sqrt{\frac{SS_{Error}}{df_{Error}}}$$

is known as the *standard error of estimate* and is simply the standard deviation of the $\widehat{Y}$ scores, *taken around the regression line* instead of the mean. In short, it's a two-dimensional measure of spread, like the standard deviation in a single variable, based on our two-dimensional center, the regression line. For the example data,

$$s_{est} = \sqrt{s^2{}_{Error}} = \sqrt{2.17}$$
$$= 1.47.$$

Subdividing Variability. Earlier we mentioned that a variance could be divided into separate parts, each representing a contributor to the overall variation. The ability to subdivide variance is a powerful tool in statistics. In this section we will introduce this process as it's related to linear regression. In Chapters 15–20, the same principles lead to a powerful inferential analysis procedure, known appropriately as the *analysis of variance*.

Let's go back to the scatterplot of the X and Y variables that we have been using throughout this section and think about an "alternative" linear model, one with the equation

$$\widehat{Y} = 0X + \overline{Y}.$$

This model has zero slope, and the intercept is at the mean of the Y values. Clearly, this model will predict $\overline{Y}$ for any X; the plot and the line, with two example residuals, appear in Figure 10.12. With this simple linear model, we're just predicting values of Y by using $\overline{Y}$, and that's not much of a regression at all. In fact, that's just what we'd do if we didn't know anything about the correlation between X and Y.

The residuals in Figure 10.12 are, as usual, the differences between the predicted Y values and the actual scores. But since the model predicts $\overline{Y}$ for all values, what we're really showing in Figure 10.12, of course, is the differences $(Y - \overline{Y})$ and not differences from a predicted Y value at all. Or are we? One way of looking at these $Y - \overline{Y}$ differences is as "errors of prediction" if we were to use $\overline{Y}$ as a best guess at the values of Y. In other words, if we had no information about the relationship between X and Y, and if we were to try to predict a Y value, then our best guess would be $\overline{Y}$, since it's the least squares center of Y. In this sense, the variance is a measure of the error in our prediction because it's an average of the differences between scores and their "predicted" value—in this case, the arithmetic mean.

Suppose that a linear model predicting Y from X improves the "goodness" of the estimate over using $\overline{Y}$; that is, the least squares line modeling the X, Y relationship comes closer to the data than does the "line" represented by $\overline{Y}$. In this case, the variability around the regression line should be less than the

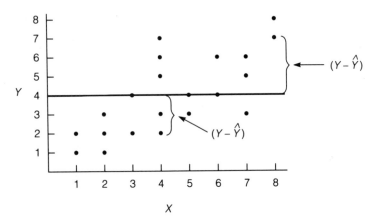

Figure 10.12

variability of Y around its mean (measured as s_Y). In other words, if the least squares line is a better predictor of Y than is $\bar{Y}$, then s_{est} should be less than s_Y. The ability to predict Y from X has reduced the variability of Y and done so to an extent that's related to the correlation between the variables. In fact, we can compute the standard error of estimate in the following way:

$$s_{est} = s_Y\sqrt{1 - r^2}\sqrt{\frac{N}{N - 2}},$$

where r is the Pearson product-moment correlation coefficient.*

In the example, we have

$$s_{est} = s_Y\sqrt{1 - r^2}\sqrt{\frac{N}{N - 2}}$$

$$= 2.02\sqrt{1 - .72^2}\sqrt{\frac{21}{21 - 2}}$$

$$= 1.47,$$

which is the same value obtained earlier.

The preceding formulas use the squared Pearson r. In fact, r^2 is an important value. To see why, let's return to the example data once more, and look carefully at just one subject, the one with $X = 8$ and $Y = 7$.

---

* Many statistics texts present the formula as

$$s_{est} = s_Y\sqrt{(1 - r^2)},$$

since for most sets of data the fraction

$$\frac{N}{N - 2}$$

will be very close to 1.0.

10 Regression and Linear Prediction

X	Y	$\hat{Y}$	$Y - \hat{Y}$	$Y - \bar{Y}$
3	4	3.03	0.97	−0.05
5	4	4.39	−0.39	−0.05
1	1	1.67	−0.67	−3.05
.	.	.	.	.
.	.	.	.	.
.	.	.	.	.
8	7	6.43	0.57	2.95
4	6	3.71	2.29	1.95
4	2	3.71	−1.71	−2.05

For this subject, the predicted Y value is 6.43, so that the residual for this subject —showing how far the prediction "missed" the actual value of 7—is 0.57. On the right side of the table, we also show that the difference between original Y value and $\bar{Y}$—that is, $(Y - \bar{Y})$—is 2.95 since for these data, $\bar{Y} = 4.05$. Graphically, the values are represented in Figure 10.13.

Now recall that if we didn't have a regression formula and were predicting Y values we would use $\bar{Y}$ as the best guess. In that case, we would have "guessed" a value of 4.05 for the subject, "missing" the actual value by $(7 - 4.05) = 2.95$, as shown in Figure 10.13. Also recall that the quantity $(Y - \bar{Y})$ is a component of the variance of Y. The illustration thus shows that that quantity—$(Y - \bar{Y}) = (7 - 4.05) = 2.95$—is made up of two individual parts. One part is the difference between the actual Y value and that predicted by the linear model, namely $Y - \hat{Y}$; the other part is the difference between the predicted value and the mean, specifically $\hat{Y} - \bar{Y}$. As illustrated, the two smaller components add together to make up the quantity $(Y - \bar{Y})$. Algebraically,

$$(Y - \bar{Y}) = (\hat{Y} - \bar{Y}) + (Y - \hat{Y})$$
$$(7 - 4.05) = (6.43 - 4.05) + (7 - 6.43)$$
$$2.95 = 2.95.$$

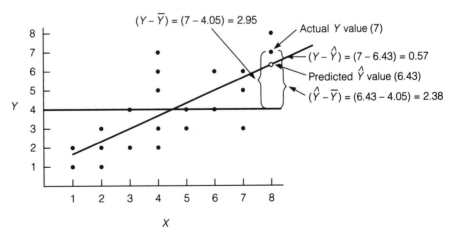

Figure 10.13

The left-hand side of the equation, $(Y - \bar{Y})$, is part of the numerator of the formula for the variance of Y. To complete the variance numerator and obtain the sum of squares for Y, we square the $(Y - \bar{Y})$ quantities, and then sum them to obtain $\Sigma(Y - \bar{Y})^2$.

What would happen (algebraically) if we were to square and sum both sides of the subdivided $(Y - \bar{Y})$ expression? After some algebra that we'll leave to others, we would have

$$\Sigma(Y - \bar{Y})^2 = \Sigma(\hat{Y} - \bar{Y})^2 + \Sigma(Y - \hat{Y})^2.$$

Two of the elements of this expression should already be familiar; the sum of squares (SS) for Y is on the left side, and the right-most term is the sum of squares for error. The remaining quantity, $\Sigma(\hat{Y} - Y)^2$, is often called the sum of squares for Y, or for regression. So now we have

$$\Sigma(Y - \bar{Y})^2 = \Sigma(\hat{Y} - \bar{Y})^2 + \Sigma(Y - \hat{Y})^2,$$
$$SS_Y = SS_{\hat{Y}} + SS_{Error}$$

or, using the more common name for the sum of squares based on the differences between the predicted $\hat{Y}$ values and the mean of Y,

$$SS_Y = SS_{Regression} + SS_{Error}.$$

Just what does this expression tell us? It says that the variability around $\bar{Y}$ (expressed as a sum of squares instead of a variance) can be thought of as having two parts, an error part and a regression part. The error part is based on the amount by which the linear model "misses" the actual values of the Y variable. The other component is the difference between the "error" part and the overall variation around $\bar{Y}$; it is the part of the variability in Y that represents an *improvement* in our predictability as a function of the model. Since the sum of squares for error will generally be less than the original sum of squares for Y, the difference represents the reduction in the variability that can be attributed to the regression.

We can express the improvement as a proportion of the total Y variability by writing the ratio

$$\frac{SS_{Regression}}{SS_Y}.$$

This fraction, the ratio of the sum of squares for regression to the sum of squares for Y, is an important quantity. It tells us that a proportion of the variability in Y can be accounted for if we have knowledge of X and can use the relationship between X and Y in predicting Y values.

The ratio is also important because it's related to the Pearson product-moment correlation coefficient; in fact,

$$r^2 = \frac{SS_{Regression}}{SS_Y}.$$

In other words, the square of Pearson's r gives the proportion of the variance of Y that is predictable from X. For this reason, the square of Pearson's r assumes considerable importance in understanding the strength of a relationship. A

Table 10.2

X	Y	$\hat{Y}$	$Y - \hat{Y}$	$(Y - \hat{Y})^2$	$(Y - \bar{Y})^2$	$(\hat{Y} - \bar{Y})^2$
3	4	3.03	0.97	0.94	0.00	0.94
5	4	4.39	-0.39	0.15	0.00	0.15
1	1	1.67	-0.67	0.45	9.00	5.43
.	.	.	.	.		
.	.	.	.	.		
.	.	.	.	.		
8	7	6.43	0.57	0.32	9.00	5.90
4	6	3.71	2.29	5.24	4.00	0.08
4	2	3.71	-1.71	2.92	4.00	0.08
				41.16	86.00	44.84
				$\Sigma(Y - \hat{Y})^2$	$\Sigma(Y - \bar{Y})^2$	$\Sigma(\hat{Y} - \bar{Y})^2$
				SS_{Error}	SS_Y	$SS_{Regression}$

correlation between two variables of, say, 0.6, represents a moderate, positive relationship. But a correlation of 0.6 means that the relationship between the two variables can account for only $0.6^2 = 0.36$, or 36%, of the Y variation.

In our example, we may illustrate the relationships by returning once again to the data set shown in Table 10.2. Two additional columns are shown, illustrating the computation of the sum of squares for Y and the sum of squares for regression. With these figures, we can illustrate that the components do sum properly:

$$SS_Y = SS_{Regression} + SS_{Error}$$
$$86.00 = 44.84 + 41.16.$$

Finally, we can complete the demonstration by computing the ratio of the two sum of squares:

$$r^2 = \frac{SS_{Regression}}{SS_Y}$$

$$= \frac{44.84}{86.00} = 0.52 = .72^2 = r^2.$$

Using Residuals. In addition to using residuals to help to explain a subdivision of variability and a measure of spread, we can use them in several ways in an actual analysis. Here we'll talk only about using residual plots to check on the linearity of the relationship.

Everything that we have developed so far is based on the assumption that a linear model is an appropriate representation for the relationship between variables. While there are precise techniques for testing whether that is the case, they would take us too far afield. Instead, we'll recommend two visual checks on linearity. The first check, which we advocated earlier, was to merely look at the scatterplot of the two variables and let the eyeball be the judge. The second check, though it still relies on the eye, is more likely to reveal a departure from linearity.

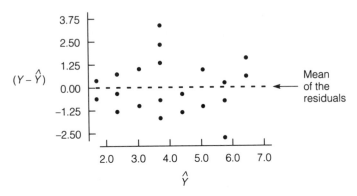

Figure 10.14

If a linear model adequately describes the relationship between X and Y, then there should be no relationship between the residuals and the predicted values. A scatterplot of the residuals against $\widehat{Y}$, as shown in Figure 10.14, should show the points centered on the residual's mean of zero and a roughly even spread above and below the zero line. A nonlinear pattern of the points, a sloping pattern in the points, or an uneven distribution above and below the zero line indicates that the linear model was not appropriate.

Predicting the "Other Way"— X from Y

Throughout our discussion, we have been calling the variable whose values are to be predicted "Y," and we've called the variable used for predicting "X." While this naming of the variables follows a statistician's standard procedure, there's no reason for us to limit our thinking to Y as the predicted variable. Let's reverse the variables and think of predicting an X for a given Y. In other words, instead of using the linear model

$$\widehat{Y} = bX + a,$$

yielding a Y value, we would use

$$\widehat{X} = bY + a.$$

But be careful; this isn't the same b and a that was used in predicting Y from X. Remember that in our original development of the least squares model we defined the criterion for b and a to be that $\Sigma(Y - \widehat{Y})^2$ was a minimum. In other words, we wanted the predicted Y's to be as close to the actual Y's as possible. The illustrations of the differences between Y and $\widehat{Y}$ were shown as vertical distance (Figure 10.15). In predicting X, though, the criterion must be that the fits to *the X values* are as good as possible—that is, they minimize $\Sigma(X - \widehat{X})^2$—and the differences are in the other direction. For example, suppose that we want to predict the X value for $Y = 6$. If the regression line is as shown in Figure 10.16, then the $\widehat{X}$ value is 5.98; the predicted value overestimates one of the values and underestimates the other.

In addition, the line that best fits the X values won't usually be the same one that best fits the Y values. In fact, for our example data, the formula is

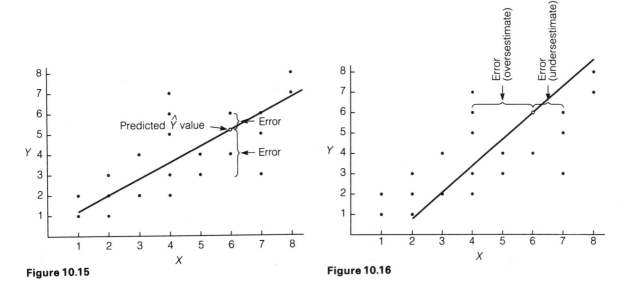

Figure 10.15

Figure 10.16

$$\widehat{X} = 0.77Y + 1.36.$$

For predicting Y, the formula was

$$\widehat{Y} = 0.68X + 0.99.$$

In other words, we have two different formulas, with two different a and b values. Until now, we've been able to just use the letters b and a for slope and intercept without confusion; but since two values for each can be confusing, statisticians developed a simple scheme for keeping their symbols clearly separate—subscripts. When we must differentiate between the intercept and slope for predicting Y from X and the a and b for predicting X from Y, we'll use the two-letter subscript scheme

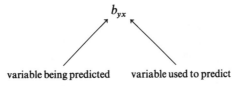

variable being predicted   variable used to predict

When Y is the predicted variable, the subscript is yx, and when X is predicted, the subscript is xy. Thus the two linear models are

$$\widehat{Y} = b_{yx}X + a_{yx}$$
$$\widehat{X} = b_{xy}Y + a_{xy}.$$

The first model that we developed was for Y predicted from X, and thus the a and b that we have been using all along are correctly known as a_{yx} and b_{yx}, while those for predicting the "other way" are a_{xy} and b_{xy}.

The formulas for predicting X are easily obtained from the formulas of a_{yx} and b_{yx} by simply replacing every X with a Y and vice versa. The original formulas, those for predicting Y from the values of X, are

$$b_{yx} = \frac{\text{cov}(X, Y)}{s^2_X} = r\frac{s_Y}{s_X} = \frac{N\Sigma XY - (\Sigma X)(\Sigma Y)}{N\Sigma X^2 - (\Sigma X)^2}.$$

For predicting the "other way," the corresponding formulas are

$$b_{xy} = \frac{\text{cov}(X, Y)}{s^2_Y} = r\frac{s_X}{s_Y} = \frac{N\Sigma XY - (\Sigma X)(\Sigma Y)}{N\Sigma Y^2 - (\Sigma Y)^2}.$$

In a similar fashion, the formulas for the intercept are

$$a_{yx} = \overline{Y} - b_{yx}\overline{X}$$

for our original formula (predicting Y from X), and

$$a_{xy} = \overline{X} - b_{xy}\overline{Y}$$

for predicting the "other way."

The two regression lines for the example data, those for $\hat{Y}$ and for $\hat{X}$, are graphed in Figure 10.17. The reason that there are two formulas, and therefore two lines, is that there is a difference in the criteria for fit. Had all of the points in the scatterplot been along a single line, then the two lines would have been identical. If there's any variation about such a hypothetical line of perfect agreement, then there will always be two different slopes.

There is a very close relationship between the slopes of the lines and the correlation coefficient. The Pearson product-moment correlation coefficient was defined in several ways in Chapter 9, and now we'll conclude with two additional ways of looking at it. First, given the slopes of the two lines, one for predicting Y from X and the other for predicting X from Y, Pearson's r may be defined as

$$r = \sqrt{b_{yx}b_{xy}}.$$

The Pearson product-moment correlation coefficient is the square root of the product of the two slopes. The square root of the product of two values is called the geometric mean, a form of "average" that we didn't introduce in Chapter 6. Thus r is an average of the two slopes. If the slopes of both lines are equal to 1.0, then the correlation will be also. But any other values for the slopes will imply less than perfect correlation.

And finally, a nice geometric interpretation of the relationship between regression and correlation is provided by the fact that the correlation coefficient is a function of the angle between the two regression lines. If the correlation between the two variables is zero, then knowledge of one variable would in no way help in predicting the other. In that case, the best prediction of Y would be $\overline{Y}$, and the best prediction for X would be $\overline{X}$. The plot of those two lines are at right angles to each other (Figure 10.18) with the two "best-fitting" lines intersecting at right (90°) angles. On the other hand, a perfect correlation of 1.0 has the two lines coinciding completely, with an angle of 0° separating them. The trigonometric *cosine* function will transform the 0° to 90° angular measurement into a 0–1 value, so that we can define

$$r = \cos(\theta),$$

where θ is the angle between the two regression lines.

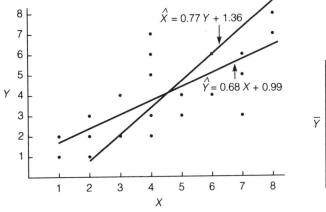

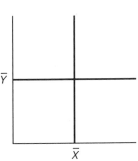

Figure 10.17

Figure 10.18

The Idea of Multiple Regression

The preceding pages in this chapter developed a logic for predicting one variable from another. We used the linear equation for modeling the relationship between the two variables. The equation that defined the line was then used for making predictions about one variable. Suppose that, instead of a single X (*predictor* or *independent*) variable, we had two of them, and a single Y (*criterion* or *dependent*) variable.* We now are in a *multiple regression* situation, instead of a *bivariate* one. In multiple regression there is one Y (dependent) variable but multiple X variables. The X variables are normally called X_1, X_2, and so forth. In any given research setting, naturally, Y and all of the X's would have more descriptive names (for example, Final exam score, Quiz 1, Quiz 2, Midterm exam, etc.).

In bivariate linear regression, a linear model is constructed for predicting Y from X. The same is true in multiple regression, except that the prediction is done from a linear combination of all of the X variables.

We might represent a relationship between three variables (Y, X_1, and X_2) as a three-dimensional plot (see Figure 10.19). Here, the points are in a three-dimensional space defined by two X variables and a single Y variable. As in the two-dimensional case, each point represents a score of a single subject. For example, if all three of the variables have values in the range 1–5, then a subject with $X_1 = 4$, $X_2 = 3$, and $Y = 4$ might appear in the plot as illustrated in Figure 10.20.

In two dimensions, the model of the relationship between two variables was the line. If we were to model this relationship in three dimensions, the natural extension of the line into two dimensions is a plane, so that a best-fitting plane might look like that in Figure 10.21. The equation for this particular plane is

---

*Note the use of the words *independent variable* and *dependent variable* in a different sense than we have used before. In regression, the variable to be predicted (Y) is often called the *dependent variable* (or sometimes the criterion variable), while the variables that do the predicting (X variables) are called *predictors* or *independent variables*.

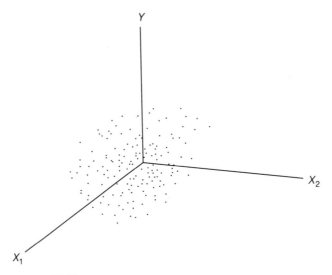

Figure 10.19

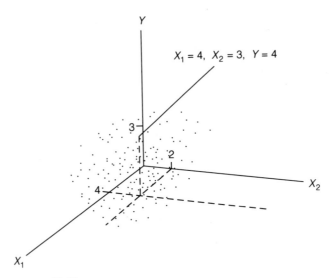

Figure 10.20

$$Y = 0.007703X_1 + 0.616280X_2 + 36.7333.$$

In the equation, there are two "slopes," one for each of the two X variables, and an intercept. The equation is linear, but in three dimensions. For any pair of X values, the equation gives the predicted value on the Y axis.

There's no reason why, other than computational difficulty (and that can be considerable), we need consider only two X's and one Y. In principle, there can be any number of X variables, combined to predict a single Y variable. We can't draw a space of greater than three dimensions, of course, but we can conceive of it, and the appropriate mathematics can provide both a representation and a way to carry out the computations.

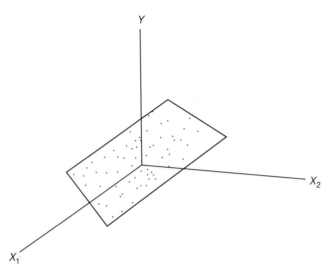

Figure 10.21

The mathematics of fitting a multidimensional plane so that it minimizes $\Sigma(Y - \widehat{Y})^2$ is difficult, and the computations are cumbersome. But if there's a computer nearby to do the computations for us, we don't have to worry. (No one ever does a multiple regression "by hand" anymore.) Most statistical programs can compute the regression coefficients (slopes) and the constant (the intercept) that will produce the best-fitting plane for any set of data. While we won't illustrate the formulas (they're best expressed using matrix algebra) or the computations (they're best done by computer), you should be aware that it's a very short step from the bivariate situation that we have presented in this chapter to the multivariate case. We'll not pursue the matter further in this text; as you continue your study in psychology, you will often encounter multivariate research. You should be prepared to take a course in which you learn about multivariate statistics, and the different ways of approaching research that they permit.

S U M M A R Y

- Predicting one variable from another is usually called "regression."
- Regression uses a linear model to predict values on one variable from another variable.
- A linear equation has two components: the slope gives the rate of climb of the line, and the intercept shows where the line intersects the ordinate.
- The linear model developed in this chapter fits the data "best" in terms of a least squares criterion—the quantity $\Sigma(Y - \widehat{Y})^2$ is minimized.
- The linear model may be used to predict values on the Y variable by entering an X into the equation and computing the value of $\widehat{Y}$.
- A residual is the difference between a predicted and an actual value; the sum of the squared residuals gives a sum of squares for error.

- The standard error of estimate gives the spread around the regression line and is a measure of how well the model fits the data.
- The square of the Pearson product-moment correlation coefficient gives the proportion of the Y variability that can be predicted from the X variable.

KEY TERMS

b_{xy}	Regression
b_{yx}	Residual
Intercept	Slope
Least squares	SS_{Error}
Linear model	$SS_{Residual}$
Multiple regression	SS_Y
r^2	Standard error of estimate

EXERCISES

Solutions to asterisked (∗) exercises appear at the back of the book. Exercises preceded by a section symbol (§) must be solved using a computer. Exercises preceded by a dagger (†) can be solved by hand.

∗†1. Use the data from Exercise 9.1 for these questions.
  a. Find the linear model for predicting Quiz 2 from Quiz 1 using the least squares method.
  b. Compute the predicted Quiz 2 values using the least squares models that you developed in part (a).
  c. Calculate the residuals from the predictions in part (b).
  d. Find the sum of squares $[\Sigma(Y - \hat{Y})^2]$ for the residuals from part (c).
  e. Calculate the standard error of estimate for your least squares model by using the residuals.
  f. Find the least squares model for predicting Quiz 1 from Quiz 2. Calculate Pearson's r as the geometric mean of the two slopes. How well does that value agree with the answer that you had for Exercise 9.1?
  g. Plot the residuals from the least squares model against the predicted values. Does it look like the linear model is acceptable for these data, based on the discussion in this chapter? Why or why not?

†2. Use the data from Exercise 9.3 for these questions.
  a. Find the linear model for predicting Y from X, and compute Pearson's r.
  b. Compute the predicted Y values using the model that you developed in part (a).

  c. Calculate the residuals from the predictions in part (b).
  d. Find the sum of squares $[\Sigma(Y - \hat{Y})^2]$ for the residuals from part (c).
  e. Calculate the standard error of estimate for your model by using the residuals.
  f. Find the least squares model for predicting X from Y. Calculate Pearson's r from the two slopes. How well does that value agree with the answer that you had for part (a)?
  g. Plot the residuals from the least squares model against the predicted values. Does it look like the linear model is acceptable for these data, based on the discussion in this chapter? Why or why not?
  h. In part (d) in Exercise 9.3, you tried several transformations, one of which may have made the relationship more linear than it was in the raw data. Repeat that transformation, and then repeat the computation from parts (a), (b), and (c) of this exercise (that is, get the residuals from a least squares model). Plot the residuals against the predicted values. Compare the results with those from part (g). Is the fit better now? Why or why not?

§3. Repeat Exercise 1 using the computer.

§4. Repeat Exercise 2 using the computer.

Statistical Inference and Classical Experimental Design

In Part One, we discussed the logic of science and presented some of the mechanical details involved in actually conducting research.

Part Two showed ways of presenting research results, using descriptive statistics, graphics, and words.

In Part Three, the focus is twofold. First, we continue to develop statistics, moving into the realm of inferential techniques. Inferential statistics let us infer beyond the data at hand to a larger world of subjects that haven't been observed or tested.

The second focus in Part Three is on classical experimental design, those ways of designing research that have served as the foundation for most of the work in psychology since its emergence as a scientific discipline. You're already familiar with some of the terms in this part of the book—experimental conditions, independent variable and dependent variable, control condition, and the like. Others will be less familiar—factorial design, analysis of variance, main effects and interactions, and so forth.

The presentations of inferential statistics and experimental design are intertwined to a considerable degree. Chapters 11 and 12 will develop the logical foundation for statistical inference. Then Chapters 13 through 19 develop increasingly sophisticated experimental designs along with their analyses. In Chapter 13, we apply the logic of inference in an experimental arrangement with a single condition. Chapter 14 expands the logic and the analysis to experiments with two distinct conditions. Chapters 15 through 17 develop experimental design further to incorporate multiple conditions, but with a single independent variable, for between-subjects and within-subjects experiments. The powerful inferential procedures of analysis of variance are first presented along with this material. Finally, Chapters 18 through 20 introduce designs with two independent variables for between-subjects and within-subjects experiments, along with their analyses.

Probability and Sampling Distributions

The preceding chapters explored techniques for describing the results of research investigations. Whether the focus was on the relationships among personality variables, as in Dr. Campbell's research, or on the effect of aversion conditioning on Dr. Stewart's animals, the intent was the same: to use the data to answer the researcher's question. But we have been limited in our conclusions, since we can't generalize beyond the individual set of data at hand.

How may we generalize beyond a single set of data? Are we confident that these data are correct? How certain are we that, if we repeated the observations with the same, or even different, subjects, we'd obtain essentially the same results?

To answer these questions, we need to turn to the methods of statistical inference. We rarely want our conclusion to apply to *only* the observations that we have at hand. Instead, we'll want to generalize to *all* students, to *all* rats, or to *all* people. Together, the techniques that allow such generalization are known as *inferential statistics*, and they are of several different kinds, in terms of both their logic and their methods. This chapter provides the foundation for an understanding of inference. In Chapter 12, we develop the logic of inference, and most of the remainder of the book applies the inference procedures in different experimental designs.

There are three common inferential procedures: point estimation, interval estimation, and hypothesis testing. Point estimation uses a single sample statistic as the "best guess" about a population parameter. Point estimates serve as the foundation for both of the other inference methods and will occupy an important place in our discussion. Interval estimation specifies a range of values and defines a confidence statement that the parameter falls in that range. Finally, hypothesis testing, the most widely used inferential technique, establishes pairs of hypothesized conditions and allows us to infer which is most likely to be true.

Populations and Samples

In Chapter 1 we discussed samples and populations. A sample is a small group of observations; for example, the group of 10 animals that were given aversion conditioning in Dr. Stewart's study was a *sample* drawn from the large population of animals that he might have used in his experiment. In the same way, Dr. Campbell's 84 individuals were also a sample of a very large number of people who might conceivably have participated in his research. In both cases, the word *sample* refers to a small group chosen from some larger group that we either didn't choose to observe or didn't have available to us. In Dr. Stewart's case, we may think of the 10 aversion-conditioned animals as a sample from a *population* of potentially studied rats, all of whom were aversion-conditioned. Likewise, the 10 animals in Dr. Stewart's control group are a sample from a population of animals not given aversion conditioning.

While Dr. Stewart is certainly interested in the difference between his two groups' consumption of various taste substances, his main concern is not just the behavior of the few animals that he happens to have. He wants to be able to draw a general conclusion about the difference between his two experimental conditions, not just between his particular subjects. He wants to say something about the similarity between the tastes of sugar and saccharin. But even beyond that, since the experiment was designed to study taste—a process known to be similar among a large number of animals, including humans—he wants to be able to draw a general conclusion about the similarity of the two sweet tastes. The task of inference is to draw a conclusion about a population, or populations, on the basis of the particular sample that we happen to have. Then, if the experiment is solidly conducted (that is, if it has internal validity), we can draw a conclusion beyond the specific variables and situation and make a statement about the underlying processes.

In common parlance, a population is a set of people who make up a well-defined (usually geographically defined) group. As such, we might speak of the population of the United States or the population of Seattle. In inferential statistics, though, the word has a more precise and limited meaning. Until now, our use of the terms *population* and *sample* have been a little careless. But now we need to be more precise in our definitions of samples and populations to avoid possible confusion later.

In statistical usage, a *population* is a *set of observations* that we might observe. Thus a population might consist of the midterm exam scores of the students in your statistics class; the IQ scores of all of the third-grade students in the state of Pennsylvania; the number of trials required to learn a certain list of 20 words by all college students past, present, and future; or the amounts of sucrose consumed by all rats who might ever be given aversion conditioning. You'll notice that there is little of the usual meaning of *population* here; the populations are sets of *scores*, not people or animals. In a sense, the people and the rats "carry" the test grades, the IQ scores, the number of words recalled, or the amounts consumed. But the members of the population are possible data values, not people or animals that happen to be associated with them.

Populations vary in size from small and finite (like the test scores in one class) to very large but finite (the IQs of all Pennsylvania third-grade students) to infinite in size (introversion/extraversion scores for all students . . .). With a very small population, there's usually little need for inference, since we can conceivably obtain all of the values. The population of IQ scores of all Pennsylvania third-grade students is very large, but not infinite; there are a fixed number of third-graders in the state on any given day, and so in theory we could obtain all of their IQ scores. As a practical matter, though, we'd never really be able to obtain them all—kids are absent, sick, or otherwise unavailable during the testing period. So, although the population is real, finite, and in principle "knowable," we would never really have all of the test scores. But if you're an educational researcher, it could be very important to have a good estimate of the IQ score of Pennsylvania third-graders, and so an inferential procedure is necessary. In order to make an inference, we begin with a sample.

A *sample* is a *subset* of *a population*. That definition means that a sample is a set of observations, typically those that we have in hand during a research investigation. In keeping with our discussion, though, remember that a sample does not consist of individual animals or third-grade children, but rather consists of the set of scores taken from the larger population. Note that nothing in the definition of *sample* says anything about whether a sample is representative of the population—a sample is just a subset. In addition, the definition of a sample doesn't imply anything about *how* a sample was selected.

Numerical characteristics of a population, such as a mean, a median, a skewness measure, or a standard deviation, are called *parameters*. Every population has measures that describe its center, its spread, and its form. Those values are parameters, since they pertain to the population. Usually we can't ever know the values directly. The mean IQ score for all Pennsylvania third-grade students, for example, is an actual value. We can't know it with absolute certainty, but it certainly exists. And that's why we need inferential statistics. In inferential statistics, the goal is to gain information about a parameter value—perhaps the form of the population distribution—or often to draw a conclusion about differences in parameters in two or more populations.

Just as there are numerical characteristics of populations, a sample also has summary values; a numerical characteristic of a sample is called a *statistic*. Thus both a population and a sample can have a median, a mean, a standard deviation, and so forth; the population values are *parameters*, while the *sample* values are *statistics*.

Statistical inference makes statements about parameters and does so on the basis of statistics. For example, the population might consist of all of the introversion/extraversion scores of all college students—an infinite population that we can't hope to study. Yet the values in that population define something of interest—namely, the personality structure of all college students. In order to draw conclusions about all students, we need to be able to say something about that population. But all we can ever hope to test is a few students—those in our sample. From the sample, we may compute the mean score; from that mean—the sample statistic—we want to be able to make an inference about the corresponding population parameter. The procedures of inference thus let us generalize to the population and also give us an indication of how comfortable we should be in the conclusions that we draw.

Statisticians customarily use Greek letters as symbols for population parameters and Roman letters for statistics. For example, the sample mean $\overline{X}$ is an estimate of the population mean μ (mu), and the sample product-moment correlation coefficient r estimates ρ. The sample standard deviation s estimates the parameter σ; and here we come to a slight problem.

In Chapter 7, we used the symbols s and s^2 to indicate the standard deviation and variance, respectively. The descriptive value for variance from Chapter 7,

$$s^2 = \frac{\Sigma(X - \overline{X})^2}{N},$$

was called the *sample* variance. And it is the correct variance for a sample. But it's not the best statistic to use for an estimate of σ^2.* In other words, the value given by this formula and its square root (the sample standard deviation) are suitable as descriptive values only. To compute a sample statistic to be used as an estimate of a parameter, we need a slightly modified formula; we'll provide such a formula in Chapter 12, where we'll also explain just why there's a difference.

For some parameters, statisticians don't seem to have a standard Greek letter. Rather than invent yet another idiosyncratic symbol system, we'll simply acknowledge that no agreed-upon symbol exists for the population median (and some other values as well) and just use words to describe those parameters.

A Brief Introduction to Probability

Statistical inference is based on the mathematics of probability. While we don't have to know much about probability for our purposes here, we do need to understand a little of its logic and terminology, as well as some of its important concepts before we can proceed further into inference.[†]

The term *probability* generally refers to the likelihood that some particular event will occur. While that's the sense in which we commonly use the word, there is somewhat more to it than that.

We often hear weather forecasts that contain the phrase "the probability of precipitation today is . . . ." Just what does that number mean? How did the weather bureau determine it? How should we interpret it?

Relative Frequency as Probability

A very useful way of thinking about probability is in terms of a long-run relative frequency. If your chemistry instructor has a favorite question (and most in-

---

[*]The Chapter 7 formula given here assumes that its data set is in fact the entire population. As such, the formula is a fine summary measure. But we'll usually need an estimate of σ, and so this formula isn't used very often.

[†]If you are interested in learning a bit more about probability theory, Lowry (1989) gives a very readable introduction. His book is intended for people who are using a book like this one and want to know a little more about probability theory.

structors do), the chances are that she keeps track of how students perform on that item. Suppose that over the years, the question has been used on many tests for a total of 300 students. If 180 of those students answered the item correctly, then the proportion, or *relative frequency*, of students scoring correctly is $180/300 = .60$ or 60%. We might also say that the probability of a student answering the item correctly is .60.

The "precipitation probabilities" that weather forecasters report are the same kinds of numbers. They're really relative frequencies and represent the proportion of the times when a weather situation similar to the present one has been followed by precipitation. (In fact, weather probabilities are not really probabilities at all, but descriptive statistics that communicate the fact that, in the recorded cases of the present weather patterns, a certain percentage was followed by precipitation.)

The relative frequency interpretation of probability is a useful one. It's not only a convenient and easily understood summary of past data, but it also suggests a reasonable way to predict future occurrences. Our instructor has every reason to expect that, if the same 60% question is used again, roughly 60% of the students will answer correctly.* In the same way, a weather forecaster's "80% chance of rain" means that on about 80% of the days following such a forecast, there should be rain. Weather forecasts don't come with a guarantee of accuracy; probabilities don't, either, but they provide some guidance in deciding on a wardrobe or test questions or even, as we'll see, on drawing a conclusion about a parameter.

Mathematical (or Axiomatic) Probability

If a mathematician is asked to define probability formally, the answer will probably go something like "A number between zero and one, inclusive, that attaches to an event, and is assigned in such a way that the sum of all of the probabilities of all of the events within a given situation is 1.0." That's not a very satisfying answer to most psychologists, but it's accurate from a mathematical point of view.

This mathematical definition has two important elements. Probabilities are generally expressed as numbers between 0 and 1, though sometimes a percentage figure ("80% chance of rain," for example) is more understandable. The important rule here is that the value can't be negative (though zero is certainly permissible) and can't exceed 1.0 (or 100%). The second part of the probability statement requires that probabilities add up to 1.0 (100%) over a certain set of possible occurrences. If you flip a coin, only two possible things can happen;† and if you assign a probability to "heads," the probability assigned to "tails" must be such that the two numbers sum to 1.0. Similarly, if past history suggests that the probability of getting a particular question right is .60, then the probability of "wrong" must be .40.

---

* If she is willing to assume that copies of her old exams aren't generally available to current students, that is.
† Coins never *really* land on edge, do they?

Table 11.1   Categories of Statistics Questions

Kind of question	Number of questions	Probability
Measures of center	18	.144
Measures of spread	16	.128
Frequency distributions	17	.136
z scores	10	.080
Normal curve areas	9	.072
Scatterplots	12	.096
Correlation	18	.144
Percentiles	15	.120
Percentile ranks	10	.080

Notice that the mathematical rules about probabilities don't say anything at all about the numbers being representative of a "likelihood" that some particular event will happen, nor do they give any guidance about how the probability values should be assigned. The mathematics of probability don't require any likelihood interpretation and proceed without any such possible real-world meaning. But that's part of the beauty of mathematics; its truths stand apart from any particular application that may be made of them.

Some Probability Rules. Let's suppose that you're a statistics instructor and that you have a file of 125 test questions on descriptive statistics. The questions can be categorized into groups as shown in Table 11.1. Now suppose that you decide to test your students individually. When a student comes to your office, you'll reach into a hat and pull out a question at random.

When the first student comes in, what is the probability that you ask a z-score question? Since there are 125 test items in the hat and since 10 of them are z-score questions, if you really are picking randomly, the probability of drawing a z-score question is 10/125, or .080. Likewise, the probability of picking a correlation question is 18/125 or .144.

To the mathematician, each question that you might draw is called an *outcome*. In the testing example, an *outcome* is one of the possible occurrences when one item is drawn from the hat. There are 125 possible outcomes—any one of the questions could be drawn.

Suppose that the possible scores on the sensation-seeking scale that Dr. Campbell uses are the integer values 1–50, inclusive. There are 50 possible values, and each of them can be regarded as an outcome. When Dr. Campbell administers that scale to a student, the score is an outcome.

An *event* is a collection of one or more outcomes. Thus there are 10 outcomes in the event "z-score question," 18 outcomes in the event "correlation question," and so forth. If Dr. Campbell defines a score of 10 or less to be "non-adventurous," then any time he finds a score of 10 or less, he has observed the event "non-adventurous."

If all of the outcomes are equally likely (the questions that you might ask on a statistics quiz are all on the same size index cards, the cards are well

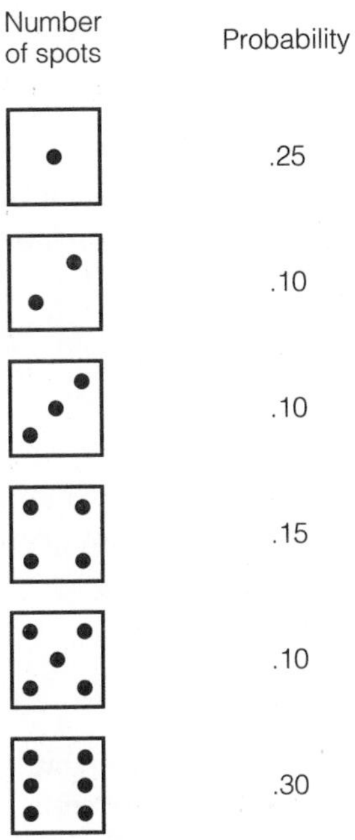

Number of spots	Probability
•	.25
(2 spots)	.10
(3 spots)	.10
(4 spots)	.15
(5 spots)	.10
(6 spots)	.30

Figure 11.1

scrambled in the hat, and so forth), we may define the simplest of the probability rules: when the outcomes are equally likely, the probability of an event is

$$\frac{\text{number of outcomes in the event}}{\text{total number of outcomes}}.$$

The probability of the event "ask a correlation question" then is

$$\frac{18}{125} = .144.$$

If we make a rule that each outcome can be a part of only one event (there are no questions that ask about both z-scores and correlations, for example), then defining events in this way meets the two requirements that we stated previously—the events have a probability between 0 and 1, and the probabilities sum to 1.0. (If there are outcomes that can be members of more than one event, the rules become more complicated.)

If the outcomes aren't equally likely (as is probably the case on Dr. Campbell's sensation-seeking scale), we would have to change the rule a bit:

sum of the individual probabilities of outcomes in the event.

Suppose we had a loaded die* with the probabilities of each of the six sides as shown in Figure 11.1. The probability of the event "even number of spots" is

$$.10 + .15 + .30 = .55$$

---

*That's the singular form of dice—in this example, we're only throwing one of them.

since the three outcomes have different probabilities. The probability of "less than 3 spots" is

.25 + .10 = .35.

Returning to drawing statistics questions out of a hat, suppose we want to find the probability of the event "we ask a correlation or scatterplot question." There are 12 outcomes in "correlation" and 18 in "scatterplot," so the number of outcomes in the event is

$$\frac{12 + 18}{125} = \frac{30}{125} = .240.$$

Note that we could also express this as the sum of the two separate events. That is, the probability of "correlation or scatterplot question" is

$$\frac{12}{125} + \frac{18}{125} = .240$$

$$= \text{Prob(correlation)} + \text{Prob(scatterplot)}.$$

This brings us to the next important probability rule, the *addition rule*: the probability of either of two non-overlapping events occurring is the sum of their separate probabilities. The addition rule is often called the *or* rule, since it deals with the occurrence of either "scatterplot" *or* "correlation."

Suppose that we ask two statistics questions, drawing each one randomly. (To keep the example simple, assume that you put the first question back into the hat after you ask it, so that the second pick is from the same 125 questions. We wouldn't really do it that way, of course, but it simplifies the example.) What's the probability, within the two questions, of asking either a correlation or a regression question? The probability is the sum of the two probabilities, as before.

What if we ask the probability of the event "asking *two* correlation questions"? Now we must introduce the *multiplication rule*: The probability of two independent* events occurring jointly is the product of their separate probabilities. (This is sometimes called the *and* rule, since it defines the probability that both of two events occur.) For our example, the probability is

Prob(correlation) × Prob(correlation) = (.144)(.144) = .021.

In the same way, we can find the probability of asking both a percentile and a percentile rank question. That probability is found by the multiplication rule as

Prob(percentile) × Prob(percentile rank) = (.120)(.080) = .0096.

As one more example, the probability of the event "z score and correlation" is

Prob(z scores) × Prob(correlation) = (.080)(.144) = .0115.

---

*The term *independent* here means that one event has no effect on the probability of the other. That is, the fact that we've drawn and asked a z-score question, for example, shouldn't change the probability of drawing a correlation question. If the first question is returned to the hat after it's been asked, then that requirement is met.

Table 11.2   Descriptive or Normal Curve Questions

Kind of question	Number of questions	Probability
Measures of center	18	.144
Measures of spread	16	.128
Frequency distributions	17	.136
z scores	10	.080
Normal curve areas	9	.072
Total	70	

Let's define two new events: "ask descriptive statistics question" and "ask a normal curve question." The first event is made up of the separate events "center," "spread," "frequency distributions," and "z scores," and its probability is

$$\frac{18}{125} + \frac{16}{125} + \frac{17}{125} + \frac{10}{125} = \frac{61}{125} = .488.$$

The second event contains the separate events "z scores" and "normal curve areas," and so its probability is

$$\frac{10}{125} + \frac{9}{125} = \frac{19}{125} = .152.$$

Now the probability of the event "Ask either a descriptive or a normal curve question" might appear to be

Prob(descriptive question) + Prob(normal question)

= .488 + .152

= .640,

but that's incorrect. To see why, let's list the separate events that go into the event "Ask either a descriptive or a normal curve question" (Table 11.2). There are a total of 70 outcomes in the event, and

$$\frac{70}{125} = .560 \neq .640.$$

What happened? We included one set of questions (z scores) twice, since it was included in both events. The situation is diagrammed in Figure 11.2. The numbers of outcomes for each of the events is shown. Calculating the probability for the "normal curve" event, for example, sums the outcomes in "normal areas" and "z scores." In the same way, calculating the probability for "descriptives" summed the outcomes in "center," "frequency," "spread," and "z scores." Thus when the probabilities of those two events were added, the 10 outcomes in "z scores" were included twice. Correcting this difficulty leads to the complete statement of the addition rule: *The probability of either of two events occurring is the sum of their separate probabilities, minus the probability of their joint*

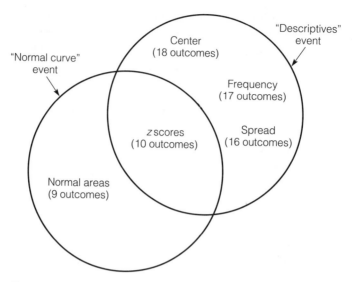

Figure 11.2

occurrence. In this case, we have

$$\text{Prob(descriptives)} + \text{Prob(normal)} - \text{Prob(descriptives and normal)}$$

$$= \underbrace{\frac{18}{125} + \frac{16}{125} + \frac{17}{125} + \frac{10}{125}}_{\text{Descriptives}} + \underbrace{\frac{10}{125} + \frac{9}{125}}_{\text{Normal}} - \underbrace{\frac{10}{125}}_{\substack{\text{Descriptives} \\ \text{and Normal}}}$$

$$= \frac{70}{125} = .560.$$

Bernoulli's Theorem. The seventeenth-century Swiss mathematician Jakob Bernoulli is perhaps best known for his contributions to the development of the calculus. He also made a major contribution to probability mathematics in the theorem that bears his name. Bernoulli's Theorem, also known as the *Law of Large Numbers*, provides a mathematical basis for the frequency interpretation of probability. In essence, the theorem states that if some event has a probability P, then, over a series of N trials, the frequency with which the event occurs approaches $P \times N$ as N increases. In terms of the statistics quiz example, this means that, if the instructor continues to sample from his hatful of questions over a very large number of testing occasions, he should ask a "centers" question about 14.4% of the time (since the probability of "centers" is .144), a "spread" question about 12.8% of the time, and so forth.

Bernoulli's theorem applies only over the "long run." There's no requirement that out of, say, 1,000 draws from the hat, there will be *exactly* 144 "centers" questions. The theorem is phrased mathematically as a limit theorem, meaning that as N increases indefinitely, the frequency approaches its theoretical (or limiting) value.

Sampling Distributions

Suppose that you and your classmates write your weights on individual slips of paper. Those values constitute a small population of weights. The mean of the weights, μ, is a parameter, since it is a characteristic of a population. Now put all of the slips with weights on them into a hat and pull out two of them at random. Those two slips contain weights and are a sample of size $N = 2$ from the population. We could compute the mean for that sample of $N = 2$. Now return the two weights to the hat, repeat the random sampling, and calculate the mean. If we did that simple sampling and calculating exercise a number of times, we would have a number of sample means, each based on samples of size 2 and each drawn from the same population.

Unless everyone in your class weighs exactly the same, the sample means won't all be equal; even though the population mean weight doesn't change, the samples won't be identical. There will be a distribution of values of the sample mean.

For example, suppose your population of weights contained the 30 values

129	149	127	137	162	113
145	145	138	130	129	161
128	155	120	152	127	154
156	129	147	153	111	163
150	126	145	181	102	133

The mean of these weights is 139.9 pounds. Since the entire set of student weights constitutes a population, 139.9 is the population mean μ.

Here's a list of several of the possible samples of $N = 2$ that we could obtain from the population, with the mean of each sample given:

Sample	Mean
(129, 155)	142.0
(149, 120)	134.5
(127, 152)	139.5
(137, 127)	132.0
(162, 154)	158.0
(113, 156)	134.5
(145, 129)	137.0
(145, 147)	146.0
(138, 153)	145.5
(130, 111)	120.5
(129, 163)	146.0
(161, 150)	155.5
(128, 126)	127.0

Even though all of the means come from the same population, the samples are different, and so are their means. In fact, the means of the samples have a distribution themselves. Figure 11.3 shows that there is variability among the sample means. The sample means do cluster around the population mean of 139.9.* But none of the individual means is equal to μ.

---

*The mean of this set of 13 sample means is 139.85.

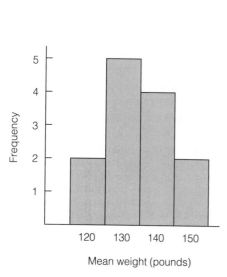

Mean weight (pounds)

Figure 11.3

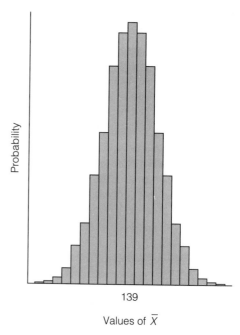

139

Values of $\overline{X}$

Figure 11.4

The example showed only a few of the possible samples of $N = 2$ that we could have taken from the population. We could have written out *all* of the possible samples of $N = 2$ (there are 435 such samples), but we won't. If we had, though, we would have been able to find the mean for each sample. Each mean would be an outcome, just as picking a question to ask is an outcome. Since each of the 435 samples is as likely as any other, each possible mean (or outcome) would have the probability of $1/435 = .0023$. We could group the sample means into convenient intervals, each comprising an event (for example, $\overline{X}$ between 100 and 105, $\overline{X}$ between 105 and 110, and so forth). By summing the probabilities of the means within each event, we could find the probability for each event. A plot of the probabilities might look something like Figure 11.4. This distribution gives the probability of each possible mean that we could observe by taking samples of $N = 2$ from the population of 30 student weights. A distribution that gives the probabilities of possible values of a statistic is called a *sampling distribution*.

A sampling distribution is a formal and abstract way of describing the probability of all of the possible values of a statistic. It is usually a theoretical distribution, meaning that we don't normally actually list all of the possible values of a statistic and find their probabilities. If we have some way to know the form, the spread, and the center of all possible sample statistic values, then we can specify probabilities of various events precisely. And that will be valuable, since it's the sampling distribution that allows us to make inferences.

An Example Sampling Distribution

Suppose that you're an instructor and you write a short quiz containing four true-false items. Let's assume that your students haven't read their assignment and will be guessing at each answer. Under these conditions, it's reasonable to

Table 11.3   Possible Patterns of T-F Answers

Question				
1	2	3	4	#Correct
T	T	T	T	2
T	T	T	F	3
T	T	F	T	3
T	F	T	T	1
F	T	T	T	1
T	T	F	F	4
T	F	T	F	2
T	F	F	T	2
F	F	T	T	0
F	T	F	T	2
F	T	T	F	2
F	F	F	T	1
F	F	T	F	1
F	T	F	F	3
T	F	F	F	3
F	F	F	F	2

assign a probability of .5 to the answer True and .5 to False. Some specific pattern (for instance, T-T-F-F) will be correct, but it's just one of 16 such possible patterns (like T-T-T-T, or T-F-T-T, or F-F-T-T, for example) that a student might guess.

If we were to write down the 16 possible patterns of T and F answers, they would look like Table 11.3. Assuming that the correct answers are T-T-F-F, the number of correct answers for each possible pattern is also shown. If we score a student's paper for the number of items correct, the possible scores are 0, 1, 2, 3, or 4. Only the T-T-F-F pattern represents a correct quiz paper. All of the others lead to one or more errors. There are four patterns that lead to a single error, six ways to make two errors, and so forth.

The 16 patterns of answers are outcomes in the simple experiment "give a student the quiz." If a student taking the quiz is really guessing, then each of the 16 outcomes is as likely as any other, giving a probability of 1/16 for each. Since that's the case, we can easily find the probabilities of several events. For example, the probability of the event "get three correct answers" is 4/16, since four of the 16 outcomes (T-T-T-F, T-T-F-T, F-T-F-F, and T-F-F-F) are in the event. We could define a set of events like "get zero right," "get 1 right," etc., and determine the probability of each by applying the counting rule. Table 11.4 shows the probabilities of the five possible "events" (actually, test scores). What we have succeeded in doing is developing a measurement rule ("Count the number of answers correct") and associating a probability with each possible measurement value (assuming, of course, that the students are actually guessing).

The probability distribution could be represented by a histogram that clearly shows the symmetry of the probabilities (Figure 11.5). This distribution represents the probabilities of a single student's receiving each possible grade, assuming that he or she is guessing. Getting two questions correct is the most

Table 11.4 Probabilities of Five Possible Events

Number of correct answers	Number of ways to get them	Probability
0	1	1/16 = .0625
1	4	4/16 = .2500
2	6	6/16 = .3750
3	4	4/16 = .2500
4	1	1/16 = .0625
	16	16/16 = 1.000

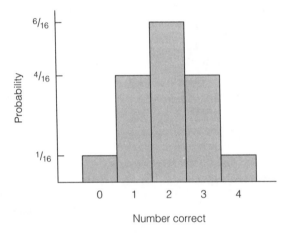

Figure 11.5

likely, and one and three are quite likely as well. But there's only a 1/16 probability that the students will guess correctly on all four. And it's just as likely that the student will guess wrong all four times.

In addition to having the unimodal, symmetric form illustrated, the distribution of possible test scores has a center and a spread. Computing the mean and standard deviation is straightforward. Using Table 11.3, compute the mean number of items correct (see Figure 11.6). Since we're dealing with a population of potential test scores, this value is a parameter. In words, this parameter tells us that if the students are merely guessing on the quiz, on the average they should have a score of 2.0 items correct.

But they won't all get 2.0 on the quiz, because there is spread in the distribution. We can also compute the standard deviation of the population by applying the formula:

$$\sigma = \sqrt{\frac{\Sigma(X - \bar{X})^2}{N}}$$

$$= \sqrt{\frac{(2 - 2)^2 + (3 - 2)^2 + \cdots + (3 - 2)^2 + (2 - 2)^2}{16}}$$

$$= 1.0.$$

1	2	3	4	#Correct
T	T	T	T	2
T	T	T	F	3
T	T	F	T	3
⋮		⋮		
F	F	T	F	1
F	T	F	F	3
T	F	F	F	3
F	F	F	F	2

$$\mu = (2 + 3 + 3 + \cdots + 1 + 3 + 3 + 2)/16 = 2.0$$

Figure 11.6

Table 11.5   Some Possible Outcomes for Two Students

Some possible samples		Mean correct	Probability of sample
John	Fred		
0	0	0.0	.0039
0	1	0.5	.0156
0	2	1.0	.0234
⋮			
2	2	2.0	.1406
2	3	2.5	.0937
⋮			
4	4	4.0	.0039

And again, this is a parameter since it is based on all of the possible values—we use the correct Greek letter symbol for the population standard deviation.

Now let's consider a sample of size $N = 2$ from the class of students taking this four-item quiz. With two students, both could happen to get all four questions right, giving a sample of (4, 4) and a sample mean of 4.0. Or, conceivably, both could miss everything, giving a sample of (0, 0) and $\overline{X} = 0.0$. Any other combination of right and wrong answers is also possible. Table 11.5 shows some possible outcomes for two hypothetical students, John and Fred. The probabilities are computed by using the multiplication rule. Since John is just guessing, the probability that he gets a score of 0 is 1/16, and the same holds for Fred. The probability that John gets 0 and that Fred also gets 0 is the product of the two probabilities. So the probability of getting a sample mean of 0.0 is $1/16 \times 1/16$ or $1/256 = .0039$. The same logic can be applied to all of the possible values of the sample mean; a few examples are shown.

Table 11.6 Probabilities for all Possible Mean Values for Two Students

Mean correct	Probability
0.0	.0039
0.5	.0312
1.0	.1093
1.5	.2186
2.0	.2734
2.5	.2186
3.0	.1093
3.5	.0312
4.0	.0039
	1.0000

We could define each possible value of the mean as an event; the possible events are 0.0, 0.5, 1.0, 1.5, ..., 3.5, 4.0. We may compute the probability of each event by using the multiplication and addition rules. For example, (1, 1), (0, 2), and (2, 0) are the three possible ways of obtaining $\overline{X} = 1.0$. The probability of the (1, 1) outcome is $4/16 \times 4/16 = .0625$ ($4/16 \times 4/16$, since the probability of each "1" is $4/16$). The probability of (0, 2) is $1/16 \times 6/16 = .0234$, as is the probability of (2, 0). By summing the probabilities, the probability of obtaining $\overline{X} = 1.0$ is found to be .1093. In a similar way, we could find the probabilities for all of the possible mean values (of course, still assuming that the students are guessing). That distribution is shown in Table 11.6. Note that we have followed the mathematical probability rules that require each event (each possible sample mean, in this case) to be assigned a probability value between 0 and 1. The rule requiring that the probability values sum to 1.0 is followed as well.

What we have just constructed is a distribution that gives the probability of all possible values of the sample mean. In other words, we have just developed the *sampling distribution of the mean* for samples of size 2. Nothing was required except the application of the addition and multiplication rules and the assumption that the students taking the quiz were guessing.

The sampling distribution of the mean provides the probability of all possible values of the mean for samples of size $N = 2$ from the population of individuals who are guessing. If we give the quiz to two randomly selected students who are guessing, then the distribution tells us the probability of obtaining any possible mean score. The mean is most likely to be in the 1.5 to 2.5 range. A mean of 0.0 or of 4.0, for example, is quite unlikely, but still possible. A histogram of the sampling distribution shows the values easily (Figure 11.7). In the illustration, each rectangle shows the probability of a possible $\overline{X}$ value. For example, if the students are guessing, the probability of the event "the mean score is between 1.5 and 2.5, inclusive" is graphed in Figure 11.8.

We may calculate the probability by applying the addition rule once more:

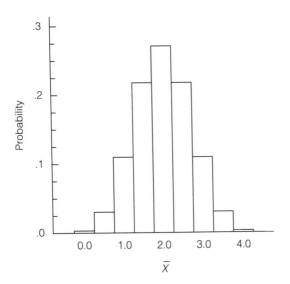

Figure 11.7

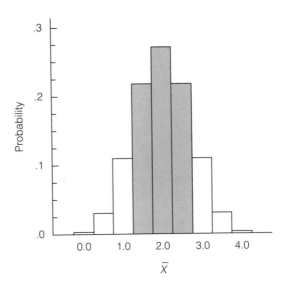

Figure 11.8

$$\text{Prob}(\overline{X} = 1.5) + \text{Prob}(\overline{X} = 2.0) + \text{Prob}(\overline{X} = 2.5)$$
$$= .2186 + .2734 + .2186$$
$$= .7106.$$

The probability that two students score a mean of 3.0 or greater if they're guessing is graphed in Figure 11.9. Computationally, the probability is

$$\text{Prob}(\overline{X} = 3.0) + \text{Prob}(\overline{X} = 3.5) + \text{Prob}(\overline{X} = 4.0)$$
$$= .1093 + .0312 + .0039$$
$$= .1444.$$

Finally, define the event "the mean score is extreme" (where we regard 0.0 and 4.0 as extreme). The area is shown in Figure 11.10, and the probability is

$$\text{Prob}(\overline{X} = 0.0) + \text{Prob}(\overline{X} = 4.0)$$
$$= .0039 + .0039$$
$$= .0078.$$

We could also define the event "$\overline{X}$ is not extreme" as $\overline{X} = 0.5, 1.0, 1.5, 2.0,$ 2.5, 3.0, and 3.5. The probability of this event is graphed in Figure 11.11. Or, in numbers,

$$\text{Prob}(\overline{X} = 0.5) + \text{Prob}(\overline{X} = 1.0) + \text{Prob}(\overline{X} = 1.5) + \text{Prob}(\overline{X} = 2.0)$$
$$+ \text{Prob}(\overline{X} = 2.5) + \text{Prob}(\overline{X} = 3.0) + \text{Prob}(\overline{X} = 3.5)$$
$$= .0312 + .1093 + .2186 + .2734 + .2186 + .1093 + .0312$$
$$= .9922.$$

We could also calculate the probability of "$\overline{X}$ is not extreme" by noting that it is the complement of "$\overline{X}$ is extreme" and that those two events together account for all of the possible means. That is,

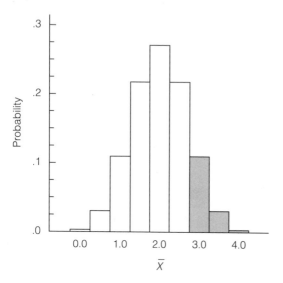

Figure 11.9

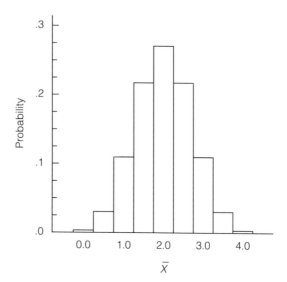

Figure 11.10

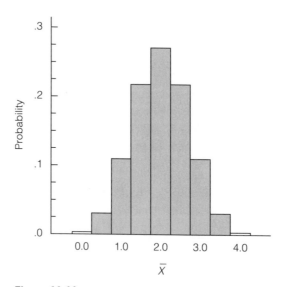

Figure 11.11

$$\text{Prob}(\overline{X} \text{ is extreme}) + \text{Prob}(\overline{X} \text{ is not extreme}) = 1.0000$$

so that

$$\text{Prob}(\overline{X} \text{ is not extreme}) = 1.0000 - \text{Prob}(\overline{X} \text{ is extreme})$$
$$= 1.0000 - .0078$$
$$= .9922.$$

At the start of this example, we made an assumption about the students' behavior—they are guessing. From that assumption, we developed the probabilities of each possible quiz score. Those probabilities were graphed in Figure 11.5. This is a population distribution of the scores on the quiz, assuming that the students are guessing.

The next step developed that sampling distribution of $\overline{X}$ for samples of $N = 2$. The sampling distribution of $\overline{X}$, though, has a somewhat different appearance, looking like Figure 11.7, which shows that the probabilities in the extreme tails have become smaller and that those in the central area occupy more of the distribution. This indicates that, with two students, obtaining an extreme mean score is less likely, while means near the center of the range of possible values are more likely.

Following procedures similar to those illustrated, we could compute the mean and the standard deviation of the sampling distribution of $\overline{X}$. If we did, we would find that

$$\mu_{\overline{X}} = 2.0$$

and that

$$\sigma_{\overline{X}} = 0.707.$$

Note the subscripted $\overline{X}$ to remind us that these values pertain to the distribution of the mean, not to the original values. What we have here are the center (the arithmetic mean) and the spread (the standard deviation) of the sampling distribution of $\overline{X}$ for samples of $N = 2$.

The last value, the standard deviation of the sampling distribution of the means, needs some special attention. The value is also equal to

$$\sigma_{\overline{X}} = \frac{\sigma}{\sqrt{N}}$$

or, in this case,

$$\sigma_{\overline{X}} = \frac{1}{\sqrt{2}} = 0.707.$$

The mean of the sampling distribution is equal to the mean of the population (2.0). But the standard deviation of the sampling distribution of $\overline{X}$ is equal to the standard deviation of the population divided by the square root of the sample size. This important relationship bears repeating:

$$\sigma_{\overline{X}} = \frac{\sigma}{\sqrt{N}}.$$

The standard deviation of the sampling distribution of the means is equal to the standard deviation of the population divided by the square root of N. This relationship formalizes an important fact about the mean—as a sample size becomes larger, the variability of the sampling distribution becomes smaller. As a consequence, the sample means cluster tightly around μ, and values far from μ become less likely.

The standard deviation of the sampling distribution of the mean is related to the degree to which a sample mean may differ from the population mean. Clearly, the larger the value of N, the closer $\overline{X}$ is likely to be to μ. Because of this relationship between sample size and the probable error in the sample mean, the standard deviation of the sampling distribution is often called the *standard error of the mean*. Indeed, the standard deviation of the sampling distribution of any statistic is often called the *standard error* of that statistic.

For the arithmetic mean, the mean of the sampling distribution is always equal to the mean of the population. And for the arithmetic mean, the standard error of the mean is always equal to

$$\sigma_{\bar{X}} = \frac{\sigma}{\sqrt{N}}.$$

For a given sample size, then, we know two of the important defining features of the sampling distribution of the sample mean—its mean and standard deviation. If we also knew the form of the sampling distribution, then we would be able to use a completely known distribution to make inferences.

If we were to repeat the four-item quiz exercise with samples of size $N = 3$, the distribution of $\bar{X}$ would become even more "normal-looking," with more of the probability concentrated near the center and very little in the extremes. We could also construct the sampling distribution for $\bar{X}$ with $N = 4$, with $N = 5$, and so forth. If we did so, we would discover three things: (1) that the mean of the sampling distribution remains equal to 2.0, (2) that the standard error of the mean continues to be equal to

$$\sigma_{\bar{X}} = \frac{\sigma}{\sqrt{N}},$$

and (3) that the form of the sampling distribution approaches the normal distribution in form. This latter characteristic of the sampling distribution of the mean is important and has been formalized in a theorem that serves as an important step in the development of inference logic.

The Central Limit Theorem. In a powerful statement known as the *Central Limit Theorem*, mathematicians can prove that the form of the sampling distribution of the means of the samples in fact becomes normal as the sample size increases. The only real requirement is that the population sampled have a finite mean and variance. Given those conditions, the mean of the sampling distribution of the mean will be equal to μ, and the standard deviation of the sampling distribution will be equal to

$$\sigma_{\bar{X}} = \frac{\sigma}{\sqrt{N}}.$$

Note that it's not necessary that the population from which observations are sampled be normal. The central limit theorem applies to the sampling distribution of the mean, regardless of population form.

The Central Limit Theorem provides an important foundation for making inferences. Because of it, we know the form of the sampling distribution of the mean, at least for sufficiently large samples. If the form of the underlying population is normal, then the sampling distribution of the mean will be normal in form regardless of sample size. For small samples from a normal population, therefore, we know the form of the sampling distribution of the mean. When the population distribution is not normal, the Central Limit Theorem tells us the form of the sampling distribution if the sample size is large enough.* That is, with a large sample, we may assume that the sampling distribution is normal in form, whatever the form of the population.

Drawing Samples

Knowing the parameters and form of a sampling distribution will let us determine the probabilities of values of a mean (and other statistics) from randomly drawn samples. The important word here is *randomly*; if the sample is not picked at random, then the probability rules won't necessarily apply. In particular, if the samples aren't picked randomly, there's no assurance that the Central Limit Theorem will describe the form of the sampling distribution.

In the example that we've followed so far, we used a very small sample size. Usually we'll want to talk about larger samples than $N = 2$. But whatever the sample size, random sampling assures that the distribution of statistics follows certain known distribution forms, of which the normal is the most important. How do we assure that we can have a random sample? In order to answer that question, we must first define just what a random sample is.

A sample of size N is a *random sample* if it was chosen from its population in such a way that *every other sample of the same size had the same chance of being selected.*

Notice that the definition of a random sample refers only to the process by which it was selected and says nothing about its "representativeness." In fact, random sampling guarantees that some samples will be "unrepresentative." The random sampling process merely assures that any sample is as likely (or unlikely) as any other so that a statistic based on a random sample, while it may not be "representative" of its parameter, has not been systematically biased in any way.

How do we select random samples? Making up numbers mentally is not a very good way to do it, since humans are poor random number generators. Taking every fifteenth name in the phone book until you have N names isn't very good either, unless you're intentionally limiting your population to those people with telephones (with listed numbers); even then, the sample is random only if you pick your starting name randomly.

One obvious sampling procedure, which follows directly from the definition, would be to write each possible sample on a slip of paper, put them all into a hat (or barrel, or cement mixer, depending upon the size of the population), mix them thoroughly, and have a blindfolded assistant pick one. Obviously, that's an impractical method for all but the very smallest of populations and sample sizes.

Another procedure would be to assign a unique number to each observation in the population and then draw the numbers out of a hat in handfuls of size N. If the numbers are mixed well, then any handful is as likely as any other, and the sample would be random.

---

* $N = 30$ is usually regarded as "large enough."

A variant of the handful sampling process is often used. Assign a number to each observation in the population and then obtain a set of N random numbers between 1 and the largest value assigned to a population member. The observations whose numbers have been selected randomly then constitute the random sample. The random numbers can be obtained from a table of random numbers such as Appendix B, or they may be computer-generated. Many statistics programs offer the ability to generate samples of numbers in the range 1, 2, ... N such that all numbers are equally likely.

When a researcher needs a random order for presenting stimuli, for ordering questionnaire items, or for similar purposes, a random number table or generator is usually pressed into service. But what of selecting subjects for research? How are they normally chosen? You'd like to think that a careful process was followed, but in fact researchers rarely have the luxury of *actually* randomly sampling from their population. If Dr. Stewart needs a group of animals, he doesn't really assign a number to all of the laboratory rats in the world and follow the rules for random samples. To be literally correct, of course, he should do just that in order to assure that the sample that he will use is as likely as any other of the same size. But practicality rules the day, and he will use a group of rats that he has raised in the laboratory colony, or perhaps he will order new animals from a commercial supplier. He will, of course, assign them randomly to experimental conditions.

What we're saying is that the real world of research recognizes that really and truly random samples occur relatively rarely outside of the statistics classroom. But it's also true that any group of animals is just as likely as any other to have arrived at the laboratory for a given research project. Commercial animal suppliers take considerable pains to assure that the rats that you buy today are genetically highly similar to those shipped last year and the year before, and to those that will be shipped next year and the year after that too, and that each batch of animals shipped is an unbiased (if not truly random) sample of the animals in their stock.

The situation is considerably more complex with human subjects. A great deal of psychological research is done using college students as "volunteer" subjects. Not only are college students not typical of all humans everywhere, but also those who participate in research are probably atypical of the entire population of college students in unknown ways. The unrepresentativeness of the subjects is troublesome to many, and indeed does place some limits on the ability of our experimental results to generalize. With some care, though, and with attention to the experiment's external validity, generalization is usually not problematic.

SUMMARY

- Inferential statistics let us generalize beyond the immediate set of data.
- A population is a set of potential observations, while a sample is the set of observations available.
- Statistical inference makes statements about parameters on the basis of statistics.

- The probability of an event may be computed by dividing the number of equally likely outcomes in the event by the number of possible outcomes.
- The probability of an event is the sum of the probabilities of the outcomes in it.
- The standard error of the mean is equal to the standard deviation of the population divided by the square root of the sample size.
- Greek letters are used for parameters and Roman letters for statistics.

KEY TERMS

Addition rule	Population
Bernoulli's Theorem	Probability
Central Limit Theorem	Random sample
Event	Sample
Law of Large Numbers	Sampling distribution
Multiplication rule	Standard error of the mean
Parameter	Statistic

EXERCISES

Solutions to asterisked (∗) exercises appear at the back of the book. Exercises preceded by a section symbol (§) must be solved using a computer. Exercises preceded by a dagger (†) can be solved by hand.

†1. A psychologist interested in taste preferences places five different substances before his experimental animals. If the animals have no taste preferences among the substances, what proportion of the time would you expect each substance to be the first one tasted? Why? Are your numbers probabilities or relative frequencies?

∗†2. In the hypothetical exam situation described earlier in the chapter (see page 222), find each of the following probabilities (remember that a question is returned to the hat after it is asked):

a. If one question is asked, what is the probability that it will be either a center or a spread question?

b. If two questions are asked, what is the probability that both of them are normal-curve-area questions?

c. If two questions are asked, what is the probability that they are the same question?

d. Suppose that the instructor makes up a 50-item test by selecting questions at random from his test file. How many of the 50 questions are likely to be from each of the question groups?

†3. Continuing from Exercise 2, define the event "relative location" as the events "z scores," "percentiles," and "percentile ranks."

a. Find the probability of "relative location."

b. Find the probability of "relative location" or "normal curve."

c. Find the probability of "relative location" or "descriptive."

†4. Construct a simple population with five values (the weights of five friends, your scores on the last five weekly quizzes, the number of words on the last five postcards you've received, or the number of your cousins plus those of four of your friends are all possible examples). Write the population elements on slips of paper.

a. Find the mean (μ) of the population.

b. With the population values on separate slips of paper, shuffle them thoroughly. Select a sample of two values randomly from the population. Find the mean and the sample standard deviation for the sample, and return the two slips to the population. Shuffle again, randomly pick two more, and find their mean and sample standard deviation. Repeat the process until you have picked 40 samples of size 2. You will now have 40 means and 40 sample standard deviations, one of each from each sample.

c. Construct the frequency distribution of your sample means.

d. Find the mean of your sample means.

e. Describe what the distribution looks like.

§5. Use your computer's random-number facility to generate 20 sets of 2 numbers between 0 and 1. These numbers are 20 samples of size $N = 2$ from a population whose distribution form is rectangular (all values are equally likely). That population has a mean μ of 0.5 and its standard deviation $\sigma = 0.289$.

a. Compute the mean for each of your samples of two.

b. Construct the frequency distribution of the sample means.

c. Find the mean of your set of 20 means.

d. What do you conclude about the form of the distribution of means as compared to the form of the population from which the samples were drawn?

e. What do you conclude about the mean of the distribution of means as compared with the mean of the population from which the samples were drawn?

§6. Repeat Exercise 5 with samples of $N = 3$ and with $N = 5$.

*†7. The sampling distribution for the mean of samples of size $N = 3$ from the four-item quiz example is:

Mean correct	Probability
0.00	0.0002
0.33	0.0029
0.67	0.0161
1.00	0.0537
1.33	0.1208
1.67	0.1934
2.00	0.2256
2.33	0.1934
2.67	0.1208
3.00	0.0537
3.33	0.0161
3.67	0.0029
4.00	0.0002
	1.0000

Using the probability distribution, find the probabilities of the following events (remember the addition and multiplication rules):

a. $\bar{X} \leq 3.0$.

b. $1.3 \leq \bar{X} \leq 2.0$.

c. $\bar{X} > 2.0$.

d. $\bar{X} \geq 2.0$.

e. $\bar{X} \leq 1$ or ≥ 3.0.

f. $\bar{X} < 1$ or > 3.0.

g. $\bar{X} \leq 0.5$ or ≥ 3.5.

h. $0.33 \leq \bar{X} \leq 1.0$ or $3.0 \leq \bar{X} \leq 3.67$.

*†8. If we were to give the four-item exam to a sample of 25 students, what would be μ and $\sigma_{\bar{x}}$ for the sampling distribution of $\bar{X}$?

†9. Suppose that we give the four-item exam to a sample of 30 students, what would be μ and $\sigma_{\bar{x}}$ for the sampling distribution of $\bar{X}$? What can you say about the form of the sampling distribution? Why?

*†10. If 30 students take the four-item exam and are all truly guessing, find the probabilities of each of the following:

a. $1.5 \leq \bar{X} \leq 2.5$.

b. $\bar{X} < 3.0$.

c. $1.5 \leq \bar{X}$.

d. $1.64 \leq \bar{X} \leq 2.36$.

e. $\bar{X} < 1.64$ or $\bar{X} > 2.36$.

f. $1.82 \leq \bar{X} \leq 2.18$.

g. $\bar{X} < 1.82$ or $\bar{X} > 2.18$.

†11. If you were to actually have 20 random samples of 30 students each who were randomly guessing on a four-item test, how many of the means of those 20 samples would you expect to fall in each of the intervals defined in Exercise 8?

*†12. Suppose that the instructor who gives our hypothetical four-item quiz awards 10 points for each correct answer. For the sampling distribution of $\bar{X}$ for $N = 2$ scores on the test, what will be μ and $\sigma_{\bar{x}}$? For $N = 3$? For $N = 30$?

CHAPTER 12

Estimates and Hypothesis Tests

If we want to estimate how long it will take for participants in a problem-solving experiment to complete the task, we might select a few pilot subjects, have them do the task, and record their times. We could use the arithmetic mean of their times as our "best guess" as to how long it will take people to solve the problem. Using a statistic in this way, as a best-guess estimate of a parameter, is an inference procedure called the *point estimate*.

If we computed the standard deviation of the problem-solving times and did a simple additional computation, we could construct an *interval estimate*. An interval estimate would give a range of times in which we expect most people to finish. For example, we might conclude our pilot study by stating, "I expect that the subjects will complete my task in 22.5 to 26.3 minutes, and I'm 95% confident of that being true."

The preceding examples illustrate two ways to estimate the parameter "mean time to complete the task." The first procedure was a *point estimate*. Point estimates are single values that are used as best-guess approximations of parameters. On the other hand, an interval estimate provides a range of values and indicates a confidence statement (often expressed as a percentage) that the parameter falls within that range. An interval estimate abandons the precision of the point estimate in return for a statement of confidence that repeated sampling from the same population will produce values in the same range. In this chapter, we apply the knowledge of probability and sampling distributions from Chapter 11 to the task of actually making inferences.

There are several forms of statistical inference. We have introduced point and interval estimation already. We will also consider the most widely used inference procedure—hypothesis testing.

Estimation

Estimation uses sample data to make a direct inference about a parameter. The hypothesis test also makes a parameter inference but its logic is indirect, as we will learn later. Because the two estimation procedures yield values presumed to be close to the parameter, we may think of their logic as making a direct inference.

Point Estimation

When we make a point estimate, we use a statistic whose single value is taken as a single "best guess" as to the value of the parameter that it is estimating. We all use point estimates regularly in daily life. ("When will the mail arrive?"—"Around 10:30" or "How late will the instructor be this morning?"—"Five minutes" both employ point estimates to answer everyday questions. An answer like "Between 10:00 and 11:00" provides an interval estimate.) While we don't understand how humans intuitively combine past evidence to produce such answers, we do it easily and can make use of point estimate information.

Point estimates form the basis for both interval estimates and hypothesis tests, and so we should look at them in a bit more detail.

Characteristics of Good Point Estimators. What makes a good point estimator? For one thing, the estimator should not consistently overestimate or underestimate its target parameter. That is, while any individual values of the statistic might be either too high or too low, they wouldn't be consistently on one side or the other. Another way of saying the same thing is that we would hope that the mean of a large number of the values of the statistic would equal the parameter being estimated. A statistic that is, on the average, neither too high nor too low is called *unbiased*. If a statistic is unbiased, then the mean of its sampling distribution is equal to the parameter being estimated. (And, of course, that's just another way of saying that it's neither too high nor too low, on the average.)

Suppose that we had two unbiased statistics to estimate the same parameter. In other words, the means of the sampling distributions are equal to each other and to the parameter. Are there still differences between the two estimators? Certainly—for one thing, they might differ in variability. Suppose that there are two estimators for μ—for example, $\overline{X}$ and the midrange.* The two sampling distributions, based on the same sample size, might look like Figure 12.1. The statistics have similar sampling distributions, and both are centered on μ since they're unbiased. But the distribution for the midrange is more variable. The sampling distribution for $\overline{X}$ is much more compact, and thus $\overline{X}$ is more likely to be closer to μ than is the midrange. The statistic with the smaller variability in its sampling distribution is more *efficient*.

Two other characteristics of good estimators are often cited, namely *sufficiency* and *consistency*. A *sufficient* statistic uses all of the information in the sample in making its estimate. Another way to say the same thing is that a

---

*The midrange, the mean of the largest and smallest values, is an unbiased estimate of μ in a symmetric population.

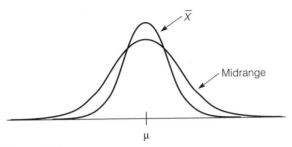

Figure 12.1

sufficient estimator can't be improved by adding additional information from the same sample. The arithmetic mean is sufficient as an estimator of μ; it uses not only all of the scores in the data but also their number. A midrange, on the other hand, is not sufficient since it omits all but the smallest and the largest values. The median is also not sufficient, because it uses only the ordinal information in the data and not distance information. Of course, that characteristic is a benefit in a skewed distribution because the median is less influenced by extreme scores.

A *consistent* statistic is one whose accuracy increases as sample size increases. In other words, taking a larger sample will give greater likelihood that the sample estimate is close to the parameter. All of the statistics that we will use are consistent, the sample standard deviation notably so. As we'll note soon, the sample standard deviation is slightly biased as an estimator of σ, but the bias diminishes as the sample size increases. This is the most notable instance of consistency in the statistics that we'll encounter.

Characteristics of Common Statistics. How do the descriptive statistics that we know fare as point estimates? Before we can answer that, we need to clarify just what each is estimating. We have talked of measures of center, for example, as if there were only a single *population* measure of center. In fact, there's the population mean, as well as the population median, population midrange, and so forth.

Measures of center and proportion. All of the measures of center discussed in Chapter 6 are adequate as measures of their respective parameters. The decision whether to use the population mean or median as the measure of center, though, isn't usually dictated by the characteristics of the estimator nearly so much as it is by characteristics of measurement and by the data themselves. In a skewed distribution, the median is the better measure, and that's a decision that can be made easily; fortunately, the sample median is an excellent estimator on all counts. Likewise, sample proportions are unbiased and otherwise good estimators for their respective parameters.*

---

* A sample proportion is the arithmetic mean of a sample from a population of 0, 1 values and is thus unbiased. For example, if we're estimating the proportion of males in a population, the sample proportion of males may be computed as (number of males)/N, or by scoring males = 1 and females = 0 and calculating the mean.

243

Measures of spread. Of the measures of spread, only two have parameters that are usually of inferential concern. Estimations of the variance and the standard deviation present special problems and need consideration.

In Chapter 7 we defined the sample variance and sample standard deviation as

$$s^2 = \frac{\Sigma(X - \overline{X})^2}{N},$$

and

$$s = \sqrt{\frac{\Sigma(X - \overline{X})^2}{N}},$$

respectively. These definitions are important for understanding the variance as the mean of the squared deviations from the arithmetic mean. And they're perfectly correct descriptive values for a set of numbers. But, as we pointed out earlier, they're not the appropriate statistics to use in making an inference about the population values σ and σ^2.

A population, in those rare instances when we really have all of the values, has parameters σ and σ^2, which may be found by the formulas

$$\sigma^2 = \frac{\Sigma(X - \overline{\mu})^2}{N}$$

and

$$\sigma = \sqrt{\frac{\Sigma(X - \overline{\mu})^2}{N}}$$

for the variance and the standard deviation. We rarely have complete populations available (except, of course, in some examples that statistics book authors make up).

Let's consider now the problem of making an inference about an unknown value of σ^2 from a sample statistic. The statistic

$$s^2 = \frac{\Sigma(X - \overline{X})^2}{N}$$

is the arithmetic mean of the squared deviations of the data about the mean. We've defined it as the variance of a sample of data, and as such it's an acceptable descriptive statistic. But as an estimate of σ^2, it's biased. In fact, it's too small by a factor of

$$\frac{N - 1}{N},$$

so that

$$\frac{N}{N - 1} \frac{\Sigma(X - \overline{X})^2}{N} = \frac{\Sigma(X - \overline{X})^2}{N - 1}$$

forms an unbiased estimate of σ^2. To differentiate between the two statistics, we'll use a special symbol, $\hat{s}^2$, to indicate the unbiased estimator for σ^2:

$$\hat{s}^2 = \frac{\Sigma(X - \overline{X})^2}{N - 1}.$$

Computationally, we can use the formula

$$\hat{s}^2 = \frac{\Sigma X^2 - \dfrac{(\Sigma X)^2}{N}}{N - 1}.$$

The statistic most frequently used to estimate the population standard deviation is simply the square root of the unbiased variance estimate,

$$\hat{s} = \sqrt{\frac{\Sigma(X - \overline{X})^2}{N - 1}}$$

$$= \sqrt{\frac{\Sigma X^2 - \dfrac{(\Sigma X)^2}{N}}{N - 1}}.$$

As it happens, this statistic is very slightly biased, but the bias is rarely enough to make any practical difference, and so we recommend $\hat{s}$ as an estimate of σ.*

The existence of two formulas for the standard deviation and the variance has caused grief for generations of students, and will continue to do so. The "N form" that was presented in Chapter 7 is used when the data are regarded as *the* population while the "$N - 1$ form" given here is for use when the data are used to estimate a parameter. The two forms for the computations are the reason why many calculators have two alternate ways to compute standard deviation and variance, as described in the footnote on page 142.

As an example of calculating the unbiased estimators $\hat{s}$ and $\hat{s}^2$, here are some data from a simple learning study; the values are the number of trials to a criterion of one correct recall of a list of words:

9	17	15	23	12
18	11	21	16	16
20	19	26		

For these data, $\Sigma X = 223$, and $\Sigma X^2 = 4103$, so that

$$\overline{X} = \frac{\Sigma X}{N}$$

$$= \frac{223}{13}$$

$$= 17.15$$

---

*The actual unbiased statistic is

$$\left(1 + \frac{1}{4(N - 1)}\right)s$$

(see Dixon and Massey, 1983). The bias gets progressively less as N increases, and thus $1/4(N-1)$ becomes smaller. An estimator whose bias decreases may, at an indefinitely large sample size, be unbiased. Such is the case here, and the sample standard deviation s is known as an *asymptotically unbiased* estimator for its parameter σ.

and

$$\hat{s} = \sqrt{\frac{4103 - \frac{(223)^2}{13}}{13 - 1}}$$

$$= 4.81.$$

The standard error of the mean (see p. 236) is a statistic that we will need often. Its population value is defined by

$$\sigma_{\bar{X}} = \frac{\sigma}{\sqrt{N}},$$

and the sample estimate may be computed as

$$\hat{s}_{\bar{X}} = \frac{\hat{s}}{\sqrt{N}},$$

simply replacing the parameter σ by its estimate $\hat{s}$.

Measures of relationship. The most common parameter estimated is the population product-moment correlation coefficient, symbolized by ρ. The sample estimate is, naturally, r. As an estimator, r is an asymtotically unbiased estimator,[*] meaning that as the sample size increases, the bias becomes progressively less.[†] The slope and intercept values in regression are likewise unbiased estimators for their population counterparts. The other measures of relationship that we discussed in Chapter 9 are normally just descriptive and are not used to estimate parameters.

Interval Estimation
Point estimates use a single sample value to make an estimate of the parameter. An unbiased point estimate will, on the average, equal the parameter. But usually we have only a single statistic, and we can never know just how close it is to its parameter. Think about playing darts, where the bull's-eye is the parameter. Unless you're a very good darts player, every throw won't hit the bull's-eye. If you throw a lot of darts and keep track of how far off-center you hit each time, you might find that over a lot of throws, your average "miss" was zero. But each individual throw might be a distance off. That's like an unbiased point estimator—any individual statistic might not be right on the mark, but "on the average" it will be.[‡]

An interval estimate, in contrast to the point estimate, establishes a range of values that should contain the parameter. Instead of presenting a single value,

---

[*] See Stilson (1966); Cramer (1946).
[†] Although the sample r is slightly biased, no one ever seems to worry about it, probably because with a reasonable sample size, the degree of bias is negligible.
[‡] You might also find that you consistently hit too low, or too far to the left, or somewhere else off the mark. Such performance is the equivalent of a biased estimator—it's off the mark and in a consistent direction.

an interval estimate is often presented as a value "plus or minus" some amount. Political polls are often presented in the news media as interval estimates: "The polls show Smith the leader over Jones by 32% to 41%, with a margin of error of 3.4%." That's an interval estimate. What it means is that Smith's "true" proportion (the parameter) is probably between 28.6% and 35.4%, while that for Jones is most likely between 37.6% and 44.4%. The "probably" indicates that an interval estimate is accompanied by a probability value (which isn't usually reported by the press). The inclusion of a probability with an interval estimate is a second difference between it and the point estimate. A point estimate offers a single value as a "best guess" at the parameter; an interval estimate, on the other hand, establishes a range of values *and* attaches a probability to it.

Parameter

Interval estimate

Figure 12.2

If a point estimate can be likened to throwing darts, then interval estimation is a little like playing horseshoes. The goal in horseshoes is to throw the U-shaped horseshoe at the target post (called the pin) in the hopes that the U of the horseshoe will "ring" the pin. The parameter is like the pin, and the estimate is the horseshoe. (Actually, the estimate is more like the opening of the horseshoe, since the estimate is a distance, not unlike the width across the open end of the horseshoe.) If you are a reasonable horseshoe player, you may expect to ring the pin in a percentage of your tosses that is proportional to the width of the horseshoe—the wider the shoe, the more "ringers."

An interval estimate gives an interval into which the parameter is "likely" to fall. Just as in horseshoes, the wider the interval, the more likely it is to capture the parameter (Figure 12.2). The interval is normally computed by using a point estimate as the starting point and then going an equal distance on either side of it. The distance out from the point estimate is determined by several things, including the probability that we want to have of "capturing" the parameter (Figure 12.3).

Suppose that the point estimate for μ was 78.2, that we wanted a probability level of .9, and that the distance on each side was 1.5. The estimate would then say, in effect, "We have a certainty of 90% that the parameter is within the interval 78.2 ± 1.5." Another way to phrase the estimate that more nearly describes the real meaning is roughly this: "If we repeat the sampling procedure a very large number of times and follow the same computational logic each time, we would expect that the interval that we compute, which this time is 78.2 ± 1.5, will enclose the parameter 90% of the time." Or, to continue our horseshoe analogy, "With a horseshoe whose width on this computation is 3, I expect a ringer 90% of the time."

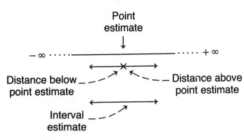

Point
estimate

$-\infty$ ..... ————————— ..... $+\infty$

Distance below — — — — Distance above
point estimate   point estimate

Interval — — —
estimate

Figure 12.3

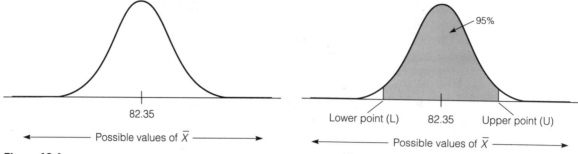

Figure 12.4

Figure 12.5

An interval estimate is often understood as an expression of how confident you are that the value of the parameter is within the interval. For this reason, interval estimates are frequently called *confidence intervals*.

Computing an interval estimate (or confidence interval) depends upon four factors—a point estimate for the parameter, a measure of spread, a desired probability (confidence level), and an assumption about the form of the population. The population mean is the most common target for an interval estimate, and we'll present the logic using it. And for now, we assume that the form of the population from which the data were sampled is normal.

Suppose that we have a set of test scores with $N = 15$, $\overline{X} = 82.35$, and that we know that $\sigma = 8.5$.* We'll compute the 95% confidence interval for μ. We first compute the standard error of the mean as

$$\sigma_{\overline{X}} = \frac{\sigma}{\sqrt{N}} = \frac{8.5}{\sqrt{15}} = 2.19.$$

The values for the mean and the standard error let us make a guess about the center and spread of that sampling distribution. If we could really see the sampling distribution, it might look like Figure 12.4.

Since we've assumed that the population distribution is normal, then the sampling distribution is normal, too. Of course, we can't know if the distribution is *really* centered on 82.35, but it's the best guess that we have. Now let's define an area of the sampling distribution that should contain the middle 95% of the possible sample means. (Remember that we're looking for the interval estimate that will make a ringer 95% of the time.) Figure 12.5 diagrams the area that we're looking for. By looking in the table of z scores (Appendix A), we can determine that the points (marked L and U in Figure 12.5) that define the 95% central area are ± 1.96. Using the standardizing formula as applied to this distribution

$$z = \frac{X - \overline{X}}{\sigma_{\overline{X}}}$$

and inserting numbers where we have them, letting U be an unknown value, we have

---

*Most of the time, of course, we don't actually know σ; we're assuming that we do to simplify the example. We'll handle the more common case of an unknown σ in Chapter 13.

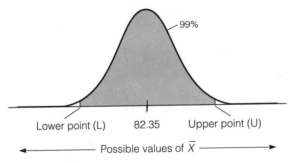

Figure 12.6

$$z = \frac{U - \overline{X}}{\sigma_{\overline{X}}}$$

$$1.96 = \frac{U - 82.35}{2.19}.$$

A little algebra results in

$$U = 82.35 + 1.96 \times 2.19$$
$$= 86.64.$$

We use the same logic for the lower bound (L) of our interval estimates:

$$z = \frac{L - \overline{X}}{\sigma_{\overline{X}}}$$

$$-1.96 = \frac{L - 82.35}{2.19}$$

and

$$L = 82.35 - 1.96 \times 2.19$$
$$= 78.06.$$

Our confidence interval, then, is 78.06 to 86.64, or 82.35 ± 4.29. We may interpret this result as an estimated relative frequency. If we were to repeat this experiment a large number of times, we should expect to make a ringer—capture the true value of μ—about 95% of the time.

In general terms, the formula for the 95% interval estimate for μ is

$$\overline{X} \pm 1.96(\sigma_{\overline{X}}).$$

Other interval estimates are computed in a similar way, substituting the appropriate value from Appendix A. For example, to find the 99% interval, the table tells us that ±2.58 defines the middle 99% of the normal distribution (Figure 12.6). Using ±2.58 instead of ±1.96 gives the 99% confidence interval; and ±1.65 would give the 90% interval, since ±1.65 enclose the middle 90% of the distribution.

Presenting Interval Estimates. There are several ways to present an interval estimate. A simple sentence format is often appropriate. The sentence "The 95%

confidence interval for the mean is 108.27 ± 6.21" is direct and to the point. A tabular format is useful if there are several intervals to report. Table 12.1 is an example. Finally, confidence intervals are often shown graphically as error bars on a plot. The data in Table 12.1 might appear as shown in Figure 12.7.

Hypothesis Testing

Point estimates and interval estimates are "direct" methods of inference because they yield values that are statements about probable values of the parameter. A hypothesis test, on the other hand, uses indirect logic. A hypothesis test establishes two opposing hypotheses about a parameter. Assuming that one of the hypotheses is true, a sampling distribution is constructed. If the obtained value of the statistic has a low probability of occurring given the sampling distribution, then the presumed hypothesis is rejected and its opposite supported. Because the tested hypothesis is often the opposite of what the researcher wants to conclude, rejecting the hypothesis gives indirect support to the conclusion that the investigator had in mind all along. ("If I reject the hypothesis that there is no difference, then there must be a difference.") It's a cumbersome logic, but it boils down to

Table 12.1 Presenting Confidence Intervals in a Table

| Age | Number recalled | | 95% interval | |
	Mean	SD	Low	High
5	13.62	6.67	11.33	15.91
8	15.74	3.15	17.63	13.85
12	16.22	2.85	17.58	14.86
:				
:				

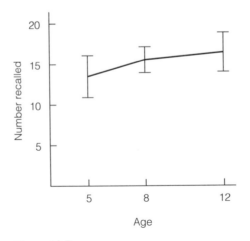

Figure 12.7

making two opposing statements about a parameter: one of the statements is tested; if it's found to be unlikely, its logical opposite is supported.

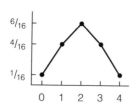

Number correct

Figure 12.8

Taking Four-Item Quizzes

In Chapter 11 we developed the sampling distribution of the mean score on a four-item true-false test. Picking up that example again, we'll test the assumption that the students are guessing. If that's true, the population distribution for "number correct" is the curve shown in Figure 12.8. For this population, $\mu = 2.0$ and $\sigma = 1.0$. That is, under the assumption that the students are guessing, the population mean is 2.0; if they're not guessing, then the mean would be something other than 2.0.

Suppose that we have a class of 35 students to whom we'll give the quiz. What do we know about the sampling distribution of the mean? For one thing, we know that if the mean number of items correct is 2.0 (that is, if the guessing hypothesis is correct), then the mean of the sampling distribution is also 2.0. We also know that the standard error of the mean (the standard deviation of the sampling distribution) is

$$\sigma_{\bar{X}} = \frac{\sigma}{\sqrt{N}}$$
$$= \frac{1.0}{\sqrt{35}}$$
$$= 0.169.$$

And by applying the Central Limit Theorem, we know that the form of the distribution is normal. The distribution looks like Figure 12.9. If the class is guessing at the quiz answers, we should find a mean number of correct answers close to 2.0; if the students are not guessing, then the class's mean should be farther from 2.0.

The next step in hypothesis testing is to define two regions of the sampling distribution, one that is "likely" given the hypothesis of a mean of 2.0 (guessing) and one that is "unlikely." For now, let's agree that anything so close to 2.0 that it should happen 95% of the time may be regarded as "likely" and will not cause us to doubt the hypothesis. On the other hand, results so far away from 2.0 as to occur by chance 5% of the time or less will be considered "unlikely" and will cause us to reject the "guessing" hypothesis.

By selecting the 95% region, we are saying that we should define the "likely" and "unlikely" areas of the standardized sampling distribution to appear as

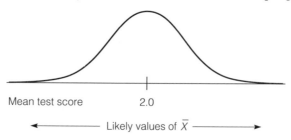

Figure 12.9

shown in Figure 12.10. Exact computations of the lower and upper bounds of the "likely" region are simple and follow the same general form as those for confidence intervals. Since we know (from Appendix A) that the critical points of the 95% region lie at $z = \pm 1.96$, the bounds are

$$\mu \pm 1.96\,\sigma_{\bar{X}}$$
$$= 2.0 \pm 1.96(0.169)$$
$$= 2.0 \pm 0.331$$
$$= 1.669 \text{ and } 2.331.$$

And now we come to the crux of the hypothesis test—if we observe a mean between 1.669 and 2.331 (that is, close enough to 2.0 to occur 95% of the time if $\mu = 2.0$), we will conclude that there is no reason to doubt that the class's behavior is anything other than guessing. On the contrary, if we observe a sample $\bar{X}$ less than 1.669 or greater than 2.331, we will *reject the hypothesis* that the population mean is 2.0, thus supporting an inference that the class is not guessing.

Suppose, for example, that we give the quiz to the 35 students in the class and find that the mean is 2.86. Since we've decided that a mean greater than 2.331 is unlikely given that the students are guessing, we reject the guessing (that is, $\mu = 2.0$) hypothesis. We conclude, therefore, that the students are not guessing. Notice that our decision makes an inference—the students are not guessing—on the basis of the data. Note also how the first of the two possible conclusions was worded: "... there is no basis for concluding that the students' behavior is anything other than random guessing." We can never really "prove" the hypothesis that we're testing is true; we can decide either to reject it and conclude that its opposite is true, or we can decide that the evidence doesn't let us reject the hypothesis of chance behavior.

More Formally ... We have just been through the entire logic of the hypothesis test, the third inference method. In particular, we completed the following steps:

Defined a null hypothesis
Defined an alternative hypothesis
Defined the population distribution
Defined the sample size
Specified the sampling distribution of the statistic under the assumption that the null hypothesis was true
Specified a decision rule and inference
Drew a conclusion

Let's take these one at a time.

Null hypothesis. The *null hypothesis* is the statement of the parameter value that we want to test. In this case, the null hypothesis is that μ is 2.0. Note that the hypothesis is about a specific parameter value and that the value comes directly from the assumption that the students' behavior is random. A value to be tested is normally established in this way—by a logical derivation from a hypothesis. In this example, we want to test the null hypothesis that the students

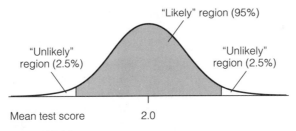

"Likely" region (95%)

"Unlikely" region (2.5%)

"Unlikely" region (2.5%)

Mean test score 2.0

Figure 12.10

are guessing. By the logic developed earlier, *if* they are guessing, then the sampling distribution would have the properties that we've assumed. It's this logical linkage between a verbal statement and a particular parameter value that establishes the hypothesis test as a powerful inference method.

The specification of the parameter also implies a statistic to be used as a point estimate. The parameter to be tested is μ, and so we use $\overline{X}$ as a point estimate. Had we been testing a hypothesis about some other parameter, σ, for example, then we'd use an appropriate estimate, such as $\hat{s}$.

Alternative hypothesis. The *alternative hypothesis* is the logical opposite to the null. In the example, the alternative is that the population mean is not 2.0 (meaning that the class is not behaving randomly). There's an important relationship between the null and the alternative: they are normally *mutually exclusive* and *exhaustive*. That is, the two can't both be true simultaneously (mutually exclusive), and together they must cover all of the possibilities (exhaustive). In our example, either $\mu = 2$, or $\mu \neq 2$. Together, the null and the alternate cover all possible values of μ, and they couldn't both be true at the same time.

Population distribution. In the example, the population distribution was specified as probabilities of obtaining the values 0, 1, ... when students were guessing. By implication, that statement contained the essentials necessary to specify the population—the center, the spread, and the form. In this case, the center is 2.0, $\sigma = 1.0$, and the form is given by the probability distribution. While a complete specification of the population distribution isn't necessary to carry out a hypothesis test, in this example we are able to do so.

Sample size. The sample size is always specified for a hypothesis test. In our example, it's $N = 35$.

Sampling distribution of the statistic. The null hypothesis implies a point estimator. Combined with our knowledge of (or assumptions about) the population distribution and the sample size, it specifies the sampling distribution of the statistic. The sampling distribution in turn provides a way to determine the probabilities of all possible values of the sample statistic.

Decision rule and inference. This is the final step in the logic of the hypothesis test. Using the sampling distribution, we decide on a set of possible observations that *supports* the null hypothesis and on a mutually exclusive and exhaustive set that *does not support* it. In our example, we decided that a sample mean between 1.669 and 2.331 supported the null hypothesis, and that sample means lower or higher than that range did not. A *decision rule* follows and defines what inference to make given any outcome. In the example, a mean less than 1.669 or greater than 2.331 would lead us to reject the hypothesis that $\mu = 2.0$ and thus conclude that the students probably were not guessing. On the other hand, means within the range 1.669–2.331 are likely to occur if the class were behaving randomly. A mean in that range wouldn't contradict the hypothesis of guessing. In either case, we make an inference about the class's behavior. In other words, we are *testing the hypothesis* that the mean number of items correct for the class is 2.0 (implying guessing) against the *alternative hypothesis* that the mean is not 2.0 (the students are not guessing).

Deciding how much of the area in the sampling distribution to allocate to the "likely" and the "unlikely" regions is a complex matter. We'll explore the choice carefully later. There are two "traditional" probability values that are used to define the "unlikely" area: .01 and .05. These values, called the *significance level* of the test, define the size of the "unlikely" region. For now, either .01 or .05 will suffice. Once one of those is defined, then the decision rule can set the critical points in the sampling distribution.

The logic of the hypothesis test, in sum, sets up two opposing hypotheses, the null and the alternative. A sampling distribution, *constructed under the assumption that the null is true*, establishes probabilities of the values of the statistic. If we observe a "likely" value (close to the null), then we retain the null hypothesis and infer that we see no evidence to conclude to the contrary. On the other hand, if we observe an "unlikely" event, then we will reject the null hypothesis, thereby indirectly supporting the alternative.

Earlier we mentioned the notion of indirect support of a hypothesis; the null is established as the *opposite* of what the investigator really wants to conclude. In our example, the instructor probably wants to conclude that the class is *not* behaving randomly. Our test is thus a test of the hypothesis that there is *no difference* between the behavior of the class and that of students who are randomly guessing. This hypothesis of no difference is what gives the null hypothesis its name. (When we learn, in Chapter 14, about testing for a difference between two experimental conditions, we will see that the usual hypothesis test is that there is no—*null*—difference. If we reject the hypothesis of no difference, then, we will conclude that there is a difference.)

Note that we could make an error in the inference. Perhaps the class *is* behaving randomly, but happens to be lucky. Perfect papers should happen, after all, roughly 1 in every 16 times when the students are guessing. Should a number of students have been so lucky or perhaps just guessed better than their colleagues, we might see an unusual number of good papers. If we see a very low mean number of errors, though, our decision rule leads to the conclusion that the behavior is nonrandom, and that could be an error.

Actually there are two kinds of errors, and we'll explore them fully later in this chapter. The first kind of error—concluding that the null hypothesis is false when it's actually true—is a Type I error. The converse kind of error (accepting the null when it is actually false) is called (what else!) a Type II error. In our

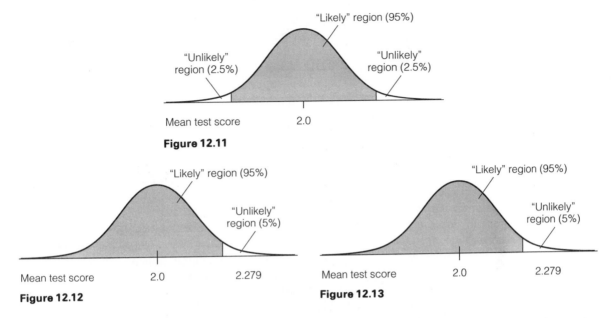

Figure 12.11

Figure 12.12

Figure 12.13

example, this kind of error could occur if, for example, a number of students who actually knew the material were distracted during the exam and pulled the class mean down far enough to be so close to 2.0 that our decision rule concluded that the class was guessing.

One Tail or Two? In the example, the "unlikely" region was divided into two pieces, with one-half of the area in each "tail" of the distribution (see Figure 12.11). Dividing the "unlikely" region this way suggests that we regard a deviation from the null hypothesis *in either direction* as evidence that the null hypothesis is incorrect. In other words, there are two ways in which the null hypothesis of $\mu = 2.0$ might be incorrect: either $\mu < 2.0$ or $\mu > 2.0$ would make us doubt the accuracy of the null hypothesis.

A test whose critical region is divided into two segments is known as a *nondirectional* or *two-tailed* hypothesis test. In most cases, we recommend a two-tailed testing procedure. Sometimes, though, we might want to use a one-tailed test. In this example, perhaps we don't want to consider the possibility that the class does worse than chance, but only that they do better. The alternative hypothesis then would be $\mu > 2.0$ or, in words, that the students know the material. In that case, we put all of the "unlikely" area in just the upper tail (see Figure 12.12). In Appendix A we can find that the z value of 1.65 defines the one-tailed .05 area, from which we can calculate

$$\mu + 1.65\,\sigma_{\bar{X}}$$
$$= 2.0 + 1.65(0.169)$$
$$= 2.0 + 0.279$$
$$= 2.279,$$

and our decision rule now becomes one that will reject the null hypothesis if we observe any $\bar{X}$ greater than 2.279 (Figure 12.13).

Hypothesis Testing

255

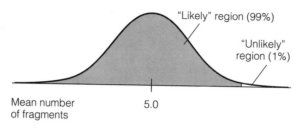

"Likely" region (99%)

"Unlikely"
region (1%)

Mean number
of fragments   5.0

Figure 12.14

As compared with the two-tailed test, a one-tailed test requires *less* difference between the null value and the obtained $\overline{X}$ to reject the null. That's a consequence of placing the entire critical region in just one tail. It makes it easier to reject the null hypothesis, because the critical point is closer to the null value than it is in a two-tailed test. Critics of the one-tailed logic often suggest that such a test is sometimes used to obtain a rejection of the null hypothesis when a two-tailed test would not have come to the same conclusion.

A better argument against one-tailed tests is that, at least in our example, you really do want to know whether your class is guessing; and if they're not, you want to know whether they score above 2.0 or below. The argument continues that we shouldn't limit ourselves (with a one-tailed test) to looking only at too-high values, but should consider too-low values to be equally suggestive of nonrandomness. A two-tailed test allows us to find effects in *either* direction, where a one-tailed test might not.

Before you conclude that you should always use a two-tailed test, you should know that there are some situations where a one-tailed test makes perfect sense. Consider an example from industrial quality control, a major employer of statistical methods. You're a quality-control statistician for a company that manufactures the breakfast cereal *Yummy Crunchies*. Federal standards, and company policy, allow a certain level of "insect fragments" to be present in the *Yummy Crunchies* sold, and your task is to assure that each batch of cereal doesn't exceed that standard. There's no penalty for having fewer than the standard, but the production line could be shut down and the company subjected to legal action if the acceptable level is exceeded.

You draw a random sample from each batch of *Yummy Crunchies* and use it to test the hypothesis that the level of insect fragments is equal to the acceptable level. The hypothesis tested is actually that the level of fragments is at, *or less than*, the acceptable value. You'll also use the significance level of .01 for the test. If we let the acceptable value be 5.0* fragments per box of *Yummy Crunchies*, then the sampling distribution for the mean number of fragments per box under the null hypothesis would look like Figure 12.14.

In this situation, any mean value close to 5.0, or less than 5.0, is likely to occur if the null hypothesis is true; and so the unlikely critical region is placed

---

* Actually, if the legal standard were really 5.0, you'll be happy to know that most manufacturers would set a company standard of something less than that—3.0 or 4.0, perhaps—just to be on the safe side.

entirely in the upper tail. We want to reject the hypothesis that the batch is acceptable (that is, that the level of fragments is 5.0 or less) only if the observed mean is far enough above 5.0 to be very unlikely to occur by chance. We could state the two hypotheses as $\mu \leq 5.0$ for the null, and $\mu > 5.0$ for the alternate, making it clear how the hypotheses are again mutually exclusive and exhaustive.

To continue this example just a little further, suppose that Yummy Inc., the parent company of *Yummy Crunchies*, is installing new equipment that may have an effect on the level of insect fragments in the finished product. You are asked to determine whether there is any change in the acceptable fragment level using the new equipment. Since you need to know if there is *any* change in the number of fragments, either more or fewer, you would use a two-tailed test for this analysis.

Most uses of one-tailed tests are in applied situations like the example. For research purposes, such as those discussed throughout this book, though, we'll recommend nondirectional, or two-tailed, tests. There are, however, situations in which a theoretical prediction is clearly a directional one ("Increasing the amount of practice should lead to *increased* learning"). Here a one-tailed test is appropriate. In fact, in such cases, not using a one-tailed test may lead to a lessened ability to detect the predicted effect.

An Example. A psychologist employed by a school district has been asked to evaluate a class of second-grade students for their performance on a standard test of intelligence. She administers an IQ test to the 27 children; the scores are

98	114	102
119	90	98
113	101	100
107	110	86
121	101	103
88	104	95
105	128	96
110	102	113
123	127	110

The psychologist wants to know whether this class differs significantly from the norm for IQ scores (IQ = 100 is the mean for the general population). Since we have a single set of data, and the question is whether these data fit with a known parameter, the single-sample hypothesis test is the proper way to proceed. We may address the question by testing the hypothesis that $\mu = 100$ against the alternative of $\mu \neq 100$. We will set the significance level at .05 for the test.

The population standard deviation for IQ scores is 15, and the distribution is normal in form. (Because of the way that standard intelligence tests are constructed and scored, working with IQ data is one of the few times where we can assume that we know a parameter value and a population form! Most of the time we don't have that luxury.)

The mean IQ score for the class of 27 children is 106.07. The sampling distribution of the mean for samples of $N = 27$ is normal in form (because the population distribution is normal), with a standard error of

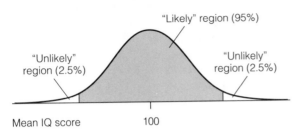

"Likely" region (95%)

"Unlikely"
region (2.5%)

"Unlikely"
region (2.5%)

Mean IQ score   100

Figure 12.15

"Likely" region (95%)

"Unlikely"
region (2.5%)

"Unlikely"
region (2.5%)

−3   −2   −1   0   1   2   3

z scale   1.96   2.10

Figure 12.16

$$\sigma_{\bar{X}} = \frac{\sigma}{\sqrt{N}}$$

$$= \frac{15}{\sqrt{27}}$$

$$= 2.89.$$

We will accept the hypothesis of $\mu = 100$ if the sample mean is close enough to that value to happen by chance 95% of the time (see Figure 12.15). To find out if that's the case, we refer to the standardized normal distribution in Appendix A. To see where the mean of 106.07 falls in the sampling distribution that's centered on 100, calculate the z value corresponding to the sample $\bar{X}$ of 106.07:*

$$z = \frac{\bar{X} - \mu}{\sigma_{\bar{X}}}$$

$$= \frac{106.07 - 100}{2.89}$$

$$= 2.10.$$

From Appendix A, we know that z values between -1.96 and 1.96 are in the "likely" region (Figure 12.16). Since the obtained z value is 2.10, it falls outside of the central "likely" region and is in the upper "unlikely" tail; we reject the hypothesis that the mean of the population from which this class is drawn is 100. This conclusion allows us to answer the original question ("Does this class differ from the norm where the mean IQ = 100?"). The null hypothesis was that $\mu = 100$; we have rejected that hypothesis because the obtained value of the mean

---

* Note how the formula for the z value has changed to adapt it for use with this distribution. It follows the basic form

$$z = \frac{\text{value} - \text{mean}}{\text{standard deviation}}.$$

Since we're referring to the sampling distribution of the mean in this case, the value of interest is an individual mean ($\bar{X}$), the mean of the distribution is μ, and the standard deviation is the standard error of the mean, leading to the formula

$$z = \frac{\bar{X} - \mu}{\sigma_{\bar{X}}}.$$

(106.07) fell outside of the "likely" region of the sampling distribution. Thus we conclude that it's unlikely that the population represented by this class's data has a mean IQ of 100. In other words, we conclude that these students differ from the norm of 100.

In Sum ... We have been through the logic of the hypothesis test twice, showing the logic and the procedure in two different ways. For both examples, the process began with a statement of a hypothesis representing a question about a parameter. In the four-item test example, we presented the test in a form that was intended to clarify the logic. From the hypothesized value, we computed the upper and lower critical bounds on the "likely" region and compared the obtained mean to them. Investigators sometimes conduct the test in this way and compute the actual upper and lower critical bounds for the "likely" region as we did. But more often they follow a procedure like that in the second example.

In the second example, a hypothesis asked a question about the mean of the population represented by a class of students. Then data were collected and the mean computed. Using knowledge of the normal distribution, the obtained $\overline{X}$ was standardized to find its location in the sampling distribution. Because the standardized value of the sample mean fell outside the ± 1.96 range in the standardized sampling distribution, the null hypothesis was rejected. That's the usual way of testing the hypothesis; computing the actual upper and lower bounds of the "likely" area is rarely done outside of the classroom and statistics texts.

Presenting Hypothesis Test Results. Presenting the results of a hypothesis test is usually a simple matter. A sentence format is ideal for the simple tests that we've illustrated. The sentence contains the conclusion, the name and value of the test statistic, and an indication of the significance level. APA has a standard form for presenting the results of hypothesis tests. Using it, the school psychologist might write, "Finally, we conclude that the mean IQ for this class differs from 100: $\underline{z} = 2.10, \underline{p} < .05$." Notice that the sentence states the conclusion ("... differs from 100"), the test statistic and its value ($\underline{z} = 2.10$), and the significance level ($\underline{p} < .05$). The symbol for the statistic and the letter "p" are underscored. The null hypothesis isn't normally stated because it's implied, and the critical value (such as 1.96, taken from Appendix A) also doesn't appear because it, too, is easily obtainable by a reader.

Two Sides of a Coin: Hypothesis Tests and Interval Estimates	Let's pursue the IQ example a bit more and use the same data to calculate an interval estimate for μ. The formula that we presented earlier for the 95% confidence interval was

$$\overline{X} \pm 1.96(\sigma_{\overline{X}}).$$

Using the values from earlier, we have

$$106.07 \pm 1.96(2.89)$$
$$= 100.41 \text{ and } 111.73.$$

Thus the 95% confidence interval for μ, based on the sample mean of 106.07, is 100.41 to 111.73. Pictorially, the interval is

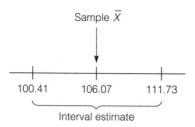

showing the interval estimate centered on the sample $\overline{X}$ of 106.07.

Earlier, we tested the null hypothesis that $\mu = 100$. To do that, we assumed that the sampling distribution of $\overline{X}$ was centered at 100, so that the distribution was that shown in Figure 12.17. Note that the null hypothesis value 100 is not included in the 95% interval estimate for μ.

Now consider the same example, but using the 99% interval estimate. For the 99% interval, we substitute 2.58 for 1.96 in the formula, and calculate

$$\overline{X} \pm 2.58(\sigma_{\overline{X}})$$
$$= 106.07 \pm 2.58(2.89)$$
$$= 98.61 \text{ and } 113.53.$$

The interval is shown in Figure 12.18. In this case, the confidence interval *includes* the null hypothesis value from the hypothesis test.

As the final step in this example, let's test the hypothesis that $\mu = 100$, but use the .01 significance level. We compute the z value as before:

$$z = \frac{\overline{X} - \mu}{\sigma_{\overline{X}}}$$
$$= \frac{106.07 - 100}{2.89}$$
$$= 2.10.$$

Consulting Appendix A, the critical value is 2.58 (you should have anticipated that!), and so we do not reject the hypothesis that $\mu = 100$. But we already knew

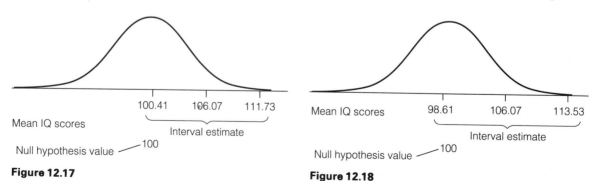

Figure 12.17

Figure 12.18

12   Estimates and Hypothesis Tests

as much from the 99% confidence limit. The 99% confidence interval includes the value 100, meaning that it's a probable value for μ. Since that's the case, then it shouldn't be rejected in a hypothesis test. And the hypothesis test computation has us conclude that, at the .01 level, we don't reject the null hypothesis of $\mu = 100$.

The point of this illustration is to show that interval estimation and hypothesis testing are two ways to do the same thing. If the null hypothesis value is inside the interval at the chosen confidence level, then the null is not rejected. If the null is outside of the interval, then the null would be rejected. This alternate means of conducting the hypothesis test is preferred by some investigators because it provides both the interval estimate and the hypothesis test in one simple and easy-to-understand operation.

Errors in Making Inferences

Any time we leave the certainty of a sample to make an inference about a parameter, we may come to an incorrect conclusion. While it would be nice to avoid making any errors, some wrong inferences are more serious than others ("I should have brought an umbrella" or "I thought the other driver was going to stop.") In statistics, too, some errors are more serious than others, but the situations are usually less clear-cut than those that concern weather or driving safety. Before we can intelligently weigh the consequences of inferential errors, we need to see just what kinds of wrong inferences we can make.

In the four-item test example, suppose that the class *really* was guessing randomly and just got lucky. In fact, they got so lucky that, on the average, their mean was 2.85 questions correct. If that happened, following the rules of our hypothesis test, we would reject the null hypothesis that the population mean was 2.0 and support the alternative hypothesis. In other words, we would reject the null hypothesis when it was actually true. We earlier indicated that such an error would be called a Type I error, and now we can formally define a *Type I error* as rejecting a *true* null hypothesis. Of course, we can never know if we make such an error, since to know it, we would have to know the value of the population mean; and if we did, then we wouldn't have to be making an inference about it. But, and this is important, we can know the *probability* of making a Type I error. If the significance level is .05, then 5% of the time, by chance alone, we'll observe a sample $\overline{X}$ that is too high or too low; if we do, then we reject the null hypothesis and make a Type I error. If the null is true, of course, 95% of the time we will find an $\overline{X}$ "close to" 2.0 and accept the null, making a correct inference.

If .05 is too large a probability of making a Type I error, it's easy to make the value as small as desired—just pick the significance level and find the appropriate critical z from Appendix A. So we can set the probability of making a Type I error by simply adjusting the "likely" and "unlikely" regions. And this is often done, leading to different "significance" levels, of which .05 and .01 are by far the most common.

A Type II error is the converse of a Type I error; it is the error of accepting a null hypothesis that is actually false. If, for example, the students in the

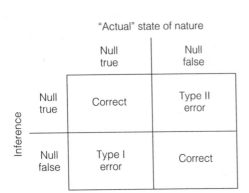

Figure 12.19

	"Actual" state of nature	
Inference	Null true	Null false
Null true	Correct	Type II error
Null false	Type I error	Correct

Figure 12.20

	"Actual" state of nature	
Inference	Students guessing μ = 2.0	Students not guessing μ ≠ 2.0
Students guessing μ = 2.0	Correct	Type II error
Students not guessing μ ≠ 2.0	Type I error	Correct

Figure 12.21

	"Actual" state of nature	
Inference	Students guessing μ = 2.0	Students not guessing μ ≠ 2.0
Students guessing μ = 2.0	**Correct**	**Type II error**
Students not guessing μ ≠ 2.0	Type I error Prob = α	**Correct**

Figure 12.22

	"Actual" state of nature	
Inference	Students guessing μ = 2.0	Students not guessing μ ≠ 2.0
Students guessing μ = 2.0	Correct Prob = 1 − α	**Type II error**
Students not guessing μ ≠ 2.0	**Type I error**	**Correct**

four-item quiz example aren't actually guessing, but we conclude that they are, then we've made a Type II error. In more general terms, then, if the null hypothesis is not true, to make a correct inference, we should reject it (Figure 12.19). Figure 12.20 summarizes the four-item quiz. The "actual" state of nature is what we're trying to make an inference about—are the students guessing or are they not? Of course, we don't know what the state of nature really is, so we can never know if we're correct or if we've made an inferential error. But we can nevertheless weigh the meaning and importance of the two kinds of error in a particular situation and decide to make either or both of the kinds of error more or less probable.

The significance level of a hypothesis test is *the probability of making a Type I error*. Statisticians often use the Greek letter α to symbolize this probability, a tradition that we will continue here. Thus α is the probability that we will reject a null hypothesis that is actually correct (Figure 12.21). If the null hypothesis is correct, the probability of *not* rejecting the null hypothesis—that is, of being correct—is 1 − α, as indicated in Figure 12.22. Usually α is set at some small value, with .05 and .01 being the two most frequent choices. These two significance levels indicate, respectively, 1 and 5 chances in 100 that a hypothesis test will reject a true null hypothesis. But there is nothing magical or sacred about

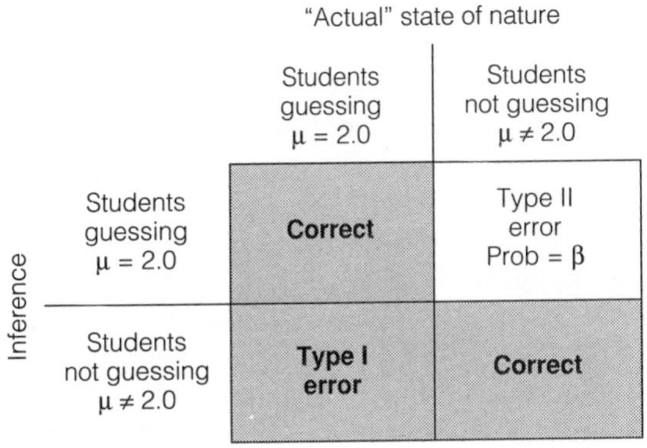

Figure 12.23

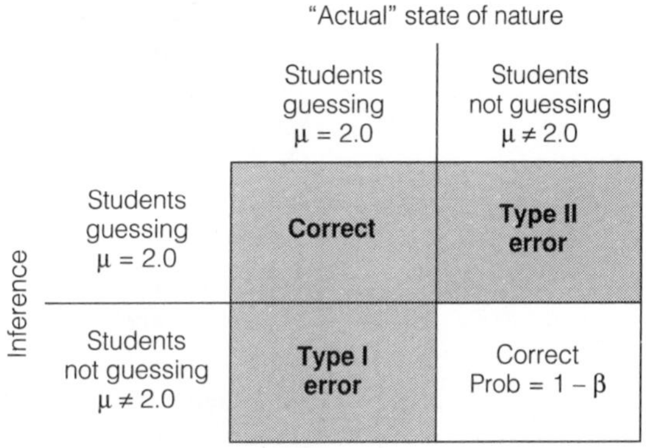

Figure 12.24

those two significance levels, and there is sometimes good reason to use some other value.

We may let the symbol β represent the probability of making a Type II error, that of failing to reject the null hypothesis when it is actually false (Figure 12.23). Naturally, if the null is false, then the probability of concluding that it really is false is $1 - \beta$, a quantity known as the *power* of the test (Figure 12.24).

We'll return to power soon. First, though, let's consider the costs of making the two kinds of error, because the cost of making an error is a factor in deciding on how to approach the matter of Type I and Type II errors.

Relative Costs

It's easy to make a Type I error less likely—just select a smaller value of α. That's such a simple adjustment that perhaps we should run all of our tests at $\alpha = .01$, or even at $\alpha = .001$. The problem is that, all other things being equal, *if we decrease the probability of a Type I error, we increase the probability of a Type II error*. In other words, Type I and Type II errors are inversely related; decreasing the probability of one of them increases the probability of the other.

It's not nearly as easy to change the probability of a Type II error. And since the two kinds of error are inversely related, opting to reduce the probability of one kind of error increases the probability of the other. Even worse, there's no universal rule to help you decide which is the more important to avoid. A decision on balancing the error probabilities has to be made in each piece of research. To illustrate the considerations involved, let's consider the consequences of the two kinds of error in several situations.

Taking Tests. In our hypothetical four-item test example, a Type I error would lead us to the erroneous conclusion that the students knew the material when actually they didn't and were just guessing. Obviously, we would like to avoid that sort of error if possible; an instructor might conclude wrongly that the students understood the material and would then offer no additional explanatory materials. That would result in the students' learning less than they would have if their instructor had correctly inferred that they were guessing.

Concluding that the students didn't know the material when in fact they did would be a Type II error. Perhaps that's not too bad an error to make, at least in this situation. It might result in the instructor's spending some additional time and effort on the material, at the risk of boring the class. That's a relatively small price to pay, and so the instructor might opt to reduce the risk of a Type I error, letting the probability of a Type II error increase, since the cost associated with the latter doesn't seem too bad.

The Class IQ. In the second example, we asked whether a class seems to have been drawn from a population whose mean IQ is 100; that is, is the class normal in intelligence? The errors are summarized in Figure 12.25. In this example, a Type I error leads the psychologist to conclude that the class's mean IQ is not 100 when it really is (the class is normal in intelligence, and the psychologist would conclude that it is not). If the class mean was above 100, as in the example, the teacher, assuming that she had a brighter-than-normal class, might present new "enrichment" materials and exercises, push the class faster than usual, and otherwise expect more from the class. A Type II error, on the other hand, would result in concluding that the class was normal in intelligence when it wasn't. In this case, that error would probably result in little change in teaching methods on the teacher's part.

In Active Research. In contrast to the previous two examples, let's consider an active research project, one dealing with infant perception.

How do you ask questions of very young children and infants? Using words doesn't work very well, but there is a technique that works quite well. Research with infants was advanced greatly with the discovery that they prefer looking at a novel stimulus (see Werner & Perlmutter, 1979, for a summary of the research). For example, if you let an infant look at a particular picture for a time and then present that picture along with a different one, the infant will spend more time looking at the novel picture than at the familiar one. This "preference for novelty" has led to the development of powerful techniques in the study of infant cognition as we mentioned in Chapter 4. Dr. Tyrrell studies what perceptual abilities are born with the child, as opposed to those that develop early in life, using the preference for novelty technique.

But for now, let's consider the original research on preference for novelty summarized by Werner and Perlmutter (1979), because it's had an enormous impact on infant research. A preference may be demonstrated by presenting two objects (pictures, patterns, lights, movements, and so forth), one of which is familiar and the other novel. If the novel stimulus is looked at for more than half of the time, then the infant has a preference for that stimulus. A hypothesis test can be used to decide whether a group of infants looked at a stimulus for more than half the time. The experiment is simple—record the proportion of time that infants look at the novel stimulus, and use the data to test the hypothesis of $\mu = .5$ (or 50%). The hypothesis and the possible conclusions may be diagrammed as in Figure 12.26.

Rejecting the hypothesis of $\mu = 50\%$ means concluding not only that infants can detect a difference between the two stimuli, but also that they prefer one over the other. This was an important finding, since it provides a way for infants to "tell" us if they can detect a difference—and without using words or requiring any training of the infant. That finding opened a vast new world of studies in

Inference	"Actual" state of nature: $\mu = 100$ (class from a normal population)	"Actual" state of nature: $\mu \neq 100$ (class from a non-normal population)
$\mu = 100$ (class from a normal population)	Correct Prob = $1 - \alpha$	Type II error Prob = β
$\mu \neq 100$ (class from a non-normal population)	Type I error Prob = α	Correct Prob = $1 - \beta$ = Power

Figure 12.25

Inference	"Actual" state of nature: $\mu = 50\%$ (infants don't have a preference)	"Actual" state of nature: $\mu \neq 50\%$ (infants have a preference)
$\mu = 50\%$ (infants don't have a preference)	Correct Prob = $1 - \alpha$	Type II error Prob = β
$\mu \neq 50\%$ (infants have a preference)	Type I error Prob = α	Correct Prob = $1 - \beta$ = Power

Figure 12.26

infant behavior. (We should note that what was important for future research was to establish that infants can detect a difference and look at one pattern for longer. A preference for familiarity would serve just as well as an indicator that an infant could tell the difference.)

What if the first research to find a preference for novelty had made a Type I error? That is, what if the first investigators had reported a preference when there really was none? The most likely outcome of such a result would probably have been a brief flurry of excitement and research activity, most of which would not find the preference for novelty. As other investigators jumped to pursue this interesting and important new research area, the first results would not be replicated, and the whole matter would soon be dropped as a fruitless endeavor. In other words, a Type I error in an active research area is likely to be self-correcting by failures to replicate.* Following that logic, then, in an active research field, Type I errors assume a less bothersome role. We shouldn't increase α too high, but we need not feel compelled to keep it at the traditional very low levels of .05 and .01.

Let's consider the effects of a Type II error. What if the investigators had made a Type II error? That is, what if there actually was a preference for novelty, but the research failed to show it? What would be the effect on other research workers? Their likely response would be something like "Well, there's certainly nothing interesting here—it looks like infants can't distinguish between two patterns; at least, they look at them for equal lengths of time." There the matter might die. And a new, important, and exciting research technique might never be developed because of an error in inference. So, to follow this logic to its conclusion, in an active research area it's generally better to avoid a Type II error—such errors often have the effect of closing off new and promising areas.

What have we just concluded about Type I and Type II errors? In one example, we decided that the cost of a Type I error was too great and, in another, that the cost of a Type II error was too great. In short, we can't come to the simple conclusion that just avoiding one or the other will suffice as a rule to live

* The argument here is essentially that of Keppel (1973).

by. We have to consider the consequences in each situation individually, weighing the consequences of each kind of error in context.

| **Dealing with Error** | There is one simple way to change the probability of making a Type I error—change the significance level of the hypothesis test. It's just that simple. But changing the probability of making a Type II error is quite a different matter. We know one way, namely increasing α. All things being equal, if we increase the probability of making a Type I error (α), then we lower the probability of making a Type II error. |

Again, all things being equal, a larger sample size leads to a lower probability of making a Type II error. So why not use a very large sample size for all research? Because it's costly in one way or another. There are more subjects to recruit, pay, or house; there are more data to be processed; there's the need for research assistants and so forth.

And besides, you might wind up with a test that's *too* powerful. What's needed in research is for the important effects to become visible, while trivial ones don't need to be discovered. In the classroom IQ example, if the teacher decides that the class is above average in intelligence, she will use the new "enrichment" materials and exercises. But maybe she shouldn't. Perhaps she discovered a "real" effect; that is, the mean IQ *really is* above 100, but not far enough to warrant introducing the new material. What the teacher wants is a test that is powerful enough to find a meaningful difference. Maybe she wouldn't want to introduce the enrichment materials if the true IQ of her class was 101. (If it *is* 101, the null hypothesis that $\mu = 100$ is actually false, and so failing to reject it would be a Type II error.) Perhaps the teacher would like to begin using the new materials, but only if she were reasonably certain that the true IQ of her class were, for example, 110 or more. So she wants the test to have the power to detect a 10-point difference; increasing the sample size to locate a difference of less than that would mean that the test was overpowered. With a large enough sample size, the probability of making a Type II error can be reduced greatly and the test given excessive power.

There are procedures for determining the necessary sample size and α values to detect the differences of specified sizes. We won't present them here, but the interested reader is referred to Bailey (1971), Cohen (1988), or Kupper and Hafner (1989).

The best advice on dealing with Type I and Type II errors is to think carefully about the consequences of each in the context of a specific research situation. We illustrated that kind of analysis when we discussed the testing, IQ, and active research situations. A decision reached about the relative costs and consequences of the two types of error can then be used to guide the selection of α and N. To lower the risk of a Type I error, just select a lower significance level. To guard against Type II errors, increase the sample size and/or increase the value of α.

SUMMARY

- Point estimates are single values that represent the "best guess" at a parameter.
- A good point estimator is unbiased, efficient, sufficient, and consistent.
- The arithmetic mean is an unbiased estimator of μ.
- The sample variance and standard deviation as defined earlier are biased estimators of σ and σ^2, respectively. The bias is corrected by defining new statistics, $\hat{s}$ and $\hat{s}^2$, which are computed by using $N - 1$ instead of N.
- Interval estimates are found by defining a region around a point estimate that should contain the parameter a fixed percentage of the time.
- A hypothesis test specifies a parameter value; the hypothesis is rejected if the obtained statistic is "unlikely" to occur given that the hypothesis is correct.
- The tested hypothesis (the null hypothesis) is established to be the logical opposite of what the researcher wants to support; rejecting the null thus indirectly supports the alternative hypothesis.
- A Type I error is made if the null is true and it is rejected.
- A Type II error is made if the null is false and it is not rejected.
- Interval estimates and hypothesis tests are alternative ways of making the same inference.
- All other things being equal, increasing the probability of making a Type I error decreases the probability of making a Type II error, and vice versa.

KEY TERMS

α	One-tailed test
Alternate hypothesis	Point estimate
β	Power
Confidence interval	$\hat{s}$
Consistent estimator	$\hat{s}^2$
Decision rule	Significance level
Efficient estimator	Sufficient estimator
Hypothesis test	Two-tailed test
Interval estimate	Type I error
Nondirectional test	Type II error
Null hypothesis	Unbiased estimator

EXERCISES

Solutions to asterisked (*) exercises appear at the back of the book. Exercises preceded by a section symbol (§) must be solved using a computer. Exercises preceded by a dagger (†) can be solved by hand.

§1. Return to the data that you have from Exercise 11.5. For each of the 20 samples of size $N = 2$, find:
   a. The 95% confidence interval for μ.
   b. The 90% confidence interval for μ.
   c. The 60% confidence interval for μ.

§2. In Exercise 1, how many of the 20 interval estimates actually contained the true value of μ (for the rectangular population sampled, $\mu = 0.5$, and $\sigma = 0.289$):
   a. In part (a)? How many would you expect?
   b. In part (b)? How many would you expect?
   c. In part (c)? How many would you expect?

†**3.** You're sampling from a normal distribution whose standard deviation is 15.

   a. What is the standard error of the mean for samples of size $N = 10$? For $N = 15$? For $N = 23$? For $N = 32$?

   b. If $N = 15$, find the 95% confidence interval (interval estimate) for μ if $\overline{X} = 105$? If $\overline{X} = 97$? If $\overline{X} = 84.6$?

   c. For $N = 23$ and $\overline{X} = 108.6$, find the 70%, 90%, 95%, and 99% interval estimates for μ.

†**4.** Here's a set of data. These data come from a population where σ is 12. Find the 95% and 99% confidence intervals for μ.

66.67	47.52
73.96	75.33
43.64	60.41
42.82	71.16
71.81	65.90

§**5.** Generate 20 samples from a normal population with N, μ, and σ of your own choosing. Compute the 60, 75, and 90% confidence intervals for the mean for each of your samples. You should find that about 60% (that is, 12) of your 60% intervals should include your known μ, about 15 of your 75% intervals, and about 18 of your 90% intervals. Prepare a table that shows both the expected numbers and the actual numbers that you obtained.

§**6.** Generate 40 samples of size $N = 10$ from a normal population where $\mu = 20$ and $\sigma = 5$. Find the mean and median of each.

   a. Plot all of your measures of center on the same set of axes.

   b. Which measure appears to have the largest spread?

   c. Which measure has the smallest spread?

§**7.** Using the samples from Exercise 6, find the sample standard deviation of each of your distributions of sample statistics (that is, compute s for the set of 25 means, for the 25 medians, and so forth). Which of the standard deviations is the smallest? What does this tell you about the efficiency of the various statistics?

*†**8.** Here's a set of scores on a four-item quiz for a class in statistics. You may assume that these scores come from a population with $\sigma = 1.0$. Using the .01 significance level, test the hypothesis that students are guessing (that is, that $\mu = 2$). Show your logic.

1	2	3	0	0
3	2	1	4	0
0	1	2	2	2
1	1	2	0	3
1	0	3	3	1
0	2			

†**9.** In Chapter 4 we introduced Dr. Tyrrell. Here's a set of his data. Infants were shown a videotape of a person walking and then were shown a pair of videotapes of people moving at the same rate of speed as the walker was. The data give the percent of the time that the infants watched the left-hand display.

   a. What descriptive statistics are appropriate? Why?

   b. What is your null hypothesis? Why?

   c. If you assume that you know that the population from which the scores were taken is normal in form with $\sigma = 9.5$, what is your conclusion from the hypothesis test?

38.48	49.04	37.23	43.89	69.34
53.99	40.79	49.44	54.47	47.45

*†**10.** Using the following data and a significance level of .05, test the hypothesis that the population mean is 125. The population is normally distributed with a standard deviation of 30.

   a. What are the null and alternative hypotheses?

   b. What is the *population* standard error of the mean $\sigma_{\overline{X}}$?

   c. What is the *sample* standard error of the mean and how does it compare to the *population* value?

   d. What is your conclusion in the hypothesis test?

   e. Find the 90, 95, and 99% confidence intervals for the population mean, using $\sigma_{\overline{X}}$ that you calculated in part (b).

110	162	124	163	133
100	135	49	100	109
136	166	162	151	191
142	136	74	96	151
87	186	122	100	177
153	97	182		

†**11.** Using the following data, test the hypothesis that the population mean is 5. The population standard deviation is 3.0, and the population is normally distributed. Do three hypothesis tests, using the .10, .05, and .01 significance levels.

   a. What are the null and alternative hypotheses?

   b. What is the sample standard error of the mean?

   c. What is your conclusion in each hypothesis test?

   d. Find the 90, 95, and 99% confidence intervals for the population mean. Do they agree with the hypothesis tests?

4.7	3.5	2.4	7.8	6.2
2.7	3.1	7.1	7.5	2.6
3.6	7.3	3.4	4.3	0.1
2.2	0.7	2.4	1.2	0.9
4.3	4.1	5.8	1.9	3.9
8.6	5.3	1.2	5.5	4.8
6.2	2.7	4.9	6.5	0.5

*†12. An instructor gives an examination to his class. From past experience, he knows that the population mean on the exam is 50 with $\sigma = 15$, and that the distribution is normal in form. The data give the scores for this year's class. Using a significance level of .05, should he conclude that this class differs from those of past years?

53	64	37	32	60
49	62	52	78	29
25	51	49	41	88
57	40	62	74	53
69	58	85	53	63
65	49	24	58	65
69	46	65	67	60
67				

†13. Find the 99% confidence interval for μ using the data in Exercise 12.

§14. Repeat Exercises 1 through 6 using the computer.

§15. Using the random-number generator, generate 20 samples of size $N = 15$ from a population with $\mu = 75$ and $\sigma = 15$. Find the sample mean and standard deviation for each sample.

a. For each sample, and at the .10 significance level, use the mean and standard deviation to test the hypothesis that $\mu = 75$. How many times did you reject the null hypothesis? Since you're testing a true null hypothesis, at the .10 level, you should expect to reject the null hypothesis about 10% of the time (that is, about two out of the 20 samples).

b. Using the same 20 samples, find the 90% confidence interval for μ for each sample. How many of those intervals do not include the true μ value of 75? (You should find that about 10%, or 2, of your 20 intervals don't include μ; they should be the same samples where you rejected the null hypothesis in part (a).)

§16. Repeat Exercise 8 using the .05 significance level and the 95% confidence interval.

§17. Repeat Exercise 8 using the .25 significance level and the 75% confidence interval.

CHAPTER 13

Experiments with One Condition

Are Dr. Campbell's subjects "normal" in their introversion/extraversion scores? Are their introversion/extraversion scores positively correlated with their scores on a measure of impulsivity? Are they negatively correlated with a measure of susceptibility to boredom? Can Dr. Tyrrell's infants tell the difference between two patterns of movement on the video screen? Does the aversion to sugar that Dr. Stewart's animals learned generalize to other sweet substances? To tastes other than sweet? The goal of research is to ask questions, and this chapter presents the first of the experimental designs and inferential statistics that let us answer questions.

A Preview

This and the next seven chapters share a common outline, although the detail will differ so much that you may miss it. Each chapter will focus on a single kind of experimental design, addressing several features about it. In particular, for each experimental design, we will look at:

- Basic nature of the design
  - Questions the design can address
  - Key features of each design
- Data analysis techniques
  - Descriptive statistics
  - Inferential statistics
  - Reporting conclusions
- Relationships to other experimental designs

This chapter explores the single-condition experimental design. Chapter 14 deals with designs with two separate experimental conditions (as in Dr.

Stewart's research), and then in Chapters 15, 16, and 17 we proceed to designs with more than two conditions but a single independent variable (one-way ANOVA designs). In Chapters 18, 19, and 20, we turn to designs that combine two or more independent variables into a single powerful experiment (factorial ANOVA designs). The bulk of each chapter will focus on the logic and computations for the inferential statistics, but what will always be most important will be the way that the procedures relate to the questions asked. We'll illustrate why particular experimental designs are appropriate for certain sorts of questions and emphasize how we are able to get answers and draw inferences.

The One-Condition Design

When we talk about the number of "conditions" in an experimental design, we are referring to the number of distinct ways in which subjects are treated. In this chapter, the experimental design has a single condition. Figure 13.1 is a diagram of the single-condition design. The illustration indicates that a sample of subjects is taken from some population, presented with some experimental condition, and then measured on some dependent variable. The data are then used to make an inference, typically about a value of a parameter. That inference provides the answer to the research question being addressed. In Dr. Campbell's experiment, he will make an inference about whether the subjects in his experiment are normal in their introversion/extraversion—that is, are their scores average, or not?

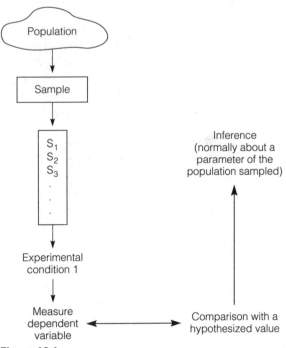

Figure 13.1

The research question in a one-condition or single sample design asks about the degree of "fit" between data and a previously known or assumed parameter. Dr. Campbell would ask if his subjects' mean differs from the population mean on the introversion/extraversion scale. Or he might ask whether the correlation between an introversion/extraversion score and a sensation-seeking score was different from 0. Or he might even ask if his subjects are more or less variable than are typical undergraduate students. This kind of question—do the data come from a population with a particular parameter or relationship?—is the place to employ the one-condition experimental design.

Strengths and Weaknesses of One-Condition Designs

In a single-condition design there is no "manipulation" of an independent variable, and the question is whether the present data agree with some standard. In that limited situation, the design provides a simple and direct way of asking and answering the question. The single-condition design obviously can't compare two or more experimental conditions. But that weakness aside, it's a simple, clear, and straightforward way to ask and answer a question.

Inferential Statistics Overview

The most common inference in the one-condition experiment is about the population mean. We may also make inferences about population spread, about population proportions, and about population correlations; but they are far less frequent than those about the population mean.

As we developed it in Chapter 12, inference takes one of several forms—point estimation, interval estimation, or hypothesis testing. We won't explore point estimation any further, since we've said about all there is to say. Point estimates are available for all parameters, and Chapter 12 discussed the criteria for estimators. Interval estimation procedures are available for some parameters, and we'll discuss them here as appropriate. By far the most frequently employed inferential technique is the hypothesis test and especially that for the population mean. We have already developed the logic for that hypothesis test rather fully, but we made a couple of simplifying assumptions that we'll need to clarify. In addition, we'll look at ways of testing hypotheses about parameters other than μ.

Distribution Form. All inference procedures use a sampling distribution to establish probabilities. The statistics differ in the sampling distribution that they employ, but fall into two general categories—those that assume that some distribution is normal in form, and those that do not. For example, Dr. Tyrrell's usual dependent variable is "looking time," a measure of how long infants spend looking at a particular stimulus. If Dr. Tyrrell could see the population of "looking time" scores, would its form be normal? If it is or if he is willing to assume that it is, then he will choose a normal-based inference procedure. If the population distribution of "looking time" is not normal, then he might want to employ a technique that does not assume normality in the dependent variable.

Inference procedures that make an assumption about an underlying normal distribution are often called *parametric*, since they assume certain parameters to be those of a normal distribution. Inferential statistics that do not have an assumption of normality are called *nonparametric*. The word *nonparametric* really isn't quite correct, since in nearly every case we will make an inference about a parameter. But the common alternative phrase, *distribution-free*, isn't correct either. In order to make any inference, *some* underlying distribution must be employed—it just isn't the normal distribution.

Some nonparametric statistics, especially those based on the binomial distribution, might be called "exact-probability" statistics, since they result in specific probabilities. But that name isn't necessarily correct either, because the probabilities might be approximations. Since we need some generic phrase for this class of procedures, we'll use the common word *nonparametric*, but we'll have to remember that what we really mean is "procedures that let us make inferences about a parameter without invoking the normal distribution." We'll present the most common parametric and nonparametric inference procedures in this chapter and discuss some of the issues involved in deciding which kind of technique to use.

Parametric Inferences About Center

The most frequent use of the one-sample experiment is in making an inference about the center of a population. And the parameter most often used is the population arithmetic mean. Inferences about a population median are much less common, but useful nonetheless. Inferences about other measures of center are almost never encountered and we won't even consider them.

Not only is μ the most common parameter in single-condition inference, but the inference generally is done when three additional conditions are present: the sample is relatively small, the population is normal in form, and we don't know the population variance σ. In this very common situation, the sampling distribution of the statistic $(\overline{X} - \mu)/\hat{s}_{\overline{X}}$ is not normal, and we must introduce a new distribution.

**Student's *t*
Distribution**

When we know that the population distribution of the independent variable is normal in form (or are willing to assume that it is), then the sampling distribution of the mean is also normal. Thus, in Chapter 12, we were able to use the statistic

$$z = \frac{\overline{X} - \mu}{\sigma_{\overline{X}}}$$

to refer to the standardized normal distribution in Appendix A to find critical values and probabilities. But a difficulty occurs when we don't know σ, and thus can't compute $\sigma_{\overline{X}}$. In such a case, the normal distribution doesn't apply.

In cases where the population is normal, and in those rare cases where we actually *do* know σ, we can use the procedures developed in Chapter 12 to make inferences. We illustrated inference using the normal distribution twice in that chapter. But knowing σ is very rare, and we must deal with the very common case where we have a small sample size and don't know σ (and so we use $\hat{s}$ to estimate it).

The problem of finding an appropriate distribution for the common research conditions of unknown σ and small N was explored by a famous statistician named W. S. Gosset during the early years of this century. Gosset studied the problem of small samples while trying to develop interval estimation procedures for μ. He published his research using the pseudonym "Student."* Student's distribution, usually called the t, or *Student's t* distribution, defines the sampling distribution of the statistic

$$t = \frac{\overline{X} - \mu}{\hat{s}_{\overline{X}}},$$

when the sampled population is normal. Note the similarity between this formula and that used in Chapter 8:

$$z = \frac{\overline{X} - \mu}{\sigma_{\overline{X}}}.$$

The formulas are nearly identical, the difference being the population standard error of the mean in the z formula and its estimate in the other. Apart from that, the formula carries out the standardizing operation by subtracting a population mean from a sample value, and then dividing by the standard deviation of the sampling distribution. In this case, though, the distribution follows a form known as Student's t.

There is but a single standardized normal distribution, but there is an entire family of t distributions. The Student's t distributions are all symmetrical and unimodal, resembling the normal in form. They differ from the normal in being relatively higher in the tails and lower and flatter in the middle.

The t distribution is controlled by a parameter called its *degrees of freedom* or simply *df*, which must be specified to define the form completely.

Degrees of Freedom. The term *degrees of freedom* (usually abbreviated df) will continue to come up as we move further into inferential statistics, and we take this opportunity to elaborate on it briefly.

In general, the number of degrees of freedom of a statistic is the number of data values that are free to vary in the face of some constraint. Write down any five values. Let's try 3, 5, -2, 4, and 8 just as an example. We could write down any five values we choose. But now we place a constraint on the problem: the five values must sum to 15. If we begin again by writing 3, 5, -2, 4, we find that we have no "degree of freedom" in picking the last value—it must be 5. By placing the constraint—the sum must be 15—on the problem, only four of the five values could be freely chosen. In the first case, we had five degrees of freedom—all five values were free to vary. In the second case, the single constraint reduced the degrees of freedom by one. In general, a statistic will have a number of degrees of freedom that corresponds to the number of data values less the number of constraints.

---

*William Sealy Gosset (1876–1938) worked as a brewer and statistician at the Guinness Brewery in Dublin nearly all of his adult life. Guinness's policy on research prevented his publishing under his own name except for one publication late in his life. The distribution that we're discussing here was described in a classic paper ("Student," 1908) that also introduced the convention of using Greek and Roman letters for parameters and statistics. For more information on Gosset, see Tankard (1984).

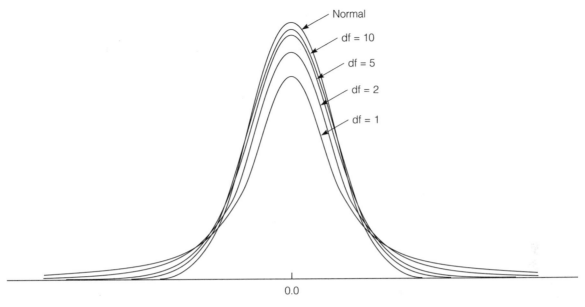

Normal
df = 10
df = 5
df = 2
df = 1

0.0

Values of Student's *t*

Figure 13.2

How does this apply to Student's *t*? The formula

$$t = \frac{\overline{X} - \mu}{\hat{s}_{\overline{X}}}$$

involves two statistics—the sample mean and the sample standard error of the mean. And there's a constraint involved in the latter statistic. In order to compute $\hat{s}_{\overline{X}}$ it was necessary to compute $\hat{s}$, and its formula

$$\hat{s} = \sqrt{\frac{\Sigma(X - \overline{X})^2}{N - 1}}$$

depends upon having the value of $\overline{X}$. Thus the fixed value of the sample mean "costs" a degree of freedom—of the N scores available in computing $\hat{s}$, only $N - 1$ are free to vary because their mean (and hence their sum) is already determined.

The Student's *t* formula above has $N - 1$ degrees of freedom. For N scores, there is one constraint placed on the computation of the standard error of the mean, leading to the value $N - 1$. A common formula is df $= N - 1$. This computation will reappear in several guises as we proceed.

A series of *t* distributions, superimposed on a normal distribution, would appear something like Figure 13.2. Note that as df increases, the *t* distributions become more and more normal in form until, at a very large value, the two converge. In fact, the normal distribution is the limiting form of Student's *t* as df increases.

Appendix A gives the probability values for a very large number of *z* values for a normal distribution. To construct a similar table for Student's *t* would mean

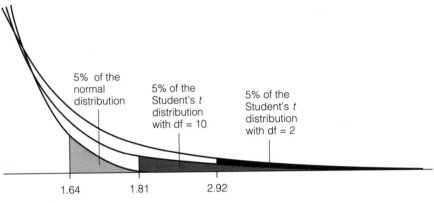

Figure 13.3

a separate multiple-page table for each value of df. Many computer programs now compute the probabilities as needed, and abbreviated tables appear in many books, including this one. Appendix C presents a table of critical values of the *t* statistic for a number of selected significance levels. To understand how such a table is constructed, consider Figure 13.3, which represents an enlargement of three of the curves from Figure 13.2.

Here, the one-tailed .05 critical value is shown for the normal distribution (1.64), and for df = 2 and df = 10 Student's *t* curves. Since the *t* curve is higher in the tails than the normal, the .05 critical point is farther away from the center than 1.64, getting progressively farther out as df decreases. Those values were taken from Appendix C, using the column headed ".05" under the heading "One tail." That column gives the critical values for a selection of df values, including the points on the df = 2 and 10 curves that were illustrated in Figure 13.3. Notice that the bottom entry in the table for the column gives the value (1.64) for df = ∞; in other words, at an indefinitely large number of degrees of freedom, the *t* curve and the normal are identical.

By including only a selected set of significance levels, the *t* table can be a great deal shorter than that for the normal curve. Of course, Appendix C includes only the critical points for the two-tailed significance levels of .002, .005, .01, .02, .05, .10 and .20. This selection is usually satisfactory, although larger tables are available. Tables are becoming less necessary since many computer programs compute the exact probability of an obtained *t* value.

Hypothesis Testing: The One-Sample *t* Test

Let's use a set of Dr. Campbell's data for an illustration. The following data are scores on the Sociability scale of the Eysenck Personality Inventory. The norm for Sociability scores in the college population is 6.0; does this sample seem to come from that population?

9	10	7	8	10
7	8	4	10	7
4	7	7	6	8
11	10	10	8	9

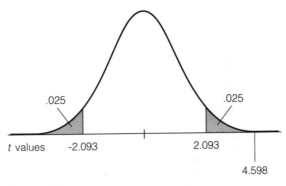

Figure 13.4

To answer that question, we'll use a single sample t test, testing the hypothesis that $\mu = 6.0$. We'll use a significance level of .05 for the test.

For these data we have $\overline{X} = 8.00$ and $\hat{s} = 1.947$ so that

$$\hat{s}_{\overline{X}} = \frac{\hat{s}}{\sqrt{N}}$$

$$= \frac{1.947}{\sqrt{20}}$$

$$= 0.435.$$

We are willing to assume that the population distribution is normal in form, and so we may use Student's t to test the null hypothesis that $\mu = 6.0$:

$$t = \frac{\overline{X} - \mu}{\hat{s}_{\overline{X}}}$$

$$= \frac{8.0 - 6.0}{0.435}$$

$$= 4.598.$$

Now we have the t value of 4.598. Is that value sufficiently far away from 0 to cause us to reject the null hypothesis that the population mean of sociability scores is 6.0? Consulting Appendix C, using the column for a two-tailed test at .05 and the row for df $= 19$ (since df $= N - 1 = 20 - 1 = 19$), we find that the critical t value is 2.093. As Figure 13.4 shows, the obtained t value of 4.598 exceeds the critical value of 2.093. Thus we reject the null hypothesis that the population mean is 6.0 and conclude its opposite, that the population mean is not 6.0.

Presenting Student's t Results. The sentence format for presenting a hypothesis test can be used to report the Student's t result as well; we need add only the degrees of freedom. Dr. Campbell might write, "We may conclude, therefore, that these students have a mean Sociability score that is greater than the population norm of 6.0; $t(19) = 4.598$, $p < .05$." Note that the degrees of freedom are placed in parentheses immediately after the name of the statistic; the remainder of the format is identical to that introduced in Chapter 12.

Interval Estimation Using Student's *t*   Instead of testing a hypothesis about μ, suppose that we use the Campbell data to form a confidence interval for μ. We learned in Chapter 7 that the 95% confidence interval for μ could be computed as

$$\overline{X} \pm 1.96 \, \sigma_{\overline{X}}$$

and that for the 99% interval as

$$\overline{X} \pm 2.58 \, \sigma_{\overline{X}}.$$

To make these same computations in the situation where we're estimating σ, obviously we can't use $\sigma_{\overline{X}}$ since we don't know σ. Further, the 1.96 and the 2.58 values were taken from the normal curve table, not the *t* table. There are two adjustments to make, then, to obtain the formula for using Student's *t*: substitute $\hat{s}_{\overline{X}}$ for $\sigma_{\overline{X}}$, and replace the normal-curve values with those for the appropriate *t* distribution. As a formula, we may write

$$\overline{X} \pm t_{1-\alpha, \, df} \, \hat{s}_{\overline{X}},$$

where $t_{1-\alpha, \, df}$ indicates the critical value for a test at the significance level α (taken from Appendix C) and df $= N - 1$. For example, to compute the 95% confidence interval from the Campbell data, we would obtain the critical *t* value of 2.093 from Appendix C and use the $\hat{s}_{\overline{X}}$ value of 0.435, so that the interval is

$$\overline{X} \pm t_{1-\alpha, \, df} \, \hat{s}_{\overline{X}}$$
$$8.0 \pm 2.093 \times 0.435$$
$$= 8.0 \pm 0.910$$
$$= 7.09 \text{ and } 8.91.$$

To calculate the 99% confidence interval, we would substitute the *t* value of 2.861 from Appendix C for the 2.093 in the formula, giving 6.755 and 9.245 for the upper and lower bounds of the interval.

Nonparametric Inferences About Center

The measure of center that is most often used by psychologists is the arithmetic mean. But, as we noted in Chapter 6, the mean is not the only measure of center; and in some cases it's not even the preferred measure. Other measures of center may sometimes be appropriate given the characteristics of the research situation. Of the statistics that we have discussed, only the median has readily available inferential procedures; it requires that we use the binomial distribution, and we turn our attention there next.

The Binomial Distribution   The binomial is a probability distribution of a variable that is based on the number of outcomes in a simple two-outcome experiment. We've already met such a variable, but we need to be a little more explicit about it.

In Chapter 11 we developed an example involving a four-item quiz, with the assumption that the students are guessing. We also developed the distribution of the variable "number of questions answered correctly" under the assumption of guessing. We saw that the distribution had the probability distribution shown in Figure 13.5. This is a binomial distribution. There are two outcomes that underlie the distribution—the student gets the question either correct or incorrect. We developed the distribution under the assumption that the student was guessing at each question; that is, the probability of getting an answer correct was equal to the probability of getting it incorrect, and thus both were equal to 0.5. From that assumption, we developed the probabilities of the events "0 correct," "1 correct," and so forth by using the multiplication and addition rules for probabilities.

In the usual terminology of probability, each of the outcomes is called the result of a *Bernoulli trial*. In a Bernoulli trial, one of two outcomes occurs; one of the outcomes is usually called a "success" and the other a "failure," although they need have nothing to do with succeeding or failing. (Flipping a coin is a Bernoulli trial; we could call "heads" a success and "tails" a failure.)

The binomial distribution gives the probability of each possible number of "successes" in N independent Bernoulli trials, with the probability p of success on each trial. Thus our four-item test example is a binomial distribution with $N = 4$ and $p = .5$.

Nothing requires that the probability of a success be .5. Binomial probabilities may be determined readily by following the elementary probability rules. For example, suppose that we are drawing a sample of $N = 2$ from an undergraduate class that is 75% women. The probability of choosing two females, calculated by using the multiplication rule, is $.75 \times .75 = .5625$. The four possible outcomes, with their probabilities, are

Possible outcome	Probability
F F	$.75 \times .75 = .5625$
F M	$.75 \times .25 = .1875$
M F	$.25 \times .75 = .1875$
M M	$.25 \times .25 = .0625$

Defining the variable "number of females," we can easily calculate the binomial probabilities by following the addition rule:

Number of females	Probability
0	.0625
1	$.1875 + .1875 = .3750$
2	.5625

Figure 13.6 illustrates this distribution as a histogram.

Appendix G gives the binomial probabilities for a range of values of N and p. For example, looking at the $N = 2$, $p = .75$ entry, you can find the values .0625, .3750, and .5625, exactly as we computed. If you check for $N = 4$ and $p = .5$, you will find the probabilities that we used in Chapter 11 for the four-item test example. In both cases, we calculated the probabilities by applying the multiplication and addition rules for probabilities, when all we would have had to do was look in Appendix G.

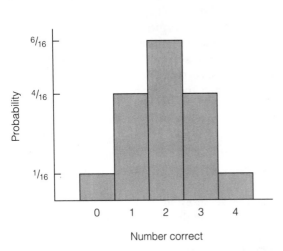

Figure 13.5

Figure 13.6

The binomial is a useful distribution for finding probabilities of events, where the events are counts of the number of occurrences of something to which you can assign a probability p of happening. The distribution is surprisingly versatile, since a large number of events can be categorized into "success" and "failure." Male-female, alive-dead, pass-fail, completed-noncompleted, young-old, and so on are all possible Bernoulli events that could serve as the foundation for a binomial distribution.

For any binomial distribution, the population mean μ is equal to Np. Thus for the four-item test when students are guessing, $\mu = Np = 4 \times .5 = 2.0$, which we already knew. For the number of females in the preceding example, the population mean number of females is $Np = 2 \times .75 = 1.50$.

The population variance of a binomial variable is

$$\sigma^2 = Np(1 - p)$$

so that for the four-item quiz, we have

$$
\begin{aligned}
\sigma^2 &= Np(1 - p) \\
&= 4(.5)(.5) \\
&= 1.0,
\end{aligned}
$$

while for the number-of-females distribution, it is

$$
\begin{aligned}
\sigma^2 &= Np(1 - p) \\
&= 2(.75)(.25) \\
&= .375.
\end{aligned}
$$

The form of the binomial varies with p. When $p = .5$, the binomial is symmetric,

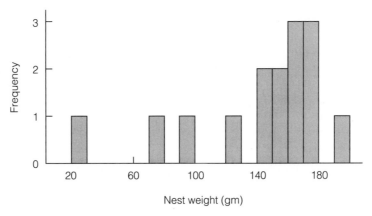

Figure 13.7

while for any other value it is skewed with a mode at approximately* the value of the mean.

The binomial distribution leads easily to a hypothesis test for the population median, which is why we introduced it here.

Inferences About the Median

We could consider both hypothesis testing and interval estimation for the median, but in fact median interval estimates are rarely used. Calculating them isn't difficult but leads to probability computations that are unnecessarily complex for our purposes since inferences about medians are needed so infrequently. For our purposes, we'll be content with hypothesis tests.

A simple and exact test for the value of the median comes from the binomial distribution. If the population median is, for example, 150, then 50% of a sample should be above 150 and the remainder below. Another way to say the same thing is that, if the null is true, then the probability of a score falling above the population median is .50. To test the hypothesis of Mdn = 150, simply count the number of data values above 150. Then you can determine the probability of obtaining a value that large or larger by consulting the binomial probabilities in Appendix G.

As an example, suppose that the following data were obtained from an experiment in which 15 birds were allowed to build nests and then the nesting material was weighed. Under normal circumstances, this species builds nests weighing about 150 grams. Does this group seem to differ from the norm? The weights are

70	190	145	172	173
168	161	155	141	178
121	163	92	24	158

Since the distribution is severely skewed (Figure 13.7), the median is the

---

*"Approximately" because in some cases the binomial has two adjacent modes.

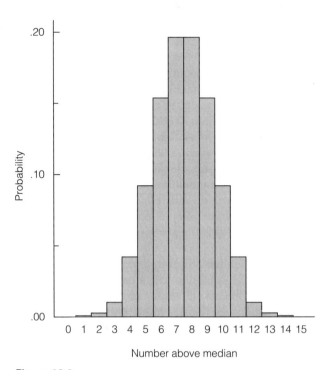

Figure 13.8

appropriate measure of center. For the sample, the median is 158 grams. We want to test the hypothesis that the population median is 150 grams.

Let's choose a significance level of .05. We first count the number of scores above the population median of 150; in the example, there are nine such scores (155, 158, 161, 163, 168, 172, 173, 178, and 190). (Note that we count above the *population* median—the null hypothesis value—and not above the sample median.) Since the median is the midpoint of the population, there are as many scores above it as below it. In other words, if we were to pick a value at random from a population whose median was 150, it's as likely that we would observe a larger score as it is a smaller score. Using probability terms, then, the probability of a value greater than 150 is equal to the probability of a value less than 150, or .5 for each event.

With a sample of size $N = 15$ from the population, how likely is it that we would observe seven or fewer scores greater than 150 sampled randomly from a population with a median of 150? The probabilities are given by the binomial distribution and can be found in Appendix G. Consulting Appendix G, we use the entry for $N = 15$, and the $p = .50$ column. This column gives the probability of getting 0, 1, 2, . . ., 15 scores above the median, assuming that the null hypothesis (median = 150) is true. The distribution appears in Figure 13.8.

What is the probability of observing nine or more scores greater than 150, if the null is true? It's the probability of exactly 9 scores, plus the probability of exactly 10 scores, plus the probability of 11, etc. (we're applying the addition

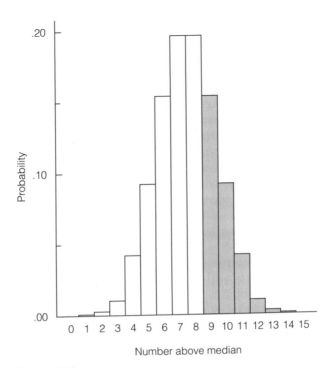

Figure 13.9

rule again). For this set of data, the values are $.1527 + .0916 + .0417 + .0139 + .0032 + .0005 = .3036$ (see Figure 13.9). Since this probability is considerably greater than the chosen significance level of .05, the conclusion is that we have observed a "likely" event given that the true median is 150. In short, the data do not permit us to reject the null hypothesis that this flock of birds builds nests that differ in weight from the norm for the species.

In this example, the possible outcomes for the Bernoulli trials are based on the data values. Each data value is either above or below the population (null hypothesis) median. If the null is correct, then each outcome has a probability of .5 of exceeding the median. The binomial distribution then gives the probabilities of all possible numbers of items falling above the median. By summing the probabilities, we determine whether we have observed an "unlikely" event given the assumed value of the median. If we observe so many actual observations falling above the median that the probability is below what we choose as α, then it's unlikely that the population median is what the null hypothesis claims.

For a large sample test of a hypothosis about the median, we follow the same logic; but instead of using the binomial distribution directly, we use the normal distribution to approximate it. When $p = .5$, as is the case in tests about the median, the binomial is symmetric on its center. Since the binomial has a standard deviation of

$$\sigma = \sqrt{Np(1 - p)}$$

and a mean $\mu = Np$, we can use the usual standardizing formula to convert the observed number of values greater than the null hypothesis median to a z score and then refer to Appendix A to determine the probability.

To take our bird nest example further, suppose that we weigh a larger number of bird nests and find that of the 39 nests, 12 of them were heavier than 150 grams. If the null hypothesis is true, then that value is a sample from a population whose mean is $39/2 = 19.5$, with a standard deviation of

$$\sqrt{39(.5)(1 - .5)} = 3.12$$

and whose form is approximately normal. Using the standardizing formula, we find that

$$z = \frac{12 - 19.5}{3.12}$$

$$= -2.40.$$

Since at $\alpha = .05$, a z of ± 1.96 represents a significant departure from chance, we reject the null hypothesis that the median weight of nests is 150 grams. This larger flock appears to build nests that are lighter in weight than is normal for this sort of bird.

Inferences About the Variance

The following set of data is taken from Dr. Campbell's research, and gives the scores of 10 students on a scale designed to measure their impulsiveness, a frequently studied personality characteristic:

2	3	4	16	9
2	6	12	2	8

For scores on this particular scale, σ^2 is typically about 36.0 (so that $\sigma = 6.0$). For this set of data, $\hat{s} = 4.81$. We want to make an inference, at the .05 significance level, about the variance of the population from which these data were drawn.

The inference for σ^2 requires that we make two assumptions: (1) that our data are a random sample from their underlying population and (2) that the population is normal in form.*

The procedure uses yet another sampling distribution that we haven't encountered, the Chi square (χ^2). A χ^2 distribution frequently comes from summing the squares of several values, and the df is often the number of items summed, less one. Like Student's t, χ^2 is a family of different distributions, depending upon the df. Examples of several χ^2 distributions are shown in Figure 13.10. The value of χ^2 must be zero or greater, and the curves are positively

---

*The normality assumption is very important in this test and in the interval estimate that follows from it. If there is any hint—from a frequency polygon or from a skewness measure—that the distribution may not be very close to normal in form, don't use this procedure. Hollander and Wolfe (1973) present some alternate methods.

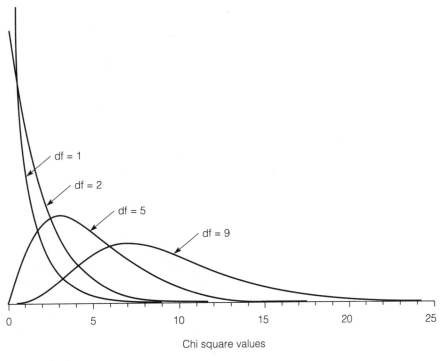

Figure 13.10

skewed, becoming less so as df increases. If the df is large enough, the χ^2 curve can be approximated by the normal distribution.

The statistic for testing the null hypothesis that $\sigma^2 = \sigma^2{}_0$ is

$$\chi^2 = \frac{(N-1)\hat{s}^2}{\sigma^2{}_0},$$

where $\hat{s}^2$ is the obtained sample value and $\sigma^2{}_0$ is the null hypothesis value. The statistic is distributed as Chi square with df $= N - 1$.

Using the Campbell data from page 285, we make the computation as

$$\chi^2 = \frac{(N-1)\hat{s}^2}{\sigma^2{}_0}$$

$$= \frac{(10-1)4.81^2}{36.0}$$

$$= 5.78.$$

Appendix D contains a table of the critical values of χ^2 for a range of df values, but determining the significance of the calculated statistic is a little more complex than with t or z since the χ^2 curve is asymmetric and the entries in the table are one-tailed, upper-tail values. For testing the null hypothesis of $\sigma^2 = \sigma^2{}_0$ against the two-tailed alternative $\sigma^2 \neq \sigma^2{}_0$, we need to determine the critical point on the curve for both the upper and lower values; if the obtained value is between those two points, we don't reject the null hypothesis. In Appendix D, we look

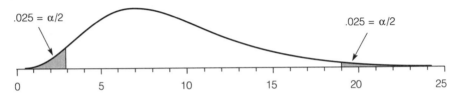

Figure 13.11

up the two critical points separately, finding the upper and the lower χ^2 values that cut off the tails at $\alpha/2$; the illustrations at the top of the table should help you to find the appropriate columns.

For the test of the Campbell data with $\alpha = .05$, and df $= 9$, the critical points obtained from Appendix D are 2.70 and 19.02 (see Figure 13.11). In this illustration, any χ^2 value of 2.70 or less or 19.02 or more would lead us to reject the null hypothesis. The value that we calculated for the Campbell data was 5.78, and we cannot conclude that Campbell's subjects are significantly more (or less) variable than is the norm for this particular personality scale.

An interval estimate for the population variance may be constructed by building on the hypothesis test that we just presented. In particular, the bounds for the interval estimate may be computed as

$$\text{Upper bound} = \frac{(N-1)\hat{s}^2}{\chi^2_L}$$

and

$$\text{Lower bound} = \frac{(N-1)\hat{s}^2}{\chi^2_U},$$

where χ^2_L and χ^2_U are the points on the χ^2 distribution that cut off the upper and lower $1 - \alpha/2$ points. For the example data, the values for a 95% confidence interval are

$$\text{Upper bound} = \frac{(N-1)\hat{s}^2}{\chi^2_L} = \frac{(10-1)4.81^2}{2.70} = 77.12$$

and

$$\text{Lower bound} = \frac{(N-1)\hat{s}^2}{\chi^2_U} = \frac{(10-1)4.81^2}{19.02} = 10.95.$$

In words, with 95% confidence, we estimate that the population variance lies between 10.95 and 77.12.

An interval estimate for the standard deviation may be constructed by taking the square root of the upper and lower variance bounds. For these data,

$$\text{Upper bound} = \sqrt{\frac{(N-1)\hat{s}^2}{\chi^2_L}} = \sqrt{77.12} = 8.78$$

and

13   Experiments with One Condition

$$\text{Lower bound} = \sqrt{\frac{(N-1)\hat{s}^2}{\chi^2_U}} = \sqrt{10.95} = 3.31.$$

In other words, with 95% confidence, we estimate that the population standard deviation is between 3.31 and 8.78.

Inferences About Relationship

Chapter 9 introduced several measures of relationship, including one for data measured on ordinal scales (the Spearman rho coefficient) and one for interval and ratio measurement (the Pearson product-moment correlation coefficient). In this section, we present inference procedures appropriate to these two statistics. There are inference procedures for many of the other measures of association in Chapter 9 as well, but covering them would take us too far afield; see Siegel and Castellan (1988).

Inferences About Pearson's r

The product-moment correlation coefficient, r, is a point estimate for the population correlation coefficient ρ. Many computer packages offer a test of the hypothesis that $\rho = 0$, but interval estimates and tests for other values are rarely available.

A common hypothesis test is that the population correlation coefficient is zero. This is usually the only hypothesis test that computer programs offer, if they offer any test about ρ at all. The test is usually conducted by using a formula that results in a value that is distributed approximately as Student's t, namely

$$t = \frac{r\sqrt{N-2}}{\sqrt{1-r^2}}.$$

The value of r is entered into the formula, and the result is referred to a standard t table with df $= N - 2$, where N is the number of pairs of scores. As a practical matter, it's usually easier to test the hypothesis that $\rho = 0$ by using a table of critical values for the significance of r; one is presented in Appendix K.

As an example, we take data from Dr. Campbell's studies of introversion/extraversion (I/E). Another trait that he often measures is impulsivity, the tendency of an individual to give in to sudden urges. He has used several measures of impulsivity, including the Impulsivity subscale of the Eysenck Personality Inventory. A second impulsivity measure is provided by the Impulsiveness scale on Eysenck and Eysenck's Impulsiveness-Venturesomeness-Empathy (IPE) questionnaire. You would expect that the two measures of impulsivity would correlate. For a sample of 84 college students, he found a correlation of $r = .425$ between EPI and the IPE scores. The value is not high, but does it differ from zero, using a significance level of .01? This question may be answered with the one-sample hypothesis test formula developed earlier, or we may simply look in Appendix K. There we find that a Pearson r of 0.256 or greater is significantly different from zero for $N = 80$ and $\alpha = .01$. (If the necessary df isn't in the table, choose the next lower entry, which gives a *higher* critical value.)

Using the formula with the Campbell data, we have

$$t = \frac{r\sqrt{N-2}}{\sqrt{1-r^2}}$$

$$= \frac{.425\sqrt{84-2}}{\sqrt{1-.425^2}}$$

$$= 4.25.$$

Appendix C does not have an entry for df $= N - 2 = 82$. Using the next smaller df (60), we obtain the critical value at $\alpha = .01$ of 2.66. The hypothesis that $\rho = 0$ is rejected; while the correlation between the two impulsivity measures is small, it *is* significantly greater than zero. Remember, though, that the square of the correlation gives the proportion of the variance in one variable that is predictable from the other. In this example, $r^2 = .425^2 = .18$; 18% is not a large amount of the variability in a variable that can be predicted from the other. While the correlation may be significantly different from zero, as in this example, that fact needs to be tempered by a knowledge of the proportion of shared variability.

Hypothesis testing becomes more complicated if we want to test a hypothesis other than $\rho = 0$. Most computer programs don't even offer the option. To test a hypothesis about a nonzero population value, we must know something about the sampling distribution of the product-moment correlation coefficient. When $\rho = 0$ and when N is large enough (greater than 50), the form of the sampling distribution can be regarded as being normal with

$$\sigma_r = \sqrt{\frac{1}{N-3}}.$$

But when $\rho \neq 0$, the distribution of r is markedly skewed, becoming more so as the absolute value of r approaches 1.0. As r approaches $+1.0$, the distribution becomes negatively skewed; the skew is positive for r approaching -1.0. Fortunately, the great early statistician R. A. Fisher (about whom we'll hear more later) developed a formula that transforms r into a z value that is normally distributed when N is greater than about 10. That formula, known appropriately as *Fisher's r-to-z transformation*, has been used to compute the values in Appendix L, which provides the transformed values of a large number of r values. To test a hypothesis about ρ, we use the sampling distribution for the transformed r; it is normal in form, centered on the transformed null hypothesis value, and has a standard deviation of

$$\sigma_r = \sqrt{\frac{1}{N-3}}.$$

To test a hypothesis, we form the test statistic

$$z = \frac{z_r - \mu_\rho}{\sigma_r},$$

which may be referred to an ordinary normal curve table like Appendix A.

As an example, let's take yet more data from Dr. Campbell. Among his data, Dr. Campbell has a measure of impulsivity derived from Zuckerman's Sensation

Seeking Scale. We'll look particularly at a subscale that Dr. Campbell calls "Experience Seeking." Another measure is a score on the Barratt Impulsivity Scale. Suppose that previous research suggests that the correlation between those two measures is likely to be about .60. For Campbell's 84 students, $r = .51$. Do Dr. Campbell's subjects differ from the assumed population, where $\rho = .6$?

To answer this question, we use the r-to-z transformation table in Appendix L to convert the obtained and the null hypothesis values of r and ρ into z, obtaining the values $z_r = 0.5627$ and $\mu_\rho = 0.6931$.

We compute the standard deviation of the sampling distribution as

$$\sigma_r = \sqrt{\frac{1}{N-3}} = \sqrt{\frac{1}{84-3}} = .111.$$

Finally, we calculate the z score for the transformed values:

$$z = \frac{z_r - \mu_z}{\sigma_r} = \frac{.5627 - .6931}{.111} = -1.175.$$

Since a z must be 1.96 or greater to reject the null hypothesis at the .05 level, we conclude that this group of subjects does not differ from the norm with regard to the correlation between the Barratt and Zuckerman scores.

Note that there is no reasonable way to test the hypothesis that $\rho = 1.0$ or that $\rho = -1.0$, as students sometimes want to do. The reason why we can't make those tests is that we must assume that the null is true to construct the sampling distribution. But if it were true, then all of the points in the scatterplot would be on a single straight line, and there could be no variability around that line. Because that's the case, *any* deviation from the single-line scatterplot would result in an automatic rejection of the hypothesis at *any* significance level.

In Chapter 10 we developed the regression equation for predicting the variable Y from the variable X. The equation was

$$\hat{Y} = bX + a.$$

The slope coefficient b, which we also called the regression coefficient, is a statistic that estimates a population parameter β. In some circumstances we may want to test the hypothesis that $\beta = 0$ in the population. This hypothesis is identical to saying that there is no predictability from X to Y.

In the two-variable situation, with a single X predicting Y, the test of the hypothesis that $\rho = 0$ is identical to a test of the hypothesis that $\beta = 0$, so we need not pursue the matter further here. We do bring it up to note that, in multiple regression, where there are two or more X variables, it would make sense to be able to test the hypothesis of predictability for each X separately. Indeed, just such tests are available and are very valuable in the multivariate situation.

| Inferences About Spearman's rho | We rarely need to use any inference for Spearman's rank-order correlation (rho) other than a test of the null hypothesis that the population value is zero. There are two procedures, depending upon sample size. The test for small samples ($N \leq 10$) is simple and requires only a table, while the second makes use of an approximation using the normal distribution. |

For small samples, Appendix E gives the values of rho that are significant at the .01 and the .05 levels for several sample sizes. The table is used by simply finding the entry for the sample size and significance level desired; if the obtained correlation exceeds that value, then we reject the hypothesis of no association.

For larger samples, the statistic

$$t = r_S \sqrt{\frac{N-2}{1 - r_S{}^2}},$$

where r_S is the Spearman's rho value is distributed as Student's t with $df = N - 2$ where N is the number of pairs of ranks. Thus for a case where $r_S = .72$ and $N = 16$, we have

$$t = r_S \sqrt{\frac{N-2}{1 - r_S{}^2}}$$

$$= .72 \sqrt{\frac{16 - 2}{1 - .72^2}}$$

$$= 3.88.$$

With $df = 16 - 2 = 14$, the critical value for .01 is 2.977; we conclude that the correlation is significantly different from zero.

Normality (and Other) Assumptions

Four common requirements underlie a great many statistical procedures. Let's look at them in some detail.

Normality and Equality of Variance

To use Student's t, and to test hypotheses about σ^2, we must assume that the population distribution of the variable being measured is normal in form. The nonparametric tests introduced earlier and those that we will meet later were developed at least partly to deal with data in which the normality condition seems not to be met. How important is the normality assumption? What happens if we violate the assumption and use the t test for data that are not normally distributed? These questions are important to the σ^2 and r tests, as well as to the single-sample t test. But they're important well beyond the applications discussed in this chapter, because they continue with us through two-sample t tests, and into the most widely used inferential technique, analysis of variance.

Because so many tests assume the normal distribution and equal variances in multiple condition designs, those assumptions have received a great deal of attention from statisticians in the past several years. We won't try to survey this expanding area of statistical literature in detail, but will summarize what seems to be an emerging consensus of opinion and offer guidelines for researchers. (Kerlinger [1986, pp. 265–269] offers a short overview of some of the literature.)

Much current opinion, but by no means all of it, is that, in general, you shouldn't worry a lot about normality and equal variance. Research seems to indicate that most of the parametric (that is, normal-curve-based) inference procedures are fairly well-behaved in the face of moderate departures from both normality and equality of variance. Tests and estimates that are relatively uninfluenced by violations in their assumptions are known as *robust* procedures, and a substantial literature has developed in the field of robust statistics.

A well-equipped statistician has a number of tools to draw upon at different stages of the analysis. In the initial stages, when you're trying to get a general "feel for" the data, all of the descriptive procedures are useful. When it comes to actually making inferences, though, parametric procedures are often the best because they are frequently more powerful.* The nonparametric tests are presented here, too, because they can be extremely useful in cases of small sample size, severe departures from normality, and/or unequal variances.

Measurement Level

In Chapters 5 through 9 we discussed the importance of the measurement characteristics when selecting descriptive procedures. Those considerations apply equally to selecting inferential statistics. Parametric inference generally requires measurement at least at the interval level. Parametric statistics make use of means and standard deviations, and those statistics require interval or ratio measurement to be meaningful. When measurement is ordinal, the measure of center is typically the median; and the inferential procedure for a median is, as we noted, nonparametric.

Independence of Observations

Unless the experimental design and its analysis are specifically designed for repeated measures, an individual subject should contribute no more than one observation to the data. Repeated observations on the same individual are not independent of each other, and most inferential techniques require that they be. While one-sample experiments such as those discussed in this chapter are not likely to violate the independence assumption, they could. We could accidentally include the same subject several times, or we could enter some data values into a computer more than once. Even worse, our subjects might tell future subjects something about the experiment. That will result in a most subtle form of nonindependence, where an individual subject's data may not be independent of others' data.

While independence is a requirement of the statistical techniques, the means of dealing with it are not; instead, the independence requirement places constraints on the conduct of the experiment itself. The remedy for independence problems is a procedural matter and is really a part of an experiment's internal validity.

The best way to deal with the independence of observations is by careful research technique. Once you understand that each observation on a variable should be independent of every other, reasonable experimental control should assure that the condition is met. This is not to say, of course, that you can never have more than one observation on each subject in an experiment; you certainly

---

*Since power is the probability of rejecting a false null hypothesis, you usually want as much power as you can have.

Normality (and Other) Assumptions

can. You may measure each subject on a large number of variables, as Dr. Campbell does. But within each variable, each of Campbell's subjects contributed only a single observation. And you can measure the same variable repeatedly for each subject; researchers in the field of learning would be in serious trouble if they could not measure, for example, the number of items recalled on each of a series of experimental trials. In both of these two examples, the research design is explicitly planned to allow a particular form of nonindependence of observations, and the analysis procedures are designed for repeated measures.

The effect of violating any of the assumptions is a change in the probability of making a Type I or a Type II error, and you won't usually know whether the change has made you more, or less, likely to commit an inferential error. When the problem is in the level of measurement, the effect of using a statistic that isn't meaningful for the measurement is to make any conclusions at least highly suspect, if not completely meaningless.

The concluding advice, then, is to use any available descriptive statistics in order to fully understand the data. When it comes to making inferences, both parametric and nonparametric procedures can be applied, with the parametric ones usually given first attention. Nonparametric procedures deserve careful consideration when there is reason to worry about parametric assumptions, or when measurement considerations demand them.

The Relationship Between the One-Condition Design and Other Experimental Designs

We have just explored the simplest of all experimental designs, the one-sample experiment. We have one set of observations, collected under a single condition, and are attempting to make an inference from it. In such research, the question addressed is typically one of how well the current data agree with previous information or with some assumed parameter.

Often, a single condition will not be sufficient to address the questions that hold our interest. Suppose that Dr. Tyrrell wants to ask whether five-week-old babies differ from ten-week-old babies. If that's his research question, a single research condition won't provide the answer. For that question, he will need two groups, one a group of five-week-olds, and the other a group of ten-week-olds. (Of course, he might just wait for five weeks and observe the same babies, using a within-subjects analysis.) A two-condition analysis is the subject of Chapter 14; there the inferential logic and procedures in this chapter form the basis of a new, but similar, group of procedures for answering questions about two experimental conditions.

Perhaps even two ages of infants wouldn't be enough to satisfy Dr. Tyrrell. As we move beyond two conditions in an experimental design, the inferential statistics become more complex. Beginning in Chapter 15 we'll have to discuss a new analysis technique, that of analysis of variance, that will let us draw conclusions from multiple-condition designs.

Once we have developed the analysis of variance for a multiple-condition experiment, ways of asking even more complicated and interesting questions will be open to us. An important question to someone interested in child development

Table 13.1   Single-Condition Hypothesis Testing Summary

Data condition	Use
INFERENCES ABOUT CENTER	
With data that may be assumed to come from a normal population	Student's t to test for a value of μ or A t-based interval estimate
With data that probably do not come from a normal population	Binomial test for the population median
INFERENCES ABOUT VARIANCE	
With data that may be assumed to come from a normal population	Chi-square test for a value of σ^2 or A χ^2-based interval estimate
With data that probably do not come from a normal population	No test available
INFERENCES ABOUT RELATIONSHIP	
Data are interval or ratio scales and roughly linearly related	Appendix K to test the hypothesis that $\rho = 0$ or The r-to-z transformation t formula for ρ other than 0
Data are ranks	Student's t formula to test the hypothesis that $r_s = 0$ in the population

might be whether boys and girls develop their perceptual abilities at the same rate. To address that kind of question, we will need an experimental design that will allow us to look at and make inferences about how two different variables—age and sex—operate together to influence perceptual ability. This experimental design combines two independent variables in a factorial experiment; these designs occupy Chapters 17 and 18.

But regardless of the complexity of the experimental designs that are developed in the following chapters, the single-condition experiment is the foundation of them all.

Table 13.1 summarizes the hypothesis testing and interval estimation procedures that we have presented in this chapter.

SUMMARY

- A one-condition experiment asks about the "fit" between the single set of data and a single known or assumed parameter; it may be used to ask about center, spread, or relationship.
- Asking whether the center of a set of data differs from some hypothesized value is the most frequent use of the one-sample design.
- Student's t is used for making inferences about the mean when sampling is from a normal population with unknown σ.
- The degrees of freedom of a statistic gives the number of values free to vary; it is often $N - 1$.
- To make an interval estimate for μ using Student's t, the value of $\hat{s}_{\bar{x}}$ is substituted for $\sigma_{\bar{x}}$ in the formula, and a value from the t table is used in place of one from the z table.
- The binomial distribution gives the probabilities of a variable based on a two-outcome experiment; the variable is the count of the number of occurrences of one of two outcomes.
- The binomial distribution may be used to test a hypothesis about the value of the population median.
- A hypothesis about a population variance in a normal distribution may be tested using the Chi-square distribution.
- A common hypothesis about a correlation coefficient is that the population value is zero.
- Parametric tests often assume normal population distributions, equal variances, and interval or ratio measurement; a variety of nonparametric alternatives are available when those conditions aren't met.
- The measurement level is very important in interpreting the results of inferential statistics.
- The one-sample experiment is the foundation of all other experimental designs.

KEY TERMS

Bernoulli trial

Binomial distribution

Chi square

Degrees of freedom

Distribution-free

Fisher's r-to-z transformation

Nonparametric

Parametric

Student's t

EXERCISES

Solutions to asterisked (∗) exercises appear at the back of the book. Exercises preceded by a section symbol (§) must be solved using a computer. Exercises preceded by a dagger (†) can be solved by hand.

∗†1. The following data represent Reading Achievement Test scores from a group of first-grade children. The national norm (that is, μ) on this test is 200. Using the 5% significance level, do these children differ from the norm?

177	206	221	195	232
222	196	205	231	213
189	195	222	204	209

†**2.** Using the data from Exercise 1, find the 80, 90, 95, and 99% confidence intervals for μ.

†**3.** Write a summary paragraph to present the results from Exercises 1 and 2.

*†**4.** It's possible to buy "maze-bright" and "maze-dull" rats. Such animals have been highly selected for generations, and the "maze-bright" animals can be counted upon to learn a 10-element T-maze quickly, perhaps in about 5 trials. A new shipment of rats has just arrived in the lab, and the label has been misplaced; the rats might be normal animals, or they might be maze-bright. From the 40 animals in the shipment, a sample of 10 was selected and taught the maze to a criterion of one error-free trial. The trials to reach that criterion for each animal are shown below; based on the data and using $\alpha = .05$, do you conclude that these are normal animals, or are they maze-bright?

```
5   9   4   8   12
7  10   7   9    4
```

†**5.** In Exercise 4, the significance level was set at .05, meaning that there is a 5% chance that we could conclude that the animals are not maze-brights when in fact they actually are. Since it is very important to the experimenter who will use the remaining 30 rats to know whether they are maze-bright or not, he suggests that a 5% chance of making a Type I error is too high. Conduct the analysis again, using $\alpha = .01$. What is your conclusion this time?

*†**6.** On a standard test of impulsiveness, a score of 50 is regarded as neutral. For the following set of data, determine whether the students who supplied the scores are neutral in impulsiveness. (Use $\alpha = .05$.)

```
66  45  55  64  75
44  63  61  59  52
55  49  57  55  58
57  65
```

*†**7.** The weight of 90-day-old rats is typically about 125 grams. For the following data, test the hypothesis that the median weight is 125. Use $\alpha = .10$.

```
 90   98  132  103  106
116  112  128
```

†**8.** For the following data, test the hypothesis that the population median is 75, using $\alpha = .05$:

```
63  66  59  33  87
31  83  67  68  81
88  88  61  68  82
58  85  49  76  96
79  85  48  83  83
95  90  85
```

*†**9.** Using the Campbell Sociability data from page 276, find the 90% and 99% confidence intervals for σ and σ^2.

†**10.** Using the following data, find the 90% and 99% confidence intervals for σ and σ^2.

```
121  265  442  275  331
196  205  386  119  401
431  335  185  398
```

*†**11.** Here's another set of Dr. Campbell's data, this representing scores on an extraversion scale.

```
14   7  11  10  19
12  14  11  15  17
```

Write a paragraph, with supporting statistics and hypothesis tests, that communicates the following information:

a. Do these data seem to represent a population whose mean score on the scale is 10 (use $\alpha = .01$)?

b. Do these data seem to represent a population whose variance is 36 (use $\alpha = .01$)?

c. An interval estimate (95%) for μ.

d. An interval estimate (95%) for σ.

†**12.** Is the Spearman rank correlation .63 significantly different from zero for $N = 8$, using $\alpha = .05$?

†**13.** Is the Spearman rank correlation .85 significantly different from zero for $N = 5$?

The next six questions are based on the following subset of data selected from Dr. Campbell's research.

Personality Scale

Student	EPIE	SSST	BIS	V	I	TAS	ES
1	15	13	36	3	2	2	10
2	14	22	42	13	3	9	17
3	6	17	37	11	4	9	14
4	20	33	89	14	16	10	26
5	14	18	41	9	9	6	13
6	14	18	48	14	2	9	15
7	16	27	42	12	6	7	19
8	15	13	61	6	12	2	7
9	12	15	40	11	2	9	11
10	14	21	34	9	8	4	14
11	14	27	76	13	13	8	20
12	14	17	65	9	6	7	13
13	12	8	59	3	10	4	6
14	11	13	31	5	8	6	9

Student	EPIE	SSST	BIS	V	I	TAS	ES
15	12	20	49	5	6	5	16
16	11	14	52	4	6	0	8
17	14	21	60	14	13	10	16
18	4	11	43	5	4	5	5
19	17	25	44	14	7	9	21
20	13	25	85	15	12	10	18

The personality test scales are:

EPIE   Extraversion scale from the Eysenck Personality Inventory (EPI)

SSST   Total score on Zuckerman's Sensation Seeking Scale, Version 5 (SSS-V)

BIS   Total score on the Barratt Impulsivity Scales

V   Venturesomeness scale on the Eysenck & Eysenck Impulsiveness-Venturesomeness-Empathy questionnaire (IVE)

I   Impulsiveness on the IVE

TAS   Thrill and Adventure Seeking subscale of the SSS-V

ES   Experience Seeking subscale of the SSS-V

†14. Compute the rank-order correlation between V and I. Is it significant at $\alpha = .05$?

*†15. Both SSST and V appear to measure similar personality traits. Obtain the correlation between them and determine whether it is significantly different from zero at the .10 level.

†16. What is the correlation between BIS and I? Is it significantly different from .5 at the .05 level?

*†17. Some theorists suggest that, because of differences in their internal states of arousal, persons with low scores on the EPIE scale (often called introverts) tend to avoid external sources of additional stimulation, while extraverts tend to seek external stimulation. Obtain the correlation between EPIE and TAS and test it for significant difference from zero at .05. What do you conclude?

†18. The same theorists would suggest a relationship between EPIE and ES. Do the same computations as you used for Exercise 17. Are your conclusions the same or different?

*†19. Compute the correlation between TAS and ES. Is it significantly different from zero using $\alpha = .01$? From .6 (also using .01)?

CHAPTER 14

Experiments with Two Conditions

The prototypical "experiment" consists of two groups, one called the "control" group and the other the "experimental." Never mind that the literature of psychology shows very few such experiments; it's the classic "real" experiment. In this chapter we'll look first at the nature of the two-condition design itself, referring back to Chapter 4 to show how the control techniques introduced there are applied in the two-condition experiment. Then, of course, we'll present the data-analysis procedures for the two conditions; and, finally, we'll sketch the relationships between this experimental design and the others that we'll be exploring in later chapters.

The Design

The two-condition experiment has a single independent variable and a single dependent variable. All extraneous variables are controlled, and so a change in the dependent variable can be causally connected to the change in the independent variable.

The Independent Variable

The independent variable is manipulated so that there are two distinct "amounts" of it. Dr. Stewart's two experimental conditions are an "aversion" condition where animals are given a lithium injection preceded by saccharin and a "control" where the injection was preceded by plain water. The single independent variable in the experiment is the substance to which an aversion is formed (saccharin or plain water), and there are two variants of it in the two conditions.

Dr. Tyrrell uses a two-condition experiment too; the infants are shown two visual patterns, "novel" and "familiar." In his experiment, each infant sees both patterns, and so the manipulation is within subjects, while for Dr. Stewart the manipulation is between subjects.

In both Dr. Stewart's and Dr. Tyrrell's experiments, as in many others, the research question often reduces to asking whether an independent variable has an effect. The simplest way to answer that question is with the two-condition experiment where two "amounts" or "levels" are given to two different experimental conditions.

The Dependent Variable

The research question addressed in the two-condition design asks about the relationship between the independent variable and the dependent variable. The dependent variable is specified as a part of the design. Logically, it must be linked to the independent variable by the researcher's question. You wouldn't measure consumption of sugar water in Dr. Tyrrell's infants, any more than you would measure "looking time" in Dr. Stewart's rats. The independent variable and the dependent variable form a logical pair. The relationship between them stems from theory and is tied closely by the internal logic of the research.

We'll be talking throughout as if there were but a single dependent variable. Our descriptive statistics and our inferential procedures will deal with only a single dependent variable. In fact, most experiments actually involve several variables at once. Thus, while Dr. Stewart is collecting data on the amount of each of four solutions consumed, he might also be measuring weight gain/loss, aggressiveness, activity level, and so on. Dr. Tyrrell records not only "time looking at the novel pattern" but also "time looking at familiar pattern," "time spent crying," and "time looking elsewhere," as well as measurements of activity level and so forth.

Since multiple variables are typically recorded, why do we make it appear that we are looking at only one dependent variable at a time? In most cases, the question or questions can be stated most easily in single variable form. While Dr. Tyrrell might hypothesize that there will be a relationship between a moving pattern and both looking time and activity level, the two relationships are probably related to different theoretical constructs; and it's simply easier to phrase the questions individually. Second, the statistics for multiple-variable analysis tend to be correlational and thus not suitable for drawing causal inferences. And, finally, the inferential statistics for multiple-dependent-variable experiments are complex, and their conclusions are often less than crystal clear.

Dealing with Extraneous Variables

The two-condition experimental design provides the most straightforward way of investigating an independent variable. In the two-condition experiment, the independent variable is manipulated in two different ways, represented by the two conditions; and all other variables are controlled or held constant. With only the independent variable varying, a difference in the dependent variable between conditions strongly indicates a causal connection between the independent and the dependent variable.

In a between-subjects manipulation of the independent variable, subjects are assigned at random to the two experimental conditions. This random assignment assures that there is no systematic difference between the two groups before the independent variable is applied (see Figure 14.1 and Chapter 4).

It is often possible to guard against some kinds of random variations between experimental conditions by placing constraints on the randomizing. A common procedure is to match subjects on a related variable and use that variable to equate two experimental groups. Suppose that you want to study the effect of computerized drill-and-practice on vocabulary development in young children. In one experimental condition, you want a group of children to practice with the computer for a period of time; the other condition would have the children spend an equivalent amount of time with a computer on some unrelated task (arithmetic drill, perhaps). After the prescribed training time, you would then measure the dependent variable.

In such an experiment, the students' reading ability would be an extraneous variable. Certainly, reading ability is related to the dependent variable in the experiment, and we wouldn't want to confound the independent variable by accidentally (but randomly) assigning good readers to one condition and poor readers to the other. We can deal with reading ability easily by using it to match the two groups of children. Pretest all of the children for reading ability. Using those scores, form pairs of children who are roughly equal in reading ability. One child in each pair is then randomly assigned to the "practice" condition and the other to the "no practice" condition. Now the two groups are balanced with respect to a potential confounding variable. The groups contain a similar range of reading abilities, and we're sure that any differences that we observe later aren't due to that variable. This procedure, of course, is *precision matching* as described in Chapter 4. Figure 14.2 diagrams this two-condition design.

When we use precision matching, we have an experiment that is not clearly either a between-subjects or a within-subjects design. In this case, the analysis will follow the plan for a within-subjects design, since subjects weren't assigned to groups independently. There is random assignment within each pair, but the students were certainly not assigned independently to the two conditions. When one member of each pair was given to one condition, his or her pair-mate was automatically placed in the other condition—clearly not independent assignment.

Precision matching nicely controls the single extraneous variable of reading ability, but it doesn't address other variables such as age, IQ-test score, or even eye color. Presumably, we could pretest for many other variables and try to make the best pairings we could by taking them all into account. But that procedure soon becomes cumbersome and impractical with many extraneous variables. In such a case, we can use a frequency-distribution matching procedure as described in Chapter 4. Figure 14.3 diagrams the frequency-distribution matching design. The analysis for this design will be the same as that for the between-subjects design, since there is no pairing of subjects. Here the subjects are assigned at random to the two conditions, with the constraint that the groups are to be balanced with regard to the frequency distributions on the matching variables.

Naturally, the best match for any individual is that individual himself or herself. Thus pairing an individual with himself achieves perfect matching. If we do that, then we have a within-subjects experiment (see Figure 14.4). As we discussed earlier, sometimes a within-subjects design is impossible. For example, we can't give the same person both practice with a computerized drill program

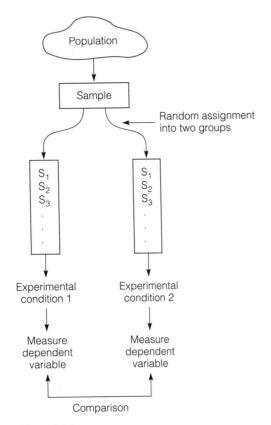

Figure 14.1

Figure 14.2

and not give it to him. But in other cases, like Dr. Tyrrell's familiar and unfamiliar patterns, we can certainly use both experimental conditions on the same subject. Of course, order effects are normally present in within-subject designs, but they can be attenuated with appropriate counterbalancing.

Inference in the Two-Condition Design	Inference in the two-condition design is about the effect of the experimental conditions on the dependent variable. Usually we're interested in a difference between the centers of the two experimental conditions. Since the researcher's interest is usually in establishing that the independent variable has an effect (that is, the two conditions differ), the null hypothesis is normally that the conditions are identical. We can test other hypotheses about centers, such as that the two conditions differ by some specific amount.

Sometimes the research question may be about spread and not center. Some drugs, for example, exert their influence by making certain behaviors more variable, while not changing the average on some variables. In such a case, the question asked might very well be one of variability: "Does the administration of Drug X change the variability in activity level?" A hypothesis test about the equality of variances is appropriate in that case.

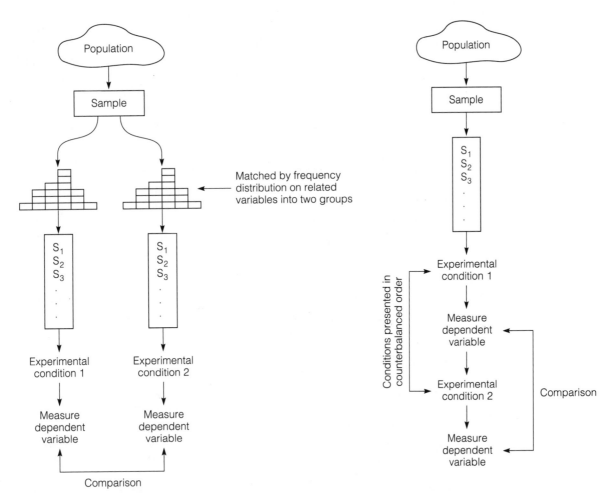

Figure 14.3

Matched by frequency distribution on related variables into two groups

Figure 14.4

Conditions presented in counterbalanced order

Strengths and Weaknesses of the Two-Condition Design

This design is the prototype of "good" experimental design: it's the design that is held up as the goal of research design, and for good reason. When you can simplify a research concept to two distinct conditions and when you find a difference or a lack of a difference, the results are clear and unambiguous. No other design offers such a clear interpretation of its results. Indeed, most of the more complicated designs that we will introduce provide only a "first look" at overall results and leave it to two-condition comparisons to clarify the results.

Besides the clarity of interpretation, the two-condition design offers the best approach to inferring causality. While we cautioned in Chapter 2 about the logical problems connected with making causal inference, if such inference is possible, the two-condition design is where it best can be done. In a well-controlled experiment, where the only variability present is that of the independent variable, the argument for causality can be made the most strongly.

On the negative side, it's sometimes difficult to force research ideas into a two-condition experiment. The design is limited to a single independent variable and further restricted to but two conditions of that variable. Systematically exploring the range of a quantitative variable such as loudness or dosage is not within the capabilities of two conditions, nor are explorations of large numbers of different stimuli. In addition, some research ideas involve more than a single independent variable, and many theories specifically predict interactions between independent variables; such investigations are beyond the scope of a two-condition experiment.

The main reason why few simple two-condition experiments actually appear in the literature is that most investigators design more complex experiments, typically involving several independent variables simultaneously. Conducting such research is more economical of time and allows exploration of the interactions between variables. Variables in psychology rarely operate independently of one another, and sometimes particular combinations of variables have unexpected consequences. Limiting research to single independent variable designs like the two-condition experiment makes finding such interactions impossible. Nevertheless, the two-condition experiment remains the prototype of "good" research.

Analyzing the Data

A two-condition experiment asks about similarities or differences in the center or spread of two sets of data, one from each condition. The data analysis uses both descriptive measures and inferential statistics to communicate the characteristics of the two data sets. There's little to add here to previous discussions of choosing descriptive procedures, except to repeat that the aim is to clearly present the answer to the question asked in the experiment. Thus a question about differences in the centers of two data sets will dictate descriptive statistics that are appropriate measures for the center of the data. Choosing statistics relies upon the same measurement considerations that we discussed earlier.

Inferential Techniques for Centers

The logic of inference for the two-condition experiment follows the same hypothesis testing steps that we presented in Chapters 12 and 13. We begin with a null hypothesis about the population. We then develop the sampling distribution of some statistic under the assumption that the null hypothesis is true. Once that's done, we define a decision rule and then draw a conclusion about a difference between the two conditions.

The hypothesis tests and interval estimates, as in the single-condition experiment, fall into two general classes, depending upon whether they assume that the underlying distribution is normal or not. We'll begin our presentation with the procedures that rely on the normal distribution—the parametric tests—and then present those that don't. In general, the parametric tests are used to make inferences about means and variances, while the nonparametric tests deal with medians or entire distributions.

Parametric Tests for Between-Subjects Designs. The most common inference to be made in this design is about the difference between the centers of the two experimental conditions. Let's take Dr. Stewart's research as an example and develop the logic of an inference procedure. The animals in his research that are given water followed by lithium chloride injection shouldn't develop a conditioned aversion to sweet tastes, because no taste other than plain water is present. We could call these animals the "control" animals, since they aren't given an aversion. Dr. Stewart's other condition gives the animals saccharin before the lithium, and they should develop a conditioned aversion to sweet tastes; we might call this condition the "experimental" condition.

The saccharin-consumption scores of the rats in Dr. Stewart's control group may be thought of as a random sample drawn from the population "saccharin consumption of all rats that might ever be given the water-lithium (control) treatment." For simplicity, let's call this population the "control" population. We might even just call it "population 1." This population of saccharin-consumption values has a mean symbolized as μ_1. In the same way, the sample of sucrose-consumption data from the aversion-conditioned group can be regarded as a random sample from the population "consumption of all rats that might ever be given the saccharin-lithium (conditioned aversion) treatment." We might call this population the "experimental" or the "aversion" population, or perhaps just "population 2," and we might symbolize its mean as μ_2.

The most important question in Dr. Stewart's experiment asks whether the introduction of a taste aversion has an effect on later consumption of various substances; for this example, we're looking at just the consumption of saccharin, but the actual experiment gave the animals a choice of several different tastes. To address the question of consumption, we need to be able to make an inference about the differences in the amounts of sucrose consumed. If the populations don't differ in their means, then we would infer that there is no effect of the conditioned taste aversion on the consumption of sucrose. On the other hand, if we can infer a difference between the two population means, then we will conclude that the aversion conditioning has caused a difference in sucrose consumption.

The question of a difference between two populations usually leads to a test of the null hypothesis of a zero difference between the two population means; that is, that $\mu_1 - \mu_2 = 0$.

So far, we've taken only the first steps in the underlying logic of the hypothesis test by noting that we have two conceptual populations, one corresponding to each of the two experimental conditions. The experiment is conducted by drawing two random samples from the two populations and obtaining two sets of data, one collected under each of the two conditions. We might assume that each sample is the same size, but we don't need to make that assumption. We can have a sample of size n_1 from the first population, and of size n_2 from the second. The mean of each sample is a point estimate of the mean of its population.

We could use each sample mean to test a hypothesis or make an interval estimate about its population mean. There are two population distributions, and there are two separate sampling distributions, one based on samples of size n_1 from population 1, and the other based on samples of size n_2 from population 2

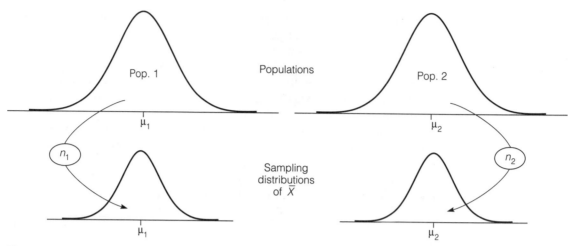

Figure 14.5

(see Figure 14.5). If you look at just one side or the other, we have a single sample design, just like those in Chapter 13. The sampling distribution for the means $\overline{X}_1$ and $\overline{X}_2$ each have a form, a center, and a spread. Since we're considering the normal-population case now, each sampling distribution is normal and its center is equal to the center of its population, μ_1 and μ_2, since the sample mean is an unbiased estimator. The spreads of the two sampling distributions, $\sigma_{\overline{X}_1}$ and $\sigma_{\overline{X}_2}$, may be estimated from the two sample standard errors, just as in Chapter 13. So far, aside from the presence of two populations and sampling distributions, there's nothing different here.

But there is something different—we're not interested in the values of μ_1 and μ_2 themselves, but specifically in the difference between them, namely $\mu_1 - \mu_2$. In particular, for the present example, we're interested in testing the hypothesis that $\mu_1 - \mu_2 = 0$. To make that test, we must define a different sampling distribution, one based on the differences between pairs of means, one mean taken randomly from each population. In other words, we must add another level to our conceptual diagram of the distributions (see Figure 14.6). This is a new sampling distribution. It consists of differences in means, one mean drawn randomly from each population. Like any sampling distribution, this one has a form, a center, and a spread. The form of the distribution is normal, since its parent distributions are both normal, and the center is $\mu_1 - \mu_2$. If the null hypothesis is correct, the center is zero. The spread of the sampling distribution of mean differences between pairs of means is a function of the two sample sizes and the spreads of the two original populations.

If the variances of the two populations, σ^2_1 and σ^2_2, are equal, then the standard deviation of the sampling distribution of the mean differences may be estimated by the statistic

$$\hat{s}_{\overline{X}_1 - \overline{X}_2} = \sqrt{\frac{(n_1 - 1)\hat{s}_1^{\,2} + (n_2 - 1)\hat{s}_2^{\,2}}{n_1 + n_2 - 2}\left[\frac{1}{n_1} + \frac{1}{n_2}\right]}.$$

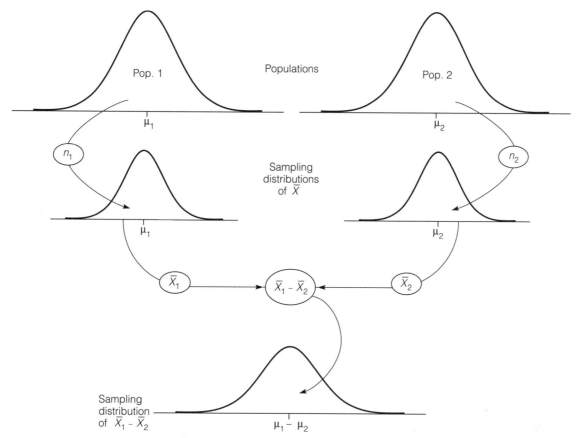

Figure 14.6

This statistic, often called the *standard error of the difference*, is an estimator of the standard deviation of the sampling distribution of the differences in means. This formula is often called a *pooled* estimate, since it "pools" the two sample variances to make an estimate of the population standard error. The pooled formula is appropriate only when the population variances are equal (or nearly so); in later discussions, we'll present tests of the equality of variance assumption.

As introduced in Chapter 8, the formula for standardizing is

$$\frac{\text{obtained value} - \text{mean of distribution}}{\text{standard deviation}}.$$

We saw that formula most recently in its adaptation to Student's *t*, as

$$t = \frac{\overline{X} - \mu}{\hat{s}_{\overline{X}}}.$$

We can make one more adaptation of the same formula, this time to the distribution of mean differences; the statistic

$$t = \frac{(\bar{X}_1 - \bar{X}_2) - (\mu_1 - \mu_2)}{\hat{s}_{\bar{X}_1 - \bar{X}_2}}$$

is distributed as Student's t with df $= n_1 + n_2 - 2$, and is used to test the two-sample hypothesis. As in the single sample test, the right-hand part of the numerator gives a null hypothesis value. In most cases, the null hypothesis is that the two population means are identical, but that needn't be the case. We could test a hypothesis about any value for the difference of μ values. But since the null hypothesis value is usually 0, you will sometimes see the formula written as

$$t = \frac{(\bar{X}_1 - \bar{X}_2)}{\hat{s}_{\bar{X}_1 - \bar{X}_2}},$$

but we'll continue to use the full formula as a reminder that we're doing the same standardizing operation

$$\frac{\text{value} - \text{mean}}{\text{estimated standard deviation}}$$

that we introduced in Chapter 8.

Our hypothesis test, then, is a test for the differences between two population means. Figure 14.7 thus becomes our diagram for the two-condition between-subjects experiment.

Let's take an example of this two-sample test before we move on to the case of unequal variances. The following data represent quinine consumption (milliliters drunk in a 15-minute test period) by two groups of rats in Dr. Stewart's lab. We will use the .05 significance level.

	Control	Aversion
	7.0	7.5
	14.0	5.0
	10.0	5.0
	11.0	6.0
	8.5	1.0
	5.0	6.0
	4.5	9.0
	11.0	3.0
	9.0	6.0
	10.0	7.0
Mean	9.00	5.55
St. Dev.	2.90	2.27
Variance	8.41	5.15

The estimate of the standard error of the difference is

$$\hat{s}_{\bar{X}_1 - \bar{X}_2} = \sqrt{\frac{(n_1 - 1)\hat{s}_1^2 + (n_2 - 1)\hat{s}_2^2}{n_1 + n_2 - 2}\left[\frac{1}{n_1} + \frac{1}{n_2}\right]}$$

$$= \sqrt{\frac{(10 - 1) \times 8.41 + (10 - 1) \times 5.15}{10 + 10 - 2}\left[\frac{1}{10} + \frac{1}{10}\right]}$$

$$= 1.16.$$

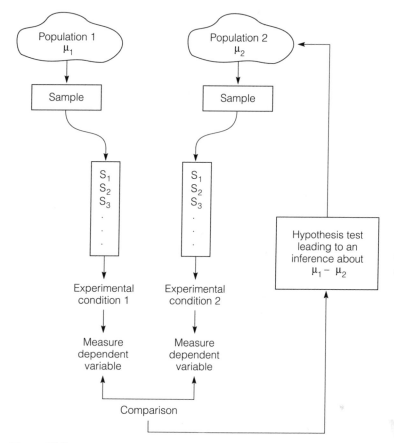

Figure 14.7

The Student's t value is calculated as

$$t = \frac{(\bar{X}_1 - \bar{X}_2) - (\mu_1 - \mu_2)}{\hat{s}_{\bar{X}_1 - \bar{X}_2}}$$

$$= \frac{(9.00 - 5.55) - 0}{1.16}$$

$$= 2.97.$$

With $\alpha = .05$ and with df $= 10 + 10 - 2 = 18$, the critical value of t from Appendix C is 2.101. We reject the null hypothesis of no difference between the two conditions in the amount of quinine solution consumed. We conclude that the aversion-conditioned animals consume significantly less quinine than do their non-conditioned peers.

When the population variances are not equal, two adjustments are made in the computations. First, instead of using the pooled formula to estimate the standard error of the difference, we use the formula

$$\hat{s}_{\bar{X}_1 - \bar{X}_2} = \sqrt{\frac{\hat{s}_1^2}{n_1} + \frac{\hat{s}_2^2}{n_2}}$$

$$= \sqrt{\hat{s}_{\bar{X}_1}^2 + \hat{s}_{\bar{X}_2}^2}.$$

With this computation done, the hypothesis test proceeds as just illustrated through the same t formula. But then an adjustment is made in the df. The formula that we recommend (Welch, 1947) is

$$\text{df} = \frac{\left[\frac{s_1^2}{n_1} + \frac{s_2^2}{n_2}\right]^2}{\frac{\left[\frac{s_1^2}{n_1}\right]^2}{n_1 + 1} + \frac{\left[\frac{s_2^2}{n_2}\right]^2}{n_2 + 1}} - 2.$$

This computation will probably result in a fractional value that should be rounded to the nearest integer.

As an example of the computations for the unequal variance case, consider these hypothetical data:

	Condition 1	Condition 2
	2	1
	3	7
	3	15
	3	13
	4	6
	4	8
Mean	3.00	8.33
St. Dev.	0.71	5.05
Variance	0.50	25.47

Clearly, these data show a substantial difference in variance. If we were to compute the pooled estimate of the standard deviation of the sampling distribution and complete the t computation, we would have $t = -2.323$ with 9 df. The critical value of t for df $= 9$ and $\alpha = .05$ is 2.262, and so we would reject the null hypothesis that the two sets of data come from populations with equal means.

On the other hand, if we follow the computations for unequal variances, as we should, we have

$$\hat{s}_{\bar{X}_1 - \bar{X}_2} = \sqrt{\frac{\hat{s}_1^2}{n_1} + \frac{\hat{s}_2^2}{n_2}}$$

$$= \sqrt{\frac{0.50}{5} + \frac{25.47}{6}}$$

$$= 2.08,$$

so that

$$t = \frac{(\overline{X}_1 - \overline{X}_2) - (\mu_1 - \mu_2)}{\hat{s}_{\overline{X}_1 - \overline{X}_2}}$$

$$= \frac{(3.5 - 8.33) - 0}{2.08}$$

$$= -2.32.$$

The Student's t value is only slightly different from that obtained using the pooled estimate of $\hat{s}_{\overline{X}_1 - \overline{X}_2}$, though the df is quite different:

$$df = \left[\frac{\left[\dfrac{s_1^2}{n_1} + \dfrac{s_2^2}{n_2} \right]^2}{\dfrac{\left[\dfrac{s_1^2}{n_1} \right]^2}{n_1 + 1} + \dfrac{\left[\dfrac{s_2^2}{n_2} \right]^2}{n_2 + 1}} \right] - 2$$

$$= \left[\frac{\left[\dfrac{0.50}{5} + \dfrac{25.47}{6} \right]^2}{\dfrac{\left[\dfrac{0.50}{5} \right]^2}{5 + 1} + \dfrac{\left[\dfrac{25.47}{6} \right]^2}{6 + 1}} \right] - 2$$

$$= 7.33 - 2$$

$$\simeq 5.$$

With df = 5, the critical value of t at $\alpha = .05$ is 2.571, so that we do not reject the null hypothesis, an opposite conclusion from that drawn earlier with the same data.

The example data were constructed specifically to show different conclusions from the two forms of the t test in order to illustrate the fact that they can differ. In fact, the two procedures often come to the same conclusion. To be on the safe side, though, you might test for equality of variances (see pp. 323–325), or (preferably) use the unequal variance computations.

Interval Estimates for $\mu_1 - \mu_2$. Sometimes it's important to obtain a confidence interval for the difference between two population means. The logic of the procedure follows directly from that developed in Chapter 12, except that we're dealing with the distribution of $\overline{X}_1 - \overline{X}_2$ and not $\overline{X}$.

In Chapter 13, we had the formula

$$\overline{X} \pm t_{1-\alpha, df}\hat{s}_{\overline{X}}$$

for an interval estimate for μ. For the difference between two population means, we can modify the formula appropriately:

$$(\overline{X}_1 - \overline{X}_2) \pm t_{1-\alpha, df}\hat{s}_{\overline{X}_1 - \overline{X}_2},$$

where $t_{1-\alpha, df}$ is the critical value taken from Appendix C for a test at the desired confidence level with the df for the analysis. For example, in Dr. Stewart's data on quinine consumption from earlier, the two means were 9.00 and 5.55, with

$\hat{s}_{\bar{X}_1 - \bar{X}_2} = 1.16$. The 95% interval estimate is computed as

$$(9.00 - 5.55) \pm 2.101 \times 1.16$$

$$3.45 \pm 2.44,$$

giving the interval estimate

$$1.01 \leq \mu_1 - \mu_2 \leq 5.89.$$

Parametric Tests for Within-Subjects (or Precision-Matched) Data. When we have manipulated the independent variable within subjects, or when we have precision-matched subjects by some pretest score, the two conditions aren't independent, and the preceding methods are inappropriate. As an example, let's take some data from Dr. Tyrrell (Table 14.1). To collect these data, an infant was shown a videotape of a person either walking or jogging. After a short interval, the infant was shown two moving stimuli, one at the same walking or jogging speed just seen (the "familiar" stimulus) or at a different speed (the "novel" stimulus). As usual, Dr. Tyrrell's dependent variable is "time spent looking" and is measured in seconds. The question is whether the infants can distinguish between the two speeds of movement; if they can, then they should look longer at the unfamiliar pattern. If they can't distinguish between them, the times should be the same for the two patterns.

The data in Table 14.1 look like those for a correlation analysis, but in this design our interest is not in the relationship between the familiar and the unfamiliar times, but in whether their means differ. We could compute the Pearson product-moment correlation coefficient, of course, but that's not what we want to know.

A reasonable null hypothesis is that there is no difference—that is, the infants look at the unfamiliar pattern for as much time as they look at the familiar

Table 14.1   Looking-Time Data from Dr. Tyrrell's Experiment

Infant	Familiar	Unfamiliar
1	38.48	66.67
2	49.04	73.96
3	37.23	43.64
4	43.89	42.82
5	69.34	71.81
6	53.99	47.52
7	40.79	75.33
8	49.44	60.41
9	54.47	71.16
10	47.45	65.90
Mean	48.412	61.922
Median	48.245	66.285
St. Dev.	9.489	12.715

one. If this hypothesis were correct, the two means should be close to the same. Not only should that be true, but also each individual infant should spend about the same amount of time looking at each of the two different patterns. That is, the difference in the time spent looking at the two patterns should be about zero for each infant.

We start the analysis by computing the difference between the looking times for each infant (see Table 14.2). We now use only the difference data and proceed as if we have a single sample experiment, testing the hypothesis that $\mu = 0$. To make it clear what we're testing, we use the symbol μ_{diff} so that it's obvious that we're talking about the differences between the pairs of scores.

The Student's t formula from Chapter 13, modified to specify the differences, is

$$t = \frac{\overline{X}_{\text{diff}} - \mu_{\text{diff}}}{\hat{s}_{\overline{X}_{\text{diff}}}}.$$

The μ_{diff} value is 0, since the null hypothesis is that there is no difference between the familiar and the unfamiliar conditions in the looking times.

The standard error of the mean is calculated as

$$\hat{s}_{\overline{X}_{\text{diff}}} = \frac{\hat{s}_{\text{diff}}}{\sqrt{N}}.$$

Putting the numbers into the formulas, we have

$$\hat{s}_{\overline{X}_{\text{diff}}} = \frac{13.387}{\sqrt{10}} = 4.23,$$

so that

$$t = \frac{-13.51 - 0.0}{4.23} = -3.19.$$

Table 14.2   Differences in Looking Times from Table 14.1

Infant	Familiar	Unfamiliar	Difference
1	38.48	66.67	−28.19
2	49.04	73.96	−24.92
3	37.23	43.64	−6.41
4	43.89	42.82	1.07
5	69.34	71.81	−2.47
6	53.99	47.52	6.47
7	40.79	75.33	−34.54
8	49.44	60.41	−10.97
9	54.47	71.16	−16.69
10	47.45	65.90	−18.45
		Mean	−13.510
		Median	−13.830
		St. Dev.	13.387

Table 14.3   Scores on Two Weekly Quizzes

Student	Quiz 1	Quiz 2
1	1	1
2	2	3
3	2	3
4	3	3
5	3	4
6	4	5
7	5	6
$\overline{X}$	2.86	3.57
$\hat{s}$	1.34	1.62

This statistic is distributed as Student's t with df $= N - 1$. If we choose to use $\alpha = .05$, Appendix C shows the critical value for t with df $= 10 - 1 = 9$ is 2.262; we reject the null hypothesis that the infants look at the two speeds of motion for equal lengths of time. Returning to the original means, it's clear that they watch the unfamiliar pattern for a greater amount of time.

The hypothesis-testing procedure that we've just illustrated is the simplest way to conduct the t test for the two-condition within-subjects or matched-groups design. Some statistics books present a different formula for the t test, one that involves the correlation between the two sets of scores:

$$t = \frac{\overline{X}_1 - \overline{X}_2}{\sqrt{\hat{s}_{\overline{X}_1}^2 + \hat{s}_{\overline{X}_2}^2 - 2r\hat{s}_{\overline{X}_1}\hat{s}_{\overline{X}_2}}}.$$

While this is definitely the hardest way to do the computation, the formula makes it clear that the effect of the correlation between the two sets of scores is to reduce the denominator of the formula. If there's no correlation between the two sets of scores, the denominator term

$$\sqrt{\hat{s}_{\overline{X}_1}^2 + \hat{s}_{\overline{X}_2}^2 - 2r\hat{s}_{\overline{X}_1}\hat{s}_{\overline{X}_2}}$$

reduces to

$$\sqrt{\hat{s}_{\overline{X}_1}^2 + \hat{s}_{\overline{X}_2}^2},$$

which is $\hat{s}_{\overline{X}_1 - \overline{X}_2}$ in the independent-groups t test when $n_1 = n_2$. Thus, if there's zero correlation between the sets of scores, the test statistic reduces to that for the independent-groups design.

To illustrate the effect of a nonzero correlation on the test for the within-subjects design, let's take a simple example. Suppose that we have two sets of scores on two weekly quizzes for a class of seven students, as in Table 14.3. Is there a difference between the means of the two quizzes? Since the two sets of scores come from the same students, this is a within-groups design. The computations are shown in Table 14.4. The standard error of the sampling distribution of the mean differences is

Table 14.4 Differences in Means for Scores in Table 14.3

Student	Quiz 1	Quiz 2	Difference
1	1	1	0
2	2	3	−1
3	2	3	−1
4	3	3	0
5	3	4	−1
6	4	5	−1
7	5	6	−1

$\overline{X}_{\text{diff}}$	−0.71
$\hat{s}_{\text{diff}}$	0.49

$$\hat{s}_{\overline{X}_{\text{diff}}} = \frac{\hat{s}_{\text{diff}}}{\sqrt{N}}$$

$$= \frac{.49}{\sqrt{7}} = 0.185$$

and

$$t = \frac{\overline{X}_{\text{diff}} - \mu_{\text{diff}}}{\hat{s}_{\overline{X}_{\text{diff}}}}$$

$$= \frac{-0.71 - 0.0}{0.185} = -3.84.$$

With df = 6 and $\alpha = .01$, this value is significantly different from zero, and we reject the hypothesis that the scores on the two exams are equal.

The correlation between the two sets of scores is 0.962, and we could compute the t test using this formula,

$$t = \frac{\overline{X}_1 - \overline{X}_2}{\sqrt{\hat{s}_{\overline{X}_1}^2 + \hat{s}_{\overline{X}_2}^2 - 2r\hat{s}_{\overline{X}_1}\hat{s}_{\overline{X}_2}}},$$

by first calculating the two standard errors of the mean as

$$\hat{s}_{\overline{X}_1} = \frac{\hat{s}_1}{\sqrt{N}} = \frac{1.34}{\sqrt{7}} = .506$$

$$\hat{s}_{\overline{X}_2} = \frac{\hat{s}_2}{\sqrt{N}} = \frac{1.62}{\sqrt{7}} = .612.$$

Then the t formula gives

$$t = \frac{\overline{X}_1 - \overline{X}_2}{\sqrt{\hat{s}_{\overline{X}_1}^2 + \hat{s}_{\overline{X}_2}^2 - 2r\hat{s}_{\overline{X}_1}\hat{s}_{\overline{X}_2}}}$$

$$= \frac{2.86 - 3.57}{\sqrt{.506^2 + .612^2 - 2(.96)(.506)(.612)}}$$

$$= \frac{-.710}{\sqrt{.630 - .596}}$$

$$= \frac{-.710}{.184}$$

$$= -3.86,$$

giving, within rounding, the same answer as before.

To illustrate the difference between the within- and the between-subjects analyses, suppose that we treat these data as coming from a between-subjects design. (Please note that this is an *incorrect* analysis because the design here is clearly within subjects.)

The summary data, from Table 14.3, are

	Quiz 1	Quiz 2
$\overline{X}$	2.86	3.57
$\hat{s}$	1.34	1.62

We use the unequal variances formula (which is the best for routine applications, even though in this case the variances don't seem to differ) and calculate

$$\hat{s}_{\overline{X}_1 - \overline{X}_2} = \sqrt{\hat{s}_{\overline{X}_1}^2 + \hat{s}_{\overline{X}_2}^2}$$

$$= \sqrt{.506^2 + .612^2}$$

$$= .794,$$

so that

$$t = \frac{(\overline{X}_1 - \overline{X}_2) - (\mu_1 - \mu_2)}{\hat{s}_{\overline{X}_1 - \overline{X}_2}}$$

$$= \frac{2.86 - 3.57}{.794}$$

$$= -.894.$$

With df $= 7 + 7 - 2 = 12$, and $\alpha = 0.01$, we do not reject the hypothesis that the two means are equal. Note that this is a different conclusion from that we came to in the first analysis (and remember, the first analysis was the correct one) using the repeated measures computations. What made the difference? It wasn't the difference in the means of the two tests—the second test remains .71 higher than the first in each analysis. The difference, then, must be in the denominator. Let's look at the difference carefully, because it illuminates the effect of the relationship between the two sets of scores.

Note that the formula for the standard deviation of the sampling distribution of the mean differences for the (incorrect) between-subjects analysis looks just like *part* of the denominator for the within analysis, calculated with the correlation formula:

$$\hat{s}_{\overline{X}_1 - \overline{X}_2} = \sqrt{\hat{s}_{\overline{X}_1}^2 + \hat{s}_{\overline{X}_2}^2 - 2r\hat{s}_{\overline{X}_1}\hat{s}_{\overline{X}_2}}.$$

If we ignore the term that involves the correlation,

$$\hat{s}_{\bar{X}_1-\bar{X}_2} = \sqrt{s_{\bar{X}_1}{}^2 + \hat{s}_{\bar{X}_2}{}^2 \left(- 2r\hat{s}_{\bar{X}_1}\hat{s}_{\bar{X}_2}\right)},$$

we have the value from the between-groups analysis.

Comparing the two formulas for the standard error of the difference, we have

Between groups	Within groups
$\hat{s}_{\bar{X}_1-\bar{X}_2} = \sqrt{\hat{s}_{\bar{X}_1}{}^2 + \hat{s}_{\bar{X}_2}{}^2}$	$\hat{s}_{\bar{X}_1-\bar{X}_2} = \sqrt{\hat{s}_{\bar{X}_1}{}^2 + \hat{s}_{\bar{X}_2}{}^2 - 2r\hat{s}_{\bar{X}_1}\hat{s}_{\bar{X}_2}}$
$= \sqrt{.506^2 + .612^2}$	$= \sqrt{.506^2 + .612^2 - 2(.96)(.506)(.612)}$
$= \sqrt{.630}$	$= \sqrt{.630 - .596}$
$= .794$	$= \sqrt{.034}$
	$= .184$

The difference between the two is solely in the right-hand term of the denominator, where the within-subjects computation uses the correlation between the two sets of data to reduce the standard error of the difference. That allowed the mean difference between the two quizzes to stand out clearly (and significantly). The ability to match subjects, or in this case to use the same subjects in two conditions, eliminates a source of variability—the variability between the two different groups—that is present in the independent-groups analysis. The standard error of the difference is a measure of the overall error in the experimental situation, and the error can be reduced by using the relationship between the two sets of scores.

The difference between the two analyses is important. In the between-subjects experimental design, a comparison between the two means is also a comparison, in some sense, of two different groups of subjects. The within-subjects analysis, on the other hand, excludes the differences between two subject groups and reduces the overall variability. We've talked about the difference between the two designs in terms of experimental control, and here we can see that that control provides a direct reduction in the variability in the data. Some part of the overall variance in the data, as reflected in the standard error in the between-subjects case, must therefore be due to differences between the two subject groups.

If there were a difference between the two experimental conditions, the within-subjects analysis is more likely to find it. That is, the within-subjects analysis is less likely to make a Type II error. Thus it has more power. The gain in the power of the t test is directly attributable to the better control of extraneous variables achieved by the within-subjects design.

Nonparametric Tests for Center. In many cases, especially with small sample sizes, there's enough concern about the normality of the underlying distributions that a nonparametric alternative to the t test is needed. We'll present two common nonparametric procedures for making inferences about differences in center without making normal-distribution assumptions. Both tests are due to Wilcoxon, one for matched pairs, and the other for two independent groups. Both tests are appropriate when the data are measured on at least an ordinal scale; they are often used with interval and ratio data when the normal distribution assumptions of the t test aren't met.

Table 14.5   Differences in Looking Times from Tyrrell's Experiment

Infant	Familiar	Unfamiliar	Difference
1	38.48	66.67	−28.19
2	49.04	73.96	−24.92
3	37.23	43.64	−6.41
4	43.89	42.82	1.07
5	69.34	71.81	−2.47
6	53.99	47.52	6.47
7	40.79	75.33	−34.54
8	49.44	60.41	−10.97
9	54.47	71.16	−16.69
10	47.45	65.90	−18.45

The Wilcoxon test* for matched groups. We'll illustrate the computations with Tyrrell's data (Table 14.5). Normally, we don't use two different tests on the same data. We're doing it in this case only to compare the two analyses; you should decide on whether to use parametric or nonparametric tests on the basis of measurement level or the form of the distributions, and then do either one or the other analysis, but not both.

Table 14.5 presents the Tyrrell data again, showing the time spent looking at the familiar and unfamiliar patterns. The differences between the pairs of values for each infant are also shown. The Wilcoxon test uses the differences, and the null hypothesis is that the differences are from a population centered on zero, as they would be if the two sets of scores actually came from the same population.

The first step in the analysis is to arrange the differences in order from smallest to largest, *disregarding their sign*, so that the absolute values are ranked as in Table 14.6. Now we attach the ranks (1, 2, . . .) to the sorted scores and mark the ranks that were formerly positive with a + and those that were negative with a − sign as shown in the rightmost column of the table. Now sum to two sets of values—those with the + sign and those with the − sign, giving two sets of rank sums:

$$\text{Sum}(+) = 1 + 4 = 5$$
$$\text{Sum}(-) = 2 + 3 + 5 + \cdots + 10 = 50.$$

The test statistic, often called T, is the *smaller* of the two values—in this case, 5. To determine whether the obtained value leads to a conclusion of a significant difference, we consult a table of the critical values of the Wilcoxon T statistic. Appendix H gives critical values for several significance levels and for a small set of values of N (the number of pairs of scores). In contrast to nearly every other table of critical values, tables of T typically show lower-tail values, so that *if the obtained value is less than* the tabled value, then *we have a significant difference* between the two conditions.[†] In our example, the critical value for T

---

*This test was originally developed by the statistician Frank Wilcoxon and described by him (Wilcoxon, 1945). It is equivalent to the other commonly-cited test for two independent samples, the Mann-Whitney U test; we present the Wilcoxon version here.
[†]The other Wilcoxon test that we introduce shares this characteristic.

Table 14.6   Ranking of Data from Table 14.5

Infant	Absolute difference	Rank	Signed rank
4	1.07	1	+1
5	2.47	2	−2
3	6.41	3	−3
6	6.47	4	+4
8	10.97	5	−5
9	16.69	6	−6
10	18.45	7	−7
2	24.92	8	−8
1	28.19	9	−9
7	34.54	10	−10

at $\alpha = .05$ and for $N = 10$ from Appendix H is 8. The calculated value is 5; since that's less than 8, we conclude that the distributions of looking times from the walking and the jogging patterns most likely come from two different populations. In other words, there's a significant difference between the two speeds. And that's the same conclusion that we reached using the t test.

When the number of pairs is fairly large, greater than 25 or so, we may use a normal-curve approximation for the Wilcoxon test. The T statistic has the two parameters

$$\mu_T = \frac{N(N + 1)}{4}$$

$$\sigma_T = \sqrt{\frac{N(N + 1)(2N + 1)}{24}}.$$

Given those two values, the statistic

$$z = \frac{T - \mu_T}{\sigma_T}$$

is approximately normally distributed. For example, suppose that we have a set of $N = 36$ pairs of values with a computed value of T equal to 515. We would calculate

$$\mu_T = \frac{36(36 + 1)}{4} = 333$$

$$\sigma_T = \sqrt{\frac{36(36 + 1)(2 \times 36 + 1)}{24}}$$
$$= 63.65$$

and then

$$z = \frac{515 - 333}{63.65}$$
$$= 2.86.$$

If we use a .01 significance level, the critical value in the normal distribution is 2.58, and we reject the hypothesis that the two sets of scores are the same.

Tied scores in the Wilcoxon test for matched pairs need special attention. There are two kinds of ties, zeros and nonzeros. A zero difference occurs when the subject's (or pair's) scores are the same in both conditions. The usual advice is simply to exclude any pairs of data that have a zero difference, reducing N by 1 for each pair discarded, since a zero difference really doesn't help to decide the question of a possible difference between the conditions. A nonzero tie occurs when there are two (or more) differences with the same absolute value. In this case, we assign each the mean rank. For example, in this set of data,

Difference	Rank
0.0	
−2.9	1
3.6	2
4.1	3.5
−4.1	3.5
5.4	5
−8.2	6.5
−8.2	6.5

we would drop the 0 difference, leaving us with $N = 7$ pairs of scores. The two largest values, −8.2, are tied for the highest rank, namely positions 6 and 7 in the list. They are assigned the mean of the ranks that they occupy, 6.5. Also, since the differences are ranked without regard to sign, the differences 4.1 and −4.1 are also tied and assigned the mean rank of 3.5.

The Wilcoxon test for two independent groups. There are two common procedures for testing a hypothesis of equality when the two conditions are represented by two independent groups. The Mann-Whitney U test is frequently cited, as is another test developed by Wilcoxon (similar to the one just presented). The Wilcoxon and the Mann-Whitney are identical in logic, and in fact the critical value of one can be easily converted to the other. We'll present the Wilcoxon version of the test. There are two forms of the test, depending upon the sample sizes. If both samples are less than 10, then we use the small sample method; if the groups are larger than 10, a normal-curve approximation is applicable.

The small sample example uses the hypothetical data set in Table 14.7. The dependent variable is weight (in pounds), and the independent variable is two colors of Labrador Retrievers in an animal laboratory. The first step in the Wilcoxon test is to rank all of the weights from smallest to largest, keeping track of the group membership (Table 14.8). Now find the sum of the ranks, which we'll call R, for the smallest group. In the example, that's for the chocolate Labs, and we find

$$R = 1 + 5 + \cdots + 16 = 59.$$

Appendix I gives a table of the largest value of R that would be significant at the level shown. In other words, if R is *less than or equal to* the tabled value, the difference is significant. The table is entered by using the two group sizes.

Table 14.7 Weights of Labrador Retrievers
Having Different Coat Colors

	Weight in pounds	
	Black coat	Chocolate coat
	53	58
	76	66
	69	68
	72	71
	70	78
	52	47
	50	56
	61	
	67	
Mean	63.33	63.43
St. Dev.	9.64	10.42
Variance	93.00	108.62

Table 14.8 Ranking of Weights from Table 14.7

Rank	Weight	Color
1	47	Chocolate
2	50	Black
3	52	Black
4	53	Black
5	56	Chocolate
6	58	Chocolate
7	61	Black
8	66	Chocolate
9	67	Black
10	68	Chocolate
11	69	Black
12	70	Black
13	71	Chocolate
14	72	Black
15	76	Black
16	78	Chocolate

Select the subtable for the smallest group size (7 in the example), and use the row for the larger sample (9). In the example, the critical value with $\alpha = .05$ is 43. Since the obtained value is 59, we do not reject the null hypothesis that the weights of the two kinds of Labs are equal.

Appendix I gives one-tailed values. To complete the test, we should compute a second sum of ranks for the other tail and look it up as well. The second sum is calculated as

Table 14.9 Hypothetical Data from Two-Condition Experiment

	Condition 1	Condition 2
	2	1
	5	7
	3	15
	4	13
	4	6
	3	8
	8	6
	6	12
	10	2
	7	3
		14
Mean	5.20	7.91
St. Dev.	2.53	4.95
Variance	6.40	24.49

$$R' = n_1(n_1 + n_2 + 1) - R.$$

For the example, the value is

$$R' = n_1(n_1 + n_2 + 1) - R$$
$$= 7 \times (7 + 9 + 1) - 59$$
$$= 60.$$

That value is also greater than the critical value, and there is no significant difference.

Of course, we just tested for significance in two one-tailed tests at $\alpha = .05$, and so we have really done a two-tailed test at $.05 + .05 = .10$. To have the probability at .05 overall, we would have needed to use the .025 critical value. In Appendix I, that value is 40, and there is still no significant difference between the two groups of dogs.

The table for the Wilcoxon two-sample test in Appendix I includes values only up to $N = 10$ for the smallest sample size. While there are larger tables available, there is a good normal-distribution approximation available for large samples. To illustrate it, we can use the hypothetical data set from an experiment with two conditions found in Table 14.9. The first step is just as it was in the small-sample analysis. The ranked data are in Table 14.10. For condition 1 (the smaller group), $R = 93.5$. The sum of the ranks for the smaller group is distributed approximately normally with

$$\mu_R = \frac{n_1(n_1 + n_2 + 1)}{2}$$

and

$$\sigma_R = \sqrt{\frac{n_1 n_2(n_1 + n_2 + 1)}{12}},$$

Table 14.10   Ranked Data from Table 14.9

Score	Rank	Condition
1	1	2
2	2.5	1
2	2.5	2
3	5	1
3	5	1
3	5	2
4	7.5	1
4	7.5	1
5	9	1
6	11	1
6	11	2
6	11	2
7	13.5	1
7	13.5	2
8	15.5	1
8	15.5	2
10	17	1
12	18	2
13	19	2
14	20	2
15	21	2

so that

$$z_R = \frac{R - \dfrac{n_1(n_1 + n_2 + 1)}{2}}{\sqrt{\dfrac{n_1 n_2(n_1 + n_2 + 1)}{12}}}$$

may be referred to the z table in Appendix A. For our example, then, we have

$$z_R = \frac{R - \dfrac{n_1(n_1 + n_2 + 1)}{2}}{\sqrt{\dfrac{n_1 n_2(n_1 + n_2 + 1)}{12}}}$$

$$= \frac{93.5 - \dfrac{10(10 + 11 + 1)}{2}}{\sqrt{\dfrac{10 \times 11(10 + 11 + 1)}{12}}}$$

$$= \frac{93.5 - 110}{\sqrt{201.67}}$$

$$= \frac{-16.5}{14.20}$$

$$= -1.16.$$

Since we would require a value of 1.96 or greater in absolute value to reject a hypothesis of no difference between the two conditions at the .05 level, we conclude that there is no evidence to suggest that the two conditions differ.

Like the Wilcoxon test for matched pairs, this test requires some additional computations when there are ties (as there are in this case). In particular, we must change the computation for the denominator (that is, for σ_R). The formula changes to

$$\sigma_R = \sqrt{\frac{n_1 n_2}{12}\left[(n_1 + n_2 + 1) - \frac{\Sigma t(t^2 - 1)}{(n_1 + n_2)(n_1 + n_2 - 1)}\right]},$$

where t is the number of scores in a tied group, and the summation is over all of the groups of ties. In the example, we have the ties shown in Table 14.11. There are six sets of tied scores, four of them containing two values and two with three values. The computation thus becomes

$$\sigma_R = \sqrt{\frac{n_1 n_2}{12}\left[(n_1 + n_2 + 1) - \frac{\Sigma t(t^2 - 1)}{(n_1 + n_2)(n_1 + n_2 - 1)}\right]}$$

$$= \sqrt{\frac{10 \times 11}{12}\left[(10 + 11 + 1) - \frac{2(2^2 - 1) + 3(3^2 - 1) + 2(2^2 - 1) + 3(3^2 - 1) + 2(2^2 - 1) + 2(2^2 - 1)}{(10 + 11)(10 + 11 - 1)}\right]}$$

$$= 14.14.$$

Using this value, the z computation, corrected for ties, becomes

$$Z_R = \frac{R - \dfrac{n_1(n_1 + n_2 + 1)}{2}}{\sqrt{\dfrac{n_1 n_2}{12}\left[(n_1 + n_2 + 1) - \dfrac{\Sigma t(t^2 - 1)}{(n_1 + n_2)(n_1 + n_2 - 1)}\right]}}$$

$$= \frac{93.5 - \dfrac{10(10 + 11 + 1)}{2}}{14.14}$$

$$= \frac{93.5 - 110}{14.14}$$

$$= \frac{-16.5}{14.14}$$

$$= -1.17,$$

which scarcely differs from the original answer; there is still no significant difference between the two conditions.

All of the tests so far in this chapter answer one question—do the two conditions differ? In the two t tests, the question is specifically about the population means. The two Wilcoxon tests ask more broadly "Do the two conditions differ?" and are sensitive primarily to differences in center.

Questions about equality of center are by far the most common research questions asked. Such questions occur in both the two-condition experiment that we're discussing here, and also in more complicated designs. The two-condition experiment provides the ideal situation in which to investigate the effect of an

14   Experiments with Two Conditions

Table 14.11   Ties in Ranked Data from Table 14.10

Score	Rank	Condition	
1	1	2	
2	2.5	1	$t = 2$
2	2.5	2	
3	5	1	
3	5	1	$t = 3$
3	5	2	
4	7.5	1	$t = 2$
4	7.5	1	
5	9	1	
6	11	1	
6	11	2	$t = 3$
6	11	2	
7	13.5	1	$t = 2$
7	13.5	2	
8	15.5	1	$t = 2$
8	15.5	2	
10	17	1	
12	18	2	
13	19	2	
14	20	2	
15	21	2	

independent variable manipulation since it allows an uncomplicated causal inference to be made in the event of a significant difference between conditions.

But the two-condition experimental design isn't limited to asking about centers. While much less common, the design can also ask about spread, form, or correlation.

Inference for Spread, Form, and Correlation

Using the same design that we've explored for differences in center, we can investigate whether the two conditions have different variabilities or whether two distributions differ in form. We might even want to know whether the correlation between two variables differs across two experimental conditions. In this section we'll present inferential procedures directed toward all of these questions.

Hypotheses About Variances (Normal Distributions). A simple and well-known test for the equality of two variances when both populations are normal is computed by forming the ratio

$$F = \frac{\text{larger variance}}{\text{smaller variance}}.$$

The null hypothesis for the test is $\sigma_1{}^2 = \sigma_2{}^2$. If the hypothesis is true *and* if both distributions are normal, then the ratio should be about 1.0. If it's false, then the ratio should not be equal to 1.0. Since the ratio is calculated by dividing the larger variance by the smaller, it will be larger as the difference in variances increases. For that reason, we will use only the upper tail of the F distribution for the critical region in the hypothesis test.

If the distributions of the two experimental groups are normal, then the ratio of the two variances is distributed as F, a statistic with which we'll become much more familiar in Chapters 15 and 16. Appendix F gives tables of the critical values of F. To find a value, you enter the table with two different df values, one for the numerator of the ratio and one for the denominator. In each case, the df is the $N - 1$, where N is the number of observations that forms the basis for the variance.

As an example, let's return to the unequal variance form of the independent groups t test (p. 308). There we had two groups of 6 observations each, with sample variances of 0.50 and 25.47. The ratio of these two variances is

$$F = \frac{25.47}{0.50} = 50.94.$$

The numerator of the F ratio is based on a sample with $N = 6$; the df for the numerator is thus $N - 1 = 5$. We follow the same rule for the denominator, $df = 4$, and we thus enter the table in Appendix F with $df = 5, 4$. We'll use a significance level of .05 for the test.*

The F distribution is a family of unimodal, positively skewed distributions, having a form that varies with the df. A typical distribution looks like Figure 14.8. Appendix F gives the upper critical points in the F scale for several common α levels. We want $\alpha = .05$; entering Appendix F with $df = 5$ for the numerator and $df = 4$ for the denominator, we find that the critical value of F is 9.36. Pictorially, the critical point is as shown in Figure 14.9. Since the obtained F value for the example is 50.94, we reject the null hypothesis of equal population variances at a significance level of .05.

Hypotheses About Variances (Non-Normal Distributions). When the populations are non-normal, and that's very common in psychology, the previous test for equality of variances is decidedly the *wrong* test to use, although it appears in the literature regularly. Instead of that test, we'll recommend one based on the procedure described by O'Brien (1981). The test is done by transforming the original data values, and then performing an independent groups t test on the transformed scores.

You begin by computing $\overline{X}$ and $\hat{s}$ for each group as usual. Then, for each group separately, transform the scores according to the formula

$$r_i = \frac{(n_1 - 1.5)n_1(X_i - \overline{X}_1)^2 - .5\hat{s}_1{}^2(n_1 - 1)}{(n_1 - 1)(n_1 - 2)}$$

for group 1, and

---

* Because we're dividing the *larger* variance by the *smaller* one, the effect is to test a two-tailed hypothesis by using a single tail. We'll thus use the critical value of $\alpha/2$, or .025, instead of .05.

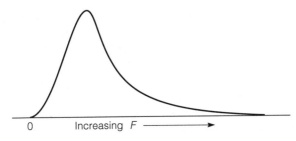

Figure 14.8

Figure 14.9

$$r_i = \frac{(n_2 - 1.5)n_2(X_i - \overline{X}_2)^2 - .5\hat{s}_2{}^2(n_2 - 1)}{(n_2 - 1)(n_2 - 2)}$$

for group 2. Once these transformations have been computed for each score in both groups, compute the mean for each set of transformed r scores; you should find that the mean of each group is equal to the variance of the original data for that group. (If they're not, check your computations.) The test for equality of variance is now a two-sample t test, using the r values and the unequal variance estimate of the standard error of the difference in means.

As an example, let's return to the same example. For the first group, $n_1 = 5$, $\overline{X}_1 = 3.00$, and $\hat{s}^2{}_1 = 0.50$. The score for the first subject is 2, and it is transformed to r as

$$r_i = \frac{(n_1 - 1.5)n_1(X_i - \overline{X}_1)^2 - .5\hat{s}_1{}^2(n_1 - 1)}{(n_1 - 1)(n_1 - 2)}$$

$$= \frac{(5 - 1.5)5(2 - 3)^2 - .5(0.50)(5 - 1)}{(5 - 1)(5 - 2)}$$

$$= 1.375.$$

Completing the computations for all scores, the transformed r values are

1.375	69.417
−0.083	−0.783
−0.083	56.817
−0.083	26.217
1.375	4.167
	−3.033

Applying the t test to these data, we compute $t(5) = -1.959$, $p > .05$. In this case, we do not reject the hypothesis of equal variance.

This test for equality of variances has two major advantages over the earlier ratio of largest-to-smallest. First, it is not particularly sensitive to violation of the normality assumption that underlies the ratio test. Thus it is nearly always the more appropriate test to use, although is it computationally more tedious. (However, if you have a computer to do the work, it's not much trouble.) And second, it generalizes very easily to those more complex designs that use the analysis of variance.

The test that we just presented deals with independent variances; that is, variances of data from independent groups. How about the case where we want

Analyzing the Data

to test a hypothesis of equal variances when the data are from a matched-pairs or repeated-measures design? Unfortunately, the situation here is complex, and treating it would take us too far afield. You may run across a test based on the F ratio from above, but that test is extremely sensitive to departure from normality and should not be used.

Hypotheses About Correlations. In Chapter 13 we presented a test of whether a Pearson product-moment correlation coefficient differs significantly from zero. Now we expand that question to the two-condition design and ask whether two Pearson's r values are different from each other.

The question addressed, of course, is whether the manipulation of some independent variable changes the relationship between a pair of dependent variables. For example, many high school students invest time and money taking courses that prepare them to take the Scholastic Aptitude Test (SAT), a test that is required for admission to many colleges. While there seems little doubt that such courses increase the score on the SAT, there are other questions to be answered. The SAT is used as a screening tool by colleges because it tends to predict academic success, often as measured by college grades. Let's suppose, completely hypothetically, that the correlation between the SAT total score and the freshman year grade point average (GPA) for a large university is .6 for students who have not taken an SAT training course. (As discussed in Chapter 10, that means that about 36% of the variance in freshman GPA can be predicted from SAT scores.) If we looked at students who have taken SAT training courses, we would expect to see a higher mean SAT total, but what of the correlation? Perhaps the SAT courses succeed in raising students' ability to *take the test*, but not their academic ability; in that case, we would expect to see a *weaker* relationship between SAT and freshman GPA since scores on the SAT were artificially inflated by the training program.

Independent groups. For two independent groups, the statistic

$$z = \frac{z_{r_1} - z_{r_2}}{\sqrt{\dfrac{1}{N_1 - 3} + \dfrac{1}{N_2 - 3}}},$$

where z_{r_1} and z_{r_2} are the Fisher's r-to-z transformed values of the two correlation coefficients, is a normally distributed variable that tests the hypothesis that the two population correlation coefficients (ρ_1 and ρ_2) are equal.

Suppose that a large university offers free SAT training to a random selection of high school seniors and not to others. The university could then compute the two correlations between SAT and GPA for the two groups of students. (Of course, some students in the nontraining group might have taken a similar course at their own expense; they could be excluded from the analysis.) Suppose further that for the SAT-trained students ($N = 360$) $r = .22$, while for nontrained students ($N = 425$) $r = .68$. Do these correlations differ? Consulting Appendix L, the values are .829 for the nontraining group and .224 for the training group. Substituting in the formula for z, we have

$$z = \frac{z_{r_1} - z_{r_2}}{\sqrt{\dfrac{1}{N_1 - 3} + \dfrac{1}{N_2 - 3}}}$$

$$= \frac{.829 - .224}{\sqrt{\dfrac{1}{425 - 3} + \dfrac{1}{360 - 3}}}$$

$$= 8.43$$

Since the z value required for significance at the .05 level is 1.96, we may conclude that there is a difference in the relationship between SAT total score and freshman GPA caused by taking the SAT training course.

Matched groups. When the correlations to be tested result from a matched-group or a within-subjects design, the situation is considerably more complicated than it was with independent groups. Howell (1987, pp. 243–244) gives a procedure and an example, but only in the case where there are a total of three correlations and you want to know if two of them are different. To pursue the matter further would take us too far afield for this book.

Summary of Techniques

This chapter has presented a number of procedures for testing hypotheses that arise in experiments with two conditions. Table 14.12 summarizes the tests that we've discussed.

Relationship to Other Designs

To wrap up our presentation of the two-condition experimental design, let's see briefly how it's related to other common designs.

The two-condition design differs from a single-condition design in the obvious way—there's another condition. But their logic is often very similar. Both involve a single independent variable, although it's not usually manipulated in the single-condition experiment. In both cases as well, there's a single dependent variable, although experimenters often measure more than one variable at a time.

In the single-condition experiment, the question is typically about the degree of fit between obtained data and a known external value. That is, we may ask if the students in a particular class differ from those of previous years in terms of their exam grades. In a way, the "previous years'" data serve as a "control" condition to be compared with the current "experimental" condition, thus making the one-condition experiment similar to a two-condition experiment with an explicit control condition.

The next group of experimental designs we consider expands the two-condition design into a multiple-condition experiment. In that design, there is a single independent variable, but it is manipulated in more than two "amounts,"

Table 14.12   Summary of Two-Condition Tests

	Independent variable is manipulated	
	Between subjects	Within subjects
INFERENCES ABOUT CENTER		
Parametric (normal distribution) test	Student's t for independent groups	Student's t for matched groups
Nonparametric test	Wilcoxon test for independent groups	Wilcoxon for matched pairs
INFERENCES ABOUT SPREAD		
	t test on r_i scores	No test
INFERENCES ABOUT CORRELATION		
	z test with transformed r values	No test

"levels," or "kinds." As in the two-condition design, manipulating the levels can be done between subjects, with one group of subjects per condition, or within subjects, with one group receiving all of the conditions.

The analysis of the multiple-condition experiment is considerably more complex than was the two-condition design, as you might suspect. And the distinction between the between- and the within-subjects manipulation becomes increasingly important. The overall analysis will be done by the technique of analysis of variance (ANOVA), but more detailed analyses will be conducted by looking at just two conditions at a time. Thus the two-condition experiment will remain the most fundamental, the cleanest, and the easiest to understand of all of the experimental designs.

SUMMARY

- The experimental design with two conditions is the prototypic experiment.
- The two experimental conditions can be manipulated either by using different groups of subjects for each condition ("between subjects") or by applying the two conditions to the same subjects ("within subjects").
- The most frequent inference method tests the hypothesis that two experimental conditions don't differ.
- The two-condition test assumes that there are two populations and that the data in the two samples are samples from them.
- The sampling distribution for the between-groups Student's t test gives the differences in means of samples taken from the two populations.
- We can make an interval estimate of the difference between two population means, but it's not done often.
- The Student's t test for within subjects uses the differences between the scores for each subject and then applies a single sample t test to those differences.

- Applying the between-groups t test to within-groups data results in a possible loss of power.
- The Wilcoxon test for matched groups uses differences between scores and tests the hypothesis that the population of differences sampled is centered on zero.
- A t test on transformed data values may be used to test for equality of variance in a between-subjects design.

KEY TERMS

F

Pooled estimate

Standard error of the difference

Wilcoxon test for matched groups

Wilcoxon test for two independent groups

EXERCISES

Solutions to asterisked (∗) exercises appear at the back of the book. Exercises preceded by a section symbol (§) must be solved using a computer. Exercises preceded by a dagger (†) can be solved by hand.

∗†1. Subjects in a verbal learning study learned two equivalently difficult words to a criterion of one complete trial through the list without error. In one condition, the subjects were tested with a vocal of the song "Tomorrow" from the musical *Annie* as background music; in the other condition, the song and its loudness were the same, but the music was an instrumental arrangement. The dependent variable was trials to criterion. Conditions were counterbalanced so that half of the subjects had the instrumental condition first and half had the vocal first. Data for the experiment follow.

Subject	Vocal	Instrumental
1	18	13
2	13	9
3	22	17
4	9	13
5	10	10
6	18	14
7	16	21
8	18	11
9	8	5
10	19	13
11	22	16
12	16	11
13	25	19
14	20	15
15	9	7

a. Conduct the appropriate t test to see if the difference between the two experimental conditions is statistically significant. (Use $\alpha = .05$.)

b. Conduct the appropriate nonparametric test on the same data. (Use $\alpha = .05$.) Do the results agree with those of part (a)?

†2. Two groups of chickens were raised from hatching either singly or in a group of five hatch-mates. At the age of six weeks, all subjects were placed in a small cage with a same-aged, group-reared chicken (in the case of group-reared subjects, the test chicken was from a different group). The dependent variable was amount of grain consumed (in grams) during a 30-minute test period.

Group reared	Individually reared
35	9
27	16
29	13
9	13
37	26
25	11
28	5
26	
45	
19	

a. Conduct the appropriate t test to see if the difference between the two experimental conditions is statistically significant. (Use $\alpha = .01$.)

b. Conduct the appropriate nonparametric test on the same data. (Use $\alpha = .01$.) Do the results agree with those of part (a)?

*†3. Here are some data from Dr. Stewart's research, representing the consumption of a dilute solution of hydrochloric acid (sour taste). The data give amount consumed in milliliters in a 15-minute test period.

Aversion	Control
7	9
14	8
9	9
12	7.5
9	9
9	10
12	10.5
10	8
9	10
11	6.5

a. Conduct the appropriate t test to see if the difference between the two experimental conditions is statistically significant. (Use $\alpha = .10$.)

b. Conduct the appropriate nonparametric test on the same data. (Use $\alpha = .10$.) Do the results agree with those of part (a)?

†4. Here's another set of Dr. Tyrrell's data, again giving "looking time" for each of the two patterns:

Familiar	Unfamiliar
55.87	60.85
53.76	65.33
54.90	54.66
48.33	59.45
34.76	54.55
56.99	47.10
68.91	71.13
61.84	56.61
67.33	44.73
42.41	56.73
68.21	46.93

a. Conduct the appropriate t test to see if the difference between the two experimental conditions is statistically significant. (Use $\alpha = .05$.)

b. Conduct the appropriate nonparametric test on the same data. (Use $\alpha = .05$.) Do the results agree with those of part (a)?

§5. Use your computer program to repeat as many of the previous exercises as you can.

†6. Using the data from Exercise 1, determine whether the variability in the number of trials to learn the list under the "Vocal" condition is significantly different from that in the "Instrumental" condition. (Use $\alpha = .05$.)

†7. Do the number of grams of grain consumed by the two groups of chickens in Exercise 2 differ in their variability? Use $\alpha = .05$.

*†8. The correlation between the amount of sucrose consumed and the amount of quinine consumed by Dr. Stewart's animals are $-.096$ for the aversion group and $.409$ for the control animals. Recall that there are 10 animals in each condition. Do the correlations differ using $\alpha = .10$?

†9. The correlation between the amount of salt consumed and the amount of quinine consumed by Dr. Stewart's animals are $-.559$ for the aversion group and $.430$ for the control animals. There are still 10 animals in each condition. Do the correlations differ using $\alpha = .05$?

Experiments with More Than Two Between-Subjects Conditions (Principles)

S uppose that Dr. Campbell selects three groups of subjects on the basis of their scores on an introversion/extraversion scale, choosing a group from each extreme of the personality scale and a third group of subjects from the center. He intends to use those three conditions to explore the relationship between introversion/extraversion and interpersonal attraction. He has a single independent variable—degree of introversion/extraversion—but he has more than two conditions in his experiment. This experimental design is often called a one-variable, single-factor, or one-way design and is widely used in psychology. As we did with the two-condition design, we'll first discuss the design itself, then move on to the analysis. The material is lengthy and divided into two chapters, since we'll develop the whole logic of analysis of variance. In this chapter, we develop the logic and show its relationship to the experimental design. The computations for the analysis of variance appear in Chapter 16.

The Design

The one-way design is a straightforward extension of the two-condition experiment. In principle there's no limit on the number of conditions that the design may have; in practice, one-way designs rarely have more than five or six conditions or levels. The analysis procedures and formulas are completely general, with no limit on the number of conditions in which they may be used.

As in the two-condition design, we have a single independent variable, manipulated according to a logic based on the research question. The manipulation might be in terms of qualitatively different stimuli, such as different patterns for Dr. Tyrrell or different lists of words in a cognitive psychology experiment. A social psychologist might use different sets of instructions to influence subject expectancy, or a comparative psychologist might use different

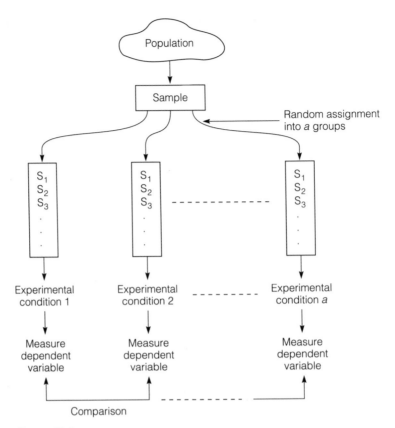

Figure 15.1

species to explore the learning process. Then again, the manipulation might be one of quantitatively different amounts of some variable like drug concentrations, hours of deprivation, the score on a pretest, or the number of practice trials.

As in the two-condition design, we can choose to manipulate the independent variable either between subjects or within subjects. In a between-subjects design, a different group of subjects is randomly assigned to each of the conditions; this design is a direct extension of the two-independent-groups design from Chapter 14. In such a design, often called a *randomized groups* or *completely randomized* design, the analysis looks at the differences between conditions and also at differences between subject groups; this point will become important when we develop the inferential procedures.

The single-factor design might be diagrammed as in Figure 15.1, where the letter *a* will indicate the number of different treatment conditions. The research question invariably asks about differences among the experimental conditions, as illustrated in Figure 15.1. Notice that the illustration suggests that the comparison among the conditions is done simultaneously. The analysis is usually done in two stages, with the first stage comparing all of the conditions at the same

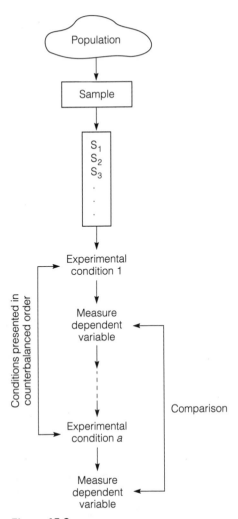

Figure 15.2

time. If that test concludes that there is a difference among the conditions, then the second stage seeks to determine just which conditions differ from the others.

A "repeated measures" design can be constructed with multiple conditions. In this design, each subject receives each of the *a* conditions in the design. Naturally, the repeated use of the same subjects poses the problem of order effects, and careful counterbalancing is required. The one-way design with repeated measures is diagrammed in Figure 15.2.

Instead of using the same subjects for all experimental conditions, it's possible to match subjects into groups (or *blocks*), where each block is formed through a precision or frequency-matching procedure as discussed in Chapter 4. Within each block (group), subjects are assigned at random to the experimental conditions. This design is called the *randomized blocks design* (*RBD*) by some analysis of variance texts. A randomized blocks design is illustrated in Figure 15.3.

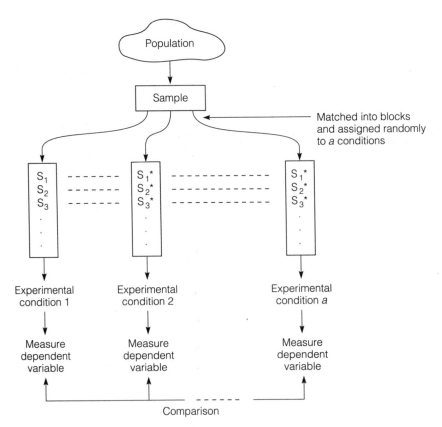

Figure 15.3

The inferential procedure most often used for multiple-condition designs is the analysis of variance (ANOVA). In the two-condition experiment, the inferential statistics differ depending upon whether the design used a between- or a within-subjects manipulation of the independent variable. It shouldn't come as any surprise, then, to learn that the ANOVA also varies depending upon the way that the independent variable was manipulated. This chapter presents the analyses for the between-subjects design. Analyses for the repeated measures design and for the randomized blocks design will be presented in Chapter 17.

In ANOVA designs, we usually assume that the dependent variable is measured on an interval or a ratio scale and that its distribution is normal in form. There are nonparametric tests that can be applied when those assumptions don't hold; we'll discuss them after we develop the parametric procedures.

Strengths and Weaknesses in the Multiple-Condition Design

The two-condition design was limited, obviously, to two conditions. The multiple-condition design increases the scope of relationships that can be studied. It is especially valuable with quantitative independent variables where the interest is often in exploring a range of possible treatment values. Exploring the effects of varying drug dosages, of age, or of practice are all quantitative variables whose ranges could be explored in a multiple-condition design.

Some research questions can't be fit into a one- or two-condition design. A typical learning experiment, for example, involves repeatedly measuring some behavior over a series of trials. Such an experiment is inherently a within-subjects design and normally involves many more than two trials. In Chapter 4 we briefly mentioned research by Dr. Owens and some students (Leer, Salvador, Goldberg, & Owens, 1986) that had subjects do three different tasks to study the effect of task on visual accommodation. The tasks (a bean bag toss at near and far distances while wearing prism glasses, and a computer game) were established to involve different visual tasks at different distances. A "toss" game and a computer game or the "toss" game at two distances just wouldn't have been enough conditions to show the visual effects that they thought should be present, and so they needed a design with three conditions.

Experimentation in psychology is sometimes criticized because its laboratory situations tend to be artificial. Sometimes that criticism is well founded, but a multiple-condition design will allow a range of different situations to be used. While nothing about multiple conditions assures realism, being able to use several different situations is sometimes helpful in establishing at least face validity in the experiment.

A final advantage of the multiple-condition design is that it, like the two-condition design, is able to come close to the conditions necessary to infer causality. The two-condition experiment controls all variables and varies only the single independent variable, thus allowing for clear inference. The same clear logic is shared with the multiple-condition design.

Naturally, there's a price to be paid for the flexibility of the multiple-condition design—the analysis is more complex. For one thing, the first hypothesis test that is done in an ANOVA design is nonspecific. That is, if the test shows a difference among four experimental conditions, it doesn't say which conditions are different. In some cases, only one condition might be different from the others, while in others, each condition might differ from every other. The way to resolve the ambiguity is with a series of follow-up tests, often reducing the analysis to a set of two-condition comparisons. When a series of tests is conducted, the probability of making a Type I error can increase, and our follow-up test procedures must take that complication into account.

While a multiple-condition design can investigate an independent variable in some detail, it is limited to exactly one variable. There is no way in the design to study the way one variable might work with a second variable to influence behavior. Research questions involving the interactions of two (or more) independent variables are the most common in psychological research. But we'll have to put off their study a little longer.

Introduction to the Analysis of Variance

In developing the logic for making inferences in the two-condition design, we stressed that there are two conceptual populations; the two samples are regarded as samples from them. The same is true in a multiple-condition experiment. Each set of data is regarded as a sample from a population of scores that might be observed under a particular experimental treatment. The null hypothesis in the analysis of variance is that there is no difference among the means of all of the populations. If it seems strange that we test hypotheses about *means* by using analysis of *variance*, we'll clear up that mystery soon. For now, let's remind ourselves just what variance really is.

Variance is a measure of the variability or spread among values. Each population has a variance σ^2, and we defined a statistic to estimate σ^2 as

$$\hat{s}^2 = \frac{\Sigma(X - \overline{X})^2}{N - 1}.$$

This formula, of course, is for a statistic. As we've said, the numerator part of the formula is a sum of the squared differences between the scores and their mean. We call such a term a *sum of squares*, or simply an SS. The denominator is the number of items summed in the numerator, minus one, and is a df. As a whole, then, a variance estimate is the average of the squared differences between the scores and their mean.

The variance measures the variability in the data. What causes that variability? In previous discussions (see pp. 136–138), we listed three major sources:

- Error in measurement
- Error in control
- Individual differences

That is, imperfections in measuring instruments, uncontrolled extraneous variables, and individual differences in subjects all contribute to variability. In the analysis of variance, all three of these sources of variability will be collectively called error variance. While the goal of careful experimentation is to minimize these sources of variation, they can never be completely eliminated.

Earlier, we also mentioned another source of variance, though we didn't explore it at the time:

- Effects of an independent variable

If we combine all of the data in an experiment, then some of the variability may be due to differences among the conditions. That is, if we have three different experimental conditions and if those conditions differ among themselves, then in the combined data, some of the variability among scores—that is, some of the variance—must be related to differences among the experimental conditions. On the other hand, if the conditions are identical, then the experimental conditions wouldn't contribute to the variance.

Here's a set of data:

10	12	15
7	10	11
11	11	14
9	11	10
8	11	12
11	13	13
10	12	13
10	12	12
9	11	13

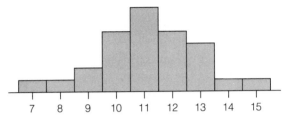

Figure 15.4

Condition 1
$\overline{X} = 9.44$
$\hat{s} = 1.33$
$\hat{s}^2 = 1.77$

Figure 15.5

Condition 2
$\overline{X} = 11.44$
$\hat{s} = 0.88$
$\hat{s}^2 = 0.77$

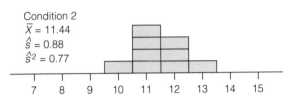

Figure 15.6

Condition 3
$\overline{X} = 12.56$
$\hat{s} = 1.51$
$\hat{s}^2 = 2.28$

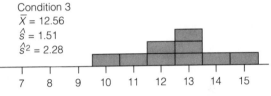

Figure 15.7

Table 15.1   Three-Condition Experiment

	Condition 1	Condition 2	Condition 3
	10	12	15
	7	10	11
	11	11	14
	9	11	10
	8	11	12
	11	13	13
	10	12	13
	10	12	12
	9	11	13
Mean	9.44	11.44	12.56
Std. Dev.	1.33	0.88	1.51
Variance	1.77	0.77	2.28

The histogram of the data (Figure 15.4) shows the variability. This distribution has a mean, standard deviation, and variance of $\overline{X} = 11.13$, $\hat{s} = 1.79$, and $\hat{s}^2 = 3.20$. The distribution is approximately symmetric and is not particularly interesting. Except, of course, that there's something special about it—it really represents the *combined* distribution of three separate groups of data for a three-condition experiment (Table 15.1). Each of the three separate conditions has its own mean, standard deviation, and form; the statistics are shown in Table 15.1, and the histograms are shown in Figures 15.5, 15.6, and 15.7. Presenting the data this way shows that each group has its own spread and center. In the three separate conditions, the standard deviation is based on a quantity $\Sigma(X - \overline{X})^2$, as always. But notice that the mean is different for each set of data and that each

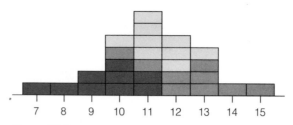

Figure 15.8

of those three means is different from what we know to be the mean of all of the data together ($\overline{X} = 11.15$). Also note that the variability of the overall distribution ($\hat{s} = 1.79$) is greater than that for any individual group of scores.

We could combine all groups into a single histogram again, as in Figure 15.8, showing the center and spread of the entire set of data across experimental conditions. In this illustration, the separate identities of the three groups are maintained, yet the overall picture of the combined data is evident as well. The picture makes it clear that, while each group is clustered reasonably close to its individual center, the spread of the combined data is somewhat greater. ANOVA analyzes this latter variability, that present in all of the scores.

Partitioning Variance in a Between-Subjects Design

The total variability in the data is based on, as usual, the differences between each score and the mean of all of the scores, so that the quantity ($X - \overline{X}$), where $\overline{X}$ is the mean of all of the scores, forms the basis of what we can think of as the *total variability* in the data. That is, if we were to compute

$$\hat{s}^2 = \frac{\Sigma(X - \overline{X})^2}{N - 1},$$

summing the differences between all of the scores in all of the experimental conditions and the overall mean, we would have the total variance: $\hat{s}^2 = 3.20$.

At this point, we need to introduce a little more terminology, since we're developing a general notation for the analysis of variance. Let's let a stand for the number of experimental conditions (or groups of subjects in a between-subjects design), so that the experimental conditions can be called Condition 1, Condition 2, and so on, through Condition a. Since this is a between-subjects design, there are a groups of subjects. When we want to talk about a particular group or condition without explicitly naming one, we'll just refer to it as group j; j as a subscript, then, can refer to any experimental condition.

We'll use the letter n to represent the number of observations in an experimental group (for now we'll keep matters simple and assume that the groups are equal in size). The formula for variance will use the value of na in place of N (there are n scores in each group, and there are a groups, so that $N = na$) to indicate the total number of values summed. The rewritten variance formula now is

$$\hat{s}^2 = \frac{\Sigma(X - \overline{X})^2}{na - 1}.$$

In all of the variance formulas that we've introduced so far, the scores are in just one group and not different groups. But now we must remember that the summation must include all groups. That won't be hard to remember; unless we indicate otherwise in a formula, the summation will simply be taken to be over all scores in all groups.

Many of the ANOVA computations are done with condition (group) totals instead of with means. For each individual set of scores in the experiment, we designate its sum as T and use a subscript to distinguish between them. The sum of the scores in the first experimental condition, then, will be T_1, while that for the second is T_2. T_j will be the sum of the scores in an arbitrary (the jth) group, and the total for the last condition will be T_a. The sum of all of the scores in all of the conditions will be called the grand total and symbolized as GT. The grand total is often calculated as the sum of the group totals; that is, as

$$GT = \sum_j T_j.$$

In a two-condition experiment we used subscripts on the means ($\overline{X}_1$ and $\overline{X}_2$) to indicate which condition the mean was from; that notation can continue here. Thus $\overline{X}_1$ is the mean of the first experimental condition, $\overline{X}_2$ is that for the second, and so on, with $\overline{X}_j$ being the mean for the jth condition, and (naturally) $\overline{X}_a$ indicating the mean of the last (the ath) condition.

Since we have a symbol for the mean of each condition, we will need a separate symbol for the overall mean. We'll call it the grand mean and use the symbol GM to indicate it. It's calculated, of course, as

$$GM = \frac{GT}{na} = \frac{\sum_j T_j}{na}.$$

Making one final modification to the formula for variance, we use GM to stand for the mean of all of the data, giving the total variance the formula

$$\hat{s}^2 = \frac{\Sigma(X - GM)^2}{na - 1}.$$

The notation so far is summarized in Table 15.2. Computations for the example data that we introduced previously are shown in Table 15.3.

The discussion so far has focused on the total variation, that around the mean for all of the scores in all of the conditions. But we also showed that each condition has its own mean and its own variance. The variance for an individual group of scores is based on the difference between a score and the mean of its group, $(X - \overline{X}_j)$. The differences $(X - \overline{X}_j)$, notice, are differences *within* each group of data. Using them we can calculate $\hat{s}^2_j$, the variance for each individual experimental condition. We can also calculate the standard deviation for each of the groups, calculated as

$$\hat{s}_j = \sqrt{\frac{\Sigma(X - \overline{X}_j)^2}{n - 1}},$$

where the subscript indicates the group. Note again that the formula uses differences within each group to compute that group's variance and standard deviation.

Table 15.2   Notation for Analysis of Variance

	Experimental conditions				
	1	2	...	j	...	a
	X	X	...	X	...	X
	X	X	...	X	...	X
n subjects per condition	.	.		.		.
	.	.		.		.
	.	.		.		.
	X_n	X_n	...	X_n	...	X_n
Group totals ⟶	T_1	T_2	...	T_j	...	T_a
Group means ⟶	$\overline{X}_1$	$\overline{X}_2$	...	$\overline{X}_j$	...	$\overline{X}_a$

$$N = na \qquad \overline{X}_j = \frac{T_j}{n}$$

$$GT = \sum_j T_j \qquad GM = \frac{GT}{na}$$

Table 15.3   Computation of GT and GM for Example Data

	Condition 1	Condition 2	Condition 3
	10	12	15
	7	10	11
	11	11	14
	9	11	10
	8	11	12
	11	13	13
	10	12	13
	10	12	12
	9	11	13
T_j	85	103	113
$\overline{X}_j$	9.44	11.44	12.56

$$N = na = 9(3) = 27$$
$$GT = \sum_j T_j = 85 + 103 + 113 = 301$$
$$GM = \frac{GT}{N} = \frac{301}{27} = 11.15.$$

In the example data, no two of the three group means were equal, and the grand mean was different from all of the group means. In real data, rarely will any of the group means be exactly equal, and they'll probably all be different from the grand mean. As a consequence, the difference between the group mean and the grand mean—that is, $(\overline{X}_j - GM)$—will be nonzero in each group of data.

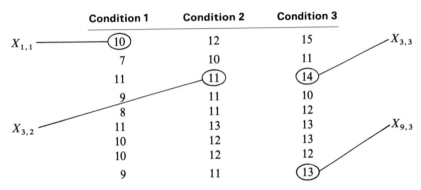

Figure 15.9

The original formula for the overall variance as rewritten in new notation, recall, was

$$\hat{s}^2 = \frac{\Sigma(X - GM)^2}{na - 1}.$$

The numerator expression $(X - GM)$ is the difference between an individual score and the overall mean. Note that this is a *different* quantity from $(X - \bar{X}_j)$; this quantity is a difference between a score and its group mean.

In the preceding discussion, we presented three sets of differences:

$(X - GM)$ between individual scores and the overall mean
$(X - \bar{X}_j)$ between individual scores and their group mean
$(\bar{X}_j - GM)$ between group means and the overall mean

These three differences provide an important step toward analyzing the total variance into two separate segments.

Let's continue now to the next step in developing the analysis of variance, one where we consider a possible way of looking at the score of a single subject in one of the experimental conditions in the experiment. Don't forget those three differences—they'll reappear very soon.

The Model of a Score

Up until now, we have kept the notation simple by not attaching subscripts to individual data values. And we'll be able to keep it simple for the most part—there's no point in complicating our notation when it's not necessary. But for the present discussion, we'll need a way to distinguish an individual score—that is, any particular X value—from all others. To do that, we'll use a simple scheme of attaching two subscripts to the X. Any score in any experimental group can be symbolized by $X_{i,j}$, where the values of the two subscripts tell us which subject (the first subscript—i) and which group (j—the second subscript). Thus the first score in the first group would be symbolized as $X_{1,1}$; in the example data, $X_{1,1} = 10$, while $X_{3,2} = 11$ (the third score in the second group), and $X_{9,3} = 13$ (the ninth score in the third group). Figure 15.9 illustrates this notation system.

Let's consider one particular score, $X_{3,3}$ (which has the value 14). It is located some distance above its group mean and above the grand mean (see

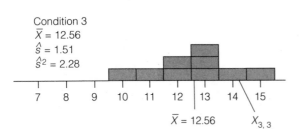

$\overline{X} = 12.56$ $X_{3,3}$

Figure 15.10

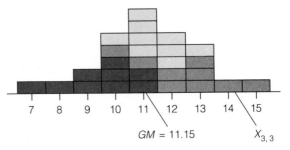

$GM = 11.15$ $X_{3,3}$

Figure 15.11

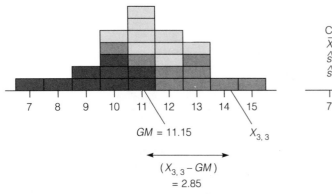

$GM = 11.15$ $X_{3,3}$

$(X_{3,3} - GM)$
$= 2.85$

Figure 15.12

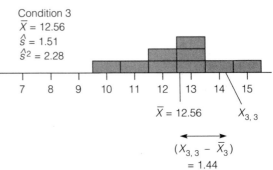

Condition 3
$\overline{X} = 12.56$
$\hat{s} = 1.51$
$\hat{s}^2 = 2.28$

$\overline{X} = 12.56$ $X_{3,3}$

$(X_{3,3} - \overline{X}_3)$
$= 1.44$

Figure 15.13

Figures 15.10 and 15.11). In computing the overall variance, $X_{3,3}$ contributed its difference from the grand mean $(X - GM) = (14 - 11.15) = 2.85$ (Figure 15.12). In computing the variance within Group 3, though, $X_{3,3}$ contributes a different amount (see Figure 15.13).

The difference between the score of 14 and the grand mean of 11.15, we saw, was $(14 - 11.15) = 2.85$. Of that, 1.44 is the difference between 14 and its group mean $(14 - 12.56)$, and the balance is the difference between the group mean and the grand mean (Figure 15.14). We represent the same equivalences schematically in Figure 15.15.

The differences between a score and the overall mean $(X_{ij} - GM)$ can be expressed as two additive components, one expressing the deviation of the score from its group mean $(X_{ij} - \overline{X}_j)$, and the other the deviation of the group mean from the overall mean $(X_j - GM)$. For $X_{3,3}$, we have

$$(X_{3,3} - GM) = (\overline{X}_3 - GM) + (X_{3,3} - \overline{X}_j)$$
$$\downarrow \qquad\qquad \downarrow \qquad\qquad \downarrow$$
$$(14 - 11.15) = (12.56 - 11.15) + (14 - 12.56)$$
$$2.85 = 1.41 + 1.44.$$

More generally, in symbols, we have

$$(X_{ij} - GM) = (\overline{X}_j - GM) + (X_{ij} - \overline{X}_j).$$

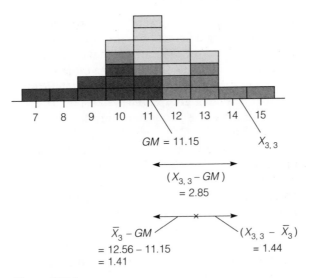

$GM = 11.15$

$X_{3,3}$

$(X_{3,3} - GM)$
$= 2.85$

$\overline{X}_3 - GM$
$= 12.56 - 11.15$
$= 1.41$

$(X_{3,3} - \overline{X}_3)$
$= 1.44$

Figure 15.14

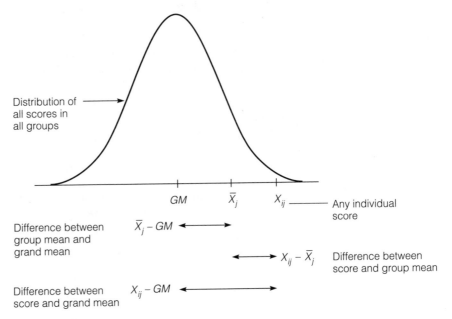

Distribution of all scores in all groups

GM $\overline{X}_j$ X_{ij} — Any individual score

Difference between group mean and grand mean $\overline{X}_j - GM$

$X_{ij} - \overline{X}_j$ Difference between score and group mean

Difference between score and grand mean $X_{ij} - GM$

Figure 15.15

This expression represents the difference between the score and the mean of all of the scores as a sum of two values. One of those two values gives a measure of how different a score is from the average of its group ($X_{ij} - \overline{X}_j$). Since all of the subjects in a group are treated exactly the same, the differences within each group represent error. The difference between group mean and grand mean ($\overline{X}_j - GM$) gives a measure of how different the group is from the others. This difference is due to the effect of the treatment that a group receives. Clearly, if an independent

Introduction to the Analysis of Variance

variable has an effect, that effect should be seen as at least one of the experimental conditions being different from the others; the quantity $(\overline{X}_j - GM)$ is a measure of that effect. On the other hand, if an experimental treatment has no effect, the group mean shouldn't differ from the other means.

So far, we have been dealing with statistics based on the data in the a different treatment groups. Since statistics are usually used to estimate parameters, let's define the parameter equivalents of the various statistics.

The statistic GM, the grand mean of all scores in all groups, is an unbiased estimate of the population parameter μ, the mean of the population of all scores that might ever be observed in this particular experiment. The group mean $\overline{X}_j$, on the other hand, estimates μ_j, the mean of the population of all possible observations under the jth experimental treatment. The difference between the two means, again, is a measure of the effect of treatment j.

The difference between the overall population mean and the mean of a treatment condition is called a *treatment effect*. A treatment effect is represented by the symbol α_j, so we can then write the expression

$$\alpha_j = \mu_j - \mu$$

as a definition of the parameter α_j. In words

treatment effect = mean of the jth population − overall mean.

One statement of the null hypothesis tested in ANOVA is that all of the treatment effects equal zero; that is, that no experimental treatment has any effect or, written a little more formally, that $\alpha_j = 0$ for all values of j. In ANOVA, any differences between scores and the population mean of all subjects treated in the same way are regarded as error. The other difference, that between a score and the mean of a treatment condition $(X_{ij} - \mu_j)$, must therefore represent error. The source of the error is unimportant in ANOVA—individual differences between subjects, measurement error, or the influence of extraneous variables are all regarded the same.

As we did with statistics in Figure 15.15, we might express the parameter relationships as shown in Figure 15.16.

We now have three quantities expressing differences between various components of the population mean and the individual score value. How do we turn all of this into a procedure for making an inference about differences among experimental treatments? To do that, let's continue to look at the difference between the score and the overall mean and use that difference in the variance formula.

Sums of Squares. We began our development of the analysis of variance by expanding the familiar formula for variance into

$$\hat{s}^2 = \frac{\Sigma(X - GM)^2}{na - 1}.$$

The single summation symbol is adequate for most purposes, but to be really complete, the summation should be a double one, indicating that we should sum within each set of scores (that is, over the i subscript) and also across all of the sets of scores (over the j subscript). That is, if we write

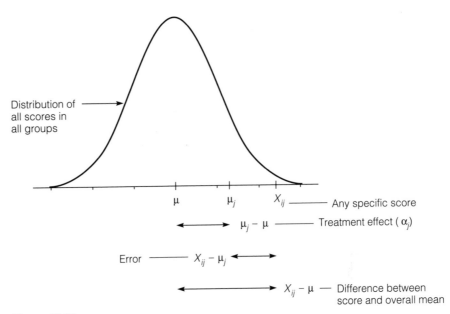

Distribution of all scores in all groups

μ μ_j X_{ij} ——— Any specific score

$\mu_j - \mu$ ——— Treatment effect (α_j)

Error ——— $X_{ij} - \mu_j$

$X_{ij} - \mu$ — Difference between score and overall mean

Figure 15.16

Condition 1		Condition 2		Condition 3	
10		12		15	
7		10		11	
11		11		14	
9		11		10	
8	$\sum_i X_{i1}$	11	$\sum_i X_{i2}$	12	$\sum_i X_{i3}$
11		13		13	
10		12		13	
10		12		12	
9		11		13	
85		103		113	
85	+	103	+	113 = 301	

$\sum_j$ $= \sum_j \sum_i X_{ij}$

Figure 15.17

$$\sum_j \sum_i X_{ij},$$

the symbols instruct us to sum first across the i subscript (subjects within each condition) and then to sum those sums across the j subscript (see Figure 15.17). As illustrated, the first set of summations are down the columns, first for $j = 1$, then for $j = 2$, and finally for $j = 3$. Once that is done, then the summation is across the j subscript, resulting in the grand total.

To symbolize the summation, within each group and then across groups, of the deviations of the individual scores for the grand mean, then, we would write

$$\sum_j \sum_i (X_{ij} - GM)^2.$$

This formula for the sum of the squared deviations around the grand mean still says "find the differences, square 'em, and then add 'em all up," just as does $\Sigma(X - \bar{X})^2$, but now says it much more explicitly. Fortunately, we won't often have to work with double summations; sometimes, though, they're best for clarity.

The modified version of the overall variance, using the modified sum of squares expression, now finally becomes

$$\hat{s}^2 = \frac{\sum_j \sum_i (X_{ij} - GM)^2}{na - 1}.$$

This formula is nothing but the overall variance in the data for all experimental conditions. As in all variances, the deviations are calculated around a mean—the grand mean in this case—and are then squared and summed to give a sum of squares or SS. The denominator, again, like all variances, is the degrees of freedom associated with the numerator.

The numerator of the variance expression—the sum of squares—involves deviations between the grand mean and the individual scores $(X_{ij} - GM)$. Earlier, we developed the expression

$$(X_{ij} - GM) = (\bar{X}_j - GM) + (X_{ij} - \bar{X}_j)$$

for that difference. Substituting the right-hand half of this expression into the overall sum of squares gives

$$\sum_j \sum_i (X_{ij} - GM)^2 = \sum_j \sum_i [(\bar{X}_j - GM) + (X_{ij} - \bar{X}_j)]^2.$$

Applying a little algebra on the right side (which we'll mercifully omit), the result is this expression for sums of squares:

$$\underbrace{\sum_j \sum_i (X_{ij} - GM)^2}_{\substack{\text{Differences of} \\ \text{scores from the} \\ \text{grand mean}}} = \underbrace{n \sum_j (\bar{X}_j - GM)^2}_{\substack{\text{Differences between condition} \\ \text{means and the grand mean}}} + \underbrace{\sum_j \sum_i (X_{ij} - \bar{X}_j)^2}_{\substack{\text{Differences of} \\ \text{scores from their} \\ \text{condition mean}}}.$$

These three quantities are all sums of squares, or SSs, and they represent variation of three different kinds. Let's look at them a bit more carefully.

The first, based on variations around the overall mean, is usually called the total sum of squares or SS_{Total}:

$$SS_{Total} = \sum_j \sum_i (X_{ij} - GM)^2.$$

It is the numerator of the formula for the overall variance as expanded with analysis-of-variance notation. It represents the total variation that is present among all of the data values.

The second component of the expression represents variation of the group means about the overall mean:

$$SS_{Between} = n \sum_j (\overline{X}_j - GM)^2.$$

It is called the sum of squares between groups, or $SS_{Between}$. This quantity is a portion of the overall variability. In particular, it is that part of the overall variation that represents differences between the experimental treatments.

The last term in the expression represents variance within the experimental conditions:

$$SS_{Within} = \sum_j \sum_i (X_{ij} - \overline{X}_j)^2.$$

It is called the sum of squares within groups (SS_{Within}) and represents a measure of error.

Putting them all together, we have

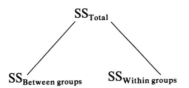

Symbolically,

$$SS_{Total} = SS_{Between} + SS_{Within}.$$

What we have just accomplished is the division of the total sum of squares, which represents all of the variation in the data, into two separate and additive components. One component represents variation within each group and thus is a measure of error. The other component measures variation between the experimental conditions and thus represents treatment effects:

$$SS_{Total}$$

$$SS_{Between\ groups} \qquad SS_{Within\ groups}$$

Degrees of Freedom. We may subdivide the degrees of freedom just as we did the sum of squares to obtain a df that corresponds to each sum of squares. The total number of degrees of freedom in the analysis is, as usual, $N - 1$. In this case, replacing N by the quantity na we have

$$df_{Total} = na - 1.$$

For $SS_{Between}$, we follow the familiar rule and use the number of values summed minus 1, or

$$df_{Between} = a - 1.$$

Finally, for the SS_{Within}, note that we have a groups, each with n observations, giving $n - 1$ degrees of freedom for each group. Combining those two facts, we have a groups, each with $n - 1$ degrees of freedom, so that

$$df_{Within} = a(n - 1) = na - a.$$

We have now completed the separation of the total degrees of freedom into two segments as

$$df_{Total} = df_{Between} + df_{Within}.$$

It's easy to see that the equation is correct:

$$df_{Total} = \underbrace{a - 1}_{df_{Between}} + \underbrace{na - a}_{df_{Within}} = \underbrace{na - 1}_{df_{Total}}.$$

Forming Variance Estimates. Any sum of squares divided by its degrees of freedom yields an estimate of a variance. Let's first look at the variance estimates in the analysis of variance and then define the parameters that they estimate. Once we take the last step, it will be clear how to test a hypothesis about equality of means.

During the early twentieth century, when most of today's statistics were being developed, the mean of the squared differences about the arithmetic mean was universally called a *mean square*. That practice continues in the analysis of variance. We know, of course, that dividing a sum of squares by its degrees of freedom gives an estimate of a variance. But the practice of calling these variances by their earlier name—mean square—continues. Thus, dividing the sum of squares Between by its degrees of freedom gives the mean square between groups:

$$\frac{SS_{Between}}{df_{Between}} = MS_{Between}$$
$$= \text{"Variance" between groups.}$$

Likewise, dividing the sum of squares Within by its degrees of freedom gives a mean square:

$$\frac{SS_{Within}}{df_{Within}} = MS_{Within}$$
$$= \text{"Variance" within groups.}$$

There's no point in computing the mean square based on the total sum of squares and its df. It would give the overall variance of all of the data, but it's not useful as a descriptive statistic. (The standard deviation of each individual group is much more important.) Moreover, it's not independent of the other two mean squares.

With two mean squares (variances) defined, we now come to the question of just what parameter(s) they estimate. In the case of the MS_{Within}, it's easy; MS_{Within} is an unbiased estimate of σ^2_e, the overall error variance.

Recall that ANOVA regards all variation (*except* that due to the independent variable) as error. In addition, the mean error across all experimental conditions is assumed to be zero, and the variance of the error is σ^2_e. MS_{Within} provides an unbiased estimate of that error variance:

MS_{Within} estimates σ^2_e.

If MS_{Within} estimates σ^2_e, then what does $MS_{Between}$ estimate? It estimates the quantity

$$MS_{Between} \quad \text{estimates} \quad \sigma^2_e + \frac{n\Sigma\alpha_j^2}{a-1}.$$

Look at these formulas carefully. Both of the two mean squares estimate error variance. But $MS_{Between}$ *also* estimates a quantity based on the treatment effects, α_j. The null hypothesis in the analysis of variance is that all of the treatment effects are zero. If the null hypothesis is true, then the right-hand part of the latter formula will equal zero, so that *both* MS_{Within} and $MS_{Between}$ estimate the same quantity, namely error variance. On the other hand, if the null hypothesis is false —that is, if at least one of the treatment effects is nonzero—then $MS_{Between}$ includes a nonzero second factor and so will be larger than MS_{Within}. This fact leads to the test of the null hypothesis of no treatment effects.

The *F* Ratio. Consider the ratio of the two mean squares

$$F = \frac{MS_{Between}}{MS_{Within}}.$$

In terms of the parameters, the ratio represents

$$F = \frac{\sigma^2_e + \dfrac{n\Sigma\alpha_j^2}{a-1}}{\sigma^2_e}.$$

If the null hypothesis of no treatment effects is true (that is, all population means are equal, and thus all $\alpha_j = 0$), then the second term in the numerator equals zero (Figure 15.18), and the numerator and the denominator of the ratio are independent estimates of the same parameter. In this case, the ratio should have a value of approximately 1.0.

On the other hand, if the hypothesis is false, then the treatment effects would be nonzero (Figure 15.19), and the numerator would exceed the denominator, giving the ratio a value greater than 1.0.

The ratio of the two variances is called the *F* ratio and is used to test the hypothesis of no treatment effects.* The ratio and its distribution is the same as

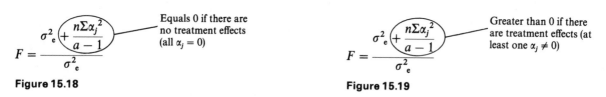

$$F = \frac{\sigma^2_e + \dfrac{n\Sigma\alpha_j^2}{a-1}}{\sigma^2_e}$$

Equals 0 if there are no treatment effects (all $\alpha_j = 0$)

Figure 15.18

$$F = \frac{\sigma^2_e + \dfrac{n\Sigma\alpha_j^2}{a-1}}{\sigma^2_e}$$

Greater than 0 if there are treatment effects (at least one $\alpha_j \neq 0$)

Figure 15.19

---

* The name *F* was given to the statistic by the American statistician George Snedecor to honor Sir Ronald Fisher, a British agricultural statistician who developed the logic underlying ANOVA as we know it. Among his many contributions, Fisher also introduced the concepts of *statistical significance* and the *null hypothesis*. (See Tankard, 1984, for additional biographical information on the remarkable Sir Ronald.)

the F that we introduced in Chapter 14, but is used here as a test of the hypothesis that all population means are equal.

| Testing the Null Hypothesis | There are two ways of expressing the null hypothesis that we want to test. The most straightforward expression is |

Testing the Null Hypothesis

There are two ways of expressing the null hypothesis that we want to test. The most straightforward expression is

$$\mu_1 = \mu_2 = \cdots = \mu_j = \cdots = \mu_a = \mu.$$

This is the direct extension of the two-sample Student's t test to the multiple-condition design (although we usually expressed the $\mu_1 = \mu_2$ hypothesis as $\mu_1 - \mu_2 = 0$). A more useful expression when it comes to understanding the F ratio, though, is

$$\alpha_j = 0 \qquad \text{for all } j = 1, 2, \ldots, a.$$

This expression declares that all treatment effects are zero and that a single nonzero effect means that the null hypothesis is false. Since MS_{Between} estimates the parameter

$$\sigma^2_e + \frac{n\Sigma\alpha_j^2}{a - 1}$$

when the null hypothesis is true, the F ratio consists of two statistics that both estimate σ^2_e:

$$F = \frac{\sigma^2_e}{\sigma^2_e}.$$

Thus, when the null hypothesis is true, the value of F should be about 1.0,* while it should be greater than 1.0 when the null hypothesis is false and there are between-conditions differences.

Note that the values of α_j are squared in the parameter expression. This means that any difference between μ and μ_j, whether it is greater or less than zero, makes the mean square increase when treatment effects are nonzero. In other words, the values of the F ratio should be greater than 1.0, regardless of whether the treatment effects are positive or negative.

The sampling distribution for F when the null hypothesis is true is controlled by two df parameters, one for the numerator of the ratio and one for the denominator. In general, the F distribution is asymmetric and positively skewed as shown in Figure 15.20, which shows the F distribution with numerator df $= 4$ and denominator df $= 16$. The values of the ratio must necessarily be positive, since both the numerator and the denominator are sums of squared values. When the null hypothesis is true, most of the values of F will cluster around 1.0. When the null hypothesis is false, though, the ratio will tend to be larger than 1.0, so that the critical region of the curve is in the extreme right-hand tail. Appendix F gives the critical values for the F distribution for a large number of sets of df values and for several significance points. With df $= 4$ for the numerator and 16

---

*Actually, this statement is a considerable simplification, but it's convenient to think of the distribution in this way and won't lead you astray in using the distribution and making inferences.

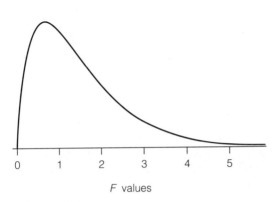

F values

Figure 15.20

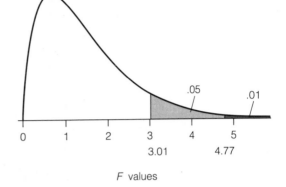

.05

.01

0   1   2   3   4   5

3.01   4.77

F values

Figure 15.21

for the denominator, two critical points given in Appendix F are 3.01 and 4.77 for $\alpha = .05$ and $\alpha = .01$, respectively (Figure 15.21). With 4 and 16 degrees of freedom, any obtained F ratio of 3.01 or larger represents a significant difference among the group means at the .05 level, while at the .01 level, a difference of 4.77 or more will result in rejecting the null hypothesis.

But just what does it mean in ANOVA to reject a null hypothesis? It means that we're rejecting the hypothesis that all of the treatment population means are equal. By rejecting the null, the alternative hypothesis that we support states that all of the means are not equal (or, alternatively, that not all of the treatment effects are zero). But that's not a very satisfying conclusion, since there are a number of ways that the means can be unequal. Consider, for example, Dr. Campbell's hypothetical three-condition study. If he concludes that his high, middle, and low introversion/extraversion conditions are not all alike, where is he left? It could be that high and middle are alike but different from low. Or maybe middle and low are alike but different from high. Or perhaps high and low are the same but different from middle. Or maybe all three are mutually different from each other.

In a three-condition experiment, the null hypothesis can be incorrect in any of four possible ways:

$$\mu_1 = \mu_2 \neq \mu_3$$
$$\mu_1 \neq \mu_2 = \mu_3$$
$$\mu_1 = \mu_3 \neq \mu_2$$
$$\mu_1 \neq \mu_2 \neq \mu_3$$

Merely rejecting the null hypothesis doesn't provide any indication as to which of the possible alternatives is likely to be correct. And if there are four conditions in the design, the situation becomes more complex, because the null hypothesis can be incorrect in any of 14 different ways; more conditions lead to even more possibilities.

It's clear, then, that the hypothesis test provides only an overall indication about the null hypothesis. For this reason, the hypothesis test just presented is

351

called an *omnibus* test; it gives only a general indication about the equality of conditions. The next step in an analysis uses a variety of techniques, often called *post hoc* or *follow-up* tests, which we'll present soon. Of course, if we conclude that there are no differences among conditions, then the analysis is completed and there's no need to pursue the data further.

A Final Comment

This chapter has presented the characteristics of the multiple-condition experimental design, as well as the conceptual foundation of the analysis of variance. The design involves multiple groups, and the analysis of variance allows us to test the hypothesis that the populations that they represent have equal means. This chapter has presented only the concepts of the design and its analysis. No exercises are provided, since all of the computations appear in the next chapter.

S U M M A R Y

- The one-way design expands the two-condition design by adding additional experimental conditions.
- In a one-way design, the independent variable can be manipulated either between or within subjects.
- The null hypothesis for the analysis of variance is that there is no difference among the means of the populations.
- The variance in experimental data comes from four sources: measurement error, control error, individual differences, and the independent variable.
- A treatment effect is the difference between a population mean and the overall mean.
- Differences within each experimental condition represent error.
- The difference between a group mean and the grand mean represents a treatment effect.
- Dividing a sum of squares by degrees of freedom gives a variance estimate; variance estimates are called mean squares in the analysis of variance.
- If the null hypothesis is true, then the mean square for between groups and the mean square for within groups should be roughly equal, and their ratio should be about 1.0. If the null hypothesis is false, the ratio should tend to be greater than 1.0.

K E Y   T E R M S

Analysis of variance (ANOVA)
Blocks
Completely randomized design
Grand mean (GM)
Grand total (GT)
Mean square

Multiple group design
Randomized blocks design
Randomized groups design
Sum of squares
T_j
Treatment effect (α_j)

Experiments with More Than Two Between-Subjects Conditions (Analysis)

$\mathbf{M}$ost investigators rely heavily on computers for doing ANOVA computations, even in the simplest of cases like the design that we presented in Chapter 15. With the one-way design there's no necessity for computers, and we'll illustrate the computation fully here. In more complex experimental designs, computers are almost universal.

The formulas that we gave in Chapter 15 are definitional; they help to show what each sum of squares actually represents. But you wouldn't want to calculate the values using definitional formulas, and so now we'll introduce the computational formulas for the quantities that we need.

The definitions of the three sums of squares and their computational equivalents are

Quantity	Definition	Computations
SS_{Total}	$\displaystyle\sum_j \sum_i (X_{ij} - GM)^2$	$\displaystyle\sum_j \sum_i X_{ij}^2 - \frac{GT^2}{na}$
$SS_{Between}$	$\displaystyle n\sum_j (\bar{X}_j - GM)^2$	$\displaystyle\frac{\sum_j T^2}{n} - \frac{GT^2}{na}$
SS_{Within}	$\displaystyle\sum_j \sum_i (X_{ij} - \bar{X}_j)^2$	$\displaystyle\sum_j \sum_i X_{ij}^2 - \frac{\sum_j T^2}{n}$

These formulas will become much clearer as we proceed through an example.

Equal Group Sizes

Suppose that we are studying the effect of three different drugs on headache pain. To the three drugs, which we'll just call drugs A, B, and C, we'll add a fourth, a placebo (sugar pill) as a control condition. Our independent variable is kind of

Table 16.1   Hypothetical Pain-Relief Data

	Drug condition			
	A	B	C	Placebo
	5	13	15	10
	7	12	11	8
	11	12	13	5
	10	8	10	9
	10	7	10	6
	6	8	16	13
	4	12	14	11
	8	11	11	16
$\overline{X}_j$	7.62	10.38	12.50	9.75
Std. dev.	2.56	2.33	2.33	3.62
T_j	61	83	100	78
ΣX^2	511	899	1288	852

drug, and the dependent variable a rating of pain relief. We'll ask our subjects, chronic headache sufferers all, to take the drug during their next headache, wait 30 minutes, and then rate the degree of relief on a 1 to 20 scale, where 20 represents complete relief and 1 means no relief at all. The hypothetical data and some summary values for the four groups of subjects are listed in Table 16.1.

Let's look first at the descriptive statistics. From the group means, it's evident that Drug C produced the most pain relief, followed by Drug B and the placebo, and finally by Drug A. The standard deviations appear generally similar, although the placebo condition is slightly more variable, suggesting that perhaps some individuals experience pain relief from the mere belief that they're taking a drug, while others don't.

Proceeding to the analysis of variance, we'll use a .05 significance level. The first step in the analysis is to compute the sum of the scores (T_j) in each condition as well as the sum of squared scores (ΣX^2) for each. These values are shown in Table 16.1.

Let's begin the computations with the total sum of squares. Following the computational formula from page 353,

$$SS_{Total} = \sum_j \sum_i X_{ij}^2 - \frac{GT^2}{na},$$

we can first calculate the grand total as

$$GT = \sum_j T_j = 61 + 83 + 100 + 78 = 322.$$

Next, we sum the squared scores across all conditions and then subtract the squared grand total divided by the total number of observations. That is,

$$SS_{Total} = \sum_j \sum_i X_{ij}^2 - \frac{GT^2}{na}$$
$$= (511 + 899 + 1288 + 852) - \frac{322^2}{8 \times 4}$$
$$= 3550 - 3240.12$$
$$= 309.88.$$

For the sum of squares between groups, we have

$$SS_{Between} = \frac{\sum_j T^2}{n} - \frac{GT^2}{na}$$
$$= \frac{61^2 + 83^2 + 100^2 + 78^2}{8} - \frac{322^2}{8 \times 4}$$
$$= 3336.75 - 3240.12$$
$$= 96.63.$$

Finally, for the within-groups sum of squares,

$$SS_{Within} = \sum_j \sum_i X_{ij}^2 - \frac{\sum_j T^2}{n}$$
$$= (511 + 899 + 1288 + 852) - \frac{61^2 + 83^2 + 100^2 + 78^2}{8}$$
$$= 3550 - 3336.75$$
$$= 213.25.$$

As a computational check (always a good idea), we can make sure that our component sums of squares really do add up to the total sum of squares:

$$SS_{Total} = SS_{Between} + SS_{Within}$$
$$309.88 = 96.63 + 213.25 = 309.88.$$

Following the formulas that we presented in Chapter 15 (pp. 347–348), we next find the degrees of freedom for each sum of squares as

$$df_{Total} = na - 1 = 8 \times 4 - 1 = 31$$
$$df_{Between} = a - 1 = 4 - 1 = 3$$
$$df_{Within} = a(n - 1) = na - a = 8 \times 4 - 4 = 28.$$

A convenient way to keep your computations neatly is to construct a summary table to hold the values. We may begin with the entries that we have so far, with headings for the values:

Summary Table

Source	SS	df	MS	F
Drugs	96.63	3		
Error	213.25	28		
Total	309.88	31		

Following the usual ANOVA custom, we have identified the sources of variation in the table with descriptive terms. The source of the between-groups sum of squares is the independent variable in the experiment (drugs), and that for within-groups is error. The sum of squares and the degrees of freedom are entered in the appropriate columns.

The variance estimates (the mean squares) are computed by dividing the $SS_{Between}$ and SS_{Within} by the degrees of freedom, and the results are placed in the summary table. For the mean square for drugs, we thus have the sum of squares for drugs divided by its df, or

$$MS_{Drugs} = \frac{SS_{Drugs}}{df_{Drugs}}$$

$$= \frac{96.63}{3}$$

$$= 32.21.$$

For error, we have

$$MS_{Error} = \frac{SS_{Error}}{df_{Error}}$$

$$= \frac{213.25}{28}$$

$$= 7.62.$$

Note that the mean square for "Total" isn't computed. While we know that value to be the total variance of all subjects in all conditions, it's not a meaningful number in the analysis of variance. The MS_{Total} isn't the sum of the two mean squares above it, and so calculating it doesn't serve as a computational check; it's never reported in the summary table.

Source	SS	df	MS	F
Drugs	96.63	3	32.21	
Error	213.25	28	7.62	
Total	309.88	31		

Finally, we calculate the F ratio as

$$F = \frac{MS_{Between}}{MS_{Within}}$$

$$= \frac{32.21}{7.62}$$

$$= 4.23$$

and complete the summary table:

Source	SS	df	MS	F
Drugs	96.63	3	32.21	4.23
Error	213.25	28	7.62	
Total	309.88	31		

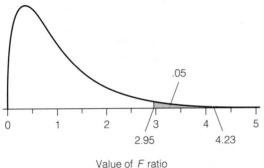

Figure 16.1

Value of *F* ratio

Figure 16.2

Value of *F* ratio

The next task is to determine whether the *F* value is large enough to make us reject the hypothesis that the four drug conditions represent populations with equal means. With $\alpha = .05$, consult Appendix F with df = 3 for the numerator and df = 28 for the denominator. The tabled critical value is 2.95. If we picture the sampling distribution of *F* as shown in Figure 16.1, then we can easily determine that there's a significant difference among the four drug conditions.

If you're using a computer, you'll find that most programs eliminate the need for a table like Appendix F by providing an exact probability for the obtained *F* value. For our example, the program might give the probability value .0138. This means that, if the null hypothesis were actually true, then we would observe an *F* value this extreme or more, with a probability of .0138. Graphically, what the program has told us is that the area beyond the obtained *F* of 4.23 is .0138 (see Figure 16.2). Since .0138 is less than the significance level (.05) that we had chosen, we may reject the null hypothesis.

Our conclusion, whether we reach it by an exact probability or by consulting a table, is to reject the hypothesis that all treatment conditions produce the same effect. By drawing that conclusion, we make the inference that at least one of the treatment effects is nonzero—that is, that at least one of the four drug conditions is different from the others.

Unequal Group Sizes

Research in psychology normally begins with equal group sizes, but ends with unequal sizes. Most often, subject loss is accidental—a subject forgets the appointment, the equipment fails, the experimenter makes a mistake, or an animal dies. Such subject loss, as long as it's not related to the manipulation of the independent variable, is of no serious consequence.

Two different approaches have been used for computations with unequal group sizes. Current opinion is that one method is preferred (we'll call the preferred method the *weighted means* procedure). The preferred method is computationally more difficult; probably prohibitively so in designs more complicated than the simple one that we're discussing here. We'll present computations for both methods, and urge you to use the weighted means computations.

We've used n to indicate the number of subjects in each group; with unequal group sizes, we let n_j designate the number of scores in group j. This means that the total number of observations is $N = \Sigma n_j$, instead of na. The total number of degrees of freedom is the total number of subjects, minus 1, as always, but we use the notation

$$\Sigma n_j - 1.$$

We turn first to the weighted means analysis.

Weighted Means Analysis

The adjustment of the equal-group-size formulas to those for weighted means is simple. In the computational formula for the between-groups sum of squares, which was originally

$$\text{SS}_{\text{Between}} = \frac{\sum_j T^2}{n} - \frac{GT^2}{na},$$

we divide by each group size *before* summing, and the formula for weighted means becomes

$$\text{SS}_{\text{Between}} = \sum_j \left(\frac{T_j^2}{n_j}\right) - \frac{GT^2}{\Sigma n_j}.$$

There's another simple adjustment, as well—wherever the quantity na appeared in the previous formulas, we substitute Σn_j, since it now represents the total number of observations.

The formula for $\text{SS}_{\text{Within}}$ originally was

$$\text{SS}_{\text{Within}} = \sum_j \sum_i X_{ij}^2 - \frac{\sum_j T^2}{n}.$$

Its adjusted version for unweighted means is

$$\text{SS}_{\text{Within}} = \sum_j \sum_i X_{ij}^2 - \sum_j \left(\frac{T_j^2}{n_j}\right).$$

The SS_{Total} formula follows from the same adjustments

$$\text{SS}_{\text{Total}} = \sum_j \sum_i X_{ij}^2 - \frac{GT^2}{\Sigma n_j}.$$

As an example of the computations, let's take the previous example, but with a few scores deleted to give unequal group sizes. The raw data and the first sums are listed in Table 16.2.

Beginning the analysis, we have

$$GT = 36 + 64 + 63 + 70 = 233$$

and then

$$\text{SS}_{\text{Between}} = \sum_j \left(\frac{T_j^2}{n_j}\right) - \frac{GT^2}{\Sigma n_j}$$

$$= \frac{36^2}{5} + \frac{64^2}{6} + \frac{63^2}{5} + \frac{70^2}{7} - \frac{233^2}{5+6+5+7}$$

$$= 2435.67 - 2360.39$$

$$= 75.28.$$

For the within-group sum of squares, the value is

$$SS_{Within} = \sum_j \sum_i X_{ij}^2 - \sum_j \left(\frac{T_j^2}{n_j} \right)$$

$$= 298 + 706 + 823 + 788 - \frac{36^2}{5} + \frac{64^2}{6} + \frac{63^2}{5} + \frac{70^2}{7}$$

$$= 2615 - 2435.67$$

$$= 179.33.$$

Finally, the total sum of squares is

$$SS_{Total} = \sum_j \sum_i X_{ij}^2 - \frac{GT^2}{\Sigma n_j}$$

$$= 298 + 706 + 823 + 788 - \frac{233^2}{5+6+5+7}$$

$$= 2615 - 2360.39$$

$$= 254.61.$$

The degrees of freedom are calculated using the same logic as previously. For $df_{Between}$, the value is one less than the number of groups of scores summed; that is, $a - 1$. For the example, $df_{Between} = 4 - 1 = 3$. The df_{Within} follows the same rule as well: there are $n_j - 1$ degrees of freedom for each group, or $df_{Within} = \Sigma n_j - a$. For the example, the value is $5 + 6 + 5 + 7 - 4 = 19$.

Table 16.2 Pain-Relief Data with Unequal Groups

	Drug condition			
	A	B	C	Placebo
	5	13	15	10
	11	12	11	5
	10	8	10	9
	6	8	16	6
	4	12	11	13
		11		11
				16
$\overline{X}_j$	7.20	10.67	12.60	10.00
Std. dev.	3.11	2.16	2.70	3.83
n_j	5	6	5	7
T_j	36	64	63	70
ΣX^2	298	706	823	788

The summary table for the analysis is completed as

Source	SS	df	MS	F
Drugs	75.28	3	25.09	2.66
Error	179.33	19	9.44	
Total	254.61	22		

With df $= 3,19$ and with $\alpha = .05$, the critical F from Appendix F is 3.13, and we thus do not reject the null hypothesis that the four drug conditions have identical means. In this case, our conclusion is that there is no difference among the four drug conditions.

Unweighted Means Analysis

Before computational equipment became available, a simplified procedure was developed to lessen the arithmetic burden of the weighted means computations. At this point in our progress, the computations aren't too formidable, but they will become much more difficult as we continue to other forms of analysis of variance. This simplified computational method, called the *unweighted means* method, proceeds as follows.

For unweighted means, a simple adjustment is made to the group totals T_j, and the analysis continues as if it were an equal-size procedure. The modification to the group sums consists of multiplying each group mean by an "average" of the group sizes to give a value that we'll symbolize as T_j^*. In symbols,

$$T_j^* = \bar{X}_j \times \tilde{n},$$

where $\tilde{n}$ is a special kind of average group size. Specifically, it is the *harmonic mean* of the sizes of all of the groups. The harmonic mean is a measure of center that we didn't present in Chapter 6 because it is rarely used as a descriptive statistic in psychology (although some other disciplines use it). In the context of the analysis of variance, the harmonic mean of the group sizes is defined as

$$\tilde{n} = \frac{a}{\sum_j \dfrac{1}{n_j}}.$$

With these definitions completed, the between-groups sum of squares is computed with the formula

$$SS_{\text{Between}} = \frac{\sum_j T_j^{*2}}{\tilde{n}} - \frac{\left(\sum_j T_j^*\right)^2}{\tilde{n}a},$$

which is the original formula, modified to use T_j^* instead of the actual group sums T_j, and $\tilde{n}$ in place of n. The sum of squares for within groups is computed as it was in the weighted means calculation, namely

$$SS_{\text{Within}} = \sum_j \sum_i X_{ij}^2 - \sum_j \left(\frac{T_j^2}{n_j}\right).$$

As an example of the computations for unweighted means, we'll use the same data as we used for the weighted means; see Table 16.3. First, compute the

Table 16.3 Pain-Relief Data for Weighted Means

	A	B	C	Placebo
		Drug condition		
	5	13	15	10
	11	12	11	5
	10	8	10	9
	6	8	16	6
	4	12	11	13
		11		11
				16
$\overline{X}_j$	7.20	10.67	12.60	10.00
T_j	36	64	63	70
n_j	5	6	5	7
ΣX^2	298	706	823	788

harmonic mean group size:

$$\tilde{n} = \frac{a}{\sum\limits_{j} \dfrac{1}{n_j}}$$

$$= \frac{4}{\dfrac{1}{5} + \dfrac{1}{6} + \dfrac{1}{5} + \dfrac{1}{7}}$$

$$= 5.64.$$

Continuing, we calculate the modified group sums T_j^*:

$$T_j^* = \overline{X}_j \times \tilde{n}$$
$$T_1^* = \overline{X}_1 \times \tilde{n} = 7.20 \times 5.64 = 40.61$$
$$T_2^* = \overline{X}_2 \times \tilde{n} = 10.67 \times 5.64 = 60.18$$
$$T_3^* = \overline{X}_3 \times \tilde{n} = 12.60 \times 5.64 = 71.06$$
$$T_4^* = \overline{X}_4 \times \tilde{n} = 10.00 \times 5.64 = 56.40.$$

Now we use the formula for the between-groups sum of squares:

$$SS_{\text{Between}} = \frac{\sum\limits_{j} T_j^{*2}}{\tilde{n}} - \frac{\left(\sum\limits_{j} T_j^*\right)^2}{\tilde{n}a}$$

$$= \frac{40.61^2 + 60.18^2 + 71.06^2 + 56.40^2}{5.64}$$

$$- \frac{(40.61 + 60.18 + 71.06 + 56.04)^2}{5.64 \times 4}$$

$$= \frac{13501.29}{5.64} - \frac{228.25^2}{22.56}$$

$$= 2393.84 - 2309.31$$

$$= 84.53.$$

Now SS_{Within} is calculated as

$$SS_{Within} = \sum_j \sum_i X_{ij}^2 - \sum_j \left(\frac{T_j^2}{n_j} \right)$$

$$= 298 + 706 + 823 + 788 - \frac{36^2}{5} + \frac{64^2}{6} + \frac{63^2}{5} + \frac{70^2}{7}$$

$$= 2615 - 2435.67$$

$$= 179.33.$$

The degrees of freedom for $SS_{Between}$ are, as expected, $a - 1$. For SS_{Within}, the df are $\Sigma n_j - a$, and so the summary table is

Source	SS	df	MS	F
Drugs	84.53	3	28.18	2.98
Error	179.33	19	9.44	

In these computations, the sums of squares for Between and Within don't sum to SS_{Total}, and so they're not computed.

Consulting Appendix F, we find the critical value of F at .05 is 3.13 (since the df were the same as in the weighted-means analysis, the critical value is the same as well), and again we don't reject the hypothesis that the drug conditions differ.

Both of our two example unequal group-size computations resulted in a failure to reject the null hypothesis, while the original analysis of similar data (with equal group sizes) did find a significant difference. You shouldn't conclude from this that unequal group sizes will *necessarily* result in nonsignificance. That's not the case. It *is* true, though, that an experiment with a small sample size will have less power than one with a large sample size and may thus be less likely to find a significant difference.

Choosing Between Weighted and Unweighted Analyses

As we indicated earlier, the weighted means procedure is normally recommended as the preferred method of computation in analysis of variance with unequal group sizes. The unweighted procedure is primarily a computational shortcut that is falling into disuse in these days of computer availability. We include it here for those who may wish to use it.

Presenting ANOVA Results

As usual, the most important results to be presented for any experimental design are those descriptive statistics that directly address the questions raised by the design. The results of the analysis of variance provide support for conclusions about differences, or the lack of differences, among the experimental conditions. In our example data, then, the presentation of results should focus on the descriptive data that show the differences among the conditions. Tables of means, medians, and standard deviations are common. When the independent variable is a quantitative one, such as age, weight, amount, loudness, concentration, or something similar, a plot of the function relating the independent variable and the dependent variable is often instructive.

The tabular format for ANOVA results is very common in the research literature, although there are several minor variations. The most common variation is how the significance is noted. The exact probability may be presented, as here for the equal group size case;

Source	SS	df	MS	F	Prob
Drugs	96.63	3	32.21	4.23	0.0138
Error	213.25	28	7.62		
Total	309.88	31			

Or we might find either of the following:

Source	SS	df	MS	F	
Drugs	96.63	3	32.21	4.23	$p < .05$
Error	213.25	28	7.62		
Total	309.88	31			

Source	SS	df	MS	F
Drugs	96.63	3	32.21	4.23*
Error	213.25	28	7.62	
Total	309.88	31		

*$p < .05$

The summary table is a reasonable way to present the result of the omnibus F test, though it's a bit complex and consumes more space than many journal editors will permit. A popular substitute is a simple sentence, which contains (or implies) all of the tabular data. For our example, we might write the sentence "The analysis shows a significant difference among the drug conditions, $F(3, 28) = 4.23$, $p < .05$, $MS_e = 7.62$." The sentence follows the APA model, and allows complete reconstruction of the summary table from the values given in the sentence. (If you don't believe that statement, try it.)

After the Analysis

As we've said, the test of the overall null hypothesis is just a part of the data analysis. If we reject the null hypothesis, the next task is to locate just where the differences are among the conditions. If the overall analysis shows no significance, on the other hand, we stop the analysis, present the summary statistics and ANOVA results, and conclude that there are no differences among the conditions that are worth pursuing.

Comparisons

In Chapter 14, we noted that the two-condition experiment provides the clearest results in an experimental design—when two conditions are pitted against each other, a significant (or non-significant) result is unambiguous. The two-condition design also provides us with an example of the meaning of the phrase "a comparison."

The two sample t test (for a between-groups design) has the formula

$$t = \frac{(\overline{X}_1 - \overline{X}_2) - (\mu_1 - \mu_2)}{\hat{s}_{\overline{X}_1 - \overline{X}_2}}.$$

The second term is often dropped, leaving

$$t = \frac{(\overline{X}_1 - \overline{X}_2)}{\hat{s}_{\overline{X}_1 - \overline{X}_2}}.$$

The numerator is the difference between the two sample means. It's also called a *comparison* between the two statistics. Since the two sample means are estimates of population values, the difference is also an estimate of $\mu_1 - \mu_2$, the difference between the population means.

In the analysis of variance, the null hypothesis is that all population means are equal. If that null hypothesis is correct, then the difference between any two pairs of means should be zero, as should the difference between any combinations of means. For example, the arithmetic mean of any two population means should be equal to the mean of a third population. For example,

$$\frac{\mu_1 + \mu_2}{2} - \mu_3 = 0.$$

This expression suggests the average of the first two population means should be equal to the mean of the third, if the null hypothesis is true.

In both of our examples of comparisons, $(\mu_1 - \mu_2)$ and

$$\frac{\mu_1 + \mu_2}{2} - \mu_3,$$

there was a subtraction, with the elements on one "side" compared to the other. In addition, the expected value of the comparison is zero when the null hypothesis is true.

We'll ordinarily talk about comparisons of sample means and not population means, so that comparison will be written using statistics. But we'll always be taking sample values as point estimates, and so the conclusions will be about parameters, as always in statistical inference. But regardless of whether we're explicitly discussing parameters or statistics, the comparisons will involve subtraction, and the null hypothesis value of the comparison will normally be zero.

Suppose that we wanted to compare the three drug conditions (Drugs A, B, and C) with the placebo condition. We can write

$$\frac{\mu_1 + \mu_2 + \mu_3}{3} - \mu_4$$

to represent the population comparison. Naturally, we'll be using sample means, so that we calculate the value as

$$\frac{\overline{X}_1 + \overline{X}_2 + \overline{X}_3}{3} - \overline{X}_4.$$

We can also write

$$\frac{1}{3}\overline{X}_1 + \frac{1}{3}\overline{X}_2 + \frac{1}{3}\overline{X}_3 - \overline{X}_4$$

with exactly the same meaning. We have accomplished something with this notation, though; we can now define a comparison as a sum of the products of means and appropriate coefficients, or

$$C = \sum c_j \overline{X}_j,$$

where C stands for the value of a comparison and c is a coefficient. In the example, the coefficient values are 1/3, 1/3, 1/3, and -1. A comparison of this form is often called a *linear contrast*, or a *linear comparison* among the means, since the formula is an ordinary linear equation.

The values of the coefficients are arbitrary, but they must sum to zero. For computational simplicity, whole numbers are usually suggested, so the previous comparison can be written as 1, 1, 1, -3. The coefficients shouldn't all be zero; such a comparison would be meaningless. But whatever its values, the comparison will always be between all of the positively signed means and all those with the opposite sign.

Any experimental condition that is not part of a comparison has a coefficient of zero, so that the coefficients 0, 0, 1, -1 indicate a comparison between the third and fourth means, ignoring the first and second means. Many of the comparisons that will be of interest will involve pairs of means, while others—like the difference between all drug conditions and the placebo—will involve more than two means.

A priori and post hoc Comparisons. Experiments are designed, and data collected, to answer specific questions. In a multiple-condition experiment, we normally have expectations about the answers to at least some of the questions. But experiments often present unexpected results too. Perhaps the drugs differ in ways that you didn't anticipate, or maybe the placebo condition is just as effective as one of the drugs. In any event, the data may offer answers to questions that you didn't even ask.

Like questions, comparisons may be separated into two broad categories: those comparisons that you had planned on from the beginning of the experiment and those that you decide upon after seeing the data. In the first category are comparisons addressing such questions as the difference between a control condition and a combination of several experimental conditions, or between several different experimental drugs, or the like. These *a priori* comparisons, and the questions that they ask, are probably the most important, since they are what you were looking for all along. The other category of comparisons, often called the *post hoc* tests because of their after-the-fact nature, includes those that are suggested by the data themselves—often by unanticipated results.

The two categories of comparisons are handled differently, with the first often treated as a part of the overall analysis, and the others conducted only if an omnibus F ratio is significant. The two categories of procedures have different Type I and Type II error properties, which is a very important consideration in choosing comparison procedures. After we've discussed both classes of comparisons, we'll discuss how to choose among them.

Planned (a priori) Comparisons

We defined a comparison among condition means as

$$C = \sum c_j \overline{X}_j.$$

We may now define the sum of squares for a comparison as

$$SS_{A\,comparison} = \frac{nC^2}{\sum c_j^2},$$

where C is the value of the comparison and the c's are the coefficients in the comparison equation. The value has one degree of freedom, and may be used to test the null hypothesis that the population value of the comparison,

$$\sum c_j \mu_j,$$

is equal to zero.

Since the sum of squares has one degree of freedom, the mean square is computed easily by dividing by the df:

$$MS_{A\,comparison} = \frac{SS_{A\,comparison}}{1}.$$

Finally, we construct the F ratio to test the hypothesis by using the MS_{Within} from the overall analysis as the denominator:

$$F = \frac{MS_{A\,comparison}}{MS_{Within}}.$$

The ratio has df $= 1$ for the numerator, and df_{Within} for the denominator.

As an example of the computation, let's use $\alpha = .05$ and ask if the placebo treatment in the equal n drug example has the same mean as the mean of the three drug conditions. That is, is

$$\frac{\mu_1 + \mu_2 + \mu_3}{3} = \mu_4?$$

Clearly, the coefficients implied here are 1/3, 1/3, 1/3, and -1.0, but we'll use 1, 1, 1, and -3 because the calculations are simpler. Using the means from the original analysis (Table 16.1, p. 354), the comparison value is

$$\sum c_j \overline{X}_j = (1)7.62 + (1)10.38 + (1)12.50 - (3)9.75 = 1.25.$$

We compute the sum of squares for the comparison as

$$SS_{A\,comparison} = \frac{nC^2}{\sum c_j^2} = \frac{8 \times 1.25^2}{1^2 + 1^2 + 1^2 + (-3)^2} = 1.042.$$

We next calculate the mean square for the comparison simply as

$$MS_{A\,comparison} = \frac{SS_{A\,comparison}}{1} = \frac{1.042}{1} = 1.042.$$

And finally, using MS_{Within} from the overall analysis, the F ratio for the comparison is

$$F = \frac{MS_{A\,comparison}}{MS_{Within}}$$
$$= \frac{1.042}{7.62}$$
$$= 0.137.$$

Since the ratio is less than 1.0, it is clearly not significant, and we conclude that there is no difference in pain relief between the placebo condition and the mean of the three drug conditions.

If we ask about the difference between Drug C and the mean of Drugs A and B, for example, the coefficients for the comparison would be 1, 1, -2, 0, and the comparison value is

$$\sum c_j \overline{X}_j = (1)7.62 + (1)10.38 + (-2)12.50 - (0)9.75 = -7.0.$$

The sum of squares is

$$SS_{A\,comparison} = \frac{nC^2}{\sum c_j^2} = \frac{8 \times (-7.0)^2}{1^2 + 1^2 + (-2)^2 + (0)^2} = 65.33,$$

yielding an F of

$$F = \frac{MS_{A\,comparison}}{MS_{Within}}$$
$$= \frac{65.33}{7.62}$$
$$= 8.57.$$

This F ratio has df $= 1, 28$; the critical value from Appendix F at the .05 level for those df is 4.20. The obtained value exceeds the tabled critical value, and we may thus conclude that there is a significant difference between the Drug C condition and the mean of Drugs A and B.

The procedure just illustrated can handle any form of comparison among experimental conditions. While sometimes we ask about the differences among more than two experimental conditions, the questions are often about pairs of means. When only two means are involved, we may use a modified form of Student's t:

$$t = \frac{\overline{X}_1 - \overline{X}_2}{\sqrt{\dfrac{2\,MS_{Within}}{n}}}.$$

This is the ordinary t test formula, except that the pooled estimate for the standard error of the difference is replaced by the mean square within groups. The t has df_{within} degrees of freedom.

Returning to the drug example once more, to test for a difference between Placebo ($\overline{X} = 9.75$) and Drug A ($\overline{X} = 7.62$), we would have

$$t = \frac{\overline{X}_1 - \overline{X}_2}{\sqrt{\dfrac{2\,MS_{Within}}{n}}} = \frac{7.62 - 9.75}{\sqrt{\dfrac{2(7.62)}{8}}} = -1.54.$$

The critical value for t at a significance level of .05, with $df = 28$, is 2.048, and we conclude that there is no difference between the Placebo and the Drug A conditions.

Unplanned (post hoc) Comparisons

Planned comparisons are normally used to address important research questions. But what about questions that we didn't ask? That is, how should we address the unexpected results that often turn up in a multiple-condition experiment? A look into the research literature will reveal a number of different tests that are used after a significant omnibus F test. The Scheffé test, the Tukey test, the Newman–Keuls test, Duncan's test, the Dunnett test, the Dunn test, and others all appear in the literature. All such tests are designed to follow a significant omnibus F test and investigate specific hypotheses about differences among population means. They differ in a number of respects, but they all attempt to control the probability of a Type I error.

We won't try to present all of the tests, but instead offer just two that seem to offer a reasonable choice and refer to other easily available sources for other tests. We'll illustrate the Scheffé test because it is one of the best-known procedures, and then recommend the Tukey HSD procedure for most research purposes.

The Scheffé Test. The Scheffé procedure is a widely known post hoc test, but has fallen from favor recently because of its lack of power. It is applicable to any form of post hoc hypothesis test, including both pairs of conditions and more complicated comparisons such as those illustrated for planned comparisons. (The Tukey procedure that we'll present later is limited to pairs of means comparisons.)

In the Scheffé test, a comparison among means is defined and the F ratio for the comparison is computed just as with a planned comparison. Then the critical value of F is calculated as

$$F_{crit} = (a - 1)F_{(df_{between},\, df_{within})},$$

where $F_{(df_{between},\, df_{within})}$ is the critical value that was used to establish the significance of the overall F ratio and a is the number of experimental conditions.

As an example, let's investigate the comparison

Drug A	Drug B	Drug C	Placebo
−2	1	1	0

with the Scheffé test at $\alpha = .05$. First we calculate the comparison value and its sum of squares as

$$\sum c_j \overline{X}_j = (-2)7.62 + (1)10.38 + (1)12.50 + (0)9.75 = 7.64$$

$$SS_{A\,comparison} = \frac{nC^2}{\sum c_j^2} = \frac{8 \times 7.64^2}{(-2)^2 + 1^2 + 1^2 + 0^2} = 77.83.$$

Using the MS_{Within} from the overall analysis as the denominator, we compute the F for the comparison as

$$F = \frac{77.83}{7.62} = 10.21.$$

Instead of looking in Appendix F for the critical F, we now compute the Scheffé critical value from the F used in the overall analysis (with df = 3, 28, at $\alpha = .05$, the tabled value is 2.95) by substituting it into the formula

$$F_{crit} = (a - 1)F_{(df_{between},\, df_{within})}$$
$$= (4 - 1) \times 2.95 = 8.85.$$

Since our obtained value of 10.21 exceeds the Scheffé critical value of 8.85, we may reject the hypothesis that the population mean for Drug A is equal to the average of Drugs B and C.

The Tukey Test. The American statistician John Tukey developed several techniques for conducting post hoc tests. The one we'll present here is sometimes called the *Tukey A* test, or sometimes the *Tukey Honestly Significant Difference* (*HSD*) test. The test is widely used and is appropriate for exploring differences in pairs of means after a significant omnibus F.

The Tukey procedure establishes a value for the smallest possible significant difference between two-condition means; any mean difference greater than that value is significant. The Tukey critical mean difference is calculated as

$$D = \frac{q_{(\alpha,\, df,\, a)} \sqrt{MS_{within}}}{\sqrt{n}},$$

where $q_{(\alpha,\, df,\, a)}$ is a studentized range value from Appendix J. Appendix J is entered using the number of degrees of freedom for within groups and the number of groups, a.

The Tukey test is usually carried out by constructing a matrix containing the differences between all pairs of means. The table of mean differences is frequently constructed by listing the conditions in order of increasing mean value:

	Experimental condition			
	Drug A	Placebo	Drug B	Drug C
Mean	7.62	9.75	10.38	12.50

The means are arranged from smallest to largest and serve as column headers in the table of differences. The experimental conditions are next written as table rows, and the differences between the row and column means are entered. For example, the difference between Placebo and Drug A is 2.13. For the complete example data, we have

	Experimental condition			
	Drug A	Placebo	Drug B	Drug C
Mean	7.62	9.75	10.38	12.50
Placebo	2.13			
Drug B	2.76	0.63		
Drug C	4.88	2.75	2.12	

The critical difference for the Tukey test is calculated as

$$D = \frac{q(\alpha, df, a)\sqrt{MS_{within}}}{\sqrt{n}} = \frac{3.85\sqrt{7.62}}{\sqrt{8}} = 3.76.$$

The mean differences are next compared to the critical value. In the example, only one of the differences in pairs of means exceeds the Tukey critical value; we conclude therefore that the only significant difference between pairs of conditions is between Drugs A and C. Those two drug conditions differ by 4.88, and thus the Tukey test concludes that they are significantly different.

In the case of unequal sample sizes, a procedure known as the Tukey-Kramer test is applicable. In this test, the critical difference for means based on samples of sizes n_i and n_j is calculated as

$$D_{ij} = q(\alpha, df, a)\sqrt{\frac{MS_{within}}{2}\left(\frac{1}{n_i} + \frac{1}{n_j}\right)}.$$

Note that D bears the subscripts i and j, indicating that this value is used for a specific group comparison—that between groups i and j. When n_i and n_j are equal, the Tukey-Kramer formula reduces to the ordinary Tukey critical value.

Other post hoc Tests. A large number of tests exist other than the Scheffé and the Tukey. Tukey proposed at least one other (the Wholly Significant Difference—WSD—test). There are also tests from Dunnett, Duncan, Newman–Keuls, and many others. The computational differences among the various tests are slight; the Newman–Keuls test is just like the Tukey, except that different critical values are computed for testing means that are farther apart in the smallest-to-largest ordering.

Choosing a Comparison Procedure

With so many possible comparison procedures, how should we decide which one, or which several, we should use? There are almost as many answers to those questions as there are authors who address them. The answer invariably hinges on the trade-offs between Type I and Type II errors. We'll make a couple of recommendations here and suggest some sources for additional reading.

Types of Errors. Until Chapter 15, experimental designs asked only a single question and thus had only a single null hypothesis. In those designs, picking a significance level defines the probability of rejecting the null hypothesis when it's true (Type I error). In the multiple-condition designs that we started discussing in Chapter 15, there are several hypothesis tests, and so establishing the probability of a Type I error becomes more complicated.

In a single-hypothesis design, the probability of making a Type I error is whatever we choose as our value for α. When we make a number of tests in a single experiment, though, we can consider Type I error in two ways: the probability of making a Type I error *on each hypothesis test*, or of making a Type I error *somewhere in all of the tests*. For example, suppose that we have a three-condition experiment. The omnibus test might be conducted with a significance level of .05. So far, the probability of making a Type I error is .05. Now suppose that we conduct a post hoc test at the .05 level. The probability that we make a Type I error in *that comparison* is .05. Now suppose that we carry out yet another test, again at the .05 level, and then stop the analysis. We made three hypothesis tests, each at the .05 level. For each test, the probability of making a Type I error was .05. But what is the probability that we have made a Type I error somewhere in the analysis of the full experiment? It could be as high as .15, or .05 for each of the three tests.

What we have just illustrated is the difference between thinking about Type I errors on a *per-comparison* (PC) basis and on an *experiment-wise* (EW) basis. In an experiment with a single-hypothesis test, the two probabilities are the same; when there's more than one test in the same experiment, the probability of erroneously concluding that a comparison is significant increases.

The probability of making a Type I error experiment-wise is given

Type I error probability $\leq m\alpha$,

where m is the number of comparisons and α is the per-comparison significance level of each. That is, the probability of making a Type I error somewhere in the analysis could be as high as α for each test, times the number of tests. Note that this isn't a statement of equality; the expression gives an upper limit for the probability.

There is yet another basis for error rates, and that's the family-wise (FW) error rate. For now, we can regard the PC and FW rates as the same. In Chapters 18 and 19, though, we'll present the factorial experimental design. In those designs, there will be at least three omnibus tests. In factorial designs, it makes sense to think of families of planned and post hoc tests, each family centered on an omnibus F ratio.

Bonferroni adjustments and the Dunn test. Since the experiment-wise error probability is roughly the per-comparison rate times the number of comparisons, it may have occurred to you that there is a simple way to set an EW rate for a number of comparisons. Suppose that you want to conduct five tests, while keeping your EW error probability at .05. You could simply conduct each test at $\alpha = .01$; with five tests, you would then have $\alpha_{EW} = 5 \times .01 \approx .05$. You can easily make this adjustment; just use the .01 level for each comparison. Such an adjustment is often called a Bonferroni procedure, since it relies on an inequality postulated by Bonferroni.*

The only real difficulty with using the Bonferroni procedure is that tables of the appropriate critical values aren't likely to be available. We invented an easy example earlier, but suppose that you wanted to conduct four tests while keeping α_{EW} at .05. Each test would have to be conducted at the $.05/4 = .0125$ level; tables with $\alpha = .0125$ are very hard to find. The difficulty was eliminated by Dunn (1961), who presented a set of tables that allow the Bonferroni adjustment to be made easily. Howell (1987) presents similar tables. The Bonferroni/Dunn procedure offers an easy way to adjust for multiple comparisons, as long as there are only a few of them. With a substantial number of comparisons, the Bonferroni adjustment makes the PC error probability very small. As a consequence, there is a substantial loss of power for each comparison, making a Type II error quite likely.

Many computer programs make using a Bonferroni adjustment easier, since they report the actual probability associated with a comparison. Summing the probabilities over all of the analyses will give the EW probability of Type I error; if it's within the bounds desired for the EW rate, then no further adjustment is required.

Deciding upon the comparison technique depends in large part upon control of the error rate. While probably the most important aim of most research is in finding differences among experimental conditions if they exist, most people would also agree that the probability of making a Type I error should be kept from increasing without bound. If you recall our discussion of the trade-off of Type I and Type II errors—as the probability of one goes down, the probability of the other increases—you remember that the ability to detect a difference among conditions, if one exists, is known as the power of the test. One simple means of increasing power (that is, decreasing the probability of a Type II error) is to increase the probability of making a Type I error by increasing the significance level to .05, or to .10, or perhaps even to .20. While such a strategy will certainly increase the power of the test, it does so at the cost of increasing the risk of making a Type I error.

We argued in Chapter 12 that in active research areas the interest is frequently on increasing power, which argues for using comparison techniques (such as planned comparisons) that provide maximum power and ignore the consequences of compounding Type I errors. On the other hand, there are techniques (Bonferroni adjustments or the Scheffé test) that will allow you to avoid increasing EW error rate at all, but at a cost of considerable loss of power.

In active research of the sort that we're addressing in this text, avoiding a Type II error is probably more important than focusing too narrowly on Type I errors. The logic of this recommendation is that making a Type II error,

---

*The Bonferroni inequality states that the probability of one or more of a set of events occurring cannot be greater than the sum of the individual probabilities of the events.

not finding a difference if there really is one, may tend to discourage further research.*

If we accept the overall guideline of avoiding Type II errors, then we want to select the most powerful procedure for each test. This would argue for the use of planned comparisons, since they are uniformly the most powerful tests available. But we must remember that using the comparisons without correction results in a greatly increased EW error rate. If we conduct enough comparisons, the probability that we will make a Type I error somewhere in the experiment becomes very large, and even the most anxious data explorer will usually want to put some EW (or FW) cap on the error rate.

A good general procedure that will keep the EW error rate reasonable and at the same time allow sufficient power in the comparisons follows: In any experiment, there are probably several important hypotheses that are known before any data are collected. If there aren't more than $a - 1$ such specific comparisons, conduct them as planned comparisons and don't make any adjustment for multiple tests. If there are more than just a few such tests, make a Bonferroni adjustment to the significance level, either directly by dividing α by the number of tests, or by using the Dunn procedure.[†] For questions that arise after the planned analyses, use the Tukey procedure for pairs of means, or the Scheffé for more complicated comparisons.

Remember, though, that these recommendations are for an active research area, one in which we want to explore interesting differences, even those that may ultimately appear to have been Type I errors, and where Type I errors will be discovered in further research. The rules will change in different situations. If you were conducting quality-control testing for a manufacturer or studying the efficacy of a new drug for treating cancer, you would have to carefully assess the importance of Type I and II errors in your own situation.

Howell (1987) has an extensive and readable discussion of the considerations in choosing a comparison procedure. Keppel (1973, 1982) is another authority on comparisons.[‡] Both of these texts contain numerous references to the ongoing debate concerning comparison procedures.

Presenting Comparison Results

For comparisons other than pairs of means, a sentence format is probably the best. For example, to summarize the data from the drug example, we might write "There is no difference between the placebo condition and the mean of the three drug conditions, $F(1, 28) = 0.137, p > .05$."

For pairs of means, several different techniques are used in the literature. We introduced one earlier—the table of mean differences. With one addition—marking the significant differences—the table serves very well:

---

*It might be advisable to return to Chapter 12's discussion of Type I and Type II errors at this point to review the arguments.

[†] Keppel (1982) recommends that the EW error rate used as the basis for the Bonferroni adjustment should be the one that would result from applying $a - 1$ comparisons, namely $(a - 1) \times \alpha_{PC}$. Thus if you had an experiment with four conditions and $\alpha = .05$ and you wanted to do five comparisons, then each comparison would be done with $\alpha_{PC} = [(4 - 1) \times .05]/5 = .03$.

[‡] Between the two editions of his text, Keppel changed his mind; you should read both versions.

	Experimental condition			
	Drug A	Placebo	Drug B	Drug C
Mean	7.62	9.75	10.38	12.50
Placebo	2.13			
Drug B	2.76	0.63		
Drug C	4.88*	2.75	2.12	

*$p < .05$

The table can also show significant differences that are at different levels—a single * can mean .05 and a double ** indicates .01, for example. The table has the added advantage of including the individual means.

An underlining scheme is sometimes used to show pairwise differences. We might present the same results as

Drug A	Placebo	Drug B	Drug C
7.62	9.75	10.38	12.50

Fig. 1. Pairwise mean differences; conditions sharing a commom underline do not differ (Tukey test, $p < .05$).

Concluding Comments

This chapter has dealt with the computations for a single experimental design—the multiple condition, between-subjects design. Only a single overall analysis technique was developed—the analysis of variance. The next chapter will develop the analysis of variance for within-subjects designs, and will also present nonparametric alternatives to ANOVA.

Table 16.4 summarizes the comparison procedures.

S U M M A R Y

- The *weighted means* procedure is usually the most appropriate when there are unequal sample sizes; the *unweighted means* procedure is sometimes used for computational convenience.
- In writing comparisons, the values of the coefficients are arbitrary but must sum to zero.
- A comparison is always between the groups with positive signs and those with negative signs.
- Post hoc comparisons are those that you decide to make after looking at the data.
- In the one-way design, you have multiple hypothesis tests and can think about the probability of a Type I error for each test or over the entire experiment.

Table 16.4 Comparison Techniques

Technique	Comments
PLANNED COMPARISONS	
Individual comparisons	Powerful and versatile technique
Bonferroni (Dunn)	Very flexible technique
	Powerful
	Best for only a few comparisons
POST HOC COMPARISONS	
Scheffé test	Conservative; little power
	Can accommodate complex (other than pairs) comparisons
	Protects EW error rate at α for all possible comparisons
Tukey (HSD) test	Protects EW error rate at α for all paired comparisons
	Useful with unequal group sizes
	More powerful than Scheffé, but less than the planned tests

- The probability of making a Type I error somewhere in the analysis ("experiment-wise" or EW) is no more than the probability of making an error on any test times the number of tests.
- The various post hoc tests are designed to guard against an increase in the experiment-wise probability of making a Type I error.

KEY TERMS

Bonferroni adjustment
Comparison
EW error rate
Harmonic mean
Linear comparison
n_j
$\tilde{n}$
PC error rate

Planned comparison
Post hoc comparison
Scheffé test
Tukey HSD test
Tukey-Kramer test
Unweighted means
Weighted means

EXERCISES

Solutions to asterisked (∗) exercises appear at the back of the book. Exercises preceded by a section symbol (§) must be solved using a computer. Exercises preceded by a dagger (†) can be solved by hand.

∗†1. The following data are from an experiment with three age groups of animals. The dependent variable is the number of trials required to reach a criterion of one error-free run through a maze. Calculate appropriate descriptive statistics, carry out the overall analysis of variance, and present the results appropriately.

90 Days	120 days	150 days
25	7	1
26	15	7
33	37	27
55	24	4
19	3	3
33	2	25
6	7	19
41	23	9
18	17	29
31	15	15
18	11	28
6	14	19
24	9	13
23	1	14

[†]2. Following is a set of data from the example drug experiment, but now there are unequal group sizes. Calculate appropriate descriptive statistics and carry out the overall analysis of variance. Compute the analysis of variance using both the weighted and unweighted means formulas.

A	B	C	Placebo
5	13	15	10
7	12	11	8
10	12	13	5
10	8	10	9
8	7	10	6
4	8	10	11
	12		12
	11		

[*†]3. The following data give the time, in minutes, that it took students to complete four different lengths of tests. The tests consisted of either 10, 15, 20, or 25 four-choice multiple-choice items. Conduct the analysis of variance and obtain the appropriate descriptive statistics.

Number of test items

10	15	20	25
13	17	18	16
10	5	17	21
13	13	10	28
5	14	23	32
6	11	24	24
6	12	17	12

Number of test items

10	15	20	25
2	3	10	9
12	16	27	18
17	18	21	18
12	8	24	9
12	14	23	5
2	7	8	15
17	13	14	10
3	16	1	7
7	14	8	30
1	18	10	5

[§]4. Use the random-number generator to obtain three sets of $n = 12$ values from a population where $\mu = 10$ and $\sigma = 4$. Conduct the analysis of variance using those three groups. Write down the F value. Repeat the process 25 or more times, recording the F value for each analysis. Now find the frequency distribution and the mean of the set of 25 (or more) F values. You should have a distribution that is positively skewed, with a mean F of approximately 1.0. Since each F was computed with the null hypothesis actually true, your distribution is an approximation of the sampling distribution of the F statistic with df $= 2, 33$. If you combine your data with those values from your fellow students, you'll have an even better approximation of the F distribution.

[*§]5. Using the data and the overall analysis from Exercise 1, define any two comparisons.
   a. Find the sum of squares for each comparison.
   b. Complete the analysis for the comparisons and present the results in sentence form.

[†]6. Using the data from Exercise 1 again, use the Tukey procedure to test for pairwise mean differences.

[*†]7. Use the Tukey-Kramer procedure to investigate all possible mean differences using the data in Exercise 2. Present the results in a table.

[*†]8. Using the data in Exercise 3, use the Scheffé test to test the significance of the following comparisons:
   a. The 10- and 12-item tests compared with the 20-item test.
   b. The 20-item test compared with the 25-item tests.
   c. The 20- and the 25-item tests compared with the 10- and the 15-item tests.

[§]9. Repeat Exercise 1 using the computer.

[§]10. Repeat Exercise 2 using the computer.

[§]11. Repeat Exercise 3 using the computer.

Experiments with More Than Two Within-Subjects Conditions (Principles and Analysis)

Chapters 15 and 16 presented the first look at the multiple-condition experimental designs. In those chapters, the independent variable was manipulated between subjects, so that each condition in the design contained a different group of subjects. In the between-subjects design, variation in the data can come from only two sources—the independent variable, measurement error, control error, and individual differences. If there are effects due to the independent variable, then those differences will contribute to the total variability in the data. In addition, measurement error contributes variability, as do individual differences between subjects. Finally, extraneous variables in the experiment contribute variation as well.

As we know, we can reduce between-groups variability by making the groups more homogeneous. Two common techniques for reducing subject variability are matching subjects or using the same subject in multiple conditions. In the two-condition design, we learned that we could cut down variability by using repeated measures on the same subject. The same logic holds in multiple-condition experiments; if we can use the same subject in multiple conditions (with suitable counterbalancing, naturally) we can reduce the error variation and thus make the effect of the independent variable stand out more clearly. (Multiple-condition designs that involve precision or frequency-distribution matching, where groups of subjects are matched with regard to an extraneous variable and then assigned to treatments in matched sets, are called *randomized block* designs.

The multiple-condition experiment with repeated measures is a powerful and a widely used design. In this chapter we'll illustrate the computations for the analysis of variance in such a design and also present appropriate follow-up analyses. The chapter concludes with a look at the nonparametric tests that parallel the analysis of variance for both between- and within-subjects designs.

The Hass Data

$$\begin{array}{cccc} \text{A} & \text{X} & \text{H} & \text{G} \\ \text{O} & \text{B+W} & \text{K} \\ \text{V} & \text{I} & \text{M} & \text{R} \end{array}$$

Figure 17.1

Dr. Hass, a cognitive psychologist, contributed data for an example that we will meet in several levels of complexity as we pursue various forms of within-subjects designs. The experiment studies the properties of visual short-term (often called *iconic*) memory.* The experiment presents subjects with an array of 12 letters on a computer screen. A typical array might look like Figure 17.1.

Edward Hass received his Ph.D. in psychology from Rutgers University and taught at Oberlin and Franklin & Marshall Colleges from 1982 to 1988. His research interests focused on brain organization as it influences both verbal and spatial processing. He is a private pilot and an FAA-certified ground school instructor; his current research interests are in the psychology of flight training. Dr. Hass publishes in journals such as *Brain and Cognition* and *Journal of General Psychology*. His coauthors are often undergraduate students.

Subjects were instructed to fixate on the + in the center of the screen, and the matrix of letters flashed for a short time (200 msec). Then the subjects were asked to recall as many letters as possible from one of the three rows. The subject was told which row to recall by either a visual presentation of a number beside the row to be recalled, or by an auditory cue—a high tone meant the top row, a low tone meant the bottom row, and an intermediate tone signaled the center row.[†] The presentation was repeated multiple times, and each subject has three scores: the mean total number of letters recalled from row 1, from row 2, and from row 3 over a series of trials. In other words, the experiment has three different conditions—the subject is to recall from the top, middle, or bottom row—and each subject appears in each condition the same number of times. The raw data are shown in Table 17.1.

Analyzing the Variance

In developing the analysis of variance for the between-subjects design, we began by looking at the total variation in the data. We broke down that total variation, as represented by a sum of squares, into a between-conditions part and a within-conditions part, as

$$\underbrace{\sum_j \sum_i (X_{ij} - GM)^2}_{SS_{\text{Total}}} = \underbrace{n \sum_j (\overline{X}_j - GM)^2}_{SS_{\text{Between}}} + \underbrace{\sum_j \sum_i (X_{ij} - \overline{X}_j)^2}_{SS_{\text{Within}}}.$$

---

*This experiment is essentially a replication of a classic investigation in cognition conducted by Sperling (1960).

[†]The fundamental question in the experiment was whether the memory is coded visually or auditorally; if it's visual, then recall should be better with a visual cue, and vice versa for auditory storage. In later presentations of this experiment, we'll look at a more complete design. For this chapter, we'll look only at recall differences between the three rows of the stimulus display.

Table 17.1   Raw Data from Visual Short-Term Memory Study

Subject	Recall from		
	Row 1	Row 2	Row 3
1	14.7	13.8	12.9
2	13.5	50.1	16.8
3	39.9	58.2	27.0
4	23.4	46.5	18.3
5	27.9	46.5	32.1
6	26.4	51.6	26.1
7	27.3	44.1	17.4
8	36.3	49.8	36.6
9	23.4	43.4	17.1
10	30.9	33.6	13.5
11	9.9	43.8	12.0

In that analysis, the "within" part of the variation was based on the differences between subjects and the mean of the group that each subject was in. Those differences represent error; when divided by its df, the "within" part estimates σ^2_e, the error variance. The "between" part of the variation is based on the differences between the means of the experimental conditions and the grand mean. The $SS_{Between}$ contains the differences between the experimental conditions *and also* differences between the groups of subjects. When divided by its df, the "between" part estimates a combination of error variance and treatment effects:

$$\sigma^2_e + \frac{n \sum \alpha_j^2}{a - 1}.$$

Since different subjects receive the different treatments, variation between the experimental conditions is completely confounded with variation between the groups of subjects. That is, the between-subjects variation is included in the between-conditions component. The repeated-measures design allows us to separate the two, removing the between-subjects variation from the between-experimental-conditions variation.

Let's develop the notation for the within-subjects design a little more fully so that we can see how to partition the variation in the repeated-measures design. Modifying the definitions from Chapter 15, we represent the basic data as shown in Figure 17.2. We've added subject totals (S) and subject means ($\bar{S}$) to the earlier illustration. There are n subjects, and each of them appears under each of the a conditions in the experiment. There are a total of na values in the data, as before, but representing only the single set of n subjects.

The total variation present in the experiment, expressed as a sum of squares (SS_{Total}), just like in the between-subjects analysis, is

$$SS_{Total} = \sum_j \sum_i (X_{ij} - GM)^2,$$

where GM is still the grand mean. In the between-subjects design, we partitioned this total variation (SS_{Total}) into two components, $SS_{Between}$ and SS_{Within}. In the

		Experimental conditions						Subject sum	Subject mean
		1	2	$\cdots$	j	$\cdots$	a	↓	↓
n subjects	1	X	X	$\cdots$	X	$\cdots$	X	S_1	$\bar{S}_1$
	2	X	X	$\cdots$	X	$\cdots$	X	S_2	$\bar{S}_2$
	$\vdots$	$\vdots$	$\vdots$		$\vdots$		$\vdots$	$\vdots$	$\vdots$
	i	$X_{i,1}$	$X_{i,2}$	$\cdots$	$X_{i,j}$	$\cdots$	$X_{i,k}$	S_i	$\bar{S}_i$
	$\vdots$	$\vdots$	$\vdots$		$\vdots$		$\vdots$	$\vdots$	$\vdots$
	n	X_n	X_n	$\cdots$	X_n	$\cdots$	X_n	S_n	$\bar{S}_n$
Condition totals →		T_1	T_2	$\cdots$	T_j	$\cdots$	T_a	GT (Grand total)	
Condition means →		$\bar{X}_1$	$\bar{X}_2$	$\cdots$	$\bar{X}_j$	$\cdots$	$\bar{X}_a$		GM (Grand mean)

Figure 17.2

within-subjects design, we'll follow a similar logic, but in two separate steps. First, we partition the overall variation into two segments, one representing variation *between subjects* and the other the variation *within subjects.* The second step partitions the within-subjects variation into two segments—*between conditions* and *error*.

A subject's mean across all conditions is a point estimate of that individual's overall performance in the task. The difference between a subject's mean and the grand mean,

$$(\bar{S}_i - GM),$$

is that part of the variation around the grand mean that can be attributed to a subject difference. Summing across all of the n subjects and multiplying by the number of conditions gives a sum of squares:

$$SS_{\text{Between subjects}} = a \sum_i (\bar{S}_i - GM)^2.$$

This sum of squares is that portion of the total variation that is due to the differences between the subjects and the grand mean. Since subjects differ from one another, those differences contribute to the total variation present, and this sum of squares provides a measure of that variation.

The difference between a subject and his *own* mean in all of the conditions in the experiment, $(X_{ij} - \bar{S}_i)$, gives an indication of the variation *within a subject.* Squaring that quantity and summing across all subjects and conditions gives a sum of squares for within subjects:

$$SS_{\text{Within subjects}} = \sum_j \sum_i (X_{ij} - \bar{S}_i)^2.$$

These two sums of squares together sum to the total variation present in the experiment:

$$\sum_j \sum_i (X_{ij} - GM)^2 = a \sum_i (\bar{S}_i - GM)^2 + \sum_j \sum_i (X_{ij} - \bar{S}_i)^2$$

or

$$SS_{\text{Total}} = SS_{\text{Between subjects}} + SS_{\text{Within subjects}}.$$

We have completed the first step of the analysis. Pictorially, what we have just done is

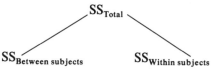

Since all subjects receive all of the experimental conditions, all of the differences among experimental conditions are included in the within-subjects variation. The second step of the analysis partitions that sum of squares into two parts.

The variability due to the different conditions in the experiment can be assessed as the differences between condition means and the grand mean $(\bar{X}_j - GM)$. Squaring and summing across the a experimental conditions and multiplying by the numbers of subjects, we have

$$SS_{\text{Conditions}} = n \sum_j (\bar{X}_j - GM)^2.$$

This is the part of the overall variation that is due to differences between the conditions, just as it was in the between-subjects analysis.

You may notice that we haven't mentioned error variation yet, and it assumed an important role in Chapter 15. In the between-subjects design, the measure of error was based on the differences between an individual score and the mean of the particular group that the score was in. In the present analysis, though, the logic of the error estimate is somewhat more complex. The estimate for error is that part of the variation that's "left over" after the effects of conditions and subjects have been removed:

$$(X_{ij} - GM) - (\bar{S}_i - GM) - (\bar{X}_j - GM).$$

Squaring and summing this complicated expression over subjects and experimental conditions gives the remaining sum of squares:

$$SS_{\text{Error}} = \sum_j \sum_i [(X_{ij} - GM) - (\bar{S}_i - GM) - (\bar{X}_j - GM)]^2.$$

The SS_{Error} and the $SS_{\text{Conditions}}$ sum to the $SS_{\text{Within subjects}}$:

$$\sum_j \sum_i (X_{ij} - \bar{S}_i)^2 = n \sum_j (\bar{X}_j - GM)^2 + \sum_j \sum_i [(X_{ij} - GM) - (\bar{S}_i - GM) \\ - (\bar{X}_j - GM)]^2$$

or

$$SS_{\text{Within subjects}} = SS_{\text{Conditions}} + SS_{\text{Error}}.$$

Now we have completed the second step. Finally, combining the two steps, we have completed the division of SS_{Total}.

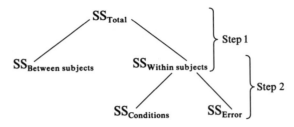

The full expression for the partition is

$$\sum_j \sum_i (X_{ij} - GM)^2 = a \sum_i (\bar{S}_i - GM)^2 + n \sum_j (\bar{X}_j - GM)^2$$
$$+ \sum_j \sum_i [(X_{ij} - GM) - (\bar{S}_i - GM) - (\bar{X}_j - GM)].$$

Labeling the segments for clarity, we have

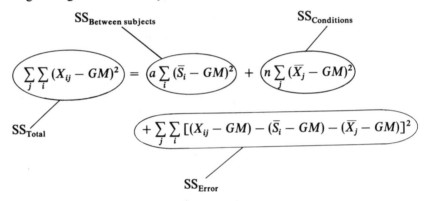

or, most simply,

$$SS_{Total} = SS_{Between\ subjects} + SS_{Conditions} + SS_{Error}.$$

Now that we have conceptually analyzed the variance in the within-subjects design, we can proceed to describing the computations.

Computations. Naturally, the defining formulas aren't the ones best suited for computations. The more convenient computational formulas are

Quantity	Definition	Computations
SS_{Total}	$\sum_j \sum_i (X_{ij} - GM)^2$	$\sum_j \sum_i X_{ij}^2 - \dfrac{GT^2}{na}$
$SS_{Between\ subjects}$	$a \sum_i (\bar{S}_i - GM)^2$	$\dfrac{\sum_i S_i^2}{a} - \dfrac{GT^2}{na}$
$SS_{Conditions}$	$n \sum_j (\bar{X}_j - GM)^2$	$\dfrac{\sum_j T_j^2}{n} - \dfrac{GT^2}{na}$
SS_{Error}	$\sum_j \sum_i [(X_{ij} - GM) - (\bar{S}_i - GM)$ $- (\bar{X}_j - GM)]^2$	$\sum_j \sum_i X_{ij}^2 - \dfrac{\sum_i S_i^2}{a} - \dfrac{\sum_j T_j^2}{n} + \dfrac{GT^2}{na}$

Table 17.2   Preliminary Calculations for Data from Table 17.2

Subject	Recall from stimulus row			S_i	ΣX_i^2
	1	2	3		
1	14.7	13.8	12.9	41.4	572.94
2	13.5	50.1	16.8	80.4	2974.50
3	39.9	58.2	27.0	125.1	5708.25
4	23.4	46.5	18.3	88.2	3044.70
5	27.9	46.5	32.1	106.5	3971.07
6	26.4	51.6	26.1	104.1	4040.73
7	27.3	44.1	17.4	88.8	2992.86
8	36.3	49.8	36.6	122.7	5137.29
9	23.4	43.4	17.1	83.9	2723.53
10	30.9	33.6	13.5	78.0	2266.02
11	9.9	43.8	12.0	65.7	2160.45
T_j	273.6	481.4	229.8	984.8	
$\sum_i X_j$	7676.64	22430.56	5485.14		35592.34

As a first step in the analysis, Table 17.2 shows Hass's raw data from earlier in the chapter, with the sums for each row (subject) and column (stimulus row), and the sum of squared values for each row and column. The means for the three stimulus rows are

Top row	24.87
Middle row	43.76
Bottom row	20.89

which shows better recall from the middle row.

We may begin the analysis of variance by computing the total sum of squares:

$$SS_{\text{Total}} = \sum_j \sum_i X_{ij}^2 - \frac{GT^2}{na}$$

$$= 35592.34 - \frac{984.8^2}{11 \times 3}$$

$$= 35592.34 - 29388.82$$

$$= 6203.52.$$

Then, for the sum of squares between subjects,

$$SS_{\text{Between subjects}} = \frac{\sum_i S_i^2}{a} - \frac{GT^2}{na}$$

$$= \frac{41.4^2 + 80.4^2 + \cdots + 65.7^2}{3} - \frac{984.8^2}{11 \times 3}$$

$$= 31388.95 - 29388.82$$

$$= 2000.13.$$

And

$$SS_{Conditions} = \frac{\sum_j T_j^2}{n} - \frac{GT^2}{na}$$

$$= \frac{273.6^2 + 481.4^2 + 229.8^2}{11} - \frac{984.8^2}{11 \times 3}$$

$$= 32673.72 - 29388.82$$

$$= 3284.90.$$

Finally, the error sum of squares is calculated as

$$SS_{Error} = \sum_j \sum_i X_{ij}^2 - \frac{\sum_i S_i^2}{a} - \frac{\sum_j T_j^2}{n} + \frac{GT^2}{na}$$

$$= 35592.34 - \frac{41.4^2 + 80.4^2 + \cdots + 65.7^2}{3}$$

$$- \frac{273.6^2 + 481.4^2 + 229.8^2}{11} + \frac{984.8^2}{11 \times 3}$$

$$= 35592.34 - 31388.95 - 32673.72 + 29388.82$$

$$= 918.49.$$

Combining the figures in a summary table, we can verify that the three component sums of squares add up to SS_{Total}:

Source	SS
Subjects	2000.13
Stimulus row	3284.90
Error	918.49
Total	6203.52

The degrees of freedom for Subjects, Conditions, and Total are determined by following the usual rule: the number of elements summed, minus 1, so that

$$df_{Total} = na - 1$$

$$df_{Between\ subjects} = n - 1$$

$$df_{Conditions} = a - 1.$$

The degrees of freedom for the error term is

$$df_{Error} = (n - 1)(a - 1).$$

We complete the summary table as follows:

Source	SS	df	MS	F
Subjects	2000.13	10	200.01	
Stimulus row	3284.90	2	1642.45	35.77
Error	918.49	20	45.92	
Total	6203.52	32		

With 2 and 20 degrees of freedom and $\alpha = .01$, the critical value for F is 5.85, so we clearly may reject the hypothesis that the row where the letters were presented has no effect on the recall. Note that there is no F given for "Subjects." In most cases, we're not interested in testing the between-subjects variation for significance (everyone will agree that subjects differ); this entry represents the variation in the data "removed" by the repeated measures analysis.

Follow-Up Analyses

From the means, it's clear that the middle row leads to far better recall than do either the top or the bottom rows. While in these data the differences are obvious, we should support the "eyeball" conclusions with follow-up analyses, as we did for the between-subjects design.

Follow-up analyses for the repeated-measures design may be separated into two general kinds, those for pairs of means and those for more complex comparisons, just as in the case of the between groups.

The major difference between conducting comparisons among conditions in the between- and the within-subjects designs is the statistic used to estimate error variance. In the between-subjects design, the within-groups mean square was used as the "error term" both in the overall analysis and in the follow-up tests. That statistic was appropriate there because it offers the most stable estimate of the overall error variance available. In the within-subjects design, though, each subject appears in all conditions and thus contributes to SS_{Error} multiple times. If each subject responded to every experimental condition in exactly the same way, the overall MS_{Error} would again provide the best available estimate of σ^2_e, just as it did before. However, subjects typically respond differently to the conditions of the experiment. In that case, then, as Keppel (1982, pp. 393–398) emphasizes, the appropriate "error term" is not an overall estimate of σ^2_e, but rather an estimate based on only those conditions involved in a particular comparison. For example, to compare the top and the middle stimulus rows in the Hass experiment, we would base our error estimate on just those two conditions.

The computations for follow-up tests can be quite cumbersome. Keppel (1982, pp. 395–398), for example, shows a detailed computational procedure for this situation. While his analysis is correct, it has some features that we don't need for most purposes. We can easily replace the cumbersome calculations suggested by both Keppel (1982) and Kirk (1982, pp. 263–266) with simple t tests with exactly equivalent results. In this way, the analysis for both pairs of means and complex comparisons consists of defining comparison coefficients, forming the product of coefficient and data for each subject, and then applying a single sample t test to the resulting values. Adjustments for multiple comparisons using Bonferonni, Tukey, or Scheffé procedures are easy to accomplish.

Pairs of Means and Complex Comparisons. All comparisons are computed by applying comparison coefficients to each subject's raw data and then conducting a single sample Student's t test with the resulting values. As an example, let's compare the middle row with the mean of the top and the bottom rows in the Hass data. (From what we already know of the data, we expect that the comparison will be significant.)

Table 17.3   Comparison Values for Raw Data from Table 17.1

Subject	Recall from Row 1	Row 2	Row 3	Comparison value
1	14.7	13.8	12.9	0.0
2	13.5	50.1	16.8	−69.9
3	39.9	58.2	27.0	−49.5
4	23.4	46.5	18.3	−51.3
5	27.9	46.5	32.1	−33.0
6	26.4	51.6	26.1	−50.7
7	27.3	44.1	17.4	−43.5
8	36.3	49.8	36.6	−26.7
9	23.4	43.4	17.1	−46.3
10	30.9	33.6	13.5	−22.8
11	9.9	43.8	12.0	−65.7

First, define the comparison among the stimulus rows with the coefficients 1, −2, 1. Now compute the comparison score by applying the comparison to *each subject's data*, forming the sum of the products of the comparison coefficients and data values for each subject. For example, the second subject has recall scores of 13.5, 50.1, and 16.8). His comparison score is computed as

$$1 \times 13.5 + (-2) \times 50.1 + 1 \times 16.8 = -69.9.$$

For all of the subjects, the raw data and the comparison values are listed in Table 17.3.

The test is conducted as a single sample Student's t test of the hypothesis that the population mean of the comparison variable (that is, the right-hand column in Table 17.3) is zero. The computations are straightforward and follow the procedure given in Chapter 13. The null hypothesis is that, in the population, the middle row is equal to the average of the top and the bottom rows. Another way to state the null hypothesis is that the population value for the comparison is 0. The mean of the comparison values is −41.76, and their standard deviation is 20.07. Applying the single sample t from Chapter 13, we have

$$\hat{s}_{\overline{X}} = \frac{\hat{s}}{\sqrt{N}} = \frac{20.07}{\sqrt{11}}$$
$$= 6.05,$$

so that

$$t = \frac{\overline{X} - \mu}{\hat{s}_{\overline{X}}}$$
$$= \frac{-41.76 - 0.0}{6.05}$$
$$= -6.90.$$

We can conclude that the recall from the middle row is significantly better than the average of the top and the bottom rows; $t(10) = -6.90$, $p < .05$.

Comparing two conditions can be done easily in the same way. Suppose that we want to ask whether the top row and the bottom row have equal recall. We define the comparison coefficients as $1, 0, -1$ and apply them to the original data. After making those computations, the single sample t test shows that the difference between the two rows is not significant: $t(10) = 1.88$, $p > .05$. On the other hand, the top and the middle rows differ significantly in recall scores: $t(10) = 18.89$, $p < .05$. The difference between the middle and the bottom rows is also significant: $t(10) = 7.68$, $p < .05$.

The latter three tests are *exactly* equivalent to conducting three separate two-sample tests with repeated measures. For example, the comparison coefficients $1, -1, 0$ form differences between rows 1 and 2 for each subject—ignoring row 3—just as if you had the data only on the top two rows and were conducting a repeated-measures t test. Of course, the tests aren't independent of each other. As a result, we need to consider the impact that doing repeated tests has on the probability of making a Type I error.

Adjusting EW Error Rates. Multiple tests cause the experiment-wise probability of a Type I error to increase with each test. If we're uncomfortable with the experiment-wise error rate that results from repeated analyses, we can make one of several adjustments. The simplest is to make a Bonferroni adjustment, lowering the significance level of each test. The Bonferroni is especially recommended for comparisons that were planned before the data were collected; conducting three comparisons at a significance level of .01 each will result in an EW probability of .03, which is an acceptable error rate for most people.

A Scheffé or Tukey adjustment can be made easily. To do either, convert the t value from the test into an F, taking advantage of the relationship between the two statistics:

$$t(\mathrm{df}_n) = \sqrt{F(1, \mathrm{df}_n)}$$

or, conversely,

$$t(\mathrm{df}_n)^2 = F(1, \mathrm{df}_n).$$

By converting the Student's t value into the corresponding F, we can easily make Scheffé or Tukey adjustments, thus limiting the EW error rate according to the rules for those two procedures.

To make the Scheffé correction for EW errors, square the t value, converting it to an F. Then compare the obtained F to the Scheffé critical value given by

$$F_{\mathrm{crit}} = (a - 1)F_{(\mathrm{df}_{\mathrm{between}}, \, \mathrm{df}_{\mathrm{error}})},$$

where the F value is the one that was used in the overall analysis to test for significance. For example, to test the difference between the recall from the middle and the bottom lines in the example, we obtain the t value of 7.68 as before and square it, giving $F = 58.98$. This F value has $\mathrm{df} = 1, 20$. The Scheffé critical value is given by

$$F_{\mathrm{crit}} = (a - 1)F_{(\mathrm{df}_{\mathrm{between}}, \, \mathrm{df}_{\mathrm{error}})} = (3 - 1) \times 4.35 = 8.70.$$

Since 58.98 exceeds the critical value, we conclude, using the Scheffé procedure, that recall from the middle line is significantly better than from the bottom line.

The modification to use the Tukey HSD criterion may be accomplished easily as well. First, square the obtained Student's t value to convert it to an F. Second, compare it to the Tukey critical value, which is calculated as

$$F_{\text{Tukey}} = \frac{q^2}{2},$$

where q is the Studentized t value from Appendix J for a conditions and df = df_{error} from the overall analysis. For the comparison between the middle and the top rows that we just used, the F value is 58.98, and the Tukey critical value is

$$F_{\text{Tukey}} = \frac{q^2}{2} = \frac{3.58^2}{2} = 6.41.$$

Again, this time using the Tukey procedure, we conclude that the middle and the bottom rows differ significantly.

Nonparametric Alternatives to ANOVA

There are two well-known nonparametric tests that are sometimes used as alternatives to ANOVA. They are often employed in cases where the group sizes are fairly small and when the distributions seem not to be normal. They are also especially appropriate when the measurement of the dependent variable is ordinal, since the analysis of variance assumes interval or ratio measurement.

  The two nonparametric tests to be presented here are excellent alternatives to the analysis of variance in terms of their power. They are highly recommended when there is doubt about the applicability of analysis of variance.

The Kruskal–Wallis Test for Independent Groups

The Kruskal–Wallis test is a nonparametric alternative to the between-groups analysis of variance. It is computed by ranking all of the data in all of the conditions, keeping track of group membership. (This process is identical to that for the Wilcoxon two-sample test from Chapter 14.) Then a sum of the ranks is calculated for each experimental condition, and the sums are entered into the test statistic:

$$H = \frac{12}{N(N+1)} \sum \frac{R_j^2}{n_j} - 3(N+1),$$

where R_j is the sum of the ranks in a group, n_j is the group size, and N is the total number of observations in all groups. The null hypothesis tested by the Kruskal–Wallis test is that the population distributions represented by the groups sampled are identical. The test is especially sensitive to differences in center, and so it is appropriate as a parallel to the analysis of variance.

  As an example, suppose that subjects are asked to solve ten arithmetic problems under one of three different conditions: quiet room, rock music, and "elevator" music. The data, in terms of the number of problems solved within a 5-minute test period might resemble those shown in Table 17.4.

Table 17.4 Raw Data for Study Conditions Experiment

	Rock	Quiet	"Elevator"
	5	6	3
	5	5	4
	7	4	4
	6	6	4
	3	6	2
	5	8	3
	7	7	4
	7	7	2
	1	5	
	2	6	
	2		
	3		
Median	5.00	6.00	3.50
Interquartile range	4.50	2.00	1.75
Mean	4.42	6.00	3.25
St. Dev.	2.15	1.15	0.89
Pearson Skewness	−0.81	0.00	−0.84

The analysis begins by combining all of the data and assigning ranks to each value; the scores and the ranks assigned to them are listed in Table 17.5, and the data are summarized further in Table 17.6.

Entering the sums of the ranks and the group sizes, the Kruskal–Wallis statistic is computed as

$$H = \frac{12}{N(N+1)} \sum \frac{R_j^2}{n_j} - 3(N+1)$$

$$= \frac{12}{30(30+1)} \left(\frac{177^2}{12} + \frac{218^2}{10} + \frac{70^2}{8} \right) - 3(30+1)$$

$$= .0129(7975.65) - 93$$

$$= 9.98.$$

The Kruskal–Wallis H value is distributed as χ^2 with df $= a - 1$. In Appendix D, we find that the critical value for df $= 3 - 1 = 2$ at the .05 significance level is 5.99; we thus reject the null hypothesis that the population distributions represented by the three experimental groups are identical.

A follow-up procedure for comparing any pair of experimental groups is given by Siegel and Castellan (1988, pp. 213–215).

The Friedman Test for Correlated Groups

The distribution-free analog to the within-groups analysis of variance is the Friedman test for correlated (or matched) groups. It is appropriate for repeated measures designs. It may also be used in a randomized blocks design where matched sets of subjects are assigned to the different conditions. The null

Table 17.5 Scores and Ranks from Data in Table 17.4

Rank	Problems solved	Music group
1	1	Rock
3.5	2	Elevator
3.5	2	Elevator
3.5	2	Rock
3.5	2	Rock
7.5	3	Elevator
7.5	3	Elevator
7.5	3	Rock
7.5	3	Rock
12	4	Elevator
12	4	Elevator
12	4	Elevator
12	4	Elevator
12	4	Quiet
17	5	Quiet
17	5	Quiet
17	5	Rock
17	5	Rock
17	5	Rock
22	6	Quiet
22	6	Quiet
22	6	Quiet
22	6	Quiet
22	6	Rock
27	7	Quiet
27	7	Quiet
27	7	Rock
27	7	Rock
27	7	Rock
30	8	Quiet

hypothesis in the Friedman test is that the data in all conditions come from the same population. You may also think of the null hypothesis as saying that all population medians are equal.

The test statistic for the Friedman is computed in a similar fashion to the Kruskal–Wallis statistic, using the formula

$$\chi^2{}_F = \frac{12}{na(a+1)} \sum R_j{}^2 - 3n(a+1),$$

where R is the sum of ranks for a condition, a is the number of experimental conditions, and n is the number of subjects. In this test, as opposed to the Kruskal–Wallis test, ranking is done *within each subject*, and then the ranks are summed across subjects to give the R_i value for each condition.

Table 17.6 Summary of Data from Table 17.5

Rock		Quiet		"Elevator"	
Score	Rank	Score	Rank	Score	Rank
5	17	6	22	3	7.5
5	17	5	17	4	12
7	27	4	12	4	12
6	22	6	22	4	12
3	7.5	6	22	2	3.5
5	17	8	30	3	7.5
7	27	7	27	4	12
7	27	7	27	2	3.5
1	1	5	17		
2	3.5	6	22		
2	3.5				
3	7.5				
Sum of ranks	177.0		218		70.0

Suppose that a group of 18 subjects was asked to rate each of five fragrances according to their perceived pleasantness, with a rating of 10 representing a pleasant odor and 1 representing a noxious odor. There would be five ratings for each subject, one for each odor.

The first step in the analysis is to rank each subject's data. The data and their associated ranks shown in parentheses are listed in Table 17.7. Note that the ranking is within each subject. For subject 1, for example, the ratings of the odors are

	Odor				
Subject	A	B	C	D	E
1	5	7	2	4	3

The smallest value (2) is assigned rank 1, the next largest (3) is given the rank 2, and so forth through the largest value (7), which receives the rank of 5, as shown:

| 1 | 5 (4) | 7 (5) | 2 (1) | 4 (3) | 3 (2) |

As usual, when there are ties, they receive the mean rank of the tied values. An example occurs for subject 4:

| 4 | 2 (2.5) | 7 (5) | 1 (1) | 2 (2.5) | 4 (4) |

where both odors A and D were rated 2. The two "2's" are tied for ranks 2 and 3; each receives the mean rank of 2.5.

Once the subjects' ranks are computed, they are summed for each condition (odor, in this case), as shown. The sums are entered into the formula, giving

Table 17.7   Data from Rating of Fragrances

Subject	Odor A	B	C	D	E
1	5 (4)	7 (5)	2 (1)	4 (3)	3 (2)
2	5 (4)	9 (5)	4 (3)	2 (1)	3 (2)
3	9 (4)	10 (5)	3 (2)	7 (3)	2 (1)
4	2 (2.5)	7 (5)	1 (1)	2 (2.5)	4 (4)
5	6 (4)	7 (5)	1 (1)	4 (2.5)	4 (2.5)
6	6 (4)	8 (5)	4 (2)	5 (3)	3 (1)
7	4 (4)	8 (5)	2 (1)	3 (2.5)	3 (2.5)
8	2 (1)	5 (4.5)	4 (3)	3 (2)	5 (4.5)
9	2 (1)	7 (4.5)	4 (3)	7 (4.5)	3 (2)
10	2 (1.5)	2 (1.5)	3 (3.5)	3 (3.5)	4 (5)
11	5 (4)	8 (5)	3 (2)	3 (2)	3 (2)
12	5 (3.5)	9 (5)	4 (1.5)	5 (3.5)	4 (1.5)
13	2 (1.5)	9 (5)	2 (1.5)	4 (4)	3 (3)
14	8 (4.5)	8 (4.5)	1 (1)	6 (3)	2 (2)
15	1 (1)	4 (2.5)	4 (2.5)	9 (5)	5 (4)
16	4 (2.5)	10 (5)	2 (1)	8 (4)	4 (2.5)
17	4 (2.5)	6 (5)	2 (1)	5 (4)	4 (2.5)
18	10 (5)	6 (3.5)	4 (1)	6 (3.5)	5 (2)
ΣR_j	54.5	81.0	32.0	56.5	46.0

$$\chi^2{}_F = \frac{12}{na(a + 1)} \sum R_j{}^2 - 3n(a + 1)$$

$$= \frac{12}{18 \times 5 \times (5 + 1)}(54.5^2 + 81.0^2 + 32.0^2 + 56.5^2 + 46.0^2)$$

$$- 3 \times 18(5 + 1)$$

$$= .0222(15863.5) - 324$$

$$= 28.17.$$

The Friedman $\chi^2{}_F$ is distributed as χ^2 with df $= a - 1$; consulting Appendix D, we find that the critical value at the .05 level is 9.49, and we may thus reject the hypothesis that the five odors are identical in pleasantness.

A follow-up procedure for comparing pairs of experimental conditions is given by Siegel and Castellan (1988, pp. 180–183).

Some Final Considerations

As we complete our discussion of the multiple-condition design, there are two final matters to present briefly. While we have more than scratched the surface of the analysis of variance, we've by no means covered the subject completely, even for the multiple-condition experiment.

Some Other ANOVA Matters	We have spent numerous pages on the analysis of variance, and you may be tempted to believe that there's nothing more left to cover. But there are several important issues (beyond the expansion of ANOVA into other experimental designs that will occupy the following three chapters).

Group Sizes. The matter of how to handle unequal group sizes is not as simple and as straightforward as we have implied so far. In Chapter 16, we suggested two modifications to the formulas for the between-groups computations using either weighted or unweighted means solutions. The implication there was that one of those two solutions would suffice for any analysis with unequal group sizes. But the modifications that we suggested are not universally accepted, and yet other solutions are sometimes recommended. And in this chapter, we tacitly assumed that all subjects would appear in all conditions in the within-subjects design. While we hope that all subjects will complete all conditions, that's sometimes an unrealistic hope in real research.

Most of the time, there's no serious problem with unequal group sizes as long as you choose the appropriate analysis of variance procedure. But there's one instance where you should be careful, and that's when the variances are unequal and/or the populations seem to be non-normal. In such a case, it's very likely that the probabilities of Type I and Type II errors will be dramatically different from what you expect. If you have unequal variances or non-normal distributions, then, it's well worth the effort to have equal group sizes. The best way to get them is to run a few more subjects. If that's impossible, then randomly discard subjects from the larger groups to obtain equal sample sizes.

Transformations. One simple way to change the form of a distribution is to apply a transformation (a square root, for example) to all of the data values. Transformations are often used in the analysis of variance, especially when they seem necessary to overcome violations of assumptions.

Random and Fixed Variables. There are two ways in which the "levels" of an independent variable may be selected for use in an experiment. Until now, we have assumed that they are chosen arbitrarily by the experimenter for reasons related to the basic questions addressed by the design. And that's the way experimental treatments are usually defined. But there is another way; we might conceive of a "population" of possible experimental conditions, all related to a single independent variable, and then sample randomly from that population. A researcher interested in childhood development might decide arbitrarily to use 1-, 3-, and 5-year-old children because of a desire to represent those specific ages in the research. Or she might decide that she's interested in the ages 1 through 10 years, and randomly choose three ages from that range. There is a difference in the inferences that can be drawn in the two situations; in the first, the researcher could draw conclusions only about 1-, 3-, and 5-year-old children, but in the latter, she could draw conclusions about the range of ages sampled. There are also differences in the analysis of variance that accompany the two situations.

Multiple-Condition Experiments and Other Designs

The experimental design discussed in Chapters 15 through 17 uses a single independent variable and three or more conditions. It is a direct extension of the two-condition design that we presented in Chapter 14. But the analysis of two conditions remains fundamental. While the overall analysis indicates differences among the conditions, the detailed understanding in both planned and post hoc comparisons comes from two-condition comparisons. All of the comparison techniques reduce the design to simple "something versus something." In pairs of means comparisons, the simplification to two conditions is direct. Complex comparisons combine two or more conditions to contrast with one or more others. In either case, though, the comparison is always between two elements, which is of course the nature of the two-condition experiment in the first place.

In the next chapter we extend our understanding of experimental designs by combining two (or more) single independent variables in one experiment. Such an arrangement is known as a factorial experimental design and is probably the most widely used design in psychology. As we will learn, in a factorial experiment it's possible to explore each independent variable separately; but in addition we can study the way two variables combine or interact to influence the dependent variable. The ability to study interaction is a major advance in the power of our designs and explains the factorial design's wide application. Yet, for all of its power, the detailed analyses that follow the overall analysis of the factorial design will reduce to simple two-condition comparisons. And the two-condition experiment will remain our prototype of "good" design.

SUMMARY

- The within-subjects multiple-condition experiment is a powerful design because of its ability to control for individual differences.
- The analysis of variance for the within-subjects multiple-condition design partitions the variation into two segments—between subjects and within subjects. The within-subjects component is further partitioned into between-condition and error components.
- Follow-up comparisons are made by applying the comparison coefficients to each subject's raw data; a single sample t test then tests the hypothesis that the mean comparison value is zero.
- Follow-up tests for within-subjects analyses often use a Bonferroni adjustment to the significance level.
- The Kruskal–Wallis test is a nonparametric alternative to the analysis of variance for between-groups designs.
- The Friedman test is a nonparametric alternative to the analysis of variance for within-groups designs.
- Unequal group sizes are especially troublesome when they occur along with unequal variances and/or non-normal distributions.

Between conditions
Between subjects
Friedman test

Kruskal–Wallis test
Within subjects

Solutions to asterisked (∗) exercises appear at the back of the book. Exercises preceded by a section symbol (§) must be solved using a computer. Exercises preceded by a dagger (†) can be solved by hand.

∗†1. Return to Exercise 16.1 and analyze those data using the Kruskal–Wallis procedure.

†2. Analyze the data from Exercise 16.2 using the Kruskal–Wallis test.

∗†3. The following data give the number of words recalled correctly on trials 3, 5, 7, and 9 of a learning experiment. Use the analysis of variance to test for differences among the trials of the experiment. Follow up with Student's t tests, using a Bonferroni adjustment to keep the EW error rate below .06.

Trial 3	Trial 5	Trial 7	Trial 9
4	10	12	14
10	16	20	19
9	11	13	15
9	7	13	16
8	6	14	17
5	6	9	13
5	18	18	11
6	7	9	14
10	11	20	20
3	4	10	13
7	15	20	20
5	9	11	19

†4. Using the data from Exercise 3, compare trial 3 with the average of trials 5 and 7. Assess the significance in three different ways: with no EW adjustment, using the Tukey adjustment, and using the Scheffé adjustment.

†5. Return to Exercise 3 and use the Friedman test to see if there are differences among the conditions.

†6. Subjects were asked to take multiple-choice tests under three different conditions of crowding. In one condition (alone), the subject worked alone at a table. In another (three other subjects), each subject was at the same table with three other individuals who were all working at the same task. In the third condition (seven other subjects), there were seven other people at the table. The presentation order of the tasks was counterbalanced and each subject participated in all three conditions. The dependent variable was the number of items correct out of a total of 50 questions. The data follow. Does crowding have an effect on the number correct? Complete any necessary follow-up tests and use a Bonferroni adjustment to keep the EW error rate below .10.

Subject	Alone	Three others	Seven others
1	31	13	26
2	49	34	24
3	33	21	23
4	34	35	33
5	37	19	20
6	29	25	21
7	29	16	26
8	30	43	20
9	17	21	22
10	29	23	12
11	41	30	16
12	50	10	29
13	32	28	16
14	44	18	27
15	30	18	25

Factorial Experimental Designs: Between Subjects (Principles)

$\mathcal{C}$hapters 15 through 17 presented the multiple-condition experimental design in depth. That design features a single independent variable manipulated in three or more distinct ways, giving rise to the several experimental conditions. The multiple-condition experimental design, with its single independent variable, is often called a *one-way* experimental design. Since an independent variable is often called a *factor*, it is also called a *single-factor* design to contrast it with the multiple-factor designs introduced in this chapter.

In Chapter 16 we explored the effect of three hypothetical drugs and a placebo on rated pain relief. The independent variable was drug, and the dependent variable was a rating of the degree of relief on a 1-to-20 scale, where 20 represented complete relief and 1 meant no relief at all. Here's a very simple selection of data from that experiment:

Drug				
A	8	9	11	13
B	12	11	8	9
C	13	15	6	7
Placebo	9	8	8	10

You'll recognize that there are few subjects, but that's all we need for this demonstration.

With these data, the means are

Drug	Mean pain relief
A	10.25
B	10.00
C	10.25
Placebo	8.75

There seem to be no differences between the four drugs, though the placebo may show a little less pain relief.

But there's something hidden in the data. Each group of four subjects contains two young subjects and two old subjects; the design and data actually are

Drug	Age			
	Young		Old	
A	8	9	11	13
B	12	11	8	9
C	13	15	6	7
Placebo	9	8	8	10

The means of the age groups for each drug are

Drug	Age	
	Young	Old
A	8.5	12.0
B	11.5	8.5
C	14.0	6.5
Placebo	8.5	9.0

With the data in this form, we can see that the ratings for pain relief are quite different for the young and the old subjects. For example, the old subjects rate Drug A more highly, while the young subjects rate C highly, rating A equal to the placebo.

What we just did was introduce a second independent variable, age, into the experiment. Instead of four drug conditions, we now have eight, the original four drug conditions for each level of the age variable. An experimental design with two independent variables (or factors), arranged so that all combinations of their treatments are presented, is called a *two-factor factorial experimental design*. It is a very widely used design and very powerful. This chapter and the next two deal with this design.

The Factorial Design

The factorial is probably the most widely used design in psychology. This is so because of its unique ability to study the effect of two or more variables operating together.

The Variables The independent variables in a factorial design are normally chosen because of a particular interest in their interaction. In the drug-by-age example, we might have reason to believe that the drugs would have different effects at different ages. We could look at either drug or age separately; but if we did, we could never learn anything about how the variables work together, or interact, to influence the pain relief. This ability to study the interaction of two variables is a kind of bonus in the factorial. We can still look at the effect of each independent variable alone ("Do the two ages differ?" "Do the four drugs differ?"), but only the factorial lets us also study the two variables together.

Each independent variable can be manipulated as either a between-subjects or a within-subjects variable. In the factorial design, this can lead to several combinations of between- and within-subjects designs. In the drug-age example, we've suggested that there are eight independent groups of subjects, where each group has a particular age and drug. But we could easily have just two groups of subjects (young and old) and use each subject under all four drug conditions. In this case, the age variable would be manipulated between subjects, while drug was a within-subjects variable.

We could also set up the experiment so that each subject receives only a single drug (making drug a between-subjects variable), but received it over a lifetime with testing done at two ages. Under this plan, the age variable is within subjects. Or both variables could be manipulated within subjects, with every subject receiving each drug at each age. The latter plan uses only a single group of subjects.*

A factorial design is often described in a phrase indicating the independent variables and the number of their levels. The example, with four drugs and two ages, is called a "4 by 2 factorial design" (often indicated with a multiplication sign, 4×2). If there were three ages, it would be a "4 by 3" design, and so forth. In addition, a "between-within" description is also used. Our design would then be a "4 by 2 between-subjects" experiment. A completely within design might be called "4 by 2 within." And a design having one between-subjects and one within-subjects variable could be called a "4 by 2 mixed" design, indicating a mixture of between- and within-subjects factors. More precisely, if the design used two different ages (between subjects) and four drug conditions (within subjects), we would say that the design was a "2 between, 4 within" factorial.

The arguments for using between-subjects and within-subjects manipulations remain the same as those we have already discussed several times. In short, between-subjects manipulations permit us to assign subjects randomly to conditions so that we may assume that the effects of extraneous variables will be randomly distributed across conditions and will thus not be confounded with an independent variable. Within-subjects manipulation adds control over subject variables, but adds concern over order effects.

The factorial design offers a way of dealing with an extraneous variable not available in a single-factor experiment—use a troublesome extraneous variable as a part of the experiment. For example, suppose that we are interested in the effect of drug on pain relief, but we're concerned with the age of the subject. We could handle the extraneous variable of age by holding it constant (using only a single age) or by at least assuring that the groups were balanced with regard to age. Alternatively, we could make age into an independent variable, giving us the experimental design that we have been discussing. We not only can eliminate

---

*Clearly, using age as a within-subjects variable will require either a great deal of patience on the part of the experimenter or subjects with short life spans!

the extraneous variable, but we can also look at the differences between ages and also at the interaction between age and the drugs.

Strengths and Weaknesses of the Factorial Design

Since the factorial design is built of two single-factor designs, it shares their advantages. With multiple levels, we can explore the range of the variable more effectively, can accommodate independent variables that don't lend themselves to a two-condition experiment (although a variable in a factorial can certainly have just two levels), and are able to make reasonably sound causal inferences.

The factorial design adds more advantages to those of one-way experiment, and we've already mentioned them. Incorporating an extraneous variable into the design is a considerable advantage. The ability to study the interaction of the independent variables is a second major benefit of the design. Also using more than one independent variable in an experiment increases the possibility for realism in the experimental situation. Finally, the economy of the factorial design is an advantage. By using two independent variables in the same experiment, you can look at both in a single experiment, in addition to exploring the interaction.

Are there disadvantages to the factorial design? Certainly. For one, some questions simply can't be addressed by a manipulated variable. In such cases, a correlation design is often more reasonable. In addition, the analysis for a factorial is more complicated than is that for the single-factor experiment. The detailed follow-up procedures can sometimes be confusing and laborious, even with electronic assistance. In addition to the computational difficulties, choosing follow-up procedures is more complex because of the more involved Type I and Type II error considerations.

Descriptive Analysis of a Factorial Experiment

Let's return to the drug and age example. The design has three pain-relieving drugs and a placebo as one independent variable. The second independent variable is the age (young and old) of the subjects. The dependent variable is a rating of severity of headaches 30 minutes after taking the medication; a rating of 20 indicates complete pain relief, and a rating of 1 means no relief at all. Table 18.1 is a set of hypothetical data with $n = 10$ subjects per condition.

Before we even begin to develop the inferential statistics for the factorial, let's look at the results descriptively. The place to begin is with means and standard deviations (see Table 18.2). The table presents the mean pain-relief ratings for the ten subjects in eight experimental conditions. For example, the mean pain-relief rating for young people using drug A is 8.00 with a standard deviation of 2.21. The table also gives, on its right margin, the means and standard deviations for each drug averaged over the age of the subjects (see Table 18.3). As an example, the mean of the 10 young and 10 old subjects receiving the placebo is indicated: the mean is 9.65 with a standard deviation of 2.30.

The means and standard deviations for the two ages, averaged across all drug conditions appear on the bottom margin (see Table 18.4). (The mean pain relief for all 40 of the young subjects is 10.70, for example, and its standard deviation is 2.95.)

The grand mean (*GM*) and standard deviation, based on all 80 subjects, are shown in the lower right-hand corner (see Table 18.5). From the means, it seems

Table 18.1 Hypothetical Drug-Age Data

| | Drug | | |
A	B	C	Placebo
YOUNG SUBJECTS			
11	14	14	9
8	10	13	8
6	10	11	9
8	12	15	12
11	12	13	13
6	13	13	8
10	11	15	10
9	11	12	6
5	10	15	8
6	10	18	13
OLD SUBJECTS			
10	9	7	8
9	8	6	11
9	7	6	6
15	9	6	10
10	8	5	8
11	7	6	8
13	7	8	9
13	8	7	12
13	7	7	14
14	7	6	11

Table 18.2 Means and Standard Deviations for Data in Table 18.1

| | | Age | | Drugs across ages |
		Young	Old	
Drug A	$\overline{X}$	8.00	11.70	9.85
	s.d.	2.21	2.16	2.85
Drug B	$\overline{X}$	11.30	7.70	9.50
	s.d.	1.42	0.82	2.16
Drug C	$\overline{X}$	13.90	6.40	10.15
	s.d.	1.97	0.84	4.12
Placebo	$\overline{X}$	9.60	9.70	9.65
	s.d.	2.37	2.36	2.30
Ages across	$\overline{X}$	10.70	8.88	9.79
drugs	s.d.	2.95	2.61	2.92

Table 18.3 Means and Standard Deviations for All Drug Conditions

		Age		Drugs across ages
		Young	Old	
Drug A	$\overline{X}$	8.00	11.70	9.85
	s.d.	2.21	2.16	2.85
Drug B	$\overline{X}$	11.30	7.70	9.50
	s.d.	1.42	0.82	2.16
Drug C	$\overline{X}$	13.90	6.40	10.15
	s.d.	1.97	0.84	4.12
Placebo	$\overline{X}$	9.60	9.70	9.65
	s.d.	2.37	2.36	2.30
Ages across	$\overline{X}$	10.70	8.88	9.79
drugs	s.d.	2.95	2.61	2.92

Means and s.d.s for all subjects in drug conditions

Mean and s.d. for all placebo subjects

Table 18.4 Means and Standard Deviations for All Ages

		Age		Drugs across ages
		Young	Old	
Drug A	$\overline{X}$	8.00	11.70	9.85
	s.d.	2.21	2.16	2.85
Drug B	$\overline{X}$	11.30	7.70	9.50
	s.d.	1.42	0.82	2.16
Drug C	$\overline{X}$	13.90	6.40	10.15
	s.d.	1.97	0.84	4.12
Placebo	$\overline{X}$	9.60	9.70	9.65
	s.d.	2.37	2.36	2.30
Ages across	$\overline{X}$	10.70	8.88	9.79
drugs	s.d.	2.95	2.61	2.92

Means and s.d.s for all subjects by age

Mean and s.d. for all young subjects

that the young subjects overall received slightly greater pain reduction (a mean rating of 10.70 compared with 8.88 for the older subjects). In addition, Drug C seems to have, overall, the greatest effect. The analysis of variance will let us conclude whether such differences are significant, but for now we're looking only at the descriptive statistics.

From these results, we might conclude that Drug C should be recommended for pain, since its overall mean is highest. But look at the two individual group means for Drug C. While the young subjects did rate Drug C highly, the old subjects rated their relief with the same drug much lower. Clearly, there is

Table 18.5 Grand Mean and Standard Deviation for All 80 Subjects

		Age		Drugs across ages
		Young	Old	
Drug A	$\overline{X}$	8.00	11.70	9.85
	s.d.	2.21	2.16	2.85
Drug B	$\overline{X}$	11.30	7.70	9.50
	s.d.	1.42	0.82	2.16
Drug C	$\overline{X}$	13.90	6.40	10.15
	s.d.	1.97	0.84	4.12
Placebo	$\overline{X}$	9.60	9.70	9.65
	s.d.	2.37	2.36	2.30
Ages across	$\overline{X}$	10.70	8.88	9.79
drugs	s.d.	2.95	2.61	2.92

Grand mean and s.d. for all subjects in all conditions

something going on here that is not evident from the overall means of drugs and ages.

Comparing the relief ratings for the age groups shows differences between the drugs. Drug A gives high relief to the older subjects, while the same drug receives the lowest mean rating given by the young subjects. Drug B, on the contrary, shows a pattern similar to that for Drug C, with the young subjects giving both higher ratings. Only in the placebo condition do the two ages of subjects rate the pain relief similarly. The differences in the responses of the two ages can be seen clearly if we plot the mean pain relief ratings for the ages separately (see Figure 18.1). Seen this way, it's clear that the two ages react very differently to the three drugs. Only the placebo produces similar ratings from young and old subjects. The young subjects receive the most relief from Drugs B and C and rate Drug A below the placebo. For the older subjects, exactly the opposite pattern holds. From the figure, it is clear that if you were a young person, you should use Drug C. If you were older, your choice should be anything but B or C—even the placebo is more effective.

Figure 18.2 also makes it easy to see that three of the drug-age combinations are more successful at pain relief than the placebo, and three are less successful than the placebo. What we are illustrating here is the *interaction* between the two independent variables, age and drug. We could never have learned about the age differences in drug response if we didn't have an opportunity to study the way the two variables act in different combinations. There was nothing in the overall drug means that suggested an age difference in the drug response. In fact, if we hadn't looked specifically for an age-drug interaction, we would have concluded that there was very little age effect and not much drug effect.

When two variables interact, the effect of one variable changes with a change in the other. In the example, for Drug A, the effect of age is that old subjects rate their pain relief as greater. However, when we look at age with regard to Drug

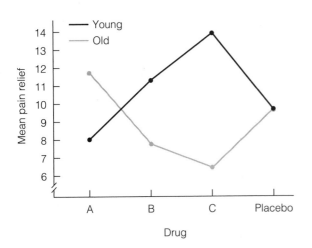

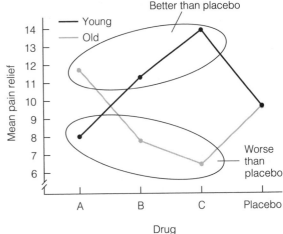

Figure 18.1

Figure 18.2

B, the effect changes. In particular, as we move from Drug A to Drug B to Drug C, the effect of the subjects' age changes; where under Drug A the old subjects rated their relief as higher, young subjects rate the relief greater under B and C.

What if the plot of the means looked like Figure 18.3? Here the lines are flat and parallel, indicating that there is no change due to the drug conditions. There *is* an effect of age—young subjects report greater pain relief than do old subjects, and that's uniformly true for *all* drug conditions. Since there are no differences between the drugs, if you wanted to obtain maximum pain relief, any drug would be as good as any other. The only relief would be to be young (and that's hard to do if you're already past the age of the younger group!). Figure 18.3 shows no interaction; the effect of age is the same for all drug conditions, including the placebo. This pattern of the means shows a *main effect*, the effect of one variable alone. Specifically, this illustration shows a main effect for age, but no effect for drug and no interaction.

Contrast Figure 18.3 with Figure 18.4. There is virtually no difference between two ages, but the drugs differ in their effects. This pattern shows a main effect for the drug variable, because there certainly are effects of that variable. Given these results, you'd want to take Drug A; it wouldn't matter whether you were young or old. But there's no effect for age, since young and old are exactly the same under all drug conditions. And there's no interaction, either—young and old are the same relative to each other under each drug.

It's possible to have a pattern that shows main effects of both age and drug, but no interaction (see Figure 18.5). Here there are effects of both age and drug—young is consistently above old, but the lines aren't flat, indicating a drug effect. But the ages don't change relative to each other under different age conditions—the lines are parallel—so there's no interaction.

We could also have a pattern like that shown in Figure 18.6. This shows both an interaction and a main effect for age. The ages aren't the same across the drugs; as is characteristic of an interaction, the relationship between the ages

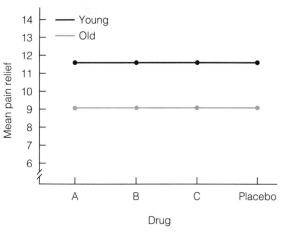

Figure 18.3

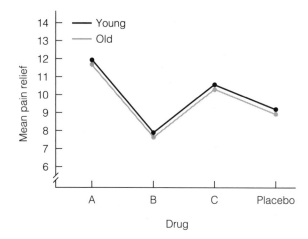

Figure 18.4

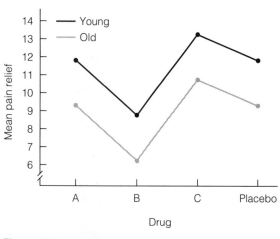

Figure 18.5

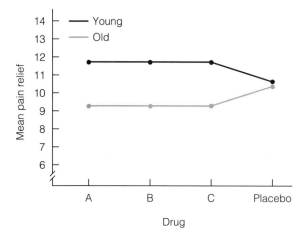

Figure 18.6

changes as a function of the drug. A main effect, though, looks at the average across the conditions of the other variable. In this case, the mean pain relief, averaged across the four drug conditions, is higher for young than for old, despite the fact that they're the same in the placebo condition.

Figure 18.7 and Figure 18.8 show other possible interactions. There's an interaction in both cases (and a main effect for age as well), but in Figure 18.7, the older subjects consistently rate their pain relief as higher. The amount of difference between the two ages changes with different drugs (that's the interaction), but the *order* of the difference is always such that old is greater than young. In Figure 18.8, the positions of the young and the old subjects reverse with different drugs, and the order of the two age groups is not maintained across the four drugs.

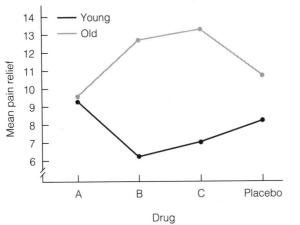

Figure 18.7

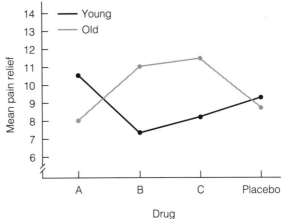

Figure 18.8

Figure 18.7, where the order of the two age groups remains the same, shows an *ordinal interaction*. Figure 18.8, indicating a change in the ordering of the age conditions, illustrates a *disordinal interaction*. These two different forms of interaction call for different handling during follow-up analyses. With an ordinal interaction there is a main effect, and it can be interpreted unambiguously. In Figure 18.7, the older subjects consistently rate pain relief higher than do the younger ones. Thus the main effect of age is clear, regardless of its interaction with drug; an ordinal interaction leads to a clear interpretation of the main effect. The same can't be said of a disordinal interaction, like that in Figure 18.8. While the old subjects might also give higher mean ratings when averaged across the drugs, the interpretation is much less clear. In a disordinal interaction, there is always a crossing of the lines in the interaction plot, indicating that one independent variable has opposite effects at different levels of the other independent variable.*

We've discussed two components to interpreting factorial results. There are the two independent variables separately—these are the two main effects. And there is also the interaction. It should come as no surprise to learn, then, that there are three hypothesis tests in the omnibus analysis of variance, one for the main effect of each independent variable and a third for the interaction. The three tests are independent of one another, meaning that there can be an effect of either one, both, or neither independent variable. And the interaction can occur whether or not either main effect is significant.

The example experiment had eight groups of subjects, representing the factorial combination of two different ages and four different drugs. A somewhat more realistic approach to research in drug effects might be to have each subject use all of the drugs, perhaps for a week at a time. If we did that, with appropriate counterbalancing of the order of the drugs, then we would have just two groups

---

*We have presented a traditional view of interaction. Rosnow and Rosenthal (1989) argue that the interpretation of an interaction is most correctly done by the use of *residuals*, those values that remain after removing the main effects of the independent variables. While their point is correct and well taken, their interpretation is not sufficiently common in the literature to warrant our attention here.

of subjects, young and old. But in that design, the manipulation of the drug variable is done *within subjects* and the age variable remains *between subjects*. Combining a between-subjects variable with a within-subjects variable leads to a very common kind of the factorial, the *mixed design* that we mentioned earlier.

In addition to the mixed factorial, both variables could be manipulated within subjects, leading to the completely within design. In a within design, a single group of subjects participates in all experimental conditions. Within-subjects factorial experiments, like mixed designs, are very common in psychology. Since the analysis of variance is different for between- and within-subjects single-factor experiments, you might expect a difference in factorial designs too; and you're correct. For now, though, we turn to the simplest design—both variables between subjects—to develop the analysis of variance.

Inference in the Two-Factor, Between-Subjects Design

In the factorial design, the three overall hypotheses are tested using the analysis of variance. The total variation present in the entire experiment forms the basis of the analysis. By partitioning it properly, we can estimate the portion contributed by each independent variable, by the interaction, and by error. In this section, we'll develop the logic of the analysis of variance in the factorial. The computations appear in Chapter 19.

Partitioning the Total Variance

In analyzing the variance in the factorial experiment, we follow the same plan as in Chapter 15. First we consider a theoretical model of a single score and the statistics that estimate the parts of it. Next we look at sums of squares. Finally we convert the sums of squares into mean squares and use them to test the three hypotheses.

The Model of a Score. In Chapter 15, we discussed contributions to a subject's score. There we said that a score, X_{ij}, has three constituents—the overall mean, a treatment effect, and error. In symbols, we said that

$$X_{ij} = \mu + \alpha_j + \varepsilon_{ij},$$

where X_{ij} is the score, μ is the overall population mean, α_j is the effect of the jth treatment (defined as $\mu_j - \mu$), and ε_{ij} is the error for individual i in treatment condition j. Chapter 15 also introduced sample estimates for the parameter values, using the difference between the mean of a particular condition and the grand mean of all conditions, specifically $(\overline{X}_j - GM)$, to estimate the treatment effect α_j, and the difference between a condition mean and an individual score, $(X_{ij} - \overline{X}_j)$ to estimate the individual error.

Before we can introduce the comparable expression for the factorial experiment, we have to develop the symbolic notation of the design. Schematically, we may represent the two-factor experiment as

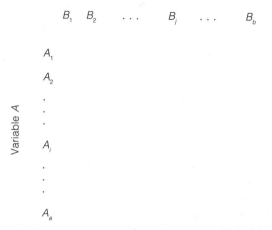

Variable *B*

B_1 B_2 . . . B_j . . . B_b

The letters *A* and *B* stand for the two independent variables; in any specific experiment, obviously, they represent real variables, like age and drug in our example. In the single-factor experiment, we used the letter *a* to stand for the number of experimental treatments. The same scheme can work with two variables; independent variable *A* has *a* treatment levels associated with it, while there are *b* conditions related to the *B* variable. In our example, $a = 4$ and $b = 2$, since *A* is drug and *B* is age (see Figure 18.9).

When we need to distinguish between specific rows and columns in the design, the letter *i* will stand for a row and *j* for a column. A specific treatment combination, then, is designated by a row and a column: row 3 and column 2 in the example would be the condition "old subject, Drug C." Each combination of treatments represents a single group of subjects since this is a completely between-subjects design. Each group is of the same size, *n* (for now, anyway), and represents a set of scores from individuals treated the same way with regard to the two independent variables. Schematically, the design, with some notation, is shown in Figure 18.10.

To indicate an individual score, we need a third letter, *k*, to indicate position in a group. Thus an individual score is

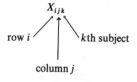

For example, in the design shown in Figure 18.11, the eighth score in the group "Drug C, old subject" would be written as $X_{3,2,8}$. And the third score in "Drug B, young" is $X_{2,1,3}$. In other words, the *k*th subject in the group receiving the *i*th treatment of the *A* variable and the *j*th treatment of the *B* variable would be $X_{i,j,k}$.

The letter *T* indicates the total of a set of scores, with two subscripts indicating what is being summed. The total of all of the scores in row 1, column

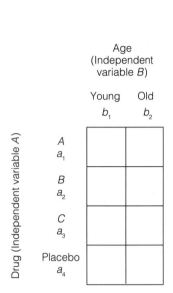

Age
(Independent
variable B)

Young   Old
b_1 b_2

Drug (Independent variable A)

A a_1

B a_2

C a_3

Placebo a_4

Figure 18.9

Independent variable B

| | 1 | 2 | ⋯ | j | ⋯ | b |

Independent variable A

$X_{1,1,1}$ ⋮ $X_{1,1,n}$ $X_{1,2,1}$ ⋮ $X_{1,2,n}$ $X_{1,j,1}$ ⋮ $X_{1,j,n}$ $X_{1,b,1}$ ⋮ $X_{1,b,n}$

$X_{2,1,1}$ ⋮ $X_{2,1,n}$ $X_{2,2,1}$ ⋮ $X_{2,2,n}$ $X_{2,j,1}$ ⋮ $X_{2,j,n}$ $X_{2,b,1}$ ⋮ $X_{2,b,n}$

$X_{i,1,1}$ ⋮ $X_{i,1,n}$ $X_{i,2,1}$ ⋮ $X_{i,2,n}$ $X_{i,j,1}$ ⋮ $X_{i,j,n}$ $X_{i,b,1}$ ⋮ $X_{i,b,n}$

$X_{a,1,1}$ ⋮ $X_{a,1,n}$ $X_{a,2,1}$ ⋮ $X_{a,2,n}$ $X_{a,j,1}$ ⋮ $X_{a,j,n}$ $X_{a,b,1}$ ⋮ $X_{a,b,n}$

Figure 18.10

1 is $T_{1,1}$, while the total in row i, column j is T_{ij}. The sum across all of the scores in the first row (that is, the first treatment of the A independent variable) is T_{A_1}, while the sum of the ith row will be T_{A_i}. The subscript A indicates that the total is for an A treatment, and the second subscript indicates the specific A condition. The same scheme applies to the B totals; T_{B_j} is the sum of all of the scores in the jth column. The sum of all of the scores in the entire data set is, as before, the grand total, or GT. In terms of sums, the design is shown in Figure 18.12.

In the one-factor experiment, the group receiving experimental condition j was regarded as a sample from a population with mean μ_j. And we defined the effect of the jth treatment, α_j, as the difference between the mean of the jth population and the overall mean μ. In the factorial design, we define the effect of the jth treatment (column j, since the j subscript always represents columns) of the B variable similarly as

$$\beta_j = \mu_j - \mu,$$

using β_j as the population treatment parameter. We make the parallel definition for the A variable, by letting α_i stand for the effect of an A treatment, just as we did in a one-way design:

$$\alpha_i = \mu_i - \mu.$$

We will know that we're talking about a row treatment (that is, the A variable) because i will always indicate a row and not a column.

In a similar fashion, we define an interaction treatment effect, an effect that is unique to a particular combination of experimental conditions i and j, using

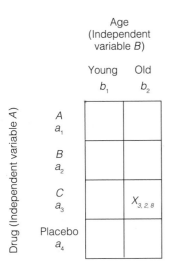

Figure 18.11

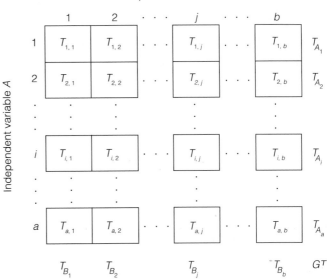

Figure 18.12

the Greek letter γ (gamma) as

$$\gamma_{ij} = \mu_{ij} - \mu_i - \mu_j + \mu.$$

Here μ_{ij} is the mean for the population of all subjects treated according to the combination of A_i and B_j; it's different from both μ_i and μ_j, the row and column population means.

In the single-factor experiment, there were three contributors to an individual score: the population mean, a treatment effect, and error. In the two-factor experiment, there's not just a single independent variable influencing a score; there are two independent variables and the interaction between them as well. In the factorial, then, we define a score as

$$X_{ijk} = \mu + \alpha_i + \beta_j + \gamma_{ij} + \varepsilon_{ijk}.$$

An individual score is made up of the overall mean, effects of the two independent variables and their interaction, and an error component unique to each subject.

Naturally, we can define sample estimates for each parameter by substituting statistics into the definitions. We use the mean of all subjects in all conditions, GM, as the estimate of μ.

The mean of all subjects given treatment A_i is the sum of all of the subjects who receive that treatment: T_{A_i} divided by the number of subjects summed. Since there are n subjects per group, and there are b groups who all receive the same A treatment, the mean is calculated as

$$\overline{X}_{A_i} = \frac{T_{A_i}}{bn}.$$

This mean, naturally, estimates μ_i, and we can estimate the effect of the ith A

treatment as

$$\text{est } \alpha_i = \overline{X}_{A_i} - GM,$$

the difference between the mean of all observations in row i and the grand mean.

In the same way, the mean of all subjects in column j is

$$\overline{X}_{B_j} = \frac{T_{B_j}}{an}$$

and estimates μ_j. An estimate of a B effect is then

$$\text{est } \beta_j = \overline{X}_{B_j} - GM.$$

A mean of a single group of subjects,

$$\overline{X}_{ij} = \frac{T_{i,j}}{n},$$

is an estimate of its population value μ_{ij}. Now we can estimate the population interaction effect as

$$\text{est } \gamma_{ij} = \overline{X}_{ij} - \overline{X}_{A_i} - \overline{X}_{B_j} + GM.$$

Finally, the estimate of error is the difference between the individual score and the mean of all subjects treated in the same way, or

$$\text{est } \varepsilon_{ijk} = X_{ijk} - \overline{X}_{ij}.$$

Substituting the estimates into the parameter expression for a score,

$$X_{ijk} = \mu + \alpha_i + \beta_j + \gamma_{ij} + \varepsilon_{ijk},$$

we can write the score of any particular individual subjects in any specific group as shown in Figure 18.13.

Sums of Squares. Let's remind ourselves once more that the variation that we're analyzing is

$$\hat{s}^2 = \frac{\Sigma(X - \overline{X})^2}{N - 1}.$$

Rewritten into notation appropriate for the two-factor design, we have Figure 18.14. Consider only the numerator, the total sum of squares. If we substitute the expression of parameter estimates for X_{ijk} and complete some very tedious algebra, we arrive at the division of the sum of squares shown in Figure 18.15. Looking carefully at the four parts of the right-hand expression in Figure 18.15, it's evident they represent four distinct sources of variation. The first term sums the differences between the A_i means and the overall mean; we call this quantity the sum of squares for the A variable, or simply SS_A. Likewise, the second term deals with the B_j means, and so it is the sum of squares for B, or SS_B. The third term is the sum of squares for interaction ($SS_{Interaction}$ or simply SS_{AB}). The final component sums differences within each group; it is thus the SS_{Within} or simply SS_{Error}. In short, we have

$$SS_{Total} = SS_A + SS_B + SS_{AB} + SS_{Error}.$$

$$X_{ijk} = GM + (\overline{X}_{A_i} - GM) + (\overline{X}_{B_j} - GM) + (\overline{X}_{ij} - \overline{X}_{A_i} - \overline{X}_{B_j} + GM) + (X_{ijk} - \overline{X}_{ij})$$

| Estimate of μ | Estimate of A effect α_i | Estimate of B effect β_j | Estimate of interaction γ_{ij} | Estimate of error ε_{ijk} |

Figure 18.13

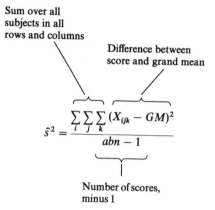

Sum over all subjects in all rows and columns

Difference between score and grand mean

$$\hat{s}^2 = \frac{\sum_i \sum_j \sum_k (X_{ijk} - GM)^2}{abn - 1}$$

Number of scores, minus 1

Figure 18.14

$$\sum_i \sum_j \sum_k (X_{ijk} - GM)^2 = nb \sum_i (\overline{X}_{A_i} - GM)^2 + na \sum_j (\overline{X}_{B_j} - GM)^2$$

$\mathrm{SS_{Total}}$ — SS_A — SS_B

$$+ n \sum_i \sum_j (\overline{X}_{ij} - \overline{X}_{A_i} - \overline{X}_{B_j} + GM)^2 + \sum_i \sum_j \sum_k (X_{ijk} - \overline{X}_{ij})^2$$

$\mathrm{SS_{Interaction}}$ — $\mathrm{SS_{Within}}$ (Error)

Figure 18.15

With this expression, we have analyzed the numerator of the variance ($\mathrm{SS_{Total}}$) into four separate parts. We're now ready to turn to the mean squares and their parameter expressions.

Mean Squares. Just as we subdivided the total sum of squares into four segments, we can also partition the degrees of freedom into corresponding parts. This is done as follows:

$$\mathrm{df}_A = a - 1$$
$$\mathrm{df}_B = b - 1$$
$$\mathrm{df}_{AB} = (a - 1)(b - 1)$$
$$\mathrm{df}_{Error} = ab(n - 1)$$
$$\mathrm{df}_{Total} = abn - 1$$

We now form variance estimates in the usual way—dividing a sum of squares by the appropriate degrees of freedom. This yields four statistics, along with the parameters that they estimate:

Mean square	Parameter estimated
$MS_A = \dfrac{SS_A}{df_A}$	$\sigma^2_e + \dfrac{bn \sum \alpha_i^2}{a - 1}$
$MS_B = \dfrac{SS_B}{df_B}$	$\sigma^2_e + \dfrac{an \sum \beta_j^2}{b - 1}$
$MS_{AB} = \dfrac{SS_{AB}}{df_{AB}}$	$\sigma^2_e + \dfrac{n \sum \sum \gamma_{ij}^2}{(a - 1)(b - 1)}$
$MS_{Error} = \dfrac{SS_{Error}}{df_{Error}}$	σ^2_e

Each mean square estimates the error variance σ^2_e. In addition, three of the mean squares estimate a single additional parameter. In each case, that additional parameter contains exactly one of the hypothesized effects: the A effect (α_i), the B effect (β_j), and the interaction effect (γ_{ij}).

Null Hypotheses

With the parameter expressions identified, we can now define three null hypotheses and illustrate how they may be tested. In single-factor analysis of variance, we tested the null hypothesis that all treatment effects were zero; that is,

$$\alpha_j = 0, \qquad j = 1, 2, \dots, k.$$

In the factorial experiment we identify three separate and independent hypotheses:

$$\alpha_i = 0, \qquad i = 1, 2, \dots a$$
$$\beta_j = 0, \qquad j = 1, 2, \dots b$$
$$\gamma_{ij} = 0, \qquad i = 1, 2, \dots a, \qquad j = 1, 2, \dots b.$$

In words, the three hypotheses are: the effects of independent variable A all equal 0, the effects of independent variable B all equal 0, and all interaction effects equal 0.

Forming F Ratios. Returning to the parameter estimates, note that, except for the error MS, each MS estimates error variance plus one null hypothesis term. For example, the value of

$$\frac{bn \sum \alpha_i^2}{a - 1}$$

in the MS_A expression would equal zero if the null hypothesis about the A variable is true. In that case, both MS_A and MS_{Error} estimate only σ^2_e, and their ratio,

$$F = \frac{MS_A}{MS_{Error}},$$

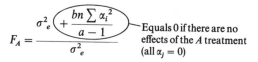

$$F_A = \dfrac{\sigma^2_e \left(+ \dfrac{bn \sum \alpha_i^2}{a-1} \right)}{\sigma^2_e} \quad \begin{array}{l}\text{Equals 0 if there are no}\\ \text{effects of the } A \text{ treatment}\\ \text{(all } \alpha_j = 0)\end{array}$$

Figure 18.16

$$F_{AB} = \dfrac{\sigma^2_e \left(+ \dfrac{n \sum \sum \gamma_{ij}^2}{(a-1)(b-1)} \right)}{\sigma^2_e} \quad \begin{array}{l}\text{Equals 0 if there is no}\\ \text{interaction effect}\\ \text{(all } \gamma_{ij} = 0)\end{array}$$

Figure 18.17

should have a value close to 1.0, since both numerator and denominator are estimating only error variance. On the other hand, if the A null hypothesis is false, then the numerator of the F ratio will be larger than the denominator because the null hypothesis term would be greater than zero.

The ratio of the two variances is distributed as F, with df = df_A, df_{Error}, and the ratio may be used to test the hypothesis that the effect of the A variable is zero. It is exactly equivalent to the hypothesis tested in the single-factor experiment. F ratios for testing the B and the interaction hypotheses are formed in the same way; the MS for B or for AB is divided by MS_{Error}, and the resulting F value is tested for significance as in Chapter 15.

By this time, the general rule for forming an F ratio should be apparent. An F ratio for any hypothesis is selected by finding two statistics whose parameter value differs only by a single term, and that term is one that should be zero if the null hypothesis to be tested is true. For example, the F for the A variable, in terms of parameters is shown in Figure 18.16, while that for interaction is shown in Figure 18.17. In the case of the factorial design, each of the mean squares for the three effects has exactly two elements, error variance and a null hypothesis term. In this design, forming the F ratios is a simple matter of placing each MS over the MS for error.

But matters won't always be quite that simple. As we continue into factorial designs where one, or maybe both, of the independent variables are manipulated within subjects, the choice of the correct "error term" for the mean squares will not be as obvious. But even in those designs, the basic rule for forming an F ratio remains the same: the numerator and the denominator differ by only a null hypothesis term.

Chapter 19 will present the analysis of variance for the factorial design. There we will consider both overall and follow-up computations for equal and for unequal group sizes.

S U M M A R Y

- A factorial design combines two independent variables so that all levels of one are paired with all levels of the other.
- A factorial design lets you test hypotheses about each independent variable alone and about the interaction.
- When two variables interact, the effect of one variable changes at different levels of the other variable.
- The effect of one variable alone is known as its main effect.
- When the interaction is ordinal, the main effects may be interpreted unambiguously.

- The total variation in a factorial design is partitioned into four components: the A variable, the B variable, interaction, and error.
- F ratios are always formed so that their value should tend to be greater than 1.0 if the null hypothesis being tested is false.

KEY TERMS

Disordinal interaction
Factorial design
Interaction

Main effect
Ordinal interaction

CHAPTER 19

Factorial Experimental Designs: Between Subjects (Analysis)

This chapter presents the computations for the factorial design with two independent variables. As in the single-factor experiment, the computations for the analyses differ depending upon whether or not there are equal group sizes. We'll take the simplest (equal) case first.

Computations for Equal Group Sizes

The first analysis tests three omnibus hypotheses: that there is no effect of the two independent variables alone (specifically, that $\mu_i = 0$ and that $\mu_j = 0$), and that there is no interaction (that is, that $\gamma_{ij} = 0$). Once those hypotheses are tested, the analysis proceeds to follow-up tests.

Overall Analysis   The most convenient computational formulas for the sums of squares are

Quantity	Definition	Computations
SS_{Total}	$\sum_i \sum_j \sum_k (X_{ijk} - GM)^2$	$\sum_i \sum_j \sum_k X_{ijk}{}^2 - \dfrac{GT^2}{abn}$
SS_A	$nb \sum_i (\overline{X}_{A_i} - GM)^2$	$\dfrac{\sum_i T_{A_i}{}^2}{nb} - \dfrac{GT^2}{abn}$
SS_B	$na \sum_j (\overline{X}_{B_j} - GM)^2$	$\dfrac{\sum_j T_{B_j}{}^2}{na} - \dfrac{GT^2}{abn}$
SS_{AB}	$n \sum_i \sum_j (\overline{X}_{ij} - \overline{X}_{A_i} - \overline{X}_{B_j} + GM)^2$	$\dfrac{\sum_i \sum_j T_{ij}{}^2}{n} - \dfrac{\sum_j T_{B_j}{}^2}{na} - \dfrac{\sum_i T_{A_i}{}^2}{nb} + \dfrac{GT^2}{abn}$
SS_{Error}	$\sum_i \sum_j \sum_k (X_{ijk} - \overline{X}_{ij})^2$	$\sum_i \sum_j \sum_k X_{ijk}{}^2 - \dfrac{\sum_i \sum_j T_{ij}{}^2}{n}$

Drug (Independent variable *A*)	Age (Independent variable *B*): Young b_1	Old b_2		
A a_1	80 684	117 1411	197	T_{A_1}
B a_2	113 1295	77 599	190	T_{A_2}
C a_3	139 1967	64 416	203	T_{A_3}
Placebo a_4	96 972	97 991	193	T_{A_4}
	428 T_{B_1}	355 T_{B_2}	783	*GT*

Figure 19.1

We'll look at two computational examples of the factorial design. The first will be the drug and age study that we examined descriptively in Chapter 18. The second example will be a variation of the first, but with a third age condition.

The raw data for the 4 by 2 factorial appear in Table 18.1 (p. 400). We begin the analysis by finding the total T_{ij} and the sum of the squared values ($\Sigma X_{ijk}{}^2$) in each experimental condition. The totals for the *A* (T_{A_i}) and *B* (T_{B_j}) conditions and the grand total are also shown in Figure 19.1.

Beginning with SS_A (drugs), we have

$$\begin{aligned} SS_A &= \frac{\sum_j T_{A_j}{}^2}{bn} - \frac{GT^2}{abn} \\ &= \frac{197^2 + 190^2 + 203^2 + 193^2}{2 \times 10} - \frac{783^2}{4 \times 2 \times 10} \\ &= 7668.35 - 7663.61 \\ &= 4.74. \end{aligned}$$

For SS_B (age), the computations are

$$\begin{aligned} SS_B &= \frac{\sum_j T_{B_i}{}^2}{an} - \frac{GT^2}{abn} \\ &= \frac{428^2 + 355^2}{4 \times 10} - \frac{783^2}{4 \times 2 \times 10} \\ &= 7730.23 - 7663.61 \\ &= 66.62. \end{aligned}$$

Table 19.1

Summary Table for Drug-Age Data

Source	SS	df	MS	F	
Drugs	4.74	3	1.58	0.45	$p > .05$
Age	66.61	1	66.61	19.03	$p < .01$
Interaction	347.94	3	115.98	33.14	$p < .01$
Error	252.10	72	3.50		
Total	671.39	79			

Computing SS_{AB}, we have

$$SS_{AB} = \frac{\sum_i \sum_j T_{ij}^2}{n} - \frac{\sum_i T_{A_i}^2}{bn} - \frac{\sum_j T_{B_j}^2}{an} + \frac{GT^2}{abn}$$

$$= \frac{80^2 + 113^2 + \cdots + 64^2 + 97^2}{10} - \frac{428^2 + 355^2}{4 \times 10}$$

$$- \frac{197^2 + 190^2 + 203^2 + 193^2}{2 \times 10} + \frac{783^2}{4 \times 2 \times 10}$$

$$= 8082.90 - 7730.22 - 7668.35 + 7663.61$$

$$= 347.94.$$

For SS_{Error}, the calculations are

$$SS_{\text{Error}} = \sum_i \sum_j \sum_k X_{ijk}^2 - \frac{\sum_i \sum_j T_{ij}^2}{n}$$

$$= 684 + 1295 + \cdots + 416 + 991 - \frac{80^2 + 113^2 + \cdots + 64^2 + 97^2}{10}$$

$$= 8335 - 8082.90$$

$$= 252.10.$$

Finally, we compute the total sum of squares as

$$SS_{\text{Total}} = \sum_i \sum_j \sum_k X_{ijk}^2 - \frac{GT^2}{abn}$$

$$= 684 + 1295 + \cdots + 416 + 991 - \frac{783^2}{4 \times 2 \times 10}$$

$$= 8335 - 7663.61$$

$$= 671.39.$$

Table 19.1 is the summary table for the analysis, using the degrees of freedom formulas from Chapter 18. The significance values are shown; there is no difference among the four drugs, while both the age effect and the interaction are significant.

We looked at these data carefully in Chapter 18, and the analysis of variance results only confirm what we learned there. The interaction, remember, is dis-

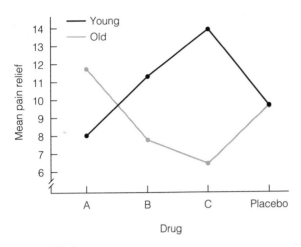

Figure 19.2

Age

Young Middle Old

Figure 19.3

ordinal (Figure 19.2). With a significant disordinal interaction, we shouldn't try to interpret the main effect of age even though it is significant because it is distorted by the interaction. If the interaction had been ordinal, then we could look at the main effects meaningfully.

As a second, and briefer, example of the between-subjects factorial, suppose that we obtain a group of middle-aged subjects and have them rate headache relief following one of the four drugs. In other words, we take our 4 × 2 (drug × age) design and expand it to a 4 × 3, with three ages and the familiar four drugs (Figure 19.3). Table 19.2 is a set of data for this enlarged design. The mean and the standard deviation of each of the twelve groups of data, along with the main effect and grand means are listed in Table 19.3.

Figure 19.4 is the plot of the individual group means—the interaction plot. It illustrates that the middle and old subjects show similar patterns of response, rating their pain relief from Drug A higher than for any other conditions (except for the middle-aged subjects who received the placebo). The young subjects show a pattern opposite to that we saw previously. Note here that there seems to be an effect of the placebo on the middle-aged individuals that wasn't there for the young and the old—young and old don't differ on their ratings for the placebo, but the middle subjects rate the placebo's relief as higher.

To begin the analysis, we compute the table of sums and summed squared values as shown in Figure 19.5. Now we apply the computational formulas to calculate the sums of squares, starting with SS_A (the sum of squares for drug):

$$SS_A = \frac{\sum_i T_{A_i}^2}{bn} - \frac{GT^2}{abn}$$

$$= \frac{302^2 + 262^2 + 296^2 + 318^2}{3 \times 10} - \frac{1178^2}{4 \times 3 \times 10}$$

$$= 11619.60 - 11564.03$$

$$= 55.57.$$

Table 19.2 Hypothetical Data for Enlarged Drug-Age Design

Young	Middle	Old		Young	Middle	Old
	Age of subject				**Age of subject**	
DRUG A				DRUG C		
11	9	10		14	9	7
8	12	9		13	7	6
6	10	9		11	10	6
8	11	15		15	8	6
11	13	10		13	4	5
6	9	11		13	14	6
10	11	13		15	10	8
9	8	13		12	13	7
5	8	13		15	10	7
6	14	14		18	8	6
DRUG B				PLACEBO		
14	5	9		9	12	8
10	5	8		8	16	11
10	10	7		9	10	6
12	8	9		12	16	10
12	5	8		13	14	8
13	9	7		8	12	8
11	9	7		10	12	9
11	8	8		6	9	12
10	6	7		8	11	14
10	7	7		13	13	11

Table 19.3 Means and Standard Deviations for the Data in Table 19.1

		Age of subject			
		Young	Middle	Old	Drugs across ages
Drug A	$\overline{X}$	8.00	10.50	11.70	10.07
	s.d.	2.21	2.07	2.16	
Drug B	$\overline{X}$	11.30	7.20	7.70	8.73
	s.d.	1.42	1.87	0.82	
Drug C	$\overline{X}$	13.90	9.30	6.40	9.87
	s.d.	1.97	2.87	0.84	
Placebo	$\overline{X}$	9.60	12.50	9.70	10.60
	s.d.	2.37	2.32	2.36	
Ages across drugs	$\overline{X}$	10.70	9.88	8.88	9.82

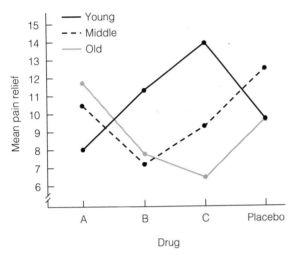

Age
(Independent
variable B)

		Young b_1	Middle b_2	Old b_3		
A a_1		80 684	105 1141	117 1411	302	T_{A_1}
B a_2		113 1295	72 550	77 599	262	T_{A_2}
C a_3		139 1967	93 939	64 416	296	T_{A_3}
Placebo a_4		96 972	125 1611	97 991	318	T_{A_4}
		428 T_{B_1}	395 T_{B_2}	355 T_{B_3}	1178	GT

Drug (Independent variable A)

Figure 19.4

Figure 19.5

For SS_B (age), we have

$$SS_B = \frac{\sum_j T_{B_j}^2}{an} - \frac{GT^2}{abn}$$

$$= \frac{428^2 + 395^2 + 355^2}{4 \times 10} - \frac{1178^2}{4 \times 3 \times 10}$$

$$= 11630.85 - 11564.03$$

$$= 66.82.$$

Calculating the sum of squares for interaction:

$$SS_{AB} = \frac{\sum_i \sum_j T_{ij}^2}{n} - \frac{\sum_i T_{A_i}^2}{bn} - \frac{\sum_j T_{B_j}^2}{an} + \frac{GT^2}{abn}$$

$$= \frac{80^2 + 113^2 + \cdots + 64^2 + 97^2}{10} - \frac{302^2 + 262^2 + 296^2 + 318^2}{3 \times 10}$$

$$- \frac{428^2 + 395^2 + 355^2}{4 \times 10} + \frac{1178^2}{3 \times 4 \times 10}$$

$$= 12131.20 - 11619.60 - 11630.85 + 11564.03$$

$$= 444.75.$$

The error sum of squares is

$$SS_{Error} = \sum_i \sum_j \sum_k X_{ijk}^2 - \frac{\sum_i \sum_j T_{ij}^2}{n}$$

Table 19.4   Summary Table

Source	SS	df	MS	F	Prob.
Drugs	55.57	3	18.52	4.50	< .05
Age	66.82	2	33.41	8.11	< .01
Interaction	444.75	6	74.12	17.99	< .01
Error	444.80	108	4.12		
Total	1011.97	119			

$$= 684 + 1295 + \cdots + 416 + 991 - \frac{80^2 + 113^2 + \cdots + 64^2 + 97^2}{10}$$
$$= 12576 - 12131.20$$
$$= 444.80.$$

Finally, the total sum of squares is

$$SS_{Total} = \sum_i \sum_j \sum_k X_{ijk}^2 - \frac{GT^2}{abn}$$

$$= 684 + 1295 + \cdots + 416 + 991 - \frac{1178^2}{4 \times 3 \times 10}$$
$$= 12576 - 11564.03$$
$$= 1011.97.$$

Summarizing and computing the remaining values, we have Table 19.4. In this analysis, we find that all three effects are significant—the three ages differ, the four drug conditions differ, and there is an interaction. We'll explore this example in detail as we present the ways to follow up significant effects in the factorial.

The follow-up procedures for a factorial experiment are guided first, of course, by the questions being asked by the experiment. They follow two different paths depending upon whether the interaction is significant. If it is not significant, then the main effects are explored, treating each main effect as a separate one-way analysis. If the interaction is significant, then the interaction is addressed first, and the main effects are considered later. If the interaction is disordinal, the main effects may not even be considered again.

Follow Up:
Interaction Not
Significant

When the interaction is not significant, the follow-up analysis simplifies to two independent one-way analyses, one for each independent variable. Establishing that there's no interaction means that each variable can be explored alone and that conclusions about one variable will hold regardless of the value of the other variable. The analysis for each variable follows the procedures illustrated in Chapter 16. There are two differences. First, the error term used for follow-up comparisons, or in Scheffé or Tukey post hoc tests, is MS_{Error} from the full analysis. Second, the value of n changes; it is the number of values entering into the means compared. For example, had our interaction been nonsignificant, and we wished to compare the drug conditions, we would have to remember that the four drug means are based not on $n = 10$, but rather on $n = 3 \times 10 = 30$, since each drug mean was taken across the three age conditions. Apart from the adjustments to the sample size, all planned and post hoc analyses of the main effects proceed exactly as in a single-factor experiment.

In a factorial design, we can distinguish between experiment-wise (EW) and family-wise (FW) error rates. The EW error rate refers, as it did in one-way analysis, to the probability of making a Type I error *somewhere* during the entire analysis. The FW error rate refers, on the other hand, to the probability of making a Type I error somewhere within a *family* of analyses. A family is the set of the follow-ups of one (or more) of the three overall effects tested. In the factorial, we have three families of analyses—for the two main effects and for the interaction. Follow-up tests of a nonsignificant interaction are in two families—those pursuing the A main effect and those pursuing the B main effect. In a one-way analysis there is only a single "family" of effects, namely the main effect of the single independent variable.

In psychology, the recommended procedure is to control Type I error on an FW basis. While we'll discuss error rates again later in this chapter, for now the recommendation is to establish an error rate for the A and the B main effect families of tests and proceed with the follow-up analyses as if you were carrying out two unrelated single-factor experiments. The EW error rate, naturally, will be no greater than the sum of the FW rates.

Follow Up: Interaction Significant

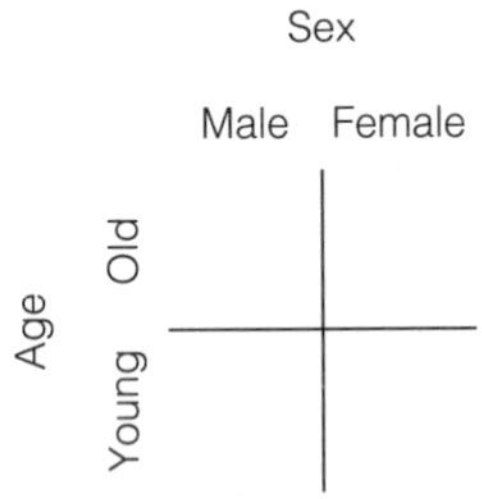

Sex

Male   Female

Figure 19.6

When the interaction is significant, we need to look at its form before deciding on the next analysis. Let's take a very simple example—a factorial with two levels of each factor, like male-female, and young-old (Figure 19.6).

Let's look at two simple sets of data, both with an interaction between sex and age, that illustrate two forms of interaction. First, consider the group means and their interaction plot as shown in Figure 19.7. These data show a classic disordinal interaction pattern of crossing lines. In the old condition, males score three points higher than do the females. In the young condition, the situation is just the opposite, with females scoring higher than males (but only by one point). The effect of age, then, is to reverse the male-female difference; the two sexes are exactly opposite for the two ages. But that's the only effect of age, since the means for age are identical. This is so because the mean (across sex) for old subjects is $(10 + 7)/2 = 8.5$ and is equal to the mean (again across sexes) for the young subjects—$(8 + 9)/2 = 8.5$. In these data, there is no main effect for age; its effect shows up only in the interaction. But that's an important effect. If you concluded that age has no effect at all, you'd be wrong; it has a strong effect, but it operates differently on males and females.

Contrast the data from Figure 19.7 with those in Figure 19.8, where the male-female differences are exactly the same within each age condition; old males score three points above females, while young females outscore their male counterparts by one point. That's exactly the same pattern as in the first example. But now the main effect of age is substantial; the old subjects are consistently above the young. Averaging across sex, the old subjects score 7.5 as previously, but now the young subjects (again averaged across sex) score 3.5, a difference of 4.0 between the two age conditions.

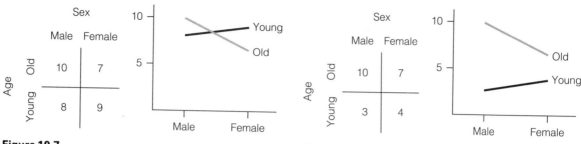

Figure 19.7

Figure 19.8

What we have just illustrated is the difference between disordinal and ordinal interactions. In Figure 19.8, the interaction is present to the same extent as in the first, but the overall ordering of the old-young distinction is preserved—old subjects, both males and females, are consistently above the young of both sexes. In the first data set, the ordering of the ages is not preserved with a change in sex. The second interaction is an *ordinal* interaction, since it preserves the rank ordering of one independent variable over changes in the other variable. The other form of interaction, illustrated by the first data set, is a *disordinal* (or *crossover*) interaction. It does not preserve a rank ordering across the other variable—males and females switched positions as age changed.

Interpretations of main effects and interactions, as well as the follow-up tests to accompany each, vary with the form of the interaction. If the interaction is ordinal, the main effect can be interpreted unambiguously, as we have seen. The presence of the age-sex interaction in the second set of example data doesn't change the conclusion that we might draw about age—old subjects have higher scores. But in the disordinal interaction, any overall conclusion about age could be seriously misleading. In the example, if we looked only at the age main effect, we would wrongly conclude that the variable had no effect. In fact, it has a strong effect, but the effect changes for the two sexes in such a way as to mask the overall effect.

There are several inferential procedures that can be used for detailed analysis of significant interactions. We'll present two and refer the industrious student to other sources for other analyses.

The first analysis is exactly comparable to the omnibus analysis in the single-factor design; it uses a single level of one independent variable and conducts an analysis of variance on the other independent variable. The second analysis, analogous to follow-up comparison in the one-way design, looks at differences within a single level of an independent variable. We'll follow Keppel's (1982) terminology in this presentation, designating the first analysis a *simple-effects* analysis and calling the second *simple comparisons*.

Simple Effects. A simple effect is conceptually just a slight modification to a one-way analysis, conducted at a single level of the other independent variable. In our drug by age example, we would conduct the equivalent of a single-factor analysis of variance using just the young subjects, then another using only the middle subjects, and a third with just the old subjects. Each analysis would

Table 19.5   Table of Means for Drug-Age Study

	Age			
	Young	Middle	Old	Drugs across ages
Drug A	8.00	10.50	11.70	10.07
Drug B	11.30	7.20	7.70	8.73
Drug C	13.90	9.30	6.40	9.87
Placebo	9.60	12.50	9.70	10.60

contain four drug conditions, and a significant result would merely mean that at least one comparison among the four groups is significant. That analysis would be followed by simple comparisons, which are the equivalent of post hoc tests.

We'll continue to use the drug by age example. The first test will be for the simple effect of age at Drug A. Returning to the table of means (Table 19.5), we will conduct a one-way analysis of the three conditions indicated. In the plot of the interaction (Figure 19.9), the analysis compares the three means indicated in Table 19.5. From looking at the plot, we might guess that if there's a significant difference, it will probably be that the young subjects differ from the combined middle and old subjects. A simple comparison can address just that question; for now, we look at the "omnibus" simple-effects analysis.

Simple-effects computations proceed from a table of group sums (*not* group means), such as that shown in Figure 19.10. The first step in testing for the simple effect is to form the sum of squares for the effect of interest. In general terms,

$$SS_{B \text{ at } A_i} = \frac{\sum_j T_{ij}^2}{n} - \frac{T_{A_i}^2}{bn}.$$

Or, in this case, for just Drug A, we have

$$SS_{\text{Age at Drug A}} = \frac{\sum_j T_{1j}^2}{n} - \frac{T_{A_1}^2}{bn}.$$

Actually, the formula is much simpler in practice than it is in symbols. It instructs us to square the group sums and sum them, divide by the group size, and subtract from that the sum of the sums, squared and divided by the product *bn*. Using the values from Figure 19.10, we have

$$SS_{\text{Age at Drug A}} = \frac{\sum_j T_{1j}^2}{n} - \frac{T_{A_1}^2}{bn}$$

$$= \frac{80^2 + 105^2 + 117^2}{10} - \frac{302^2}{30}$$

$$= 71.27.$$

This sum of squares has df = $b - 1$ (as usual, the number of elements summed, minus one), so that the mean square is

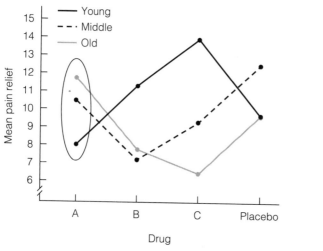

Figure 19.9

	Young b_1	Middle b_2	Old b_3		
A a_1	80	105	117	302	T_{A_1}
B a_2	113	72	77	262	T_{A_2}
C a_3	139	93	64	296	T_{A_3}
Placebo a_4	96	125	97	318	T_{A_4}
	428 T_{B_1}	395 T_{B_2}	355 T_{B_3}	1178	GT

Drug (Independent variable A)

Figure 19.10

$$MS_{\text{Age at Drug A}} = \frac{SS_{\text{Age at Drug A}}}{df_{\text{Age at Drug A}}}$$

$$= \frac{71.27}{2} = 35.63.$$

Finally, we compute an F, using the MS_{Error} from the overall analysis:

$$F = \frac{MS_{\text{Age at Drug A}}}{MS_{\text{Error}}} = \frac{35.63}{4.12} = 8.65.$$

With df = 2, 108,* the critical value for F at $\alpha = .01$ is 4.98[†], we may reject the null hypothesis that the three age groups have identical population means under Drug A.

We continue with the parallel analysis for Drug B, looking at the ages under the second drug condition (see Figure 19.11). The sum of squares for this effect is calculated as

$$SS_{\text{Age at Drug B}} = \frac{\sum_{j} T_{2j}^2}{n} - \frac{T_{A_2}^2}{bn}$$

$$= \frac{113^2 + 72^2 + 77^2}{10} - \frac{262^2}{30}$$

$$= 100.07.$$

---

*We use the closest lower df entry, which is for df = 2, 60.
[†]Note that the error term is taken from the overall analysis, and so this analysis is not quite the same as if we had done a one-way analysis using *only* the Drug A data. Conceptually it's the same, but the overall error term provides the better estimate of σ^2_{error}. This analysis assumes that the variances of all experimental groups are equal. If there is evidence that they are not, then an ordinary one-way analysis should be run using only the Drug A data.

Computations for Equal Group Sizes

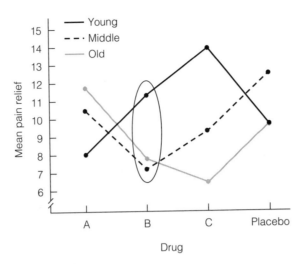

Figure 19.11

Table 19.6 Computing *F* Ratios for Drug-Age Data

Source	SS	df	MS	F
Drug	55.57	3	18.52	4.50
Age at Drug A	71.27	2	35.64	8.65
Age at Drug B	100.70	2	50.35	12.22
Age at Drug C	286.07	2	143.04	34.72
Age at Placebo	54.20	2	27.10	6.58
Error	444.80	108	4.12	
Total	1012.61	119		

We continue the analysis and compute the simple effects of age under each of the remaining drug conditions as

$$SS_{\text{Age at Drug C}} = \frac{139^2 + 93^2 + 64^2}{10} - \frac{296^2}{30} = 286.07$$

$$SS_{\text{Age at Placebo}} = \frac{96^2 + 125^2 + 97^2}{10} - \frac{318^2}{30} = 54.20.$$

We can summarize all of the computations in a table and compute the *F* ratios easily; see Table 19.6. In the summary table, the entries for age and for interaction from the overall analysis have been replaced by the simple-effects values. The sum of the set of sums of squares is close (identical, within rounding) to the SS_{Total} from the original analysis. That's no coincidence; the simple-effects analysis has merely partitioned the variability differently, so that the variation that was previously partitioned into drugs and interaction has been redistributed into the four simple-effect sums of squares. To be explicit about this relationship,

$$\sum_i SS_{B \text{ at } A_i} = SS_B + SS_{\text{Interaction}}.$$

Table 19.7   Possible "Other Way" Analysis

	Age of subject			
	Young	Middle	Old	Drugs across ages
Drug A	8.00	10.50	11.70	10.07
Drug B	11.30	7.20	7.70	8.73
Drug C	13.90	9.30	6.40	9.87
Placebo	9.60	12.50	9.70	10.60

This relationship will always hold, within rounding, and serves as an easy check of the accuracy of the computations.

The simple-effects analyses so far have examined the effects of age at each level of drug. The same procedure is equally applicable "the other way"; that is, looking at the effects of drug at each age. The table of means (Table 19.7) shows one possible "other way" analysis that looks at the effect of drug for only the old subjects. Graphically, the analysis uses only the old line from the plot (see Figure 19.12). The formulas for this analysis are

$$SS_{A \text{ at } B_j} = \frac{\sum_i T_{ij}^2}{n} - \frac{T_{B_j}^2}{an}$$

$$df = a - 1$$

$$\sum_j SS_{A \text{ at } B_j} = SS_A + SS_{\text{Interaction}}.$$

As an example, let's look at the effect of the four drug conditions for just the old subjects. Returning to Figure 19.10 for the relevant sums, we have

$$SS_{A \text{ at } B_3} = \frac{\sum_i T_{i3}^2}{n} - \frac{T_{B_3}^2}{an}$$

$$= \frac{117^2 + 77^2 + 64^2 + 97^2}{10} - \frac{355^2}{40}$$

$$= 161.68.$$

With $df = a - 1$, the mean square is

$$MS_{A \text{ at } B_3} = \frac{SS_{A \text{ at } B_3}}{a - 1}$$

$$= \frac{161.68}{3}$$

$$= 53.89.$$

Using the MS_{Error} from the overall analysis, we have

$$F = \frac{MS_{A \text{ at } B_3}}{MS_{\text{Error}}} = \frac{53.89}{4.12} = 13.08.$$

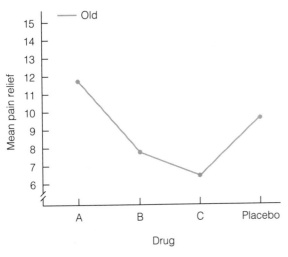

Figure 19.12

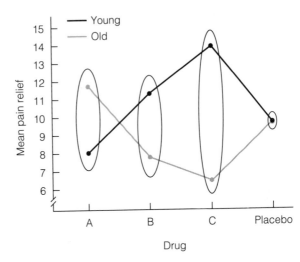

Figure 19.13

This ratio has df = 3, 108; the critical value at $\alpha = .01$ from Appendix F is 4.13, and we conclude that there are significant differences among the four drug conditions for the old subjects.

To be complete, we would also compute the sums of squares for the young and the middle conditions and check the accuracy of the computations by following the formula

$$\sum_j SS_{A \text{ at } B_j} = SS_A + SS_{\text{Interaction}}.$$

We'll save that for an exercise.

Simple Comparisons. When a simple-effects analysis involves only two conditions, such as the illustration of the 4×2 drug example in Figure 19.13, no additional analyses are needed. The simple-effects analysis is sufficient (either the two ages differ for each drug or they don't). If there are more than two conditions and the simple effect shows a significant difference, then the analysis should be pursued further. We're left with the same dilemma as in a one-way design—there's a difference, but the omnibus test can't pinpoint it. In the single-factor design, we followed an omnibus test with comparisons and post hoc tests; the same procedures are applicable in the factorial design, with only slight modification. Since these comparisons follow a simple-effects analysis, we call them *simple comparisons*.

Simple comparisons are conducted by removing a single row or column from the table of means and applying the comparison just as if the column listed the results for a one-way design. The only difference in the procedure comes in the F ratio: the MS_{Error} from the overall analysis is used in the denominator. To illustrate, let's pursue the simple effect of age at Drug B. We concluded earlier that the simple effect was significant. Table 19.8 shows the entries we need (note that it's the means, not the sums, that we use here).

Table 19.8   Means for Simple Effect of Age at Drug B

| | Age of subject | | | |
	Young	Middle	Old	Drugs across ages
Drug A	8.00	10.50	11.70	10.07
Drug B	11.30	7.20	7.70	8.73
Drug C	13.90	9.30	6.40	9.87
Placebo	9.60	12.50	9.70	10.60

Let's first look at the comparison of the young subjects with the mean of the middle and the old animals, using coefficients of 2, -1, -1. Following the formula from Chapter 16 for the sum of squares for a comparison, we have

$$SS_{A \text{ comparison}} = \frac{nC^2}{\Sigma c_j^2}$$

$$= \frac{10[2(11.30) + (-1)(7.20) + (-1)(7.70)]^2}{2^2 + (-1)^2 + (-1)^2}$$

$$= 98.82.$$

This sum of squares has df $= 1$, so that its mean square has the same value. Thus we form the F for testing the hypothesis that the comparison has a value of zero as

$$F = \frac{MS_{A \text{ comparison}}}{MS_{\text{Error}}} = \frac{98.82}{4.12} = 23.99.$$

If we adopt a significance level of .01 for this comparison, the critical F for df $= 1$, 108 is 6.63, and we may reject the hypothesis that the population mean pain-relief rating for young under Drug B is the same as the mean of the middle and old ages also under Drug B. From the means, it's clear that the young rate pain relief of Drug B more highly than do the middle and old subjects.

Simple comparisons offer a highly versatile way to explore a significant interaction in detail. They allow comparisons within a level of an independent variable and are ideally suited for following a significant simple effect. Together, simple-effect analyses and simple comparisons are the most frequent procedures used in a factorial design. There are other procedures; Keppel (1982) and others describe them fully.

Unequal Group Sizes

We turn now to the case of unequal group sizes. In Chapter 16 we discussed two different procedures for handling unequal group sizes, the weighted- and the unweighted-means computations. In the factorial design, the situation becomes exceptionally complicated, and we'll illustrate the computations for only the unweighted-means analysis.

In the factorial, to compute using the weighted-means procedure—probably the most correct way to do the analysis—virtually requires computer assistance. The computations are best handled by employing a regression-like approach called the *general linear model*. Developing that procedure would take us much too far afield for this text. We'll also omit the weighted-means analysis because it normally requires a very sophisticated computer program, and a computer is assumed not to be necessary for carrying out any of the analyses in this book. You should know, though, that in the near future, unweighted-means computations in factorial designs may go the way of the dinosaur.

Overall Analysis

The unweighted-means analysis is computed by multiplying each individual mean by the harmonic mean of all of the group sizes $\tilde{n}$, where $\tilde{n}$ is defined as

$$\tilde{n} = \frac{ab}{\sum_i \sum_j \dfrac{1}{n_{ij}}},$$

and where n_{ij} is the number of observations in an experimental condition. Each group mean, $\overline{X}_{ij}$, is multiplied by $\tilde{n}$ to give a new group "total," T_{ij}^*. That sum is then used in all further calculations.

To illustrate the unweighted-means analysis, consider the following data from a hypothetical* study of the visibility of three different coating materials for highway signs: normal paint, "reflective" paint, and a new paint called

Table 19.9   Hypothetical Data for Paint Visibility Study

	Paint type	
Ordinary	Reflective	Retro
DAY		
126	121	114
116	93	119
79	123	111
96	105	104
	109	
NIGHT		
68	52	99
41	70	104
32	59	115
65	94	97
69	85	118
58		108

*While the study is hypothetical, the "new" paint is a real product. The data values are based on actual visibility studies and have approximately the values that they would have if this experiment were actually done.

Figure 19.14

Paint type

	Ordinary	Reflective	Retro
Day	417 4	551 5	448 4
Night	333 6	360 5	641 6

Figure 19.14

Figure 19.15

Paint type

	Ordinary	Reflective	Retro	
Day	104.25	110.20	112.00	108.82
Night	55.50	72.00	106.83	78.11
	79.88	91.10	109.42	93.46

Figure 19.15

"retroflective." Subjects viewed the signs under either daylight or night conditions (with simulated automobile headlights). The dependent variable was the distance (in meters) at which a word on the sign could be read. The data are listed in Table 19.9.

A good place to start the analysis is with the group totals and sizes, since we'll need them later (see Figure 19.14). The means of the six conditions, along with the main effect and grand means, are shown in Figure 19.15. The plot of the means suggests a strong interaction (Figure 19.16).

We begin by calculating the harmonic mean sample size as

$$\tilde{n} = \frac{ab}{\displaystyle\sum_i \sum_j \frac{1}{n_{ij}}}$$

$$= \frac{2 \times 3}{\dfrac{1}{4} + \dfrac{1}{5} + \dfrac{1}{4} + \dfrac{1}{6} + \dfrac{1}{5} + \dfrac{1}{6}}$$

$$= 4.86.$$

The next computation is to obtain the T^* for each condition as

$$T_{ij}^* = \overline{X}_{ij} \times \tilde{n}$$

so that

$$T_{1,1}^* = \overline{X}_{1,1} \times \tilde{n}$$
$$= 104.25 \times 4.86 = 506.66.$$

Completing the computations, the T^* values are

$$T_{1,2}^* = \overline{X}_{1,2} \times \tilde{n}$$
$$= 110.20 \times 4.86 = 535.57$$
$$T_{1,3}^* = \overline{X}_{1,3} \times \tilde{n}$$
$$= 112.00 \times 4.86 = 544.32$$
$$T_{2,1}^* = \overline{X}_{2,1} \times \tilde{n}$$
$$= 55.50 \times 4.86 = 269.73$$
$$T_{2,2}^* = \overline{X}_{2,2} \times \tilde{n}$$
$$= 72.00 \times 4.86 = 349.92$$

$$T_{2,3}^* = \bar{X}_{1,1} \times \tilde{n}$$
$$= 106.83 \times 4.86 = 519.19.$$

Arranging the T^* values in a table will help to keep our numbers well organized (Figure 19.17). For SS_A, the formula makes a slight modification in the formula for equal group sizes to reflect the use of $\tilde{n}$ and the T_{ij}^* values:

$$SS_A = \frac{\sum_i T_{A_i}^{*2}}{b\tilde{n}} - \frac{GT^{*2}}{ab\tilde{n}}$$
$$= \frac{1586.55^2 + 1138.84^2}{3 \times 4.86} - \frac{2725.39^2}{2 \times 3 \times 4.86}$$
$$= 261597.90 - 254723.96$$
$$= 6873.94.$$

A corresponding change is made in SS_B:

$$SS_B = \frac{\sum_j T_{B_j}^{*2}}{a\tilde{n}} - \frac{GT^{*2}}{ab\tilde{n}}$$
$$= \frac{776.39^2 + 885.49^2 + 1063.51^2}{2 \times 4.86} - \frac{2725.39^2}{2 \times 3 \times 4.86}$$
$$= 259046.04 - 254723.96$$
$$= 4327.08.$$

The pattern repeats for the interaction sum of squares:

$$SS_{AB} = \frac{\sum_i \sum_j T_{ij}^{*2}}{\tilde{n}} - \frac{\sum_i T_{A_i}^{*2}}{b\tilde{n}} - \frac{\sum_j T_{B_j}^{*2}}{a\tilde{n}} + \frac{GT^{*2}}{ab\tilde{n}}$$
$$= \frac{506.66^2 + \cdots + 519.19^2}{4.86} - \frac{1586.55^2 + 1138.84^2}{3 \times 4.86}$$
$$- \frac{776.39^2 + 885.49^2 + 1063.51^2}{2 \times 4.86} + \frac{2725.39^2}{2 \times 3 \times 4.86}$$
$$= 268432.18 - 261597.90 - 259046.04 + 254723.96$$
$$= 2512.20.$$

In the single-factor analysis for unequal group sizes, we used the formula

$$SS_{\text{Within}} = \sum_j \sum_i X_{ij}^2 - \sum_j \left(\frac{T_j^2}{n_j} \right)$$

to compute the SS_{Error} term. Note that the T^* and the $\tilde{n}$ values aren't used here; instead we use the actual group totals and sizes. The formula is easily modified for the two-factor experiment:

$$SS_{\text{Within}} = \sum_i \sum_j \sum_k X_{ijk}^2 - \sum_i \sum_j \left(\frac{T_{ij}^2}{n_{ij}} \right).$$

The logic of the formula is exactly the same; the value is the sum of the squared raw scores, and the sum of all of the squared group sums divided by the group sizes. Again, note that computations use actual group totals and sizes—T^* and $\tilde{n}$ are not used.

Employing the formula, we have

$$SS_{\text{Within}} = \sum_i \sum_j \sum_k X_{ijk}^2 - \sum_i \sum_j \left(\frac{T_{ij}^2}{n_{ij}} \right)$$

$$= 126^2 + 116^2 + \cdots + 118^2 + 108^2 - \left(\frac{417^2}{4} + \frac{551^2}{5} + \cdots + \frac{641^2}{6} \right)$$

$$= 272072 - 267250.12$$

$$= 4821.88.$$

With the sums of squares completed (we don't compute SS_{Total} in unweighted-means analysis), we proceed to the degrees of freedom:

$$df_A = a - 1$$
$$df_B = b - 1$$
$$df_{AB} = (a - 1)(b - 1)$$
$$df_{\text{Error}} = \sum_i \sum_j n_{ij} - ab.$$

The only change here is in the degrees of freedom for error, where we must sum the group sizes. Now we can complete the analysis with the summary table (Table 19.10). All of the three effects are significant using $\alpha = .01$.

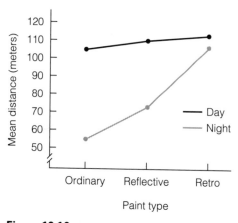

Figure 19.16

Paint type

	Ordinary	Reflective	Retro		
Day	506.66	535.57	544.32	1586.55	$T_{A_1}^*$
Night	269.73	349.92	519.19	1138.84	$T_{A_2}^*$
	776.39	885.49	1063.51	2725.39	GT^*
	$T_{B_1}^*$	$T_{B_2}^*$	$T_{B_3}^*$		

Figure 19.17

Table 19.10 Summary Table

Source	SS	df	MS	F
Light	6873.94	1	6873.94	34.21
Paint	4327.08	2	2161.04	10.76
Interaction	2512.20	2	1256.10	6.25
Error	4821.88	24	200.91	

Unequal Group Sizes

Follow-up analyses for the unequal groups factorial design parallel those for equal group sizes. For simple effects, we have the modified formulas

$$SS_{A \text{ at } B_j} = \frac{\sum_i T_{ij}^{*2}}{\tilde{n}} - \frac{T_{A_i}^{*2}}{a\tilde{n}}$$

and

$$SS_{B \text{ at } A_i} = \frac{\sum_i T_{ij}^{*2}}{\tilde{n}} - \frac{T_{A_i}^{*2}}{b\tilde{n}}.$$

Figure 19.18 illustrates the procedure for our example by examining the simple main effect of day-night lighting at the reflective paint condition. Figure 19.19 gives the relevant T values. The sum of squares for the effect of day/night for the reflective paint is

$$SS_{A \text{ at } B_2} = \frac{\sum_i T_{i2}^{*2}}{\tilde{n}} - \frac{T_{A_2}^{*2}}{a\tilde{n}}$$

$$= \frac{535.57^2 + 349.92^2}{4.86} - \frac{885.49^2}{2 \times 4.86}$$

$$= 3545.88.$$

The degrees of freedom for the sum of squares, as usual, equals the number of items summed minus one, so that the df here is $2 - 1 = 1$. The mean square is thus

$$MS_{A \text{ at } B_2} = \frac{3545.88}{1} = 3545.88.$$

Using the MS_{Within} from the overall analysis, we have

$$F = \frac{MS_{A \text{ at } B_2}}{MS_{\text{Within}}} = \frac{3545.88}{200.91} = 17.65.$$

With df $= 1, 24$, the difference is significant. We can thus conclude that the reflective paint leads to word recognition at a significantly greater distance in daylight than in darkness. (An exercise asks you whether the retroreflective paint shows a similar difference.)

If we ask about differences among the paint conditions at night, then we're asking about a simple main effect of B at A. As an example of the analysis, we take the values indicated in Figure 19.20 and use the formula listed earlier:

$$SS_{B \text{ at } A_2} = \frac{\sum_i T_{ij}^{*2}}{\tilde{n}} - \frac{T_{A_i}^{*2}}{b\tilde{n}}$$

$$= \frac{269.73^2 + 349.92^2 + 519.19^2}{4.86} - \frac{1138.84^2}{3 \times 4.86}$$

$$= 95628.92 - 88954.50$$

$$= 6674.42.$$

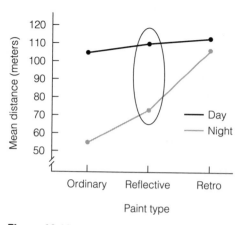

Figure 19.18

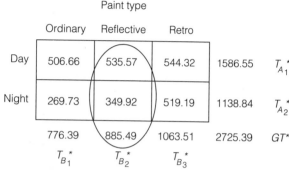

Figure 19.19

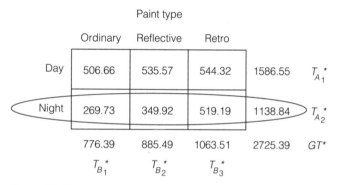

Figure 19.20

Since there were three items summed, this sum of squares has df = 2, so that

$$MS_{B \text{ at } A_2} = \frac{6674.42}{2} = 3337.21.$$

Dividing by the MS_{Within} from the overall analysis, we have

$$F = \frac{MS_{B \text{ at } A_2}}{MS_{\text{Within}}} = \frac{3337.21}{200.91} = 16.61.$$

With df = 2, 24, this is a significant value. We conclude that there are significant differences among the three paints at night. Naturally, since there are three paints involved, we need to follow up this test with a more specific comparison, which we turn to now.

As a last example, let's look at the simple comparison of the reflective and the retroreflective paints in the dark. The two points are shown in Figure 19.21. Following the procedure for a simple comparison that we developed for the equal-group-size case, and substituting the harmonic mean sample size, we have the formula

$$SS_{A \text{ comparison}} = \frac{\tilde{n}C^2}{\Sigma c_j^2},$$

where C is the value of a comparison among the set of means. Figure 19.22 is a table of means for this example; the comparison 0, 1, -1 will define the comparison of the two paints. We make the computation as

$$
\begin{aligned}
SS_{A \text{ comparison}} &= \frac{\tilde{n}C^2}{\Sigma c_j^2} \\
&= \frac{4.86[0(55.50) + (1)(72.00) + (-1)(106.83)]^2}{0^2 + (1)^2 + (-1)^2} \\
&= 2947.90.
\end{aligned}
$$

Since all comparison sums of squares have df = 1, the mean square for the comparison is also equal to 2947.90. The F for the comparison is computed in the usual way, dividing the mean square for the comparison by the SS_{Within} from the overall analysis:

$$
\begin{aligned}
F &= \frac{MS_{\text{Comparison}}}{MS_{\text{Within}}} \\
&= \frac{2947.90}{200.91} \\
&= 14.67.
\end{aligned}
$$

With df = 1, 24, this F is significant. We may conclude that the retroreflective paint is significantly more visible than the reflective paint in darkness.

By applying the examples just given, you should be able to completely analyze the results of any between-subjects factorial experiment. Table 19.11 summarizes the follow-up procedures described in this chapter.

Error Control in Factorial Designs

In Chapter 16 we discussed control of Type I and Type II errors extensively, and we won't review the arguments here. While they still hold, current practice in psychological research is to do little to deal with error rates in the factorial design (Keppel, 1982). Just why this should be the case is unclear, but the literature contains very few references to Scheffé or Tukey procedures in factorials. Of course, there's absolutely nothing wrong with applying post hoc tests in factorial designs. If they seem the best way to address research questions, and additionally offer a reasonable approach to managing a Type I error, then they can certainly be employed.

When adjustments are made, they're made on an FW basis, with the two main effects and the interaction as the families. When the interaction is not significant, it's easy to treat the two independent variables separately and control Type I error family-wise within each of the two "one-way" analyses that result. But it's unclear how best to proceed in following up a significant interaction. The active literature suggests ignoring the problem of the compounding Type I error.

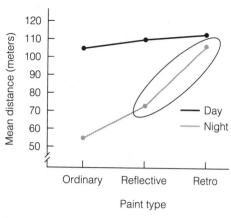

Mean distance (meters)

— Day
— Night

Paint type: Ordinary, Reflective, Retro

Figure 19.21

	Paint type			
	Ordinary	Reflective	Retro	
Day	104.25	110.20	112.00	108.82
Night	55.50	72.00	106.83	78.11
	79.88	91.10	109.42	93.46

Figure 19.22

Table 19.11   After the Overall Factorial Analysis

If the interaction IS NOT significant

Each independent variable is treated as a single-factor analysis of variance; the follow-up procedures are those presented in Chapter 16, but using MS_{Error} from the overall analysis as the error term. The value of n is the number of scores that are in the means being compared (the number of observations per group times the number of groups combined to compute the mean).

If the interaction IS significant

Simple-effects analyses are used to find the differences of one independent variable at each individual level of the other variable. These may be followed by simple comparisons within a single independent variable level.

If the interaction is disordinal (crossover), explore it first since conclusions about the main effects of the variables can be distorted by the interaction. In an ordinal interaction, the main effects are meaningful by themselves.

If you're uncomfortable with that, the reasonable approach is to decide on a basis for controlling error and apply Bonferroni adjustments within those limits. For example, in following up the drug example, we might decide to let the drug variable constitute one "family" and the combined age and interaction variables another. Suppose that we want to hold Type I error at about .05 for each of the three original hypothesis families (age, drug, and interaction). Combining age and interaction as a single family allows a .10 FW error rate (.05 each for the age and the interaction effects) for our simple-effects analyses. Now conduct the four simple-effect tests at a Bonferroni-adjusted PC rate of .10/4 = .025. We might then follow any significant simple effects with simple comparisons, using an uncorrected .05 level for each. If you're particularly concerned with Type I error, make a Tukey or even a Scheffé adjustment to the critical F value for the simple comparisons as illustrated in Chapter 16.

Presenting the Results of a Factorial Experiment

Presenting the results of a factorial experiment normally follows a standard outline. First, descriptive statistics are shown, usually as tables of mean and standard deviations. If the interaction is significant, the plot often appears, too. Then the overall analysis of variance summary table is shown, with accompanying verbal statements about the data. Finally, follow-up tests are presented, again with accompanying verbal materials. When the interaction isn't significant, follow-up results look very much like the results of one-way analyses and normally present pairwise tests on the main effect means. If the interaction is significant, simple-effects tests appear as standard summary tables. Pairwise simple-effect tests are normally described verbally: for example, "The mean of the middle-aged, placebo animals differed from that of the old, Drug B animals (Newman–Kuels test, $p < .05$), but there were no other significant differences."

SUMMARY

- When the interaction is not significant, the follow-up tests are conducted as if there were two separate analyses, one for each independent variable.
- When the interaction is significant, both simple effects and simple comparisons are used as follow-up tests.
- A simple-effect analysis is similar to a one-way analysis of variance that is conducted using a single level of one independent variable.
- Simple comparisons are just like follow-up analyses in a one-way design except that they deal with one row or one column of a factorial design.
- The computations for unequal group sizes are best done by computer following the *general linear model*; the unweighted-means procedure is often used for computational ease.

KEY TERMS

Simple comparison   Simple effect

EXERCISES

Solutions to asterisked (∗) exercises appear at the back of the book. Exercises preceded by a section symbol (§) must be solved using a computer. Exercises preceded by a dagger (†) can be solved by hand.

∗†1. Tonic immobility (TI), often called death-feigning, is a common response among some birds to threatening situations. In this hypothetical study, two different species of birds—chickens and quail—were subjected to one of four different stimulus conditions just before an experimental manipulation that typically induces TI. The stimuli were presented for 60 seconds, following which the experimenter grasped the bird firmly and held it on its side until it stopped struggling. At that point a timer was started and stopped when the bird regained its feet. The data give duration of TI (in seconds). The stimulus conditions were (1) silence (control condition), (2) sound of species-specific "distress call," (3) sound of species-specific feeding/contented call, (4) visual appearance of a stuffed hawk. Carry out the analysis, including appropriate follow-up tests.

Stimulus condition

Silence	Distress call	Comfort call	Hawk
CHICKENS			
30	55	20	50
26	65	32	43
39	33	28	65
31	49	18	39
28	59	25	52
QUAIL			
40	45	30	70
35	50	24	72
47	48	32	53
38	30	30	68
42	42	27	74

†2. Here are the (hypothetical) results of a study of kindergarten, second-grade, and fourth-grade boys and girls on a vocabulary test. The scores are assumed to be standardized; that is, each group is compared with a set of norms for children of their own ages. (Since children's vocabularies normally increase with age, using raw scores would result in a main effect solely because of that. Using standard scores eliminates that problem.) Conduct the analysis of variance, along with any appropriate follow-up procedures.

Kindergarten	Grade 2	Grade 4
BOYS		
60	63	55
55	68	64
66	72	48
56	58	57
62		

Kindergarten	Grade 2	Grade 4
GIRLS		
60	45	55
58	54	53
66	55	48
52	50	59
57		60

*†3. Use the 4×3 drug by age data and complete the analysis of the factorial the "other way." That is, compute the simple effects for the simple effects of drug at each age level. Be sure to check your computations by assuring that the sum of the SS for the simple effects of drug equals the total of the SS_{Drugs} and $SS_{Interaction}$ from the original analysis. (We illustrated the analysis for the old subjects on p. 427.)

†4. In the discussion of ordinal and disordinal interactions, we presented sets of means tables and plots (see Figures 19.7 and 19.8, p. 423). Plot each interaction the "other way," using young and old on the abscissa with male and female as lines in the figure.

*†5. For each of the interaction means tables and plots from Exercise 4, compute the simple-effects analysis for the effect of sex at each age level, assuming that there were five subjects in each group. (Use $\alpha = .05$, $MS_{Error} = 3.86$, and $df_{Error} = 16$.) Interpret the results verbally.

*†6. Using the data from the day/night by paint example, which of the following pairs of means are different (use $\alpha = .01$):
   a. Ordinary paint and reflective paint in daylight?
   b. Ordinary paint and retroreflective paint in daylight?
   c. Ordinary paint and reflective paint at night?
   d. Retroreflective paint in darkness and retroreflective paint in daylight?

*†7. Write a paragraph that summarizes the light/dark by paint study, making use of both the original analysis of the data and those in Exercise 6. Pay particular attention to recommendations that you might make concerning paint choice and driving safety.

Factorial Experimental Designs: Within Subjects (Principles and Analysis)

Apopular variant of the factorial design manipulates both of the independent variables within subjects. This leads to a two-factor design with a single group of subjects. This design is especially popular in perception and cognitive research. Indeed, the first example will be a more complete version of the iconic memory experiment that we introduced in Chapter 17.

The completely within-subjects factorial is a very powerful design since it controls subject variables by using the same subjects in all conditions of the experiment. Of course, this control comes at the expense of complicating the experiment by concern for order and carryover effects. In some cases it's impossible to use a completely within-subjects design because of carryover. But when the design is practical, it's very efficient since it can collect a great deal of data, often quickly, and with comparatively few subjects.

A X H G
O B+W K
V I M R

Figure 20.1

In case you've forgotten, Dr. Hass had his subjects recall letters that were flashed on a computer display screen. Subjects were asked to fixate a point that was in the center of the middle row of a briefly presented stimulus array like the one in Figure 20.1. The matrix of letters is flashed for a short time (200 msec). Then the subjects are asked to recall as many letters as they can from one of the three rows. The subject is told which row to recall by either a visual presentation of a number beside the row to be recalled or an auditory cue.

The experiment studied the properties of visual short-term (iconic) memory. One important question was whether short-term memory operates as a visual or as an auditory storage area. If it's visual, then recall should be better following a visual cue; if the storage is auditory, then recall should be best under the auditory cue. Using cue modality as one independent variable addresses this question. The factorial design also looks at the question of location within the stimulus array and the interaction of cue and location.

440

ANOVA for the Completely Within Factorial

The 11 subjects that Dr. Hass used were presented with a number of trials in each of the six experimental conditions in the completely within-subjects factorial design that is diagrammed in Figure 20.2. On each trial, the number of letters recalled correctly was recorded. The data were averaged across three different delay intervals and a number of trials for use in our example. The total recall data for the 11 subjects are listed in Table 20.1.

Row in the stimulus display

	Top	Middle	Bottom
Auditory			
Visual			

Cue modality

Figure 20.2

Table 20.1 Raw Data for Visual-Auditory Recall Experiment

Subject	Top	Middle	Bottom
AUDITORY CUE			
1	10.2	6.0	13.9
2	6.3	22.8	10.5
3	22.2	29.4	17.4
4	11.1	19.5	11.7
5	15.9	24.6	15.3
6	15.3	27.0	13.2
7	15.0	22.8	11.1
8	20.1	28.5	23.1
9	15.6	21.5	9.0
10	18.6	19.2	9.0
11	15.1	22.5	7.2
VISUAL CUE			
1	7.5	7.8	4.0
2	7.2	27.3	6.3
3	9.7	28.8	9.6
4	10.3	27.0	9.6
5	12.0	21.9	10.8
6	11.1	24.6	8.9
7	12.3	21.3	6.3
8	11.2	21.3	12.5
9	6.8	21.9	8.1
10	12.3	14.4	3.5
11	4.8	21.3	4.8

Table 20.2   Means for Data in Table 20.1

	Row in stimulus pattern			
	Top	Middle	Bottom	Across rows
Auditory cue	15.04	22.16	12.85	16.68
Visual cue	9.56	21.61	7.67	12.94
Across cues	12.30	21.88	10.26	14.81

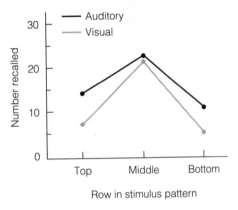

Figure 20.3

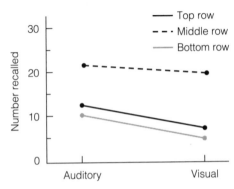

Figure 20.4

The means for the 11 subjects in the experiment serve as the starting point for our analysis; they are listed in Table 20.2. In Figure 20.3 the plots of the six condition means suggest an interaction. Figure 20.4 shows the same data plotted the "other way," with the cue conditions on the abscissa. Clearly, the middle row leads to the best overall recall, a finding that we noted in the analysis of these data in Chapter 17. But note that the effect of the cue mode seems different for the different positions, having no effect on the middle row, but a substantial effect in both the upper and the lower stimulus rows. In those two rows, the auditory cue leads to the better recall. It isn't clear in this descriptive analysis, of course, whether the interaction is significant and whether the auditory cue presentation is really superior to the visual in the top and bottom stimulus rows. To address those questions, we must develop the analysis of variance for the completely within-subjects design.

Computations for the Overall Analysis

The analysis of variance for the completely within-subjects factorial is very similar to that for the between-subjects design, so we'll omit much of the development of the sums of squares and move quickly to the computational formulas.

As in the single-factor experiment with repeated measures, the overall variation can be broken into two segments, between subjects and within subjects (Figure 20.5). Again, as in the single-factor experiment, all of the differences among all of the conditions in the experiment are within subjects; there is no between-subject independent variable. In Chapter 17, the next diagram in the

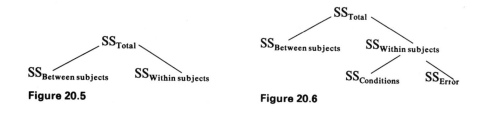

Figure 20.5

Figure 20.6

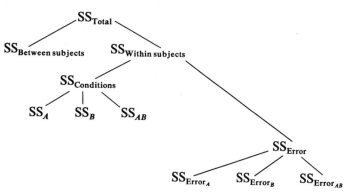

Figure 20.7

sequence (Figure 20.6) showed that the variation within subjects was broken into two parts, experimental conditions and error.

In the factorial design, the same breakdown can be done. But now, there are three different "conditions" and three different sources of "error," so the "conditions" and "error" variation is broken into two sets of three sources of variation (Figure 20.7). There are three sources of "between-conditions" variation—from the two independent variables and from their interaction. Each source has a unique "error term" associated with it.*

The computational formulas for the various sums of squares begin with the following:

Quantity	Computations
SS_{Total}	$\sum_i \sum_j \sum_k X_{ijk}^2 - \dfrac{GT^2}{abn}$
SS_A	$\dfrac{\sum_i T_{A_i}^2}{bn} - \dfrac{GT^2}{abn}$
SS_B	$\dfrac{\sum_j T_{B_j}^2}{an} - \dfrac{GT^2}{abn}$
SS_{AB}	$\dfrac{\sum_i \sum_j T_{ij}^2}{n} - \dfrac{\sum_i T_{A_i}^2}{bn} - \dfrac{\sum_j T_{B_j}^2}{an} + \dfrac{GT^2}{abn}$

---

*The "error term" for each source of between-conditions variation actually represents an interaction of subjects and that treatment; we won't explore that complication here.

Table 20.3   Sums and Summed Square Values for Data in Table 20.1

| | Stimulus row | | | |
	Top	Middle	Bottom	T_{A_i}
Auditory	165.40	243.80	141.40	550.60
cue	2693.02	5803.84	2022.10	
Visual	105.20	237.60	84.40	427.20
cue	1072.78	5497.38	732.70	
T_{B_j}	270.60	481.40	225.80	977.80 GT

These formulas need no introduction, since they're the same as they were in the completely between-subjects analysis; we'll illustrate them later.

These quantities may be calculated from the basic sums. Returning to the original data, Table 20.3 lists the sums and summed squared values in each experimental condition, along with the row, column, and grand totals. These values are all that are required to compute the sums of squares defined earlier.

For the total sum of squares, we have

$$SS_{Total} = \sum_i \sum_j \sum_k X_{ijk}{}^2 - \frac{GT^2}{abn}$$

$$= 2693.02 + 5803.84 + \cdots + 732.70 - \frac{977.80^2}{2 \times 3 \times 11}$$

$$= 17821.82 - 14486.26$$

$$= 3335.56.$$

Continuing with SS_A and SS_B, the values are

$$SS_A = \frac{\sum_i T_{A_i}{}^2}{bn} - \frac{GT^2}{abn}$$

$$= \frac{550.60^2 + 427.20^2}{3 \times 11} - \frac{977.80^2}{2 \times 3 \times 11}$$

$$= 14716.98 - 14486.26$$

$$= 230.72$$

and

$$SS_B = \frac{\sum_j T_{B_j}{}^2}{an} - \frac{GT^2}{abn}$$

$$= \frac{270.60^2 + 481.40^2 + 225.80^2}{2 \times 11} - \frac{977.80^2}{2 \times 3 \times 11}$$

$$= 16179.82 - 14486.26$$

$$= 1693.56.$$

Finally, for interaction,

$$SS_{AB} = \frac{\sum_i \sum_j T_{ij}^2}{n} - \frac{\sum_i T_{A_i}^2}{bn} - \frac{\sum_j T_{B_j}^2}{an} + \frac{GT^2}{abn}$$

$$= \frac{165.40^2 + \cdots + 84.40^2}{11} - \frac{550.60^2 + 427.20^2}{3 \times 11}$$

$$- \frac{270.60^2 + 481.40^2 + 225.40^2}{2 \times 11} + \frac{977.80^2}{2 \times 3 \times 11}$$

$$= 16493.98 - 14716.98 - 16179.82 + 14486.26$$

$$= 83.44.$$

In addition to the sums of squares listed, there are four new formulas—for SS_{Subjects} and for the three error terms. These formulas all require some new quantities and are based on different sums from those previously.

The formulas are

Quantity	Computations
SS_{Subjects}	$\dfrac{\sum_k T_{S_k}^2}{ab} - \dfrac{GT^2}{abn}$
SS_{Error_A}	$\dfrac{\sum_i \sum_k T_{A_i S_k}^2}{b} - \dfrac{\sum_i T_{A_i}^2}{bn} - \dfrac{\sum_k T_{S_k}^2}{ab} + \dfrac{GT^2}{abn}$
SS_{Error_B}	$\dfrac{\sum_j \sum_k T_{B_j S_k}^2}{a} - \dfrac{\sum_j T_{B_j}^2}{an} - \dfrac{\sum_k T_{S_k}^2}{ab} + \dfrac{GT^2}{abn}$
$SS_{\text{Error}_{AB}}$	$\sum_i \sum_j \sum_k X_{ijk}^2 + \dfrac{\sum_i T_{A_i}^2}{bn} + \dfrac{\sum_j T_{B_j}^2}{an} + \dfrac{\sum_k T_{S_k}^2}{ab} - \dfrac{\sum_i \sum_j T_{ij}^2}{n}$ $- \dfrac{\sum_i \sum_k T_{A_i S_k}^2}{b} - \dfrac{\sum_j \sum_k T_{B_j S_k}^2}{a} - \dfrac{GT^2}{abn}$

These formulas all involve various sums of scores for individual subjects. Figure 20.8 shows the sum of the scores for subject 1. Each subject appears in all six experimental conditions, and to find each subject's total, we sum six values, as shown in Figure 20.8. The symbol T_S will denote a subject's total across some set of conditions; an A or B subscript will be used when needed to indicate a sum of just A or B scores. The third subscript, in the expression X_{ijk}, denotes the subject, and so we'll call the subject sums, across all conditions, T_{S_k}. Thus the total for the first subject across all conditions, shown above, is T_{S_1}. The total for the second subject is 80.4, and so forth.

We'll also need the sum of scores for each subject in each of the A and B variable conditions (see Figure 20.9). The sum of the first subject's scores in the auditory condition would be symbolized $T_{A_1 S_1}$ as indicated, since it's a total (T), in the A_1 condition, and for subject 1 (S_1).

In a similar fashion, the sums for each subject in the B conditions (row of the stimulus display) are calculated as shown in Figure 20.9. For the eleven subjects

Auditory cue

Subject	Row 1	Row 2	Row 3	
1	10.20	6.00	13.90	
2	6.30	22.80	10.50	
3	22.20	29.40	17.40	
4	11.10	19.50	11.70	
.	.	.	.	
.	.	.	.	$T_{S_1} = 49.4$
.	.	.	.	
11	15.10	22.50	7.20	

Visual cue

Subject	Row 1	Row 2	Row 3
1	7.50	7.80	4.00
2	7.20	27.30	6.30
3	9.70	28.80	9.60
4	10.30	27.00	9.60
5	12.00	21.90	10.80

Figure 20.8

in the experiment the sums across all conditions (subject totals) and the sums in the two cue conditions and in the three display rows are listed in Table 20.4. With these subject totals, we can proceed with the computations for the remaining sum of squares. For the sum of squares between subjects:

$$
\begin{aligned}
SS_{\text{Subjects}} &= \frac{\sum\limits_{k} T_{S_k}^2}{ab} - \frac{GT^2}{abn} \\
&= \frac{49.4^2 + 80.4^2 + \cdots + 75.7^2}{2 \times 3} - \frac{977.8^2}{2 \times 3 \times 11} \\
&= 15121.68 - 14486.26 \\
&= 635.42.
\end{aligned}
$$

The remaining sums of squares, all error terms, are computed as

$$
\begin{aligned}
SS_{\text{Error}_A} &= \frac{\sum\limits_{i}\sum\limits_{k} T_{A_i S_k}^2}{b} - \frac{\sum\limits_{i} T_{A_i}^2}{bn} - \frac{\sum\limits_{k} T_{S_k}^2}{ab} + \frac{GT^2}{abn} \\
&= \frac{30.1^2 + 39.6^2 + \cdots + 30.9^2}{3} - \frac{550.60^2 + 427.20^2}{3 \times 11} \\
&\quad - \frac{49.4^2 + 80.4^2 + \cdots + 75.7^2}{2 \times 3} + \frac{977.8^2}{2 \times 3 \times 11} \\
&= 15482.88 - 14716.98 - 15121.68 + 14486.26 \\
&= 130.48
\end{aligned}
$$

20   Factorial Experimental Designs: Within Subjects

Auditory cue

Subject	Row 1	Row 2	Row 3
1	(10.20)	(6.00)	13.90
2	6.30	22.80	10.50
3	22.20	29.40	17.40
4	11.10	19.50	11.70

$T_{A_1 S_1} = 30.1$
= Sum of scores for Subject 1 in auditory (A_1) condition

Visual cue

Subject	Row 1	Row 2	Row 3
1	(7.50)	(7.80)	4.00
2	7.20	27.30	6.30
3	9.70	28.80	9.60
4	10.30	27.00	9.60
5	12.00	21.90	10.80

$T_{A_2 S_1} = 19.3$
= Sum of scores for Subject 1 in visual (A_2) condition

$T_{B_1 S_1} = 17.7$
= Sum of scores for Subject 1 in the top row (B_1)

$T_{B_2 S_1} = 13.8$
= Sum of scores for Subject 1 in the middle row (B_2)

Figure 20.9

Table 20.4 Sums

Subject	Subject totals under the two cue conditions		Subject totals for the three stimulus rows			Subject totals
	Visual $T_{A_1 S_k}$	Auditory $T_{A_2 S_k}$	Top $T_{B_1 S_k}$	Middle $T_{B_2 S_k}$	Bottom $T_{B_3 S_k}$	T_{S_k}
1	30.1	19.3	17.7	13.8	17.9	49.4
2	39.6	40.8	13.5	50.1	16.8	80.4
3	69.0	48.1	31.9	58.2	27.0	117.1
4	42.3	46.9	21.4	46.5	21.3	89.2
5	55.8	44.7	27.9	46.5	26.1	100.5
6	55.5	44.6	26.4	51.6	22.1	100.1
7	48.9	39.9	27.3	44.1	17.4	88.8
8	71.7	45.0	31.3	49.8	35.6	116.7
9	46.1	36.8	22.4	43.4	17.1	82.9
10	46.8	30.2	30.9	33.6	12.5	77.0
11	44.8	30.9	19.9	43.8	12.0	75.7

$$SS_{Error_B} = \frac{\sum_j \sum_k T_{B_j S_k}^2}{a} - \frac{\sum_i T_{B_j}^2}{an} - \frac{\sum_k T_{S_k}^2}{ab} + \frac{GT^2}{abn}$$

$$= \frac{17.7^2 + 13.5^2 + \cdots + 12.0^2}{2} - \frac{270.60^2 + 481.40^2 + 225.40^2}{2 \times 11}$$

$$- \frac{49.4^2 + 80.4^2 + \cdots + 75.7^2}{2 \times 3} + \frac{977.8^2}{2 \times 3 \times 11}$$

$$= 17286.17 - 16179.82 - 15121.68 + 14486.20$$

$$= 470.93$$

$$SS_{Error_{AB}} = \sum_i \sum_j \sum_k X_{ijk}^2 + \frac{\sum_i T_{A_i}^2}{bn} + \frac{\sum_j T_{B_j}^2}{an} + \frac{\sum_k T_{S_k}^2}{ab}$$

$$- \frac{\sum_i \sum_j T_{ij}^2}{n} - \frac{\sum_i \sum_k T_{A_i S_k}^2}{b} - \frac{\sum_j \sum_k T_{B_j S_k}^2}{a} - \frac{GT^2}{abn}$$

$$= 2693.02 + 5803.84 + \cdots + 732.70 + \frac{550.60^2 + 427.20^2}{3 \times 11}$$

$$+ \frac{17.1^2 + 13.5^2 + \cdots + 12.0^2}{2} + \frac{49.4^2 + 80.4^2 + \cdots + 75.7^2}{2 \times 3}$$

$$- \frac{165.40^2 + \cdots + 84.40^2}{11} - \frac{30.1^2 + 39.6^2 + \cdots + 30.9^2}{3}$$

$$- \frac{17.7^2 + 13.5^2 + \cdots + 12.0^2}{2} - \frac{977.8^2}{2 \times 3 \times 11}$$

$$= 17821.82 + 14716.98 + 16179.82 + 15121.68 - 16493.98$$

$$- 15482.88 - 17286.17 - 14486.26$$

$$= 91.01.$$

The degrees of freedom for the various sums of squares are:

SS_A	$a - 1$
SS_B	$b - 1$
SS_{AB}	$(a - 1)(b - 1)$
$SS_{Subjects}$	$n - 1$
SS_{Error_A}	$(a - 1)(n - 1)$
SS_{Error_B}	$(b - 1)(n - 1)$
$SS_{Error_{AB}}$	$(a - 1)(b - 1)(n - 1)$
SS_{Total}	$abn - 1$

The formulas are used to construct the summary table (Table 20.5).

As in the single-factor design, subject variability is removed as a separate component and the balance of the variability apportioned to other sources. The same three between-condition sources are here—the two main effects and their interaction—as in the between-subjects factorial. The major difference in this totally within-subjects analysis is an error term for each hypothesis. The three individual error terms are placed immediately under the effect that they are used

Table 20.5   Summary Table

Source	SS	df	MS	F	
Subjects	635.42	10	63.54		
Cue mode(A)	230.72	1	230.72	17.68	$p < .01$
Error(A)	130.48	10	13.05		
Stimulus row(B)	1693.56	2	846.78	35.96	$p < .01$
Error(B)	470.93	20	23.55		
Interaction	83.44	2	41.72	9.17	$p < .01$
Error(AB)	91.01	20	4.55		
Total	3335.56	65			

to test.* As noted earlier, these error terms reflect not only the overall error variance σ^2_e but also subject interaction with each treatment.

The F ratios for testing the three null hypotheses are formed by dividing the mean square for an effect (cue mode, stimulus row, or interaction) by its individual error mean square. In the previous presentations of the analysis of variance, we have presented the exact parameter expressions for each mean square. In this case, developing those expressions would lead us unnecessarily far afield. Nevertheless, the F's are formed so that the numerator and the denominator differ by only a null hypothesis term as they have previously, and so the ratios will tend to be close to 1.0 when there is no effect.[†]

In this experiment, all three effects are significant—there are differences in cue modality and in the position of the stimulus in the array of letters, and there is an interaction between position and cue modality. Look again at Figures 20.3 and 20.4 (p. 442); we can make some sense out of the results. First, it is clear that the greatest recall is from the middle row (the row where the fixation point is located); it's not clear whether the difference between the top and the bottom rows is significant, since they appear very similar. The interaction is ordinal with the auditory condition producing greater recall across all stimulus positions except perhaps the middle row, where the difference is probably not significant.

The main effect of the cue modality is significant as well, with the auditory cue showing a slight overall advantage. From the interaction plot, though, that advantage seems to hold only for the top and the bottom rows. Since the interaction is significant, the cue differences for the three rows seem worth some additional attention. We'll explore these differences more fully in the follow-up analyses.

---

*The df for the F for cue mode effect are thus 1, 10, while those for the row and interaction effects are 2, 20 each.

[†]You may encounter another way to conduct the analysis of variance for the completely within-subjects factorial. That method uses a single error term for the three hypothesis tests and is much simpler computationally. However, it assumes that no interaction occurs between subjects and experimental conditions. Since that assumption is unlikely to be met in psychology, we don't recommend that analysis. If you want to find out about it, Winer (1971) and Collyer and Enns (1986) present the computations.

Follow-up analysis for the two-factor, completely-within subjects is straight-forward and quite simple, since there's really nothing new to learn. The simple-effect analyses are conducted by extracting a single level of one independent variable and carrying out a one-way, within-subjects analysis of variance. Simple comparisons are done as if they were in a single-factor design. We'll illustrate both kinds of analysis by using the Hass data set.

Simple Effects. Let's begin by looking at the simple effects of stimulus row at each cue mode. For the auditory mode, this corresponds to a one-way analysis using just the means indicated in Figure 20.10. The analysis is accomplished easily by extracting just the *auditory* data from the full data set and submitting it to a single-factor, repeated-measures analysis. The data thus are those listed at the top of Table 20.1 (p. 441).

The analysis follows the procedures presented in Chapter 17, giving the summary table (Table 20.6). The results indicate a significant difference among the three rows for the auditory condition.

Continuing with the analysis, the simple effects of stimulus row for the *visual* cue condition, using the data from the bottom of Table 20.1, gives the summary table (Table 20.7). Again, the results indicate a significant difference among the three rows for the visual cues.

We could also conduct the simple-effect analysis of cue for each of the three rows; that is, the three tests indicated in Figure 20.11. Each analysis would be conducted as *t* tests between the visual and auditory conditions for each row; we'll leave that task to an exercise. For now, we'll move on to explore further the simple effects that we have just established through the use of simple comparisons.

Simple Comparisons. Simple comparisons following a significant simple effect are computed just as were comparisons in Chapter 17 following a significant one-way, within-subjects analysis. We'll illustrate only one simple comparison here.

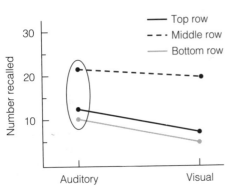

Figure 20.10

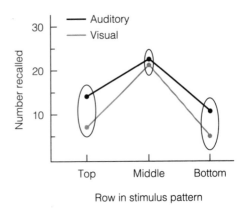

Figure 20.11

Table 20.6 Summary Table for Auditory Condition

Source	SS	df	MS	F	
Subjects	504.30	10	50.43		
Row	521.46	2	260.73	17.01	$p < .01$
Error	306.52	20	15.33		
Total	1332.28	32			

Table 20.7 Summary Table for Visual Condition

Source	SS	df	MS	F	
Subjects	261.60	10	26.16		
Row	1255.54	2	627.77	49.16	$p < .01$
Error	255.42	20	12.77		
Total	1772.56	32			

Table 20.8 Applying the Comparison to Visual Data

Stimulus row			
Top	Middle	Bottom	Comparison value
7.5	7.8	4.0	−4.1
7.2	27.3	6.3	−41.1
9.7	28.8	9.6	−38.3
10.3	27.0	9.6	−34.1
12.0	21.9	10.8	−21.0
11.1	24.6	8.9	−29.2
12.3	21.3	6.3	−24.0
11.2	21.3	12.5	−18.9
6.8	21.9	8.1	−28.9
12.3	14.4	3.5	−13.0
4.8	21.3	4.8	−33.0

We concluded earlier that there was a difference among the three stimulus rows for both the visual and the auditory cues. To illustrate a simple comparison following such a simple-effects analysis, let's look at the comparison of the middle row with the average of the top and the bottom rows in the visual condition. The coefficients for the comparison are 1, −2, 1 for top, middle, and bottom respectively. Using only the visual cue data, we apply the comparison to each subject's data individually (see Table 20.8). The comparison is tested by applying a single sample t test (of the null hypothesis that $\mu = 0$) to the comparison values. The mean comparison value is −25.96 and $\hat{s} = 11.14$, so that the standard error of the mean is

$$\hat{s}_{\bar{X}} = \frac{11.14}{\sqrt{11}} = 3.36$$

and thus

$$t = \frac{-25.96 - 0.0}{3.36}$$

$$= -7.73.$$

We reject the hypothesis that the mean recall from the top and bottom rows is equal to that from the middle row: $t(10) = -7.73$, $p = < .01$.

One additional analysis will clarify the situation in the visual data; do the top and the bottom rows themselves differ? The comparison coefficients are 1, 0, -1; using those values with the visual data and following our earlier computation, we conclude that there is no difference between the top and the bottom rows; $t(10) = 2.01$, $p > .05$. We may thus conclude that, in the visual cue condition, recall from the middle row leads to significantly better recall than does recall from either of the other two rows, and those rows don't differ from each other.

The Two-Factor Mixed Factorial Design

The final factorial design that we'll present is commonly called the *mixed design*, since it combines a between-subjects variable with a within-subjects variable. The mixed design is probably the most widely used experimental design in psychology. Our example will be Dr. Stewart's full experiment. He induced a conditioned aversion to saccharin in a group of animals and then allowed those animals and the control animals free access to four taste solutions for a 15-minute test period. The design combines a between-subjects independent variable (aversion conditioning) with a within-subjects variable (four tastes), and is diagrammed in Figure 20.12.

The key question in Dr. Stewart's research is whether or not the sweet taste of saccharin used in the aversion conditioning generalizes to sucrose and is an interaction question—does the consumption of sucrose differ between the conditioned and the control animals? Does it differ for the other tastes? If there is a main effect for conditioning and no interaction—aversion-trained animals

Taste presented

	Sucrose	Salt	HCl	Quinine
Yes				
No (Control)				

Aversion conditioning

Figure 20.12

drink either more or less of *all* solutions—then the conditioning has affected drinking and the sweet taste hasn't generalized. On the other hand, if there is no overall effect of aversion, but only a simple effect in the sucrose condition, then conditioning to saccharin is generalized.

The data for the experiment give the amount of solution consumed in the test period (see Table 20.9). The means and standard deviations are listed in Table 20.10. The interaction plot (Figure 20.13) shows clearly that the aversion-conditioned animals consume much less sucrose. They don't differ much from

Table 20.9   Raw Data for Taste Aversion Study

| | Test solution | | | Subject |
Sucrose	Salt	HCl	Quinine	Total
AVERSION				
2.5	24.0	7.0	7.0	40.5
2.0	23.0	14.0	14.0	53.0
5.0	11.0	9.0	10.0	35.0
1.0	12.0	12.0	11.0	36.0
7.0	21.5	9.0	8.5	46.0
4.0	30.0	9.0	5.0	48.0
4.0	24.5	12.0	4.5	45.0
5.0	17.0	10.0	11.0	43.0
1.0	16.0	9.0	9.0	35.0
9.0	18.0	11.0	10.0	48.0
CONTROL				
26.0	30.0	9.0	7.5	72.5
19.0	19.0	8.0	5.0	51.0
23.0	20.0	9.0	5.0	57.0
24.0	19.0	7.5	6.0	56.5
15.0	16.0	9.0	1.0	41.0
20.0	19.5	10.0	6.0	55.5
15.0	22.0	10.5	9.0	56.5
16.0	19.0	8.0	3.0	46.0
18.0	20.0	10.0	6.0	54.0
27.5	13.5	6.5	7.0	54.5

Table 20.10   Means and Standard Deviations for Taste Aversion Study

Condition		Sucrose	Salt	HCl	Quinine	Over tastes
Aversion	$\overline{X}$	4.05	19.70	10.20	9.00	10.74
	s.d.	2.59	5.97	2.04	2.90	
Control	$\overline{X}$	20.35	19.80	8.75	5.55	13.61
	s.d.	4.56	4.28	1.25	2.27	
Across conditions	$\overline{X}$	12.20	19.75	9.48	7.28	12.18

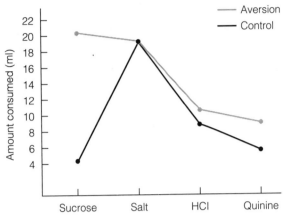

Figure 20.13

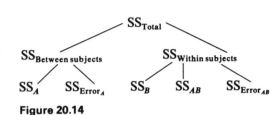

Figure 20.14

the control animals in the other three tastes, except perhaps for quinine. We'll use these data to illustrate the analysis of variance for the mixed design.

Analysis of Variance for the Two-Factor Mixed Design

In developing the notation and symbols for the mixed design, we'll let A indicate the between-subjects variable (aversion in the example). B will symbolize the within-subjects variable (taste substance). The overall variation (in terms of sums of squares, as usual) is partitioned first into between- and within-subject segments as in the other designs containing within-subjects variables. The between-subjects component contains the variation between the groups of subjects and error. Since one independent variable is between subjects (aversion conditioning, in the example), its effects must be a part of the between-subjects variation. The within-subject variation contains the effects of the repeated-measures variable (taste in the example), as well as the interaction and error. In short, the total variation is partitioned as shown in Figure 20.14.

There are thus five component sums of squares, plus SS_{Total}. In contrast to the completely within factorial, note that there is no $Error_B$ component in this analysis. The computational formulas for the analysis are:

Quantity	Computations
SS_{Total}	$\sum_i \sum_j \sum_k X_{ijk}^2 - \dfrac{GT^2}{abn}$
SS_A	$\dfrac{\sum_i T_{A_i}^2}{bn} - \dfrac{GT^2}{abn}$
SS_B	$\dfrac{\sum_j T_{B_j}^2}{an} - \dfrac{GT^2}{abn}$
SS_{AB}	$\dfrac{\sum_i \sum_j T_{ij}^2}{n} - \dfrac{\sum_i T_{A_i}^2}{bn} - \dfrac{\sum_j T_{B_j}^2}{an} + \dfrac{GT^2}{abn}$

		Sucrose	Salt	HCl	Quinine	T_{A_i}
Aversion conditioning	Yes	40.50 224.25	197.00 4201.50	102.00 1078.00	90.00 885.50	429.50
	No (Control)	203.50 4328.25	198.00 4085.50	87.50 779.75	55.50 354.25	544.50
	T_{B_j}	244.00	395.00	189.50	145.50	974.00

GT

Figure 20.15

Quantity	Computations
SS_{Error_A}	$\dfrac{\sum_k T_{S_k}^2}{b} - \dfrac{\sum_i T_{A_i}^2}{bn}$
$SS_{Error_{AB}}$	$\sum_i \sum_j \sum_k X_{ijk}^2 + \dfrac{\sum_i T_{A_i}^2}{bn} - \dfrac{\sum_i \sum_j T_{ij}^2}{n} - \dfrac{\sum_k T_{S_k}^2}{b}$

The first several terms are familiar and are calculated from the basic sums and sums of squared values. The sums for each condition, the marginal and grand totals, and the within-condition sums of squared values are shown in Figure 20.15.

The first sums of squares are

$$SS_{Total} = \sum_i \sum_j \sum_k X_{ijk}^2 - \frac{GT^2}{abn}$$

$$= 224.25 + 4201.50 + \cdots + 354.25 - \frac{974^2}{2 \times 4 \times 10}$$

$$= 15937.00 - 11858.45$$

$$= 4078.55$$

$$SS_A = \frac{\sum_i T_{A_i}^2}{bn} - \frac{GT^2}{abn}$$

$$= \frac{429.50^2 + 544.50^2}{4 \times 10} - \frac{974^2}{2 \times 4 \times 10}$$

$$= 12023.76 - 11858.45$$

$$= 165.31$$

$$SS_B = \frac{\sum_j T_{B_j}^2}{an} - \frac{GT^2}{abn}$$

$$= \frac{244.00^2 + 395.00^2 + 189.50^2 + 145.50^2}{2 \times 10} - \frac{974^2}{2 \times 4 \times 10}$$

The Two-Factor Mixed Factorial Design **455**

$$= 13632.08 - 11858.45$$
$$= 1773.63$$

$$SS_{AB} = \frac{\sum_i \sum_j T_{ij}^2}{n} - \frac{\sum_i T_{A_i}^2}{bn} - \frac{\sum_j T_{B_j}^2}{an} + \frac{GT^2}{abn}$$

$$= \frac{40.50^2 + 203.50^2 + \cdots + 55.50^2}{10} - \frac{429.50^2 + 544.50^2}{4 \times 10}$$

$$- \frac{244.00^2 + 395.00^2 + 189.50^2 + 145.50^2}{2 \times 10} + \frac{974^2}{2 \times 4 \times 10}$$

$$= 15030.60 - 12023.76 - 13632.08 + 11858.45$$
$$= 1233.21.$$

The next two sums of squares require the total for each individual subject (T_{S_k}). Those values appear in Table 20.9 and the computation is completed as

$$SS_{Error_A} = \frac{\sum_k T_{S_k}^2}{b} - \frac{\sum_i T_{A_i}^2}{bn}$$

$$= \frac{40.5^2 + 53.0^2 + \cdots + 54.5^2}{4} - \frac{429.50^2 + 544.50^2}{4 \times 10}$$

$$= 12261.88 - 12023.76$$
$$= 238.12$$

$$SS_{Error_{AB}} = \sum_i \sum_j \sum_k X_{ijk}^2 + \frac{\sum_i T_{A_i}^2}{bn} - \frac{\sum_i \sum_j T_{ij}^2}{n} - \frac{\sum_k T_{S_k}^2}{b}$$

$$= 224.25 + 4201.50 + \cdots + 354.25 + \frac{429.50^2 + 544.50^2}{4 \times 10}$$

$$- \frac{40.50^2 + 203.50^2 + \cdots + 55.50^2}{10} - \frac{40.5^2 + 53.0^2 + \cdots + 54.5^2}{4}$$

$$= 15937.00 + 12023.76 - 15030.60 - 12261.88$$
$$= 668.28.$$

The degrees of freedom for the sums of squares are

SS_{Total}	$abn - 1$
SS_A	$a - 1$
SS_B	$b - 1$
SS_{AB}	$(a - 1)(b - 1)$
SS_{Error_A}	$a(n - 1)$
$SS_{Error_{AB}}$	$a(b - 1)(n - 1)$

With these values, we complete the summary table (Table 20.11). There are three F ratios, one for each independent variable and one for the interaction. All three null hypotheses are rejected, and we conclude that the aversion conditioning has an effect, that the taste substances differ in amount consumed, and that conditioned taste aversion and taste solution interact.

Table 20.11   Summary Table

Source	SS	df	MS	F	
Conditioning (A)	165.31	1	165.31	12.50	$p < .01$
Error (A)	238.12	18	13.23		
Taste (B)	1773.62	3	591.21	47.76	$p < .01$
Interaction (AB)	1233.21	3	411.07	33.20	$p < .01$
Error (AB)	668.28	54	12.38		
Total	4078.54	79			

There are two different "error terms" in Table 20.11. Recall that the total variation in the data was partitioned first into between- and within-subjects segments. Each of those was then partitioned, and there was an error component between subjects and another within subjects. The between-subjects error term is used to test the between-subjects variable (aversion conditioning, which we symbolized as A). The within-subjects error term is used to test both the within-subjects variable (taste—B) and the interaction. The summary table is arranged so that the between- and the within-subjects components are together. That arrangement makes determining degrees of freedom easy; the F ratio for conditioning has df = 1, 18, while the F's for taste and for interaction have df = 3, 54.

To complete the analysis of Dr. Stewart's experiment, we need to be able to carry out follow-up analyses. Of particular interest will be the simple effects of aversion conditioning for each taste solution; if the sweet taste generalizes, there should be a difference in sucrose consumption.

Follow-Up Procedures for the Mixed Factorial

The follow-up techniques for the mixed design again are of two familiar varieties—those that explore the main effects of the independent variables and those that explore the interaction. The former look at marginal means and are especially useful if the interaction is not significant. The other set of follow-up tests are the simple effects and simple comparisons that are used to look in detail at the interaction. The procedures differ depending upon which variable we're looking at. Thus to look at the effect of taste (the within-subjects variable), we would follow a different procedure from that used in investigating the effect of conditioning (the between-subjects variable).

Main Effect Comparisons. If the interaction is not significant, the analysis looks at the two independent variables separately. Or if the interaction is ordinal, post hoc analyses of the independent variables by themselves may be helpful. We consider the between- and the within-subjects variables individually.

Between-subjects main effect comparisons. For the between-subjects variable, comparisons are defined as they were in Chapter 16, the mean square for a comparison is computed, and the between-subjects error term is used to test for the significance. In short, the analysis proceeds much like the follow-up to any between-subjects analysis.

The Two-Factor Mixed Factorial Design

Table 20.12   Means for Taste Aversion Study, Comparison over Tastes

Condition		Sucrose	Salt	HCl	Quinine	Over tastes
Aversion	$\overline{X}$	4.05	19.70	10.20	9.00	10.74
	s.d.	2.59	5.97	2.04	2.90	
Control	$\overline{X}$	20.35	19.80	8.75	5.55	13.61
	s.d.	4.56	4.28	1.25	2.27	
Across conditions	$\overline{X}$	12.20	19.75	9.48	7.28	12.18

To illustrate, suppose that we wanted to test the main effect comparison of "conditioned versus control." That is, we want to compare the marginal means listed in Table 20.12. The coefficients to be applied to the conditioned and the control means are 1 and −1. (Note that this is a redundant comparison, since there are only two levels of the between-subjects variable; this result should duplicate the analysis of variance for the main effect of condition. We conduct the analysis only for illustration purposes.)

The formula for the sum of squares for a comparison (from Chapter 16) is

$$SS_{A \text{ comparison}} = \frac{nC^2}{\Sigma c_j^2}.$$

A marginal mean in a factorial design is based on the number of observations in a cell multiplied by the number of levels of the variable averaged across. There are n observations in each condition in the design, and there are b sets of them, so we rewrite the formula as

$$SS_{A \text{ comparison}} = \frac{bnC^2}{\Sigma c_j^2}.$$

For Dr. Stewart's data, the two main effect means are 10.74 (aversion) and 13.61 (control). Each mean is based on four taste conditions with 10 observations in each. The sum of squares for the comparison is computed as

$$
\begin{aligned}
SS_{A \text{ comparison}} &= \frac{bnC^2}{\Sigma c_j^2} \\
&= \frac{4 \times 10 \times ((1) \times 10.74 + (-1) \times 13.61)^2}{1^2 + (-1)^2} \\
&= 164.74.
\end{aligned}
$$

Since this sum of squares has df = 1, its mean square is equal to the sum of squares. The "error term" is the between-subjects error from the summary tables, and so the F for the comparison is

$$F = \frac{MS_{A \text{ comparison}}}{MS_{\text{Error}_A}} = \frac{164.74}{13.23} = 12.45.$$

With df = 1, 18, this F ratio is significant. Note that, within rounding, this value is precisely the value obtained in the full analysis for the effect of conditioning,

Table 20.13 Table of Means, Comparison Across Conditions

Condition		Sucrose	Salt	HCl	Quinine	Over tastes
Aversion	$\overline{X}$	4.05	19.70	10.20	9.00	10.74
	s.d.	2.59	5.97	2.04	2.90	
Control	$\overline{X}$	20.35	19.80	8.75	5.55	13.61
	s.d.	4.56	4.28	1.25	2.27	
Across conditions	$\overline{X}$	(12.20)	(19.75)	9.48	(7.28)	12.18

This compared with the mean of these

illustrating that the overall F is a test of the hypothesis of no effect of the aversion conditioning.

Within-subjects main effect comparisons. Comparisons among the marginal means of the within-subjects variable are most easily done by ignoring the between subjects variable and treating the data as if it were from a one-way experiment. The analysis is then just like a comparison in Chapter 17. Comparison coefficients are applied to raw data, and the resulting values used in a single sample Student's t test of the hypothesis that $\mu = 0$. As an example, let's compare the overall mean sucrose consumption with the mean consumption of salt and quinine; the mean values are listed in Table 20.13. The comparison coefficients are 2, -1, 0, -1. The raw data for the experiment and the comparison values are given in Table 20.14. The mean comparison is -2.62 and $\hat{s} = 20.15$. Applying a single-sample Student's t, we have

$$\hat{s}_{\overline{X}} = \frac{20.15}{\sqrt{20}} = 4.51$$

so that

$$t = \frac{-2.62 - 0.0}{4.51}$$

$$= -0.58.$$

This value leads to the conclusion that the consumption of saccharin does not differ from the average of salt and quinine: $t(19) = 0.583, p > .05$.

Simple Effects and Simple Comparisons. Simple-effects analyses and their follow-up simple comparisons take two different forms depending upon whether we're dealing with the repeated or the between-subjects variable. In both cases, the analysis reduces to a familiar procedure.

Effects of the repeated variable. The simple effect of the repeated factor is analyzed by extracting a single level of the between-subjects variable and conducting a standard repeated-measures analysis on those data. As an example, consider the effect of taste solution for the control condition. The analysis asks whether the means circled in Table 20.15 are significantly different.

Table 20.14 Raw Data and Comparison Values for Taste Aversion

Sucrose	Salt	HCl	Quinine	Comparison
AVERSION-CONDITIONED				
2.5	24.0	7.0	7.0	−26.0
2.0	23.0	14.0	14.0	−33.0
5.0	11.0	9.0	10.0	−11.0
1.0	12.0	12.0	11.0	−21.0
7.0	21.5	9.0	8.5	−16.0
4.0	30.0	9.0	5.0	−27.0
4.0	24.5	12.0	4.5	−21.0
5.0	17.0	10.0	11.0	−18.0
1.0	16.0	9.0	9.0	−23.0
9.0	18.0	11.0	10.0	−10.0
CONTROL				
26.0	30.0	9.0	7.5	14.5
19.0	19.0	8.0	5.0	14.0
23.0	20.0	9.0	5.0	21.0
24.0	19.0	7.5	6.0	23.0
15.0	16.0	9.0	1.0	13.0
20.0	19.5	10.0	6.0	14.5
15.0	22.0	10.5	9.0	−1.0
16.0	19.0	8.0	3.0	10.0
18.0	20.0	10.0	6.0	10.0
27.5	13.5	6.5	7.0	34.5

Table 20.15 Table of Means, Effect of Repeated Variable

Condition		Sucrose	Salt	HCl	Quinine	Over tastes
Aversion	$\overline{X}$	4.05	19.70	10.20	9.00	10.74
Control	$\overline{X}$	20.35	19.80	8.75	5.55	13.61
Across conditions	$\overline{X}$	12.20	19.75	9.48	7.28	12.18

Using only the data from the control subjects in a single-factor analysis of variance for a within-subjects design, and following the computations given in Chapter 17, the summary table (Table 20.16) shows a significant effect for the tastes. We thus conclude that, among the control subjects, there are significant differences in the amounts of the two taste substances consumed. A follow-up analysis for this simple effect would be conducted by following the procedures in Chapter 17.

We can illustrate a follow-up analysis by calculating the simple comparison of sucrose versus salt, using the control subjects. The coefficients for the comparison are 1, −1, 0, 0. When these coefficients are applied to each control subject's data, the results show no difference between the consumption of sucrose

Table 20.16   Summary Table

Source	SS	df	MS	F	
Subjects	151.56	9	16.84		
Taste	1723.27	3	74.42	59.44	$p < .01$
Error	260.92	27	9.66		
Total	2135.74	39			

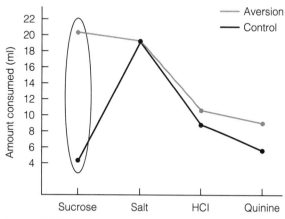

Figure 20.16

and salt for the control animals; $t(9) = 0.298$, $p > .05$. We could continue to define other simple comparisons within the control condition; all would be follow-up analyses to the simple effect of taste for the control subjects.

To complete the analysis, we might look at the simple effect of taste for the aversion-conditioned subjects, and, if that analysis shows significance, follow it with simple comparisons within that subject group. We'll leave those analyses as exercises.

Effects of the nonrepeated variable. As you might expect, the simple effect of a between-subjects variable is computed by selecting a level of the within-subjects variable and performing a between-subjects one-way analysis on the data. In Dr. Stewart's data, for example, we might ask about the effects of the aversion conditioning on sucrose ingestion. The means of interest are plotted in Figure 20.16. For Dr. Stewart's experiment, of course, this is the crucial question; is the reduction in sucrose consumption by the aversion-conditioned animals significant?

We conduct the analysis by extracting the sucrose-consumption data for the control and the conditioned subjects and entering those values into a one-way analysis. If we do that, we obtain the summary table (Table 20.17). Clearly, the difference is significant, and we may conclude that the aversion conditioning has reduced the consumption of sucrose. We may infer, then, that the sweet taste of the saccharin used in the aversion trial has generalized to sucrose.

Table 20.17   Summary Table

Source	SS	df	MS	F	
Condition	1328.45	1	1328.45	97.00	$p < .001$
Error	247.25	18	13.74		
Total	1575.70	19			

Since the between-subjects variable in Dr. Stewart's design has only two levels, the simple-effect analysis that we just did could as easily have been a two-group t test. If we had done that, the obtained t would have been 9.85, with df = 18.*

Simple comparisons following the simple-effect analysis are carried out just as if you were conducting a one-way analysis between subjects; since those comparisons were illustrated extensively in Chapter 16, we don't need to repeat them here.

Randomized-Blocks Designs

In Chapter 4 we introduced various procedures for controlling extraneous variables. One very useful technique is the repeated use of subjects, and we have followed the use of within-subject manipulation through this chapter's presentation of within-subjects and mixed-design analysis of variance.

Instead of using repeated measures, we often match subjects on an external variable. That is, we might pretest children on an IQ test and select groups who are very similar in intelligence. The matched set of children in each group would then be randomly assigned to experimental conditions. This assures a balance with regard to IQ score and controls it as an extraneous variable. The same logic holds for a large number of potentially confounding variables—they can be measured and used in matching.

Let's take a numerical example with a matching control. Suppose that we're interested in the number of words recalled after five presentations of a list of 25 words. The raw data in Table 20.18 are for a hypothetical experiment with three groups of 18 elementary school children. Each group learned a single list, and the number of words recalled correctly after five presentations are listed. The means indicate that there may be a difference among the three word lists, but an analysis of variance summary table for this three-group, between-subjects experiment indicates otherwise (see Table 20.19).

The group standard deviations suggest that there may be considerable variability in the data. There could be an extraneous variable at work here; and there is. Suppose that, prior to the experiment, we had divided the 54 students into three groups according to their reading ability and then assigned the

---

*This is the case because

$$\sqrt{F(1, \text{df})} = t(\text{df}).$$

That is, the square root of an F with df = 1, df equals t with the same df.

Table 20.18 Raw Data for Hypothetical Experiment

	Word list		
	A	B	C
	7	4	2
	8	5	4
	10	7	5
	10	7	6
	17	8	10
	18	5	10
	5	6	1
	6	6	3
	6	7	4
	6	9	4
	8	12	8
	8	12	9
	8	13	9
	9	14	11
	13	15	11
	13	17	13
	14	18	13
	16	22	15
Mean	10.11	10.39	7.67
Std. Dev.	4.07	5.21	4.17

Table 20.19 Summary Table

Source	SS	df	MS	F	
List	80.78	2	40.39	1.98	$p > .05$
Error	1040.06	51	20.39		
Total	1120.84	53			

members of each ability group randomly (and equally) among the three word lists. In other words, we used a reading ability test to match the students roughly. Now we have the experimental design shown in Figure 20.17. This design is easy to recognize—it's just a 3 × 3 between-subjects factorial. One of the variables is the word list, and the other is reading ability. The primary interest in the experiment is presumably the differences among the lists of words. And reading ability may be an extraneous variable that is being included in the design primarily as a control measure.

Table 20.20 gives the data from the first analysis, subdivided into ability groups. The overall means for the three word lists don't change since the recall scores don't change. Note that there also appears to be an effect due to reading ability, which shouldn't be surprising considering the nature of the experimental task.

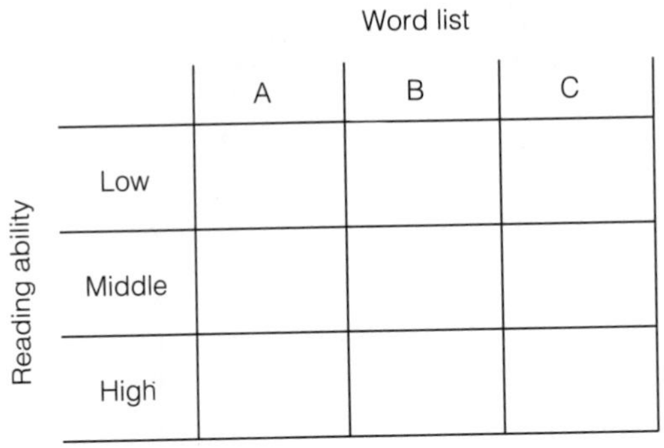

Word list

	A	B	C
Low			
Middle			
High			

Reading ability

Figure 20.17

Table 20.20 Data from Table 20.21, Subdivided into Ability Groups

	Word list			Ability group mean
	A	B	C	
LOW ABILITY				
	7	4	2	
	8	5	4	
	10	7	5	7.94
	10	7	6	
	17	8	10	
	18	5	10	
MEDIUM ABILITY				
	5	6	1	
	6	6	3	
	6	7	4	6.67
	6	9	4	
	8	12	8	
	8	12	9	
HIGH ABILITY				
	8	13	9	
	9	14	11	
	13	15	11	13.56
	13	17	13	
	14	18	13	
	16	22	15	
Means	10.11	10.39	7.67	

Table 20.21   Summary Table

Source	SS	df	MS	F	
List	80.78	2	40.39	4.66	$p < .05$
Reading ability	483.44	2	241.72	27.88	$p < .001$
Interaction	166.44	4	41.61	4.80	$p < .01$
Error	390.17	45	8.67		
Total	1120.83	53			

Table 20.22   Comparison of Analyses

Source	SS	df	MS
FIRST (ONE-WAY) ANALYSIS			
List	80.78	2	40.39
Error	1040.06	51	20.39
Total	1120.84	53	
SECOND (FACTORIAL) ANALYSIS			
List	80.78	2	40.39
Ability	483.44	2	241.72
Interaction	166.44	4	41.61
Error	390.17	45	8.67
Total	1120.83	53	

$$1040.06 = 483.44 + 166.44 + 390.06$$

The analysis of variance summary table for the 3×3 design is interesting and illuminates the ability of the analysis to separate variance into components (Table 20.21). First note that the sums of squares for the word lists and SS_{Total} are identical (when rounded off) to the first analysis. That means that the total variation in the set of data hasn't changed (obviously—because the data haven't changed!), and neither has the portion of the variability due to the differences among the word lists.

But now the word list variable is significant. In the first analysis, there was no difference, but in this analysis the lists are significantly different even though their means are unchanged. What can account for the apparent contradiction? The change is that the error variation is reduced in the second analysis. And how can it be reduced? It's reduced because we have identified two additional sources on variation—reading ability and the interaction of ability and word list. That variation was there in the first analysis, but it couldn't be accounted for separately and thus went into the error variation. To see that the same amount of variability is present in both analyses, note in Table 20.22 that the SS_{Within} (error) in the first analysis is equal to the combined sums of squares for ability, interaction, and error in the second analysis:

In the latter analysis, where the reading ability levels were identified as a second independent variable, its contribution to the overall variation could be identified. The analysis of variance then partitioned the error variation into two other segments—ability and interaction—and reduced the error component. That smaller "error term" allowed the effect of the differences in word lists to be seen. We won't pursue this example any further analytically here; it will appear as an exercise.

The Design

What we just illustrated is a very common experimental design, often called the *randomized-blocks* design. In this design, one of the independent variables is used to match subjects. Sometimes the matching variable is of interest in and of itself, but often it is simply introduced as a control factor in the experiment. In the example, the blocking variable isn't particularly interesting; differences due to reading ability shouldn't be surprising in the learning task.

Building an extraneous variable into the experimental design is a powerful technique for control and error reduction. The example illustrates the effect that an uncontrolled variable can have* and also shows how it becomes a part of the error variation unless it can be identified and removed as a part of the analysis.

The Analysis

If we control extraneous variables by using a within-subjects design, then the computations for analysis of variance change. However, if we use a randomized-blocks design, the analysis simply adds a between-subjects factor to an existing design. If we start with a single-factor, between-subjects design (like our example), then the randomized-blocks design becomes a two-factor between-subjects experiment. The analysis proceeds exactly as it would in an ordinary two-factor experiment.

We could have begun with a single-factor within-subjects experiment (if, for example, we had asked each subject to learn all three lists). In this case, adding the blocking variable of reading ability would have produced a mixed design, with reading ability the between-subjects factor and the lists the within-subjects factor. In this case, the analysis would proceed using the computations for the mixed factorial design.

In either case, there are no new analysis techniques to illustrate. The existing analyses for factorial designs are simply applied in this new experimental context. In a situation where a nonparametric test seems appropriate, the Friedman test for matched groups can be used for the randomized-blocks design.

Nonparametric Procedures and Factorial Designs

At this point in this chapter, you would expect to find a presentation of the nonparametric alternatives to the analyses discussed earlier. Except for the Friedman test in the randomized-blocks design, there are no commonly used

---

* You realize, of course, that these data were invented specifically to show the effect; you can't count on a randomized-blocks design producing significance where there might otherwise be none!

nonparametric analogues to factorial analysis of variance. If you find yourself in a situation where your data seem to violate the assumptions of analysis of variance, you have two options. First, you can separate the design into its single-variable components and apply the distribution-free procedures from Chapters 14 and 17. This approach deals only with the main effects in the design, and analyzing the interaction is difficult. If the interaction is important, nonparametric tests can be used as if they were follow-up tests. In Dr. Stewart's analysis, for example, he might choose to look at the effects of aversion condition for each taste by using four Wilcoxon two-sample tests. Each test would be equivalent to a simple effect follow-up to the analysis of variance, but without the omnibus test first. Since the tests wouldn't be independent of each other, a Bonferroni adjustment to the probabilities would probably be appropriate.

This leads us to the second alternative—ignore the problem and use the analysis of variance anyway. While this seems a silly suggestion, it has been a popular one for some years. You'll encounter situations in the literature where a nonparametric test might well have been used but wasn't. This was the case because the analysis of variance was believed to be a very robust statistical technique, meaning that it's quite insensitive to violations in its assumptions (at least in certain cases). That may change in the future. Milligan, Wong, and Thompson (1987) present evidence that, under some conditions of unequal group size coupled with unequal variances and/or non-normal distributions, neither the weighted- nor unweighted-means procedure is satisfactory. In addition, Wilcox (1987) recommends that nonparametric tests and other alternatives to the traditional analysis of variance be used almost routinely in some cases.

Relationship of the Factorial to Other Designs

The factorial is a combination of two single independent variable designs. Each independent variable in the factorial brings with it all of the considerations of control and manipulation from single-factor experiments, as well as the concept of between- and within-subjects manipulation of the variables. Each of the independent variables in the design retains its own character in the factorial and can be analyzed separately to yield the same information that could be derived from two separate single-factor experiments.

But the factorial brings interaction into research design; that increases the power of the design a great deal and allows us to study the way variables can combine to produce effects that can't be seen in single-variable experiments. This ability to study variables jointly is the feature that makes the factorial the most widely used of all experimental designs.

Detailed analysis of the interaction, though, reduced the design to a series of tests on single factors. And to fully understand an interaction, we usually made comparisons between two separate treatment conditions—the basic two-condition design in yet another guise. While the factorial provides an overall view of the interaction of two variables, the real support for research conclusions often lies in the two-condition tests that characterize simple comparisons. Thus while it's interesting to know that aversion conditioning affects consumption of various taste substances, we must look to the simple comparisons to really understand the nature of the relationship. Of particular importance are the comparisons between the two groups of animals for each taste.

If we can combine two single-factor experiments into a factorial design, can we add yet another variable? Certainly, and then we have a factorial design with three (or more) variables. We've already met one such design in passing—Dr. Hass's experiment actually has three factors—row in the display, cue modality, and delay (the cue was presented either with the display, 200 msec later, or 500 msec later). Our analysis collapsed the design into two factors by summing across the delay variable.

A multifactor design offers a great deal of flexibility and power. Each variable can be manipulated either between- or within-subjects, leading to a wide variety of combinations. The Hass experiment, for example, is a totally within-subjects design, but there can be designs with only one within-subjects variable (trials in a learning experiment, for example), or two within-subjects variables, or no within-subjects variables at all.

In addition to the various combinations of between- and within-subjects designs, the higher-order factorial gives the experimenter the ability to look at each variable individually ("What is the effect of delay interval on recall?" for example), at three two-factor interactions ("Does delay interact with cue mode?" "Does cue mode interact with row in the display?" "Does delay interact with row in the display?"), and also a three-factor interaction ("Does the form of the mode by row interaction change with the three different display intervals?").

If three variables make a good design, are four better? If four are better, might five be better still? Or perhaps six? Among the advantages that we cited earlier for factorials was the ability to investigate the way that two variables interact to influence behavior. Surely that same advantage can be generalized to higher-order designs, can't it?

To a limited extent, it's true that the more variables we use, the better we can explore their interrelations. But that ability comes at a price in terms of the complexity of the design. Quite apart from computations, the more variables in an experiment, the more complex is the task of both running the experiment and understanding its results.

With a multifactor design, the sheer logistics of the research are often burdensome. There are many stimulus conditions to prepare, counterbalancing becomes very complex with repeated measures designs, there may be many different groups of subjects, and the recordkeeping and data collection can be burdensome. But the most serious problem with complex factorials is interpreting the results.

We suggested previously how to expand the Hass experiment to three factors. Imagine what would happen if we were to add a fourth variable, age, for example. Now we would have the possibility of the *triple* interaction of delay, recall mode, and row of the display changing as a function of whether the subject is a child or an adult. If we had trouble understanding and verbalizing a three-factor interaction, a significant four-factor interaction will be even worse. Unless there is some theoretically important reason to investigate the four-way interaction, it's best to keep a design to fewer than four variables.

- For the completely within-subjects factorial, the analysis of variance partitions the variability into seven components. Between-subjects variability is one; the other six components all represent partitions of the within-subjects variation—three are due to the effects (one for each independent variable plus interaction) and three are for error (a separate error term for each independent variable plus one interaction).
- The follow-up analysis for the completely within-factorial design is done by extracting a single row or column and proceeding as if it were a one-way, within-subjects design.
- A mixed factorial design has one variable that is manipulated between subjects and another that is manipulated within subjects.
- In a mixed design, the between-subjects variation is partitioned into a component for the between-subjects variable and for its error. The within-subjects component is partitioned into components due to the repeated-measures variable, the interaction, and an error term.
- The follow-up procedures for a mixed design differ depending upon whether we're studying the effect of the between-subjects or the within-subjects variable.
- A randomized-blocks design is a factorial where one variable represents an extraneous variable that was controlled by matching.

K E Y   T E R M S

Mixed factorial design   Within-subjects factorial design
Randomized-blocks design

E X E R C I S E S

Solutions to asterisked (∗) exercises appear at the back of the book. Exercises preceded by a section symbol (§) must be solved using a computer. Exercises preceded by a dagger (†) can be solved by hand.

∗†1. Using the Hass visual cue data, conduct the following simple comparisons.
   a. The top row versus the middle row.
   b. The bottom row versus the middle row.

†2. Calculate the simple effects of cue type for the three stimulus rows using Hass's data. Describe the results verbally.

∗3. This exercise comes from a study by cognitive psychologist Tim Hubbard. Hubbard presented subjects with a moving circle on a computer screen. The circle moved in one of four directions, (left-to-right [LR], right-to-left [RL], top-to-bottom [TB], or bottom-to-top [BT], and at one of three speeds (slow, medium, and fast). At some point in its travel across the screen, the circle vanished. The subject's task was to position a pointer where the center of the circle was last seen. The following data give the distance (in inches) between the actual disappearing point and *the one indicated by the subject*. A positive value indicates that the subject overestimated where the circle was (indicated a point farther along its path than it actually was), while a negative value means an underestimate. Carry out the overall analysis of variance.

Left-Right			Right-Left		
Slow	Med.	Fast	Slow	Med.	Fast
.25	.37	.60	.15	.29	.51
.25	.41	.55	.28	.45	.57
−.01	.00	.10	.15	.33	.44
.13	.23	.18	.12	.13	.16
.20	.34	.42	.28	.49	.82
.23	.23	.39	.35	.36	.55
.18	.29	.32	.16	.23	.32
.15	.32	.24	.26	.56	.57
.07	.09	.06	.10	.17	.09
.14	.18	.38	.16	.28	.38
.27	.34	.53	.37	.47	.62
.17	.21	.32	.34	.39	.64
.20	.42	.61	.32	.61	.87
.21	.43	.53	.32	.45	.73
.29	.43	.51	.28	.45	.65

Top-Bottom			Bottom-Top		
Slow	Med.	Fast	Slow	Med.	Fast
.18	.44	.52	.05	.15	.15
.17	.52	.41	.02	.13	.07
.14	.16	.34	−.15	−.13	.06
.07	.12	.18	−.05	−.02	−.03
.14	.23	.34	.11	.25	.27
.26	.32	.41	−.01	−.10	−.11
.06	.13	.24	.01	−.01	.11
.24	.11	.40	.11	.21	.21
.05	.08	.04	.05	.04	.17
.07	.24	.41	−.10	.03	.15
.21	.33	.45	−.05	.16	.25
.15	.30	.39	.12	.14	.27
.24	.39	.63	−.02	.22	.21
.26	.42	.48	−.08	.27	.27
.03	−.04	.13	.22	.46	.53

†4. Plot the interaction of the speed and direction variables from the Hubbard data.

*†5. Find the simple effects of the interaction in the Hubbard data.

†6. In the illustration in the chapter, we computed the simple effects of taste for Dr. Stewart's control subjects. Using Dr. Stewart's data, conduct the following analyses:

　*a. Carry out the simple-effects analysis of tastes for the *aversion-conditioned* subjects.

　*b. Follow up the simple-effects analysis with a set of simple comparisons among the taste conditions.

Pay special attention to the sucrose-salt, and the sucrose-quinine comparisons.

§c. In the text, the simple comparison of sucrose-salt was not significant for the control animals. Compare that result with your analysis from part (b). What do you conclude?

†7. In a study of meaningfulness of nonsense syllables, three groups of subjects were given different syllable lists to learn to a criterion of two perfect recall trials. The dependent variable recorded was the number of trials required to reach that criterion. The order of presentation was counterbalanced within each group. All stimuli were presented by a computer and were visible on screen for 0.5 sec. The groups differed in the inter-item presentation time, with one group having 0.5 sec between each succeeding syllable, another group having 1.0 sec, and the third group having 2 sec. One hypothesis of the study was that the short interval will prevent or curtail rehearsal, leading to slower learning; there is also a suspicion that the variables of meaningfulness and inter-item presentation interval will interact.

Meaningfulness

High	Medium	Low
0.5 sec		
10	18	21
8	16	22
17	27	33
17	23	35
13	26	27
16	22	34
20	22	32
1.0 sec		
26	30	38
13	15	20
18	20	23
10	14	20
12	15	14
14	20	21
15	19	21
2.0 sec		
4	7	13
12	14	18
11	11	12
10	12	13
13	17	19
7	10	9
15	15	17

a. Conduct the overall analysis of variance. Plot the condition means and write a verbal description of the results.

b. Compute the simple effects of meaningfulness for each delay condition. Follow each significant analysis with appropriate simple comparisons.

c. Compute the simple effects of delay for each meaningfulness condition. Follow each significant analysis with appropriate simple comparisons.

†**8.** In Chapter 1, we indicated that full generalization of the taste aversion in Dr. Stewart's data requires that there be a difference in consumption in the sucrose condition and *no* differences in the consumption of other taste substances. Using the data from Dr. Stewart's experiment, determine whether there are differences in consumption of the other three tastes.

*†**9.** Complete the analysis of the treatments by blocks example by conducting the appropriate simple effects and simple comparisons. What do you conclude about the difference in the three lists? About the interaction between reading ability and the lists?

†**10.** Pretend that the treatments by blocks example given was actually a repeated-measures design with all subjects learning each of the three lists. (Naturally, you may assume that there was appropriate counterbalancing to deal with order effects.) Conduct the complete analysis of the data. Do your conclusions differ from those in Exercise 9?

PART FOUR

Other Research Techniques

At this point in their studies, most students are ready to conclude that they are ready to tackle most research problems in psychology by applying a suitable analysis of variance design. But ANOVA isn't the only "true way" to do research in psychology. In this final section of the book, we consider some popular alternatives.

As widely applicable as ANOVA designs are, they can't be applied everywhere that we might wish. Sometimes important research questions arise in settings where we are presented with already-collected data, or with data where certain experimental conditions are not available, or where there is but a single subject.

The chapters in this final section of the book offer a selection of research procedures that fall outside of "classical" experimental design. In Chapter 21, we introduce procedures for data that consist of frequency counts rather than measured values. In Chapter 22, we discuss several research strategies other than the experiment—quasi-experiments, surveys, case studies, research with a single subject, and historical research.

Dealing with Category
and Frequency Data

Research conducted in the classical experimental designs discussed in Chapters 13 through 20 assume that measurement is at least at the ordinal level. The analysis of variance assumes interval or ratio measurement; the non-parametric tests assume at least ordinal measurement. In every case so far, the research question has concerned center or occasionally spread. But sometimes our research question is one of frequency, and the statistics that we've introduced so far aren't appropriate. Research questions about frequency may arise from the distribution of a numeric variable (that's how to test a hypothesis about form). But more often questions about frequency arise when the data represent nominal measurement. We might, for example, ask how many dogs, cats, mice, and rats were seen in the sample neighborhood. Or we might want to know how many people fall into each of ten different occupational categories. Or we might be interested in how males and females intend to vote on certain ballot issues. In all of these examples, the measurement is category: dog, cat, teacher, lawyer, mechanic, artist, male, female, pro, or con. Data of this sort are very frequent in many social science disciplines, psychology included.

In this chapter we will present inferential procedures for frequency information. We won't have to deal with descriptive statistics much, though we will introduce two "correlation" statistics for category data. Traditional descriptive statistics as measures of center or spread are irrelevant here.

We covered the descriptive techniques for presenting frequency data in Chapter 5. Tables remain the basic technique. Graphics, including polygons and histograms, are particularly useful for frequency data. While we won't discuss them more here, thorough and informative presentation of the frequency data itself is essential in communicating frequencies.

Two general kinds of data sets arise in frequency data. In some cases, the data address a unidimensional question like "Are the proportions of people in the 'Agree' and 'Disagree' categories the same or different?" or "Is this set of frequencies different from the one suggested by theory?" In other cases, the data are two-dimensional: "Is there an association between sex and voting intentions?" or "Are freshmen, sophomores, juniors, and seniors equally likely to live in various kinds of housing?".

Inference with a Single Category Variable

Suppose that we ask a sample of 45 senior psychology majors about their postgraduation plans. We give the students five choices of response and obtain the results in Table 21.1. (Ignore the "'Chance' frequency" column for now.) This table is a descriptive summary of the 45 students' responses. We could present this table in a report; we could convert the data to percentages, or we could use a bar graph to present the results. And if all we're interested in is merely describing what our 45 seniors plan, then we could leave it with the descriptive results.

But we want to ask if these data show a "real" preference, or if the unequal frequencies are just chance fluctuations. To ask the question differently, how confident are we that if we were to repeat our survey with 45 different students we'd get something similar to this pattern? In short, are these frequencies really different from each other, or are the underlying population frequencies really equal and this distribution occurred just by chance? If the students *really* have no preference (and that's the null hypothesis that we'll test), then they should choose response categories at random. If they did, then we should find roughly the same number of responses in each category. Since we have 45 students in the survey and five choices, then we might expect $45/5 = 9$ observations in each category. Those "expected" frequencies are shown in the "Chance" frequency column. They constitute the "expected" frequencies under a null hypothesis that states that the students are behaving randomly in choosing a response. If the students actually have preferences, then the frequencies should depart from the "chance" values indicated.

The Chi-Square Test for Fit

To answer the question about preference, we need a way to test the null hypothesis that the population frequency distribution has the numbers shown in the "Chance" frequency column. What we'll use is a statistic whose distribution is approximately the Chi-square distribution introduced in Chapter 13 to test the agreement between two columns of frequencies. As we'll illustrate in a second example, this test procedure is very general and can be applied to any two sets of hypothetical and observed frequencies.

The test statistic is

$$\chi^2 = \sum \frac{(f_o - f_e)^2}{f_e},$$

where f_o and f_e are the observed and expected frequencies, respectively, and the summation is taken over all pairs of frequencies. The number of degrees of freedom for the χ^2 value is the number of categories (pairs of frequencies) minus 1.

Table 21.1   Hypothetical Postgraduation Plans

Choice	Frequency	"Chance" frequency
Grad school	13	9
Professional school	7	9
Family business	5	9
Other job	15	9
Undecided	5	9
Total	45	45

While the Chi-square distribution correctly applies only to a continuous variable, the formula just given (properly called a *Pearson Chi square*) is a reasonable approximation under the right conditions. Many texts present this formula as the *only* Chi-square formula, which it is not; we'll label it appropriately as the Pearson* approximation.

The conditions for using the Chi-square distribution are:

1. The categories must be mutually exclusive. (In the example, students aren't permitted to check two or more alternatives.)
2. Observations must be independent (that is, student A's response can't influence that of student B).
3. The expected frequencies must be large enough (usually five or so) to allow the Chi-square distribution to be a reasonable approximation.

For our example set of data, the computation proceeds as

$$\chi^2 = \sum \frac{(f_o - f_e)^2}{f_e}$$

$$= \frac{(13 - 9)^2}{9} + \frac{(7 - 9)^2}{9} + \frac{(5 - 9)^2}{9} + \frac{(15 - 9)^2}{9} + \frac{(5 - 9)^2}{9}$$

$$= \frac{88}{9} = 9.78.$$

The statistic has $5 - 1 = 4$ degrees of freedom. In Appendix D we find that the critical value at $\alpha = .05$ with $df = 4$ is 9.49. Figure 21.1 shows the sampling distribution.

In order to reject the null hypothesis that the two sets of frequencies come from the same population, the obtained χ^2 must exceed 9.49. In the case of our example data, it does, and we conclude that our seniors aren't responding randomly when asked about their postgraduation plans.

The next logical question concerns just what the differences between the obtained and the theoretical frequencies actually tell us. In this regard, it's often helpful to look at the residuals from the analysis. The residual is defined as

$$\frac{(f_o - f_e)}{\sqrt{f_e}}.$$

---

*Yes, it's the same Pearson as in the product-moment correlation coefficient.

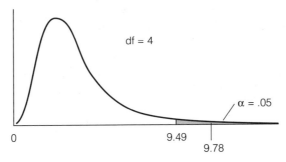

Figure 21.1

Table 21.2 Residuals for Data in Table 21.1

Choice	Observed	Expected	Residual
Grad school	13	9	1.33
Professional school	7	9	−0.67
Family business	5	9	−1.33
Other job	15	9	2.00
Undecided	5	9	−1.33

For our example, the residuals are shown in Table 21.2. The residuals show how much each of the obtained frequencies differs from the expected. The larger values, then, indicate where the greatest discrepancies are between the two sets of frequencies. For the example data, the largest difference is in the "Other job" category, while the smallest is for "Professional school."

Employing residuals to interpret Chi-square computations is a useful procedure and one too often overlooked by students. Students often stop an analysis with a statement like "These frequencies differ significantly from those expected by chance" without any further interpretation. Looking at the residuals can help a great deal in understanding the nature of the differences and is an analysis that should always be done.

Squaring and summing the residuals gives the Chi-square value. For that reason, the residuals directly reflect a contribution to the statistic and are good to use for interpretative purposes. It also makes a handy computational check. For our example,

$$\chi^2 = 1.33^2 + (-0.67)^2 + (-1.33)^2 + 2.00^2 + (-1.33)^2$$
$$= 9.76.$$

Within rounding, that's the same value as the original Chi square.

Another Example. Nothing says that the null hypothesis must specify equal frequencies in all categories. In some cases, like that of the postgraduate plans, the question is appropriately addressed by testing a "no preference" hypothesis. In other cases, though, the question might be whether the data fit with a set of frequencies derived from some other null hypothesis. For example, hair color in rats is thought to be controlled by two genes, operating in a classical dominant-recessive fashion. If that's the case, then the offspring from the mating of pairs of black and "yellow" rats should yield offspring in roughly the following proportions:

Color	Expected number
Gray	9
Black	3
Yellow	3
Cream	1
Total	16

Those frequencies come from the understanding of how genes combine to control certain features; if the genetic laws operate as expected, then the resulting body features should follow roughly those proportions.

Suppose that we have a group of 74 rats, all the offspring of black-yellow matings. The frequencies of the four colors are

Color	Observed number
Gray	47
Black	9
Yellow	12
Cream	6
Total	74

Does this distribution represent a significant departure from the expected frequencies? First, we calculate the expected frequencies. To find the expected frequencies, note that $9/16 = 0.56$ of the animals should be gray. Since there are 74 animals in our group, then, we would expect that $0.56 \times 74 \simeq 41$ gray rats. Applying the same logic to black and to yellow animals, there should be $3/16 \times 74 \simeq 14$. There should be $1/16 \times 74 \simeq 5$ cream-colored rats. Completing the calculations, we have

	Observed	Expected
Gray	47	41
Black	9	14
Yellow	12	14
Cream	6	5

so that

$$\chi^2 = \sum \frac{(f_o - f_e)^2}{f_e}$$

$$= \frac{(47 - 41)^2}{41} + \frac{(9 - 14)^2}{14} + \frac{(12 - 14)^2}{14} + \frac{(6 - 5)^2}{5}$$

$$= 3.15.$$

Inference with a Single-Category Variable

For df $= 4 - 1 = 3$, Appendix D shows a critical χ^2 value of 7.81 at $\alpha = .05$; thus we don't reject the hypothesis that this distribution is identical to that suggested by genetic theory. In this example, we may conclude that hair color in rats seems to be controlled by the classical dominant/recessive gene operation, since the obtained frequencies don't differ from those indicated by theory.

A glance at the residuals gives another indication of a good fit between the sets of values:

	Observed	Expected	Residual
Gray	47	41	0.94
Black	9	14	-1.34
Yellow	12	14	-0.53
Cream	6	5	0.45

The residuals are quite small, thus supporting our conclusion that there are no differences, other than chance variation, between the two sets of frequencies. That conclusion, in turn, leads to confidence that hair color is indeed controlled as genetic theory suggests.

Presenting Chi-Square Results. The APA style for presenting the results of a hypothesis test is used with a Chi-square statistic, with one addition. Inside the parentheses, with the degrees of freedom, give the value of N as well. Thus for the example using rats, we might write "The distribution of coat color does not differ from that expected under classical genetic theory, $\chi^2(3, N = 74) = 3.01$, $p > .05$."

Fitting a Distribution Form

Of the three characteristics of a distribution—center, spread, and form—we've presented inferential statistics for center and spread, but not for form. And in fact, inference normally focuses on the center of data and occasionally on spread. Inferences about form are unusual but are sometimes an important focus in research. In addition, tests of form may be used to determine whether a normal distribution-based procedure should be used. Several different tests may be used to test hypotheses about form. We'll illustrate one that uses the Pearson Chi-square procedure.*

Since the Pearson Chi square may be used to assess the fit between two sets of frequencies, it can be used to test whether a frequency distribution differs from a normal distribution (or from any other form). All we need to do is to find the expected frequencies for intervals under a normal distribution and compare them with the obtained frequencies using the Pearson Chi square. There's a minor modification in the df value, which we'll illustrate when we get there.

Let's illustrate the process by using Dr. Campbell's data from 84 subjects on the Sociability subscale of the Eysenck Personality Inventory (we'll call the variable EPIS for short). The frequency distribution of EPIS is shown in Figure 21.2. The skewness is -0.56, while the mean and median are 7.69 and 8.0 respectively. The standard deviation is 2.3.

---

*When the variable being counted is at least ordinal, the Kolmogorov-Smirnov one-sample test is appropriate; see Siegel and Castellan (1988).

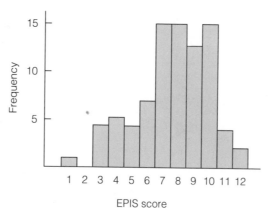

Figure 21.2

Table 21.3   Score Intervals

EPIS score	Score interval
1	below 1.5
2	1.5– 2.5
3	2.5– 3.5
4	3.5– 4.5
5	4.5– 5.5
6	5.5– 6.5
7	6.5– 7.5
8	7.5– 8.5
9	8.5– 9.5
10	9.5–10.5
11	10.5–11.5
12	above 11.5

To calculate the expected frequencies, we use $\overline{X}$ and $\hat{s}$ as point estimates of μ and σ. If the population is normally distributed with mean = 7.69 and standard deviation = 2.3, then we can calculate the proportion of the normal curve that should appear in each of the score intervals as we did in Chapter 8. For an EPIS score of 2.0, for example, we assume that 2.0 is the midpoint of an interval that extends from 1.5 to 2.5, that 3.0 is the midpoint of the 2.5 to 3.5 interval, and so on. Since 1.0 is the lowest value of EPIS, we'll assume that it represents all values below 1.5 and that the score intervals are those listed in Table 21.3.

Converting the interval limits into z scores using $\overline{X} = 7.69$ and $s = 2.3$, we can then obtain (from Appendix A) the proportions of the normal curve. For the interval 1.5 to 2.5, for example, we would compute the two z scores as

$$z = \frac{1.5 - 7.69}{2.3}$$

$$= -2.69$$

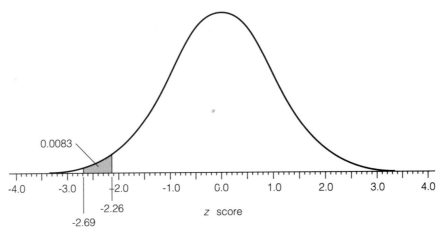

0.0083

-4.0 -3.0 ╎+2.0 -1.0 0.0 1.0 2.0 3.0 4.0

-2.26

z score

-2.69

Figure 21.3

Table 21.4   Expected Frequencies, z Intervals, Probabilities, and Obtained Frequencies

EPIS score interval	Range of z		Probability	Obtained frequency	Expected frequency
1		≤ −2.69	0.0036	1	0.30
2	−2.69	−2.26	0.0083	0	0.70
3	−2.26	−1.82	0.0225	4	1.89
4	−1.82	−1.39	0.0479	5	4.02
5	−1.39	−0.95	0.0888	4	7.46
6	−0.95	−0.52	0.1374	7	11.54
7	−0.52	−0.08	0.1666	15	13.99
8	−0.08	0.35	0.1687	15	14.17
9	0.35	0.79	0.1484	12	12.47
10	0.79	1.22	0.1036	15	8.70
11	1.22	1.66	0.0627	4	5.27
12	≥ 1.66		0.0485	2	4.05
				84	84

for the lower limit of 1.5 and

$$z = \frac{2.5 - 7.69}{2.3}$$

$$= -2.26$$

for the upper (2.5). Consulting Appendix A, we find the proportion of the curve between those two points, which is shown in Figure 21.3. The proportion is 0.0083. This means that, of Dr. Campbell's 84 subjects, $0.0083 \times 84 = 0.70$ are expected to have a score of 2.0. Following the same procedure for each of the EPIS scores, we obtain the expected frequencies in Table 21.4, listed together with the z intervals, their probabilities, and the obtained frequencies from Figure 21.2.

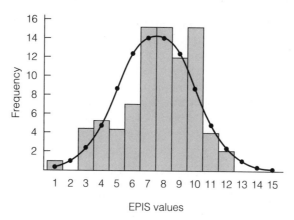

Figure 21.4

The expected frequencies are those that we would find if the form of the distribution were normal with $\mu = 7.69$ and $\sigma = 2.3$. The expected frequencies are superimposed on the histogram in Figure 21.4. Having found those expected frequencies under the null hypothesis that the distribution has a normal form, we proceed to the χ^2 formula and calculate

$$
\chi^2 = \sum \frac{(f_o - f_e)^2}{f_e}
$$
$$
= \frac{(1 - .30)^2}{.30} + \frac{(0 - .70)^2}{.70} + \cdots + \frac{(2 - 4.07)^2}{4.07}
$$
$$
= 14.36.
$$

If this were an ordinary χ^2 computation, we would compute number of intervals $- 1$ degrees of freedom and proceed to the χ^2 table to test for the significance of the statistic. But here's where the difference lies in this distribution-fitting application. From the df that we would have if this were not a test of distribution form, we must subtract *one df for each each separate parameter that we estimated*. In this case, we estimated both μ and σ so that we could compute the z scores for the intervals, and our df are thus

$$
\text{df} = \text{Number of intervals} - 1 - 2
$$
$$
= 12 - 1 - 2
$$
$$
= 9.
$$

In Appendix D, we find that the critical value for χ^2 with $\alpha = .05$ is 16.92; we may thus conclude that there is no evidence to indicate that Dr. Campbell's EPIS data come from a non-normal distribution.

Binomial Tests for Proportions

It's a very short step from considering tests about frequencies to considering tests about proportions. Suppose that we have a variable with only two categories—pass-fail, male-female, oppose-support, or something similar. We could test hypotheses about the frequencies in such a case using the Pearson Chi square, establishing the expected frequencies in each of the two categories. But there are other alternatives that are at least as accurate.

Asking whether a hypothetical sample distribution of eight males and five females differs from an expected distribution of 50/50 is equivalent to asking whether the proportion of males in the sample group differs from 0.5; for this reason, categorical inferences in the two-category case are usually called tests of proportions. When we have a small sample, Appendix G may be used to obtain a precise test of a hypothesis about a proportion.

As an example, suppose that we're developing a set of multiple-choice test items. A particular question that we're investigating has four alternatives, only one of which is correct. If the students are guessing at the answer, then 25% of them should get the answer correct by chance. Suppose that we have a sample of 15 students and find that 8 of them got the correct answer. Are the students guessing?

You'll recall from Chapter 13 that Appendix G gives binomial probabilities. In particular, it gives the probabilities of the numbers of "successes" in N trials when the probability of a success on each trial is p. Giving a four-choice question to 15 students under the null hypothesis of guessing is the same as flipping a coin whose probability of "heads" is .25 a total of 15 times. In Appendix G we find the probabilities of each of the possible number of students getting the item correct under guessing (that is, a .25 probability of being correct); these probabilities are listed in Table 21.5.

Under the null hypothesis (that is, $p = .25$), what's the probability of 8 or more students getting the question right? It's $.0131 + .0034 + .0007 + \cdots = 0.0173$. If we had chosen $\alpha = .05$, we would reject the hypothesis that the students are guessing, since the probability of seeing 8 or more correct answers by chance alone is less than .05. Note that we've used the probability of 8 *or more*, since we're really interested not in exactly 8 correct but in the probability that the students will do that well or better.

In a large sample situation, we may use the normal curve approximation to the binomial distribution that we first introduced in Chapter 13. There we pointed out that the binomial distribution can be approximated by a normal distribution with

$$\mu = Np$$
$$\sigma = \sqrt{Np(1 - p)}.$$

Suppose that instead of 15 students we have 46 of them and find that 32 have the correct answer. In this case, then, we would obtain

$$\mu = Np \qquad\qquad \sigma = \sqrt{Np(1 - p)}$$
$$= 46 \times .25 \qquad\quad = \sqrt{46 \times .25 \times .75}$$
$$= 11.5 \qquad\qquad\quad = 2.94.$$

Then, using the standardizing formula, we obtain

$$z = \frac{X - \overline{X}}{\mu} = \frac{19 - 11.5}{2.94}$$
$$= 2.55.$$

Table 21.5 Probabilities of Students Getting Item Correct by Guessing

Number	Probability
0	.0134
1	.0668
2	.1559
3	.2252
4	.2252
5	.1651
6	.0917
7	.0393
8	.0131
9	.0034
10	.0007
11	.0001
12	.0000
13	.0000
14	.0000
15	.0000

With $\alpha = .05$, we can reject the hypothesis of guessing since the obtained value of 2.55 exceeds the critical z value of 1.96. We may conclude, therefore, that the students are guessing on this test item.

Inference with Two Category Variables

Suppose that we ask members of the freshman, sophomore, and junior classes in a psychology department whether they agree with the proposed addition of a course to those required for majors. The data are

Class	Yes	No
Freshmen	1	11
Sophomores	8	4
Juniors	11	3

Here we have frequency data, certainly, but with two category variables* instead of one. We could easily investigate either of the two variables separately and ask, for example, whether the proportion of "Yeses" is different from 50% for freshmen, or for sophomores, or for juniors. We could also ask whether the distribution of "No" choices, for example, differs across the three classes. But what we really are interested in knowing is whether the classes feel the same way about the question of adding a required course. The frequencies suggest otherwise, but can we test a hypothesis that will give us some confidence in our

---

* If you're being really strict, year in school is ordinal; that's unimportant for the example.

judgment? The answer, naturally, is yes, which brings us to probably the most common application of the Pearson Chi square—the test for association or contingency.

Testing for Contingency

The contingency test investigates the null hypothesis that there is no relationship or dependency between the "row" variable (class in our example) and the "column" variable (opinion on adding a course). If there is no association between the two—if the three classes have the same opinion—then student opinion is not contingent upon the class of the student, which gives the procedure the name "contingency test."

As with a single-variable Pearson Chi square, the test looks at the difference between obtained and expected frequencies in that table. If there is no contingency or relationship, then the proportion of freshmen who answer "yes" should represent the same proportion for freshmen as it does of sophomores and juniors. Let's look at the row and column totals for the example data:

Class	Yes	No	Total
Freshmen	1	11	12
Sophomores	8	4	12
Juniors	11	3	14
Total	20	18	38

Each individual frequency is often called a "cell" in the frequency table. Let's first obtain the expected frequencies for two freshmen cells, under the null hypothesis that there is no contingency. If there's no association between opinion and year in school, the 12 freshmen should divide themselves between "Yes" and "No" in the same proportions as the total Yes/No vote for all classes combined. Of the 38 students, 20 answered "Yes"; in each of the three classes, then, 20/38 of the students should say "Yes." To calculate the expected number of freshmen saying "Yes," then, we have

$$\text{Number of freshman "Yeses"} = 12 \times \left(\frac{20}{38}\right) = 6.32$$

Number of freshmen

Proportion of students answering "Yes"

By changing the form of the equation a little, we can write

$$\text{Number of freshman "Yeses"} = \frac{12 \times 20}{38} = 6.32.$$

The same logic holds for freshmen answering "No," so that

$$\text{Number of freshman "Nos"} = 12 \times \frac{18}{38} = \frac{12 \times 18}{38} = 5.68,$$

since 18 of the 38 total responses are "No."

We can generalize the logic to all rows and columns and summarize the rule: the expected frequency for each cell may be calculated as the product of the row and column sums divided by the total number of observations. As a formula,

$$f_e = \frac{R \times C}{N},$$

where R and C are row and column sums corresponding to the cell being calculated. Thus the computation for juniors answering "No" would be

Class	Yes	No	Total
Freshmen			12
Sophomores			12
Juniors		$\frac{14 \times 18}{38} = 6.63$	⑭
	—		—
Total	20	⑱	㉈

or, using the formula,

$$f_e = \frac{R \times C}{N}$$

$$= \frac{14 \times 18}{38}$$

$$= 6.63.$$

The full matrix of expected frequencies is

Class	Yes	No
Freshmen	6.32	5.68
Sophomores	6.32	5.68
Juniors	7.37	6.63

Once we have the expected frequencies for each cell, the χ^2 statistic is calculated as:

$$\chi^2 = \sum \sum \frac{(f_o - f_e)^2}{f_e},$$

where the $\sum \sum$ merely means to sum over both the rows and the columns of the table. For our example, then, the value is

$$\chi^2 = \sum \sum \frac{(f_o - f_e)^2}{f_e}$$

$$= \frac{(1 - 6.32)^2}{6.32} + \frac{(11 - 5.68)^2}{5.68} + \cdots + \frac{(3 - 6.63)^2}{6.63}$$

$$= 14.17.$$

The degrees of freedom for the Pearson Chi square for contingency are

$$df = (\text{number of rows} - 1)(\text{number of columns} - 1).$$

For this example,

$$df = (\text{number of rows} - 1)(\text{number of columns} - 1)$$
$$= (3 - 1)(2 - 1) = 2.$$

From Appendix D we determine that the critical value for χ^2 with df $= 2$ at $\alpha = .05$ is 5.991. Since the obtained statistic exceeds that value, we reject the hypothesis that there is no association between the year in school and the students' opinions of the additional course. The hypothesis that we support is that there is a relationship between year and opinion; the next task is to understand that relationship.

Residuals Analysis. Let's look at the residuals from the analysis. We define the residual in the same way as before, namely

$$\frac{(f_o - f_e)}{\sqrt{f_e}}.$$

For our data, the residuals are

Class	Yes	No
Freshmen	−2.12	2.23
Sophomores	0.67	−0.70
Juniors	1.34	−1.41

The residuals highlight what was visible in the raw data, specifically that the differences are primarily between freshmen and juniors and that they respond in opposite ways; the freshmen are opposed to adding another course while the juniors generally favored the addition. The sophomores are less divided, but tend to vote like the juniors, as can be seen from the signs of the residuals. In a table with two category variables, we may estimate the standard deviation of each residual, making it possible to compute a z score for each.* The formula for the standard deviation of a residual is

$$\text{s.d.}_{\text{resid}} = \sqrt{\frac{N - R}{N - C}},$$

where R and C are the row and column totals for the cell whose residual is being computed. For the "freshman-yes" cell, we would have

$$\begin{aligned}
\text{s.d.}_{\text{resid}} &= \sqrt{\frac{N - R}{N - C}} \\
&= \sqrt{\frac{38 - 12}{38 - 20}} \\
&= 1.20.
\end{aligned}$$

The standardized residual for any cell is computed as

$$\begin{aligned}
z_{\text{resid}} &= \frac{\text{residual}}{\text{s.d.}_{\text{resid}}} \\
&= \frac{\dfrac{(f_o - f_e)}{\sqrt{f_e}}}{\sqrt{\dfrac{N - R}{N - C}}}.
\end{aligned}$$

---

* See Siegel and Castellan (1988).

A computationally simpler form is given by

$$z_{\text{resid}} = \frac{(f_o - f_e)}{\sqrt{f_e}} \sqrt{\frac{N - C}{N - R}}.$$

For the "freshman-yes" cell, the standardized residual is

$$\begin{aligned}
z_{\text{resid}} &= \frac{(f_o - f_e)}{\sqrt{f_e}} \sqrt{\frac{N - C}{N - R}} \\
&= \frac{(1 - 6.32)}{\sqrt{6.32}} \sqrt{\frac{38 - 20}{38 - 12}} \\
&= -1.76.
\end{aligned}$$

Applying the formula to all of the cells, the full table of standardized residuals is

Class	Yes	No
Freshmen	−1.76	1.96
Sophomores	0.56	−0.62
Juniors	1.16	−1.29

If N is reasonably large, we may regard the standardized residuals as coming from a standardized normal distribution. In the normal distribution, any z value of 1.96 or greater is significantly different from the mean; thus freshmen answering "No" is a significantly large residual. Looking at the overall pattern of the standardized residuals, it's clear that there are substantial differences between the freshmen and the juniors in their opinions, with the freshmen being in general quite opposed to the new course requirement.

The 2 × 2 Table

When there are only two categories in both the row and the column categories, the χ^2 computation simplifies a great deal. If we let the letters a, b, c, and d stand for the frequencies in the table as

$$\begin{array}{c|c} a & b \\ \hline c & d \end{array}$$

then we may compute the Chi-square value as

$$\chi^2 = \frac{N(|ad - bc| - N/2)^2}{(a + b)(c + d)(a + c)(b + d)}.$$

As an example, suppose that we have counted the number of males and females in two campus organizations, the Camera Club and the Marching Band, with these results:

	Camera	Band	Grand total
Male	11	54	65
Female	19	34	53
Grand total	30	88	118

Inference with Two-Category Variables

Using the formula given, the Chi-square value is

$$\chi^2 = \frac{N(|ad - bc| - N/2)^2}{(a + b)(c + d)(a + c)(b + d)}$$

$$= \frac{118(|(11 \times 34) - (54 \times 19)| - 118/2)^2}{(11 + 54)(19 + 34)(11 + 19)(54 + 88)}$$

$$= 4.56.$$

If we choose $\alpha = .05$, the critical value for Chi square with df $= (2 - 1)(2 - 1) = 1$ is 3.84, and we reject the hypothesis that there is no relationship between sex and choice of these two extracurricular activities. By inspection of the data, it appears that women are more likely to join the Camera Club, while men join the Marching Band more often.

"Correlation" with Category Data

Several statistics have been developed to index the relationship between two-category variables on a 0–1 scale like that of correlation coefficients. The most common of these "correlation coefficients" is the *contingency coefficient*, defined as

$$C = \sqrt{\frac{\chi^2}{\chi^2 + N}},$$

where χ^2 is the value obtained from a contingency analysis and N is the number of observations. For our class opinion example, then,

$$C = \sqrt{\frac{\chi^2}{\chi^2 + N}}$$

$$= \sqrt{\frac{14.17}{14.17 + 38}}$$

$$= .52.$$

This value may be interpreted as a correlation coefficient, with a value of .52 indicating a modest degree of relationship between class in school and opinion. While the contingency coefficient is a very common measure of the association, it's not an especially good one because it doesn't behave quite the way you'd like a correlation coefficient to behave. A serious problem with C is that it can never obtain a value of 1.0, even with perfect agreement. Even worse, the maximum value of C is a function of the number of observations; the larger N, the smaller the largest possible value of C.

Some of the problems with the contingency coefficient are addressed by *Cramer's phi* (Cramer, 1946), which is a very widely used statistic. The phi coefficient is defined as

$$\Phi = \sqrt{\frac{\chi^2}{N(k - 1)}}.$$

Here, χ^2 and N have the meanings that they had for the contingency coefficient, and k is the smaller of the number of rows or columns. For our example, there are three rows and two columns, so that $k = 2$. The value of Φ for the example is

$$\Phi = \sqrt{\frac{\chi^2}{N(k-1)}}$$
$$= \sqrt{\frac{14.18}{38 \times (2-1)}}$$
$$= .61.$$

This value is slightly higher than was the contingency coefficient based on the same data.

The Φ coefficient solves the problem that plagues the contingency coefficient, since it has 1.0 as an upper limit regardless of the sample size. But neither Φ nor C offers another feature that helps in the interpretation of the Pearson product-moment correlation coefficient—the square of the coefficient gives a proportion of variance explained by the relationship. A measure proposed by Light and Margolin (1971; see also Berenson, Levine, & Goldstein, 1983) does offer such an interpretation.

More Than Two Category Variables

The procedures that we have described so far are limited to two separate tasks: fitting of frequency data to one set of expected frequencies (that is, a single-category variable) or to assessing the contingency between two category variables. But frequently we have more than two variables, often many more than two. Can we extend the notion of contingency analysis to multivariate data? The answer is "yes," but not nearly as simply as you might hope. We can't just construct a three-dimensional frequency table, generalize an expected frequency procedure, and proceed. Instead, we must rely on a much more complicated process, known as log-linear modeling. We won't explore the point here because it would take us too far afield. For a short introduction see Berenson et al. (1983, pp. 488–498). For an advanced treatment, see Fienberg (1980). Marascuilo and Serlin (1988) present a nice single-chapter introduction.

S U M M A R Y

- Sometimes data are just counts of the number of occurrences of discrete events.
- The Pearson Chi-square statistic may be used to test the "fit" between sets of obtained and theoretical frequencies.
- In order to use the Chi-square distribution to approximate the sampling distribution of the Pearson Chi-square statistic, be sure that (1) the categories are mutually exclusive, (2) the observations are independent, and (3) the expected frequencies are greater than or equal to 5.0.
- Exploring the residuals from a Pearson Chi-square analysis is usually a good way to understand the data.
- The Pearson Chi square may be used to test whether the form of a frequency distribution differs from the normal.

- When there are just two possible responses, the binomial distribution may be used to test a hypothesis about a proportion.
- If there are two category variables, the Pearson Chi square may be used to determine whether a significant contingency exists between them.
- The contingency coefficient and Cramer's phi are correlation-like measures for two-category variables.

KEY TERMS

Binomial test
Contingency coefficient
Contingency test

Cramer's phi
Pearson Chi square

EXERCISES

Solutions to asterisked (∗) exercises appear at the back of the book. Exercises preceded by a section symbol (§) must be solved using a computer. Exercises preceded by a dagger (†) can be solved by hand.

∗†1. The academic department described early in the chapter has always been viewed as highly preprofessional, with many more of its students planning to attend graduate or professional school than planning on other future endeavors. This suggests that perhaps the null hypothesis distribution of equal frequencies that we tested earlier might not have been appropriate. Use the following data (and $\alpha = .01$) to test the revised hypothesis:

Choice	Frequency	"Chance" frequency
Grad school	13	14
Professional school	7	13
Family business	5	6
Other job	15	6
Undecided	5	6
Total	45	45

State your conclusions verbally. (You might want to look at residuals.)

†2. A count of students in a Computers in Psychology class showed that 7 out of 11 students were female. Does that proportion differ significantly (with $\alpha = .05$) from 50%?

∗†3. A count of students in an Abnormal Psychology class showed that 32 out of 48 students were male. Does that proportion differ significantly (with $\alpha = .05$) from 50%?

†4. A table of random numbers, like that in Appendix B, should not favor any digit over any other. That is, if you would count the number of 0's, 1's, and so forth, they should all occur an equal number of times. Take a random sample of 100 values from Appendix B and count the number of times each digit occurs. Test whether your sample differs from what would be expected if the table really contained random values. Use $\alpha = .05$.

§5. This problem investigates the behavior of the random-number generator in your statistics program. Generate a sample of 100 values from a rectangular distribution in the range 0.0–1.0. If your random-number generator is performing correctly, 10% of the values should be in the range 0.0–0.1, 10% in the 0.1–0.2 range, and so forth. Using $\alpha = .05$, does your distribution follow the expected pattern? Try this with at least five different samples of size 100.

∗†6. Exercise 1 used the survey of senior psychology majors' postgraduation plans. The following data give the frequencies for the same 45 seniors, but also the choices made by a group of juniors. Is there a relationship between class and choice? If so, describe it verbally. (Use $\alpha = .01$.)

Choice	Seniors	Juniors
Grad school	13	20
Professional school	7	7
Family business	5	6
Other job	15	3
Undecided	5	23

*†7. Compute C and Φ for the data in Exercise 6.

†8. Following are the data for a number of birds, categorized as to their species (A, B, or C) and whether they have built nests low or high (L, H) above the ground. Compute the Chi square for association and also C and Φ. Is there an association between species and nest location? (Use $\alpha = .05$.) Describe it verbally.

	Nest location	
	Low	High
Species A	10	3
Species B	12	14
Species C	5	18

Quasi-Experiments, Surveys, Case Studies, and Archival and Small-*N* Research

In Chapter 2, we noted that psychologists use many research strategies in their work. In this, our final chapter, we complete the survey of research techniques. We'll look first at the quasi-experiment, a widely used research approach that is *almost* an experiment but not quite. Next we'll consider two approaches to use with very small sample sizes (indeed, usually where $N = 1$). Following that, we'll present the case study (an in-depth investigation of a single subject). Next we'll discuss the widely employed survey and interview method. And finally, we'll briefly consider research that uses existing data sets and archives. There won't be any new statistics to learn in this chapter, since the analyses for all these other research methods rely on the procedures that we already know.

Quasi-Experiments

In a quasi-experiment, there are independent variable(s) just like in a "true" experiment, but they aren't actually manipulated by the experimenter. Suppose, for example, that you're interested in the effects of brain injury in two different areas of the cortex on memory. If you are able to produce the injuries surgically, you might opt to study brain injury in animals since the brain structures of humans and many animals are highly similar. Doing the research this way, you could surgically produce two groups of subjects, directly manipulating the locus of brain damage, the independent variable. Following the logic for experimental manipulation, if all variables other than the surgical procedures were constant or equivalent across the two groups of animals, differences in memory could be causally related to the locus of the brain injury.

If you're interested specifically in the difference between the two brain damage sites in humans, though, you can't do the experiment in the same way.

But through hospitals and medical records, you might be able to find two groups of individuals with damage to the two brain locations that you're interested in. If you did, then you would have two groups of subjects that are comparable to those in the animal study, at least with regard to locus of injury. But there's a critical difference in this case—you didn't do the independent variable manipulation yourself. You have no control over extraneous variables that might be introduced by the cause of the brain injury, nor by the treatment of the individuals after the trauma. For example, suppose that one of the brain-injury sites is typical of damage in automobile accidents, and the other site is normally damaged by prolonged exposure to an industrial solvent in the workplace. You have two groups of individuals in your "experiment," and they have brain injury in the locations of interest, but they probably have very different histories. One group has been involved in a traumatic vehicle accident; the other group may or may not have had such an accident, but even if they have, it did not occur in conjunction with the brain injury. There will very likely be other differences; the groups may differ in education, socioeconomic class, or intelligence as well.

An "experiment" in which the groups are formed by selection rather than by manipulation is called a *quasi-experiment*. At first glance, it "looks like" an experiment. But the independent variable was not manipulated by the investigator.

A quasi-experiment suffers from unknown biases in group assignment. There's usually no way to know what extraneous variables may be confounded with the independent variable. Such a situation obviously complicates inferences. If you find a significant difference in memory between the two brain-injury groups, for example, to what should you attribute that difference? It could be due to the location of the damage, of course, but it could just as easily be to any (or all) of the other possible differences between the two groups. Obviously, conclusions about possible causality need to be carefully qualified in this sort of research.

Quasi-experiments are far more prevalent in the literature than experimental design textbooks lead you to believe. Why? For a very simple reason: often, they're the only way possible to gain information on important practical and theoretical problems. Should we not investigate the effects of brain injury on memory just because we can't do experimental surgery with humans? Should we stop looking for effects of nutritional deficits in infancy on cognitive development just because we can't assign infants randomly to experimental deficiency conditions? Should we abandon research on AIDS just because we can't randomly assign subjects to be exposed to the disease? Certainly not; they're all important research areas.

Since much important research can only be conducted using quasi-experiments, they will continue to have an important place in the literature of psychology. They can easily pass on a quick reading for "true" experiments, but they are much more limited in their ability to clearly answer research questions. For that reason, it's important to understand exactly the manipulations that are done. If there is no manipulation, only a selection of existing groups, then you should be very cautious in interpreting generalizations of causality.

There are a large number of quasi-experimental designs. We'll present several frequently used, and useful, designs.

Nonequivalent Group Designs	A very common variety of quasi-experiment involves two groups of subjects, differing with regard to some treatment that was applied to one of them. Of these, the most common is certainly the "nonequivalent control" situation. Here, experimental and control conditions exist, but assignment to the groups was not under the control of the experimenter and generally not random.

There's no reason why the quasi-experimental designs need to be limited to only two conditions, of course. Any of the nonequivalent group designs could readily be expanded to multiple groups. Our presentation here will be in terms of two group designs, but the comments that we'll make about any of them will apply equally to multiple-condition designs.

Nonequivalent Post-Test Design. The design that we just suggested for the two brain-injury locations is a *nonequivalent post-test design*. There are two experimental conditions—two groups of subjects—differing in the locus of their brain injury. *After* the injury, the two groups of subjects are given memory tests. Figure 22.1 might represent the design. The question mark indicates that we have no way of knowing whether the subject populations are identical or not, even before any selection into two groups. The groups are nonequivalent to start with, then are administered two different "treatments," and are finally compared. Since there is no random assignment into experimental conditions, it's a good bet that any number of variables are confounded with the "independent variable." This makes the nonequivalent post-test design particularly weak in causal inference.

If we are able to add a test *before* the experimental manipulation, then we can use that information to learn something about the similarity of the two groups of subjects. The next design, a very popular one, offers that ability.

Nonequivalent Control-Group Design. This design may be represented as shown in Figure 22.2. Note that in this design, as in those two-condition designs described in Chapter 14, there are two populations. As in the nonequivalent post-test design, the relationship between those populations is unknown. This means that we don't know whether the populations are identical, as we assume that they are in the between-subjects design of Chapter 14. Thus if we conclude that there's a difference, we will never be clear whether the difference is between populations that were different to begin with or whether the difference was caused by the experimental manipulation.

The differences between this design and the nonequivalent post-test design is the first test of the dependent variable. This allows two hypothesis tests. The first, a simple test of the differences between the two groups *before* the experimental manipulation, can serve as a check of the equivalence between the groups. But even if they differ, using a change score $(X_1 - X_2)$ as the dependent variable eliminates some of the variability that might otherwise be included. It gives a direct measure of the change, or lack of it, in the two subject groups. Even if the two groups differ initially, measuring the change gives an indication of the effect of the experimental treatment.

As an example, suppose that Clayworks Manufacturing has two branches, each engaged in roughly the same activities. The company wants to assess the effect of changing the fringe benefits package on employee morale. They can't

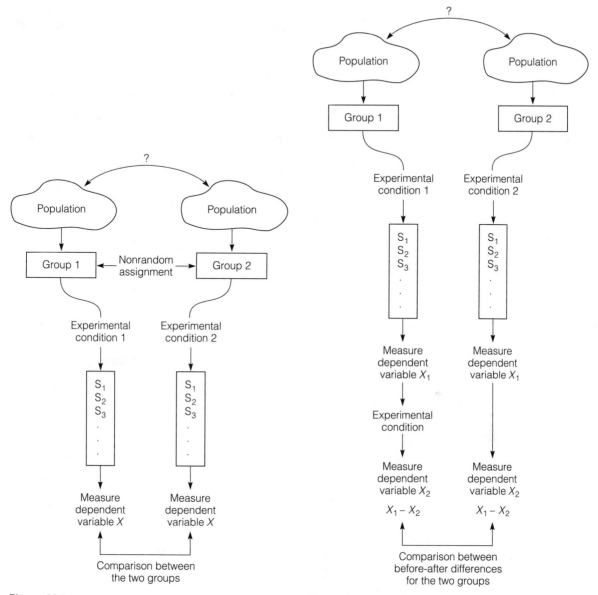

Figure 22.1

Figure 22.2

very well offer the new package to a randomly chosen group of employees and not to the other, because that could cause morale problems by itself. Instead, Clayworks offers the new package at one office but not at the other. If they take a measure of employee morale before and after the new package is introduced, then they can use the nonequivalent control group design. The manipulation in the quasi-experiment is the introduction of the new benefits package at one office. The dependent variable is the difference between the two morale measures (pre- and post-package) at the two plants. We would expect that there would be no overall change in morale at the "no-package" office. A difference at the "package" office would suggest a change due to the offer of the new package.

Causal inference isn't possible in this design, since it's impossible to randomly assign subjects to conditions. Since that's the case, there are many possible extraneous variables that could be confounded with the independent variable. In this design, particular attention needs to be paid to alternative explanations for obtained results. Differences can often be attributed to variables that affect how the participants were grouped in the first place. Suppose that Clayworks' first office is in a rural area and the second is in a large city. Though the work done is the same, there are likely to be important differences between the two groups of employees. Not only might they differ in morale before any change in benefits, but the benefits package may differ in appeal to the two groups. In this case, the groups are clearly different to begin with, with or without any change. Nevertheless, the results of the design are normally interpretable and are better than having no information at all.

The Cohort Design. In the language of behavioral science research, a *cohort* is a group of roughly the same age and background that follow one another through time. All of the people in your grade in school, for example, form a cohort; you all age at the same rate, have the same general history, and so forth. A cohort may sometimes be used as a kind of control group. The cohort design, as diagrammed in Figure 22.3, uses one group ("Cohort 1" in the illustration) as a control for its cohort ("Cohort 2"), which is given an experimental treatment. The pre-treatment measure on Cohort 1 is compared to the post-treatment measure for Cohort 2. Here again, as in the nonequivalent control group design, we don't know whether the populations are identical or not, but using a cohort control attempts to provide some degree of similarity between the two groups.

As an example of a cohort design, suppose that you wanted to study the effect of electronic calculators on a statistics course. An instructor could allow calculators in one class and forbid them in another, of course; if he could also assign students to the two conditions, he could conduct a true experiment. But that's probably not possible, nor would it be possible to forbid students to use calculators on homework. The best we can hope to do is to use some measure of statistical knowledge (final examination scores, perhaps) taken from a class taught *before* calculators were in wide use to serve as a control. Comparing those exam scores with those from an identical contemporary course would permit the comparison.

You can easily think of a number of alternative hypotheses to explain any observed change between the two classes' performance. Not only is there the possibility that calculators actually had an effect, but there have also been many other dramatic changes that occurred during the time between the two classes. During that time, computers entered the consumer market and electronics in general became much more sophisticated. College and departmental prerequisites for the statistics course could have changed. Statistics textbooks changed. The instructor could have changed the syllabus, the course content, or the lecture notes. The institution could have become more (or less) selective, the career goals of the students could have changed so that statistics became more (or less) relevant, thereby changing students' motivation, and so on. There's no

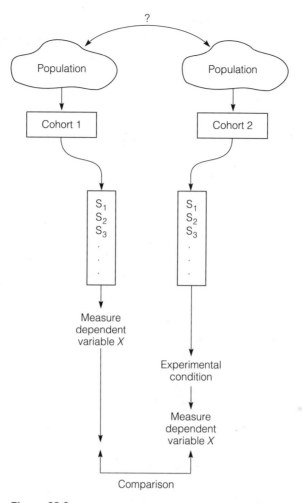

Figure 22.3

shortage of alternative explanations, indicating that this design is unable to make causal inferences.

Data Analysis for Nonequivalent Group Designs. Finding the appropriate analysis for nonequivalent group designs is problematic. One approach, and one that's probably adequate for most purposes, is straightforward: use ordinary, classical methods. Thus we could look to Student's t and the Wilcoxon test to compare the two sets of data in any of the previous designs. If the design has multiple conditions, the analysis of variance and the Kruskal–Wallis test are likely candidates for inferential tests.

Cook and Campbell (1979) consider the nonequivalent group designs carefully and find numerous problems in applying the traditional inferential analyses. They suggest several alternatives, including the analysis of covariance

(ANCOVA). The analysis of covariance is a variant of analysis of variance that allows certain extraneous variables to be dealt with by a form of statistical control. If you are considering a nonequivalent control group design, you might find Cook and Campbell helpful.

Internal and External Validity in Nonequivalent Group Designs. In Chapter 4 we discussed internal and external validity in research designs. Just to remind you, external validity refers to the ability to generalize to situations outside of the experiment, while internal validity determines whether we can infer a causal connection between the independent variable and the dependent variable. Chapter 4 distinguished three categories of threats to internal validity: physical factors, individual factors, and interpersonal factors. Let's look briefly at those categories again with special reference to the nonequivalent group quasi-experiments.

Physical factors. Included under physical factors are instrumentation and measurement problems, along with instruction and situational difficulties. There's nothing in nonequivalent control group quasi-experiments that poses unusual problems in measurement and instrumentation. The normal questions of reliability and validity apply, regardless of the form of the experimental design. But quasi-experiments often pose problems with situations and instructions. When two or more groups are tested in something other than a controlled experiment, they probably differ in several physical ways. There may be different individuals collecting the data (researchers, teachers, supervisors, and the like). Those individuals may read the instructions differently, may convey different attitudes toward the research, or take their responsibilities more or less seriously. Data may be collected in a lunchroom or a classroom, from a mailed questionnaire, or from observations on an assembly line. While these "realistic" settings increase external validity, the internal validity suffers greatly.

Interpersonal factors. These effects—from social desirability, from the demand characteristics of the experiment, and from evaluation anxiety—all appear in quasi-experiments. They are much more likely to affect two experimental groups differently when the groups are being studied at different times or by different investigators; both are often the case in quasi-experiments.

Individual factors. Of the individual factors that we discussed in Chapter 4, those having to do with subject selection are the most damaging to the nonequivalent group quasi-experiments. When we can't assign subjects to conditions directly, but must use existing groups or cohorts, we lose experimental control. The groups may be equivalent, or they may not be; and we'll never know. Subjects could have been selected into groups by chance, by self-selection, or by an arbitrary administrator. In any case, the groups probably are not equivalent, and there is no way to know the ways in which they differ. Group differences are completely confounded, of course, with the independent variable, which is what makes causal inference impossible in the quasi-experiment.

Other kinds of threats to internal validity, particularly maturation and order effects, aren't usually a problem with the nonequivalent group designs. They are, though, the major concern with the other broad class of quasi-experiment that we will discuss later.

The external validity of most quasi-experiments is quite good. This is so for the same reasons that the quasi-experiment is used—the research is done in the "real world" rather than in the "lab." Quasi-experiments often appear in applied settings where manipulation of variables is usually impossible; the research has considerable "realism" because it is in many ways more "real" than is laboratory research. Of course, the external validity is purchased at the cost of severely decreased internal validity.

Time Series Designs

In the designs just presented, two or more groups of subjects receive different treatments, as in classical between-groups experimental design. The difference between the true experiment and the quasi-experiment is, of course, that we can't randomly assign subjects to conditions and thus are not certain that they actually represent identical populations.

As in the classical experimental designs, we can improve quasi-experimental designs by using the same subjects under more than one condition. While any repeated-measures design is subject to a number of possible confounding extraneous variables, the ability to use subjects "as their own controls" is a powerful technique that can be used in quasi-experiments. In the language of quasi-experimentation, a design that uses the same subjects more than once is called a *time series* design, since that research is conducted in a series of observations over time.

The Pretest–Post-Test Design. The simplest of the time series designs is familiar (see Figure 22.4). This design is the simple repeated-measures experiment that we introduced in Chapter 14, but here there's a difference. In Chapter 14, we could control order effects by counterbalancing. In the quasi-experiment, though, the comparison is over time; specifically, it's a before-treatment–after-treatment comparison. This is a weakness of this design, since the order effect is completely confounded with the manipulation. This confounding, obviously, makes unequivocal causal inference impossible. Nevertheless, this design is often employed, if for no reason other than that it is frequently the only design possible.

The Pretest–Post-Test Control Group Design. It is often possible to have a pretest–post-test design in which you can arrange a control condition given to a separate group of subjects. This design is a very powerful one; it is diagrammed in Figure 22.5. This is exactly like the nonequivalent control group design that we presented earlier, with the exception that the assignment to experimental conditions is random. In this design, we have a control over the order effects that rendered the previous design so inadequate. This design can be considered to be a true experimental design. In fact, it's exactly like the two-condition, between-subjects design of Chapter 14, except that it uses the difference between a pretest and a post-test as its dependent variable. This is a very widely used design and

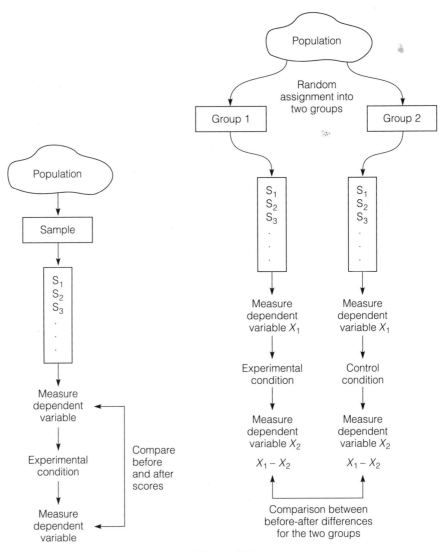

Figure 22.4

Figure 22.5

a very powerful one. But since it's identical to a standard two-condition design, we need not consider it further in this chapter.

The two designs just discussed represent the most elementary of the time series designs, comparing only two different points in time within the same subjects. As we increase the number of measurements, we come to the true time series designs. These designs are very useful, but limited to situations in which the same subjects can be measured on the same variables on multiple occasions. They are widely used in educational research, where data on the same children are readily available and in industrial settings where measures of productivity and other employee characteristics are taken frequently.

Interrupted Time Series Design. Suppose that your statistics instructor gives a weekly quiz on arithmetic problems and records the number of items correct out of 15 each week.* The subjects in the experiment remain the same over a period of weeks, as does the variable being measured. Research in a situation like this is called *time series* research and is very common in political science and economics.

In the beginning of the course, suppose that the instructor requires that all computations be done by hand. At some point later in the semester, the instructor permits the students to use calculators on the arithmetic quizzes. This experimental procedure is known as an interrupted time series design, since the series of measurements is interrupted by an experimental manipulation (introducing the calculator, in this case). The design is illustrated in Figure 22.6.

Results from time series designs are normally presented graphically. For example, suppose that Figure 22.7 shows the mean scores in the arithmetic quiz. The plot shows a steady increase in the number of problems correct over the semester. Now let's suppose that the instructor permitted calculators beginning with the quiz in the sixth week and that Figure 22.8 shows those data. Even without any inferential statistical analysis, it's clear that the introduction of the calculators led to a sudden and dramatic increase in the mean items correct. In fact, introducing the calculator led to a jump in the class's performance to nearly the final level achieved at the end of the semester.

A number of patterns might appear in the interrupted time series for our example. Figure 22.9, for example, shows no effect of the calculator at all. On the other hand, Figure 22.10 suggests an initial improvement when calculators were introduced, but then a decline after a couple of weeks, followed by an increase over the rest of the semester.

Other patterns are also possible. For example, Figure 22.11 shows no improvement until the calculators are used. One of the more interesting results in an interrupted time series is a change in the slope of the line after the interruption (see Figure 22.12). In this figure we can see a slow increase in arithmetic accuracy during the first five weeks; after calculators are permitted, though, the progress is more rapid. The slopes of the two line segments—before and after calculators—are different, which indicates a difference in rate of improvement. On the other hand, a shift in the level of the response *without* a change in slope suggests that the calculators increase the ability to solve the problems, but don't change the rate at which the class members improve their arithmetic skill. In Figure 22.13 the slope of the two segments of the curve remains the same, while the intercept changes after the calculators are introduced.

Multiple Time Series Design. The step from the interrupted time series design to the multiple time series is a short one—just introduce a control group. (Indeed, this design is sometimes called an "interrupted times series with control" design.) Suppose that our hypothetical statistics instructor teaches two sections of the

---

*Your instructor might also include statistics questions, but they increase in complexity over the semester and might be expected to be increasingly difficult. We'll consider only the kind of problems that remain relatively constant over the weeks of the class.

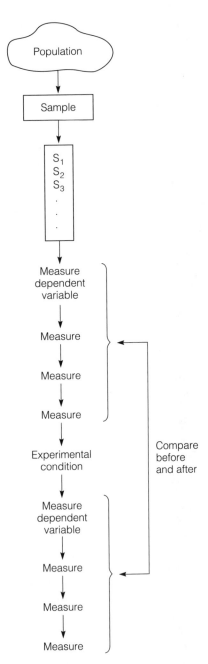

Figure 22.6

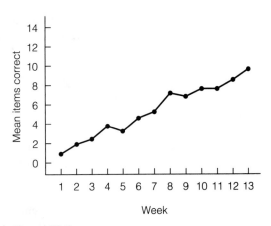

Figure 22.7

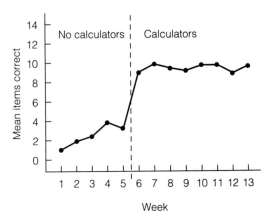

Figure 22.8

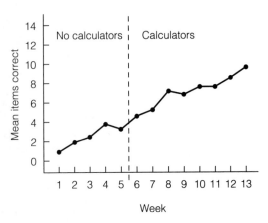

Figure 22.9

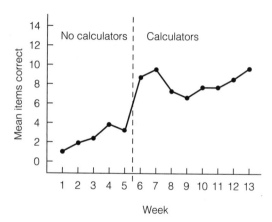

Figure 22.10

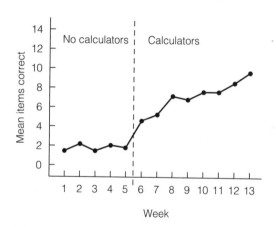

Figure 22.11

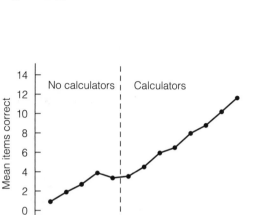

Figure 22.12

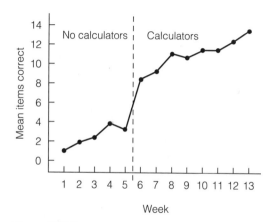

Figure 22.13

same course and permits the use of calculators beginning in week 6 in one of them. The plot of the two sets of means will clarify the effect of the interruption in the time series. Suppose that the instructor found the pattern plotted in Figure 22.14. This pattern strongly suggests that there was an effect of introducing the calculators.

Figure 22.15 illustrates the multiple time series design. This diagram implies that the two groups are drawn from the same population, as might be possible for a study of students in statistics classes. In such a case, you can have some confidence that the two groups are in fact equivalent. Usually, though, investigators are unable to assign subjects to conditions in a time series analysis, so that the control group is typically nonequivalent. Still, a dramatic change between two groups is often persuasive evidence of an effect of the experimental manipulation.

Quasi-Experiments

505

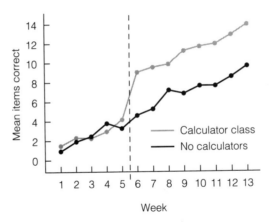

Figure 22.14

The Repeated/Removed Treatment Design. Suppose that you are interested in the effect of a particular drug on the activity level in hyperactive children. Establishing a baseline activity level and then administering the drug would constitute an interrupted time series design, with the drug administration as the interruption. After a period of time, the drug might be withdrawn and then reintroduced and so forth for several cycles of drug and no-drug. Such a design is called, for good reason, the repeated/removed treatment design. Figure 22.16 diagrams the design.

If the results of a study of drug and activity resulted in Figure 22.17, the evidence is visually clear—there is a substantial reduction in activity level during the no-drug periods, with a return to approximately the same level upon withdrawal of the drug.

Analysis of Time Series Designs. Our presentation of time series designs has been descriptive, and so it will remain. The correct analysis for time series designs, while not particularly complex, is beyond the scope of this book. The analyses might seem fairly straightforward, but the obvious solutions are incorrect. For example, it might occur to you to compare the mean for all of the drug periods in the previous example with the mean for all of the no-drug periods using a Student's t test. Or you might compare the slopes or the intercepts of the lines before and after the introduction of the calculator in an interrupted time series experiment to determine whether or not there was a change in the level of correctness or in the rate of improvement.

But both of those obvious analyses are incorrect. Why? Because they violate one or more of the fundamental assumptions of standard analyses, and in so doing they lead to dramatically increased probabilities of Type I error. Standard analyses assume that measures of variability are uncorrelated. That is, they require that the standard deviation of measurements taken at different times be unrelated to each other. But that's almost never the case in time series data. Events happening closely in time are typically more similar than are events

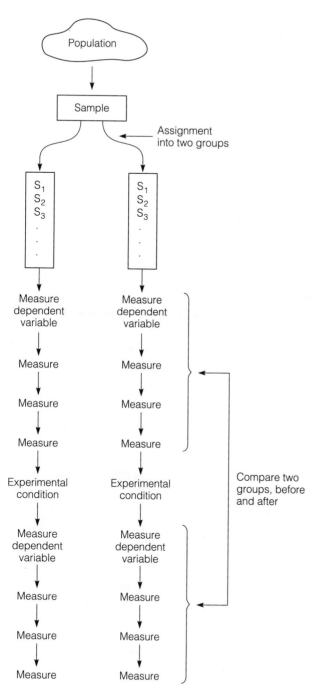

Figure 22.15

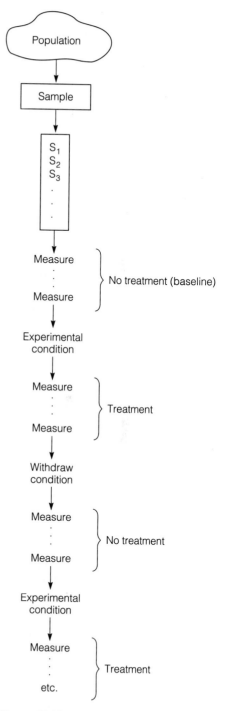

Figure 22.16

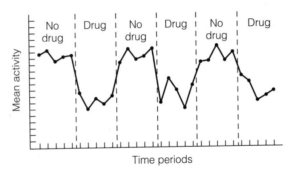

Figure 22.17

separated by longer periods, so that variabilities differ as a function of the distance in time between sets of observations. When this is the case, conventional test statistics such as t and F are often very inflated, leading to incorrect conclusions.

What are we to do with time series data? Descriptive plots are informative, as we've noted, and are often sufficient. But they don't address the issue of statistical significance. The usual inferential statistics for time series analysis rely on the work of Box and Jenkins (1976). McCain and McCleary (1979) summarize the problems with standard analyses and then provide a short and informative introduction to the Box–Jenkins ARIMA (autoregressive integrated moving average) model. Their chapter is a good starting point for the interested student.

Internal Validity and Time Series Designs. While interpersonal and physical factors can threaten the internal validity of time series research, the major weaknesses are in the personal area. In particular, order effects, maturation, and subject mortality are concerns. In addition, in the multiple time series design, subject selection bias can threaten internal validity.

Time series research takes place, by definition, in a fixed sequence over time. All subjects experience the research in exactly the same order. Counterbalancing is impossible. Thus the experimental manipulations are completely confounded with order effects. The multiple time series design offers a partial way around this weakness—both groups are exactly comparable in the order in which they take part in the research. Any differences between the groups are not likely to be order effects, since the orders are identical.

Maturation is sometimes a problem in time series research, and sometimes it isn't. When carried out over a long time interval, time series data may be influenced by subject maturation. With more limited lengths of time, that is not likely to be a major weakness. In adults, a time series study spanning several months or even a year or more is not likely to be seriously influenced by maturation. For young children, though, the same time interval could represent a major growth period for the child; and thus the research could be seriously confounded by growth.

Finally, subject attrition or mortality is frequently a serious problem in time series studies. The longer individuals remain in any situation, the greater the risk that some of them will leave the situation. Subjects can die, become ill, quit their job, move away from the area, or quit participating for almost any conceivable reason. As a result, the subjects who supply the last data points in a time series may be a small group that differs in subtle and unknown ways from the starting group. For example, think about a time series study on employee morale in an office. Over a period of time, employees will leave the work group. Some will be promoted, others will resign or be dismissed, others will remain in the group. But at the end of the research, the members of the original group will be fewer and will probably differ in important ways from the group that started the study. Perhaps some will have failed to be promoted or have failed to find other work; their morale level is likely to be quite different from that of people who left, regardless of any experimental manipulation that might have been intended to improve morale. Even replacing people who leave to keep the group the same size won't help much; there's no way to assure that replacements have the same characteristics as those who leave.

In short, time series designs have serious weaknesses in their internal validity. Causal inference is risky at best. Only a few of the designs—the pretest–post-test control and the multiple time series designs—have sufficient control over confounding variables that causal inference is sometimes possible. When the investigator can assign subjects randomly to conditions and when the time spanned is short enough that maturation and mortality are not issues, those two designs can make causal inferences. But it's rare that an investigator has that much control. Remember—these are research designs intended for use when tight experimental control is impossible. They represent a compromise between having no data at all and having a full and carefully controlled experiment.

Small-*N* Research

When we speak of small-*N* research, we don't mean just an experiment with an extremely small sample size. Small-*N* research usually has a single subject. The subject under study is often a clinical patient, a child with a learning or a behavior disorder, or sometimes an animal. Typically the research is directed at alleviating a problem in the subject's behavior; single-subject research is rarely used in theory-testing research.

The research designs for single subjects involve a series of activities involving the subject and the investigator; in fact, they're very similar to some of the time series designs just discussed.

The Before-After (A-B) Design

Your dog goes on a rampage each afternoon, chewing and destroying shoes, socks, clothing, bedding, and any other small object within its reach. After routine scolding and warning has failed, you call a specialist in animal behavior. He asks about the dog's feeding schedule. When he learns that you feed Fido at 5 P.M. each day and that the chewing usually happens between 2 P.M. and dinner time, he suggests a simple experiment. For a week, you keep track of the destructive behavior to establish a baseline rate of destruction. Then, introduce ad-lib feeding, in which a supply of food is made available all the time for the dog to eat whenever it's hungry. You continue to keep track of the undesirable behavior for a week. If you see a reduction in destructive chewing, you may be able to infer that the chewing has been eliminated by the simple expedient of changing the feeding procedure.

This procedure is a simple before-after experiment. In the first time period (A), a base rate of some behavior is established. Then an experimental manipulation is performed (B), and the behavior observed again. If there is a change in behavior, in the absence of other changes, you might be tempted to infer a causal connection between the manipulation and the change. But be careful— this is a repeated-measures experiment and is subject to the possible sources of invalidity that we know are present in such a situation. In particular, the maturation of the subject over the course of the experiment is a possible alternative explanation of the results. Perhaps your switch to ad lib feeding happened to coincide with the end of the dog's teething period, with entry into heat, or with a change of weather. The A-B design is exactly like the pretest–post-test quasi-experimental design, except that there is but a single subject involved.

An easy check on a maturation alternative hypothesis is simply to reinstate the initial condition and watch for a return to the original base rate. If we do this, we have changed the design into an A-B-A design.

The Reversal (A-B-A) Design

The A-B-A, or reversal, design simply reestablishes the initial conditions of the experiment. If the original behavior returns or its occurrence returns to the base rate, then there's good evidence that the change wasn't due to maturation but rather to the experimental intervention. If you withhold Fido's food and find that the chewing resumes, you can be reasonably sure that the destruction was related to prefeeding activity of some kind.

With our dog, we'd probably want to expand the experiment one more step, into an A-B-A-B experiment. If introducing ad lib feeding again led to a decrease in chewing, then we would be even more sure of our inference. The first change could have been just a coincidence, of course, but a second reduction in chewing would be strong evidence. Of course, for even more certainty, you could use an A-B-A-B-A-B-A-B design, repeating the A-B cycles until even the most skeptical observer was convinced. (Note that this design is just like the repeated/removed treatment design, but with a single subject.)

In the case of the destructive dog, we'd probably use an A-B-A-B design for another reason—we want to end the cycle in the most favorable situation. In this case, we want the dog's last experience to be the one that leads to decreased chewing.

Single-subject research is often employed in conjunction with behavior-modification techniques with institutionalized people. The A-B-A reversal design is a very common approach to finding which reinforcers are effective for an individual and which are not. But the A-B-A design is not the answer to all of the problems. When a reinforcer is found to be effective in, for example, reducing self-destructive behavior in a retarded person, you might not want to withdraw

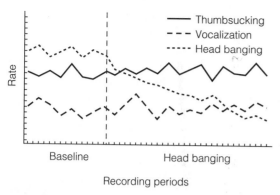

Figure 22.18

Figure 22.19

the condition as a check on a maturation hypothesis. To complete the A-B-A cycle in such a case might mean reestablishing the self-destructive behaviors; while it can be useful to rule out maturation as an explanation, it's probably not a good idea in an institutional setting. Fortunately, there is another design that can be used to rule out maturation as an alternative explanation in many cases.

The Multiple Baseline Design	A multiple baseline design records the rates for several behaviors during the baseline period. Then an intervention is directed at one of the behaviors. If target behavior changes its rate, and the others don't, then maturation is probably not causing the change, because all of the behaviors should be affected. For example, Figure 22.18 plots the hypothetical rates of three behaviors (head banging, thumbsucking, and vocalization) in a hypothetical retarded person. After the baseline period, the adult supervisors simply withdrew all attention from the individual when head banging began. Over the period of baseline recording periods, the three behaviors fluctuate somewhat, but do not change their overall levels appreciably. After the behavioral intervention, though, there is a steady reduction in head banging, but there is no accompanying decrease in the rate of thumbsucking or vocalization. Thus it's likely that the change can be causally related to the withdrawal of attention for head banging.

In most multiple baseline experiments, the procedure continues with the attempted modification of another of the chosen behaviors. In the example, the next step might be to try to increase vocalization by providing a reinforcement when the child makes a sound. Figure 22.19 shows hypothetical results. These results suggest that vocalization does increase in the third phase of the experiment, when it is reinforced. Note also that reinforcing vocalization seems to have no effect on the rate of head banging—it continues to decrease steadily.

Validity in Small-N Experiments	Experiments with very small samples often lend themselves to quite good internal validity. With reasonable care given to a single subject, conditions can often be well controlled, even if the research is often done in a non-laboratory setting such

as an institution. Extraneous variables can often be minimized, if not eliminated entirely. Subject selection is not usually a problem, since the study focuses on a single individual, often chosen because of a particular clinical or behavioral problem. (Of course, how representative that individual is of some larger population is a problem for external validity.) There is always the problem of maturation, but both the reversal and the multiple baseline designs have controls for that factor.

Analysis of Small-*N* Research	Small-*N* research typically has one of two aims. Most often, it is used to solve some particular problem, often a particular behavior problem, as we suggested in the illustrations. It is also used to demonstrate that some phenomenon or relationship exists. In either case, formal statistical analysis is rarely needed. Simple descriptive techniques are generally sufficient. Most often, simple plots of the data are sufficient to indicate whether the expected results occurred or not.

When inferential statistics are desired, small-*N* research faces the problems outlined for time series studies—because the variabilities are correlated with the time of measurement, conventional analyses are inappropriate. Even worse, since there is normally only a single subject, there can be no variability associated with a data point. In the time series quasi-experiments, each point in a plot represented the mean of a number of subjects at that time in the research. Since there was a mean, there could also be a variability around each point. In single-subject research, each point is a single value, and there can be no variability. The lack of variability makes developing inferential procedures exceptionally difficult.

Case Studies

A case study is an investigation of a single subject (or sometimes a very few subjects) just as are the small-sample experiments that we just discussed. But there's an important difference. Case studies are most often found in clinical literature and are detailed reports of a specific therapeutic case or group of cases. In Chapter 2, we mentioned the classic study of multiple personality by Thigpen and Cleckley (1957). Most case studies are not book-length as theirs is, but appear in the research literature as journal articles.

Case studies are detailed reports of a single individual or sometimes of small groups. In contrast to the small-*N* designs just explored, these are much more subjective, much less data-oriented, and much more clinically directed.

Case studies often suffer from serious defects in internal and external validity. In terms of external validity, case studies are severely limited by the cases and situations presented. In some cases, the individuals and the techniques used may generalize to other situations, while in other cases, the generality is limited. The internal validity is likewise weak. There is certainly subject selection bias, since the individual presented in the study was chosen by the researcher. At the least, the generality of the data from a single individual is often questionable. The objectivity of the data presented is open to serious question as well. If data are recorded, they are often in the form of behavioral notes and records kept by the clinician. The best data are likely to come from standardized tests given to the client.

Surveys and Interviews

The survey and the interview are very similar and are very widely used in all of the social and behavioral sciences. Both are used to obtain values on a great many variables quickly and easily. The two techniques have some similarities, and so we consider them together. They are carefully structured data collection instruments, designed to elicit information from people in response to a series of questions. The questions may take a variety of forms, but each question is asked in the same way for each subject. In the survey, the subjects read the questions and respond on paper, while in an interview, the questions and answers are delivered orally. The interactive nature of the interview allows a form of question that is not common on the survey, one where the answer to one question determines which question is asked next. In general, what we say about the survey is also true of the interview except for the manner of administration.

There are two general forms of survey. The *status survey* is the kind of survey that you probably think of first when you read the word *survey*. Its purpose is to investigate the attitudes and preferences of a large group of people, but not to test theoretical hypotheses. The well-known public opinion surveys conducted by polling organizations are status surveys. If a political party, a television producer, or a cereal manufacturer wants to know attitudes among the population, the status survey is the instrument that is employed. It is not concerned with hypothesized relationships among psychological variables, but merely describes the status of attitudes among a selected group of people. The *research survey*, on the other hand, is a scientific tool for exploring hypotheses and collecting data relevant to scholarly research. We'll be concerned only with the latter kind of survey here, though the general principles hold for status surveys just as well.

Kinds of Surveys

Surveys may be administered in any of several ways. The written survey or questionnaire is already a familiar form to most people. It is often delivered by mail or by hand, with a request for a by-mail return. Ordinary mail is often used for distributing questionnaires to geographically selected areas. Written surveys can be hand-delivered to individuals entering shopping malls or other gathering places, included with magazines or newspapers, sent through interoffice mail, or even delivered by a computer network. Surveys can also be administered verbally (in which case they're usually called interviews) either in person or by telephone. Public opinion polling organizations often use face-to-face interviews, but telephone interviews are becoming more popular. The telephone interview is widely regarded as a very good way to deliver a survey: the response rate is high, and it's inexpensive; and because of the comparative lack of demand characteristics on the subject, the data are more likely to be accurate than they are in a face-to-face interview. A telephone interview, of course, limits the possible subject population to those with telephones.

Conducting Survey Research

A research survey has four stages:

1. Developing hypotheses and writing the survey instrument
2. Planning the sampling
3. Collecting the data
4. Analyzing and interpreting the data

We'll discuss each briefly, and then turn to the validity of the survey method.

Developing Hypotheses and Writing the Survey. The research survey is directed at asking and answering theoretical questions, just as are all of the research techniques presented in this book. Why, then, do we restate that point here? Because students (and professionals, too) sometimes lose track of their research goal when they begin writing questions for a survey. The survey project should begin by writing a research proposal that specifically states the question or questions of interest. This set of questions need not be in the form that they'll have in the survey, but should be the ones that are theoretically important. Once you understand clearly just what you want to know, then write the actual survey questions. Once they're written, throw out those that don't address the research questions. This final editing will reduce the number of interesting questions that are unrelated to the research project.

There are two general forms of questions asked on surveys, open-ended and closed-ended. In a closed-ended question, the subject is given the possible answers and must select among them. A closed-ended question, taken from the survey by Lehman (1988) is

How did you learn to program (check all that apply)

_____ Self-taught (from books and/or manuals)
_____ High school course
_____ College computer science course
_____ College "Computers for psychology" course
_____ Industrial training program
_____ Other

An item like this yields category data; we could count how many people marked each alternative, but little other analysis would be possible. (Note the "check all that apply" instruction. This eliminates the use of Chi square to test a frequency hypothesis, since a subject may contribute more than a single count in the data.)

Your author, Richard S. Lehman, graduated from the University of Redlands and received his Ph.D. in psychology from the University of Colorado. He has taught at Franklin & Marshall College since 1965. His research interests are in music and the arts, computers, and statistics. When not teaching or writing this book, Dr. Lehman is a confirmed do-it-yourselfer who is equally likely to be found in his shop or in front of a computer.

Another common form of closed-ended question yields a numerical value. An example, again taken from Lehman (1988):

Below are several of the common rules of structured programming and/or "good programming style." For each, please indicate whether you agree in principle with each.

(Agree = 1, Disagree = 5)

Limit program modules to one page of code each	_____
Avoid GO TO statements	_____
Plan and build programs using top-down design	_____

These "rating scale" or *Likert scale* items are usually treated as if they yield interval-scale data. In other words, we assume that, to subjects, the difference between a "2" and a "3" is the same as the difference between a "3" and a "4," as well as that between a "4" and a "5." If that's the case, we have a set of "equal-appearing" intervals. If the measurement is on an interval scale, then the common measures of center and spread may be used.

An open-ended question, in contrast to the closed-ended question, permits the subject to elaborate on an answer. For example, these questions are from the same survey:

Major reason(s) for choosing this [computer programming] language _____

The major strength of the language is _____

Questions like these offer flexibility to the respondent, but require that the investigator deal with written responses. The investigator doesn't have to specify all possible alternatives in advance, so open-ended questions are easy to write. When the data are collected, the answers are usually grouped into categories and their frequencies tallied, as if the subjects had been given a closed-ended list of alternatives.

Once the questions are prepared, the survey instrument can be constructed. Normally, the survey begins with a series of demographic questions that allow the investigator to determine some personal characteristics. Age, educational background, sex, income, and occupation are examples of common demographic questions. Demographics is an area where students often ask too much information; what's important are those questions that address the research hypotheses.

Surveys normally progress from the demographic items to the research and attitude questions, keeping similar questions together. Save the more "personal" questions for the end, when the subjects will feel more comfortable with the process.

Planning the Sampling. In Chapter 11 we defined a random sample as a sample chosen from its population in such a way that every other sample of the same size had the same chance of being selected. To contrast it with other sampling methods, we may call this form of sample a *simple* random sample. Inferential statistics assume random sampling, but the sampling method need not be the simple procedure from Chapter 11. In conducting surveys, researchers often try to represent the population more representatively than might be possible with simple random sampling by using any of several other sampling methods.

There are two broad classes of sampling systems, *probability sampling* and *nonprobability sampling*. In probability sampling, randomness is used at some point in the process; in nonprobability sampling, it isn't. The simplest form of probability sampling is the simple random sample. If the population being sampled is small enough, it's conceivable to draw a simple random sample from it by using a random number table or generator. As we noted in Chapter 11, most experimental research simply *assumes*, for example, that a groups of rats is a random sample of those available from a breeder. Survey researchers are generally a bit more systematic in their sampling.

In most survey research, simple random sampling is neither possible nor desirable. Instead, some other form of sampling is used. In addition to simple random sampling, the two other most common forms of probability sampling are *cluster sampling* and *stratified random sampling*. In stratified random sampling, the population is divided into subsets (or strata), each of which is then sampled randomly. For example, if you wanted to survey the students at Big State U., you might define freshmen, sophomores, juniors, seniors, and graduate students as the strata. For a total sample size of 100, then, you would randomly sample 20 students from each stratum. If the sizes of the strata are quite different, you might want to make the samples proportional in size to the sizes. If graduate students constitute only 5% of the student body at Big State, you would sample five graduate students and fill the balance of the sample from the other classes.

Cluster sampling, the other common method of probability sampling, defines clusters of subjects to be sampled, often based on existing units. A national sample of college students could be developed by first randomly sampling states, then sampling campuses randomly within each of those states, randomly sampling from classes within each chosen campus, and so forth. Cluster sampling preserves randomness, but at the same time assures a broadly representative sample from well-defined existing geographic or sociopolitical groupings. Cluster sampling is probably the most widely used of all of the survey sampling methods.

Nonprobability samples are probably used in behavioral research more frequently than they should be. The most common, and least satisfactory, form of nonprobability sampling is *accidental sampling*. An accidental sample is one that is taken simply because it's convenient and available. Using your class as survey participants is an example of an accidental sample. Other accidental samples might be those obtained by using members of a club, students at a table in a dining hall, or students attending a rock concert. A *quota sample*, the other common form of nonprobability sampling, is formed by defining specific subgroups within the population and then choosing participants to fill out a "quota" of a certain number of individuals from each subgroup. Note the similarity here to a stratified random sample; the difference is that subjects are not chosen randomly from the strata.

Collecting, Analyzing, and Interpreting the Data. At this point in the book, there's little to be said about how to actually conduct research or even how to analyze the data. The general rules about conduct of research remain the same whether you are conducting an experiment in the laboratory or asking survey questions over the telephone. Courtesy, informed consent, and awareness of expectancy and other forms of bias apply to surveys as well as to laboratory research.

No data-analysis techniques are unique to surveys. In fact survey data typically call for the greatest variety of statistical tools. Many of the variables measured on a survey will be categorical in nature, and so the statistics in Chapter 21 are often used. In addition, many analyses will be correlational. Bivariate correlations are often the most important statistics in studying hypothesized relationships. Multivariate statistics, particularly multiple regression and factor analysis, are important tools in survey research.

If probability sampling was used in obtaining the subjects for the survey, then the classical inferential statistics can be employed. In fact, the classical tests are usually used even when nonprobability sampling was employed. While this actually violates the assumptions of the statistics, with careful limits on generalization, there is probably little risk of incorrect inference.

Validity in Survey Research

The external validity of a survey is typically high, since the questions asked are usually relevant to real-life situations. Surveys are often concerned with variables and questions that are of relevance and interest to the subjects and are clearly related to the world of daily interest and concern.

Internal validity in surveys is generally good, with the proviso that correlational data can't infer causation any better here than anywhere else. A carefully developed survey instrument contains a set of interrelated questions that can offer substantial construct validity to the variables being measured. Category variables are sometimes used to form "groups" within the survey respondents, and analysis of variance is used to explore differences among the groups. Such an analysis is much like that of a quasi-experiment—the investigator didn't randomly assign subjects to those groups, and so causal inference is impossible.

Archival Research

Psychologists sometimes do research without gathering any new data at all. In many institutions, where data have been collected over a period of time, a great deal of information is available, awaiting analysis. Thus it's possible to investigate the effects of admitting women at a previously all-male institution or to study trends in postgraduation careers at a university from available records at the institution.

There are also national and international repositories of computer-accessible data available to nearly every college and university. The U.S. Bureau of the Census collects a great deal of sociological and economic data, all of which is available. There are a number of indices, directories, and national organizations that make such data available. The Interuniversity Consortium for Political and Social Research (ICPSR) at the University of Michigan, and the Roper Center at the University of Connecticut are two well-known centers that provide vast quantities of data. There are numerous directories of data sets as

Analysis and Validity

There is no single technique of data analysis that is used on archival data, any more than there was for the survey. Indeed, much archival data is exactly that—survey data. Archival data typically include large numbers of variables, some of which may be appropriate to your research questions but many of which will not be. Whatever the focus of the research, the usual considerations in selecting an analysis apply—formulate the questions and then select the descriptive and inferential procedures that provide the best ways to find the answers.

Archival data usually have external validity equivalent to the survey, since it's often survey data. In most archival data sets, the data represent a great variety of individuals, have generally been collected in real-world settings, and are concerned with actual variables in problems of interest to society. An effort is usually made to have the sample be a broad and representative one, and so the results are often quite meaningful in their real-world context.

The internal validity for archival research, though, is another matter. There are several areas of concern. First, the data were collected and subjects placed in conditions (if different conditions or groups even exist in the data) by someone other than the current investigator. Thus there is the real possibility of selection bias, no way to know about it, and certainly no way to eliminate it. Second, the analyses are often correlational, which eliminates the possibility of determining causal connections between variables. And finally, the variables were defined and measured by someone else, who usually had different purposes and definitions than you will. This means that the construct validity of the measures may be low for your purposes. Suppose, for example, that you find a set of data relating childhood poverty level to career achievement. In your view, you would prefer to define the construct "poverty" in terms of several economic measures (per capita family income, number of parents in the household, number of siblings, and so forth). The earlier investigators, though, included educational level in their construct of "poverty" and collected data on variables to provide construct validity for their definition. The data available to you, then, might not have the appropriate measurements to establish the construct validity of your concept, because the earlier investigators simply hadn't collected data on those variables.

SUMMARY

- A quasi-experiment has an independent variable, but it isn't manipulated by the experimenter.
- The quasi-experiment suffers from unknown biases because of subject assignment.
- Quasi-experiments often have good external validity and very poor internal validity.

- A time series design is a form of quasi-experiment that involves a series of observations.
- In an interrupted time series design, an experimental manipulation takes place during the series of observations.
- The most serious confounding factors in time series designs are order effects, maturation, and subject mortality.
- Small-N research usually involves a single subject and is often used in applied settings.
- The internal validity in small-N research is usually very good, while the external validity is not.
- Case studies are detailed reports of single subjects or small groups.
- Surveys and interviews are standardized ways of asking questions.
- The internal and external validity of surveys and interviews is typically very good, although causal inference is limited.
- Archives of data make it possible to conduct research without actually collecting new data.

KEY TERMS

Accidental sampling	Nonequivalent post-test design
Archival research	Nonprobability sampling
Before-after (A-B) design	Open-ended question
Case study	Pretest–post-test design
Closed-ended question	Pretest–post-test control-group design
Cluster sampling	Probability sampling
Cohort design	Quasi-experiment
Demographic question	Quota sample
Interrupted time series design	Repeated/removed treatment design
Interview	Research survey
Likert scale item	Reversal (A-B-A) design
Multiple baseline design	Simple random sample
Multiple time series design	Status survey
Nonequivalent control-group design	Stratified random sampling
Nonequivalent group design	

EXERCISES

1. In the published literature (use the *Psychological Abstracts*, see pp. 33–36), identify three quasi-experiments that might easily masquerade as "real" experiments. For each, say why it is actually a quasi-experiment and identify the actual design that was used.

2. A friend who knows that you're a psychology major asks you what she can do to keep her dog from jumping up on guests. Pick a small-N strategy and write a set of instructions for your friend in which you describe the procedures that she should use and the data she should collect.

3. Develop a survey on some topic of interest to you. Your finished survey should have a few demographic questions, several closed-ended questions and one or two open-ended questions. (*Hint*: see p. 514 for a discussion of the steps in conducting a survey.)

4. Administer the survey from Exercise 3 to a sample of individuals. Summarize the data appropriately and write a report. Be sure that the report states the sampling method that you used.

5. Consult your computer center and/or reference librarian and find out what major data archives are available at your institution.

Z	Area between mean and Z	Area beyond Z	Z	Area between mean and Z	Area beyond Z
0.00	0.00000	0.50000	0.47	0.18083	0.31917
0.01	0.00400	0.49600	0.48	0.18439	0.31561
0.02	0.00798	0.49202	0.49	0.18794	0.31206
0.03	0.01198	0.48802	0.50	0.19146	0.30854
0.04	0.01595	0.48405	0.51	0.19498	0.30502
0.05	0.01995	0.48005	0.52	0.19847	0.30153
0.06	0.02392	0.47608	0.53	0.20195	0.29805
0.07	0.02791	0.47209	0.54	0.20540	0.29460
0.08	0.03188	0.46812	0.55	0.20885	0.29115
0.09	0.03587	0.46413	0.56	0.21226	0.28774
0.10	0.03983	0.46017	0.57	0.21567	0.28433
0.11	0.04381	0.45619	0.58	0.21904	0.28096
0.12	0.04776	0.45224	0.59	0.22242	0.27758
0.13	0.05173	0.44827	0.60	0.22575	0.27425
0.14	0.05567	0.44433	0.61	0.22908	0.27092
0.15	0.05963	0.44037	0.62	0.23237	0.26763
0.16	0.06356	0.43644	0.63	0.23566	0.26434
0.17	0.06751	0.43249	0.64	0.23891	0.26109
0.18	0.07142	0.42858	0.65	0.24216	0.25784
0.19	0.07536	0.42464	0.66	0.24537	0.25463
0.20	0.07926	0.42074	0.67	0.24858	0.25142
0.21	0.08318	0.41682	0.68	0.25175	0.24825
0.22	0.08706	0.41294	0.69	0.25491	0.24509
0.23	0.09096	0.40904	0.70	0.25804	0.24196
0.24	0.09483	0.40517	0.71	0.26116	0.23884
0.25	0.09872	0.40128	0.72	0.26424	0.23576
0.26	0.10257	0.39743	0.73	0.26732	0.23268
0.27	0.10643	0.39357	0.74	0.27035	0.22965
0.28	0.11026	0.38974	0.75	0.27338	0.22662
0.29	0.11410	0.38590	0.76	0.27637	0.22363
0.30	0.11791	0.38209	0.77	0.27936	0.22064
0.31	0.12173	0.37827	0.78	0.28230	0.21770
0.32	0.12552	0.37448	0.79	0.28525	0.21475
0.33	0.12931	0.37069	0.80	0.28814	0.21186
0.34	0.13307	0.36693	0.81	0.29104	0.20896
0.35	0.13684	0.36316	0.82	0.29389	0.20611
0.36	0.14058	0.35942	0.83	0.29674	0.20326
0.37	0.14432	0.35568	0.84	0.29955	0.20045
0.38	0.14803	0.35197	0.85	0.30235	0.19765
0.39	0.15174	0.34826	0.86	0.30511	0.19489
0.40	0.15542	0.34458	0.87	0.30786	0.19214
0.41	0.15911	0.34089	0.88	0.31057	0.18943
0.42	0.16276	0.33724	0.89	0.31328	0.18672
0.43	0.16641	0.33359	0.90	0.31594	0.18406
0.44	0.17003	0.32997	0.91	0.31860	0.18140
0.45	0.17366	0.32634	0.92	0.32121	0.17879
0.46	0.17724	0.32276	0.93	0.32383	0.17617

Source: Entries in this table were computed by the author.

Z	Area between mean and Z	Area beyond Z	Z	Area between mean and Z	Area beyond Z
0.94	0.32639	0.17361	1.45	0.42648	0.07352
0.95	0.32895	0.17105	1.46	0.42785	0.07215
0.96	0.33147	0.16853	1.47	0.42923	0.07077
0.97	0.33399	0.16601	1.48	0.43056	0.06944
0.98	0.33646	0.16354	1.49	0.43190	0.06810
0.99	0.33892	0.16108	1.50	0.43319	0.06681
1.00	0.34134	0.15866	1.51	0.43449	0.06551
1.01	0.34376	0.15624	1.52	0.43574	0.06426
1.02	0.34614	0.15386	1.53	0.43700	0.06300
1.03	0.34851	0.15149	1.54	0.43822	0.06178
1.04	0.35083	0.14917	1.55	0.43944	0.06056
1.05	0.35315	0.14685	1.56	0.44062	0.05938
1.06	0.35543	0.14457	1.57	0.44180	0.05820
1.07	0.35770	0.14230	1.58	0.44295	0.05705
1.08	0.35993	0.14007	1.59	0.44409	0.05591
1.09	0.36215	0.13785	1.60	0.44520	0.05480
1.10	0.36433	0.13567	1.61	0.44631	0.05369
1.11	0.36651	0.13349	1.62	0.44738	0.05262
1.12	0.36864	0.13136	1.63	0.44846	0.05154
1.13	0.37077	0.12923	1.64	0.44950	0.05050
1.14	0.37286	0.12714	1.65	0.45054	0.04946
1.15	0.37494	0.12506	1.66	0.45154	0.04846
1.16	0.37698	0.12302	1.67	0.45255	0.04745
1.17	0.37901	0.12099	1.68	0.45352	0.04648
1.18	0.38100	0.11900	1.69	0.45450	0.04550
1.19	0.38299	0.11701	1.70	0.45543	0.04457
1.20	0.38493	0.11507	1.71	0.45638	0.04362
1.21	0.38687	0.11313	1.72	0.45728	0.04272
1.22	0.38877	0.11123	1.73	0.45820	0.04180
1.23	0.39066	0.10934	1.74	0.45907	0.04093
1.24	0.39251	0.10749	1.75	0.45995	0.04005
1.25	0.39436	0.10564	1.76	0.46080	0.03920
1.26	0.39617	0.10383	1.77	0.46165	0.03835
1.27	0.39797	0.10203	1.78	0.46246	0.03754
1.28	0.39973	0.10027	1.79	0.46328	0.03672
1.29	0.40149	0.09851	1.80	0.46407	0.03593
1.30	0.40320	0.09680	1.81	0.46486	0.03514
1.31	0.40491	0.09509	1.82	0.46562	0.03438
1.32	0.40658	0.09342	1.83	0.46639	0.03361
1.33	0.40825	0.09175	1.84	0.46712	0.03288
1.34	0.40988	0.09012	1.85	0.46785	0.03215
1.35	0.41150	0.08850	1.86	0.46856	0.03144
1.36	0.41309	0.08691	1.87	0.46927	0.03073
1.37	0.41467	0.08533	1.88	0.46995	0.03005
1.38	0.41621	0.08379	1.89	0.47063	0.02937
1.39	0.41775	0.08225	1.90	0.47128	0.02872
1.40	0.41924	0.08076	1.91	0.47194	0.02806
1.41	0.42074	0.07926	1.92	0.47257	0.02743
1.42	0.42220	0.07780	1.93	0.47321	0.02679
1.43	0.42365	0.07635	1.94	0.47381	0.02619
1.44	0.42507	0.07493	1.95	0.47442	0.02558

Z	Area between mean and Z	Area beyond Z	Z	Area between mean and Z	Area beyond Z
1.96	0.47500	0.02500	2.48	0.49343	0.00657
1.97	0.47559	0.02441	2.49	0.49362	0.00638
1.98	0.47615	0.02385	2.50	0.49379	0.00621
1.99	0.47672	0.02328	2.51	0.49397	0.00603
2.00	0.47725	0.02275	2.52	0.49413	0.00587
2.01	0.47780	0.02220	2.53	0.49431	0.00569
2.02	0.47831	0.02169	2.54	0.49446	0.00554
2.03	0.47883	0.02117	2.55	0.49462	0.00538
2.04	0.47932	0.02068	2.56	0.49477	0.00523
2.05	0.47983	0.02017	2.57	0.49493	0.00507
2.06	0.48030	0.01970	2.58	0.49506	0.00494
2.07	0.48078	0.01922	2.59	0.49521	0.00479
2.08	0.48124	0.01876	2.60	0.49534	0.00466
2.09	0.48170	0.01830	2.61	0.49548	0.00452
2.10	0.48214	0.01786	2.62	0.49560	0.00440
2.11	0.48258	0.01742	2.63	0.49574	0.00426
2.12	0.48300	0.01700	2.64	0.49585	0.00415
2.13	0.48342	0.01658	2.65	0.49599	0.00401
2.14	0.48382	0.01618	2.66	0.49609	0.00391
2.15	0.48423	0.01577	2.67	0.49622	0.00378
2.16	0.48461	0.01539	2.68	0.49632	0.00368
2.17	0.48501	0.01499	2.69	0.49644	0.00356
2.18	0.48537	0.01463	2.70	0.49653	0.00347
2.19	0.48575	0.01425	2.71	0.49665	0.00335
2.20	0.48610	0.01390	2.72	0.49674	0.00326
2.21	0.48646	0.01354	2.73	0.49684	0.00316
2.22	0.48679	0.01321	2.74	0.49693	0.00307
2.23	0.48714	0.01286	2.75	0.49703	0.00297
2.24	0.48745	0.01255	2.76	0.49711	0.00289
2.25	0.48779	0.01221	2.77	0.49721	0.00279
2.26	0.48809	0.01191	2.78	0.49728	0.00272
2.27	0.48841	0.01159	2.79	0.49738	0.00262
2.28	0.48870	0.01130	2.80	0.49744	0.00256
2.29	0.48900	0.01100	2.81	0.49753	0.00247
2.30	0.48928	0.01072	2.82	0.49760	0.00240
2.31	0.48957	0.01043	2.83	0.49768	0.00232
2.32	0.48983	0.01017	2.84	0.49774	0.00226
2.33	0.49011	0.00989	2.85	0.49782	0.00218
2.34	0.49036	0.00964	2.86	0.49788	0.00212
2.35	0.49062	0.00938	2.87	0.49796	0.00204
2.36	0.49086	0.00914	2.88	0.49801	0.00199
2.37	0.49112	0.00888	2.89	0.49808	0.00192
2.38	0.49134	0.00866	2.90	0.49813	0.00187
2.39	0.49159	0.00841	2.91	0.49820	0.00180
2.40	0.49180	0.00820	2.92	0.49825	0.00175
2.41	0.49203	0.00797	2.93	0.49832	0.00168
2.42	0.49224	0.00776	2.94	0.49836	0.00164
2.43	0.49246	0.00754	2.95	0.49842	0.00158
2.44	0.49266	0.00734	2.96	0.49846	0.00154
2.45	0.49287	0.00713	2.97	0.49852	0.00148
2.46	0.49305	0.00695	2.98	0.49856	0.00144
2.47	0.49325	0.00675	2.99	0.49862	0.00138

Z	Area between mean and Z	Area beyond Z	Z	Area between mean and Z	Area beyond Z
3.00	0.49865	0.00135	3.25	0.49943	0.00057
3.02	0.49874	0.00126	3.30	0.49952	0.00048
3.04	0.49882	0.00118	3.35	0.49961	0.00039
3.06	0.49889	0.00111	3.40	0.49966	0.00034
3.08	0.49896	0.00104	3.45	0.49973	0.00027
3.10	0.49903	0.00097	3.50	0.49977	0.00023
3.12	0.49910	0.00090	3.60	0.49984	0.00016
3.14	0.49916	0.00084	3.70	0.49989	0.00011
3.16	0.49921	0.00079	3.80	0.49993	0.00007
3.18	0.49926	0.00074	3.90	0.49995	0.00005
3.20	0.49931	0.00069	4.00	0.49997	0.00003

	1	2	3	4	5	6	7	8	9	10
1	90651	67179	43389	45592	09057	38806	06873	29710	37293	04462
2	74107	35471	37272	07404	31724	05619	24288	30487	36478	08412
3	47864	24073	04782	20490	03629	15687	19691	23560	05433	45868
4	50294	05025	21530	03813	16484	20691	24757	05709	48197	15299
5	09991	04277	00758	03275	04110	04918	01134	09575	03039	06478
6	42809	03246	14030	17611	21072	04859	41023	13022	27757	24162
7	07582	02485	03119	03732	00861	07266	02306	04916	04280	02084
8	32774	13483	16133	03720	31408	09969	21251	18499	09010	23077
9	41139	20250	04670	39424	12514	26674	23220	11310	28967	04775
10	49223	05587	47171	14973	31916	27783	13532	34659	05713	35629
11	11351	10878	03453	07360	06407	03121	07992	01317	08216	04522
12	95830	29150	62135	54088	26345	67475	11122	69363	38179	22231
13	30418	19723	17169	08363	21418	03530	22017	12119	07056	01800
14	64839	36597	17825	45654	07525	46932	25832	15041	03838	53919
15	56442	15517	39742	06551	40854	22487	13093	03341	46936	18092
16	27492	19357	03191	19899	10953	06378	01627	22861	08812	09727
17	70412	08172	50965	28053	16334	04168	58552	22570	24913	48731
18	11606	08400	04624	02692	00687	09651	03720	04106	08032	02770
19	72382	28837	16791	04284	60191	23201	25610	50095	17276	38910
20	39841	09242	02358	33130	12771	14096	27573	09509	21417	03672
21	23198	01373	19291	07436	08208	16055	05537	12470	02138	10245
22	05919	04922	01897	02094	04096	01413	03182	00546	02614	03716
23	83157	26655	29423	57553	19848	44703	07665	36725	52204	21068
24	32054	11341	22184	07651	17231	02955	14156	20123	08121	11411
25	35382	24488	08445	19020	03261	15626	22212	08964	12596	20851
26	69209	16519	37205	06380	30565	43448	17535	24639	40786	49892
27	23868	12831	02200	10541	14984	06047	08497	14066	17206	04375
28	53757	04955	23741	33747	13620	19138	31679	38752	09855	11516
29	09218	04071	05787	02335	03282	05432	06645	01690	01975	06733
30	44164	27725	11189	15722	26026	31837	08096	09461	32260	00830
31	62778	15905	22349	36996	45256	11508	13449	45857	01179	54826
32	25336	09020	14931	18264	04645	05428	18507	00476	22127	10469
33	35600	20980	25664	06526	07627	26005	00669	31091	14710	29652
34	58931	42483	10803	12625	43047	01107	51467	24351	49085	04526
35	72089	13215	15444	52658	01354	62958	29788	60044	05536	54542
36	18332	03927	13391	00344	16010	07575	15269	01408	13870	03584
37	21423	15649	00402	18710	08852	17844	01645	16209	04189	05347
38	73047	01372	63795	30184	60842	05610	55267	14283	18233	24470
39	01878	01640	00776	01565	00144	01421	00367	00469	00629	00680
40	87334	36087	72742	06707	66076	17076	21799	29256	31593	17684
41	41321	34417	03173	31263	08079	10314	13842	14948	08367	06374
42	83292	06397	63018	16286	20790	27902	30131	16865	12849	81253
43	07680	05810	01502	01917	02573	02778	01555	01185	07492	06707
44	75659	14793	18885	25345	27370	15320	11672	73807	66071	14103
45	19553	04880	06550	07073	03959	03016	19074	17075	03645	00422
46	24960	08361	09030	05054	03851	24349	21797	04653	00538	10766
47	33499	12118	06783	05168	32679	29254	06244	00722	14449	14442
48	36176	07325	05581	35290	31591	06743	00780	15603	15596	31311
49	20248	03124	19753	17682	03774	00437	08734	08730	17525	19423
50	15427	15049	13472	02876	00333	06654	06651	13352	14798	15385

Source: Entries in this table were computed by the author.

	1	2	3	4	5	6	7	8	9	10
51	97552	85190	18184	02103	42076	42057	84434	93575	97291	93617
52	87328	16278	01883	37666	37649	75584	83767	87093	83804	11550
53	18640	00402	08040	08036	16133	17880	18590	17888	02465	03233
54	02156	00930	00930	01866	02068	02150	02069	00285	00374	00556
55	43132	18595	37332	41373	43016	41392	05705	07481	11123	13721
56	43112	37315	41354	42996	41373	05702	07478	11117	13715	30457
57	86552	83024	86320	83061	11448	15012	22320	27534	61146	67000
58	95923	95665	92053	12687	16637	24736	30515	67766	74253	20442
59	99731	95708	13191	17298	25718	31726	70457	77201	21253	86408
60	95966	12693	16645	24747	30528	67796	74286	20451	83145	82268
61	13226	02294	03411	04207	09344	10238	02819	11459	11339	03348
62	17345	04473	05518	12253	13426	03696	15028	14869	04391	14348
63	25787	08203	18218	19962	05495	22342	22107	06528	21332	07871
64	31812	22474	24625	06779	27562	27271	08053	26315	09710	11796
65	70647	54687	15055	61209	60563	17884	58441	21564	26196	12522
66	77409	16496	67068	66361	19596	64035	23628	28704	13721	76725
67	21310	18464	18269	05395	17629	06505	07902	03777	21122	11437
68	86641	74275	21933	71672	26446	32127	15357	85875	46500	30675
69	85727	21701	70915	26167	31788	15195	84970	46009	30352	54380
70	25314	20941	07727	09387	04487	25091	13586	08963	16058	13481
71	82722	25250	30674	14662	81992	44397	29288	52474	44054	62971
72	30524	11318	05410	30254	16382	10807	19362	16255	23236	03849
73	37080	06572	36753	19901	13128	23522	19747	28227	04675	08347
74	17725	17568	09513	06275	11243	09439	13493	02235	03990	03836
75	99117	53196	35092	62873	52784	75451	12497	22311	21449	23602
76	53670	19002	34045	28582	40855	06767	12081	11614	12780	18202
77	35405	22459	18855	26951	04464	07970	07662	08431	12007	00701
78	63434	33781	48288	07998	14279	13727	15105	21513	01255	43363
79	53255	40539	06715	11988	11524	12681	18061	01054	36405	08802
80	76123	09598	17135	16473	18127	25817	01507	52037	12582	75610
81	12608	02838	02728	03002	04276	00250	08619	02084	12523	09807
82	22510	04871	05360	07634	00445	15388	03720	22358	17509	09911
83	21640	05153	07339	00428	14793	03577	21494	16833	09528	04197
84	23813	08076	00471	16278	03936	23652	18523	10485	04618	06827
85	33914	00671	23184	05605	33685	26380	14932	06577	09723	17046
86	01979	01353	00327	01966	01539	00871	00384	00567	00995	01491
87	68359	11299	67898	53173	30098	13257	19597	34359	51493	13965
88	16528	16417	12857	07277	03205	04738	08308	12450	03376	08256
89	99326	77260	43732	19262	28475	49923	74819	20291	49614	35982
90	77785	34248	15084	22299	39097	58593	15890	38854	28178	52758
91	44029	08538	12622	22130	33166	08994	21993	15950	29863	24369
92	19392	05559	09747	14608	03962	09687	07025	13153	10733	03114
93	28668	14409	21595	05856	14320	10385	19444	15867	04603	11960
94	50262	37861	10268	25107	18208	34091	27819	08070	20969	42767
95	75327	15388	37626	27288	51090	41691	12094	31426	64094	59078
96	20428	10204	07400	13856	11306	03280	08523	17382	16022	13660
97	49951	18095	33880	27646	08020	20839	42502	39176	33400	15264
98	36226	24570	20050	05816	15113	30824	28411	24223	11070	09028
99	67825	37539	10890	28296	57711	53194	45352	20727	16904	58845
100	55347	08886	23090	47093	43408	37008	16913	13794	48019	51289
101	16055	06698	13661	12592	10735	04906	04001	13930	14878	15157
102	41719	35498	32720	27896	12749	10397	36195	38660	39384	20438
103	85088	66733	56894	26002	21206	73822	78849	80325	41684	82874
104	78429	52442	23967	19546	68045	72678	74039	38422	76388	76783
105	66866	20433	16664	58013	61963	63123	32757	65126	65463	29715
106	30559	07616	26513	28318	28848	14971	29764	29918	13580	01619

B Random Numbers

	1	2	3	4	5	6	7	8	9	10
107	24922	21622	23095	23527	12209	24274	24399	11075	01321	18260
108	86760	80399	81904	42504	84503	84940	38556	04598	63569	47224
109	92668	87482	45398	90257	90724	41181	04911	67898	50440	43765
110	94403	46248	91947	92422	41952	05003	69169	51385	44584	53378
111	48990	47715	47962	21771	02596	35895	26666	23137	27700	14936
112	97398	95355	43284	05162	71363	53015	45999	55072	29694	95934
113	97902	43507	05188	71732	53289	46237	55357	29847	96430	61580
114	44440	02355	32561	24189	20988	25128	13548	43772	27952	28947
115	05299	03883	02885	02503	02996	01616	05220	03333	03452	04897
116	73270	39882	34603	41429	22338	72168	46086	47727	67701	62474
117	54431	25706	30777	16594	53613	34237	35455	50294	46411	39883
118	47227	26704	14398	46518	29706	30763	43638	40269	34605	04229
119	56543	17238	55693	35565	36831	52245	48212	41431	05063	52062
120	30487	30029	19176	19859	28170	25995	22339	02730	28071	01664
121	98497	61954	64159	91011	83985	72171	08819	90691	05378	69702
122	62900	40972	58119	53632	46088	05632	57915	03434	44511	42886
123	65138	60187	55541	47729	05832	59976	03556	46096	44412	13142
124	92400	78786	67704	08273	85077	05045	65387	62999	18642	89399
125	85266	62477	07635	78508	04655	60339	58135	17203	82497	30324
126	73273	06561	67466	04000	51852	49958	14783	70893	26058	26193
127	08954	08244	00489	06336	06105	01806	08663	03184	03201	01599
128	92075	05027	65157	62777	18576	89085	32745	32914	16448	34829
129	05460	03864	03722	01101	05282	01942	01952	00975	02065	02964
130	70766	48249	14277	68468	25167	25296	12641	26768	38418	30038
131	68181	13756	65967	24248	24372	12179	25790	37015	28941	09488
132	20175	19520	07175	07212	03604	07632	10953	08564	02808	00669
133	96753	34409	34586	17283	36598	52526	41069	13464	03207	22836
134	35564	12713	06353	13453	19307	15096	04949	01179	08394	32655
135	35747	06386	13522	19407	15173	04975	01185	08437	32823	22953
136	17863	06757	09698	07582	02486	00592	04216	16402	11470	11171
137	37827	20536	16056	05264	01254	08928	34733	24288	23655	25581
138	54289	23044	07555	01799	12814	49849	34859	33951	36714	06579
139	42447	05907	01407	10018	38975	27255	26545	28706	05144	37231
140	13916	00461	03284	12778	08935	08703	09411	01686	12206	12431
141	03314	00782	03043	02128	02073	02241	00402	02907	02961	00223
142	23602	21672	15155	14760	15962	02860	20702	21084	01585	09521
143	91821	58958	57422	62096	11127	80538	82025	06165	37042	18583
144	64209	40154	43423	07781	56319	57359	04311	25903	12994	35980
145	62537	42292	07579	54852	55865	04199	25228	12656	35043	15801
146	67627	08195	59317	60412	04540	27282	13686	37896	17087	54410
147	12119	10629	10826	00814	04889	02453	06791	03062	09750	05064
148	87712	78354	05889	35384	17751	49151	22162	70570	36649	62409
149	89331	05998	36037	18079	50058	22571	71873	37325	63561	57293
150	06714	02708	01359	03762	01696	05402	02805	04777	04306	02811
151	40341	08164	22606	10193	32457	16856	28703	25873	16890	25617
152	20238	11340	05113	16283	08456	14399	12980	08473	12851	16429
153	56036	14159	45085	23414	39871	35939	23461	35584	45491	17456
154	25267	20329	10557	17978	16205	10579	16045	20512	07871	17524
155	80457	33617	57246	51601	33685	51091	65316	25063	55801	67001
156	41783	29729	26798	17493	26533	33920	13016	28979	34795	18091
157	71152	45634	29789	45182	57762	22164	49348	59253	30808	26396
158	64136	26852	40727	52066	19979	44482	53410	27770	23794	27479
159	41867	26586	33988	13042	29037	34865	18128	15532	17938	01025
160	63501	51551	19781	44042	52881	27495	23558	27207	01555	52885
161	81181	25289	56304	67605	35150	30117	34782	01988	67610	33764
162	31151	21605	25941	13488	11557	13347	00763	25943	12956	06287

	1	2	3	4	5	6	7	8	9	10
163	69356	57757	30030	25730	29716	01699	57761	28846	13997	62480
164	83276	36057	30894	35680	02039	69355	34635	16806	75021	74496
165	43298	16063	18551	01060	36060	18008	08738	39006	38733	03038
166	37099	15895	00909	30897	15430	07487	33421	33187	02603	18553
167	42845	01049	35683	17820	08647	38598	38328	03007	21427	22929
168	02449	02040	01019	00494	02206	02191	00172	01225	01311	01275
169	83282	34638	16807	75026	74501	05844	41650	44569	43361	60811
170	41591	08394	37468	37206	02919	20800	22258	21654	30369	06279
171	20181	18181	18053	01416	10093	10800	10507	14736	03047	10616
172	90086	80588	06322	45053	48210	46903	65779	13600	47388	03362
173	89456	06278	44738	47873	46575	65319	13505	47057	03339	41013
174	07018	03510	03755	03654	05124	01059	03691	00262	03217	04502
175	50011	26764	26038	36517	07550	26307	01867	22928	32084	19890
176	53516	27863	39076	08079	28151	01997	24535	34332	21284	30681
177	52065	38016	07860	27388	01943	23870	33401	20707	29849	35845
178	73018	11024	38410	02725	33476	46844	29041	41861	50271	19984
179	15097	07942	00563	06921	09685	06004	08655	10394	04132	12276
180	52603	01963	24117	33747	20921	30158	36216	14397	42772	06014
181	03732	01711	02394	01484	02140	02570	01021	03035	00427	02377
182	45847	29412	18234	26284	31564	12547	37278	05242	29197	21705
183	64154	25515	36780	44169	17558	52164	07335	40856	30372	54547
184	39772	22801	27382	10885	32339	04547	25328	18829	33816	13224
185	57330	39471	15690	46616	06555	36510	27141	48745	19062	12275
186	68848	18842	55981	07872	43845	32594	58538	22891	14741	42824
187	27368	22253	03129	17429	12957	23270	09100	05860	17023	09416
188	81311	09297	51782	38494	69135	27035	17410	50576	27974	43317
189	11433	07281	05413	09721	03801	02448	07112	03934	06091	07909
190	63684	30149	54147	21174	13635	39612	21910	33926	44051	47181
191	47342	40252	15741	10136	29447	16288	25220	32747	35074	38589
192	85025	28270	18205	52886	29252	45295	58813	62992	69305	67667
193	33249	07119	20681	11439	17713	22999	24633	27101	26461	00140
194	21411	13318	07366	11406	14810	15863	17452	17040	00090	16272
195	62201	21400	33136	43025	46082	50701	49503	00261	47272	16468
196	34404	18328	23798	25489	28043	27381	00144	26147	09109	25857
197	53273	36850	39468	43423	42397	00224	40487	14104	40038	46539
198	69171	51246	56382	55050	00290	52570	18313	51987	60428	41305
199	74086	60388	58962	00311	56305	19615	55681	64721	44240	10760
200	81511	64871	00342	61948	21580	61261	71208	48673	11838	12097
201	79585	00334	60484	21071	59814	69525	47523	11558	11811	29066
202	00420	00319	00111	00315	00367	00251	00061	00062	00153	00153
203	75999	20121	57119	66393	45382	11038	11279	27756	27667	39281
204	26476	19898	23129	15810	03845	03929	09669	09638	13684	02768
205	75157	65657	44879	10915	11154	27449	27361	38846	07858	27523
206	87360	52166	12688	12965	31905	31803	45153	09134	31992	86072
207	59714	08672	08862	21809	21738	30864	06243	21868	58834	21992
208	14523	02155	05304	05287	07507	01518	05319	14309	05349	12855
209	14841	05420	05403	07671	01552	05435	14622	05466	13136	11120
210	36522	13296	18877	03818	13375	35984	13451	32327	27365	10030
211	36404	18816	03806	13332	35868	13407	32223	27277	09998	02345
212	51686	05404	18928	50924	19035	45750	38728	14195	03329	36214
213	10455	03829	10301	03851	09254	07834	02871	00673	07326	10207
214	36621	36081	13487	32415	27440	10058	02359	25659	35752	10962
215	98526	36286	87210	73824	27059	06346	69033	96188	29493	35803
216	36829	32599	27595	10115	02372	25804	35955	11025	13383	25916
217	88515	66323	24310	05701	62018	86414	26497	32165	62288	37068
218	74928	20579	04826	52499	73150	22430	27228	52727	31378	47153

	1	2	3	4	5	6	7	8	9	10
219	27464	01769	19243	26813	08221	09980	19327	11501	17283	20457
220	06441	04513	06288	01928	02340	04532	02697	04053	04797	04105
221	70065	68403	20974	25461	49305	29342	44092	52188	44653	05996
222	97627	29224	35477	68701	40884	61437	72717	62218	08354	43847
223	29935	10878	21065	12536	18838	22297	19077	02562	13444	22062
224	36339	25572	15218	22868	27067	23159	03110	16321	26782	03340
225	70370	29470	44284	52415	44847	06022	31605	51864	06468	01417
226	41878	26354	31192	26689	03584	18808	30865	03849	00843	25857
227	62930	46873	40105	05385	28264	46381	05784	01268	38856	33844
228	74484	47469	06374	33453	54896	06847	01500	45990	40057	65642
229	63730	05453	28623	46970	05858	01284	39350	34274	56164	51244
230	08557	03843	06307	00787	00172	05284	04602	07541	06881	01425
231	44913	33101	04128	00905	27731	24154	39581	36113	07477	18930
232	73701	06775	01484	45507	39636	64952	59262	12270	31064	70029
233	09192	00185	05676	04943	08101	07391	01530	03874	08734	05373
234	02014	01244	01083	01775	01620	00335	00849	01914	01177	00275
235	61745	33206	54415	49647	10280	26024	58668	36095	08435	08747
236	53780	47395	43243	08954	22667	51099	31438	07347	07619	09284
237	88129	70862	14672	37144	83737	51518	12039	12485	15214	54867
238	80408	13387	33890	76401	47005	10985	11391	13881	50060	50825
239	16649	07017	15819	09733	02274	02359	02874	10365	10524	11867
240	42148	40047	24639	05758	05971	07276	26240	26641	30043	05508
241	95016	55545	12980	13460	16403	59155	60059	67728	12418	71013
242	58458	07986	08281	10092	36394	36951	41669	07640	43690	15204
243	13661	01935	02358	08505	08635	09738	01785	10210	03553	06239
244	14166	02446	08820	08954	10098	01851	10588	03684	06470	11532
245	17264	10748	10912	12306	02256	12903	04490	07884	14054	04972
246	62257	39353	44377	08137	46530	16192	28433	50682	17929	06551
247	63210	45056	08261	47241	16440	28868	51457	18203	06651	44047
248	71280	09316	53273	18539	32553	58027	20527	07500	49671	67686
249	13069	09768	03399	05969	10639	03764	01375	09107	12410	09529
250	74738	19438	34132	60842	21523	07864	52080	70970	54491	05402
251	26009	11878	21173	07490	02737	18124	24697	18963	01880	01301
252	45670	37178	13152	04806	31824	43367	33297	03301	02284	29941
253	81407	23444	08566	56728	77303	59354	05884	04071	53371	77709
254	28798	03030	20067	27346	20996	02082	01440	18880	27490	22271
255	10522	07332	09992	07672	00761	00526	06899	10044	08138	00285
256	69684	66171	50806	05037	03484	45685	66518	53891	01889	60914
257	94958	69234	06864	04748	62256	90645	73437	02575	83008	83523
258	72910	05270	03646	47800	69598	56385	01977	63734	64130	20108
259	07228	00361	04739	06900	05590	00196	06318	06358	01993	02382
260	05000	03278	04773	03867	00136	04371	04398	01379	01648	02185
261	65561	62583	50702	01778	57310	57666	18081	21608	28643	57722
262	95457	73823	02588	83444	83962	26326	31462	41704	84044	59364
263	77336	02097	67603	68023	21328	25489	33787	68089	48094	21463
264	02711	02370	02385	00748	00894	01185	02387	01686	00753	01372
265	87415	76888	24108	28811	38191	76963	54362	24260	44225	11260
266	87958	24258	28990	38428	77441	54700	24411	44500	11330	00715
267	27579	09090	12049	24281	17151	07654	13953	03553	00224	20881
268	32959	14399	29018	20497	09147	16675	04246	00268	24955	16431
269	43689	38465	27170	12125	22103	05628	00355	33079	21780	02685
270	88043	54753	24434	44543	11341	00716	66661	43893	05411	21743
271	62189	17259	31463	08011	00506	47086	31003	03822	15358	47635
272	27753	14041	03575	00226	21013	13836	01706	06854	21258	23067
273	50592	06517	00411	38305	25222	03110	12494	38752	42051	34607
274	12881	00105	09753	06422	00792	03181	09867	10707	08811	10070

B   Random Numbers

	1	2	3	4	5	6	7	8	9	10
275	00813	00616	00405	00050	00201	00623	00676	00556	00636	00056
276	75714	37746	04654	18699	57995	62932	51791	59190	05259	39440
277	49854	03064	12312	38187	41437	34102	38973	03463	25969	01712
278	06146	01518	04708	05109	04204	04805	00427	03202	00211	00902
279	24696	18917	20527	16893	19306	01715	12864	00848	03625	05102
280	76598	63666	52396	59880	05320	39900	02630	11244	15825	32881
281	83118	56856	64978	05773	43296	02854	12201	17172	35680	82892
282	68404	53475	04751	35632	02348	10041	14132	29364	68218	38293
283	78175	05430	40722	02684	11475	16151	33559	77963	43764	67752
284	06946	03618	00238	01020	01435	02982	06927	03888	06020	02067
285	52090	01788	07646	10762	22361	51949	29161	45145	15499	42852
286	03433	00504	00709	01474	03424	01922	02975	01021	02824	00824
287	14679	03033	06301	14639	08217	12722	04367	12076	03522	01198
288	20660	08869	20604	11566	17906	06147	16996	04958	01687	05468
289	42928	42811	24031	37204	12772	35314	10301	03504	11361	00632
290	99728	55829	86431	29672	82041	23931	08141	26393	01468	61137
291	55981	48517	16656	46053	13433	04570	14815	00824	34319	22237
292	86667	25786	71296	20797	07075	22936	01276	53130	34426	11442
293	29753	24476	07140	02429	07874	00438	18240	11818	03928	25135
294	82265	19740	06716	21771	01211	50431	32677	10861	69495	23503
295	23996	01959	06350	00353	14710	09532	03168	20271	06856	01960
296	08163	02160	00120	05004	03243	01078	06896	02332	00667	06713
297	26465	00390	16224	10512	03494	22357	07561	02162	21762	16098
298	01472	00903	00585	00194	01244	00421	00120	01211	00896	00758
299	61304	24351	08093	51788	17515	05007	50411	37290	31551	03293
300	39722	05244	33556	11349	03244	32664	24162	20443	02133	36891
301	13202	11153	03772	01078	10856	08030	06795	00709	12261	07428
302	84477	24136	06900	69467	51386	43477	04537	78458	47530	34028
303	28571	02334	23494	17379	14704	01535	26535	16075	11508	25948
304	08168	06717	04968	04204	00439	07586	04596	03290	07418	03336
305	82231	50019	42321	04417	76371	46266	33123	74683	33583	17752
306	60828	31306	03267	56493	34224	24501	55244	24842	13132	34774
307	51466	02764	47799	28957	20731	46742	21019	11111	29423	28198
308	05371	04988	03022	02163	04878	02194	01160	03071	02943	02866
309	92874	52254	37410	84349	37930	20050	53095	50885	49551	89513
310	56264	22663	51099	22978	12146	32165	30827	30018	54227	42655
311	40280	36583	16450	08696	23028	22069	21490	38822	30538	06678
312	90820	37091	19606	51921	49760	48455	87533	68854	15057	44195
313	40840	08817	23348	22376	21789	39362	30962	06771	19874	30322
314	21588	12342	11828	11518	20807	16367	03579	10505	16028	10157
315	57169	31323	30501	55099	43341	09478	27819	42445	26896	18561
316	54790	29232	52807	41538	09083	26662	40678	25777	17789	04336
317	53352	51421	40448	08845	25962	39611	25101	17322	04223	14226
318	96381	73069	15979	46901	71557	45345	31293	07628	25700	67451
319	75813	12569	36892	56287	35668	24615	06000	20215	53058	36980
320	16579	08067	12309	07800	05383	01312	04421	11602	08087	04348
321	48662	36129	22894	15799	03851	12976	34056	23736	12761	25575
322	74245	34930	24106	05876	19797	51960	36215	19470	39021	25005
323	47047	15275	03724	12545	32926	22949	12338	24727	15845	31354
324	32468	02570	08657	22722	15837	08514	17064	10935	21637	22640
325	07915	02110	05539	03861	02076	04160	02666	05275	05519	07133
326	26665	18661	13006	06992	14014	08980	17770	18594	24032	18673
327	69984	34137	18353	36782	23570	46640	48801	63074	49010	10280
328	48778	12791	25636	16428	32507	34013	43961	34159	07165	04285
329	26224	13783	08832	17476	18286	23634	18365	03852	02304	14738
330	52557	17701	35026	36649	47368	36806	07720	04617	29539	06065

	1	2	3	4	5	6	7	8	9	10
331	33679	22445	23485	30354	23586	04947	02959	18929	03887	22497
332	66643	46471	60062	46670	09790	05854	37455	07691	44515	48371
333	69731	62846	48833	10243	06126	39191	08047	46578	50613	12135
334	90126	63115	13239	07917	50653	10401	60201	65416	15684	07045
335	70030	10287	06152	39359	08082	46778	50830	12187	05474	69228
336	14690	01290	08256	01695	09812	10662	02556	01148	14521	08764
337	08784	04937	01014	05868	06376	01529	00687	08684	05241	01758
338	56203	06486	37542	40794	09781	04393	55559	33531	11247	31451
339	11540	07709	08376	02008	00902	11408	06885	02309	06458	03285
340	66797	48483	11624	05222	66031	39851	13367	37380	19013	02027
341	72583	12631	05674	71751	43303	14525	40618	20660	02203	24238
342	17403	01360	17203	10382	03483	09739	04953	00528	05811	10065
343	07817	07727	04664	01564	04374	02225	00237	02610	04521	07116
344	98854	58977	19783	55319	28138	03000	33011	57176	89985	26944
345	59660	11939	33386	16982	01811	19923	34507	54308	16261	15418
346	20012	11199	05696	00607	06683	11575	18216	05455	05172	07574
347	55960	15928	01698	18687	32366	50939	15253	14461	21181	32670
348	28464	00864	09505	16463	25910	07758	07356	10773	16618	11666
349	03035	01013	01755	02763	00827	00784	01149	01772	01244	01657
350	33394	19314	30398	09102	08630	12639	19496	13687	18231	21546
351	57838	52649	15765	14947	21892	33767	23705	31576	37318	12397
352	91028	24811	23524	34454	53144	37308	49695	58733	19511	52995
353	27257	07044	10317	15913	11171	14880	17587	05842	15868	23426
354	25842	09781	15087	10591	14108	16674	05539	15045	22211	02392
355	37849	22097	15513	20663	24421	08113	22035	32530	03504	01303
356	58382	23928	31872	37669	12514	33989	50177	05405	02010	32769
357	40985	22375	26444	08785	23861	35225	03794	01411	23005	33619
358	54593	35224	11701	31783	46921	05054	01879	30643	44782	27995
359	64522	13830	37564	55454	05973	02221	36216	52926	33086	37908
360	21434	12479	18422	01984	00738	12031	17582	10991	12593	16702
361	58218	50037	05390	02004	32678	47755	29854	34205	45366	39250
362	85947	07957	02959	48241	70500	44072	50496	66973	57943	81932
363	09258	00319	05196	07594	04747	05439	07214	06241	08825	01075
364	03442	01932	02824	01765	02022	02682	02321	03282	00400	01911
365	56129	46042	28782	32977	43738	37841	53508	06517	31161	41361
366	82028	42063	48194	63919	55302	78197	09524	45539	60445	73507
367	51279	30127	39958	34571	48884	05954	28468	37786	45952	12930
368	58752	45782	39610	56008	06821	32617	43293	52649	14815	56745
369	77924	52534	74284	09047	43260	57420	69829	19649	75261	64068
370	67418	64269	07827	37428	49679	60414	17000	65115	55430	38703
371	95329	11068	52923	70246	85426	24037	92072	78379	54727	70441
372	11610	06446	08555	10404	02928	11214	09546	06665	08579	01635
373	55516	40909	49749	13998	53619	45645	31871	41022	07816	23375
374	73688	66033	18580	71170	60585	42303	54450	10375	31026	61408
375	89612	22596	86550	73678	51444	66216	12617	37731	74679	36465
376	25215	24354	20732	14476	18632	03550	10617	21013	10261	06549
377	96584	79410	55447	71368	13598	40667	80489	39302	25086	58593
378	82219	47200	60753	11576	34618	68518	33457	21355	49879	17371
379	57408	42420	08083	24172	47842	23361	14911	34827	12129	53559
380	73892	10403	31112	61579	30068	19192	44827	15611	68938	16398
381	14079	05928	11733	05729	03657	08541	02975	13135	03125	12781
382	42105	35089	17133	10936	25543	08896	39282	09344	38221	32627
383	83336	33911	21645	50556	17607	77748	18494	75649	64577	76123
384	40692	10569	24686	08597	37964	09031	36939	31532	37170	25695
385	25974	15757	05488	24232	05764	23578	20127	23726	16401	24186
386	60666	12817	56598	13463	55070	47010	55415	38308	56490	16935

	1	2	3	4	5	6	7	8	9	10
387	21127	19711	04689	19179	16372	19299	13341	19673	05898	12438
388	93295	20704	84690	72295	85221	58912	86874	26043	54923	43140
389	22192	20145	17197	20272	14013	20665	06195	13065	10262	15804
390	90776	70343	82920	57321	84528	25340	53440	41975	64644	89153
391	77490	70784	48932	72156	21631	45618	35832	55183	76104	37469
392	91345	57680	85058	25498	53775	42238	65049	89712	44169	03168
393	91541	27554	17549	54662	17632	38757	01772	91109	69333	83598
394	45227	33385	06178	38615	31763	57721	21046	45374	05708	46223
395	90839	49028	16611	83546	79684	61627	71219	98711	51399	82532
396	11101	91855	10368	61313	07233	82249	82991	46671	91733	75175
397	80272	32434	25993	92273	42979	68599	57607	05008	87695	95258
398	00632	21480	33261	33644	77632	88411	35820	44562	65509	28006
399	97205	24495	91013	59111	04453	39423	79292	76451	18744	31290
400	94278	40620	24884	37779	63585	87634	79291	59431	76669	91956

APPENDIX C Critical Values for the Student's *t* Distribution

Two tails	0.20	0.10	0.05	0.02	0.01	0.005	0.002
One tail	0.10	0.05	0.025	0.01	0.005	0.0025	0.001
df							
1	3.078	6.314	12.706	31.821	63.657	127.320	318.310
2	1.886	2.920	4.303	6.965	9.925	14.089	22.327
3	1.638	2.353	3.182	4.541	5.841	7.453	10.214
4	1.533	2.132	2.776	3.747	4.604	5.598	7.173
5	1.476	2.015	2.571	3.365	4.032	4.773	5.893
6	1.440	1.943	2.447	3.143	3.707	4.317	5.208
7	1.415	1.895	2.365	2.998	3.499	4.029	4.785
8	1.397	1.860	2.306	2.896	3.355	3.833	4.501
9	1.383	1.833	2.262	2.821	3.250	3.690	4.297
10	1.372	1.812	2.228	2.764	3.169	3.581	4.144
11	1.363	1.796	2.201	2.718	3.106	3.497	4.025
12	1.356	1.782	2.179	2.681	3.055	3.428	3.930
13	1.350	1.771	2.160	2.650	3.012	3.372	3.852
14	1.345	1.761	2.145	2.624	2.977	3.326	3.787
15	1.341	1.753	2.131	2.602	2.947	3.286	3.733
16	1.337	1.746	2.120	2.583	2.921	3.252	3.686
17	1.333	1.740	2.110	2.567	2.898	3.222	3.646
18	1.330	1.734	2.101	2.552	2.878	3.197	3.610
19	1.328	1.729	2.093	2.539	2.861	3.174	3.579
20	1.325	1.725	2.086	2.528	2.845	3.153	3.552
21	1.323	1.721	2.080	2.518	2.831	3.135	3.527
22	1.321	1.717	2.074	2.508	2.819	3.119	3.505
23	1.319	1.714	2.069	2.500	2.807	3.104	3.485
24	1.318	1.711	2.064	2.492	2.797	3.091	3.467
25	1.316	1.708	2.060	2.485	2.787	3.078	3.450
26	1.315	1.706	2.056	2.479	2.779	3.067	3.435
27	1.314	1.703	2.052	2.473	2.771	3.057	3.421
28	1.313	1.701	2.048	2.467	2.763	3.047	3.408
29	1.311	1.699	2.045	2.462	2.756	3.038	3.396
30	1.310	1.697	2.042	2.457	2.750	3.030	3.385
40	1.303	1.684	2.021	2.423	2.704	2.971	3.307
60	1.296	1.671	2.000	2.390	2.660	2.915	3.232
120	1.289	1.658	1.980	2.358	2.617	2.860	3.160
∞	1.282	1.645	1.960	2.326	2.576	2.807	3.090

Source: The values in this table were obtained from *Biometrika Tables for Statisticians*, 3rd ed., Vol. 1 (Table 12, p. 138). Used by permission of Cambridge University Press.

	Lower tail values				Upper tail values			
df	.005	0.010	0.025	0.05	0.05	0.025	0.01	0.005
1	.0000393	.000157	.000982	.00393	3.841	5.024	6.635	7.879
2	.0100	.0201	.0506	.103	5.991	7.378	9.210	10.597
3	.0717	.115	.216	.352	7.815	9.348	11.345	12.838
4	.207	.297	.484	.711	9.488	11.143	13.277	14.860
5	.412	.554	.831	1.145	11.070	12.832	15.086	16.750
6	.676	.872	1.237	1.635	12.592	14.449	16.812	18.548
7	.989	1.239	1.690	2.167	14.067	16.013	18.475	20.278
8	1.344	1.646	2.180	2.733	15.507	17.535	20.090	21.955
9	1.735	2.088	2.700	3.325	13.919	19.023	21.666	23.589
10	2.156	2.558	3.247	3.940	18.307	20.483	23.209	25.188
11	2.603	3.053	3.816	4.575	19.675	21.920	24.725	26.757
12	3.074	3.571	4.404	5.226	21.026	23.337	26.217	28.300
13	3.565	4.107	5.009	5.892	22.362	24.736	27.688	29.819
14	4.075	4.660	5.629	6.571	23.685	26.119	29.141	31.319
15	4.601	5.229	6.262	7.261	24.996	27.488	30.578	32.801
16	5.142	5.812	6.908	7.962	26.296	28.845	32.000	34.267
17	5.697	6.408	7.564	8.672	27.587	30.191	33.409	35.718
18	6.265	7.015	8.231	9.390	28.869	31.526	34.805	37.156
19	6.844	7.633	8.907	10.117	30.144	32.852	36.191	38.582
20	7.434	8.260	9.591	10.851	31.410	34.170	37.566	39.997
21	8.034	8.897	10.283	11.591	32.671	35.479	38.932	41.401
22	8.643	9.542	10.982	12.338	33.924	36.781	40.289	42.796
23	9.260	10.196	11.689	13.091	35.172	38.076	41.638	44.181
24	9.886	10.856	12.401	13.848	36.415	39.364	42.980	45.558
25	10.520	11.524	13.120	14.611	37.652	40.646	44.314	46.928
26	11.160	12.198	13.844	15.379	38.885	41.923	45.642	48.290
27	11.808	12.879	14.573	16.151	40.113	43.194	46.963	49.645
28	12.461	13.565	15.308	16.928	41.337	44.461	48.278	50.993
29	13.121	14.256	16.047	17.708	42.557	45.722	49.588	52.336
30	13.787	14.953	16.791	18.493	43.773	46.979	50.892	53.672

Source: The values in this table were obtained from *Biometrika Tables for Statisticians*, 3rd ed., Vol. 1 (Table 8, pp. 130–131). Used by permission of Cambridge University Press.

Critical Values for the Spearman Rank-Order Correlation

Two tails	0.20	0.10	0.05	0.02	0.01	0.005	0.002	0.001
One tail	0.10	0.05	0.025	0.01	0.005	0.0025	0.001	0.0005
N								
4	1.000	1.000						
5	0.800	0.900	1.000	1.000				
6	0.657	0.829	0.886	0.943	1.000	1.000		
7	0.571	0.714	0.786	0.893	0.929	0.964	1.000	1.000
8	0.524	0.643	0.738	0.833	0.881	0.905	0.952	0.976
9	0.483	0.600	0.700	0.783	0.833	0.867	0.917	0.933
10	0.455	0.564	0.648	0.745	0.794	0.830	0.879	0.903
11	0.427	0.536	0.618	0.709	0.755	0.800	0.845	0.879
12	0.406	0.503	0.587	0.671	0.727	0.776	0.825	0.860
13	0.385	0.484	0.560	0.648	0.703	0.747	0.802	0.835
14	0.367	0.464	0.538	0.622	0.675	0.723	0.774	0.811
15	0.354	0.443	0.521	0.604	0.654	0.700	0.754	0.786
16	0.341	0.429	0.503	0.582	0.635	0.679	0.732	0.765
17	0.328	0.414	0.485	0.566	0.615	0.662	0.713	0.748
18	0.317	0.401	0.472	0.550	0.600	0.643	0.695	0.728
19	0.309	0.391	0.460	0.535	0.584	0.628	0.677	0.712
20	0.299	0.380	0.447	0.520	0.570	0.612	0.662	0.696
21	0.292	0.370	0.435	0.508	0.556	0.599	0.648	0.681
22	0.284	0.361	0.425	0.496	0.544	0.586	0.634	0.667
23	0.278	0.353	0.415	0.486	0.532	0.573	0.622	0.654
24	0.271	0.344	0.406	0.476	0.521	0.562	0.610	0.642
25	0.265	0.337	0.398	0.466	0.511	0.551	0.598	0.630
26	0.259	0.331	0.390	0.457	0.501	0.542	0.587	0.619
27	0.255	0.324	0.382	0.448	0.491	0.531	0.577	0.608
28	0.250	0.317	0.375	0.440	0.483	0.522	0.567	0.598
29	0.245	0.312	0.368	0.433	0.475	0.513	0.558	0.589
30	0.240	0.306	0.362	0.425	0.467	0.504	0.549	0.580
31	0.236	0.301	0.356	0.418	0.459	0.496	0.541	0.571
32	0.232	0.296	0.350	0.412	0.452	0.489	0.533	0.563
33	0.229	0.291	0.345	0.405	0.446	0.482	0.525	0.554
34	0.225	0.287	0.340	0.399	0.439	0.475	0.517	0.547
35	0.222	0.283	0.335	0.394	0.433	0.468	0.510	0.539
36	0.219	0.279	0.330	0.388	0.427	0.462	0.504	0.533
37	0.216	0.275	0.325	0.383	0.421	0.456	0.497	0.526
38	0.212	0.271	0.321	0.378	0.415	0.450	0.491	0.519
39	0.210	0.267	0.317	0.373	0.410	0.444	0.485	0.513
40	0.207	0.264	0.313	0.368	0.405	0.439	0.479	0.507
41	0.204	0.261	0.309	0.364	0.400	0.433	0.473	0.501
42	0.202	0.257	0.305	0.359	0.395	0.428	0.468	0.495
43	0.199	0.254	0.301	0.355	0.392	0.423	0.463	0.490
44	0.197	0.251	0.298	0.351	0.386	0.419	0.458	0.484
45	0.194	0.248	0.294	0.347	0.382	0.414	0.453	0.479
46	0.192	0.246	0.291	0.343	0.378	0.410	0.448	0.474
47	0.190	0.243	0.288	0.340	0.374	0.405	0.443	0.469
48	0.188	0.240	0.285	0.336	0.370	0.401	0.439	0.465

Source: The values in this table were obtained from Zar, J. H. (1972). Significance testing of the Spearman rank correlation coefficient. *Journal of the American Statistical Association, 67*, 578–580. Used by permission of the publisher.

Two tails	0.20	0.10	0.05	0.02	0.01	0.005	0.002	0.001
One tail	0.10	0.05	0.025	0.01	0.005	0.0025	0.001	0.0005
N								
49	0.186	0.238	0.282	0.333	0.366	0.397	0.434	0.460
50	0.184	0.235	0.279	0.329	0.363	0.393	0.430	0.456
52	0.180	0.231	0.274	0.323	0.356	0.386	0.422	0.447
54	0.177	0.226	0.268	0.317	0.349	0.379	0.414	0.439
56	0.174	0.222	0.264	0.311	0.343	0.372	0.407	0.432
58	0.171	0.218	0.259	0.306	0.337	0.366	0.400	0.424
60	0.168	0.214	0.255	0.300	0.331	0.360	0.394	0.418
62	0.165	0.211	0.250	0.296	0.326	0.354	0.388	0.411
64	0.162	0.207	0.246	0.291	0.321	0.348	0.382	0.405
66	0.160	0.204	0.243	0.287	0.316	0.343	0.376	0.399
68	0.157	0.201	0.239	0.282	0.311	0.338	0.370	0.393
70	0.155	0.198	0.235	0.278	0.307	0.333	0.365	0.388
72	0.153	0.195	0.232	0.274	0.303	0.329	0.360	0.382
74	0.151	0.193	0.229	0.271	0.299	0.324	0.355	0.377
76	0.149	0.190	0.226	0.267	0.295	0.320	0.351	0.372
78	0.147	0.188	0.223	0.264	0.291	0.316	0.346	0.368
80	0.145	0.185	0.220	0.260	0.287	0.312	0.342	0.363
82	0.143	0.183	0.217	0.257	0.284	0.308	0.338	0.359
84	0.141	0.181	0.215	0.254	0.280	0.305	0.334	0.355
86	0.139	0.179	0.212	0.251	0.277	0.301	0.330	0.351
88	0.138	0.176	0.210	0.248	0.274	0.298	0.327	0.347
90	0.136	0.174	0.207	0.245	0.171	0.294	0.323	0.343
92	0.135	0.173	0.205	0.243	0.268	0.291	0.319	0.339
94	0.133	0.171	0.203	0.240	0.265	0.288	0.316	0.336
96	0.132	0.169	0.201	0.238	0.262	0.285	0.313	0.332
98	0.130	0.167	0.199	0.235	0.260	0.282	0.310	0.329
100	0.129	0.165	0.197	0.233	0.257	0.279	0.307	0.326

APPENDIX F Critical Values for the *F* Distribution

df for Denominator	x	df for Numerator																	
		1	2	3	4	5	6	7	8	9	10	12	15	20	24	30	40	60	∞
1	.25	5.83	7.50	8.20	8.58	8.82	8.98	9.10	9.19	9.26	9.32	9.41	9.49	9.58	9.63	9.67	9.71	9.76	9.85
	.10	39.9	49.5	53.6	55.8	57.2	58.2	58.9	59.4	59.9	60.2	60.7	61.2	61.7	62.0	62.3	62.5	62.8	63.3
	.05	161	200	216	225	230	234	237	239	240	242	244	246	248	249	250	251	252	254
	.025	648	800	864	900	922	937	948	957	963	969	977	985	993	997	1001	1006	1010	1018
	.01	4052	5000	5403	5625	5764	5859	5928	5982	6022	6056	6106	6157	6209	6235	6261	6287	6313	6366
	.001	4053*	5000*	5404*	5625*	5764*	5859*	5929*	5981*	6023*	6056*	6107*	6158*	6209*	6235*	6261*	6287*	6313*	6366*
2	.25	2.57	3.00	3.15	3.23	3.28	3.31	3.34	3.35	3.37	3.38	3.39	3.41	3.43	3.43	3.44	3.45	3.46	3.48
	.10	8.53	9.00	9.16	9.24	9.29	9.33	9.35	9.37	9.38	9.39	9.41	9.42	9.44	9.45	9.46	9.47	9.47	9.49
	.05	18.5	19.0	19.2	19.3	19.3	19.3	19.4	19.4	19.4	19.4	19.4	19.4	19.5	19.5	19.5	19.5	19.5	19.5
	.025	38.5	39.0	39.2	39.3	39.3	39.3	39.4	39.4	39.4	39.4	39.4	39.4	39.5	39.5	39.5	39.5	39.5	39.5
	.01	98.5	99.0	99.2	99.3	99.3	99.3	99.4	99.4	99.4	99.4	99.4	99.4	99.5	99.5	99.5	99.5	99.5	99.5
	.001	999	999	999	999	999	999	999	999	999	999	999	999	999	999	1000	1000	1000	1000
3	.25	2.02	2.28	2.36	2.39	2.41	2.42	2.43	2.44	2.44	2.44	2.45	2.46	2.46	2.46	2.47	2.47	2.47	2.47
	.10	5.54	5.46	5.39	5.34	5.31	5.28	5.27	5.25	5.24	5.23	5.22	5.20	5.18	5.18	5.17	5.16	5.15	5.13
	.05	10.1	9.55	9.28	9.12	9.01	8.94	8.89	8.85	8.81	8.79	8.74	8.70	8.66	8.64	8.62	8.59	8.57	8.53
	.025	17.4	16.0	15.4	15.1	14.9	14.7	14.6	14.5	14.5	14.4	14.3	14.2	14.2	14.1	14.1	14.0	14.0	13.9
	.01	34.1	30.8	29.5	28.7	28.2	27.9	27.7	27.5	27.4	27.2	27.0	26.9	26.7	26.6	26.5	26.4	26.3	26.1
	.001	167	148	141	137	135	133	132	131	130	129	128	127	126	126	125	125	124	124
4	.25	1.81	2.00	2.05	2.06	2.07	2.08	2.08	2.08	2.08	2.08	2.08	2.08	2.08	2.08	2.08	2.08	2.08	2.08
	.10	4.54	4.32	4.19	4.11	4.05	4.01	3.98	3.95	3.94	3.92	3.90	3.87	3.84	3.83	3.82	3.80	3.79	3.76
	.05	7.71	6.94	6.59	6.39	6.26	6.16	6.09	6.04	6.00	5.96	5.91	5.86	5.80	5.77	5.75	5.72	5.69	5.63
	.025	12.2	10.6	9.98	9.60	9.36	9.20	9.07	8.98	8.90	8.84	8.75	8.66	8.56	8.51	8.46	8.41	8.36	8.26
	.01	21.2	18.0	16.7	16.0	15.5	15.2	15.0	14.8	14.7	14.6	14.4	14.2	14.0	13.9	13.8	13.8	13.6	13.5
	.001	74.1	61.2	56.2	53.4	51.7	50.5	49.7	49.0	48.5	48.0	47.4	46.8	46.1	45.8	45.4	45.1	44.8	44.0
5	.25	1.69	1.85	1.88	1.89	1.89	1.89	1.89	1.89	1.89	1.89	1.89	1.89	1.88	1.88	1.88	1.88	1.87	1.87
	.10	4.06	3.78	3.62	3.52	3.45	3.40	3.37	3.34	3.32	3.30	3.27	3.24	3.21	3.19	3.17	3.16	3.14	3.10
	.05	6.61	5.79	5.41	5.19	5.05	4.95	4.88	4.82	4.77	4.74	4.68	4.62	4.56	4.53	4.50	4.46	4.43	4.36
	.025	10.0	8.43	7.76	7.39	7.15	6.98	6.85	6.76	6.68	6.62	6.52	6.43	6.33	6.28	6.23	6.18	6.12	6.02
	.01	16.3	13.3	12.1	11.4	11.0	10.7	10.5	10.3	10.2	10.0	9.89	9.72	9.55	9.47	9.38	9.29	9.20	9.02
	.001	47.2	37.1	33.2	31.1	29.8	28.8	28.2	27.6	27.2	26.9	26.4	25.9	25.4	25.1	24.9	24.6	24.3	23.8
6	.25	1.62	1.76	1.78	1.79	1.79	1.78	1.78	1.78	1.77	1.77	1.77	1.76	1.76	1.75	1.75	1.75	1.74	1.74
	.10	3.78	3.46	3.29	3.18	3.11	3.05	3.01	2.98	2.96	2.94	2.90	2.87	2.84	2.82	2.80	2.78	2.76	2.72
	.05	5.99	5.14	4.76	4.53	4.39	4.28	4.21	4.15	4.10	4.06	4.00	3.94	3.87	3.84	3.81	3.77	3.74	3.67
	.025	8.81	7.26	6.60	6.23	5.99	5.82	5.70	5.60	5.52	5.46	5.37	5.27	5.17	5.12	5.07	5.01	4.96	4.85
	.01	13.8	10.9	9.78	9.15	8.75	8.47	8.26	8.10	7.98	7.87	7.72	7.56	7.40	7.31	7.23	7.14	7.06	6.88
	.001	35.5	27.0	23.7	21.9	20.8	20.0	19.5	19.0	18.7	18.4	18.0	17.6	17.1	16.9	16.7	16.4	16.2	15.8
7	.25	1.57	1.70	1.72	1.72	1.71	1.71	1.70	1.70	1.69	1.69	1.68	1.68	1.67	1.67	1.66	1.66	1.65	1.65
	.10	3.59	3.26	3.07	2.96	2.88	2.83	2.78	2.75	2.72	2.70	2.67	2.63	2.59	2.58	2.56	2.54	2.51	2.47
	.05	5.59	4.74	4.35	4.12	3.97	3.87	3.79	3.73	3.68	3.64	3.57	3.51	3.44	3.41	3.38	3.34	3.30	3.23
	.025	8.07	6.54	5.89	5.52	5.29	5.12	4.99	4.90	4.82	4.76	4.67	4.57	4.47	4.42	4.36	4.31	4.25	4.14
	.01	12.2	9.55	8.45	7.85	7.46	7.19	6.99	6.84	6.72	6.62	6.47	6.31	6.16	6.07	5.99	5.91	5.82	5.65
	.001	29.2	21.7	18.8	17.2	16.2	15.5	15.0	14.6	14.3	14.1	13.7	13.3	12.9	12.7	12.5	12.3	12.1	11.7
8	.25	1.54	1.66	1.67	1.66	1.66	1.65	1.64	1.64	1.63	1.63	1.62	1.62	1.61	1.60	1.60	1.59	1.59	1.58
	.10	3.46	3.11	2.92	2.81	2.73	2.67	2.62	2.59	2.56	2.54	2.50	2.46	2.42	2.40	2.38	2.36	2.34	2.29
	.05	5.32	4.46	4.07	3.84	3.69	3.58	3.50	3.44	3.39	3.35	3.28	3.22	3.15	3.12	3.08	3.04	3.01	2.93
	.025	7.57	6.06	5.42	5.05	4.82	4.65	4.53	4.43	4.36	4.30	4.20	4.10	4.00	3.95	3.89	3.84	3.78	3.67
	.01	11.3	8.65	7.59	7.01	6.63	6.37	6.18	6.03	5.91	5.81	5.67	5.52	5.36	5.28	5.20	5.12	5.03	4.86
	.001	25.4	18.5	15.8	14.4	13.5	12.9	12.4	12.0	11.8	11.5	11.2	10.8	10.5	10.3	10.1	9.92	9.73	9.33

* Multiply these entries by 100.

Source: The values in this table were obtained from *Biometrika Tables for Statisticians*, 3rd ed., Vol. 1 (Table 18, pp. 157–162). Used by permission of Cambridge University Press.

df for Numerator

df for Denominator	x	1	2	3	4	5	6	7	8	9	10	12	15	20	24	30	40	60	∞
9	.25	1.51	1.62	1.63	1.63	1.62	1.61	1.60	1.60	1.59	1.59	1.58	1.57	1.56	1.56	1.55	1.54	1.54	1.53
	.10	3.36	3.01	2.81	2.69	2.61	2.55	2.51	2.47	2.44	2.42	2.38	2.34	2.30	2.28	2.25	2.23	2.21	2.16
	.05	5.12	4.26	3.86	3.63	3.48	3.37	3.29	3.23	3.18	3.14	3.07	3.01	2.94	2.90	2.86	2.83	2.79	2.71
	.025	7.21	5.71	5.08	4.72	4.48	4.32	4.20	4.10	4.03	3.96	3.87	3.77	3.67	3.61	3.56	3.51	3.45	3.33
	.01	10.6	8.02	6.99	6.42	6.06	5.80	5.61	5.47	5.35	5.26	5.11	4.96	4.81	4.73	4.65	4.57	4.48	4.31
	.001	22.9	16.4	13.9	12.6	11.7	11.1	10.7	10.4	10.1	9.89	9.57	9.24	8.90	8.72	8.55	8.37	8.19	7.81
10	.25	1.49	1.60	1.60	1.59	1.59	1.58	1.57	1.56	1.56	1.55	1.54	1.53	1.52	1.52	1.51	1.51	1.50	1.48
	.10	3.29	2.92	2.73	2.61	2.52	2.46	2.41	2.38	2.35	2.32	2.28	2.24	2.20	2.18	2.16	2.13	2.11	2.06
	.05	4.96	4.10	3.71	3.48	3.33	3.22	3.14	3.07	3.02	2.98	2.91	2.85	2.77	2.74	2.70	2.66	2.62	2.54
	.025	6.94	5.46	4.83	4.47	4.24	4.07	3.95	3.85	3.78	3.72	3.62	3.52	3.42	3.37	3.31	3.26	3.20	3.08
	.01	10.0	7.56	6.55	5.99	5.64	5.39	5.20	5.06	4.94	4.85	4.71	4.56	4.41	4.33	4.25	4.17	4.08	3.91
	.001	21.0	14.9	12.6	11.3	10.5	9.92	9.52	9.20	8.96	8.75	8.45	8.13	7.80	7.64	7.47	7.30	7.12	6.76
11	.25	1.47	1.58	1.58	1.57	1.56	1.55	1.54	1.53	1.53	1.52	1.51	1.50	1.49	1.49	1.48	1.47	1.47	1.45
	.10	3.23	2.86	2.66	2.54	2.45	2.39	2.34	2.30	2.27	2.25	2.21	2.17	2.12	2.10	2.08	2.05	2.03	1.97
	.05	4.84	3.98	3.59	3.36	3.20	3.09	3.01	2.95	2.90	2.85	2.79	2.72	2.65	2.61	2.57	2.53	2.49	2.40
	.025	6.72	5.26	4.63	4.28	4.04	3.88	3.76	3.66	3.59	3.53	3.43	3.33	3.23	3.17	3.12	3.06	3.00	2.88
	.01	9.65	7.21	6.22	5.67	5.32	5.07	4.89	4.74	4.63	4.54	4.40	4.25	4.10	4.02	3.94	3.86	3.78	3.60
	.001	19.7	13.8	11.6	10.4	9.58	9.05	8.66	8.35	8.12	7.92	7.63	7.32	7.01	6.85	6.68	6.52	6.35	6.00
12	.25	1.46	1.56	1.56	1.55	1.54	1.53	1.52	1.51	1.51	1.50	1.49	1.48	1.47	1.46	1.45	1.45	1.44	1.42
	.10	3.18	2.81	2.61	2.48	2.39	2.33	2.28	2.24	2.21	2.19	2.15	2.10	2.06	2.04	2.01	1.99	1.96	1.90
	.05	4.75	3.89	3.49	3.26	3.11	3.00	2.91	2.85	2.80	2.75	2.69	2.62	2.54	2.51	2.47	2.43	2.38	2.30
	.025	6.55	5.10	4.47	4.21	3.89	3.73	3.61	3.51	3.44	3.37	3.28	3.18	3.07	3.02	2.96	2.91	2.85	2.72
	.01	9.33	6.93	5.95	5.41	5.06	4.82	4.64	4.50	4.39	4.30	4.16	4.01	3.86	3.78	3.70	3.62	3.54	3.36
	.001	18.6	13.0	10.8	9.63	8.89	8.38	8.00	7.71	7.48	7.29	7.00	6.71	6.40	6.25	6.09	5.93	5.76	5.42
13	.25	1.45	1.55	1.55	1.53	1.52	1.51	1.50	1.49	1.49	1.48	1.47	1.46	1.45	1.44	1.43	1.42	1.42	1.40
	.10	3.14	2.76	2.56	2.43	2.35	2.28	2.23	2.20	2.16	2.14	2.10	2.05	2.01	1.98	1.96	1.93	1.90	1.85
	.05	4.67	3.81	3.41	3.18	3.03	2.92	2.83	2.77	2.71	2.67	2.60	2.53	2.46	2.42	2.38	2.34	2.30	2.21
	.025	6.41	4.97	4.35	4.00	3.77	3.60	3.48	3.39	3.31	3.25	3.15	3.05	2.95	2.89	2.84	2.78	2.72	2.60
	.01	9.07	6.70	5.74	5.21	4.86	4.62	4.44	4.30	4.19	4.10	3.96	3.82	3.66	3.59	3.51	3.43	3.34	3.17
	.001	17.8	12.3	10.2	9.07	8.35	7.86	7.49	7.21	6.98	6.80	6.52	6.23	5.93	5.78	5.63	5.47	5.30	4.97
14	.25	1.44	1.53	1.53	1.52	1.51	1.50	1.49	1.48	1.47	1.46	1.45	1.44	1.43	1.42	1.41	1.41	1.40	1.38
	.10	3.10	2.73	2.52	2.39	2.31	2.24	2.19	2.15	2.12	2.10	2.05	2.01	1.96	1.94	1.91	1.89	1.86	1.80
	.05	4.60	3.74	3.34	3.11	2.96	2.85	2.76	2.70	2.65	2.60	2.53	2.46	2.39	2.35	2.31	2.27	2.22	2.13
	.025	6.30	4.86	4.24	3.89	3.66	3.50	3.38	3.29	3.21	3.15	3.05	2.95	2.84	2.79	2.73	2.67	2.61	2.49
	.01	8.86	6.51	5.56	5.04	4.69	4.46	4.28	4.14	4.03	3.94	3.80	3.66	3.51	3.43	3.35	3.27	3.18	3.00
	.001	17.1	11.8	9.73	8.62	7.92	7.43	7.08	6.80	6.58	6.40	6.13	5.85	5.56	5.41	5.25	5.10	4.94	4.60
15	.25	1.43	1.52	1.52	1.51	1.49	1.48	1.47	1.46	1.46	1.45	1.44	1.43	1.41	1.41	1.40	1.39	1.38	1.36
	.10	3.07	2.70	2.49	2.36	2.27	2.21	2.16	2.12	2.09	2.06	2.02	1.97	1.92	1.90	1.87	1.85	1.82	1.76
	.05	4.54	3.68	3.29	3.06	2.90	2.79	2.71	2.64	2.59	2.54	2.48	2.40	2.33	2.29	2.25	2.20	2.16	2.07
	.025	6.20	4.77	4.15	3.80	3.58	3.41	3.29	3.20	3.12	3.06	2.96	2.86	2.76	2.70	2.64	2.59	2.52	2.40
	.01	8.68	6.36	5.42	4.89	4.56	4.32	4.14	4.00	3.89	3.80	3.67	3.52	3.37	3.29	3.21	3.13	3.05	2.87
	.001	16.6	11.3	9.34	8.25	7.57	7.09	6.74	6.47	6.26	6.08	5.81	5.54	5.25	5.10	4.95	4.80	4.64	4.31
16	.25	1.42	1.51	1.51	1.50	1.48	1.47	1.46	1.45	1.44	1.44	1.43	1.41	1.40	1.39	1.38	1.37	1.36	1.34
	.10	3.05	2.67	2.46	2.33	2.24	2.18	2.13	2.09	2.06	2.03	1.99	1.94	1.89	1.87	1.84	1.81	1.78	1.72
	.05	4.49	3.63	3.24	3.01	2.85	2.74	2.66	2.59	2.54	2.49	2.42	2.35	2.28	2.24	2.19	2.15	2.11	2.01
	.025	6.12	4.69	4.08	3.73	3.50	3.34	3.22	3.12	3.05	2.99	2.89	2.79	2.68	2.63	2.57	2.51	2.45	2.32
	.01	8.53	6.23	5.29	4.77	4.44	4.20	4.03	3.89	3.78	3.69	3.55	3.41	3.26	3.18	3.10	3.02	2.93	2.75
	.001	16.1	11.0	9.00	7.94	7.27	6.81	6.46	6.19	5.98	5.81	5.55	5.27	4.99	4.85	4.70	4.54	4.39	4.06
17	.25	1.42	1.51	1.50	1.49	1.47	1.46	1.45	1.44	1.43	1.43	1.41	1.40	1.39	1.38	1.37	1.36	1.35	1.33
	.10	3.03	2.64	2.44	2.31	2.22	2.15	2.10	2.06	2.03	2.00	1.96	1.91	1.86	1.84	1.81	1.78	1.75	1.69
	.05	4.45	3.59	3.20	2.96	2.81	2.70	2.61	2.55	2.49	2.45	2.38	2.31	2.23	2.19	2.15	2.10	2.06	1.96
	.025	6.04	4.62	4.01	3.66	3.44	3.28	3.16	3.06	2.98	2.92	2.82	2.72	2.62	2.56	2.50	2.44	2.38	2.25
	.01	8.40	6.11	5.18	4.67	4.34	4.10	3.93	3.79	3.68	3.59	3.46	3.31	3.16	3.08	3.00	2.92	2.83	2.65
	.001	15.7	10.7	8.73	7.68	7.02	6.56	6.22	5.96	5.75	5.58	5.32	5.05	4.78	4.63	4.48	4.33	4.18	3.85

df for Denominator	x	1	2	3	4	5	6	7	8	9	10	12	15	20	24	30	40	60	∞
18	.25	1.41	1.50	1.49	1.48	1.46	1.45	1.44	1.43	1.42	1.42	1.40	1.39	1.38	1.37	1.36	1.35	1.34	1.32
	.10	3.01	2.62	2.42	2.29	2.20	2.13	2.08	2.04	2.00	1.98	1.93	1.89	1.84	1.81	1.78	1.75	1.72	1.66
	.05	4.41	3.55	3.16	2.93	2.77	2.66	2.58	2.51	2.46	2.41	2.34	2.27	2.19	2.15	2.11	2.06	2.02	1.92
	.025	5.98	4.56	3.95	3.61	3.38	3.22	3.10	3.01	2.93	2.87	2.77	2.67	2.56	2.50	2.44	2.38	2.32	2.19
	.01	8.29	6.01	5.09	4.58	4.25	4.01	3.84	3.71	3.60	3.51	3.37	3.23	3.08	3.00	2.92	2.84	2.75	2.57
	.001	15.4	10.4	8.49	7.46	6.81	6.35	6.02	5.76	5.56	5.39	5.13	4.87	4.59	4.45	4.30	4.15	4.00	3.67
19	.25	1.41	1.49	1.49	1.47	1.46	1.44	1.43	1.42	1.41	1.41	1.40	1.38	1.37	1.36	1.35	1.34	1.33	1.30
	.10	2.99	2.61	2.40	2.27	2.18	2.11	2.06	2.02	1.98	1.96	1.91	1.86	1.81	1.79	1.76	1.73	1.70	1.63
	.05	4.38	3.52	3.13	2.90	2.74	2.63	2.54	2.48	2.42	2.38	2.31	2.23	2.16	2.11	2.07	2.03	1.98	1.88
	.025	5.92	4.51	3.90	3.56	3.33	3.17	3.05	2.96	2.88	2.82	2.72	2.62	2.51	2.45	2.39	2.33	2.27	2.13
	.01	8.18	5.93	5.01	4.50	4.17	3.94	3.77	3.63	3.52	3.43	3.30	3.15	3.00	2.92	2.84	2.76	2.67	2.49
	.001	15.1	10.2	8.28	7.26	6.62	6.18	5.85	5.59	5.39	5.22	4.97	4.70	4.43	4.29	4.14	3.99	3.84	3.51
20	.25	1.40	1.49	1.48	1.47	1.45	1.44	1.43	1.42	1.41	1.40	1.39	1.37	1.36	1.35	1.34	1.33	1.32	1.29
	.10	2.97	2.59	2.38	2.25	2.16	2.09	2.04	2.00	1.96	1.94	1.89	1.84	1.79	1.77	1.74	1.71	1.68	1.61
	.05	4.35	3.49	3.10	2.87	2.71	2.60	2.51	2.45	2.39	2.35	2.28	2.20	2.12	2.08	2.04	1.99	1.95	1.84
	.025	5.87	4.46	3.86	3.51	3.29	3.13	3.01	2.91	2.84	2.77	2.68	2.57	2.46	2.41	2.35	2.29	2.22	2.09
	.01	8.10	5.85	4.94	4.43	4.10	3.87	3.70	3.56	3.46	3.37	3.23	3.09	2.94	2.86	2.78	2.69	2.61	2.42
	.001	14.8	9.95	8.10	7.10	6.46	6.02	5.69	5.44	5.24	5.08	4.82	4.56	4.29	4.15	4.00	3.86	3.70	3.38
22	.25	1.40	1.48	1.47	1.45	1.44	1.42	1.41	1.40	1.39	1.39	1.37	1.36	1.34	1.33	1.32	1.31	1.30	1.28
	.10	2.95	2.56	2.35	2.22	2.13	2.06	2.01	1.97	1.93	1.90	1.86	1.81	1.76	1.73	1.70	1.67	1.64	1.57
	.05	4.30	3.44	3.05	2.82	2.66	2.55	2.46	2.40	2.34	2.30	2.23	2.15	2.07	2.03	1.98	1.94	1.89	1.78
	.025	5.79	4.38	3.78	3.44	3.22	3.05	2.93	2.84	2.76	2.70	2.60	2.50	2.39	2.33	2.27	2.21	2.14	2.00
	.01	7.95	5.72	4.82	4.31	3.99	3.76	3.59	3.45	3.35	3.26	3.12	2.98	2.83	2.75	2.67	2.58	2.50	2.31
	.001	14.4	9.61	7.80	6.81	6.19	5.76	5.44	5.19	4.99	4.83	4.58	4.33	4.06	3.92	3.78	3.63	3.48	3.15
24	.25	1.39	1.47	1.46	1.44	1.43	1.41	1.40	1.39	1.38	1.38	1.36	1.35	1.33	1.32	1.31	1.30	1.29	1.26
	.10	2.93	2.54	2.33	2.19	2.10	2.04	1.98	1.94	1.91	1.88	1.83	1.78	1.73	1.70	1.67	1.64	1.61	1.53
	.05	4.26	3.40	3.01	2.78	2.62	2.51	2.42	2.36	2.30	2.25	2.18	2.11	2.03	1.98	1.94	1.89	1.84	1.73
	.025	5.72	4.32	3.72	3.38	3.15	2.99	2.87	2.78	2.70	2.64	2.54	2.44	2.33	2.27	2.21	2.15	2.08	1.94
	.01	7.82	5.61	4.72	4.22	3.90	3.67	3.50	3.36	3.26	3.17	3.03	2.89	2.74	2.66	2.58	2.49	2.40	2.21
	.001	14.0	9.34	7.55	6.59	5.98	5.55	5.23	4.99	4.80	4.64	4.39	4.14	3.87	3.74	3.59	3.45	3.29	2.97
26	.25	1.38	1.46	1.45	1.44	1.42	1.41	1.39	1.38	1.37	1.37	1.35	1.34	1.32	1.31	1.30	1.29	1.28	1.25
	.10	2.91	2.52	2.31	2.17	2.08	2.01	1.96	1.92	1.88	1.86	1.81	1.76	1.71	1.68	1.65	1.61	1.58	1.50
	.05	4.23	3.37	2.98	2.74	2.59	2.47	2.39	2.32	2.27	2.22	2.15	2.07	1.99	1.95	1.90	1.85	1.80	1.69
	.025	5.66	4.27	3.67	3.33	3.10	2.94	2.82	2.73	2.65	2.59	2.49	2.39	2.28	2.22	2.16	2.09	2.03	1.88
	.01	7.72	5.53	4.64	4.14	3.82	3.59	3.42	3.29	3.18	3.09	2.96	2.81	2.66	2.58	2.50	2.42	2.33	2.13
	.001	13.7	9.12	7.36	6.41	5.80	5.38	5.07	4.83	4.64	4.48	4.24	3.99	3.72	3.59	3.44	3.30	3.15	2.82
28	.25	1.38	1.46	1.45	1.43	1.41	1.40	1.39	1.38	1.37	1.36	1.34	1.33	1.31	1.30	1.29	1.28	1.27	1.24
	.10	2.89	2.50	2.29	2.16	2.06	2.00	1.94	1.90	1.87	1.84	1.79	1.74	1.69	1.66	1.63	1.59	1.56	1.48
	.05	4.20	3.34	2.95	2.71	2.56	2.45	2.36	2.29	2.24	2.19	2.12	2.04	1.96	1.91	1.87	1.82	1.77	1.65
	.025	5.61	4.22	3.63	3.29	3.06	2.90	2.78	2.69	2.61	2.55	2.45	2.34	2.23	2.17	2.11	2.05	1.98	1.83
	.01	7.64	5.45	4.57	4.07	3.75	3.53	3.36	3.23	3.12	3.03	2.90	2.75	2.60	2.52	2.44	2.35	2.26	2.06
	.001	13.5	8.93	7.19	6.25	5.66	5.24	4.93	4.69	4.50	4.35	4.11	3.86	3.60	3.46	3.32	3.18	3.02	2.69
30	.25	1.38	1.45	1.44	1.42	1.41	1.39	1.38	1.37	1.36	1.35	1.34	1.32	1.30	1.29	1.28	1.27	1.26	1.23
	.10	2.88	2.49	2.28	2.14	2.05	1.98	1.93	1.88	1.85	1.82	1.77	1.72	1.67	1.64	1.61	1.57	1.54	1.46
	.05	4.17	3.32	2.92	2.69	2.53	2.42	2.33	2.27	2.21	2.16	2.09	2.01	1.93	1.89	1.84	1.79	1.74	1.62
	.025	5.57	4.18	3.59	3.25	3.03	2.87	2.75	2.65	2.57	2.51	2.41	2.31	2.20	2.14	2.07	2.01	1.94	1.79
	.01	7.56	5.39	4.51	4.02	3.70	3.47	3.30	3.17	3.07	2.98	2.84	2.70	2.55	2.47	2.39	2.30	2.21	2.01
	.001	13.3	8.77	7.05	6.12	5.53	5.12	4.82	4.58	4.39	4.24	4.00	3.75	3.49	3.36	3.22	3.07	2.92	2.59
40	.25	1.36	1.44	1.42	1.40	1.39	1.37	1.36	1.35	1.34	1.33	1.31	1.30	1.28	1.26	1.25	1.24	1.22	1.19
	.10	2.84	2.44	2.23	2.09	2.00	1.93	1.87	1.83	1.79	1.76	1.71	1.66	1.61	1.57	1.54	1.51	1.47	1.38
	.05	4.08	3.23	2.84	2.61	2.45	2.34	2.25	2.18	2.12	2.08	2.00	1.92	1.84	1.79	1.74	1.69	1.64	1.51
	.025	5.42	4.05	3.46	3.13	2.90	2.74	2.62	2.53	2.45	2.39	2.29	2.18	2.07	2.01	1.94	1.88	1.80	1.64
	.01	7.31	5.18	4.31	3.83	3.51	3.29	3.12	2.99	2.89	2.80	2.66	2.52	2.37	2.29	2.20	2.11	2.02	1.80
	.001	12.6	8.25	6.60	5.70	5.13	4.73	4.44	4.21	4.02	3.87	3.64	3.40	3.15	3.01	2.87	2.73	2.57	2.23

df for Denominator	x	\multicolumn{18}{c}{df for Numerator}

df for Denominator	x	1	2	3	4	5	6	7	8	9	10	12	15	20	24	30	40	60	∞
60	.25	1.35	1.42	1.41	1.38	1.37	1.35	1.33	1.32	1.31	1.30	1.29	1.27	1.25	1.24	1.22	1.21	1.19	1.15
	.10	2.79	2.39	2.18	2.04	1.95	1.87	1.82	1.77	1.74	1.71	1.66	1.60	1.54	1.51	1.48	1.44	1.40	1.29
	.05	4.00	3.15	2.76	2.53	2.37	2.25	2.17	2.10	2.04	1.99	1.92	1.84	1.75	1.70	1.65	1.59	1.53	1.39
	.025	5.29	3.93	3.34	3.01	2.79	2.63	2.51	2.41	2.33	2.27	2.17	2.06	1.94	1.88	1.82	1.74	1.67	1.48
	.01	7.08	4.98	4.13	3.65	3.34	3.12	2.95	2.82	2.72	2.63	2.50	2.35	2.20	2.12	2.03	1.94	1.84	1.60
	.001	12.0	7.76	6.17	5.31	4.76	4.37	4.09	3.87	3.69	3.54	3.31	3.08	2.83	2.69	2.55	2.41	2.25	1.89
120	.25	1.34	1.40	1.39	1.37	1.35	1.33	1.31	1.30	1.29	1.28	1.26	1.24	1.22	1.21	1.19	1.18	1.16	1.10
	.10	2.75	2.35	2.13	1.99	1.90	1.82	1.77	1.72	1.68	1.65	1.60	1.55	1.48	1.45	1.41	1.37	1.32	1.19
	.05	3.92	3.07	2.68	2.45	2.29	2.17	2.09	2.02	1.96	1.91	1.83	1.75	1.66	1.61	1.55	1.50	1.43	1.25
	.025	5.15	3.80	3.23	2.89	2.67	2.52	2.39	2.30	2.22	2.16	2.05	1.94	1.82	1.76	1.69	1.61	1.53	1.31
	.01	6.85	4.79	3.95	3.48	3.17	2.96	2.79	2.66	2.56	2.47	2.34	2.19	2.03	1.95	1.86	1.76	1.66	1.38
	.001	11.4	7.32	5.79	4.95	4.42	4.04	3.77	3.55	3.38	3.24	3.02	2.78	2.53	2.40	2.26	2.11	1.95	1.54
∞	.25	1.32	1.39	1.37	1.35	1.33	1.31	1.29	1.28	1.27	1.25	1.24	1.22	1.19	1.18	1.16	1.14	1.12	1.00
	.10	2.71	2.30	2.08	1.94	1.85	1.77	1.72	1.67	1.63	1.60	1.55	1.49	1.42	1.38	1.34	1.30	1.24	1.00
	.05	3.84	3.00	2.60	2.37	2.21	2.10	2.01	1.94	1.88	1.83	1.75	1.67	1.57	1.52	1.46	1.39	1.32	1.00
	.025	5.02	3.69	3.12	2.79	2.57	2.41	2.29	2.19	2.11	2.05	1.94	1.83	1.71	1.64	1.57	1.48	1.39	1.00
	.01	6.63	4.61	3.78	3.32	3.02	2.80	2.64	2.51	2.41	2.32	2.18	2.04	1.88	1.79	1.70	1.59	1.47	1.00
	.001	10.8	6.91	5.42	4.62	4.10	3.74	3.47	3.27	3.10	2.96	2.74	2.51	2.27	2.13	1.99	1.84	1.66	1.00

APPENDIX G Binomial Probabilities

Entries are the probabilities of x "successes" in N trials, where p gives the probability of a "success" on each trial.

		Probability p										
N	x	0.01	0.05	0.10	0.15	0.20	0.25	0.30	0.33	0.40	0.45	0.50
2	0	0.9801	0.9025	0.8100	0.7225	0.6400	0.5625	0.4900	0.4444	0.3600	0.3025	0.2500
	1	0.0198	0.0950	0.1800	0.2550	0.3200	0.3750	0.4200	0.4444	0.4800	0.4950	0.5000
	2	0.0001	0.0025	0.0100	0.0225	0.0400	0.0625	0.0900	0.1111	0.1600	0.2025	0.2500
3	0	0.9703	0.8574	0.7290	0.6141	0.5120	0.4219	0.3430	0.2963	0.2160	0.1664	0.1250
	1	0.0294	0.1354	0.2430	0.3251	0.3840	0.4219	0.4410	0.4444	0.4320	0.4084	0.3750
	2	0.0003	0.0071	0.0270	0.0574	0.0960	0.1406	0.1890	0.2222	0.2880	0.3341	0.3750
	3	0.0000	0.0001	0.0010	0.0034	0.0080	0.0156	0.0270	0.0370	0.0640	0.0911	0.1250
4	0	0.9606	0.8145	0.6561	0.5220	0.4096	0.3164	0.2401	0.1975	0.1296	0.0915	0.0625
	1	0.0388	0.1715	0.2916	0.3685	0.4096	0.4219	0.4116	0.3951	0.3456	0.2995	0.2500
	2	0.0006	0.0135	0.0486	0.0975	0.1536	0.2109	0.2646	0.2963	0.3456	0.3675	0.3750
	3	0.0000	0.0005	0.0036	0.0115	0.0256	0.0469	0.0756	0.0988	0.1536	0.2005	0.2500
	4	0.0000	0.0000	0.0001	0.0005	0.0016	0.0039	0.0081	0.0123	0.0256	0.0410	0.0625
5	0	0.9510	0.7738	0.5905	0.4437	0.3277	0.2373	0.1681	0.1317	0.0778	0.0503	0.0313
	1	0.0480	0.2036	0.3281	0.3915	0.4096	0.3955	0.3602	0.3292	0.2592	0.2059	0.1563
	2	0.0010	0.0214	0.0729	0.1382	0.2048	0.2637	0.3087	0.3292	0.3456	0.3369	0.3125
	3	0.0000	0.0011	0.0081	0.0244	0.0512	0.0879	0.1323	0.1646	0.2304	0.2757	0.3125
	4	0.0000	0.0000	0.0005	0.0022	0.0064	0.0146	0.0284	0.0412	0.0768	0.1128	0.1563
	5	0.0000	0.0000	0.0000	0.0001	0.0003	0.0010	0.0024	0.0041	0.0102	0.0185	0.0313
6	0	0.9415	0.7351	0.5314	0.3771	0.2621	0.1780	0.1176	0.0878	0.0467	0.0277	0.0156
	1	0.0571	0.2321	0.3543	0.3993	0.3932	0.3560	0.3025	0.2634	0.1866	0.1359	0.0938
	2	0.0014	0.0305	0.0984	0.1762	0.2458	0.2966	0.3241	0.3292	0.3110	0.2780	0.2344
	3	0.0000	0.0021	0.0146	0.0415	0.0819	0.1318	0.1852	0.2195	0.2765	0.3032	0.3125
	4	0.0000	0.0001	0.0012	0.0055	0.0154	0.0330	0.0595	0.0823	0.1382	0.1861	0.2344
	5	0.0000	0.0000	0.0001	0.0004	0.0015	0.0044	0.0102	0.0165	0.0369	0.0609	0.0938
	6	0.0000	0.0000	0.0000	0.0000	0.0001	0.0002	0.0007	0.0014	0.0041	0.0083	0.0156
7	0	0.9321	0.6983	0.4783	0.3206	0.2097	0.1335	0.0824	0.0585	0.0280	0.0152	0.0078
	1	0.0659	0.2573	0.3720	0.3960	0.3670	0.3115	0.2471	0.2048	0.1306	0.0872	0.0547
	2	0.0020	0.0406	0.1240	0.2097	0.2753	0.3115	0.3177	0.3073	0.2613	0.2140	0.1641
	3	0.0000	0.0036	0.0230	0.0617	0.1147	0.1730	0.2269	0.2561	0.2903	0.2918	0.2734
	4	0.0000	0.0002	0.0026	0.0109	0.0287	0.0577	0.0972	0.1280	0.1935	0.2388	0.2734
	5	0.0000	0.0000	0.0002	0.0012	0.0043	0.0115	0.0250	0.0384	0.0774	0.1172	0.1641
	6	0.0000	0.0000	0.0000	0.0001	0.0004	0.0013	0.0036	0.0064	0.0172	0.0320	0.0547
	7	0.0000	0.0000	0.0000	0.0000	0.0000	0.0001	0.0002	0.0005	0.0016	0.0037	0.0078
8	0	0.9227	0.6634	0.4305	0.2725	0.1678	0.1001	0.0576	0.0390	0.0168	0.0084	0.0039
	1	0.0746	0.2793	0.3826	0.3847	0.3355	0.2670	0.1977	0.1561	0.0896	0.0548	0.0313
	2	0.0026	0.0515	0.1488	0.2376	0.2936	0.3115	0.2965	0.2731	0.2090	0.1569	0.1094
	3	0.0001	0.0054	0.0331	0.0839	0.1468	0.2076	0.2541	0.2731	0.2787	0.2568	0.2188
	4	0.0000	0.0004	0.0046	0.0185	0.0459	0.0865	0.1361	0.1707	0.2322	0.2627	0.2734
	5	0.0000	0.0000	0.0004	0.0026	0.0092	0.0231	0.0467	0.0683	0.1239	0.1719	0.2188
	6	0.0000	0.0000	0.0000	0.0002	0.0011	0.0038	0.0100	0.0171	0.0413	0.0703	0.1094
	7	0.0000	0.0000	0.0000	0.0000	0.0001	0.0004	0.0012	0.0024	0.0079	0.0164	0.0313
	8	0.0000	0.0000	0.0000	0.0000	0.0000	0.0000	0.0001	0.0002	0.0007	0.0017	0.0039
9	0	0.9135	0.6302	0.3874	0.2316	0.1342	0.0751	0.0404	0.0260	0.0101	0.0046	0.0020
	1	0.0830	0.2985	0.3874	0.3679	0.3020	0.2253	0.1556	0.1171	0.0605	0.0339	0.0176
	2	0.0034	0.0629	0.1722	0.2597	0.3020	0.3003	0.2668	0.2341	0.1612	0.1110	0.0703
	3	0.0001	0.0077	0.0446	0.1069	0.1762	0.2336	0.2668	0.2731	0.2508	0.2119	0.1641
	4	0.0000	0.0006	0.0074	0.0283	0.0661	0.1168	0.1715	0.2048	0.2508	0.2600	0.2461

Source: The values in this table were computed by the author.

		Probability p										
N	x	0.01	0.05	0.10	0.15	0.20	0.25	0.30	0.33	0.40	0.45	0.50
	5	0.0000	0.0000	0.0008	0.0050	0.0165	0.0389	0.0735	0.1024	0.1672	0.2128	0.2461
	6	0.0000	0.0000	0.0001	0.0006	0.0028	0.0087	0.0210	0.0341	0.0743	0.1160	0.1641
	7	0.0000	0.0000	0.0000	0.0000	0.0003	0.0012	0.0039	0.0073	0.0212	0.0407	0.0703
	8	0.0000	0.0000	0.0000	0.0000	0.0000	0.0001	0.0004	0.0009	0.0035	0.0083	0.0176
	9	0.0000	0.0000	0.0000	0.0000	0.0000	0.0000	0.0000	0.0001	0.0003	0.0008	0.0020
10	0	0.9044	0.5987	0.3487	0.1969	0.1074	0.0563	0.0282	0.0173	0.0060	0.0025	0.0010
	1	0.0914	0.3151	0.3874	0.3474	0.2684	0.1877	0.1211	0.0867	0.0403	0.0207	0.0098
	2	0.0042	0.0746	0.1937	0.2759	0.3020	0.2816	0.2335	0.1951	0.1209	0.0763	0.0439
	3	0.0001	0.0105	0.0574	0.1298	0.2013	0.2503	0.2668	0.2601	0.2150	0.1665	0.1172
	4	0.0000	0.0010	0.0112	0.0401	0.0881	0.1460	0.2001	0.2276	0.2508	0.2384	0.2051
	5	0.0000	0.0001	0.0015	0.0085	0.0264	0.0584	0.1029	0.1366	0.2007	0.2340	0.2461
	6	0.0000	0.0000	0.0001	0.0012	0.0055	0.0162	0.0368	0.0569	0.1115	0.1596	0.2051
	7	0.0000	0.0000	0.0000	0.0001	0.0008	0.0031	0.0090	0.0163	0.0425	0.0746	0.1172
	8	0.0000	0.0000	0.0000	0.0000	0.0001	0.0004	0.0014	0.0030	0.0106	0.0229	0.0439
	9	0.0000	0.0000	0.0000	0.0000	0.0000	0.0000	0.0001	0.0003	0.0016	0.0042	0.0098
	10	0.0000	0.0000	0.0000	0.0000	0.0000	0.0000	0.0000	0.0000	0.0001	0.0003	0.0010
11	0	0.8953	0.5688	0.3138	0.1673	0.0859	0.0422	0.0198	0.0116	0.0036	0.0014	0.0005
	1	0.0995	0.3293	0.3835	0.3248	0.2362	0.1549	0.0932	0.0636	0.0266	0.0125	0.0054
	2	0.0050	0.0867	0.2131	0.2866	0.2953	0.2581	0.1998	0.1590	0.0887	0.0513	0.0269
	3	0.0002	0.0137	0.0710	0.1517	0.2215	0.2581	0.2568	0.2384	0.1774	0.1259	0.0806
	4	0.0000	0.0014	0.0158	0.0536	0.1107	0.1721	0.2201	0.2384	0.2365	0.2060	0.1611
	5	0.0000	0.0001	0.0025	0.0132	0.0388	0.0803	0.1321	0.1669	0.2207	0.2360	0.2256
	6	0.0000	0.0000	0.0003	0.0023	0.0097	0.0268	0.0566	0.0835	0.1471	0.1931	0.2256
	7	0.0000	0.0000	0.0000	0.0003	0.0017	0.0064	0.0173	0.0298	0.0701	0.1128	0.1611
	8	0.0000	0.0000	0.0000	0.0000	0.0002	0.0011	0.0037	0.0075	0.0234	0.0462	0.0806
	9	0.0000	0.0000	0.0000	0.0000	0.0000	0.0001	0.0005	0.0012	0.0052	0.0126	0.0269
	10	0.0000	0.0000	0.0000	0.0000	0.0000	0.0000	0.0000	0.0001	0.0007	0.0021	0.0054
	11	0.0000	0.0000	0.0000	0.0000	0.0000	0.0000	0.0000	0.0000	0.0000	0.0002	0.0005
12	0	0.8864	0.5404	0.2824	0.1422	0.0687	0.0317	0.0138	0.0077	0.0022	0.0008	0.0002
	1	0.1074	0.3413	0.3766	0.3012	0.2062	0.1267	0.0712	0.0462	0.0174	0.0075	0.0029
	2	0.0060	0.0988	0.2301	0.2924	0.2835	0.2323	0.1678	0.1272	0.0639	0.0339	0.0161
	3	0.0002	0.0173	0.0852	0.1720	0.2362	0.2581	0.2397	0.2120	0.1419	0.0923	0.0537
	4	0.0000	0.0021	0.0213	0.0683	0.1329	0.1936	0.2311	0.2384	0.2128	0.1700	0.1208
	5	0.0000	0.0002	0.0038	0.0193	0.0532	0.1032	0.1585	0.1908	0.2270	0.2225	0.1934
	6	0.0000	0.0000	0.0005	0.0040	0.0155	0.0401	0.0792	0.1113	0.1766	0.2124	0.2256
	7	0.0000	0.0000	0.0000	0.0006	0.0033	0.0115	0.0291	0.0477	0.1009	0.1489	0.1934
	8	0.0000	0.0000	0.0000	0.0001	0.0005	0.0024	0.0078	0.0149	0.0420	0.0762	0.1208
	9	0.0000	0.0000	0.0000	0.0000	0.0001	0.0004	0.0015	0.0033	0.0125	0.0277	0.0537
	10	0.0000	0.0000	0.0000	0.0000	0.0000	0.0000	0.0002	0.0005	0.0025	0.0068	0.0161
	11	0.0000	0.0000	0.0000	0.0000	0.0000	0.0000	0.0000	0.0000	0.0003	0.0010	0.0029
	12	0.0000	0.0000	0.0000	0.0000	0.0000	0.0000	0.0000	0.0000	0.0000	0.0001	0.0002
13	0	0.8775	0.5133	0.2542	0.1209	0.0550	0.0238	0.0097	0.0051	0.0013	0.0004	0.0001
	1	0.1152	0.3512	0.3672	0.2774	0.1787	0.1029	0.0540	0.0334	0.0113	0.0045	0.0016
	2	0.0070	0.1109	0.2448	0.2937	0.2680	0.2059	0.1388	0.1002	0.0453	0.0220	0.0095
	3	0.0003	0.0214	0.0997	0.1900	0.2457	0.2517	0.2181	0.1837	0.1107	0.0660	0.0349
	4	0.0000	0.0028	0.0277	0.0838	0.1535	0.2097	0.2337	0.2296	0.1845	0.1350	0.0873
	5	0.0000	0.0003	0.0055	0.0266	0.0691	0.1258	0.1803	0.2067	0.2214	0.1989	0.1571
	6	0.0000	0.0000	0.0008	0.0063	0.0230	0.0559	0.1030	0.1378	0.1968	0.2169	0.2095
	7	0.0000	0.0000	0.0001	0.0011	0.0058	0.0186	0.0442	0.0689	0.1312	0.1775	0.2095
	8	0.0000	0.0000	0.0000	0.0001	0.0011	0.0047	0.0142	0.0258	0.0656	0.1089	0.1571
	9	0.0000	0.0000	0.0000	0.0000	0.0001	0.0009	0.0034	0.0072	0.0243	0.0495	0.0873
	10	0.0000	0.0000	0.0000	0.0000	0.0000	0.0001	0.0006	0.0014	0.0065	0.0162	0.0349
	11	0.0000	0.0000	0.0000	0.0000	0.0000	0.0000	0.0001	0.0002	0.0012	0.0036	0.0095
	12	0.0000	0.0000	0.0000	0.0000	0.0000	0.0000	0.0000	0.0000	0.0001	0.0005	0.0016
	13	0.0000	0.0000	0.0000	0.0000	0.0000	0.0000	0.0000	0.0000	0.0000	0.0000	0.0001

Probability *p*

N	x	0.01	0.05	0.10	0.15	0.20	0.25	0.30	0.33	0.40	0.45	0.50
14	0	0.8687	0.4877	0.2288	0.1028	0.0440	0.0178	0.0068	0.0034	0.0008	0.0002	0.0001
	1	0.1229	0.3593	0.3559	0.2539	0.1539	0.0832	0.0407	0.0240	0.0073	0.0027	0.0009
	2	0.0081	0.1229	0.2570	0.2912	0.2501	0.1802	0.1134	0.0779	0.0317	0.0141	0.0056
	3	0.0003	0.0259	0.1142	0.2056	0.2501	0.2402	0.1943	0.1559	0.0845	0.0462	0.0222
	4	0.0000	0.0037	0.0349	0.0998	0.1720	0.2202	0.2290	0.2143	0.1549	0.1040	0.0611
	5	0.0000	0.0004	0.0078	0.0352	0.0860	0.1468	0.1963	0.2143	0.2066	0.1701	0.1222
	6	0.0000	0.0000	0.0013	0.0093	0.0322	0.0734	0.1262	0.1607	0.2066	0.2088	0.1833
	7	0.0000	0.0000	0.0002	0.0019	0.0092	0.0280	0.0618	0.0918	0.1574	0.1952	0.2095
	8	0.0000	0.0000	0.0000	0.0003	0.0020	0.0082	0.0232	0.0402	0.0918	0.1398	0.1833
	9	0.0000	0.0000	0.0000	0.0000	0.0003	0.0018	0.0066	0.0134	0.0408	0.0762	0.1222
	10	0.0000	0.0000	0.0000	0.0000	0.0000	0.0003	0.0014	0.0033	0.0136	0.0312	0.0611
	11	0.0000	0.0000	0.0000	0.0000	0.0000	0.0000	0.0002	0.0006	0.0033	0.0093	0.0222
	12	0.0000	0.0000	0.0000	0.0000	0.0000	0.0000	0.0000	0.0001	0.0005	0.0019	0.0056
	13	0.0000	0.0000	0.0000	0.0000	0.0000	0.0000	0.0000	0.0000	0.0001	0.0002	0.0009
	14	0.0000	0.0000	0.0000	0.0000	0.0000	0.0000	0.0000	0.0000	0.0000	0.0000	0.0001
15	0	0.8601	0.4633	0.2059	0.0874	0.0352	0.0134	0.0047	0.0023	0.0005	0.0001	0.0000
	1	0.1303	0.3658	0.3432	0.2312	0.1319	0.0668	0.0305	0.0171	0.0047	0.0016	0.0005
	2	0.0092	0.1348	0.2669	0.2856	0.2309	0.1559	0.0916	0.0599	0.0219	0.0090	0.0032
	3	0.0004	0.0307	0.1285	0.2184	0.2501	0.2252	0.1700	0.1299	0.0634	0.0318	0.0139
	4	0.0000	0.0049	0.0428	0.1156	0.1876	0.2252	0.2186	0.1948	0.1268	0.0780	0.0417
	5	0.0000	0.0006	0.0105	0.0449	0.1032	0.1651	0.2061	0.2143	0.1859	0.1404	0.0916
	6	0.0000	0.0000	0.0019	0.0132	0.0430	0.0917	0.1472	0.1786	0.2066	0.1914	0.1527
	7	0.0000	0.0000	0.0003	0.0030	0.0138	0.0393	0.0811	0.1148	0.1771	0.2013	0.1964
	8	0.0000	0.0000	0.0000	0.0005	0.0035	0.0131	0.0348	0.0574	0.1181	0.1647	0.1964
	9	0.0000	0.0000	0.0000	0.0001	0.0007	0.0034	0.0116	0.0223	0.0612	0.1048	0.1527
	10	0.0000	0.0000	0.0000	0.0000	0.0001	0.0007	0.0030	0.0067	0.0245	0.0515	0.0916
	11	0.0000	0.0000	0.0000	0.0000	0.0000	0.0001	0.0006	0.0015	0.0074	0.0191	0.0417
	12	0.0000	0.0000	0.0000	0.0000	0.0000	0.0000	0.0001	0.0003	0.0016	0.0052	0.0139
	13	0.0000	0.0000	0.0000	0.0000	0.0000	0.0000	0.0000	0.0000	0.0003	0.0010	0.0032
	14	0.0000	0.0000	0.0000	0.0000	0.0000	0.0000	0.0000	0.0000	0.0000	0.0001	0.0005
	15	0.0000	0.0000	0.0000	0.0000	0.0000	0.0000	0.0000	0.0000	0.0000	0.0000	0.0000
20	0	0.8179	0.3585	0.1216	0.0388	0.0115	0.0032	0.0008	0.0003	0.0000	0.0000	0.0000
	1	0.1652	0.3774	0.2702	0.1368	0.0576	0.0211	0.0068	0.0030	0.0005	0.0001	0.0000
	2	0.0159	0.1887	0.2852	0.2293	0.1369	0.0669	0.0278	0.0143	0.0031	0.0008	0.0002
	3	0.0010	0.0596	0.1901	0.2428	0.2054	0.1339	0.0716	0.0429	0.0123	0.0040	0.0011
	4	0.0000	0.0133	0.0898	0.1821	0.2182	0.1897	0.1304	0.0911	0.0350	0.0139	0.0046
	5	0.0000	0.0022	0.0319	0.1028	0.1746	0.2023	0.1789	0.1457	0.0746	0.0365	0.0148
	6	0.0000	0.0003	0.0089	0.0454	0.1091	0.1686	0.1916	0.1821	0.1244	0.0746	0.0370
	7	0.0000	0.0000	0.0020	0.0160	0.0545	0.1124	0.1643	0.1821	0.1659	0.1221	0.0739
	8	0.0000	0.0000	0.0004	0.0046	0.0222	0.0609	0.1144	0.1480	0.1797	0.1623	0.1201
	9	0.0000	0.0000	0.0001	0.0011	0.0074	0.0271	0.0654	0.0987	0.1597	0.1771	0.1602
	10	0.0000	0.0000	0.0000	0.0002	0.0020	0.0099	0.0308	0.0543	0.1171	0.1593	0.1762
	11	0.0000	0.0000	0.0000	0.0000	0.0005	0.0030	0.0120	0.0247	0.0710	0.1185	0.1602
	12	0.0000	0.0000	0.0000	0.0000	0.0001	0.0008	0.0039	0.0092	0.0355	0.0727	0.1201
	13	0.0000	0.0000	0.0000	0.0000	0.0000	0.0002	0.0010	0.0028	0.0146	0.0366	0.0739
	14	0.0000	0.0000	0.0000	0.0000	0.0000	0.0000	0.0002	0.0007	0.0049	0.0150	0.0370
	15	0.0000	0.0000	0.0000	0.0000	0.0000	0.0000	0.0000	0.0001	0.0013	0.0049	0.0148
	16	0.0000	0.0000	0.0000	0.0000	0.0000	0.0000	0.0000	0.0000	0.0003	0.0013	0.0046
	17	0.0000	0.0000	0.0000	0.0000	0.0000	0.0000	0.0000	0.0000	0.0000	0.0002	0.0011
	18	0.0000	0.0000	0.0000	0.0000	0.0000	0.0000	0.0000	0.0000	0.0000	0.0000	0.0002
	19	0.0000	0.0000	0.0000	0.0000	0.0000	0.0000	0.0000	0.0000	0.0000	0.0000	0.0000
	20	0.0000	0.0000	0.0000	0.0000	0.0000	0.0000	0.0000	0.0000	0.0000	0.0000	0.0000
25	0	0.7778	0.2774	0.0718	0.0172	0.0038	0.0008	0.0001	0.0000	0.0000	0.0000	0.0000
	1	0.1964	0.3650	0.1994	0.0759	0.0236	0.0063	0.0014	0.0005	0.0000	0.0000	0.0000
	2	0.0238	0.2305	0.2659	0.1607	0.0708	0.0251	0.0074	0.0030	0.0004	0.0001	0.0000
	3	0.0018	0.0930	0.2265	0.2174	0.1358	0.0641	0.0243	0.0114	0.0019	0.0004	0.0001
	4	0.0001	0.0269	0.1384	0.2110	0.1867	0.1175	0.0572	0.0313	0.0071	0.0018	0.0004

N	x	0.01	0.05	0.10	0.15	0.20	0.25	0.30	0.33	0.40	0.45	0.50
	5	0.0000	0.0060	0.0646	0.1564	0.1960	0.1645	0.1030	0.0658	0.0199	0.0063	0.0016
	6	0.0000	0.0010	0.0239	0.0920	0.1633	0.1828	0.1472	0.1096	0.0442	0.0172	0.0053
	7	0.0000	0.0001	0.0072	0.0441	0.1108	0.1654	0.1712	0.1487	0.0800	0.0381	0.0143
	8	0.0000	0.0000	0.0018	0.0175	0.0623	0.1241	0.1651	0.1673	0.1200	0.0701	0.0322
	9	0.0000	0.0000	0.0004	0.0058	0.0294	0.0781	0.1336	0.1580	0.1511	0.1084	0.0609
	10	0.0000	0.0000	0.0001	0.0016	0.0118	0.0417	0.0916	0.1264	0.1612	0.1419	0.0974
	11	0.0000	0.0000	0.0000	0.0004	0.0040	0.0189	0.0536	0.0862	0.1465	0.1583	0.1328
	12	0.0000	0.0000	0.0000	0.0001	0.0012	0.0074	0.0268	0.0503	0.1140	0.1511	0.1550
	13	0.0000	0.0000	0.0000	0.0000	0.0003	0.0025	0.0115	0.0251	0.0760	0.1236	0.1550
	14	0.0000	0.0000	0.0000	0.0000	0.0001	0.0007	0.0042	0.0108	0.0434	0.0867	0.1328
	15	0.0000	0.0000	0.0000	0.0000	0.0000	0.0002	0.0013	0.0040	0.0212	0.0520	0.0974
	16	0.0000	0.0000	0.0000	0.0000	0.0000	0.0000	0.0004	0.0012	0.0088	0.0266	0.0609
	17	0.0000	0.0000	0.0000	0.0000	0.0000	0.0000	0.0001	0.0003	0.0031	0.0115	0.0322
	18	0.0000	0.0000	0.0000	0.0000	0.0000	0.0000	0.0000	0.0001	0.0009	0.0042	0.0143
	19	0.0000	0.0000	0.0000	0.0000	0.0000	0.0000	0.0000	0.0000	0.0002	0.0013	0.0053
	20	0.0000	0.0000	0.0000	0.0000	0.0000	0.0000	0.0000	0.0000	0.0000	0.0003	0.0016
	21	0.0000	0.0000	0.0000	0.0000	0.0000	0.0000	0.0000	0.0000	0.0000	0.0001	0.0004
	22	0.0000	0.0000	0.0000	0.0000	0.0000	0.0000	0.0000	0.0000	0.0000	0.0000	0.0001
	23	0.0000	0.0000	0.0000	0.0000	0.0000	0.0000	0.0000	0.0000	0.0000	0.0000	0.0000
	24	0.0000	0.0000	0.0000	0.0000	0.0000	0.0000	0.0000	0.0000	0.0000	0.0000	0.0000
	25	0.0000	0.0000	0.0000	0.0000	0.0000	0.0000	0.0000	0.0000	0.0000	0.0000	0.0000
30	0	0.7397	0.2146	0.0424	0.0076	0.0012	0.0002	0.0000	0.0000	0.0000	0.0000	0.0000
	1	0.2242	0.3389	0.1413	0.0404	0.0093	0.0018	0.0003	0.0001	0.0000	0.0000	0.0000
	2	0.0328	0.2586	0.2277	0.1034	0.0337	0.0086	0.0018	0.0006	0.0000	0.0000	0.0000
	3	0.0031	0.1270	0.2361	0.1703	0.0785	0.0269	0.0072	0.0026	0.0003	0.0000	0.0000
	4	0.0002	0.0451	0.1771	0.2028	0.1325	0.0604	0.0208	0.0089	0.0012	0.0002	0.0000
	5	0.0000	0.0124	0.1023	0.1861	0.1723	0.1047	0.0464	0.0232	0.0041	0.0008	0.0001
	6	0.0000	0.0027	0.0474	0.1368	0.1795	0.1455	0.0829	0.0484	0.0115	0.0029	0.0006
	7	0.0000	0.0005	0.0180	0.0828	0.1538	0.1662	0.1219	0.0829	0.0263	0.0081	0.0019
	8	0.0000	0.0001	0.0058	0.0420	0.1106	0.1593	0.1501	0.1192	0.0505	0.0191	0.0055
	9	0.0000	0.0000	0.0016	0.0181	0.0676	0.1298	0.1573	0.1457	0.0823	0.0382	0.0133
	10	0.0000	0.0000	0.0004	0.0067	0.0355	0.0909	0.1416	0.1530	0.1152	0.0656	0.0280
	11	0.0000	0.0000	0.0001	0.0022	0.0161	0.0551	0.1103	0.1391	0.1396	0.0976	0.0509
	12	0.0000	0.0000	0.0000	0.0006	0.0064	0.0291	0.0749	0.1101	0.1474	0.1265	0.0806
	13	0.0000	0.0000	0.0000	0.0001	0.0022	0.0134	0.0444	0.0762	0.1360	0.1433	0.1115
	14	0.0000	0.0000	0.0000	0.0000	0.0007	0.0054	0.0231	0.0463	0.1101	0.1424	0.1354
	15	0.0000	0.0000	0.0000	0.0000	0.0002	0.0019	0.0106	0.0247	0.0783	0.1242	0.1445
	16	0.0000	0.0000	0.0000	0.0000	0.0000	0.0006	0.0042	0.0116	0.0489	0.0953	0.1354
	17	0.0000	0.0000	0.0000	0.0000	0.0000	0.0002	0.0015	0.0048	0.0269	0.0642	0.1115
	18	0.0000	0.0000	0.0000	0.0000	0.0000	0.0000	0.0005	0.0017	0.0129	0.0379	0.0806
	19	0.0000	0.0000	0.0000	0.0000	0.0000	0.0000	0.0001	0.0005	0.0054	0.0196	0.0509
	20	0.0000	0.0000	0.0000	0.0000	0.0000	0.0000	0.0000	0.0001	0.0020	0.0088	0.0280
	21	0.0000	0.0000	0.0000	0.0000	0.0000	0.0000	0.0000	0.0000	0.0006	0.0034	0.0133
	21	0.0000	0.0000	0.0000	0.0000	0.0000	0.0000	0.0000	0.0000	0.0006	0.0034	0.0133
	22	0.0000	0.0000	0.0000	0.0000	0.0000	0.0000	0.0000	0.0000	0.0002	0.0012	0.0055
	23	0.0000	0.0000	0.0000	0.0000	0.0000	0.0000	0.0000	0.0000	0.0000	0.0003	0.0019
	24	0.0000	0.0000	0.0000	0.0000	0.0000	0.0000	0.0000	0.0000	0.0000	0.0001	0.0006
	25	0.0000	0.0000	0.0000	0.0000	0.0000	0.0000	0.0000	0.0000	0.0000	0.0000	0.0001
	26	0.0000	0.0000	0.0000	0.0000	0.0000	0.0000	0.0000	0.0000	0.0000	0.0000	0.0000
	27	0.0000	0.0000	0.0000	0.0000	0.0000	0.0000	0.0000	0.0000	0.0000	0.0000	0.0000
	28	0.0000	0.0000	0.0000	0.0000	0.0000	0.0000	0.0000	0.0000	0.0000	0.0000	0.0000
	29	0.0000	0.0000	0.0000	0.0000	0.0000	0.0000	0.0000	0.0000	0.0000	0.0000	0.0000
	30	0.0000	0.0000	0.0000	0.0000	0.0000	0.0000	0.0000	0.0000	0.0000	0.0000	0.0000

Critical Values for Wilcoxon's *T*

Two tails	0.10	0.05	0.02	0.01
One tail	0.05	0.025	0.01	0.005
N				
4				
5	0			
6	2	0		
7	3	2	0	
8	5	3	1	0
9	8	5	3	1
10	10	8	5	3
11	13	10	7	5
12	17	13	9	7
13	21	17	12	9
14	25	21	15	12
15	30	25	19	15
16	35	29	23	19
17	41	34	27	23
18	47	40	32	27
19	53	46	37	32
20	60	52	43	37
21	67	58	49	42
22	75	65	55	48
23	83	73	62	54
24	91	81	69	61
25	100	89	76	68
26	110	98	84	75
27	119	107	92	83
28	130	116	101	91
29	140	126	110	100
30	151	137	120	109
31	163	147	130	118
32	175	159	140	128
33	187	170	151	138
34	200	182	162	148
35	213	195	173	159
36	227	208	185	171
37	241	221	198	182
38	256	235	211	194
39	271	249	224	207
40	286	264	238	220
41	302	279	252	233
42	319	294	266	247
43	336	310	281	261
44	353	327	296	276
45	371	343	312	291
46	389	361	328	307
47	407	378	345	322
48	426	396	362	339
49	446	415	379	355
50	466	434	397	373

Source: The values in this table were obtained from McCornack, R. L. (1965). Extended tables of the Wilcoxon matched pair signed rank test. *Journal of the American Statistical Association, 60,* 864–871. Used by permission of the publisher.

One-Tailed Critical Values for the Wilcoxon Two-Group Test

Note: $N1$ is the *smaller* group size and $N2$ is the *larger*. If the obtained value is less than or equal to the tabled value, there is a significant difference between the groups.

| | $N_1 = 1$ | | | | | | $N_1 = 2$ | | | | | | |
N_2	0.001	0.005	0.010	0.025	0.05	0.10	0.001	0.005	0.010	0.025	0.05	0.10	N_2
2												—	2
3												3	3
4											—	3	4
5											3	4	5
6											3	4	6
7										—	3	4	7
8						—				3	4	5	8
9						1				3	4	5	9
10						1				3	4	6	10

| | $N_1 = 3$ | | | | | | $N_1 = 4$ | | | | | | |
N_2	0.001	0.005	0.010	0.025	0.05	0.10	0.001	0.005	0.010	0.025	0.05	0.10	N_2
3					6	7							
4				—	6	7			—	10	11	13	4
5			6	7	8			—	10	11	12	14	5
6		—	7	8	9		10	11	12	13	15		6
7		6	7	8	10		10	11	13	14	16		7
8	—	6	8	9	11		11	12	14	15	17		8
9	6	7	8	10	11		—	11	13	14	16	19	9
10	6	7	9	10	12		10	12	13	15	17	20	10

| | $N_1 = 5$ | | | | | | $N_1 = 6$ | | | | | | |
N_2	0.001	0.005	0.010	0.025	0.05	0.10	0.001	0.005	0.010	0.025	0.05	0.10	N_2
5		15	16	17	19	20							
6		16	17	18	20	22	—	23	24	26	28	30	6
7	—	16	18	20	21	23	21	24	25	27	29	32	7
8	15	17	19	21	23	25	22	25	27	29	31	34	8
9	16	18	20	22	24	27	23	26	28	31	33	36	9
10	16	19	21	23	26	28	24	27	29	32	35	38	10

| | $N_1 = 7$ | | | | | | $N_1 = 8$ | | | | | | |
N_2	0.001	0.005	0.010	0.025	0.05	0.10	0.001	0.005	0.010	0.025	0.05	0.10	N_2
7	29	32	34	36	39	41							
8	30	34	35	38	41	44	40	43	45	49	51	55	8
9	31	35	37	40	43	46	41	45	47	51	54	58	9
10	33	37	39	42	45	49	42	47	49	53	56	60	10

N_2	$N_1 = 9$						$N_1 = 10$						N_2
	0.001	0.005	0.010	0.025	0.05	0.10	0.001	0.005	0.010	0.025	0.05	0.10	
9	52	56	59	62	66	70							
10	53	58	61	65	69	73	65	71	74	78	82	87	10

APPENDIX J Critical Values for the Studentized Range

		Number of means																		
df Error	α	2	3	4	5	6	7	8	9	10	11	12	13	14	15	16	17	18	19	20
1	.05	17.97	26.98	32.82	37.08	40.41	43.12	45.40	47.36	49.07	50.59	51.96	53.20	54.33	55.36	56.32	57.22	58.04	58.83	59.56
	.01	90.03	135.0	164.3	185.6	202.2	215.8	227.2	237.0	245.6	253.2	260.0	266.2	271.8	277.0	281.8	286.3	290.4	294.3	298.0
2	.05	6.08	8.33	9.80	10.88	11.74	12.44	13.03	13.54	13.99	14.39	14.75	15.08	15.38	15.65	15.91	16.14	16.37	16.57	16.77
	.01	14.04	19.02	22.29	24.72	26.63	28.20	29.53	30.66	31.69	32.59	33.40	34.13	34.81	35.43	36.00	36.53	37.03	37.50	37.95
3	.05	4.50	5.91	6.82	7.50	8.04	8.48	8.85	9.18	9.46	9.72	9.95	10.15	10.35	10.52	10.69	10.84	10.98	11.11	11.24
	.01	8.26	10.62	12.17	13.33	14.24	15.00	15.64	16.20	16.69	17.13	17.53	17.89	18.22	18.52	18.81	19.07	19.32	19.55	19.77
4	.05	3.93	5.04	5.76	6.29	6.71	7.05	7.35	7.60	7.83	8.03	8.21	8.37	8.52	8.66	8.79	8.91	9.03	9.13	9.23
	.01	6.51	8.12	9.17	9.96	10.58	11.10	11.55	11.93	12.27	12.57	12.84	13.09	13.32	13.53	13.73	13.91	14.08	14.24	14.40
5	.05	3.64	4.60	5.22	5.67	6.03	6.33	6.58	6.80	6.99	7.17	7.32	7.47	7.60	7.72	7.83	7.93	8.03	8.12	8.21
	.01	5.70	6.98	7.80	8.42	8.91	9.32	9.67	9.97	10.24	10.48	10.70	10.89	11.08	11.24	11.40	11.55	11.68	11.81	11.93
6	.05	3.46	4.34	4.90	5.30	5.63	5.90	6.12	6.32	6.49	6.65	6.79	6.92	7.03	7.14	7.24	7.34	7.43	7.51	7.59
	.01	5.24	6.33	7.03	7.56	7.97	8.32	8.61	8.87	9.10	9.30	9.48	9.65	9.81	9.95	10.08	10.21	10.32	10.43	10.54
7	.05	3.34	4.16	4.68	5.06	5.36	5.61	5.82	6.00	6.16	6.30	6.43	6.55	6.66	6.76	6.85	6.94	7.02	7.10	7.17
	.01	4.95	5.92	6.54	7.01	7.37	7.68	7.94	8.17	8.37	8.55	8.71	8.86	9.00	9.12	9.24	9.35	9.46	9.55	9.65
8	.05	3.26	4.04	4.53	4.89	5.17	5.40	5.60	5.77	5.92	6.05	6.18	6.29	6.39	6.48	6.57	6.65	6.73	6.80	6.87
	.01	4.75	5.64	6.20	6.62	6.96	7.24	7.47	7.68	7.86	8.03	8.18	8.31	8.44	8.55	8.66	8.76	8.85	8.94	9.03
9	.05	3.20	3.95	4.41	4.76	5.02	5.24	5.43	5.59	5.74	5.87	5.98	6.09	6.19	6.28	6.36	6.44	6.51	6.58	6.64
	.01	4.60	5.43	5.96	6.35	6.66	6.91	7.13	7.33	7.49	7.65	7.78	7.91	8.03	8.13	8.23	8.33	8.41	8.49	8.57
10	.05	3.15	3.88	4.33	4.65	4.91	5.12	5.30	5.46	5.60	5.72	5.83	5.93	6.03	6.11	6.19	6.27	6.34	6.40	6.47
	.01	4.48	5.27	5.77	6.14	6.43	6.67	6.87	7.05	7.21	7.36	7.49	7.60	7.71	7.81	7.91	7.99	8.08	8.15	8.23
11	.05	3.11	3.82	4.26	4.57	4.82	5.03	5.20	5.35	5.49	5.61	5.71	5.81	5.90	5.98	6.06	6.13	6.20	6.27	6.33
	.01	4.39	5.15	5.62	5.97	6.25	6.48	6.67	6.84	6.99	7.13	7.25	7.36	7.46	7.56	7.65	7.73	7.81	7.88	7.95
12	.05	3.08	3.77	4.20	4.51	4.75	4.95	5.12	5.27	5.39	5.51	5.61	5.71	5.80	5.88	5.95	6.02	6.09	6.15	6.21
	.01	4.32	5.05	5.50	5.84	6.10	6.32	6.51	6.67	6.81	6.94	7.06	7.17	7.26	7.36	7.44	7.52	7.59	7.66	7.73
13	.05	3.06	3.73	4.15	4.45	4.69	4.88	5.05	5.19	5.32	5.43	5.53	5.63	5.71	5.79	5.86	5.93	5.99	6.05	6.11
	.01	4.26	4.96	5.40	5.73	5.98	6.19	6.37	6.53	6.67	6.79	6.90	7.01	7.10	7.19	7.27	7.35	7.42	7.48	7.55
14	.05	3.03	3.70	4.11	4.41	4.64	4.83	4.99	5.13	5.25	5.36	5.46	5.55	5.64	5.71	5.79	5.85	5.91	5.97	6.03
	.01	4.21	4.89	5.32	5.63	5.88	6.08	6.26	6.41	6.54	6.66	6.77	6.87	6.96	7.05	7.13	7.20	7.27	7.33	7.39
15	.05	3.01	3.67	4.08	4.37	4.59	4.78	4.94	5.08	5.20	5.31	5.40	5.49	5.57	5.65	5.72	5.78	5.85	5.90	5.96
	.01	4.17	4.84	5.25	5.56	5.80	5.99	6.16	6.31	6.44	6.55	6.66	6.76	6.84	6.93	7.00	7.07	7.14	7.20	7.26
16	.05	3.00	3.65	4.05	4.33	4.56	4.74	4.90	5.03	5.15	5.26	5.35	5.44	5.52	5.59	5.66	5.73	5.79	5.84	5.90
	.01	4.13	4.79	5.19	5.49	5.72	5.92	6.08	6.22	6.35	6.46	6.56	6.66	6.74	6.82	6.90	6.97	7.03	7.09	7.15
17	.05	2.98	3.63	4.02	4.30	4.52	4.70	4.86	4.99	5.11	5.21	5.31	5.39	5.47	5.54	5.61	5.67	5.73	5.79	5.84
	.01	4.10	4.74	5.14	5.43	5.66	5.85	6.01	6.15	6.27	6.38	6.48	6.57	6.66	6.73	6.81	6.87	6.94	7.00	7.05
18	.05	2.97	3.61	4.00	4.28	4.49	4.67	4.82	4.96	5.07	5.17	5.27	5.35	5.43	5.50	5.57	5.63	5.69	5.74	5.79
	.01	4.07	4.70	5.09	5.38	5.60	5.79	5.94	6.08	6.20	6.31	6.41	6.50	6.58	6.65	6.73	6.79	6.85	6.91	6.97
19	.05	2.96	3.59	3.98	4.25	4.47	4.65	4.79	4.92	5.04	5.14	5.23	5.31	5.39	5.46	5.53	5.59	5.65	5.70	5.75
	.01	4.05	4.67	5.05	5.33	5.55	5.73	5.89	6.02	6.14	6.25	6.34	6.43	6.51	6.58	6.65	6.72	6.78	6.84	6.89
20	.05	2.95	3.58	3.96	4.23	4.45	4.62	4.77	4.90	5.01	5.11	5.20	5.28	5.36	5.43	5.49	5.55	5.61	5.66	5.71
	.01	4.02	4.64	5.02	5.29	5.51	5.69	5.84	5.97	6.09	6.19	6.28	6.37	6.45	6.52	6.59	6.65	6.71	6.77	6.82
24	.05	2.92	3.53	3.90	4.17	4.37	4.54	4.68	4.81	4.92	5.01	5.10	5.18	5.25	5.32	5.38	5.44	5.49	5.55	5.59
	.01	3.96	4.55	4.91	5.17	5.37	5.54	5.69	5.81	5.92	6.02	6.11	6.19	6.26	6.33	6.39	6.45	6.51	6.56	6.61
30	.05	2.89	3.49	3.85	4.10	4.30	4.46	4.60	4.72	4.82	4.92	5.00	5.08	5.15	5.21	5.27	5.33	5.38	5.43	5.47
	.01	3.89	4.45	4.80	5.05	5.24	5.40	5.54	5.65	5.76	5.85	5.93	6.01	6.08	6.14	6.20	6.26	6.31	6.36	6.41
40	.05	2.86	3.44	3.79	4.04	4.23	4.39	4.52	4.63	4.73	4.82	4.90	4.98	5.04	5.11	5.16	5.22	5.27	5.31	5.36
	.01	3.82	4.37	4.70	4.93	5.11	5.26	5.39	5.50	5.60	5.69	5.76	5.83	5.90	5.96	6.02	6.07	6.12	6.16	6.21
60	.05	2.83	3.40	3.74	3.98	4.16	4.31	4.44	4.55	4.65	4.73	4.81	4.88	4.94	5.00	5.06	5.11	5.15	5.20	5.24
	.01	3.76	4.28	4.59	4.82	4.99	5.13	5.25	5.36	5.45	5.53	5.60	5.67	5.73	5.78	5.84	5.89	5.93	5.97	6.01
120	.05	2.80	3.36	3.68	3.92	4.10	4.24	4.36	4.47	4.56	4.64	4.71	4.78	4.84	4.90	4.95	5.00	5.04	5.09	5.13
	.01	3.70	4.20	4.50	4.71	4.87	5.01	5.12	5.21	5.30	5.37	5.44	5.50	5.56	5.61	5.66	5.71	5.75	5.79	5.83
∞	.05	2.77	3.31	3.63	3.86	4.03	4.17	4.29	4.39	4.47	4.55	4.62	4.68	4.74	4.80	4.85	4.89	4.93	4.97	5.01
	.01	3.64	4.12	4.40	4.60	4.76	4.88	4.99	5.08	5.16	5.23	5.29	5.35	5.40	5.45	5.49	5.54	5.57	5.61	5.65

Source: The values in this table were obtained from *Biometrika Tables for Statisticians*, 2nd ed., Vol. 1 (Table 29, pp. 176–177). Used by permission of Cambridge University Press.

Critical Values for Pearson's r when $\rho = 0$

Two tails	0.10	0.05	0.02	0.01	0.005	0.001
One tail	0.05	0.025	0.01	0.005	0.0025	0.0005
df						
1	.9877	$.9^2692$	$.9^3507$	$.9^3877$	$.9^4692$	$.9^5877$
2	.9000	.9500	.9800	$.9^2000$	$.9^2500$	$.9^2000$
3	.085	.878	.9343	.9587	.9740	$.9^2114$
4	.729	.811	.882	.9172	.9417	.9741
5	.669	.754	.833	.875	.9056	.9509
6	.621	.707	.789	.834	.870	.9249
7	.582	.666	.750	.798	.836	.898
8	.549	.632	.715	.765	.805	.872
9	.521	.602	.685	.735	.776	.847
10	.497	.576	.658	.708	.750	.823
11	.476	.553	.634	.684	.726	.801
12	.457	.532	.612	.661	.703	.780
13	.441	.514	.592	.641	.683	.760
14	.426	.497	.574	.623	.664	.742
15	.412	.482	.558	.606	.647	.725
16	.400	.468	.543	.590	.631	.706
17	.389	.456	.529	.575	.616	.693
18	.378	.444	.516	.561	.602	.679
19	.369	.433	.503	.549	.589	.665
20	.360	.423	.492	.537	.576	.652
25	.323	.381	.445	.487	.524	.597
30	.296	.349	.409	.449	.484	.554
35	.275	.325	.381	.418	.452	.519
40	.257	.304	.358	.393	.425	.490
45	.243	.288	.338	.372	.403	.465
50	.231	.273	.322	.354	.384	.443
60	.211	.250	.295	.325	.352	.408
70	.195	.232	.274	.302	.327	.380
80	.183	.217	.257	.283	.307	.357
90	.173	.205	.242	.267	.290	.338
100	.164	.195	.230	.254	.276	.321

Source: The values in this table were obtained from *Biometrika Tables for Statisticians*, 2nd ed., Vol. 1 (Table 13). Used by permission of Cambridge University Press.

r	z	r	z	r	z
0.00	0.0000	0.36	0.3769	0.71	0.8872
0.01	0.0100	0.37	0.3884	0.72	0.9076
0.02	0.0200	0.38	0.4001	0.73	0.9287
0.03	0.0300	0.39	0.4118	0.74	0.9505
0.04	0.0400	0.40	0.4236	0.75	0.9730
0.05	0.0500	0.41	0.4356	0.76	0.9962
0.06	0.0601	0.42	0.4477	0.77	1.0203
0.07	0.0701	0.43	0.4599	0.78	1.0454
0.08	0.0802	0.44	0.4722	0.79	1.0714
0.09	0.0902	0.45	0.4847	0.80	1.0986
0.10	0.1003	0.46	0.4973	0.81	1.1270
0.11	0.1104	0.47	0.5101	0.82	1.1568
0.12	0.1206	0.48	0.5230	0.83	1.1881
0.13	0.1307	0.49	0.5361	0.84	1.2212
0.14	0.1409	0.50	0.5493	0.85	1.2562
0.15	0.1511	0.51	0.5627	0.86	1.2933
0.16	0.1614	0.52	0.5763	0.87	1.3331
0.17	0.1717	0.53	0.5901	0.88	1.3758
0.18	0.1820	0.54	0.6042	0.89	1.4219
0.19	0.1923	0.55	0.6184	0.90	1.4722
0.20	0.2027	0.56	0.6328	0.91	1.5275
0.21	0.2132	0.57	0.6475	0.92	1.5890
0.22	0.2237	0.58	0.6625	0.93	1.6584
0.23	0.2342	0.59	0.6777	0.94	1.7380
0.24	0.2448	0.60	0.6931	0.95	1.8318
0.25	0.2554	0.61	0.7089	0.96	1.9459
0.26	0.2661	0.62	0.7250	0.97	2.0923
0.27	0.2769	0.63	0.7414	0.98	2.2976
0.28	0.2877	0.64	0.7582	0.99	2.6467
0.29	0.2986	0.65	0.7753		
0.30	0.3095	0.66	0.7928		
0.31	0.3205	0.67	0.8107		
0.32	0.3316	0.68	0.8291		
0.33	0.3428	0.69	0.8480		
0.34	0.3541	0.70	0.8673		
0.35	0.3654				

Note: The table shows positive values; the transformed value takes the sign of the original *r* (e.g., *r* = 0.81 becomes 1.1270, and *r* = −0.81 becomes −1.1270).

Source: The values in this table were computed by the author.

References

American Psychological Association. (1983). *Publication manual of the American Psychological Association* (3rd ed.). Washington, DC: Author.

American Psychological Association. (1988). *Thesaurus of psychological index terms* (5th ed.). Washington, DC: Author.

American Psychological Association. (1990). Ethical principles of psychologists. *American Psychologist, 45,* 390–395.

Bachrach, A. J. (1962). *Psychological research: An introduction.* New York: Random House.

Bailey, D. E. (1971). *Probability and statistics: Models for research.* New York: Wiley.

Bakeman, R., & Gottman, J. M. (1986). *Observing interaction: An introduction to sequential analysis.* Cambridge: Cambridge University Press.

Baron-Cohen, S., Wyke, M. A., & Binnie, C. (1987). Hearing words and seeing colours: An experimental investigation of a case of synesthesia. *Perception, 16,* 761–767.

Berenson, M. L., Levine, D. M., & Goldstein, M. (1983). *Intermediate statistical methods and applications: A computer package approach.* Englewood Cliffs, NJ: Prentice-Hall.

Box, G.E.P., & Jenkins, G. M. (1976). *Time-series analysis: Forecasting and control.* San Francisco: Holden-Day.

Cohen, J. (1988). *Statistical power analysis* (2nd ed.). Hillsdale, NJ: Erlbaum.

Collyer, C. E., & Enns, J. T. (1986). *Analysis of variance: The basic designs.* Chicago: Nelson-Hall.

Cook, T. D., & Campbell, D. T. (1979). *Quasi-experimentation: Design and analysis issues for field settings.* Chicago: Rand McNally.

Corsini, R. J. (Ed.). (1984). *Encyclopedia of psychology.* New York: Wiley.

Cramer, H. (1946). *Mathematical methods of statistics.* Princeton: Princeton University Press.

Dethier, V. G. (1962). *To know a fly.* San Francisco: Holden-Day.

Dixon, W. J., & Massey, F. J. (1983). *Introduction to statistical analysis* (4th ed.). New York: McGraw-Hill.

Dunn, O. J. (1961). Multiple comparisons among means. *Journal of the American Statistical Association, 56,* 52–64.

Eysenck, H. J., & Eysenck, S.B.G. (1968). *Manual for the Eysenck Personality Inventory.* San Diego: Educational and Industrial Testing Service.

Fienberg, S. (1980). *The analysis of cross classified categorical data.* Cambridge, MA: MIT Press.

Fitzgerald, J. M. (1988). Vivid memories and the reminiscence phenomenon: The role of a self-narrative. *Human Development, 31,* 261–273.

Hammond, K. R., Householder, J. E., and Castellan, N. J. (1970). *Introduction to the statistical method: Foundations and use in the behavioral sciences.* (2nd ed.). New York: Knopf.

Hays, W. L. (1981). *Statistics.* (3rd ed.). New York: Holt, Rinehart & Winston.

Hollander, M., & Wolfe, D. A. (1973). *Nonparametric statistical methods.* New York: Wiley.

Howell, D. C. (1987). *Statistical methods for psychology.* Boston: PWS-Kent.

Kenny, D. (1979). *Correlation and causality.* New York: Wiley.

Keppel, G. (1973). *Design and analysis: A researcher's handbook.* Englewood Cliffs, NJ: Prentice-Hall.

Keppel, G. (1982). *Design and analysis: A researcher's handbook* (2nd ed.). Englewood Cliffs, NJ: Prentice-Hall.

Kerlinger, F. N. (1986). *Foundations of behavioral research.* (3rd ed.). New York: Holt, Rinehart & Winston.

Kirk, R. E. (1982). *Experimental design: Procedures for the behavioral sciences* (2nd ed.). Monterey, CA: Brooks/Cole.

Kruzas, A. T. (Ed.). (1978). *Encyclopedia of information systems and services.* Detroit: Gale Research.

Kupper, L. L., & Hafner, K. B. (1989). How appropriate are popular sample size formulas? *The American Statistician, 43,* 101–105.

Leer, M., Salvador, A., Goldberg, L. H., & Owens, D. A. (1986). Perceptual-motor disturbance and adaptation to base-out prisms. Psychonomic Society Convention, New Orleans.

Lehman, R. S. (1988). The languages we use. *Behavior Research Methods, Instruments, and Computers, 20,* 236–242.

Light, R. J., & Margolin, B. H. (1971). An analysis of variance for categorical data. *Journal of the American Statistical Association, 66,* 534–544.

Lord, F. M. (1953). On the statistical treatment of football numbers. *American Psychologist, 8,* 750–751.

Lowry, R. (1989). *The architecture of chance: An introduction to the logic and arithmetic of chance.* New York: Oxford University Press.

Marascuilo, L. A., & Serlin, R. C. (1988). *Statistical methods for the social and behavioral sciences*. New York: Freeman.

Martin. P., & Bateson, P. (1986). *Measuring behaviour: An introductory guide*. Cambridge: Cambridge University Press.

McCain, L. J., & McCleary, R. (1979). The statistical analysis of the simple interrupted time series quasi-experiment. In T. D. Cook & D. T. Campbell, *Quasi-experimentation: Design and analysis issues for field settings*. Chicago: Rand McNally.

Mech, L. D. (1987, May). At home with the Arctic wolf. *National Geographic, 171(5)*, 562–593.

Milligan, G. W., Wong, D. S., & Thompson, P. A. (1987). Robustness properties of nonorthogonal analysis of variance. *Psychological Bulletin, 101*, 464–470.

Mook, D. G. (1983). In defense of external invalidity. *American Psychologist, 38*, 379–387.

Oakes, W. (1972). External validity of the use of real people as subjects. *American Psychologist, 27*, 959–962.

O'Brien, R. G. (1981). A simple test for variance effects in experimental designs. *Psychological Bulletin, 89*, 570–574.

Orne, M. (1962). On the social psychology of the psychological experiment: With special reference to demand characteristics and their implications. *American Psychologist, 17*, 776–783.

Owens, D. A., & Leibowitz, H. W. (1976). Night myopia: Cause and a possible basis for amelioration. *American Journal of Optometry and Physiological Optics, 53*, 709–717.

Pillemer, D. B., Goldsmith, L. R., Panter, A. T., & White, S. H. (1988). Very long-term memories of the first year in college. *Journal of Experimental Psychology: Learning, Memory, and Cognition, 14*, 709–715.

Pitman, E.J.G. (1939). A note on normal correlation. *Biometrika, 31*, 9–12.

Roethlisberger, F. J., & Dickson, W. J. (1939). *Management and the worker*. Cambridge, MA: Harvard University Press.

Rosenthal, R. (1976). *Experimenter effects in behavioral research*. (2nd ed.). New York: Irvington.

Rosnow, R. L., & Rosenthal, R. (1989). Definition and interpretation of interaction effects. *Psychological Bulletin, 105*, 143–146.

Siegel, S., & Castellan, N. J. (1988). *Nonparametric statistics for the behavioral sciences*. (2nd ed.). New York: McGraw-Hill.

Sperling, G. (1960). The information available in brief visual presentations. *Psychological monographs, 74* (Whole no. 11).

Stevens, S. (1951). Mathematics, measurement, and psychophysics. In S. Stevens (Ed.), *Handbook of experimental psychology*. New York: Wiley.

Stilson, D. W. (1966). *Probability and statistics in psychological research and theory*. San Francisco: Holden-Day.

Stine, W. W. (1989). Meaningful inference: The role of measurement in statistics. *Psychological Bulletin, 103*, 147–155.

"Student" (W. S. Gosset). (1908). The probable error of a mean. *Biometrika, 6*, 1125.

Tankard, J. W., Jr. (1984). *The statistical pioneers*. Cambridge, MA: Schenkman.

Thigpen, C. H., & Cleckley, H. (1957). *The three faces of Eve*. New York: McGraw-Hill.

Torgerson, W. S. (1958). *Theory and methods of scaling*. New York: Wiley.

United States Department of Commerce. (1989). *Statistical abstract of the United States 1989* (109th edition). Washington, DC: Government Printing Office.

von Cranach, M., Foppa, K., Lepenies, W., & Ploog, D. (1979). *Human ethology: Claims and limits of a new discipline*. Cambridge: Cambridge University Press.

Weber, W. B., & Cook. T. D. (1972). Subject effects in laboratory research: An examination of subject roles, demand characteristics, and valid inference. *Psychological Bulletin, 77*, 273–295.

Welch, B. L. (1947). The generalization of Student's problem when several different population variances are involved. *Biometrika, 34*, 28–35.

Werner, J. S., & Perlmutter, M. (1979). Development of visual memory in infants. In H. W. Reese and L. P. Lipsitt (Eds.), *Advances in child development and behavior, Vol. 14* (pp. 2–56). New York: Academic Press.

Wilcox, R. R. (1987). New designs in analysis of variance. *Annual Review of Psychology, 38*, 29–60.

Wilcoxon, F. (1945). Individual comparisons by ranking methods, *Biometrics, 1*, 80–83.

Winer, B. J. (1971). *Statistical principles in experimental design* (2nd ed.). New York: McGraw-Hill.

Wolman, B. B. (Ed.). (1977). *International encyclopedia of psychiatry, psychology, psychoanalysis, and neurology*. New York: Aesculapius.

Zuckerman, M., Eysenck, S., & Eysenck, H. J. (1978). Sensation seeking in England and America: Cross-cultural, age, and sex comparisons. *Journal of consulting and clinical psychology, 46*, 139–149.

Solutions to Selected Exercises

CHAPTER 2

1. **a.** Naturalistic observation—observe and watch for behaviors such as marking territorial boundaries, defense, etc.

   c. Questionnaire—ask about such behaviors.

   e. Case study—select an individual who shows disruptive behaviors, design a behavior modification program, and determine whether the disruption decreases.

   g. Interview—you might ask them to describe how to get from the dining hall to the Psychology Building and to describe several other paths between buildings.

   i. Survey—locate volunteer helpers and ask about their family backgrounds, time spent, etc.

2. **b.** Independent variable: music playing (or not) during study periods; dependent variable: score on an examination.

   d. Independent variable: hours of required study; dependent variable: grades.

   f. Independent variable: instruction in study strategies; dependent variable: recall.

   h. Independent variable: art training; dependent variable: ratings of various art works.

   j. Independent variable: drug/tobacco users/ nonusers; dependent variable: personality test scores.

CHAPTER 3

1. **a.** ratio **c.** ordinal **e.** ratio **g.** nominal
   i. ratio **k.** ratio **m.** ratio

2. Ordinal. (Could be regarded as interval; to do that we must assume that the intervals appear equal to the judges, so that the difference between a 3 and a 4 performance is really the same as the difference between, say, an 8 and a 9.)

4. It's reasonable only if you assume that the intervals appear equal so that the measurement is interval.

CHAPTER 4

1. You might try a few "pilot subjects" and explore the relationship between practice and problem solving;

you could then decide on optimal levels. If you want to explore the relationship more fully than is possible with two conditions, you could use several different amounts of practice.

3. Intelligence of subjects, previous experience with similar tasks, gender, instructions.

5. Have two experimenters, so that the one who administers the test problems is blind to the amount of practice that a subject has received.

7. **a.** For complete counterbalancing, construct all possible orders of the three paintings (there are $3! = 6$ of them):

A	B	C
A	C	B
B	A	C
B	C	A
C	A	B
C	B	A

   Use a number of subjects that is a multiple of six and present each order the same number of times.

   c. For a Latin square, use the orders

A	B	C
B	C	A
C	A	B

CHAPTER 5

1. Using an interval width of 3, the data are

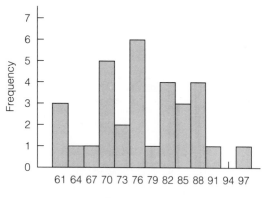

Examination scores

3. Using an interval width of 9.0, the frequencies are

Reaction time interval (.01 sec)	Frequency
9–17	1
18–26	10
27–35	2
36–44	3
45–53	1
54–62	2
63–71	0
72–80	2
81–89	2
90–98	1
99–107	1
108–116	0
117–125	1
126–134	0
135–143	0
144–152	2

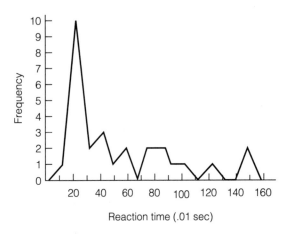

5.

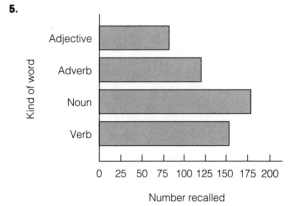

7. a.

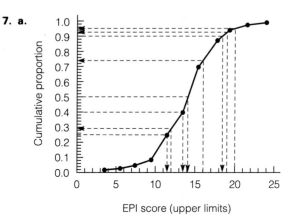

b. 50th percentile ≈ 14.00
40th percentile ≈ 13.50
25th percentile ≈ 11.50
90th percentile ≈ 18.50
c. Percentile rank of 12 ≈ 29
Percentile rank of 16 ≈ 74
Percentile rank of 20 ≈ 95
Percentile rank of 19 ≈ 92

8. a.

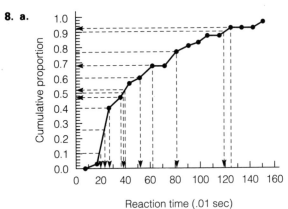

b. 10th percentile ≈ .19
25th percentile ≈ .22
40th percentile ≈ .27
50th percentile ≈ .38
60th percentile ≈ .53
75th percentile ≈ .81
90th percentile ≈ 1.18
c. Percentile rank of .40 ≈ 52
Percentile rank of 1.25 ≈ 93
Percentile rank of .63 ≈ 68
Percentile rank of .35 ≈ 46

CHAPTER 6

1. Mean = 77.22
   Median = 76.00

3. Mean = 0.54
   Median = 0.38

CHAPTER 7

1.

	Group		
	A	**B**	**C**
Mean	42.25	50.50	53.67
Median	41.50	49.50	51.50
Range	53.00	17.00	48.00
Interquartile range	5.50	7.50	22.00
s^2	17.58	27.58	216.38
s	4.19	5.25	14.71

3.

	Quiz scores			
	Week 1	**Week 2**	**Week 3**	**Week 4**
Mean	44.04	24.85	52.26	43.74
Median	44.00	23.00	52.00	46.00
s^2	349.96	71.90	37.67	219.30
s	18.71	8.50	6.14	14.81
Interquartile range	33.00	11.00	10.00	21.00

7.

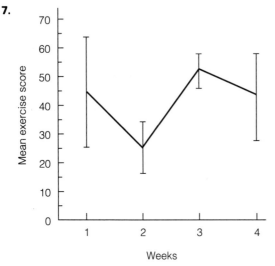

9. a.

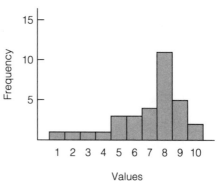

Mean = 7.00
Median = 8.00
s = 2.16
Skewness = -1.39

b. Mean = 7.00
   Median = 8.00
   s = 2.16
   Skewness = 1.39
   Changing the sign of each data value changes the sign of the measures of center and leaves the standard deviation unchanged; it changes the sign of the Pearson skewness but not its value.

c. Mean = 0.184
   Median = 0.125
   s = 0.166
   Skewness = 1.066
   All of the statistics have changed considerably; the skewness has decreased but is positive.

d. Mean = 0.809
   Median = 0.903
   s = 0.208
   Skewness = -1.356
   All of the statistics have changed once again; the skewness has increased and is negative.

CHAPTER 8

1. First exam, $z = 1.29$
   Second exam, $z = 3.06$

3. Mean = -0.0003
   Median = 0.46
   s = 1.0026
   Skewness = -1.38
   The measures of center and spread change, while the skewness (and thus the form of the distribution) remain essentially unchanged.

4. a. 0.1736   **b.** 0.4052   **c.** 0.2224   **d.** 0.8577

6. Percentile rank on exam 1 = 90.15
Percentile rank on exam 2 = 99.89

7. Lower value = 40
Upper value = 60

CHAPTER 9

1.

	Quiz 1	Quiz 2
Mean	23.50	21.94
Median	24.00	23.50
Standard deviation	4.21	4.43
Interquartile range	6.75	4.75

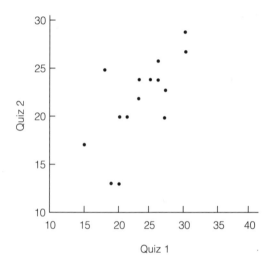

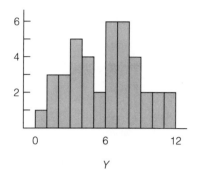

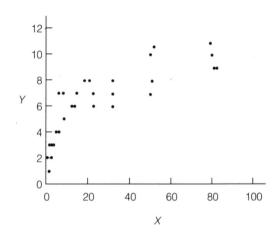

c. The relationship appears to be nonlinear.
d. The plots of Y versus $\log(X)$ and $\log(Y)$ versus $\log(X)$ are the most linear.

4. $r = .69$

3. a.

	X	Y
Mean	22.10	5.53
Median	11.00	6.00
Standard deviation	24.72	2.84
Interquartile range	29.75	4.75
Skewness	1.33	−0.49

7. a. $W = 0.448$
b. Judges 1–2, $r_S = .83$, judges 2–5 $r_S = .14$, judges 4–6 $r_S = .83$
c. Judges 1–2, $\tau = .71$, judges 2–5 $\tau = .21$, judges 4–6 $\tau = .71$

9. Point biserial correlation = .30

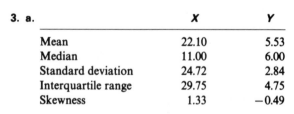

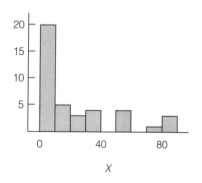

CHAPTER 10

1. a. $\hat{Y} = 0.73 \times$ Quiz 1 $+ 4.85$

b. & c.

Quiz 2 actual	Linear prediction	Residual
13	19.39	-6.39
27	26.66	0.34
22	21.57	0.43
23	24.48	-1.48
24	21.57	2.43
17	15.76	1.24
29	26.66	2.34
20	19.39	0.61
24	23.76	0.24
20	24.48	-4.48
13	18.67	-5.67
25	17.94	7.06
20	20.12	-0.12
26	23.76	2.24
24	23.03	0.97
24	23.76	0.24

d. $\Sigma(Y - \hat{Y})^2 = 164.79$

e. $s_{est} = 3.43$

f. Predicted Quiz 1 $= .66$ x Quiz 2 $+ 9.12$
$r = 0.690$ (from Exercise 9.1)
$r = \sqrt{0.73 \times 0.66} = .694$ (from geometric mean of slopes)

g.

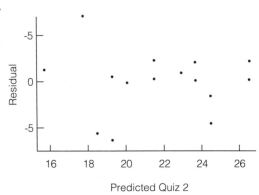

Predicted Quiz 2

There seems to be little relationship between the predicted values and the residuals; we may conclude that the linear model is probably appropriate.

CHAPTER 11

2. a. .272
   b. .005

c. .000064 $(= 1/125 \times 1/125)$

d.

Group	Probability	Probable number of questions
Measures of center	.144	7
Measures of spread	.128	6
Frequency distributions	.136	7
z scores	.080	4
Normal curve areas	.072	4
Scatterplots	.096	5
Correlation	.144	7
Percentiles	.120	6
Percentile ranks	.080	4

7. a. 0.9806   **d.** 0.6127   **g.** 0.0062
   b. 0.5398   **e.** 0.1458   **h.** 0.1454
   c. 0.3871   **f.** 0.0384

8. $\mu = 2.0$
$\sigma_{\bar{X}} = 1.0/\sqrt{25} = 0.20$

10. With N this large, $\bar{X}$ may be assumed to be normally distributed; thus we use the normal distribution with $\mu = 2.0$ and $\sigma_{\bar{X}} = 1.0/\sqrt{30} = 0.18$.
   a. Probability $= .9946$
   b. Probability ≈ 1.00
   c. Probability $= .0027$
   d. Probability $= .9545$
   e. Probability $= .455$
   f. Probability $= .6827$
   g. Probability $= .3173$

12. For $N = 2$, $\mu = 20$, $\sigma_{\bar{X}} = 7.07$
For $N = 3$, $\mu = 20$, $\sigma_{\bar{X}} = 5.77$
For $N = 30$, $\mu = 2.0$, $\sigma_{\bar{X}} = 1.83$

CHAPTER 12

8. First compute

$$\sigma_{\bar{X}} = \frac{\sigma}{\sqrt{N}}$$
$$= \frac{1}{\sqrt{27}}$$
$$= 0.19$$

so that

$$z = \frac{\bar{X} - \mu}{\sigma_{\bar{X}}}$$
$$= \frac{1.48 - 2.00}{.19}$$
$$= -2.70.$$

Now determine the significance by noting that -2.70 is beyond the "likely" region, so the null hypothesis that $\mu = 2$ is rejected:

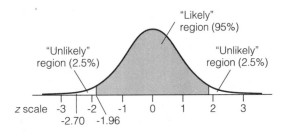

In APA sentence format, the result could be stated as, "We may conclude that the obtained mean of 1.48 differs significantly from that suggested by chance if the students were guessing, $z = -2.70$, $p < .01$".

10. a. Null: $\mu = 125$
Alternative: $\mu \neq 125$
b. $30/\sqrt{28} = 5.67$
c. $s/\sqrt{28} = 36.10/\sqrt{28} = 6.82$. Somewhat larger than the parameter.
d. Using the z formula, we obtain $z = 1.222$. Because the value must exceed ± 1.96 to be significant, we do not reject the hypothesis that $\mu = 125$.
e. 90%: 122.6–141.2
90%: 120.8–143.0
90%: 117.3–146.5

12. $\sigma_{\bar{x}} = 15/\sqrt{36} = 2.5$

so that

$$z = (56.08 - 50)/2.5 = 2.43.$$

Since 2.43 exceeds the critical value of z for $\alpha = .05$, we reject the hypothesis that $\mu = 50$. Thus we conclude that this year's class has a mean that is different from the mean of preceding classes: $z = 2.43$, $p < .05$.

CHAPTER 13

1. The scores of this class (mean $= 207.80$) do not differ significantly from the national norm of 200: $t(14) = 1.904$, $p > .05$.

4. These are probably not maze-bright animals. Their mean (7.5 trials to learn the maze) is significantly greater than the 5.0 trials required by maze-bright rats: $t(9) = 3.00$, $p < .05$.

6. This set of scores is significantly different from the neutral norm of 50.0; mean $= 57.647$, $t(16) = 4.02$, $p < .05$.

7. There are two out of the eight scores above the null hypothesis population median of 125. Consulting Appendix G with $N = 8$ and $p = .5$, we find that the probability of finding two or fewer weights more than the median is 0.1446. Thus we do not reject the hypothesis that the population median is 125, $p > .10$.

9. For σ^2: 90%: 2.39 – 7.12
99%: 1.87 – 10.52
For σ: 90%: 1.54 – 2.67
99%: 1.37 – 1.87

11. The mean of this set of extraversion data ($\bar{X} = 13.00$, $s = 3.53$) is not significantly different from that of a population whose mean is 10.00; $t(9) = 2.69$, $p > .01$. In addition, the variance of the sample does not differ from an assumed population variance of 36, $\chi^2(9) = 3.12$, $p > .01$. The 95% confidence interval for the population mean extraversion score is 10.48–15.52. The 95% confidence interval for the population standard deviation is 2.43–6.44.

15. $r = .784$. The obtained correlation is significantly different from zero: $t(18) = 5.36$, $p < .10$.

17. The correlation between EPIE and TAS ($r = .186$) is not significantly different from zero: $t(18) = 0.80$, $p > .05$.

19. The correlation between TAS and ES ($r = .692$) is significantly different from zero: $t(18) = 4.07$, $p < .01$. It is not significantly different from 0.6: $z = 0.65$, $p > .01$.

CHAPTER 14

1. a.

	Vocal	Instrumental
Mean	16.20	12.93
Std. dev.	5.32	4.33

$t(14) = 3.50$, $p < .05$.

b. Sum $(+) = 93$, Sum $(-) = 12$; thus $T = 12$, $p < .05$.

3. a.

	Aversion	Control
Mean	10.20	8.75
Std. dev.	2.04	1.25

$t(18) = 1.91$, $p > .10$.

b. $t = 84$, $z = -1.59$, $p > .10$; the t and Wilcoxon tests come to opposite conclusions.

8. $z = -1.01$, $p > .05$.

CHAPTER 16

1.

Source	df	SS	MS	F
Age	2	1231.86	615.929	5.15
Error	39	4662.14	119.542	
Total	41	5894.00		

3.

Source	df	SS	MS	F
Number of items	3	606.30	202.10	4.42
Error	59	2743.06	45.72	
Total	62	3349.36		

7. The following table gives the $\alpha = .05$ Tukey-Kramer critical values (upper value) and the mean difference (lower value) for each pair of means. The only significant difference is marked by an asterisk.

	Drug A	Drug B	Drug C	Placebo
Mean	7.33	10.38	11.80	8.71
Drug A		3.64	4.08	3.75
		3.05	4.47*	1.38
Drug B			3.84	3.48
			1.42	1.67
Drug C				3.94
				3.09

8. The Scheffé critical value is 8.28 (assuming $\alpha = .05$). The comparison between the 10- and 15-item tests and the 20-item test is not significant ($F = 6.83$); neither is the comparison between the 20- and 25-item tests ($F = 0.011$). The comparison between the two shortest tests (10- and 15-item) and the two longest (20- and 25-item) is significant ($F = 10.73$).

CHAPTER 17

1. $H = 7.93$, $p < .05$.

3.

Source	df	SS	MS	F	
Subjects	11	360.56	32.79		
Trials	3	610.23	203.41	29.76	$p < .01$
Error	33	225.52	6.83		
Total	47	1196.31			

The means for the four trials are

Trial 3	Trial 5	Trial 7	Trial 9
6.75	10.00	14.08	15.92

There are six pairwise comparisons possible among the four trials. To maintain the EW error rate at .06 or less, each pair must be tested at the .01 level. Using Student's t test for repeated measures at the .01 significance level, all pairs of trials differ significantly except between trials 3 and 5, and between trials 7 and 9.

CHAPTER 19

1.

Source	df	SS	MS	F	
Species	1	302.50	302.50	5.17	$p < .05$
Stimulus	3	5850.00	1950.00	33.31	$p < .001$
Interaction	3	953.90	317.97	5.43	$p < .01$
Error	32	1873.20	58.54		
Total	39	8979.60			

The plot indicates the nature of the interaction:

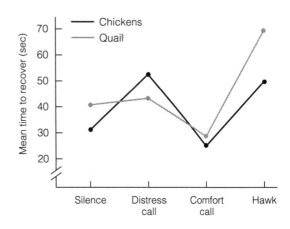

The table of simple main effects is

Source	df	SS	MS	F
Species at Silence	1	230.40	230.40	3.94
Species at Distress	1	211.60	211.60	3.61
Species at Comfort	1	40.00	40.00	0.68
Species at Hawk	1	774.40	774.40	13.23
Stimulus at Chickens	3	2824.95	941.65	16.08
Stimulus at Quail	3	3979.00	1326.32	22.66
Error	32	1873.20	58.54	

3.

Source	df	SS	MS	F	
Drug at Young	3	191.00	63.67	15.45	$p < .01$
Drug at Middle	3	147.68	49.23	11.95	$p < .01$
Drug at Old	3	161.68	53.89	13.08	$p < .01$
Age	2	66.82	33.41	8.11	$p < .01$
Error	108	444.80	4.12		
Total	119	1011.97			

For the computational check, note that $191.00 + 147.68 + 161.68 = 500.36$, and that (from the summary table) $SS_{Drug} + SS_{Interaction} = 55.57 + 444.80 = 500.37 \approx 500.36$.

5. For the first table, $SS_{Sex\ at\ old} = 22.50$, so that $F(1, 16) = 5.83$, $p < .05$, and $SS_{Sex\ at\ young} = 2.50$, so that $F(1, 16) = 0.65$, $p > .05$.

For the second table, the values are exactly the same. These results indicate that, regardless of whether the interaction is ordinal (first table) or disordinal (second table), the effect of sex is the same. In the case of old subjects, males score significantly higher than females; for young subjects, there is no difference between the sexes.

6. a. $F(1, 24) = 0.43$, $p > .05$
b. $F(1, 24) = 0.73$, $p > .05$
c. $F(1, 24) = 3.29$, $p > .05$
d. $F(1, 24) = 0.32$, $p > .05$

7. The analysis makes it clear that the retroflective paint is superior in visibility. In daylight conditions, there are no significant differences in the visibility of the three paints. At night, on the other hand, the superiority of the new paint is clear. While the reflective paint has a higher visibility than ordinary paint, that difference is not significant. The difference between the reflective and the retroflective paints is substantial and significant. In fact, the visibility of the retroflective paint in darkness is not significantly different from its visibility in daylight.

C H A P T E R 20

1. a. For the top row versus the middle row, $t(10) = -6.14$, $p > .05$.
b. For the bottom row versus the middle row, $t(10) = -9.30$, $p < .05$.

3.

Source	df	SS	MS	F	
Subjects	14	1.627	.116		
Direction	3	1.818	.606	23.09	$p < .01$
Error	42	1.102	.026		
Velocity	2	1.353	.677	56.13	$p < .01$
Error	28	.338	.012		
Interaction	6	.072	.012	3.11	$p < .01$
Error	84	.322	.004		
Total	179	6.632			

5.

Source	df	SS	MS	MS_{error}	F
Dir. at Slow	3	0.416	0.139	0.005	26.46
Dir. at Med.	3	0.512	0.171	0.012	13.95
Dir. at Fast	3	0.961	0.320	0.016	19.50
Speed at L-R	2	0.302	0.151	0.005	31.49
Speed at R-L	2	0.611	0.306	0.007	41.03
Speed at T-B	2	0.321	0.161	0.006	28.72
Speed at B-T	2	0.191	0.096	0.006	16.81

6. a.

Source	df	SS	MS	F	
Subjects	9	86.556	9.617		
Taste	3	1283.569	427.856	28.358	$p < .01$
Error	27	407.369	15.088		
Total	39	1777.494			

b. All pairs of means are significantly different (.01) except that between salt and quinine. The table gives the Student's t value for the comparison of each pair of conditions. Each t has df = 9, and the .01 critical value is 3.25.

	Sucrose	Salt	HCl
Salt	7.74		
HCl	5.59	4.67	
Quinine	3.85	4.25	1.44

9. Several approaches can be taken to explore these results. Here we begin with the interaction plot, follow that with simple effects, and then look at two simple comparisons. The interaction plot suggests the nature of the relationship:

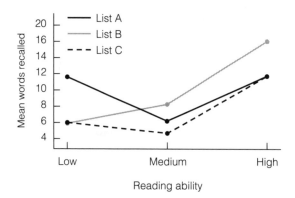

The simple effect analysis shows

Source	df	SS	MS	F	
List at Low	2	124.778	62.389	7.196	$p < .01$
List at Med.	2	44.334	22.167	2.557	$p > .05$
List at High	2	78.112	39.056	4.504	$p < .05$
Ability at A	2	118.112	59.056	6.811	$p < .01$
Ability at B	2	357.444	178.722	20.613	$p < .01$
Ability at C	2	174.334	87.167	10.053	$p < .01$
Error	45	390.150	8.670		

The plot suggests looking at List A versus List B in the low- and high-ability groups. For the simple comparison of the lists for Low, $F(1, 45) = 11.12$, $p < .01$. For the same lists in the high group, $F(1, 45) = 6.49$, $p < .05$ (but note that the positions of the two groups have reversed).

We may summarize the results as follows. There is an overall effect of reading ability: higher-reading-ability children have higher recall scores, except for List A. List A leads to significantly higher recall in the low-ability group. In the medium-ability condition, the lists are learned equally well by the fifth presentation. List B is learned by high-ability students better than are Lists A and C.

CHAPTER 21

1. The obtained distribution of student choices differs from those expected by chance, $\chi^2(4, N = 45) = 16.67$, $p < .01$. Analysis of the residuals suggests that the difference lies primarily in the "other job" category, with far more students choosing that option than expected.

3. With $N = 48$, use the normal approximation

$$\mu = Np \qquad\qquad \sigma = \sqrt{Np(1 - p)}$$
$$= 48 \times .50 \qquad\quad = \sqrt{48 \times .50 \times .50}$$
$$= 24 \qquad\qquad\quad = \sqrt{12}$$
$$\qquad\qquad\qquad\quad = 3.46$$

so that

$$Z = \frac{X - \mu}{\sigma} = \frac{32 - 24}{3.46}$$
$$= 2.31.$$

Because the two-tailed critical value for $z = 1.96$, we reject the hypothesis that the true proportion is 50%.

6. We conclude that the association between year in school and choice is significant, $\chi^2(4, N = 104) = 19.62$, $p < .01$. Inspection of the residuals suggests that the greatest change between the two classes of students is in the "Undecided" category, suggesting that the seniors are more clear in their plans than the juniors.

7. $C = 0.398$; $\Phi = 0.434$.

Credits

Index

References to tables and figures are printed in italic type.